ACTIVITIES WISE AND OTHERWISE

For Bernie

Activities
Wise and Otherwise

The Career of
Sir Henry Augustus Robinson
1898–1922

BRENDAN O DONOGHUE

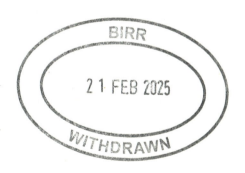

IRISH ACADEMIC PRESS

First published in 2015 by Irish Academic Press
8 Chapel Lane
Sallins
Co. Kildare

© 2015 Brendan O Donoghue

British Library Cataloguing in Publication Data
An entry can be found on request

978-07165-3299-6 (cloth)
978-07165-3300-9 (PDF)

Library of Congress Cataloging in Publication Data
An entry can be found on request

Printed and bound by CPI group (UK) Ltd, Croydon, CR0 4YY

CONTENTS

PREFACE AND
ACKNOWLEDGEMENTS

This book has taken nearly twenty years to reach publication. When I retired in 1997 as Secretary of the Department of the Environment (formerly Local Government) on completion of a seven-year term of office, I fully intended to research and write up the career of Sir Henry Augustus Robinson, who had been appointed to the nineteenth-century equivalent of my position in 1898 and who – until the Custom House fire of May 1921 – had been based in what was, for all practical purposes, the same room in which I had worked in the 1990s. However, a variety of other activities and projects pushed Sir Henry into the background until a few years ago when I convinced myself that it might be worthwhile to resume the research on the man and his career which I had planned to undertake in the late 1990s.

Robinson does not appear to have left a diary, his personal papers were destroyed in a raid on his house at Foxrock, County Dublin, in August 1922, and over a year before that the records and files of the Local Government Board for Ireland, which he headed for over twenty years, were destroyed in the Custom House fire. Fortunately, however, having kept two or three typists busy at one time, he left a substantial paper trail, much of which has survived. A large number of his formal official letters and memoranda can be found on former Treasury and other files at the National Archives in London and to a lesser extent on Chief Secretary's Office files at the National Archives in Dublin, while many hundreds of pages of his handwritten informal and semi-official letters are among collections of papers of his political masters and associates, which are held in the Manuscripts Department of the National Library of Ireland, and in various repositories in England. These collections include the papers of Gerald Balfour, Walter Long, James Bryce, Augustine Birrell, Sir Matthew Nathan, Ian Macpherson and Field-Marshal Lord French. Given the standard to which most of the papers held in England have been listed and catalogued, it has been a pleasure to work on many of these collections in different repositories and in some cases via the internet. All of the often-unnamed archivists, librarians and others who have contributed to this happy situation deserve the best thanks of researchers and students in general, but in my own case, I must mention a number of repositories and individuals who have been particularly helpful. At the Wiltshire and Swindon Archives at Chippenham, I was indebted to Andrew Crookston who catalogued the large collection of Walter Long papers and to the other staff (including Robert Jago) who facilitated access to the collection and subsequently provided photocopies. In the course of a number of visits to the Imperial War Museum, archivists Simon Robbins, Simon Offord and others facilitated access to the Sir John French papers, and Victoria Wylde dealt efficiently with subsequent requests for photocopies. At the Bodleian Library in Oxford, Colin Harris and his friendly and helpful staff at the Special Collections Reading Room made it possible for me to get through a large amount of material, and I am grateful also to Rebecca Wall and Angie Goodgame for their efficient supply of photocopies. As always, it was a pleasure to work at the British National Archives at Kew, where the already excellent cataloguing, document delivery and copying services continue to improve. Others who have assisted me include Gemma Hamilton and Garth Stewart at the National Archives of Scotland; Clare Elsey and Richard Ward at the Parliamentary Archives in London; staff at the Manuscripts Department of the British Library; and Liz Bregazzi, county archivist at Durham County Record Office.

In Ireland I have availed of the excellent services at the Public Record Office of Northern Ireland (PRONI), at the UCD Archives and at the Manuscripts and Research Library at TCD. Noelle Grothier of the Bureau of Military History kindly provided access to selected witness statements before they were available online, and at the Manuscripts Room of the National Library, my work was greatly facilitated by Colette O'Daly, Tom Desmond and Ciara Kerrigan. Mary O'Keeffe and Gerry McNamee helped in locating material held by the Department of the Environment, Community and Local Government, while Helen Kelly, professional genealogist, helped in tracing Robinson's family background and Mary Millar located his grave at Poole. Bob Montgomery of the Royal Irish Automobile Club, Berni Metcalfe of the National Library, Mairead and Dominic Lee of Priory Studios, and Aisling Dunne and Colum O'Riordan at the Irish Architectural Archive helped in acquiring suitable images. Thanks are also due to Mary Mackey, senior archivist, and to the Reading Room staff at the National Archives of Ireland, although it must be said that if the collection of Chief Secretary's Office Registered Papers held there is ever properly sorted, listed and catalogued, future researchers will almost certainly be able to revise and supplement some of the chapters which follow after this:

For advice and assistance in various ways I am grateful to Professor Ronan Fanning, Professor Eunan O'Halpin, Professor Michael Laffan, Professor James McGuire, Professor Mary Daly and Dr Kieran Rankin, but as none of them have read the manuscript in full, they cannot be held responsible for omissions or errors of fact or of interpretation. Finally, my wife, Bernie, deserves special thanks, not only for virtually having had to live with Sir Henry for some years past, but also for her help at the research stage, especially in Chippenham and at Kew, for encouraging and supporting me in pressing on with the work, and more recently for the time devoted to copy-editing and proof-reading.

ABBREVIATIONS

AOH	Ancient Order of Hibernians
AR	Annual Report of the Local Government Board for Ireland
BMH	Bureau of Military History
CB	Companion of the Order of the Bath
CDB	Congested Districts Board
CO	Colonial Office
CSORP	Chief Secretary's Office Registered Papers
DATI	Department of Agricultural and Technical Instruction
DIB	Dictionary of Irish Biography
DMP	Dublin Metropolitan Police
GPO	General Post Office, Dublin
IHS	Irish Historical Studies
IWM	Imperial War Museum
KCB	Knight Commander of the Order of the Bath
LGB	Local Government Board for Ireland
NAI	National Archives of Ireland
NAS	National Archives of Scotland
NHI	New History of Ireland
NLI	National Library of Ireland
OAP	Old Age Pension
ODNB	Oxford Dictionary of National Biography
OPW	Office of Public Works
OTC	Officers Training Corps
PC	Privy Councillor

PRO	Public Record Office, Kew (now TNA: The National Archives)
RAMC	Royal Army Medical Corps
RIC	Royal Irish Constabulary
TCD	Trinity College, Dublin
TNA	The National Archives (formerly PRO)
UCD	University College, Dublin
UIL	United Irish League
WNHA	Womens National Health Association
WRO	Wiltshire Record Office (now Wiltshire and Swindon Archives)
WS	Witness Statement (BMH)

In the chapters that follow, quotations (especially from Robinson's letters and memoranda) have been used extensively. Silent editorial amendments have been made for the sake of clarity, and typographical and other obvious errors have been corrected. Abbreviations, which appear in manuscript letters, have been written out in full and capitalisation has been standardised. Regardless of how they appear in original documents, references to Sinn Féin, Sinn Féiners, the Dáil and Dáil Éireann appear in these correct Irish language forms.

LIST OF PLATES AND MAPS

1. Grave of Sir Henry Robinson (senior) (d. 1893) and his wife, Eva, in Mount Jerome Cemetery, Dublin. (Author photo)
2. The De Dion Voiturette of Sir Henry Robinson, driven by his 17-year-old son, Christopher (right), in a parade of motor cars at the RDS, Dublin, in April 1901. (RIAC, Guinness Seagrave Archive)
3. Sir Henry Robinson (on the right) as a passenger in the white 12 hp Panhard of Sir Hickman Bacon, at Pontoon Bridge, Co. Mayo, during the IAC Motor Tour of Ireland, August 1901. (RIAC, Guinness Seagrave Archive)
4. On tour with King Edward VII in the West in July 1903 – waiting for the King to emerge from the Weaver's House in Leenane, Co. Galway. (*Memories: Wise and Otherwise*)
5. Robinson and Chief Secretary, Walter Long, in discussion with a parish priest during a tour of the West in 1905. (*Memories: Wise and Otherwise*)
6. Robinson driving Chief Secretary Augustine Birrell and Mrs Birrell on a tour of the West, c. 1910. (*Memories: Wise and Otherwise*)
7. Robinson's favourite hotel at Recess, Co. Galway, which he regularly visited with Chief Secretaries (and with King Edward VII and his Queen in 1903); the hotel was destroyed by fire in October 1922 and never rebuilt. (*National Library of Ireland, Lawrence collection, CAB 07355*)
8. The Custom House on fire, May 1921. (*Old Ireland in Pictures*, issued by Wilson Hartnell & Co. Dublin, July 1922)
9. The ruins of the Custom House after the fire of May 1921, showing what remained of the dome with the statue of Commerce which stood above it. (*Old Ireland in Pictures*, issued by Wilson Hartnell & Co. Dublin, July 1922)
10. Map of rural districts sent by Henry Robinson to Chief Secretary Birrell on 5 March 1914 showing how a northern excluded area

might be defined by reference to rural district boundaries; districts with catholic majorities were shaded green and non-catholic districts red *(The Bodleian Library, University of Oxford, Birrell Papers, MSS. Eng. c. 7034, f. 60)*. See also page 177.

11. Map sent on 6 May 1914 by Henry Robinson to Chief Secretary Birrell, at his urgent request, giving him 'a rough idea' of an area (defined by reference to poor law union boundaries and coloured yellow) which might be excluded from Home Rule arrangements; this is likely to have been 'the Irish Office map' referred to by John Redmond in his note on the Buckingham Palace Conference of July 1914 *(The Bodleian Library, University of Oxford, Birrell Papers, MSS. Eng. c. 7034, f. 71)*. See also page 180.

12. A map of Ireland similar to map 2 but showing unions in Ulster coloured green for those with catholic majorities, yellow for those with protestant majorities and blue for those 'with no majority'. This map, which survives among John Redmond's papers, is likely to have been the map presented by the nationalists at the Buckingham Palace Conference in July 1914 *(National Library of Ireland, John Redmond Papers, MS 15,266)*. See also page 184.

13. Sir Henry Robinson leaving Dublin Castle on 16 January 1922, after the 'surrender' of the government to Sinn Féin. *(British Pathe)*

14. Lisnacarrig, Brighton Road, Foxrock, Co. Dublin, home of Sir Henry Robinson until 1923. *(Irish Times, sale advertisement)*

15. Drawing, c.1915, of the proposed ground floor of the North Block of Government Buildings, Dublin, showing the room designed for Robinson as Vice-President of the LGB, but subsequently used as the Cabinet Room. *(Irish Architectural Archive)*

16. The grave of Sir Henry Robinson and his wife at Parkstone Cemetery, Poole, Dorset. (Courtesy of Mary Millar)

Introduction

Sir Henry Augustus Robinson (1857–1927) ended his career as one of the most senior civil servants in Ireland, serving as Vice-President of the Local Government Board for Ireland (LGB) from 1898 until it was replaced by the Department of Local Government in April 1922. When he published *Memories: Wise and Otherwise* in March 1923,[1] he explained that his objective had been to write something of all the happenings which made his intimate association with twenty chief secretaries so full of interest. However, Robinson was economical with the truth, as neither this first volume of memoirs nor a second 1924 volume made any reference to the advisory work and other political activity which, in breach of his civil service status, linked him at different times not just to chief secretaries but also to other government ministers and to the Cabinet itself.[2] Thus, *Activities: Wise and Otherwise* seemed to be an appropriate title for the present book, which tells the story of Robinson's official career and uncovers this other Henry Robinson who had not emerged fully from published work before now.

In November 1926, when applying for compensation of £1,000 from the British Government for expenses which he claimed had been imposed on him because of his service to the Government up to 1922, Robinson presented an account of that service, which emphasised his dual role in the administration and thus differed significantly from his published memoirs:

> ... there was no one in Ireland called upon by the Government to do more compromising and confidential work than I was, or to take greater risks without any effective protection ... my position in Ireland became one of the utmost danger and from which I barely escaped with my life, when the Government withdrew their armed forces on the establishment of the Provisional Government.

> ... I had been the permanent head of the Local Government Board and ...had been in constant communication ... with the English

Chief Secretaries. My forty years' experience of Irish government was at their disposal, and they never hesitated to call on me ... to advise them upon and to carry into effect any measures they may have had in mind, even though sometimes quite outside the scope of the work coming under the Local Government Board.

... after the Rebellion broke out ... I was called upon almost hourly to advise the Lord Lieutenant, the Chief Secretary and occasionally the Prime Ministers ... The work I did in 1916 and the prominence of my position in the public eye from then onwards had its inevitable result. I came to be looked on by the Irish Revolutionary movement as being the most dangerous and formidable ally of the British Government in Ireland, and from that time onward my life was never safe ... the moment the British Government withdrew their armed forces, and left the country in a state of anarchy which rendered these revolutionary leaders almost unchecked, my house was raided and I and my family were driven out of the country at a few hours' notice, having just escaped with our lives.

... I was entitled to retire on pension some time before events in Ireland began to look really grave ... It was only on the particular request of the English Government, who wished me not to deprive them of my knowledge and experience during the critical times the country was going through, that I reluctantly consented to remain on.

... I was driven out of the country by the rebels on account of my being regarded as a leading official of the British Government and a representative of the old British ascendancy in Ireland ... I had ... come to know intimately the people and characteristics of all parts of the country ... [and] had means of obtaining information, through local officials and others, of passing occurrences and political movements, and my knowledge was always at the service of the Government.[3]

How much of this 1926 statement was true? To what extent was Robinson called on to advise the government on strategic and policy matters well outside the area of responsibility of the LGB? Was he really seen by the public and by the forces opposed to the government as a key figure in the response to the struggle for independence? Alternatively, should the case he advanced in support of his compensation claim be dismissed in whole or in part as fantasy or, at least, as the exaggerated, embellished recollection of a possibly embittered and sick 70-year-old man?

Undoubtedly, Robinson deserves to be seen as a much more important figure than the civil service head of a busy government department. Through the 'extra-curricular' activity in which he engaged, he influenced Cabinet decisions on strategic policy matters and the information and opinions which he provided at different times had a significant effect on the administration of Ireland in the 1912–22 period. This book attempts to provide an overall assessment of the man and his career – not just his civil service work but also his other activities and advices at critical times, and on critical issues, in the last pre-independence decade.

The Official Robinson

Robinson was an effective administrator and manager under whose direction the responsibilities of the LGB itself and the size of the organisation increased substantially. In addition, the new local government system, which he was largely responsible for bringing into operation in 1899, and which operated after that under his supervision, undertook the administration and development of a growing number of infrastructural, environmental, health and social services. Looking back on it, he found the twenty-four years from 1898 to 1922 to have been 'so crowded with reforms, industrial and administrative, and so characterized by sudden and violent changes of policy under successive chief secretaries of each new administration' that there seemed to be no break in the perpetual high pressure under which he had to work.[4] As Vice-President of the LGB throughout that period he was – apart from the Under-Secretary – the most senior and best-paid civil servant in Ireland, recognised by contemporaries as an official of major capacity and influence and widely known throughout the country and among all sections of the public. Described by Ronan Fanning as the 'doyen of Irish civil servants after the turn of the century',[5] he was knighted (KCB) in 1900, appointed to be a member of the Privy Council in 1902, became a Baronet in 1919 and was considered on several occasions for appointment as Under-Secretary. An obviously well-informed special correspondent of *The Times* wrote in December 1919 that 'by general admission, [he] stands out by his ability from all other permanently employed servants of the Crown in Ireland',[6] while Maurice Headlam, the Dublin-based Treasury Remembrancer from 1912 to 1920, also considered him to be outstanding among the heads of Dublin departments 'both in ability and in knowledge of Ireland and its problems'.[7]

Historians of early twentieth-century Ireland have depicted Robinson in various ways. For Virginia Crossman, he was typical of the imperial governing elite, his knowledge of Irish localities was unrivalled within the Dublin administration and he won the respect of some nationalist politicians.[8] R. B. McDowell noted his ironic good humour and saw him as 'a highly efficient civil servant, with thirty-five years' experience of Irish public life, whose absurdities he good-naturedly enjoyed',[9] while Cormac Ó Grada called him a 'reforming unionist'.[10] George Dangerfield saw him as 'a blank Tory, with a great deal of charm and even greater prestige',[11] Lawrence McBride noted that although he was a unionist, he was on good personal terms with many nationalists and catholic priests[12] but Mary Daly's overall conclusion was that he was 'unsympathetic to nationalists'.[13] Terence de Vere White described him as 'extremely able'[14] and Leon Ó Broin considered him to be 'perhaps the ablest official of them all',[15] although he was 'reputedly a unionist and unpopular with Irish nationalists' who alleged that he was 'slim' and a 'time-server'.[16] Ó Broin noted also that Robinson had 'a talent for mimicry and a story for every occasion' but Mary Daly classifies some of these stories as caricatures, demonstrating an attitude that was 'undoubtedly racist' and a belief in the racial inferiority of the native Irishman. Andrew Gailey notes that he was one of a small number of heads of Dublin departments who began under Gerald Balfour to assume a more general advisory role,[18] a conclusion which is consistent with the experience of Elizabeth, Countess of Fingall, who noted that Balfour, with whom she was very friendly, would always listen to Robinson.[19]

Augustine Birrell, only a few months after he had taken up duty as chief secretary in 1907, spoke in the House of Commons about the gloomy portals of Dublin Castle, which was 'switched off' from the current of national life and feeling ... no pulse of real life runs through the place.[20] By contrast, Robinson and his senior Custom House officials were widely known throughout Ireland. With his own regular travels throughout the country, his family connections and years of experience in the west of Ireland, a constant flow of reports from a network of personally-chosen inspectors based around the country, and information received from a regular stream of deputations of local officials and councillors as well as other visitors to the Custom House, Robinson was probably in a better position than any other Dublin official to brief chief secretaries and others on the situation in different parts of Ireland and on sensitive political issues, even those which should not have concerned him as a civil servant. He was certainly not switched off, as Birrell described those who served at the Castle, and can be seen to have compensated to some extent for the ineffective administration at the Castle for much of the 1900–22 period and the lack of good advice and perceptive assessment of current issues available to chief secretaries from Castle officials.

The Other Robinson

Robinson has been described as a worldly-wise man with a 'cynical affection for his political masters',[21] and he was also, according to Eunan O'Halpin, a man who 'never let his obligations as a civil servant get in the way of his political activities' and whose conduct as a bureaucrat 'deviated from the apolitical British norm'.[22] As has been said of some others, this more political Robinson stalks the index to many important studies of early twentieth-century Ireland, and there are numerous references to him in monographs and journal articles, in text and in footnotes. However – as is true of many of the others who governed or administered Ireland in the nineteenth and early twentieth centuries – no detailed study or overall assessment of the man and his career has been attempted, and the extent of his influence on Irish affairs has never been fully explored. His two volumes of memoirs are primarily concerned with local and often humorous incidents and are completely silent on matters such as his involvement in the Home Rule controversy; the determination of a possible north–south border; the conscription crisis; the various ineffectual administrative reform initiatives promoted by Lord French; the framing of the Government of Ireland Act 1920; and many others.

While he was never an advocate of any form of Home Rule, Robinson came to accept that it was inescapable and he was critical in early 1918 of the 'die-hard' group 'who haven't sense enough to see that some form of Home Rule or other is sooner or later inevitable' but were disposed to adhere to a policy that was 'dust and ashes ten years ago'.[23] From 1919 onwards he was primarily concerned to avert any solution which would entail complete separation from the Empire or any solution which involved partition. He was one of the few within the administration who recognised at an early stage the political strength of the Sinn Féin movement and was able accurately to predict the outcome of the December 1918 general election long before the votes were counted. As violent incidents began to be reported from around the country, he recognised that there were different factions in the movement that were still being referred to as Sinn Féin and he went further by arguing that de Valera and others whom he regarded as 'moderates' should be released from jail early in 1919 to facilitate negotiations and to ensure that the 'wild men' at local level were restrained. With Sir John Anderson, he advised the Cabinet in May 1921 that the time had come for a truce but the treaty agreed in December

1921 went too far: it appalled him because he saw it as a British surrender to the forces of disorder.[24]

Robinson – the man

There is relatively little material to draw on for information on Robinson's private and family life, apart from what is contained in the memoirs of Christopher, his eldest son who described him as 'a tall, thin, good-looking man with an extremely pleasant old-world courtesy towards women' who had a highly developed sense of humour and was well known as a *raconteur* of original Irish anecdotes. He was very fond of cricket, a good lawn tennis player and skater, a keen yachtsman, especially in his younger days at Westport, and a really fine water-colour artist, but disliked shooting and fishing, unlike so many of the LGB inspectors. He was 'a brilliant administrator' who had 'cunning methods of getting his own way and maintaining the independence of the LGB',[25] but Christopher's description of him as 'a strong true-blue Briton' is debatable: he sensed himself to be Irish and loved Ireland – and would not have seen himself to be less Irish simply because of his attachment to the Empire. But while there can be no doubt about his unionist status, he had little time for the unionists of Ulster: they should be ignored and 'let screech and yell till they were tired' was his advice to the chief secretary in 1912.[26]

Mrs Sidney (Beatrice) Webb, the social reformer and prolific writer who got to know Robinson well when they were both members of the 1906–09 Poor Law Commission, described him in her diary at the time as lively, astute and a consummate flatterer; she considered him:

> one of the most agreeable companions I have ever run across ... he is tall and thin, with a retreating forehead, large ears, straight dark hair, long foxy nose and somewhat foxy expression in his dark grey eyes. He has an agreeable and accomplished manner and a most pleasant faculty of mimicry and an endless flow of Irish stories. He knows his Ireland through and through, and looks at its life with kindly good sense. His enemies say he is 'slim' and a 'time-server'. So he is, but he has developed these qualities without a lack of uprightness, and with a measure of good intention ... He has the characteristics of all very clever officials; he seems indiscreet and is a monument of discretion.[27]

A somewhat similar portrayal is found in the memoirs of W. J. Braithwaite, who as a young Treasury assistant secretary worked with Robinson in 1911 on the drafting of the Irish clauses of the National Insurance Act. He found Robinson to be:

> A great character, very amusing and much given to flattery ... He belonged to the governing Irish type of aristocrats, one of the finest ever bred. He was President of the Irish Local Government Board and a regular Pooh-Bah in the offices which he held. He knew Ireland inside out, having had to watch the Irish county councils. And the tales which he could tell were endless. He was of the usual tall distinguished-looking Irish type. I enjoyed seeing a great deal of him.[28]

Describing 'The Higher Official' in *Irishmen All*, published in 1913, Rev. James Owen Hannay, Church of Ireland clergyman and prolific novelist, writing under his pseudonym George A. Birmingham, portrays an imaginary official named Bates whom he describes as a typical representative of the class of half a dozen higher officials who ran Ireland. In many respects, the man he describes could well be Henry Robinson – a man who is consulted frequently by chief secretaries ... who is sent for hurriedly and made to go to London ... [who] arranges and directs the great ballet of Government. Like Robinson, Bates was able to tell the most exquisitely amusing stories about the government of Ireland, with a note of well-bred cynicism in every story but still demonstrating a tolerant amusement of the absurdities of all political and social creeds. The fictional Bates knew Ireland intimately, instructed chief secretaries, was capable not only of administering but of governing with a steady eye to the general welfare, and 'generally speaking, ran Ireland'. Irish politics he found faintly amusing, slightly wearisome, but he remained an altruist at heart, with a splendidly high sense of duty and certain hopefulness about the ultimate destiny of Ireland.[29] It would be difficult to pen as good a description of Henry Augustus Robinson.

NOTES

1   Sir Henry Robinson, *Memories: Wise and Otherwise* (London, 1923).

2   Sir Henry Robinson, *Further Memories of Irish Life* (London, 1924).

3   Letter of 3 Nov. 1926 from Robinson to the Irish Grants Committee, Colonial Office, London, and application form dated 15 Nov. 1926, TNA, CO 762/32/24 No. 478.

4   Robinson, *Memories*, p.xi.

5   Ronan Fanning, *The Irish Department of Finance 1922–58* (Dublin, 1978), p.6.

6   Reprinted in *Irish Times*, 16 Dec. 1919.

7   Maurice Headlam, *Irish Reminiscences* (London, 1947) p.58.

8   Virginia Crossman, 'Local Government in Nineteenth-Century Ireland' in Terence McDonough (ed.), *Was Ireland a Colony?* (Dublin, 2005), p.112; *DIB*, vol. 8, p.536–37.

9   R. B. McDowell, *The Irish Convention 1917–18* (London, 1970), p.187.

10   Cormac Ó Grada, 'Foreword', in Ciara Breathnach (ed.), *Framing the West* (Dublin, 2007), p.xv.

11   George Dangerfield, *The Damnable Question* (London, 1976), p.282.

12   Lawrence W. McBride, *The Greening of Dublin Castle* (Washington, 1991), p.78.

13   Mary E. Daly, *The Buffer State* (Dublin, 1997), p.22.

14   Terence de Vere White, 'Mahaffy, the Anglo-Irish Ascendancy, and the Vice-Regal Lodge' in F. X. Martin OSA (ed.), *Leaders and Men of the Easter Rising: Dublin 1916* (London, 1967), p.22.

15   Leon Ó Broin, *Dublin Castle & the 1916 Rising* (London, 1966), p.16.

16   Leon Ó Broin, *The Chief Secretary* (Connecticut, 1970), pp.31–32.

17   Daly, *The Buffer State*, pp.32, 520.

18   Andrew Gailey, *Ireland and the Death of Kindness* (Cork, 1987), p.72.

19   Elizabeth, Countess of Fingall, *Seventy Years Young* (paperback edition, Dublin, 1991), pp.231–32.

20   *Hansard* IV, 174, 7 May 1907, 83.

21   D. G. Boyce and Cameron Hazlehurst, 'The unknown chief secretary: H. E. Duke and Ireland', *IHS* xx, no. 79 (Mar. 1977), p.289.

22   Eunan O'Halpin, *The Decline of the Union* (Dublin, 1987), pp.8, 61–2.

23   Robinson to Long, 14 Mar. 1918, WRO, Long Papers, WRO 947/332.

24   Robinson, *Grant Application, 1926*.

25   Sir Christopher Lynch-Robinson, *The Last of the Irish R.M.s* (London, 1951), pp.17–18, 28, 166.

26   Robinson to Birrell, 26 Jan. 1912, TNA, CO 906/18/1.

27   Beatrice Webb (eds Barbara Drake and Margaret I. Cole), *Our Partnership* (London, 1948), pp.404–10.

28   William J. Braithwaite (ed. Henry N. Bunbury), *Lloyd George's Ambulance Wagon* (London, 1957), pp.148, 150–52.

29   G. A. Birmingham, *Irishmen All* (London, 1913), pp.3–18.

PART I

ACTIVITIES WISE:
THE OFFICIAL ROBINSON

Born in 1857 into an Anglo-Irish protestant ascendancy family, many of whose members were military men or public servants, Henry Augustus Robinson became a temporary Local Government Board (LGB) inspector in 1879 when his father was Vice-President of that same board. He soon became the board's main expert on poor relief and distress in the west of Ireland and after his father retired in 1891, he was promoted to be a member of the board while continuing his close association with western relief schemes. Between March 1897 and April 1899 he worked closely with the Chief Secretary, Gerald Balfour, in planning and implementing the Local Government (Ireland) Act of 1898, which brought about a revolution in local government by sweeping away the old aristocratic and oligarchical local authorities and substituting a more popular and democratic system.

Chapters IV to VII deal with Robinson's subsequent work as Vice-President of the LGB in the relatively peaceful period before 1914, when politics mainly revolved around the activities of the moderate Irish Party; there are chapters dealing with his relationship with the new local councils, which were largely controlled by nationalists (Chapter IV); the growth in the range of functions for which both the board and these councils were responsible (Chapter V); and the concomitant growth by a factor of three in the size of the LGB itself, making it by far the largest Dublin-based bureaucracy, where political influence, religious discrimination and nepotism was alleged to be rife (Chapter VI). Finally, Chapter VII describes Robinson's successful efforts to maintain the LGB as an independent organisation that was not subject to officials at Dublin Castle, as well as his sometimes difficult relationship with lords-lieutenant and under-secretaries and, by contrast, his exceptionally close relationship with most chief secretaries, whether conservative or liberal.

CHAPTER I

Family Background and Early Career

Henry Augustus Robinson PC, KCB, 1st Baronet, was born in 1857 into a family whose financial resources were strictly limited but whose members had managed for generations to build successful careers in the public service in Ireland and in the Empire. As Mrs Sidney (Beatrice) Webb put it, he was bred for the public service, coming 'of an Irish garrison family that has produced a bevy of admirals, governors, and army officers of considerable distinction'.[1] As the son of an Anglo-Irish protestant ascendancy family, he was a typical example of a social class who simply had to find employment outside the landed order and who 'turned quite naturally to the state, its administrative system and its attendant patronage connections' as well as taking full advantage of the opportunities the Empire offered.[2] He made such good use of the possibilities his family position opened up for him that, less than twenty years after his entry to the public service, he was to become one of the most senior and best-known civil servants in the last decades of British rule in Ireland and a trusted adviser of successive chief secretaries.

The Early Robinsons

Within the family, the belief was that Robinson's stock was 'pure Dublin', although there is no trace of them before Christopher, a medical doctor, who was buried in St Audeon's Church in Dublin in 1688.[3] Christopher's son, Bryan, was Regius Professor of Physic at TCD until his death in 1754, while Bryan's son, another Christopher, was a prominent judge of the King's Bench Division from 1758 until his death in 1787, when his large library of valuable early printed books was sold by auction. In turn, that Christopher's only surviving son, Rev. Christopher Robinson MA, became rector of Granard, County Longford, and with his wife Elizabeth, daughter of Sir Hercules Langrishe Bart., of Knocktopher, County Kilkenny, had a large family; one of their sons – later Sir Bryan Robinson (1808–87) – became a prominent judge in Canada while another son, Hercules, was to be the grandfather of Henry Augustus.

Born in 1789, Hercules joined the navy in 1800 when he was only 11 years old, fought as a midshipman at Trafalgar in 1805 and was promoted to captain in 1814. After his last ship was paid off in 1819–20 he devoted himself to what he described as the pursuits and politics of a country gentleman near Delvin, County Westmeath, where his wife – Frances Elizabeth Wood, the only child of Henry Widman Wood, whom he had married in 1822 – had inherited Rosmead House and its modest estate. He served as a magistrate for some years and was Deputy Lieutenant and High Sheriff of the county in 1842. After the estate steward was murdered 'in a most savage manner' in March 1849,[4] the senior Robinsons left Rosmead and went to live near Portsmouth, after which the house and lands were sold under the Encumbered Estates Acts.[5] According to Hercules, the estate had been valued at £128,000, exclusive of the woodlands and the house (built in the early 1700s at a cost of £10,000), but the entire estate was sold for a total of £74,000. As he described it himself in his reminiscences, *Sea Drift* (1858),[6] his estate was 'buried under a shower of parliamentary lava' just as the town of Herculaneum had been lost along with Pompeii when Vesuvius erupted in AD 79.

Hercules and his wife had one daughter and six sons, the eldest of whom, Henry, is dealt with below. Hercules George Robert (1824–97) became a successful colonial governor and was created Baron Rosmead in 1896; Loftus Christopher Hawker (1826–96) became a captain in the Royal Navy; Widman, born in 1828, died in infancy while nothing is known of Frances Elizabeth, who was born c. 1832; Sir William Cleaver Francis (1834–97) was a colonial governor until 1895; and Frederick Charles Bryan (1836–96) ended his career as a vice-admiral in the Royal Navy.[7] Although his own sea-going days were long over, Hercules was promoted to rear-admiral in 1849, vice-admiral in 1856 and admiral in 1862. He died at Portsmouth on 15 May 1864, leaving effects valued at less than £100.

The First Sir Henry

Unlike his brothers who built successful careers in the navy and the colonial service, Henry, the eldest son of Hercules Robinson, born on

13 April 1823, opted to remain in Ireland, hoping perhaps to inherit Rosmead before its forced sale in 1849. He served for a few years as adjutant of the local militia and during the Famine was engaged as an inspector under the Relief Commission, possibly through the influence of Lord Valentia, his future father-in-law, who had already arranged the appointment of Robinson's brother, Hercules, to supervise relief works in County Kildare. From February 1848 onwards he was employed by the Poor Law Commissioners as a temporary poor law inspector, serving initially in Cashel union where over 10,000 people were in receipt of outdoor relief, and also serving occasionally as a vice-guardian where boards of guardians had been dissolved. The large team of temporary inspectors was reduced in 1849 and again in 1850, but Robinson managed to retain his post. By the end of 1852, when the transition from outdoor to indoor relief was complete, most of the temporary inspectors had been let go but seven of them, including Robinson, were added to the permanent staff, bringing the total number of inspectors to sixteen, each with a district comprising from six to eighteen unions.[8] With the addition of five medical inspectors appointed under the Medical Charities Act 1851, the total inspectorate then numbered twenty-one. At management level, the organisation also changed after some years of experimentation, during which supervision of the poor law system was first exercised by a London-based body operating through officials based in Ireland, and then by a separate Irish Poor Law Commission comprising one full-time chief commissioner and two *ex-officio* members – the chief secretary and the under-secretary. The 1851 Act made provision for the appointment of two additional full-time commissioners, one of whom was to be a physician or surgeon of ten years standing, thus creating a five-member board. One of the full-time commissioners, designated Vice-President, became the dominant figure in the organisation after it had been transformed into the Local Government Board for Ireland (LGB) in September 1872.

In his position as poor law inspector, Henry Robinson was based initially in Limerick and then in the northern district before moving to a district based on Dublin. Having survived the retrenchment of the mid-1850s, when inspectors of greater experience and longer service were dismissed as an economy measure, he was still serving in Dublin when the LGB replaced the Poor Law Commissioners. At that stage, he and the other members of the permanent staff transferred to the new organisation while the three full-time members of the commission were appointed to the corresponding offices in the board: Sir Alfred Power became Vice-President, continuing to receive the salary of £2,000, which he had enjoyed since 1851; John MacDonnell became Medical

Commissioner with a salary of £1,200 a year; and Richard M. Bellew filled the third position with the same salary. In 1876, Robinson moved to the Chief Secretary's Office at Dublin Castle when he was appointed to a newly-created post of Assistant Under-Secretary for Ireland with a salary of £1,200 a year, supporting Thomas Henry Burke, who had been Under-Secretary since 1869. When he returned to the LGB as Vice-President on 6 May 1879, following the retirement of Power, Mitchell Henry MP criticised the 'scandalous haste' with which the appointment had been made – not, apparently, because he had any particular objection to Robinson himself but because he believed that the opportunity might have been availed of to appoint a member of the government to chair both the LGB and the OPW and represent them in Parliament, as had been suggested in 1878 in the report of the Chrichton Committee, of which Mitchell Henry had been a member.[9]

With Robinson's appointment as Vice-President, the three full-time members of the board were, for the first time, all Irish-born, and this continued to be the case until 1922. After almost fifteen years in office, Bellew (a member of a prominent County Louth catholic family who had resigned his seat in Parliament in 1856 to take up the commissioner position) died in January 1880, having done nothing 'but sign formal documents and draw his salary' according to E.D. Gray MP.[10] The vacancy was filled by the appointment on 12 April of George Morris who, like Bellew, was a member of a prominent catholic family, and had been elected Home Rule MP for Galway County at a by-election in 1867 and again in 1874. The Medical Commissioner, Dr Charles Croker-King, who had replaced MacDonnell in 1876, died in office in February 1888 and was succeeded by Frederick F. X. MacCabe, a catholic, son of a Dublin journalist, and who – like his two predecessors – was well qualified and experienced in medicine and was willing to forego other relatively high-profile positions in the medical world to join the board. He was knighted in 1892, an honour which neither of his medical predecessors had gained.

Robinson's term of office as Vice-President was a difficult one. For the first few years, and at intervals after that, he and his board had to cope with demands for relief measures to cater for exceptional distress in western areas. In addition, the growing numbers of nationalist poor law guardians created problems and, especially after the appointment of Arthur Balfour as Chief Secretary in 1887, there was continuous pressure on the board to take hard-line action in relation to guardians whose activities and campaigns irritated the authorities at Dublin Castle. The non-interventionist approach of the board to low-level political activity by guardians provoked considerable frustration in the Chief Secretary's Office, leading Balfour to tell Robinson that changes in the board's operating procedures were necessary and that the Under-Secretary should be consulted on all matters which might touch on politics or general administration.[11] Pressure from Balfour and his Under-Secretary forced the board between 1887 and 1890 to dissolve no less than eight boards of guardians and to issue serious warnings to nineteen others.[12]

At a meeting in September 1890 at Balfour's Scottish family home at Whittingehame, to which Robinson had been summoned to discuss failure of the potato crop in the west of Ireland, one of the participants described him as 'an old man in a very precarious state of health'.[13] The *Irish Times* reported in the following month[14] that the Vice-President had been taken suddenly ill at his residence at 55 Lansdowne Road, Dublin, where he had lived since 1882 and that his son, Henry Augustus, was also ill with typhoid fever.[15] Having been appointed CB in April 1880 and knighted, KCB, in 1886, Robinson senior resigned with effect from 1 March 1891 after the '65 rule' had come into effect in his case and was awarded a pension of £1,333 a year, two-thirds of his salary, in recognition of what the Treasury described as the eminent services he had rendered to the Government during an official career of more than forty-three years and the loss which the public service would sustain by his retirement from a department which he had directed with so much advantage to the State since 1879.[16] He died on 23 March 1893 and was buried at Dublin's Mount Jerome cemetery, where the inscription on his modest headstone declares that 'the memory of the just is blessed'.

In 1853 Robinson had married Eva, daughter of Arthur Annesley, 10th Viscount Valentia, seven years after Eva's twin sister, Nea (Ada), had married his younger brother Hercules, later Baron Rosmead. The couple had three sons, Hercules Francis Annesley (1853–1900); Henry Augustus, born on 20 November 1857; and Sydney Loftus, born in 1860 and mortally wounded at the battle of Magersfontein in South Africa on 11 December 1899, while serving as a major with the Argyll and Sutherland Highlanders. In 1882, the couple's only daughter, Eva Eleanora (born on 19 December 1858), married Joseph Hone (1850–1908) of Roebuck Grove, County Dublin, a businessman, director of the Bank of Ireland since 1883, Governor, 1892–94, and a relative of Nathaniel Hone RHA. Eva Eleanora died on 25 April 1894, a few days after giving birth to a fourth daughter, Eva Sydney (Evie) Hone (1894–1955), the distinguished painter and stained-glass artist. Eva Robinson, mother of Henry Augustus, and grandmother of Evie Hone, died on 30 June 1894.

Henry Augustus – First Appointments

Born in or around Belfast while his father was serving as LGB inspector for the northern district, nothing has emerged about any formal primary or second-level education of Henry Augustus Robinson and, unlike many of those who were later to become his contemporaries in the top levels of the Irish civil service, he never acquired a third-level qualification.[17] It was only by mischance that the navy was not his own profession, he wrote in 1924, going on to add that he was very sorry that circumstances (which he did not specify) had prevented such a career, as naval traditions were strong in the family.[18] Earning up to £800 a year in the 1870s as a permanent inspector, his father could certainly have afforded to send young Henry to one of the better schools or to TCD or one of the English universities but, instead of that, having studied 'to read up for the home civil service', Henry was sent at the age of 17 to work (initially, unpaid) in the office of a large merchant in the city of London.[19] After some two years, the firm made heavy losses and, realising that 'without capital or family connexion with merchants, the City was no place for the likes of me', he returned to Ireland in 1876 with a view to resuming studies for the upper division civil service examinations. His father had by then become Assistant Under-Secretary at Dublin Castle, working with T. H. Burke, who was to be assassinated three years later. It was Burke who arranged for the young Robinson's appointment to replace the ineffective secretary to a three-man commission of enquiry, which had been set up in August 1876 to establish the facts regarding the properties, revenue and expenditure of 110 municipal towns in Ireland. Having taken oral evidence in more than fifty of the main towns, the commission completed detailed reports on each of the towns as well as a number of general reports between February and July 1877.[20]

Still only 20 years old, Robinson moved on smoothly to become secretary to another commission, which was appointed in July 1877 to inquire into the number of poor law unions and workhouses in Ireland, with particular reference to the possibility of amalgamating unions and closing workhouses, the need for additional accommodation for the sick poor, and the possible diversion of unused workhouse accommodation to cater for some categories of lunatics. Having visited every one of the 163 unions in the country and consulted widely, the commissioners completed their report and presented it to Parliament in February 1879. They recorded their debt to Robinson for the zealous and efficient manner in which he had discharged his duties and noted the great labour he had devoted to the preparation of statistical returns.[21]

In October 1878 Robinson was appointed as secretary to a third commission – the Municipal Boundaries Commission – which was charged with the task of reviewing the boundaries of Irish cities and municipal towns. When one of the commissioners resigned in February 1879 to take up a position as a member of the General Prisons Board, Robinson – who was still only 22 years old – was promoted to replace him, his experience and ability winning for him due recognition at the hands of the government, according to the *Irish Times*.[22] After the death of the commission's Chairman, William Exham QC, in November 1881, it was left to Robinson and the remaining commissioner, Charles P. Cotton CE, to complete the work in June 1882.[23] The reports of the commissioners' visits of inspection to 113 towns, many of them prepared and signed by Robinson, provide a valuable body of information on the condition of the towns and of local services immediately before major investment in sanitary services and public housing began in most of them.[24] Significantly, too, Robinson's involvement in the work of the three commissions between 1876 and 1882 provided the foundation for the unparalleled body of knowledge of every town and poor law union in Ireland for which he was to become well known in later years and the understanding he developed of the attitudes and activities of local officials and of the different categories of local representatives.

Temporary Inspector in Distressed Unions

While still engaged in winding up his work on municipal boundaries, and by what he described as an extraordinary coincidence, Robinson entered the service of the LGB as a temporary inspector, just as his father had done more than thirty years earlier. A third year of bad weather in 1879, coupled with a poor potato harvest and falling livestock prices, had created serious subsistence problems in parts of Connacht where there were high population densities and numerous small holdings, leading to rent defaults and threats of eviction. At first, the demand for relief was thought in official circles to be no more than a move in the political agitation which followed the establishment of the Land League by Michael Davitt in October that year. Harrowing stories of distress were believed to be untrustworthy and like most others, Robinson assumed that newspaper reports of the crisis were grossly exaggerated. Late that year, however, on a private weekend visit to Recess, County Galway (which was afterwards to become his favourite holiday retreat), he was taken by a young priest to a mountain village where he was appalled to find starving people – 'living skeletons ... scarcely able to crawl ... and not a house with any food in it'. A letter reporting this experience, which he sent to Under-Secretary Burke, led directly to his appointment in December 1879, notwithstanding the reservations of his father (who had become Vice-President of the LGB a few months earlier) as one of three additional temporary inspectors assigned to relief work in connection with what the board then recognised as exceptional distress. This was the first occasion on which the authorities decided to concentrate efforts in particular areas where it was accepted that the resources of the unions could not be expected to cope with the problem. The inspectors' duties, as Robinson put it, were to supervise relief administration, to attend meetings of guardians, to act as the eyes and ears of the government, and to investigate and report upon all matters upon which the LGB required information.[25] With his new colleagues he was required to report regularly on conditions in each of the unions for which he was responsible; extracts from these reports, published in an appendix to the board's annual report for 1879–80, provide valuable first-hand accounts of living conditions in the different districts.[26]

In relation to the union of Clifden, the first of Robinson's reports dated 17 December advised that actual distress did not then exist although English newspapermen who had visited the area and were not familiar with the normal condition of the people were likely to report otherwise. However, a large section of the population would certainly be in very straitened circumstances in the coming spring. The union was 'the theatre of almost daily acts of violence', no rent was being paid even by those who could afford it, and landlords were being subjected to every kind of intimidation and to overt acts of defiance. Following a visit to Oughterard union at the end of January, he reported that the extreme poverty of the people in parts of the parish of Rosmuck was 'a lamentable illustration of how people can live with no visible means of subsistence'. A large section of the population was in actual want, he reported, for potatoes would not grow in rocks no matter how prosperous the season may be, they had few boats and so few could speak English that they could not avail of employment opportunities at the harvest in England. In cases like this, he concluded, it is 'difficult to devise any means that will prove effectual in permanently ameliorating the circumstances of the people' – relief work might be inaugurated, potato seed might be made available and rent arrears might be wiped out, but these measures could never enable the people of the area to live through any year without outside assistance.

In some of the Mayo unions, Robinson's reports suggested that there were few signs of actual want and insisted that there was no foundation whatever for rumours which had gained credence in Ballina concerning hardship and privation. While there was likely to be a considerable amount of distress within a few months, he argued that there was a wide difference between 'distress' and 'famine', and the situation would not be as alarming as the visions being conjured up by local agitators would lead one to believe. Belmullet was a special case, however: because of outbreaks of disease among pigs and fowl it deserved 'an unfortunate prominence in the category of distressed unions and the future left much to be feared'. In Castlebar union, on the other hand, the tenant-farmers were better off, so much so that he found it necessary to defend them against allegations that extravagance in dress was causing insolvency among them: if in the course of time 'they make an effort to rise out of their normal state of rags and squalor, it should rather be accepted as an index of the advancement of civilisation than as an illustration of unfortunate improvidence'. Further north in Killala, a great deal of poverty was to be expected between February and the end of July, and in Newport the powers of endurance of the population would be put to the test towards the end of February, although many were so inured to hardship that short of actual starvation there was nothing they could not endure. The situation in the district was particularly bad, he reported, because while it had been the practice for members of each family to go to work in England or Scotland for the harvest each year, returning with sufficient earnings to maintain the family during the winter, many of the men had found it difficult to obtain any employment of the kind in 1879. Besides, he had established that receipts from relatives in America that year bore no comparison with the remittances of previous years.

Presumably because he was so much younger and more active than the established inspectors, Robinson was commissioned in 1880 to prepare a special report on some twenty islands off the Galway–Mayo coast to which he was ferried by the gun-boat HMS *Goshawk* in rough weather between 10 and 24 February. His lengthy report graphically described the living conditions on the islands: on one of them he noted the 'piles of mud and stones', which people called their homes; on another, the houses were 'mostly deep holes dug in the sand', roofed but without windows; while another island was distinguished by the filth of the cabins – built of turf and sods, with scarcely head-room for the cow, they stood in a lake of filth and access except on all-fours was almost impossible. It was useless to argue, in his view, that the thick population of some of the islands could ever eke out an existence from the barren rocks, and he was sad to think of the number of children that were growing up to a life of such degrading poverty and squalor. He concluded that 'there is but one remedy – education – and it must lead to the only hope for the people – emigration,' a view shared by James Hack Tuke, the English Quaker philanthropist noted for his charitable work in the west of Ireland since the Famine.

Relief Schemes 1880–82

Robinson was heavily involved from 1880 onwards in the administration of relief measures funded by boards of guardians, the government and voluntary agencies in the areas where exceptional distress existed. Emergency legislation had allowed outdoor relief to be provided on a temporary basis in these areas, even to able-bodied persons, but subject to a requirement that those receiving relief by way of food or fuel should work for not less than eight hours each day, generally breaking stones for the roads. In addition, government loans were available to enable guardians to provide supplies of seed potatoes and seed oats, and to enable grand juries to finance work on roads, bridges and other infrastructure. Robinson's memoirs record that he saw a great deal of the more compassionate side of the Chief Secretary, William E. ('Buckshot') Forster, during these years 'as the west was the storm centre of the land agitation … and Forster was torn to pieces with the stories of evictions and distress and other miseries' which the people underwent.[27] On one occasion in 1881 Forster gave Robinson a personal cheque for £1,000 to buy seed potatoes for distribution in the Blacksod area of County Mayo, but with instructions not to disclose the source of the funds. A few weeks later, Forster's adopted daughter, Florence, recorded the pleasure it was for the Chief Secretary to read a report from Robinson about the reception of the 'seed potato gift' by the local population.[28]

A memoir of J. H. Tuke described Robinson in 1881 as one of his 'zealous collaborators' although he was apt to relieve the 'sad and wearisome' relief work by touches of humour.[29] In October that year, Florence Arnold-Forster recorded a visit by Tuke to the Chief Secretary's lodge, during which he presented a graphic picture of the state of society in the desolate regions of Mayo, having driven over 300 miles through the country on an outside car with Robinson, 'the popular poor-law inspector', who dined at the lodge the following month before going to a concert at the Vice-Regal Lodge.[30] Tuke himself, writing to his daughters from Connemara in February 1882, told them that it was delightful to see Robinson's 'kindness and desire to help these poor people'– families who had been evicted for non-payment of rent and who were then living in wretched conditions by the roadside.[31] Robinson in turn was most impressed in 1883 by the prompt and effective action of Tuke's committee in facilitating the emigration (part-funded by the government) of about

1,500 families from his Mayo district: the removal of such a large number of people was an immediate relief to the ratepayers of the unions involved because the emigrants were nearly all of a class who were overwhelmed with debt and without food, or the means of procuring it.

Sympathy for the condition of the people of particular districts and a genuine appreciation of the difficulty experienced in surviving in more remote areas without outside assistance is evident in many of Robinson's early reports, but so too are opinions and attitudes which remained with him for decades after his first experience of the West: criticism of local agitation and of exaggeration in press reports, a belief in the futility of relief measures as a solution to the underlying causes of poverty and distress in particular areas, and insistence on the need, in considering the case for relief measures, to maintain a distinction between distress and starvation. This distinction was essentially a development of the argument made in 1879 by the Poor Law Union and Lunacy Inquiry Commission (of which he had been secretary) that confounding destitution with poverty – legal relief with charity – 'is at the root ... of the maladministration of all poor laws, acting as an encouragement to imposture'.[32] And thirty years after what the Royal Commission on the Poor Laws described as the memorable winter of 1879–80, Robinson – as a member of that commission and co-author of its 1909 report on Ireland – had an opportunity of reiterating his hard-line views on relief administration: the report lamented the fact that the government had authorised outdoor relief to all destitute persons in the western unions and implemented measures wholly at variance with the first principles of the poor law as to eligibility for support at the public expense. It had 'bowed its head to the storm', after charitable organisations had 'spread the tale of suffering and misery to the ends of the earth'.[33]

Permanent Inspector, 1882–1890

Given that he was personally well known to the Chief Secretary and that his father was then serving as Vice-President of the LGB, it was hardly surprising that Robinson became a member of the permanent staff of inspectors in 1882 when he was only 24 years old. With a salary rising to the handsome figure of £800 after fifteen years, he continued to be based for some years at Westport and to have responsibility for counties Galway and Mayo, including the islands. But while he witnessed scenes of real poverty and distress in the mid-1880s, he continued to hold a cynical view of some of the efforts made by the local people and their supporters, including the priests, to persuade the government that famine conditions existed and that relief works should be instituted. His reports and advice arising from his experience in Mayo, Connemara and the islands in the 1880s were influential in convincing the authorities in Dublin to resist demands for the continuation of exceptional relief measures – and on a very different level, this experience provided colourful material for the two volumes of memoirs, which he published forty years later.

Although the LGB had been confident enough to report with much satisfaction in April 1882 that the ordinary relief arrangements had been sufficient during the past winter and that there was no longer a need for special temporary measures, demands for relief works in some areas were again being made by the end of the year.[34] At a conference in Dublin attended by the Lord Lieutenant, Chief Secretary, Under-Secretary, Vice-President of the LGB (Robinson's father) and Robinson himself, he supported the view that the normal system of poor relief should continue to be relied on[35] and, with his father, argued strongly that special measures such as those which had operated in the previous few years encouraged demoralisation and jobbery.[36] Lord Lieutenant Spencer accepted this advice and a circular, which issued from the Castle on 9 December, firmly stated the government's determination to rely solely on the administration of relief through the boards of guardians, effectively by means of the workhouses, noting that persons who were unable to procure for themselves the necessaries of life should not 'be allowed to determine the manner in which public relief is to be afforded'. The circular firmly rejected proposals for the establishment of relief works, because these were 'not only extravagant and demoralising in their effects but ... often fail to aid the most necessitous'.[37] In his memoirs, Robinson noted that the announcement of this new hard-line policy caused tremendous uproar at the time and accepted that, harsh though it seemed to be, it was his own advice on the issue that had had been most influential.[38] However, this effort to recover lost ground was not followed up and the workhouse test was never afterwards rigidly enforced, even in times of exceptional distress.

Robinson was transferred to the Dublin district towards the end of 1885 but continued to be regularly involved in dealing with reports of distress in parts of the west and to be called on to advise on how the authorities should respond. In November 1886, when it was alleged that there had been abuse in the administration by boards of guardians of funds made available for an outdoor relief scheme in six western unions, he was appointed, with another inspector, to report on the administration of the scheme.[39] The two men found that expenditure had been extravagant and careless, far exceeding the grants available, and leaving the guardians with heavy liabilities, which had to be met from borrowings and repaid over a number of years – a wholesome lesson, according to Robinson of what may follow corrupt administration.[40]

Commissioner 1891–98

Following the retirement of Robinson's father from the Vice-Presidency in March 1891, George Morris, junior commissioner since 1880, was promoted to replace him and Henry Augustus, then aged 33, was selected by Arthur Balfour to fill the consequential vacancy at commissioner level. He had been the senior inspector, except for a man who was nearly 70-years-of-age and just about to retire. According to Tim Healy MP, nobody imagined that Morris did 5,000 half-pennies worth of work for his large salary as commissioner in the 1880s,[41] and it seems that when he became Vice-President, he left much of the work (particularly work relating to the relief of distress) to the energetic new junior commissioner who recorded years later that because he was 'very slow and deliberate in his thoughts', Morris dreaded having to meet Balfour.[42]

Legislation enacted in the twenty years before Robinson became a commissioner had significantly extended the powers and functions of the poor law guardians to embrace matters such as housing, water and sewerage, and other public health and environmental services. There had also been a corresponding expansion in the supervisory and other powers of the LGB. However, the primary concern of the organisation in the 1890s was still the proper administration of the poor relief acts. At that stage the board had no responsibilities in relation to the grand juries and their functions, including roads and bridges, and Robinson personally was criticised in the House of Lords by the Marquess of Londonderry in 1898 for his lack of knowledge of the grand jury system: in giving evidence on the subject before a recent Royal Commission, Londonderry charged that 'he did not know this and he did not know that' and time after time, when he was asked a question or invited to give his opinion his answer was 'I have no knowledge'.[43]

In practice, Robinson continued throughout the 1890s to be heavily involved in dealing with distress in the west, often taking it on himself to manage particular situations and to tour areas where demands for relief operations were arising. Towards the end of February 1898, for example, when an LGB inspector and the local relieving officer who were marooned on Tory Island because of a heavy gale wired the board that the people had nearly run out of food, he took it on himself late in the day, with the glass still falling and no gunboat within reasonable distance of the island, to authorise the charter of a steamer to start out from Derry at daybreak with five tons of meal; 'I hope it won't turn out a flat calm when the steamer starts' he wryly concluded in a report to Gerald Balfour on the incident.[44] Again, in April 1898, a week after Easter, he reported that he had made a careful inspection of the Belmullet and Carraroe areas, where relief measures were operating satisfactorily; he had personally met the relieving officers and had told them that whenever they had any concern about eligibility, they should give the applicant the benefit of the doubt pending further enquiries.[45] By and large, however, the attitudes, which he had formed years earlier, continued to inform his approach to relief operations in the 1890s. He was critical of some of the representatives of philanthropic bodies and of newspaper correspondents, particularly those from England. In April 1898, he told Balfour that it was again the old story:

> ... the personally conducted visits of philanthropic Englishmen to 'show houses' – the abominable lying, and the absence of any shame when misrepresentations are exposed – the neglect of the ordinary work – the well-to-do begging and cringing for a share in the spoil – the record Easter collections in the churches, the envy, rivalry and ill-feeling engendered, the complete loss of independence and self-respect – the same wretched sordid business of the Duchess of Marlborough's fund all over again.[46]

He occasionally had cause also to complain about Irish publications; he was acutely offended by an 'absurd, shrieking sensational' article in the *Irish Field*, which wilfully misrepresented the situation in Oughterard union in February 1898 – and to make matters worse, the article was written by the then owner of the periodical, Lt Col Freddie MacCabe, a qualified doctor, who was a son of the LGB medical commissioner, Sir Francis MacCabe.[47]

Another source of regular complaint by Robinson (and of occasional amusement) were those members of the Catholic clergy who, as he saw it, brought undue pressure to bear on guardians in relation to relief works. In February 1898, he told Balfour that the competition for funds in the distressed districts was providing 'some very ornate language from PPs and CCs in the daily press' and that one old priest had written to say that his parishioners were 'subsisting entirely without food'.[48] A few months later, when telling Balfour about a Father Lavelle's system of securing a good Easter collection, he warned that there should be no mention of this in the House of Commons because 'on all religious subjects the people are so thin-skinned that their feelings would be desperately shocked at any illusion (sic) in the House to the villainy of their CC though they wouldn't mind blackguarding him privately'.[49] By 1899 he held such strong views on the subject of priests and their methods of increasing their incomes that he objected to a proposal being considered that year to allow guardians to pay old age pensions because priests would promote the scheme as a means of ensuring that Christmas and Easter offerings of reasonable amount were promptly paid. In fact, he claimed 'there are many who see in the application of an old age pension system to the congested districts nothing beyond a proposal to largely endow the catholic clergy from public funds'.[50]

Robinson was not, of course, the only official who took the view that distress could often be exploited for political or other inappropriate reasons: in December 1897, for example, Sir David Harrel, who had been under-secretary since 1893, told Balfour that 'distress is being run in the West on political lines for all it is worth' so that when measures which had already been decided on to deal with distress in the financially embarrassed unions were announced, the public would be led to believe that they were the outcome of the agitation and not a voluntary exercise of policy.[51] On that occasion, Robinson followed up by spelling out the instructions he proposed to give to his inspectors who were dealing with the unions that were in difficulty and the assurances about government financial assistance which the inspectors were empowered to give. He was irritated by John Dillon's 'vapourings' in the West about the apathy of the government, but on balance, he agreed with Harrel's view that 'we should show our hands forthwith and get credit, early, for our good intentions'.[52]

Virginia Crossman's study of poor law administration in late nineteenth-century Ireland suggests that after Gerald Balfour became Chief Secretary in July 1895, the relationship between the Chief Secretary's Office and the LGB became closer and more harmonious than it had been ... due partly to ideological and partly to personal factors.[53] The surviving correspondence between Balfour and Robinson fully supports this conclusion and suggests that even before his promotion to the Vice-Presidency in 1898 Robinson was not only relied on by Balfour as the board's expert on emergency relief but had also begun to offer comments, advice and feedback on matters well outside the area of responsibility of the LGB. In August 1896, for example, he told Balfour that everything he had heard from the board's inspectors indicated that his success in carrying the Land Act through 'in the face of the powerful combination of forces opposed to it has made a deep impression on the people ... the moral effect of such a triumph will show itself and strengthen your hand in the government of the country'.[54] Together, Robinson and Balfour devised a poor relief bill, which would have achieved a modest modernisation of the system and would have allowed for the amalgamation of unions, but this was dropped in 1898 when parliamentary time had to be made available for the Local Government (Ireland) Bill.[55] More importantly, Robinson was probably instrumental in ensuring the announcement by Balfour in the House of Commons in February 1898 of a policy change designed to bring to an end the annual 'frantic appeals to the government to start relief works at the government's expense' and the extreme demoralization created by this state of things.[56] The new policy was challenged in an adjournment debate initiated by John Dillon on 22 April during which Balfour, as he put it himself, had been charged with being callous and hard-hearted and wanting in sympathy.[57] Robinson, however, wrote to congratulate him on his 'firm stand against wholesale jobbery and demoralization'; he believed that the debate had cleared the air and would strengthen the position of the government materially, although the Irish members had been knowingly and persistently lying in a barefaced manner in the hope of bullying the chief secretary into conceding their demands.[58] Even if all of this may have been fair comment on that particular debate, it was hardly the kind of language that a non-political civil servant might have been expected to use.

The new policy was heavily criticised by nationalist and other MPs. Dillon argued (with some justification) that it was designed to transfer much of the responsibility for initiating measures to relieve exceptional distress (and much of the expense) from the authorities in Dublin to the guardians and the new county councils while Edward Carson opposed it as a 'most mischievous' provision because of the risk that impossibly heavy rates on occupiers in distressed areas would result in the reimposition of rates on landowners.[59] However, notwithstanding the devolution policy, Robinson's own hands-on involvement in dealing with distressed areas continued: in June 1898 he reported to Balfour on visits to Westport and other distressed districts, which he found to be overrun with English newspaper correspondents and gullible philanthropists. He had interviewed the PPs and the Catholic Archbishop, who happened to be at Mulrany, and had succeeded in persuading the guardians to postpone any decision to stop the relief works for three weeks. He was happy also that the relieving officers were acting reasonably: they were willing to place men with as many as five head of cattle on the works if they were heavily in debt, and he had advised them that they should not take quite so severe a view in determining eligibility as they would in a year of general prosperity.[60]

Created CB in the diamond jubilee honours in June 1897, Robinson had been working closely with Balfour throughout that year on local government reform and a strong mutual respect had clearly developed between the two men as Crossman described it.[61] With his father, he had dominated the LGB during the 1880s and 1890s when the two men steered the board through some very choppy political waters and 'despite facing some formidable obstacles in the shape of guardians chaffing at central interference on the one hand and ministers seeking more effective means of control over local boards on the other, they succeeded in maintaining a relatively steady course'.[62] Henry Augustus was therefore the obvious choice to succeed Morris as Vice-President when the latter reached retirement age.

NOTES

1 Beatrice Webb (eds Barbara Drake and Margaret I. Cole), *Our Partnership* (London, 1948), p.408.

2 D. M. Schreuder, 'Ireland and the expertise of imperial administration: Hercules Robinson, the Irish Fairs and Markets Commission (1853), and the making of a Victorian Proconsul' in Roy MacLeod (ed.), *Government and Expertise: specialists, administrators and professionals 1860–1919* (Cambridge, 1988), pp.145–165.

3 Sir Christopher Lynch-Robinson, *The Last of the Irish R.M.s* (London, 1951), p.18; there are DIB and ODNB entries for Bryan Robinson and Christopher Robinson, there is an ODNB entry for Sir Bryan Robinson and a DIB entry for Robert Robinson (c.1713–1770), lecturer in anatomy at TCD and State physician.

4 *Westmeath Guardian*, 29 Mar. 1849.

5 Rosmead has been in ruins since the 1940s but the attractive arched gateway which served the house and demesne still stood in 2012.

6 *Sea Drift*, published privately in London (1858) contains Robinson's reminiscences, snippets of family history, and an image of the author.

7 There are ODNB entries for Hercules and his sons Hercules George Robert and William Cleaver, and a DIB entry for Hercules George Robert.

8 *Sixth annual report of the Poor Law Commissioners* 1852–53, p.16.

9 *Hansard* III, 245, 5 May 1879, 1708; *Report of the committee appointed to inquire into the Board of Works, Ireland*, HC 1878 [C. 2060].

10 *Hansard* III, 248, 28 July 1879, 1430–32.

11 Virginia Crossman, *Politics, Pauperism and Power in Late Nineteenth-Century Ireland* (Manchester, 2006), pp. 59–61; A. J. Balfour to Henry Robinson, 25 May 1889, Balfour Papers, BL Add. MS 49828, f. 27.

12 *Return of the Boards of Poor Law Guardians in Ireland dissolved or warned*, HC 1892 (298).

13 William Henry Joyce, diary, quoted in Leon Ó Broin, *The Prime Informer* (London, 1971), p.101.

14 *Irish Times*, 25 Oct. 1890.

15 The Robinson residence was one of a terrace of houses dating from the 1860s, eight of which have been interconnected to form the *Sandymount Hotel* (formerly the *Mount Herbert*).

16 *Copies of Correspondence between the Irish Government and the Treasury relating to the superannuation of Sir Henry Robinson, KCB*, HC 1890–91 [c.6362].

17 Robinson gave Belfast (amended to County Antrim) as his birthplace in his 1901 census return and County Down in the 1911 return; a search of available databases has failed to locate a baptismal record.

18 Sir Henry Robinson, *Further Memories of Irish Life* (London, 1924), p.121.

19 Sir Henry Robinson, *Memories: Wise and Otherwise* (London, 1923), p.7.

20 *Local Government and Taxation of Towns Inquiry Commission (Ireland)*, HC 1877 [C.1696], [C.1755], [C.1787], [C.1787.1].

21 *Poor Law Union and Lunacy Inquiry Commission (Ireland)*, HC 1879 [C. 2239].

22 *Irish Times*, 1 July 1879.

23 In 1879, Cotton became the first LGB engineering inspector and served as chief engineering inspector until his retirement in 1898.

24 *Municipal Boundaries Commission (Ireland)*, HC 1880 [C. 2725]; HC 1881 [C.2827], [C.3089], [C.3089.I], [C.3089.II].

25 Robinson, *Memories*, pp.9–12 and 22.

26 *AR*, 1879–80, Appendix, pp.114–138; see also CSORP, 1880/13676.

27 Robinson, *Memories*, pp.28–29.

28 Moody, T. W. and Richard Hawkins (eds), *Florence Arnold-Forster's Irish Journal* (Oxford, 1988), entry for 8 May 1881.

29 Sir Edward Fry, *James Hack Tuke: a memoir* (London, 1899), pp.139–42.

30 Arnold-Forster, *Irish Journal*, entries for 10 Oct. and 4 Nov. 1881.

31 Fry, *Tuke Memoir*, p.148.

32 *Poor Law Union and Lunacy Inquiry Commission (Ireland), Report and Evidence*, HC 1878–79 [C.2239].

33 *Royal Commission on Poor Laws and Relief of Distress, Report on Ireland*, HC 1909, [Cd.4630], paras. 83–103.

34 *AR*, 1881–82.

35 Robinson, *Memories*, pp.43–48.

36 Allen Warren, 'Dublin Castle, Whitehall and the Formation of Irish Policy, 1879–92', *IHS*, 34, No. 136 (Nov. 2005), pp.412–13.

37 *Irish Times*, 16 Dec. 1882; letter of 9 Dec. 1882, printed in *AR* 1882–83, pp.119–120.

38 Robinson, *Memories*, pp.42–50.

39 *Poor Relief (Ireland) Inquiry Commissioners, Report and Evidence*, HC 1887 [C.5043].

40 Robinson, *Memories*, p.81.

41 *Hansard* III, 282, 4 Aug. 1883, 1586–87.

42 Robinson, *Memories*, pp.91, 103.

43 *Hansard* IV, 62, 21 July 1898, 564.

44 Robinson to Balfour, 25 Feb. 1898, NAS, Balfour Papers, GD 433/2/230/13.

45 Robinson to Balfour, 17 Apr. 1898, NAS, Balfour Papers, GD 433/2/114/1.

46 Ibid; the Duchess of Marlborough's fund, established in 1880 by the wife of the lord lieutenant, provided relief in distressed western areas where Robinson had served as a temporary inspector.

47 Robinson to Balfour, 6 Feb. 1898, NAS, Balfour Papers, GD 433/2/230/10.

48   Ibid; Robinson, *Memories*, p.112; at an earlier stage, shopkeepers who had become guardians and profited indirectly from the operation of outdoor relief were among his targets – see, for example, his letter of 10 Mar 1892 to A. J. Balfour, BL. ABP Add MSS 49850.

49   Robinson to Balfour, 10 May 1898, NAS, Balfour Papers, GD 433/2/230/17; the Fr Lavelle referred to may have been the radical County Mayo priest who died in 1886 and whom Robinson would have encountered when the priest was active in his district in 1879–80.

50   Memorandum on Old Age Pension Scheme dated 22 Nov. 1899 by H.A. Robinson, TNA, Balfour Papers, PRO 30/60/28.

51   Harrell to Balfour, 7 Dec. 1897, NAS, Balfour Papers, GD 433/2/230/7.

52   Robinson to Balfour, 7 Dec. 1897, NAS, Balfour Papers, GD 433/2/230/8.

53   Crossman, *Politics, Pauperism and Power*, pp.130–31.

54   Robinson to Balfour, 20 Aug. 1896, NAS, Balfour Papers, GD 433/2/230/6.

55   Poor Relief (Ireland) Bill 1896 (Bill No. 337), 7 Aug. 1896; Poor Relief (Ireland) Bill 1897 (Bill No. 197), 8 Apr. 1897.

56   *Hansard* IV, 53, 9 Feb. 1898, 206.

57   *Hansard* IV, 56, 22 Apr. 1898, 814–854.

58   Robinson to Balfour, 24 April 1898, NAS, Balfour Papers, GD 433/2/230/15.

59   *Hansard* IV, 57, 4 May 1898, 312; 5 May 1898, 482–83.

60   Robinson to Balfour, 4 June 1898, NAS, Balfour Papers, GD 433/2/230/21.

61   Crossman, *Politics, Pauperism and Power*, pp.130–31.

62   Ibid., p.19.

CHAPTER II

Planning the Local Government (Ireland) Act 1898

The years 1897 to 1899 were eventful and busy years in the life of Henry Augustus Robinson. Given the age profile of his LGB colleagues, he might well have expected when 1897 dawned that he would be called on before long to take on the most senior position in the organisation, but there was no reason to think at that stage that the role and functions of the board itself would soon be dramatically expanded, or that the environment in which it operated was about to be transformed. In the event, working with Chief Secretary Balfour, Robinson was to play a major part in planning and drafting legislation which would democratise Irish local government and provide the statutory framework for local authority activity for more than a century. Balfour was entirely justified in telling the House of Commons in June 1899 that the work of initiating this legislation 'has been a great achievement, and one of which any department of the State, whether English or Irish, might justly be proud' and he was happy to acknowledge that the principal burden of implementing the legislation had fallen on Robinson, who had 'shown through all these months a judgment, a capacity, a power of industry, and the power of putting heart into his subordinates when in difficulties, which is beyond all praise'.[1]

'A Surprise upon the Country'

The major political controversy in Ireland at the beginning of 1897 – the financial relationship between Britain and Ireland – did not appear directly to affect the LGB, while its estimates of expenditure, as presented to Parliament in January, suggested a business-as-usual scenario: spending was expected to be essentially the same as what it had been ten years earlier and the staff complement – eighty-seven in all, including the board – was only eight more than it had been in 1887–88.[2] Irish nationalist MPs availed of the Commons debate on the board's estimates on 21 May to rehearse their regular criticisms of the organisation: it was composed of gentlemen sitting in separate apartments in the Custom House in Dublin, who rarely, if ever, consulted the chief secretary, despite him being President of the board, about decisions they were making in his name. It was an out-of-date and unsympathetic body, which endeavoured to flout the wishes of the boards of guardians throughout the country, and to impose additional expenditure on the ratepayers. It was also staffed by inspectors drawn from the ranks of 'half-pay colonels and retired officers and navy captains' appointed by political favouritism, instead of men drawn from the ranks of experienced union officers or men appointed through open, public competition in whom the public could have confidence.[3]

These criticisms of the board, trenchant though they were, would probably have been more forceful and incisive but for the announcement to the House earlier that day by Arthur Balfour, First Lord of the Treasury, that instead of proceeding with the bills which had already been introduced to reform the Irish Poor Relief System and to establish a new Department of Agriculture and Industries, the government planned to bring forward a local government reform bill in the next session to set up elected county councils in place of the grand juries, and to make provision for a large grant in aid of agricultural rates.[4] These proposals did not form part of a policy of 'killing Home Rule with kindness' of which Gerald Balfour had spoken in 1895,[5] nor could they be seen as a response to the calls for reform of county government, which had been expressed – and resisted – in Parliament and elsewhere at regular intervals in the previous fifty years.[6] Instead, in presenting his twin-track approach, Arthur Balfour openly admitted that the overriding strategy had been to devise a response to the crisis which followed publication of the report of a royal commission, whose findings gave substance to the oft-repeated allegation that Ireland was overtaxed by comparison with the rest of the United Kingdom.[7] Arthur's Balfour's proposals were effectively designed to buy off both sides of a dangerous combination of Irish unionist and nationalist MPs who had been demanding action on foot of the report, and threatening to hold up the government's legislative programme. Unionists and nationalists alike welcomed Balfour's proposals: Edward Carson described the scheme as a statesmanlike one, which, as a unionist, he would gladly accept[8] and while the reaction of the nationalist, John Dillon, leader of the anti-Parnellites, was cautious, Tim Healy thought that Balfour's statement was the most hopeful and auspicious statement of policy produced by a Tory government during his time at Westminster.[9] In the same vein, the Parnellite leader, John Redmond, had no doubts – he could recall no government statement that was received with such a universal expression of agreement and satisfaction.[10]

The government's decision to go ahead with a scheme of local government reform at county level was made quite suddenly and without any kind of involvement by the LGB, whose legislative priority was the enactment of a Poor Relief Bill, which had already made progress in the Commons. The unionist view at the time was that Ireland already had a system of county government 'superior to that of England as regards simplicity, uniformity, economy and efficiency'[11] while for most nationalists, the establishment of a democratic system of local self-government was never a major objective in its own right. The unionist political writer, Michael J. F. McCarthy, was therefore able to record that the initiative 'came as a surprise upon the country', was introduced 'without precedent agitation' and 'had not been heralded in by any series of promises or by any flourish of trumpets whatsoever'.[12]

Robinson's Proposals

Robinson, despite being the junior member of the LGB, was clearly the one on whom Gerald Balfour relied most heavily. He had no advance knowledge of the government's decision and happened to be cruising in his yacht off the west coast of Scotland when contacted by Balfour about the matter. At his request, he hurriedly prepared a memorandum for submission to the government, showing how the system of county, county borough and urban and rural district councils, which had been introduced by law in the English counties in 1888, might be applied in Ireland, exploring 'how far the principles might be accepted, and what modifications, if any, were necessary'.[13] What appears to be the memorandum drafted by Robinson in 1897 has survived among the Balfour papers in the National Archives at Kew.[14] In the memorandum, he reviewed the operations of the existing local bodies – mainly the grand juries, the boards of guardians and the dispensary committees – and suggested that local government in Ireland might operate on a three-tier system, with business apportioned between county councils, rural district councils/boards of guardians and, at least in the larger areas, parish councils (like those introduced in England in 1894), operating on the basis of the dispensary districts rather than the ecclesiastical or civil parishes. He went on to suggest the specific functions which might be discharged at each level and what the relationships between the different levels should be. The rural district councils/boards of guardians would have more or less the same range of functions as the guardians already had, but with the addition of road maintenance and improvement and without responsibility for the administration of the Labourers Acts, which would pass to the parish councils. While the services to be provided directly by the county councils would be quite limited, Robinson strongly advocated the need in Irish circumstances to make rate collection a function of these councils, as they would be larger and more inaccessible bodies, thus less open to being influenced by defaulting ratepayers. In addition, he suggested that only the rural district councils should be directly elected, with a number of members from each of these councils coming together to form the county council. He believed it would be a mistake, 'in a country so split up into bitterly hostile parties, where poor law elections alone cause quite disturbance and intimidation enough', to have further elections for county and parish councillors and that this would preclude a 'concerted process of administration'.

There was nothing in Robinson's memorandum to suggest that he had any reservations about the principle of establishing an extensive, new and democratic local- government system, or that he would have supported the view of TCD historian, W. E. H. Lecky, who believed that Ireland was 'as little suited for democracy as almost any country in Europe'.[15] Neither is there any evidence that he subscribed to the controversial view of Horace Plunkett about the Irishman's defective character and political inferiority.[16] His memorandum, in fact, advocated the delegation of functions to the lowest possible level, and argued that the existing dispensary committees, which were invariably 'fully acquainted with the requirements of their districts', would be better qualified to manage some of the business, which was then dealt with at union level. In effect, he could be said to have adopted what was later referred to as the principle of subsidiarity – although he is highly unlikely to have been influenced by (or even to have known of) the statement of this key principle of catholic social policy in the encyclical *Rerum Novarum*, which had been issued by Pope Leo XIII six years earlier.

After Robinson's initial proposals had been modified in discussion with Balfour and between various ministers, work began on drafting a local government bill, which was to create for the first time an ordered and systematic set of local authorities in Ireland. Drafting continued in the autumn, with numerous printed drafts and memoranda on various points being prepared and submitted to the chief secretary between

October 1897 and February 1898.[17] It is clear from the surviving papers that Balfour was a hands-on participant in the work, presiding at round-table conferences and, according to Robinson, instrumental in personally resolving problems that arose in framing the rating and other financial clauses of the bill.[18] It is clear also that Balfour's main collaborator was Robinson – although the latter's initial suggestions concerning the establishment of parish councils and the avoidance of direct county council elections were not accepted.

Details of the Bill

For the larger, built-up areas, the Local Government (Ireland) Bill, which was finalised early in 1898, provided for county borough, borough and urban district councils without significant structural change. In the rural areas, however, there was to be an entirely new two-tier system, comprising elected county councils and a network of separately elected rural district councils:

- The county councils (thirty-three) were to take over the administrative business of the grand juries, but they were not to be entrusted with functions relating to education or with the control of the police, even though these were among the major functions of the English county councils, which had been established ten years earlier.
- The county grand juries were to continue but would revert to their original judicial role.
- The 213 new rural district councils were to take responsibility for most of the functions of the poor law guardians, including housing, sanitary services and public health matters, but not poor relief, and were to take the place of the baronial presentment sessions in making proposals to the county councils for road works, with the baronies ceasing to be administrative units.
- In most of the urban areas, the county borough councils (six), borough councils (five) and urban district councils (seventy-nine) were to take on the housing, sanitary services and public health functions of the guardians; the towns, having elected town commissioners (thirty), were largely unaffected.
- The boards of poor law guardians (by then reduced to 159) were to continue as separate legal entities, but *ex-officio* membership was abolished and in rural areas the rural district councillors were to function also as guardians. In effect, the guardians, retaining only their poor relief functions, were to return to a role close to that which they

had filled before the expansion of their activities under the sanitary, housing and other legislation of the previous five decades.

• The electorate for all local councils was to be extended to include parliamentary electors, together with peers and women who were otherwise qualified, bringing the total to almost 900,000; clergymen were disqualified for election as county or district councillors (a provision which Cardinal Logue saw as further evidence of growing anticlericalism) while women were eligible for membership of district councils and boards of guardians but not county councils.

In addition to changes in local government structures, the bill set out to affect a revolution in local financial arrangements in line with the policy which had been outlined by Arthur Balfour in May 1897. Landlords' liability for local rates was to be swept away by a new consolidated rating system, under which a transfer of liability to the occupiers in rural areas would be balanced by the Agricultural Grant, which would effectively meet the share of local costs that had formerly been levied on landlords in those areas. To achieve this, the sum of the grant was set at £727,000 – representing half the average county cess and half the average poor rate levied on land in rural areas in 1896–97. Specific grants totalling about £280,000 were also to continue. These included grants paid through the LGB to meet half the salaries of medical officers at workhouses and dispensaries, half the salaries of trained workhouse nurses, the salaries of workhouse school teachers, half the cost of medicines and appliances, and grants towards the maintenance of pauper lunatics. Before 1898 the grand juries had been raising about one million pounds through the grand jury cess. The boards of guardians raised another £750,000 annually by means of the poor rate, but Robinson's recommendation for a new unified rating system was accepted. Thus, the bill proposed that there would, in future, be a single authority for levying and collecting a new consolidated rate in rural areas. Effectively, the county councils were to raise – by means of what was, confusingly, still described as the poor rate – sufficient funds to meet their own expenditure, as well as the expenses of the rural district councils and each of the boards of guardians within the county.

The Debates in Parliament

When the bill was introduced in the House of Commons on 21 February 1898, Gerald Balfour explained that the existing system was no longer in harmony with the spirit of the age and that structural reform was a *sine qua non* for further reforms which he hoped to achieve.[19] His speech was a long but rather low-key one about which, according to his sister Alice, their elder brother Arthur had been nervous a few days earlier.[20] On the opposition side, however, the future prime minister, Herbert Asquith, was impressed by the speech: 'Nothing could have been better done', he wrote to Gerald's wife, Betty.[21] In the second-stage debate on 21 March,[22] John Dillon had very little to say about the broad principle of the bill, but concentrated largely on points of detail. While objecting to the 'bribing' of the landlords by means of the agricultural grant, he conceded that the bill, despite its faults and shortcomings, would achieve 'a most beneficial and far-reaching revolution in the condition of Irish local government and Irish life'. John Redmond welcomed the bill, noting that Irishmen were practically united on the broad principle, that no serious section of English opinion was hostile, and that it represented a step in the direction of Home Rule. For the Ulster unionists, grudging acceptance was expressed by Colonel E. J. Saunderson, who was inclined to dismiss the significance of the bill, noting that local government did not excite any emotion among the people of Ireland and that his own party had been 'perfectly indifferent' on the subject. Another approach was represented by W. E. H. Lecky, who sat for Trinity College at the time and believed that what was proposed was 'a great and perilous experiment', but he felt obliged to accept that these arrangements were inevitable because of pledges given since 1886 by all parties and 'the manifest trend of opinion both inside and outside the House'.

In addition to sweeping away the old, non-elected undemocratic system of local government in the counties, the 1898 bill also proposed to widen considerably the powers of the LGB by bringing road development and maintenance activity within its sphere of influence for the first time. This widening of powers was done by limiting county councils' spending on road works in the early years, unless the board approved, and by extending to the new county and district councils some of the controls on staffing, financial, and procedural matters, which the board had previously been able to exercise only in relation to the poor law guardians. In addition, the bill conferred on the board the power to make legally binding rules and regulations, the exercise of which was to lead to some serious controversy within a few years. The potential for conflict was, in fact, apparent from an early stage: Balfour believed that the councils were 'cribbed, cabined and confined' in every direction to ensure that they would not become legislative bodies or a substitute for Home Rule[23] whereas William O'Brien, founder of the United Irish League, believed that thirty of the thirty-three new county councils could become 'simply thirty Irish parliaments'.[24]

The *Irish Times* neatly summarized the possible outcome: 'The thirty-two parliaments, as he calls them, kill the One Parliament.'[25]

'An Obsolete Administrative Body out of Touch with the Needs of the People'

While the debates on the bill continued at Westminster, concerns began to be expressed about the suitability of the LGB for the new role it would have to play when the bill came into operation. The case for direct representation of the board in the House of Commons, instead of obliging the chief secretary to act as the mouthpiece of the organisation, was raised again, even though successive chief secretaries had taken the view in the previous thirty years that this was neither necessary nor practicable. The *Daily Chronicle*, which supported the liberal opposition, asked in February:

> How can an obsolete administrative body out of touch with the needs of the people and subject to no pressure of public opinion foster, watch over, and check the new developments? And yet it is as clear as daylight that there must be, at the head of affairs, a responsive and responsible body, a minister or a board in the closest sympathetic touch with the new councils. We hope the government will not hide this fact from themselves, or spoil the new ship out of deference to the qualms of Dublin Castle.[26]

The *Chronicle's* line was followed by some Irish members in the second stage debate.[27] Dillon spoke of the board as 'a nominated and irresponsible body', which differed radically from the English board which was headed by a minister who was kept in touch with public opinion through his membership of Parliament; he advocated the introduction of 'some popular element' into the membership of the board to decrease the danger of friction between it and the new councils. Redmond took a similar line, arguing that the board – which with its increased powers would be the most powerful board in the country – should be strengthened by the addition of suitable individuals who would command the goodwill and confidence of the people. As a compromise solution, Tim Healy suggested at a later stage that, leaving 'the paid men doing the drudgery', the board might be assisted by a panel of honorary members, drawn from all parties in the House, who would deal with 'questions of principle where local feeling arose'.[28] John Morley, who had served two terms as chief secretary in Gladstone's governments, supported the Irish members, arguing that it would be entirely anomalous for a large number of strong, local authorities to be subject to checks and controls by what he described as 'practically an alien board' out of touch with local sentiment or local demand. He also questioned the ability of any chief secretary, with the mass of business for which he was responsible, to play an active part in the operations of the board and suggested that, like any other department, it should have its own minister who would be accountable in Parliament and to the public. The need to strengthen the board was again raised some months later in the House of Lords, where a number of members, including the Earl of Mayo and a former lord-lieutenant, Earl Spencer, specifically suggested that a minister should be appointed to head the board.[29]

In advancing their criticisms of the structure of the board and suggesting new arrangements, MPs would have been aware of the proposals made in the July 1896 report of the Recess Committee relating to the governance of the proposed Department of Agriculture. They would also have been conscious of the bill that had been presented by Balfour in April 1897 to give effect to that committee's proposals.[30] The committee had argued that the head of the proposed department should be an MP, answerable as a minister to Parliament and independent of the chief secretary, not only because of the importance of the work but also to relieve the chief secretary and his office whose workload was already 'beyond the power of a single minister'.[31] While Balfour had accepted the thrust of most of the committee's recommendations and proposed to give effect to them in the 1897 bill, which set out to establish a Department of Agriculture and Industry for Ireland, he resisted the case regarding the head of the new department acting as a separate, independent minister because, he later explained, this would have involved splitting up the Irish government. Instead, the department was to be under the management of a three-man team: the chief secretary as president, a vice-president who *could be* a member of Parliament, and a civil servant to be styled the commissioner of agriculture. The position of commissioner was dropped, however, when the legislation was eventually enacted in 1899,[32] the intention being that the vice-president should be both the working head of the department and a minister with a seat in Parliament.[33]

In the case of the LGB, Balfour seemed to be willing, at least in principle, to consider an arrangement under which a separate minister would be appointed to head the board. However, he did not wish to see that happen for some time as he personally wanted to see the new local government system through to full implementation.[34] Over ten years earlier, his brother, Arthur, after he had taken up office as Chief Secretary, had arranged for the appointment of Colonel Edward

King-Harman, MP to support him in a new position of Parliamentary Under-Secretary,[35] and had brought in a bill to ensure that the new office-holder would also be a member of the LGB 'holding rank ... next after the president of the board'.[36] After that bill had been strongly opposed in the Commons by liberal members, including the previous chief secretary, John Morley, and W. E. Gladstone, who both thought that the new office was unnecessary,[37] and after bitter criticism by Irish nationalist members, who regarded King-Harman as a champion of the Orange Order, the unfortunate colonel's death in June 1888 brought the controversy to a close. The government withdrew the bill and the constitution of the LGB remained as it had been.

There is evidence that Gerald Balfour considered, at one stage, another option for the reconstitution of the LGB – providing that the MP who was to be appointed as Vice-President of his new Department of Agriculture would act also as Vice-President of the LGB and be assisted by a permanent civil service commissioner. When Henry Robinson was invited to comment on this proposal, he was in a delicate position due to the fact that he was likely himself to succeed to the Vice-Presidency before too long. He told Balfour that while he would do his utmost to make a success of whatever plan was decided on, and while the position of commissioner would be a demanding one, he would, if entrusted with adequate powers, not be afraid of the extra work and had sufficient experience 'to keep things fairly straight'. Nevertheless, he made a long, private submission to Balfour setting out a variety of reasons for not implementing the change.[38] Was it desirable, he asked, in the case of an important board, which practically controls the rating authorities, holds the balance between the conflicting interests of the classes , and has various quasi-judicial functions, to have non-working members as first and second in command, 'absentees so to speak, whose attention is principally engaged elsewhere'? Would this not give the board the character of a department neglected by its chiefs and left almost completely in the hands of an irresponsible junior commissioner? And, by giving that commissioner a lower official standing than his three predecessors as Vice-President, might not the respect of the public for his authority be lessened, his decisions be unlikely to be regarded as final and more liable to be questioned and brought before the Commons? Finally, resorting to an argument which clearly exposed his own political sympathies, he suggested that any of Balfour's 'hypercritical friends' in Ireland would realise that the existing system of appointing a permanent civil servant as Vice-President would give them 'the same security against imposition and partisan administration that they have always had', whereas it might be otherwise if the Vice-President were to be an MP 'appointed by a liberal, Home Rule government ... a gentleman, say, of the Aloysius McHugh type'.[39]

Whether convinced by Robinson's arguments or because of other considerations, Balfour eventually decided not to go ahead with this proposal for modifying the constitution of the board. He also decided against a suggestion from Robinson that the board should be 'popularized' by severing its connection with the Lord Lieutenant and Dublin Castle. Robinson's reasoning was that while Sir David Harrel remained as Under-Secretary, things would always run smoothly because he was charming to deal with and understood the character of the people, however:

> ... under permanent English officials such as Redvers Buller [Under-Secretary, 1886–87] and Sir Robert Hamilton [Under-Secretary, 1882–86] who knew nothing of the moods and management of local authorities, we never were able to pursue an even and consistent course; our administration was made subject to such violent wrenches and we were so dragged into every 'law and order' squabble that the local authorities hardly dared at the time to come to us for help and guidance.

> Under Ridgeway [1887–93] and Harrel [from 1893 onwards] we have managed to regain a good deal of our influence, but if Harrel was [sic] to be succeeded by a red-hot Orangeman, the Irish government might expect us to dissolve the boards [of guardians] whenever there was a 'sunbursty' resolution passed.[40]

Although this suggestion of Robinson's was not accepted and although Harrel's successor was not the red-hot Orangeman Robinson had feared, a new Under-Secretary was destined to create serious problems for the board within a few years. However, Balfour did give effect in the bill to another suggestion from Robinson designed to strengthen the position of the Vice-President and to speed up the operations of the board. Robinson had argued that the provision, dating from 1872, under which the junior commissioners could make decisions only by acting jointly, needed to be changed because this meant that, in practice, each member of the board devoted some time each day to the study of papers on which decisions had already been reached by his colleague. The system was thus 'an insult to common sense' and could be 'a source of embarrassment and delay' in attempting to cope with the extra work which would arise under the new bill. It was also equally harassing that so much of the board's time was taken up in approving routine work, which it should be possible to delegate to senior staff.[41] As a result, Balfour agreed that the bill should not only restate the power of the Vice-President to act on his own in making decisions of any kind, but should also allow him to appoint a person to act on his behalf. This decision considerably strengthened Robinson's position when he became Vice-President: he now had power not only to make formal decisions himself but also to authorise another individual, either a commissioner or a staff member, to act on his behalf and thus, effectively, to act in the name of the board. In a letter to Balfour on 2 May 1898, Robinson told him that he was indebted to him for 'giving me the power of nominating someone to act for me if called away on urgent business. I think you will find that it will work well'.[42] In practice, the 1898 Act meant that Robinson became the dominant personality – in effect he could almost declare, as Louis XIV is reputed to have done, that *l'etat c'est moi.*

'The Most Lasting Monument to Balfour's Term of Office'

Gerald Balfour has been described as an advanced workaholic and a master of legislative detail who was intimately involved in every aspect of the legislative programme for which he was responsible.[43] This is supported by Robinson's statement that Balfour piloted the 1898 bill through the House 'with consummate skill, and his knowledge of the object of every line of it was so clear that he was unassailable'.[44] The committee stage of the bill was taken in April and May and the report stage in July, after which the bill was debated in the House of Lords and passed with amendments towards the end of July. Balfour, however, had been unwell for much of 1898 and was obliged to take a holiday in Switzerland beginning in May.[45] According to Robinson, 'it was therefore a terrible disappointment to him that, just when the work was finished, he broke down under the strain, and the final stages had to be taken by John Atkinson, the attorney general'. In sympathising with Balfour at the time, Robinson wrote that no human 'could have gone through what you have done without being knocked up' but assured him that he would pick up like magic when he got away to some high mountain air.[46]

After amendments made in the House of Lords had been reviewed in the Commons, the 1898 Act finally received the Royal Assent on 12 August. When first brought in on 21 February the bill comprised only seventy-seven sections. After it had been amended in committee by the Commons on 24 May the number of sections grew to ninety-three and when finally signed into law, the bill had grown to 124 sections and seven schedules, running to 117 pages in the official version issued by the Queen's Printer. Despite this, it was still not enough to spell out all the details of the radical changes that were planned, and for this reason, the bill represented what Balfour described as 'a new departure in draftsmanship'[47] by delegating extensive powers, effectively to the LGB, to make orders for the application to Ireland of English and Scottish acts, for adapting existing Irish legislation so as to bring it into conformity with the act, for regulating the procedure of the new councils and for transitional arrangements of various kinds. While these unprecedented shortcuts, for which Tim Healy afterwards claimed the credit,[48] were essential because of the rush to have the bill passed before the end of the 1898 session, the pattern was adopted by parliamentary draftsmen at Westminster in the following thirty years to such an extent that Lord Chief Justice Hewart was provoked to publish his classic essay 'The New Despotism' in 1929, calling for resistance to the encroachment on the role of Parliament by the growing bureaucracy.[49] The approach adopted in drafting the act also set a precedent for Irish local government legislation in the century that followed, leading to regular complaints about the extent to which, as the politicians saw it, ministers and civil servants in the Custom House were arrogating to themselves decisions and functions which were proper to the Oireachtas. But, whatever its faults, sections of the 1898 Act were still in operation one hundred years after its enactment, which helps to justify its description by F. S. L. Lyons as the 'most lasting monument to Balfour's term of office' and an act which deservedly ranks as one of the most important measures of conciliation passed during the whole of the period of the Union.[50]

NOTES

1   *Hansard* IV, 73, 30 June 1899, 1226–27.

2   *Estimates for Civil Services, 1887–88 and 1897–98*, HC 1887 (53), HC 1897 (33).

3   *Hansard* IV, 49, 21 May 1897, 1061–1102.

4   *Hansard* IV, 49, 21 May 1897, 1040–6.

5   *Leeds Mercury*, 17 Oct. 1895; *The Times*, 17 Oct. 1895; Robinson described 'killing Home Rule by kindness' as an unfortunate phrase and insisted that what Balfour said was that 'he did not conceive that it would be possible to kill Home Rule by kindness'.

6   Brendan O Donoghue, 'From Grand Juries to County Councils: The Effects of the Local Government (Ireland) Act 1898' in Felix M. Larkin (ed.), *Librarians, Poets and Scholars* (Dublin, 2007), pp.175–184.

7   *Royal Commission appointed to inquire into the Financial Relations of Great Britain and Ireland, Final Report*, HC 1896 [C. 8262].

8   *Hansard* IV, 49, 21 May 1897, 1048.

9   *Hansard* IV, 49, 21 May 1897, 1051; in *Letters and Leaders of My Day* II (1928), p.431, Healy was later to claim that it was he who first suggested to Balfour the idea of providing an agricultural grant coupled with the replacement of grand juries by popularly elected councils.

10 *Hansard* IV, 49, 21 May 1897, 1055.

11 *Special Committee on Local Government: Report by the Secretary, Irish Unionist Alliance* (n.d.).

12 Michael J. F. McCarthy, *Five Years in Ireland: 1895–1900* (8th edn) (Dublin, 1902), p.377.

13 Sir Henry Robinson, *Memories: Wise and Otherwise* (London, 1923), pp.124–25.

14 Memorandum by H. A. Robinson as to the application of the English system of Local Government to Ireland (undated), TNA, PRO 30/60/21.

15 *Hansard* IV, 55, 21 Mar. 1898, 455–457.

16 Horace Plunkett, *Ireland in the New Century*, pp. 4, 78, 81.

17 Balfour papers, TNA, PRO 30/60/21, PRO 30/60/29, PRO 30/60/30.

18 Robinson, *Memories*, p.110.

19 *Hansard* IV, 53, 21 Feb. 1898, 1227.

20 Diary of Alice Balfour, entry for 18 Feb. 1898, NAS, Balfour Papers, GD 433/2/224.

21 H. H. Asquith to Lady Betty Balfour, 21 Feb. 1898, NAS, Balfour Papers, GD 433/2/230/11.

22 *Hansard* IV, 55, 21 Mar. 1898, 420–525.

23 *Hansard* IV, 55, 21 Mar. 1898, 510–11.

24 O'Brien's diary, 14 Aug. 1898, quoted in Philip Bull, *Land, Politics and Nationalism: A Study of the Irish Land Question* (Dublin, 1996), p.134.

25 *Irish Times*, 17 Sept. 1898.

26 Quoted in an *Irish Times* editorial, 23 Feb. 1898.

27 *Hansard* IV, 55, 21 Mar. 1898, 419–525.

28 *Hansard* IV, 58, 20 May 1898, 181–82.

29 *Hansard* IV, 62, 21 July 1898, 531–95.

30 Agriculture and Industries (Ireland) Bill, 1897 (Bill No. 204), presented 12 Apr. 1897.

31 *Report of the Recess Committee* (1896), para. 100–104.

32 Agricultural and Technical Instruction (Ireland) Act 1899, 62 & 63 Vict., c.50, 9 Aug. 1899.

33 *Departmental Committee of Inquiry into Department of Agriculture and Technical Instruction (Ireland), Minutes of Evidence*, HC 1907 [Cd. 3574].

34 *Hansard* IV, 55, 21 Mar. 1898, 511–12.

35 King-Harman, the owner of Rockingham House and its 30,000 acre estate in County Roscommon, had been elected as Home Rule MP for Sligo County in 1877 but, having been defeated in 1880, represented Dublin County as a unionist from 1883 to 1885 and was subsequently returned for the Isle of Thanet.

36 Parliamentary Under Secretary to the Lord Lieutenant of Ireland Bill, Bill No. 201, 9 Apr. 1888.

37 *Hansard* III, 324, 9 Apr. 1888, 725–30; 325, 30 Apr. 1888, 909–49; 326, 14 May 1888, 207–264.

38 Memorandum: Proposed Re-Constitution of the Irish Local Government Board, signed H. A. Robinson, undated, TNA, PRO 30/60/21.

39 Patrick Aloysius McHugh was nationalist MP for Leitrim North and for Sligo North from 1892 until 1909.

40 Robinson to Balfour, n.d. [early 1898], NAS, Balfour Papers, GD 433/2/230/9 .

41 Robinson to Balfour, 3 Nov. 1897, TNA, PRO 30/60/21.

42 Robinson to Balfour, 2 May 1898, NAS, Balfour Papers, GD 433/2/230/16.

43 David R. C. Hudson, *The Ireland that We Made* (Ohio, 2003), pp.4, 103,152.

44 Robinson, *Memories*, p.127.

45 Hudson, *The Ireland that We Made*, p.127.

46 Robinson to Balfour, 4 Aug. 1898, NAS, Balfour Papers, GD 433/2/114/4.

47 *Hansard* IV, 53, 21 Feb. 1898, 1245.

48 T. M. Healy, *Letters and Leaders of My Day*, Vol. II (London, 1928), p.432.

49 Lord Hewart of Bury, *The New Despotism* (London, 1929).

50 F. S. L. Lyons, *The Irish Parliamentary Party, 1890–1910* (London, 1951), p.67; *Ireland since the Famine* (London, 1971), p.212.

CHAPTER III

Implementing the Act – A Triumph for the Local Government Board

A New Board with Robinson as Vice-President

Although the 1898 Act was long and complex, it was, in some respects, merely a framework, leaving it to the LGB to develop an implementation programme which would enable the new local councils to be brought fully into operation in the spring of 1899. By complete coincidence, as the legislation continued its slow passage through Parliament in the early summer of 1898, the need arose to reconstitute the board.

In May, two of the three full-time members – Sir George Morris, Vice-President since March 1891, and Sir Francis F. X. MacCabe, Medical Commissioner since March 1888 – were due to retire under the '65 rule' and both men were presented with illuminated addresses from the senior staff of the board at a luncheon in Dublin's Hamman Hotel on 30 April. Membership of the board had always been a prized position and a well-paid one: the two commissioners were each paid £1,200 a year while successive Vice-Presidents had each enjoyed a salary of £2,000, equal to that paid to the Under-Secretary.[1] Board members had always been drawn from the close-knit elite which governed Ireland in the nineteenth century. Two of those who served before 1898 had resigned their seats in Parliament to take up their positions with the board. Against this background, rumours and speculation concerning possible successors were rife in the media and in political circles in early 1898. On 8 March, the *Freeman's Journal* reported

rumours that Robinson was to succeed Morris,[2] and a few weeks later, John
Dillon claimed that 'an irreconcilable section of the landlord class' had
begun a campaign to have one of their representatives with experience
of the work of the grand juries added to the board.[3] The *Irish Times* had
already carried a report that Colonel Thomas Waring, MP for North Down
since 1885, was best fitted in the judgment of the unionist landlords to
become Vice-President,[4] although the appointment of Waring (who was
to die suddenly on 12 August) would have provoked strong reaction
from nationalists because of his Ulster unionist and Orange-Institution
connections. Other unionists, assuming that Robinson was likely to be
promoted to the Vice-Presidency, sought to have his place as commissioner
filled by Gilbert De L. Willis, secretary of the County Kildare Grand Jury
and secretary of the Landowners' Convention, in whose favour the Duke
of Abercorn and others lobbied Lord-Lieutenant Cadogan in March.[5] In
the event, precedent was followed and the vacancies were filled by internal
promotions of men who had already been heavily involved in the work of
the board.

A few days before Morris was due to retire Tim Healy suggested
in the Commons that his replacement at that stage, with a new local
government system about to be brought into operation, would be like
swopping horses while crossing a stream.[6] Some weeks later, he was
regretting the disappearance of Morris from the board, as he was a man
of great common sense who understood the prejudices of the people.[7]
Morris had in fact been allowed a short extension of his service, on
foot of an application made to the Treasury by the Under-Secretary, Sir
David Harrel.[8] It appears that Harrel was asked by Balfour to explore the
possibility that both Morris and MacCabe would agree to serve until 30
August, by which time the Local Government Bill was expected to have
become law.[9] Nothing came of this, however, and there is no evidence
that Morris himself wished to have his service further extended. Healy
again suggested in 1899 that it had been a great mistake to replace a
man whose service on the board since 1880 had not caused a single
complaint [10] and although he had been assured by Balfour that Morris
had indeed expressed a desire to retire at age sixty-five, this was not
enough to prevent him from protesting again two years later that Morris
should have been continued in office for two or three years so that he
could 'take the burden of seeing in motion' the new system of local
government.[11] Healy's motives in championing Morris between 1898 and
1901 must, however, be seen to be suspect in light of his statement in the
Commons fifteen years earlier, when Morris was a commissioner, that few
people believed he ever did any work.[12]

Robinson's appointment as Vice-President was formally announced in the *Dublin Gazette* on 10 May 1898 and was welcomed by the *Irish Times* because of his experience and personal qualities.[13] He had been advised of the appointment more than a week earlier, after which he wrote to Gerald Balfour to thank him for his good wishes and for the great kindness, which had made it a pleasure to work under his presidency. Although Robinson was the obvious candidate for the Vice-Presidency, he expected to get 'a good peppering from the nationalists in the House' when the appointment became known. He told Balfour, however, that 'as I don't know any of them except Jameson, they will have to draw on their imagination, which will be interesting'.[14] If Irish Party MPs had little respect for Robinson, the feeling was mutual, at least in so far as some of them were concerned. A few weeks later, in wishing Balfour a restful holiday during the short parliamentary recess, Robinson expressed the hope that he had dismissed 'the snarling, querulous, ill-conditioned members' from his mind.[15] Looking back on his appointment twenty-five years later, he recalled that as 'the task of breaking up the old system of local government and inaugurating the new ... was considered to be such a very hazardous job, there were no applicants for the post of Vice-President and I was promoted to it without opposition from anyone'. He added, however, that because he had worked so hard on the 1898 bill and had all the strings in his hands so firmly, he would probably have held his own against any other candidate.[16]

Robinson's place as commissioner was assigned on 10 May to William Lawson Micks (1851–1928). Micks had worked with the LGB as an inspector from 1885 to 1891, before being seconded to become the first secretary of the Congested Districts Board. On the same day, the post of medical commissioner was filled by the promotion of Dr Thomas Joseph Stafford (1857–1935), who had been a medical inspector since February 1890 and whose appointment maintained the established practice of having at least one catholic on the board. Stafford had married the only daughter and heir of Colonel E. R. King-Harman, the MP who had acted as unpaid Parliamentary Under-Secretary to the Chief Secretary in 1887–88 and who, but for his untimely death, would have become an additional *ex-officio* member of the board under the controversial legislation which was dropped on his death.

The Under-Secretary, Sir David Harrel, approved of the selection of the new board members, telling Balfour that 'the men are all able and tried men. You know their strong points and their weak ones and I have no doubt the general verdict of the public would endorse the selection.' He went on to note that the new men possessed knowledge and experience, which rendered them capable of dealing with all sections and classes of people with the minimum of friction and for maintaining, at the same time, the authority of the government.[17] Another serving civil servant, Edward Ennis, Registrar of the Court of Chancery and a long-time aspirant to the post of assistant under-secretary, was less impressed, complaining to Dillon that the appointments had 'securely safeguarded the unionist preponderance'. There had previously been two catholics on the board (Morris and MacCabe) but now there was only one – Stafford, and 'he is a unionist'– and while Micks was a good appointment, there was no paucity of fully qualified catholics (including, presumably, himself) to fill the positions.[18]

In reconstituting the board, the opportunity was availed of by the Treasury to reduce the salaries payable to the new appointees: the two commissioners were placed on a scale extending from £1,000 to £1,200 over four years instead of the flat rate of £1,200, which had applied before 1898. Robinson, whose predecessors since the early 1850s had enjoyed a salary of £2,000 a year, was placed on a scale commencing at £1,500 and rising to £1,800 after three years.[19] Even with a reduced level of pay, Robinson's salary meant that he was still the highest-paid civil servant in Ireland at the time apart from the Under-Secretary.[20] Despite this, Robinson and his board colleagues asked Balfour in May 1899 to press the Treasury for an immediate advance to the maximum of their scales in view of the exceptional demands which had been made on them in the previous year. Robinson told Balfour that they were 'all very sore with the Treasury when we see what we have been through and what is before us' and argued that it was entirely wrong of the Treasury to equate their salaries with those of the permanent secretary and assistant secretaries of the English local government board who did not have to carry out their duties 'under a running fire of abuse from every MP or newspaper disapproving of his religious or political views'.[21] Stafford (whose wife, the former Frances Agnes King-Harman, was a wealthy heiress and landowner) was not so upset about the salary, according to Robinson, but Micks could not allude to it without choking. However, while Balfour seems to have done his best to support the claims of the three men, his efforts were ultimately unsuccessful. In March 1900, Robinson told him not to think anything more about the Treasury refusal: 'I am sure nothing more can be done, and we must express our indebtedness to you for your kindness in the matter.'[22]

The 'Antidote to Micks'

In reporting the appointment of the new board, the *Irish Times* suggested that without incurring any displeasure from fair-minded men, the government might have appointed 'a representative of the class from which the grand jurors are taken and of the larger cesspayers ... who are rendered uneasy by the experiment that is being entered upon'. This would ensure that the board would be one 'to command abundantly the respect of all, and to conciliate the conflicting views' that would inevitably arise in administering the new local government system.[23] Such an additional appointment became possible under a clause which was added to the 1898 bill at committee stage in the Commons.[24] This clause allowed the Chief Secretary to appoint an inspector or auditor or another person to be an additional commissioner for not more than five years in order to assist in the work of bringing the act into operation and of supervising its operation in the initial years. Aware of the argument that the membership of the board should include a person with grand jury experience, Robinson suggested to Balfour that 'if you contemplate another commissioner ... I think you would do better by giving Cotton's place, which will shortly become vacant to a county surveyor'. (Charles Philip Cotton, a former consulting engineer, had been the board's Chief Engineering Inspector since 1879 and was approaching retirement age.)

Anxious to avoid the appointment of a complete outsider, Robinson went on to offer another solution – the board's legal adviser since 1879, James H. Monahan Q C, could be made a commissioner for five years at £1,200 a year without any cost to the Treasury as Monahan was already paid two guineas 'for every paper submitted to him ... [and] he will have such a crop of knotty points to give opinions on when the bill becomes law he will certainly get three times that sum'. According to Robinson, Monahan would be most useful because – although he was useless in court – he was a very sound chamber lawyer and his knowledge of the public health, local government and poor law legislation was second to none in Ireland.[25] In a subsequent letter, Robinson reverted to the suggestion that 'a county surveyor is really the kind of article we want for the next couple of years'. This was a sensible proposal, given that the board was to have responsibility from 1898 onwards for roads. However, the fourth member should not be made permanent because it would be both wholly unnecessary and 'ruinous to a department to have any idle hands at the head of affairs'.[26]

For obvious political reasons, none of Robinson's suggestions regarding an additional commissioner found favour with Balfour; instead, he decided in August to appoint Richard Bagwell (1840–1918) as a temporary commissioner for a one-year term with an initial salary of £1,000 a year. Bagwell was a barrister, a historian of sixteenth and seventeenth-century Ireland, a County Tipperary landowner with considerable grand jury experience and an uncompromising unionist.[27] According to Tim Healy, the appointment was made to placate the House of Lords and on foot of a private understanding with the Irish landlords.[28] Irish peers had, indeed, lobbied the government to make an appointment of this kind and several of them spoke of the need for it in the course of the second stage debate. The most forthright was the Marquess of Londonderry, a former lord-lieutenant and one of the most trenchant defenders of landlords' interests. He claimed that none of the permanent members of the board had any practical experience of the grand jury system and argued that a man with such experience was essential to act as a safeguard against the 'enormous amount of extravagance, of jobbing, and of maladministration' that could arise in the new county councils.[29] Londonderry was openly critical of the appointment of Micks, recalling that, as one of the board's inspectors, he had been transferred to a new district in 1888 when his activity in relation to an estate connected with the plan of campaign created controversy. He also suggested that his political convictions, at least in the past, were not in sympathy with those of the government. If the board were to be strengthened, this should be done 'by appointing gentlemen who have always held unionist opinions, and not by a man who has only recently taken to holding those views'.[30]

Gerald Balfour had known Bagwell since 1886 when he had been a guest at Bagwell's home near Clonmel in the course of a little-publicised visit to Ireland[31] but, by his own account, Bagwell 'had never been in any department before'.[32] Nevertheless, his appointment was welcomed by the *Irish Times*, which took the view that 'no better choice could have been made than of one so thoroughly familiar with county government under the grand jury system and so capable of bringing the new scheme into harmonious and successful operation, possessing the confidence alike of the gentry and landholders and the general body of ratepayers'.[33] But Bagwell's appointment was not acceptable to nationalists: he had been a founding member of the Irish Loyal and Patriotic Union, set up by southern unionists in 1885 to oppose Home Rule. For the rest of his life he remained a prominent member of that organisation (later the Irish Unionist Alliance), regularly speaking at public meetings in England in favour of the Union, producing pamphlets on the subject for the alliance, and declaring in January 1897 that 'no price is too high to pay for the privilege of not being governed by Home Rule politicians'.[34]

Bagwell's appointment was destined to create difficulties for Robinson in managing the business of the board, given that Lord Londonderry had 'made such mischief' by insisting that Bagwell was required 'as an antidote to Micks'. He suggested, therefore, that Bagwell's appointment should be deferred until he returned from his own holidays in October. Robinson would then be in the office to 'smooth any little feeling of irritation' which may have been caused, adding that there was no urgency about it because 'until we have our machinery put together, and are ready to start the train, we really don't need the guard'. He was so concerned about the issue that when Balfour insisted on making the appointment towards the end of August, he deferred his holidays so that he would be able to keep the peace between Bagwell and Micks in the initial weeks.[35] Bagwell caused further problems in February 1899 when he told the board that when the new act came into operation, he proposed that he himself should do all of the work arising from it, because he had been appointed for that purpose on the nomination of the unionists, and would resign if prevented from doing so. Robinson was so concerned about this idea, which he thought might have been inspired by some mischief-making at the Kildare Street Club, that he told Balfour 'if I don't revise everything of importance that goes out, I can't be answerable to you'. He warned that while Bagwell was 'infinitely better read, etc than I am' he had not served as an official under eight administrations, as Robinson himself had done, and 'had no more idea of what is a safe line for his chief to take, and what would bring trouble, than the man in the moon'.[36] He was so reluctant at that stage to leave Bagwell free of restrictions in the office that he decided to postpone a visit that he had planned to make to London to discuss important matters with Balfour and his own counterparts on the English board.[37] Two months later the crisis passed when Bagwell became somewhat ashamed of the scene he had made 'or else he is alarmed at the difficulty of some of the questions arising'.[38] But Robinson was still distrustful of his new colleague and, when planning another trip to London in June, had to arrange with Micks to 'keep his eye on Bagwell' and refer any doubtful issues to himself in London. Bagwell, he told Balfour, still needed 'to get rid of the idea that he is infallible and become imbued with some of the low cunning' which, according to one of Robinson's regular clerical correspondents, was the leading characteristic of the board.[39] In July, a much more favourable report on Bagwell's performance was presented by Robinson: he had advised the board when questions arose about grand jury procedure and had assisted in every way possible in the work of carrying the act into operation, especially while Micks was ill. Robinson claimed that when Bagwell had thoroughly mastered official procedure, he would be able to relieve the other members in every department.[40]

Whatever about the improvement in his day-to-day performance as a board member, Bagwell had been in office for only six months when, at the annual dinner of the Irish Land Agents Association in April 1899, he created public controversy by commenting that the 1898 Act was 'the worst of all acts of Parliament ever drawn'.[41] Writing to Balfour about this 'wild diatribe', Robinson told him that he had 'never yet come across a man of his ability who was so utterly wanting in tact and reserve'. He asked in the letter if anything could have been more ill-judged or in worse taste than his speech: 'Here we are, inviting the councils to come to us for assistance and advice, and can we be surprised if they refuse, and see no hope of fair play, when a member of the board, who admits that he can't understand the act and that it is the worst act ever made, gives out in the course of a violent partisan speech that the act is to be administered by him?'[42] Inevitably, the matter was raised in Parliament a few days later when Dillon asked the Chief Secretary if, in view of his speech, Bagwell was to be permitted to continue in office. Balfour was able to evade the issue by pointing to an assurance from Bagwell that the newspaper report of the speech was a condensed one, which gave a totally wrong impression of what he had said, and that he strongly supported the policy enshrined in the act.[43] However, given the comments about Bagwell's role, which were appearing in certain newspapers, Balfour was urged by Robinson to take any opportunity that presented itself to explain that Bagwell did not have a free hand in the Custom House because the board was a department 'with a regular ladder of authority and responsibility, at the head of which is our parliamentary representative'. Bagwell survived that particular crisis and his appointment was continued on a year-to-year basis until August 1903. Although he appears not to have made any further controversial public statements, nationalist MPs continued to use every opportunity which presented itself in the Commons to criticize him. According to Tim Healy, he was totally unfit for the post and should be 'sent back to look after his bullocks'.[44]

Supplementing the Act

To supplement the 1898 Act and to provide for points of detail, four major orders in council were made by the board in December 1898 and January 1899. These orders applied sections of English and Scottish enactments to the county and district councils; adapted existing Irish local government law to conform to the new arrangements; provided for necessary transitional arrangements; and spelled out the procedure to be followed by the new councils in carrying out their business. Some provisions of these orders continued to have effect for much of the twentieth century. A large number of additional orders were made by the board in the following months, prescribing, among other things, rules for the conduct of elections to the different classes of local councils, setting out in detail how rates were to be collected, how accounts were to be kept and how finances were to be managed. As well as drafting these orders, Robinson and his board had to urgently complete a variety of other tasks to ensure that the new councils came into operation in April 1899. The 159 Poor Law Unions had been based on towns of reasonable size and their hinterlands, ignoring existing county and other boundaries. As a result, thirty-eight unions extended into two counties and another eight included parts of three counties. To ensure that each of the new rural districts would fall fully within a single county, it was necessary therefore (while allowing the unions themselves to continue) to alter the boundaries of sixteen counties and to begin a process of splitting up some unions and amalgamating parts of others to create a network of 213 rural districts.[45] A new system for the registration of electors and a new arrangement of electoral areas had also to be put in place. In general, the poor law electoral divisions, numbering some 3,750 and dating originally from 1838, were retained as district electoral divisions and, as a rule, it was provided that two rural district councillors would be elected from each division. There was provision also for three co-opted members of each council and, in the case of the first councils, three additional members were to represent the former *ex-officio* guardians. In all, this made for a total of 9,456 urban and rural district councillors. District electoral divisions were grouped to form new county electoral divisions, generally about twenty in each county and with average populations ranging from 2,000 to 10,000, depending on the size of the county. In general, one councillor was to be elected from each division on the traditional 'first past the post' system for a three-year term. Provision was made for two co-opted members of each council and for another three to represent the former grand jury members on the first councils. In addition, the chairman of each rural district council was to be an *ex-officio* member of the county council.

Under these arrangements, the total number of the four categories of county councillors came to 1,059, of whom 698 were to be directly elected. The 1898 Act, therefore, set up the most extensive local representative system which ever operated in Ireland, one in which individual councillors were directly elected by, and identified with, very small areas. In all, the total number of elected county and district councillors came to more than 10,000. With the 296 members of the six county-borough councils, the 670 guardians elected for urban areas and the thirty boards of town commissioners, the total number of elected local representatives was more than 11,000, or about eight times the number in the country, north and south, today. Use of the parliamentary franchise, with the addition of peers and for the first time, adult women who were householders or lodgers, brought the total number of local government electors to almost 900,000.

Balfour was actively involved in the implementation process in 1898–99 and, as President of the board, personally signed many of the necessary formal orders. Robinson kept him fully informed on the progress of the work, writing to him regularly on particular points when he was detained in London during the parliamentary sessions. In March 1898, for example, well in advance of the enactment of the bill, Robinson reported that drafting of the orders to establish the new electoral divisions had almost been completed and, while he had personally considered every change and could defend them all, he would like to spend an hour with Balfour in London to get his agreement for the new wards in county boroughs where some major changes were proposed.[46] By August, he was reporting the recruitment of additional temporary clerical staff, the steps being taken to develop a new system of grants, and progress on the drafting of the orders relating to county and rural district boundaries.[47]

From December onwards, the volume and the pace of the work increased and the correspondence being received by the board concerning the January elections for the urban authorities was very heavy – returning officers thought it 'less trouble to write to us than to read the rules'.[48] Everything was going well in early February 1899, but there were claims of 'being rushed within an inch of our lives and some of my best men are showing symptoms of a nervous breakdown'. With the new session of Parliament due to begin on 7 February, Robinson promised to send Balfour a report by Sunday's post each week. It seems that Robinson did not renege on his promise – many of his surviving hand-written letters do, in fact, carry Sunday dates, conveying an image of Robinson scribbling furiously on Sunday afternoons at his home on the seafront at Dun Laoghaire (then Kingstown) and rushing to post the letters at the nearby Carlisle Pier before the mail boat sailed to Holyhead, allowing the letters to be on Balfour's desk at the Irish Office in London the following morning.[49] By early March, the work of getting things ready for the county and district council elections was 'at fever heat' and the men were working splendidly, but Robinson was afraid he was driving them a bit too hard.[50] By 5 April the pressure had increased yet again: election correspondence had grown out of all bounds and 'telegrams [were] numerous enough to thatch the Custom House with'.[51]

The 1899 Elections

Given that the franchise had been widened considerably, that elections had never previously been held at county level, that many of the returning officers were new to the work and that the county and rural district council elections were to be held on the one day, making a total of over 4,000 separate elections in all, Robinson was naturally anxious about the electoral arrangements. The board had encouraged returning officers to 'come in and see us in their difficulties, as it is so much easier to smooth things out by personal interviews than by correspondence'. Despite this, however, there were still concerns as Robinson considered many returning officers to be 'stupid' and their deputies to be even worse, which meant that they had to be nursed and coached through the whole business.[52] Other difficulties were also arising: some of the banks were looking to the board to guarantee the overdrafts that returning officers needed to meet their expenses, and some priests were refusing to provide the keys of schoolhouses where voting was to take place. Robinson told Balfour that there was a simple solution to this last problem: 'Turnscrews are cheap'.[53]

Long before the dates set for the elections – 16 January 1899 for the urban authorities and 6 April for the rural district and county councils – the nationalists' election campaigns were well under way, but there were considerable differences of opinion as to how the elections should be fought. Speaking in Waterford in September 1898, John Redmond argued that the best men should be elected, irrespective of political or religious opinions, so as to ensure that local affairs would be administered efficiently and that the capacity of the Irish people for self-government would be demonstrated to the world.[54] While he urged his followers at a party convention to see to it that nationalist majorities were elected in every county, which would represent an enormous step in the direction of Home Rule, he was harshly critical of Dillon, who had argued that any man who was not determined to forward the principles of the United Irish League (UIL) should not be granted entry to the county councils. The United Irish League was the new political party that had been established by William O'Brien earlier in the year,[55] and which was to become the constituency organisation of the Irish Party in 1900. Dillon, along with O'Brien and Davitt, continued to advocate that the elections should be fought strictly on party political lines. He derided the 'doctrine of toleration' preached by Redmond, rhetorically asking what toleration had the grand juries shown when nationalists sought employment opportunities under them.[56] This strategy was to prevail, with resolutions pledging votes only for candidates who were declared nationalists and members of the UIL being adopted at meetings all over the country. On the other side, the unionists knew that their days in power in the counties were numbered. Their leader, Colonel Saunderson, admitted publicly as early as March 1898 that those who had held county government in their hands for decades would almost universally disappear: the gentlemen who had done the work so well would be replaced by others 'such as we now see on the poor law boards'.[57] In the Commons, Gerald Balfour had urged the gentry – 'the natural leaders of the people' – to seek election to positions which, he said, they alone were truly qualified to fill. They might meet with rebuffs at first, but if they persevered, their reward would be certain.[58] These pleas fell largely on deaf ears: most unionists opted not to stand rather than, as one of them put it, make sport for the philistines and part with what alone was left to them – their self-respect.[59]

The Election Results

According to the LGB, the January elections for 120 urban authorities passed off without a hitch.[60] The extended franchise and the participation of organised labour for the first time were to bring significant changes in membership. Within a few days, the results for county boroughs and urban districts were neatly summarised for the Chief Secretary by Sir David Harrel, who provided a tabular statement, setting out the political affiliations of those elected and comparing the results with those of the previous elections.[61] Four different categories of labour councillors were identified (nationalist, extremist, unionist and non-political) and, as well as unionists and neutrals, there were four categories of nationalists (Dillonites, Redmondites, Healyites and an undefined group). Overall, nationalists were credited with 968 of the total of 1,880 seats, having previously held 1,134, while labour councillors took another 303 (218 of them classified as nationalist labour), having previously held only 15. Unionists won 523 seats in total, 347 of them in Ulster, as against their previous total of 658, and the balance was accounted for by 86 councillors classified as neutrals. Harrel concluded that the marked feature was the introduction of a considerable number of members – one sixth of the total – who had been returned as representatives of labour interests. He went on to explain that:

> The labour representatives include amongst them persons of all religions and of every shade of politics, but by far the greatest number are nationalists not associated with any particular leadership and not holding extreme views. The labour representatives almost balance the losses of the various sections of nationalists who follow leaders.

> The unionists, the neutrals, and the moderate nationalists who do not follow any particular leader, taken together, remain almost as

they were. The electorate may on the whole be regarded as having shown a great appreciation of men of moderate views. It is too soon to express an opinion as to the business capacity of the men who have been returned, but there are no grounds for forming discouraging anticipations.

Addressing his constituents in Leeds on 3 February, Gerald Balfour clearly drew on Harrel's memorandum. He noted the 'remarkable increase in the number of representatives of labour', whose numbers 'about balanced the loss suffered by the nationalists who followed recognised leaders', while unionists had lost about one fifth. Like Harrel, he took comfort in the fact that those elected appeared to have been 'returned with less regard to strictly political considerations than those who were returned under the old electorate'. He also believed that there was no reason to form any 'gloomy anticipation' of the business capacity of the new members and dismissed as idle apprehension the suggestion by William O'Brien that the county councils, which were yet to be elected, would become thirty small parliaments.[62] Redmond was pleased with the results, although the number of nationalist councillors had fallen by fifteen per cent and those classified as Redmondites had been reduced from 436 to 391. He took comfort, however, from the fact that, except in some parts of the north, overwhelming nationalist majorities had been elected.[63]

The election campaign in the counties in the first three months of 1899 attracted far more attention and press coverage than the municipal elections had done. The campaign was marked by large public meetings and processions, with bands and rousing speeches deployed at various locations, along with the occasional outbreaks of violence. Conventions were held to select candidates with appropriate nationalist credentials and opposition to these was discouraged, so much so that there was no contest in a significant proportion of the electoral areas. Overall, the campaign helped to transform the UIL from an isolated agrarian movement into what has been described as 'one of the most influential and popular political organizations in modern Irish history'.[64] The authorities in Dublin were kept in touch with events and speeches by reports from the Royal Irish Constabulary (RIC) county inspectors that were collated and summarised in the Chief Secretary's Office. Some of these reports disclosed electioneering of an unorthodox kind: at Newport, County Mayo, for example, the local parish priest was reported to have told his congregation, in an address from the altar after Mass, that every man should vote for the principles of the UIL and that no man should delude himself with the idea that a vote against the people's candidates would remain undiscovered. He warned that such persons 'will be as well known to me as if I saw the vote recorded, notwithstanding the undoubted secrecy of the polling booth'.[65]

The elections themselves on 6 April passed off quietly almost everywhere and the poll was low, partly because the day was very wet and wild, especially towards the evening. Three days later, Robinson was able to inform Balfour that reports from all of the returning officers had indicated that 'the election arrangements went like clock-work – there wasn't a hitch'– and, to celebrate, he proposed taking two days holiday later in the week and going to the horse races at Punchestown, which were to be attended by the Duke and Duchess of York.[66] More formally, the board's annual report noted that, although more than 4,000 separate elections had taken place, there had not been the slightest disturbance of any kind.[67] Once the votes were counted, it was clear that unionists and large landowners had been swept from office in three of the four provinces and that catholic nationalist councillors, many of them representing tenant farmers, labourers, small shopkeepers and publicans, were to become the dominant force in local affairs in most parts of the country. By contrast to their success at the urban elections a few months earlier, labour candidates failed to make an impression, gaining a total of only eleven seats. While a decisive shift in the location of political power certainly took place in the counties, the view that local self-government in rural Ireland actually dated from the 1899 elections was challenged in a 1984 study by William L. Feingold. As Feingold saw it, the results of the elections simply completed a process which had been going on for some time in poor law administration, where the domination of the boards of guardians by the *ex-officio* landowners had been broken by 1886 in much of the country outside Ulster, as a result of the urgings of Parnell, the Land League and the Catholic Church.[68] In 1899, the UIL gained control of councils in areas where it was well organised, notably in the west, and many nationalist councillors were later to join the UIL as it spread into their own areas, resulting in further success at the elections in 1902.[69] Unionists and landlords who went forward for election suffered heavy defeat and humiliation in most parts of the country. The *Cork Constitution* noted with regret that not a single grand jury-man, unionist or protestant had been elected to Cork County Council.

The figures often quoted for the country as a whole give unionists no more than 25 per cent of the county council seats (265 out of 1,059), with nationalists holding 774. The scale of the electoral rout, however, is more apparent if the figures for directly elected county council members are considered separately. According to a return showing the political constitution of the new councils, which was compiled in the Chief Secretary's Office,[70] nationalists took 563, or just over 80 per cent of these seats, having held no more than 47 seats on the last set of grand juries. The return showed that Dillonites (294) constituted the majority, followed by Redmondites (147), and Healyites (67), with 55 non-aligned. A separate return compiled by the RIC Crimes Special Branch indicated that 114 of the new county councillors were members of the Irish Republican Brotherhood (IRB), along with 468 of the urban and rural district councillors.[71] Unionists, who had dominated the last set of grand juries, holding 704 seats, won only 118 seats on the county councils, 85 of them in Ulster, highlighting more sharply than ever before the division in political opinion that existed within the island. These numbers justify Tom Garvin's argument that 'in a sense, the partition of Ireland dates not from 1920 but from 1898', with a *de facto* acceptance that there were orange and green areas long before partition legislation was contemplated.[72] This may be what the writer of an editorial in the *Freeman's Journal* had in mind when suggesting that, for the nationalists, a victory of a less sweeping character would serve their purposes better.[73]

The First Meetings

The first meetings of the new rural district councils were scheduled to be held on 15 April 1899, with the first county council meetings following on 22 April. The LGB had prepared and issued a circular letter to be read out at each of these meetings, outlining the business which was to be done although, according to Robinson, they were careful not to do anything 'in the way of reading a homily'.[74] He was pleased to find that this agenda circular, as he later referred to it, was a good idea as the councils 'went right through it in nearly every case' and people who had attended meetings in all parts of the country told him the same story – 'that the councillors were desperately on their mettle and anxious to do well'.[75] He told Balfour that the minutes of the first meetings of the district councils and guardians suggested that 'the work was got through on the whole most satisfactorily', while the minutes of county council meetings that had become available were 'models of really business-like proceedings'. He took pleasure in adding that 'even our official pessimist [Bagwell] – who has been predicting at the top of his voice for the last six months, hopeless confusion, dislocation and deadlock – is unable to deny that he is mistaken and I have been taking the liberty of gently rubbing this into him'.[76]

Notwithstanding Robinson's confidential letters to the Chief Secretary and the board's official pronouncements, the first meetings of the new county councils did not entirely conform to the official guidelines. Redmond told the House of Commons in February that the very first formal act of those urban authorities, to which nationalist majorities had been elected, was to make a declaration of their adhesion to the principle of national self-government, demonstrating that the great masses of the Irish people were determined to work the act to promote the interests of Home Rule.[77] Much the same procedure was seen at the first county council meetings when many of the new councillors adopted the UIL strategy of making maximum use of existing institutions to give authority, and the appearance of legitimacy, to the activities and strategies of the league. Thus, from the beginning, most of the new councils were passing resolutions that demanded Home Rule, expressed support for the Boers, or dealt with the university question, railway rates and charges, and various other political and economic matters that did not come within their areas of responsibility. Robinson, however, was not particularly concerned with these resolutions. He reported to Balfour on 23 April that 'most councils have passed the usual resolutions about Home Rule, England's tyranny, and the money taken by England from the blood and bowels of Ireland', but suggested that 'Ireland would be a dull country without its resolutions and its romance and its delicious grievances.'[78] In the House of Commons, Balfour had already dismissed as irrelevant the political resolutions which boards of guardians had been in the habit of passing and which the county councils were also likely to pass. But there was a limit as far as he was concerned: after Dillon had advocated that the issue of reinstating evicted tenants should be taken up by the county councils, he was warned that councils would find that 'their powers are somewhat more limited and circumscribed than they imagine' and they would 'commit a great mistake if they enter upon a province which is clearly not their own'.[79]

'A Triumph for the Local Government Board'

In addition to the new appointments at board level in May 1898, there were other significant changes in the organisation of the LGB in the following two years. Charles P. Cotton, chief engineering inspector since 1879, retired at the end of December 1898 and J. H. Monahan Q C, who had served as the board's legal counsel since 1879 and had been appointed legal adviser in May 1898, died on 1 March 1900. Dr Thomas Mooney, a catholic who had been board secretary since 1887, retired at the age of 53 in October 1899, having been absent due to ill-health for almost a year, and was replaced by Henry Swaine, another catholic and formerly a first-class clerk. Robinson's rather disparaging comment mentioned that, after working for a week on implementing the act, Mooney had a nervous breakdown 'and disappeared for good from official life'.[80] These changes meant that Robinson, as the only member of the senior management team who had significant experience at that level, found himself in a particularly powerful but demanding position. It also meant that the preparatory work, which had to be undertaken to bring the new councils into operation, had to be planned and directed largely by him.

Balfour acknowledged in the House of Commons in June 1899 that the principal burden of implementing the act had fallen on Robinson and claimed that any department of State, whether English or Irish, might justly be proud of what had been achieved.[81] Robinson himself had relished the challenge of bringing the new system into operation and was proud of what had been accomplished, even though it was 'only by working from early morning till long after midnight, night after night, throughout the autumn and spring' that he had been able to get through the work. Although he was well accustomed to hard work, 'the strain has been throughout so constant and so heavy that nothing but the confident hope of being able to make the act a successful working measure has rendered my labours bearable'.[82] He acknowledged that his board colleagues had also to work long hours and Micks was obliged to take leave when 'the additional work had completely knocked him up'. They expected that the great pressure of work would continue for another two years at least, making it necessary for them to 'abandon all ideas of enjoying the few hours of leisure to which public servants are entitled'.[83]

Well over one hundred years later, and taking account of twentieth-century experience of the implementation of proposals for structural reform in the public sector, it is difficult to disagree with Balfour's conclusion: the reorganisation which was planned and fully implemented between the initial policy announcement in March 1897 and the first elections in April 1899 was indeed a significant achievement for which the LGB and Robinson in particular, deserved great credit. The smooth transition was, as Pauric Travers described it, 'a triumph for the Local Government Board'.[84] If, as R. B. McDowell remarked, the magnitude of the operation is taken into account, 'the great revolution in Irish local government was accomplished remarkably swiftly and smoothly. And if a self-congratulatory note is clearly discernible in the board's reports, a measure of official self-satisfaction is forgivable'.[85] It cannot have come as a surprise to anyone that Robinson, who had been a CB since 1897, was raised to the rank of Knight Commander (KCB) in May 1900 in recognition of his work for the previous two years. Because of his pride in what had been achieved, he was at pains to ensure that the board's annual report of more than 1,000 pages for 1898–99 contained lengthy particulars about the act and the implementation process.[86] In light of subsequent events, including the destruction of the board's records in the Custom House fire of May 1921, and the gaps in the holdings of the Chief Secretary's Office Registered Papers at the National Archives in Dublin, Robinson's almost apologetic statement to Balfour justifying the length of the report was indeed a prescient one: 'It is historical, and fifty years hence, someone may want to refer to the steps taken, and every other record will be destroyed.'[87]

NOTES

1   *Estimates for Civil Services,* various years.
2   *Freeman's Journal,* 8 Mar. 1898.
3   *Hansard* IV, 55, 21 Mar. 1898, 424–26.
4   *Irish Times,* 26 Feb. 1898.
5   Cadogan–Abercorn correspondence, March 1898, Parliamentary Archives, cited in Lawrence McBride, *The Greening of Dublin Castle* (Washington, 1991), pp.79–80.
6   *Hansard* IV, 56, 29 Apr. 1898, 1544.
7   *Hansard* IV, 58, 20 May 1898, 181–82.
8   NAI, CSORP 1898/5913 and 6360, but the original correspondence cannot be found in NAI; Harrel to Balfour, 30 Mar. 1898, TNA, PRO 30/60/15.
9   Harrel to Balfour, 19 Apr. 1898, PRO 30/60/15.
10 *Hansard* IV, 73, 22 June 1899, 365.
11 *Hansard* IV, 99, 8 Aug. 1901, 103–04.
12 *Hansard* III, 282, 4 Aug. 1883, 1586–87.
13 *Irish Times,* 11 May 1898; the original papers relating to the appointment (CSORP 1898/7871 and 8385) cannot be found in NAI.
14 Robinson to Balfour, 2 and 10 May 1898, NAS, Balfour Papers, GD 433/2/230/16 and 17; Major J. E. Jameson of Dundrum, County Dublin was nationalist MP for Clare County West from 1895 to 1906.
15 Robinson to Balfour, 29 May 1898, NAS, Balfour Papers, GD 433/2/230/18.
16 Sir Henry Robinson, *Memories: Wise and Otherwise* (London, 1923), p.127.
17 Harrel to Balfour, 30 Mar. 1898, TNA, PRO 30/60/15.
18 Ennis to Dillon, 17 Jul. 1898, TCD, John Dillon Papers, MS 6800/116
19 *Estimates for Civil Services,* 1898–1904.
20 Judges in the higher courts were paid considerably greater salaries, as were land commissioners.
21 Robinson to Balfour, 20 May, 4 June and 16 July, 1899, TNA, PRO 30/60/15; Stafford and Micks to Balfour, 30 May 1899, TNA, PRO 30/60/15.
22 Robinson to Balfour, 19 Mar. 1900, NAS, Balfour Papers, GD 433/2/114/13; the original Treasury letter setting out the new salary scales (CSORP 1898/8395) cannot be found in NAI nor can the Treasury letters (CSORP 1900/4575, 4576) rejecting the applications for increases.

23 *Irish Times*, 11 May 1898.

24 *Hansard* IV, 58, 24 May 1898, 630–31.

25 Robinson to Balfour, n.d. [May 1898], NAS, Balfour Papers, GD 433/2/230/9.

26 Robinson to Balfour, n.d. [May 1898], NAS, Balfour Papers, GD 433/2/114/14.

27 R. B. McDowell, 'Administration and the Public Services, 1870–1921' in *NHI* VI, p.593.

28 *Hansard* IV, 99, 8 Aug. 1901, 103–04.

29 *Hansard* IV, 62, 21 July 1898, 557–58, 563–65.

30 *Hansard* IV, 62, 25 July 1898, 1070–72.

31 Letters from Gerald Balfour to Lady Frances Balfour, Sept. 1886, NAS, Balfour Papers, GD 433/2.

32 *Irish Times*, 5 Dec. 1905.

33 *Irish Times*, 13 Sept. 1898.

34 *Irish Times*, 7 Jan. 1897, letter commenting on the proceedings of the Financial Relations Commission.

35 Robinson to Balfour, 16 and 19 Aug. 1898, TNA, PRO 30/60/15; it is not clear whether Londonderry had used the expression 'antidote to Micks' or whether it originated with Robinson.

36 Robinson to Balfour, 12 Feb. 1899, TNA, PRO 30/60/15.

37 Robinson to Balfour, 19 Feb. 1899, TNA, PRO 30/60/15.

38 Robinson to Balfour, 9 Apr. 1899, TNA, PRO 30/60/15.

39 Robinson to Balfour, 4 June 1899, TNA, PRO 30/60/15.

40 Robinson to Balfour, 18 July 1899, TNA PRO 30/60/15.

41 *Irish Times*, 21 Apr. 1899.

42 Robinson to Balfour, 23 Apr. 1899, TNA, PRO 30/60/15.

43 *Hansard* IV, 70, 24 Apr. 1899, 385–86.

44 *Hansard* IV, 73, 22 June 1899, 365; from 1905 until his death in 1918, Bagwell served as commissioner for national education, still a diehard uncompromising unionist who confessed in 1918, when he was one of those responsible for the split in southern unionist ranks, that he was too old to change his views.

45 *AR*, 1898–99, pp.5–6.

46 Robinson to Balfour, 30 Mar. 1898, TNA, PRO 30/60/15.

47 Robinson to Balfour, 19 Aug. 1898, TNA, PRO 30/60/15.

48 Robinson to Balfour, 27 Dec. 1898, TNA, PRO 30/60/15.

49 Robinson to Balfour, 3 Feb. 1899, TNA, PRO 30/60/15.

50 Robinson to Balfour, 6 Mar. 1899, TNA, PRO 30/60/15.

51 Robinson to Balfour, 6 Mar. and 5 Apr. 1899, TNA, PRO 30/60/15.

52 Robinson to Balfour, 19 Feb. and 5 Apr. 1899, TNA, PRO 30/60/15.

53 Robinson to Balfour, 19 Feb. and 5 Apr. 1899, TNA, PRO 30/60/15.

54 *Annual Register*, 1898.

55 *Irish Times*, 11 Oct. 1898.

56 *Irish Times*, 16 Dec. 1898.

57 *Hansard* IV, 55, 21 Mar. 1898, 494.

58 *Hansard* IV, 53, 21 Feb. 1898, 1248.

59 Letter of 26 Mar. 1898 to W. E. H. Lecky, quoted in Catherine B. Shannon, *Arthur J. Balfour and Ireland* (Washington, 1988), p.101.

60 *AR*, 1898–99, p.10.

61 Harrel to chief secretary, 24 Jan 1899, TNA, PRO 30/60/28; Numerical return of Results, TNA, CO 904/184/1.

62 *Irish Times*, 4 Feb. 1899.

63 *Hansard* IV, 66, 16 Feb. 1899, 1180–83.

64 Fergus Campbell, *Land and Revolution: Nationalist Politics in the West of Ireland 1891–1921* (Oxford, 2005), pp.39–40.

65 Extracts from a report of an altar address by Revd Canon Greally, Newport, 2 Apr. 1899, TNA, CO 904/184/1.

66 Robinson to Balfour, 9 Apr. 1899, TNA, PRO 30/60/15.

67 *AR*, 1898–99, p.12.

68 William L. Feingold, *The Revolt of the Tenantry: The Transformation of Local Government in Ireland, 1872–1886* (Boston, 1984), pp.232–8.

69 Philip Bull, 'The UIL and the Reunion of the Irish Parliamentary Party', *IHS*, xxvi, No. 101 (May 1988), p.62.

70 Numerical Return shewing political constitution of the County Councils elected in 1899 and of the last existing Grand Juries, TNA, CO 904/184/1.

71 Numerical Return of County and District Councillors reported by the Crimes Special Branch, RIC, to belong to the Irish Republican Brotherhood, TNA, CO 904/184/1; Owen McGee's study of *The IRB* (Dublin, 2005, 268) suggests, not unreasonably, that these estimates were very possibly gross exaggerations.

72 Tom Garvin, *1922: The Birth of Irish Democracy* (Dublin, 1996), p.65.

73 *Freeman's Journal*, 10 Apr. 1899.

74 Robinson to Balfour, 19 Feb. 1899, TNA, PRO 30/60/15.

75 Robinson to Balfour, 25 Apr. 1899, TNA, PRO 30/60/15.

76 Robinson to Balfour, 23 and 30 Apr. 1899, TNA, PRO 30/60/15.

77 *Hansard* IV, 66, 16 Feb. 1899, 1180–83.

78 Robinson to Balfour, 23 Apr. 1899, TNA, PRO 30/60/15.

79 *Hansard* IV, 69, 12 Apr. 1899, 921–22, 926–27.

80 Robinson, *Memories*, p.128.

81 *Hansard* IV, 73, 30 June 1899, 1226–27.

82 Robinson to Balfour, 20 May 1899, TNA, PRO 30/60/15.

83 Robinson to Balfour, 18 July 1899, TNA, PRO 30/60/28.

84 Pauric Travers, 'A Bloodless Revolution: The Democratisation of Irish Local Government, 1898–9' in Mary E. Daly (ed.), *County & Town: One Hundred years of Local Government in Ireland* (Dublin, 2001), p.14.

85 R. B. McDowell, 'Administration and the Public Services, 1870–1921' in *NHI* VI, p.594.

86 *AR*, 1898–99; the report included the text of many of the orders and circulars issued during the year.

87 Robinson to Balfour, 1 Aug. 1899, TNA, PRO 30/60/15.

CHAPTER IV

A Remarkably Harmonious Working Relationship with the Local Councils

'All the New Machinery is Working Admirably'

Having devoted so much of the previous two years to planning and implementing a revolutionary new system of democratic local government, in April 1899 Robinson found himself facing the challenge of presiding over the activities of a network of some 400 local councils, with a total of more than 11,000 elected members, most of whom (except in Ulster) were nationalists, who had never previously held office. Notwithstanding the political context, however, and the inexperience of many of the councillors, the initial transfer of power was so orderly that Robinson could tell Balfour after a few months that 'all the new machinery is working admirably in its own appointed groove'.[1] But for him the most satisfactory thing was that the new councils:

> ...in spite of their idiotic Boer resolutions and their antics over the green flag, and their violent controversies as to whether the wolfhound on the official seal should be in the centre of the rising sun or beside it, in spite of all these determined efforts to turn themselves into burlesque – when it comes to real, practical, business-like work they are doing splendidly and the jobbing of road contractors and grand jury officers is receiving a great check.

He anticipated that the winter of 1899–1900 would be a busy one, with much work still to be done 'knocking off the rough edges and filling in the gaps of last year's work'. Despite this, he was happy that nothing facing the board looked troublesome: 'We are always more or less among the breakers, but no very dangerous rocks [are] ahead.' In December, things were still 'going satisfactorily all round; the councils are not so difficult to lead as you might think from the aggressive tone of their resolutions about us. We have half a dozen struggles going on, but we shall be able to make everything right, I hope'.[2] By early 1900 it was 'a great thing to be able to look back on the nightmare of the past two years and to realise that all is running smoothly and that our doubts and uncertainties are solved and our anxieties for the result are cleared up'.[3]

Because the attitude of the new county councils to the LGB varied in the initial stages, the board was a bit at sea: 'Some councils are furious if we give them any advice as to their procedure, while others are equally indignant if we don't, and say they fail to see the use of a central authority if they don't advise the councils.'[4] Nevertheless, minor difficulties were arising: according to Robinson, there was 'a disposition among some of the new urban district councils to want to get rid of their old officers'. When a number of them asked if they could do so he felt that it would 'be rather a scandal and would look very bad if they were to want to job their friends already'.[5] A number of the county councils set about transferring their accounts from one bank to another, because in some cases, as Robinson saw it, bank managers had 'poured whiskey down the throats of the voters' on behalf of councillors who in turn had pledged themselves to vote for the establishment of the accounts at their branch.[6] He was critical too of some of the county secretaries who were 'quite hopeless'; it was 'terrible work' trying to shake them up and the board was having to get them up to Dublin one by one to explain matters to them.[7]

Compromise and Conciliation in the Late-Nineteenth-Century

When Robinson took charge of the LGB, the operating procedures of the organisation, the system of controls which it exercised, and its reliance on teams of locally-based inspectors and auditors to guide, supervise and effectively control the activities of local authorities were well settled. The extensive powers which the board had inherited from the poor law commissioners in the 1870s were without parallel in England and, from the very beginning, had been bitterly resented by many poor law guardians, regardless of their political opinions. Slight remains of this resentment still faced the LGB in the 1890s but there were additional difficulties at that stage when the board was seen by many, especially by the growing number of nationalist guardians, as the most obvious representation of British rule in every locality in Ireland. The result, as William L. Feingold saw it in *The Revolt of the Tenantry* (1984), was that 'the board's authority was to be opposed and obstructed whenever possible'.[8] Although a more recent study by Virginia Crossman suggests that this assertion is not entirely borne out by the evidence,[9] the board itself recognised in 1892 that because there was 'a new class of elected guardians ... politics became the ruling factor in the acts and decisions of the poor law boards'.[10] Robinson may well have been the author of this claim, although earlier comments of his on nationalist guardians were relatively benign, noting that they were 'intelligent enough according to their lights' and while they acted at times in a way that 'the exigencies of patriotism oblige them to' it was 'nevertheless a fact that they are extremely sensitive about the capabilities of transacting the ordinary poor law business'.[11] In his 1923 memoirs, however, he reverted to more sweeping criticism: except in Ulster, opposition to the government and the executive 'was the first principle of political life, and the determination to obstruct and make government troublesome could in great measure be effected by constant resistance to the LGB'.[12] Returning to the subject in his second volume of memoirs, he wrote that his board 'was naturally regarded by the patriotic local guardians and councillors as the statutory Saxon curse on the country and a department which could never appreciate the high-spirited Irish contempt for the restriction of dirty little English acts of Parliament'.[13] In his survey of administration and the public services up to 1921, R. B. McDowell adopted Robinson's viewpoint suggesting that, to some extent, attacks on the LGB by local councils and MPs reflected 'the hostility of Irish nationalists to Westminster legislation and the Irish executive'.[14] In a letter to local councils in 1920, W. T. Cosgrave, the Dáil Minister for Local Government, indirectly endorsed that view by suggesting that 'a more rigid observance of regulations and orders will be noticeable when the public bodies are acting under a national authority than was the case when the supervising body was of enemy origin'.[15]

In 1899, Robinson was amused rather than alarmed by what he described as 'sunbursty' resolutions passed by some of the new councils and by the 'very romantic' efforts of other councils to design their official seals. He told Balfour in one case that 'the wolfhound, the round tower, Erin with a harp, and the rising sun bursting out through a cloud of shamrocks, all these devices were put to the vote and ordered to be included'.[16] Although *The Leader* took a critical view of the councils' design efforts, damning childish efforts to exploit the flag 'in the cause of cheap and effeminate patriotism',[17] Robinson's dismissal of the significance of the patriotic and nationalist activities of the new councils in the early stages were entirely consistent with the tactics of the board in the 1880s and 1890s when, despite strong pressure from the Chief Secretary's Office, it adopted the sensible policy of generally ignoring political resolutions. Even when furious protests were made by *ex-officio* guardians and RIC officers, the board still maintained that the best response to such resolutions was to ignore them. Overall, Virginia Crossman's study of LGB activities in the last decades of the nineteenth century concludes that the board 'pursued a cautious strategy' and relied more on persuasion rather than coercion,[18] not unlike the approach of the English board which, according to historian Christine Bellamy, was flexible and pragmatic, tolerating a great deal of variation in local practice, with technical requirements mediated by political judgment.[19]

'We Must Expect to Meet with Much Organised Resistance'

Whether the policy of compromise and conciliation could continue after 1899 was clearly a matter of concern to Robinson. It was obvious that the new county and district councils would be dominated from the outset by nationalists in most parts of the country, and he anticipated that if the thousands of members of these councils were to adopt the nationalist guardians' attitude of opposing and obstructing the board, a challenging and possibly unsustainable situation would result. By December 1899, he was telling Balfour that 'we are able now to form a very fair opinion as to what our relations with these new, popularly elected bodies will be', and while the situation was reasonably satisfactory at that stage, he expected later on 'to meet with much organised resistance'.[20] However, the weight attached to these comments should be discounted to some extent, given that they were offered in the context of a submission seeking Treasury sanction for substantial additional staff numbers.

In 1898, in what might be seen as a concession to the more democratic character of the new local authorities and the spirit of the age about which Gerald Balfour had spoken,[21] the extensive powers which had been inherited by the LGB (including the drastic power to dissolve a recalcitrant board of guardians) were not, in general, extended to the new county and district councils. Robinson was anxious that the local authorities should be encouraged to come to it for help and guidance. In March 1899 he told Balfour that 'it has been our practice for the last fifty years to advise the local councils' and in spite of the views of the attorney general, he intended that this should continue because 'they need advice more than ever now – without it, everything would be in a state of hopeless confusion'.[22] A few months later, he hoped that 'when we get to know the peculiar idiosyncrasies of the different councils, we shall be able to tone our correspondence to suit each in a manner that will lessen all friction considerably'.[23] However, good intentions of this kind – even if an attempt were made to carry them into effect – were not enough to obviate criticism of Robinson and his colleagues as autocrats whose actions were dictated by political considerations. The board itself, although it was always based in the Custom House, also continued to attract criticism as a 'Castle Board'. As such, it was seen to be an essential part of the Irish government and, even if it were headed by an archangel, it would still be distrusted, as Robinson's friend, Denis Kelly, the Catholic Bishop of Ross, put it when speaking in 1906 about the Department of Agriculture and Technical Instruction, which suffered the same difficulty in its early years.[24]

'Almost Automatic Resistance [...] to Centralized, Bureaucratic Control'

Even if political considerations were never to arise, conflict between a central authority and local councils is almost always inevitable because of different views on how the system should operate. Thus, as R. B. McDowell saw it, attacks on the board represented 'the almost automatic resistance that local elective bodies are likely to show to centralized, bureaucratic control'.[25] In 1899, the potential for conflict of this kind was considerable as so few of the thousands of county and rural district councillors had previous experience in local government. Many of them were members of the UIL or had been endorsed by the league, and many others joined the league as it spread into their own areas, sometimes doing so *en masse* during council meetings.[26] In the euphoric mood that prevailed after the overwhelming success of nationalist candidates at the elections, councillors would have looked forward to implementing policies and developing services in a manner which, as they saw it, was denied to the majority of them until that moment. They would have interpreted the results of the elections as involving a real transfer of power from the grand jury regime. Those who believed, as John Dillon did, that the grand juries had shown little tolerance when nationalists sought employment opportunities under them, must have been disposed to use the levers of power to benefit nationalists, catholics, and local people, just as grand jurors were seen to have favoured their own class.[27] The new councillors would have been slow to recognise that a local government system necessarily involves a form of partnership between central and local authorities, with at least some controls and restraints being applied by the central body at key points, leaving the board open to accusations that it was attempting to take back with one hand what had been given with the other, and creating a local government system which was little better than a farce. Nevertheless, W. T. Cosgrave's 1950 comments on the board were remarkably benign: it had 'full and detailed information regarding every phase of the activities of public bodies' because of its efficient staff of inspectors, but even where it had specific powers to supervise particular services, or was subsidising services, 'care was taken ... to avoid friction and to have harmonious relations with public bodies'.[28]

Less Unpopular than 'The Mysterious Dublin Castle'

Robinson believed – and probably with more than a little justification – that the LGB was less unpopular than 'the mysterious Dublin Castle'. He argued that he and the other members of the board were well known to most members of the local councils, whereas 'the Irish government ... or Dublin Castle, as it was known, was a shadowy thing ... inaccessible phantoms and behind them ... clerks in the Castle who were somewhat out of touch with local bodies and without opportunities of meeting and knowing them'.[29] Much the same view of the Castle administration was held by Chief Secretary Birrell, who told the House of Commons in 1907 that it was 'switched off' from the current of national life and feeling; no pulse of real life ran within its gloomy portals and 'the main current of Irish life as it rushes past its walls passes by almost unheeded'.[30] By contrast to his civil service colleagues in the Castle, Robinson, like Sir Horace Plunkett at DATI, regarded his position as 'a human link' between the people and the government. Plunkett wrote about the stream of callers who arrived at his offices in Upper Merrion Street, particularly when an event like the Dublin Horse Show brought crowds from the country to Dublin, wishing to see the ultimate source of responsibility or in concrete terms 'himself'.[31] At the Custom House, Robinson was in a similar position, and recalled somewhat cynically that on the occasion of Punchestown Horse Races and the Horse Show, 'a mass of business from all parts of the country came to the fore, which was found to require personal interviews at the ratepayers' expense with the board by local councillors'.[32] But over and above these possibly contrived reasons for visits to Dublin, Robinson personally, or the board as a whole, received deputations on a regular basis from local authorities and representative bodies of various kinds. Visits by deputations were sometimes noted in an addendum to the minutes of the daily board meetings; in addition, lists of the deputations received were usually published in the board's annual report (twenty-three of them, for example, in the report for 1908–09) and detailed reports on the proceedings at meetings with particular groups, (sometimes prepared by staff of the board) often appeared in the national and provincial press.

Robinson told the Royal Commission on Local Taxation in October 1899 that while the new councils were 'strange to the work at first', they had 'done their work admirably so far as road work is concerned and the preparation of the rate books and everything of that nature'.[33] The board's annual reports for the first few years after the implementation of the 1898 Act also painted a picture of a generally harmonious relationship with local councils, conveying an impression of satisfaction, if not pride, at the manner in which the new system was working. The report for 1899–1900 recorded that the predictions of those who had affirmed the inevitable breakdown under the strain of administering a complex new system had not come true.[34] The report for the following year stated that 'further experience enables us to confirm the statement in our last report as to the satisfactory manner in which the duties of the county councils and rural district councils have been discharged'.[35] In 1902, the board was again reporting that the conduct of their affairs by local councils and their officials, and particularly their financial administration, continued to justify the delegation of substantial powers to them, although 'certain political difficulties' had been introduced by some of the smaller bodies into their business, especially in regard to appointments and the award of contracts.[36]

Getting Bad Press – and a Lecture from the *Irish Times*

In contrast to the impression conveyed in the annual reports, Robinson was alleged by a Dáil deputy in 1924 to have stated that the local government system involved 'a continual struggle or a sort of war' between the central and local authorities and that he could not 'allow local government to march but had to compel it to shamble'.[37] Reports in the national and local press of serious disputes between the board and local councils in the early years of the century suggest that a tussle of sorts was in fact going on at an early stage, at least in some areas. Robinson, however, was critical of some of these reports and seemed to believe that the board was unfairly getting a bad press: he told Balfour in July 1899 that the *Freeman's Journal* was going downhill fast and was starting a regular campaign against the board 'hoping to win back favour' – and if this continued, the other papers would be obliged to follow suit.[38] But even the *Irish Times* regularly

carried reports of criticism of the board by councils around the country
to such an extent that the newspaper's editor decided in May 1901 to
lecture the board on how it should conduct its affairs: 'Friction between
the board and the local authorities under its control should be reduced to
a minimum', and while great power had rightly been given to the board –
because without its restraining influence the administration of many rural
districts would have fallen into confusion – the local councils should not
be 'dry-nursed ... in too grand-motherly fashion'. Instead, they should be
allowed to learn through their own mistakes, to which, if not too glaring,
the board might turn a blind eye.[39] A few months later, the *Irish Times*
returned to the subject, having reported another clash between the board
and local councils:

> We have all along held that red tape should not be too tightly
> bound round the local bodies. Reasonable laxity must be allowed
> if the various boards are to be permitted to learn the art of local
> government. Mistakes will necessarily be made from time to
> time, but they will right themselves for the most part. The Local
> Government Board, therefore, while they should not in the main
> relax their control over the various boards, might very well allow
> the exercise of a considerable degree of independence, for that,
> we venture to assert, was contemplated by the act. They will not be
> blamed for the occasional blunders that will be made owing to their
> acceptance of this principle. The science of local government will
> not be learned through the medium of 'orders', and a strenuous
> endeavour to drive elected bodies, with a reasonable sense of their
> own importance, as representatives of the people, can only lead to
> incessant disputes.[40]

Some of the disputes between the board and local councils that occurred
in the years after 1899 arose from what might be classed as political factors.
Such factors included spending money on the procurement of green flags
and flagstaffs to be erected over courthouses where county councils held
their meetings or the provision of street name-plates in the Irish language.
Allowing workhouses where rural district councils held their meetings to
be also used for meetings of the UIL gave rise to major controversy in
some areas when the LGB, in which the workhouses were vested, attempted
through the courts to have the practice ended. As Robinson explained to
the Chief Secretary, the board had to keep within the very strict letter
of the law '[and] the judges have no mercy on us if – even unwittingly –
we deviate a hair's breadth from the law.'[41] When disputes such as these,

and disputes concerning more substantial matters, began to generate a significant number of court challenges by local councils, the board foolishly, and rather arrogantly, attempted to establish that its decisions were exempt from the writ of *certiorari*, but this defence was firmly denied to them by Lord Chief Baron Palles in the court of appeal in February 1901.[42] Subsequently, the board suffered an embarrassing number of reverses when the courts, much to the satisfaction, if not delight, of its critics, quashed particular decisions either as mistaken interpretations of the law or because they were made in excess of jurisdiction.

Imposing an Immense Burden of Additional Costs on the Ratepayers

Because the new councils were profoundly conservative, parsimonious, and slow to embrace change, they attached enormous significance to economy and the maintenance of low rate poundages so much so that, within a few months of the elections, one of the most frequent and most persistent font of criticism of the LGB – quickly taken up by nationalist MPs in the House of Commons – was the claim that requirements and actions of the board were imposing an immense burden of additional costs on the ratepayers now that the landlords had been relieved of the obligation to pay half the poor rate. There were objections to the administrative costs which the establishment of the new system necessarily entailed, including even the costs of compiling and printing the new registers of electors. There was also a reluctance to offer reasonable levels of salary and conditions of service to employees, and there was a lack of enthusiasm on the part of many councillors for the extra spending which was required to improve basic health and welfare services for their constituents. The board's efforts to improve standards at workhouse hospitals often met with resistance from guardians. The board's aim to introduce trained nurses at these hospitals in place of untrained staff or long-stay pauper inmates was also contested because of the expense involved and because it could force nuns to leave these hospitals. Developments like these forced Robinson to tell Balfour that councils' error on the side of economy would be the worst feature of their administration.[43]

Because of the overriding concern of the early generations of local councillors for minimising expenditure and reducing the rates, Robinson and his board had great difficulty in persuading councils to improve their services, particularly in the health and welfare fields. He also experienced difficulty in convincing parliamentarians to allow relevant English legislation to be extended to Ireland. Councillors' attitude reflected that of John Redmond, whose main reason for strongly supporting the 1898 Act had been that the new councils would be proof of the capacity of Irishmen to govern themselves. As a regular critic of what he believed to be the 'monstrous and hopelessly' extravagant and corrupt British system of administration in Ireland, Redmond saw the test of good local government not in an improvement or expansion of services but rather as a reduction in expenditure on county administration. In March 1908, in moving a Home Rule motion in the House of Commons, he declared that the competence of the Irish people to manage their own affairs was clearly demonstrated by the fact that the county councils had reduced the rates all over Ireland in the previous eight years, whereas rural rates in England had increased significantly during that period.[44] The same approach was evident in 1911 in the remarks of the Chairman of Galway County Council, who described the operation of the 1898 Act as 'magnificent proof of the administrative capacity of the Irish people' and claimed that 'all the predictions of our critics were falsified' by the financial administration of the local councils: instead of extravagance, the councils were economical and almost niggardly in their various activities.[45] Effectively endorsing the views expressed by Robinson to Balfour years earlier, L. Paul Dubois had noted in 1908 that while the 'Cassandras of reaction' had predicted all kinds of disaster, the local councils had been more economical than their predecessors.[46] Harold Spender, the liberal political journalist and author, wrote a few years later that if the county councils possessed any fault, it was that they were too thrifty and economical.[47]

Appointments, Salaries and Conditions of Service

Given that many of the councillors elected in 1899 would probably have agreed with John Dillon's view that there was little or no evidence of a 'doctrine of toleration' by the grand juries when nationalists sought employment opportunities under them,[48] it would have been naïve to expect that there would be no difficulties when appointments came to be made by the new councils. In practice, failure by particular councils to observe the rules and regulations concerning the recruitment and employment of staff regularly led to intervention by the board, with public controversy often following. Jobbery had been endemic in local government in the years before 1898, with appointments being made on the basis of political views, religion, family connections or, especially in rural areas and small towns, a simple preference for awarding to a native of the area one of the small number of permanent and pensionable jobs available locally. Most modern historians accept that in their operations, the new local councils failed to bring an end to this form of small-scale corruption, which had characterised the old regime.[49] Patrick Maume found that many of the nationalists who dominated the councils quickly developed a reputation for jobbery and petty corruption[50] or, as Professor Joe Lee more colourfully put it, they 'dutifully attended to the three "Fs" of popular politics – friends, family and favours', resulting in a situation in which non-canvassing automatically disqualified.[51]

As early as 1905, when relatively few Sinn Féin members were involved in local government, Arthur Griffith was denouncing the fact that efficient administration and moral standards were being impaired by the public appointments system. He also argued that patronage should be exercised in the interests of the nation rather than the individual.[52] Canvassing for appointments however, continued to be the order of the day in most counties. There was nothing the LGB could do about this except where the essential qualifications for certain positions were ignored, or where a council decided to restrict eligibility for particular positions by reference to unacceptable requirements, or where there were allegations of bribery. In cases of this kind, refusal by the board to endorse an appointment generated controversy, often giving rise to questions in Parliament, even where it was obvious that the board's position was fully justified. It is worth noting in this context that Catherine Shannon's study of local government in the 1899–1905 period found that if the LGB had not been efficient in its supervisory duties, councils would probably have wandered 'off the path of efficient administration on to one of agitation and consequent inefficiency'.[53]

When religious factors, directly or indirectly, came into play in making appointments, the board was slow to become involved because their functions were confined to seeing that the person selected for a particular post was properly qualified. Where a number of qualified candidates were available, they had to leave it to the vote of the councillors or guardians to determine which of them should be selected. Salary levels for staff in various grades were also a source of conflict with the new councils, especially where the salary decided on by a particular council was much less than the salary paid to the outgoing officeholder, the view being taken in some cases that the burden on the ratepayers arising from pension payments would have to be offset by the payment of a lesser salary to the new appointee.[54] The board regularly protested that proposed salary levels would not attract candidates of good calibre. Their arguments, however, generally had little effect, but they were able to withhold approval for appointments in some cases until better conditions were offered.

'Not the Best Plan ... to be Always Fulminating its Edicts against Popularly Elected Bodies'

There is ample evidence that the LGB (or at least some of its officials) occasionally adopted an excessively legalistic approach to particular issues and were reluctant to look for a way of avoiding disputes and controversy. Some chief secretaries hinted in public that they did not altogether approve of this approach. Wyndham, for example, seemed to believe that the county councils should be trusted to carry out their duties and told the Prime Minister in 1904 that the government should not revert to the view that the councils were unfit for the duties which devolved on them.[55] In January 1902, he told a deputation that Robinson 'had done a great deal of public work in recent years for which we ought to be grateful, and in nothing has he succeeded more than in the manner in which he has been able to show popularly elected bodies how they can advance the interests of those whom they represent'. But, he added, 'it is not the best plan for the LGB to be always fulminating its edicts against popularly elected bodies' and a great deal of good could be effected by pursuing another course.[56] Some years later, in an election speech in his Aberdeen constituency, Chief Secretary Bryce suggested that the administration of Ireland should avoid needless friction. While he believed that the officials at the top of the various departments were men of great capacity and high character, he felt that there was a need to bring the administration more into touch with the people, to let them feel that they have a real part in the government of Ireland, and to demonstrate that Parliament wished to conduct the government of Ireland according to Irish ideas.[57] Interventions by Bryce in certain issues in the months that followed provided clear evidence that he was attempting to give effect to these views and in a speech at Sligo in September, he led his listeners to believe that his new doctrine had been adopted by the LGB itself. He told his audience that it was the desire of the board 'to get into more intimate and friendly touch with the local bodies in Ireland. They desired co-operation with the local bodies, because in this way they would be better able to understand local needs'.[58]

Robinson and his colleagues are unlikely to have been overly impressed by the various declarations made by Bryce or by the attitude of Under-Secretary MacDonnell. MacDonnell attempted to persuade Bryce in 1906 that local bodies should be allowed to make their own mistakes in the award of contracts, even if the ratepayers, or those who were provided with medicines, were to suffer. Robinson's approach was right, he admitted, if regard were to be had only to economy, 'but what of self-government?'

Guardians might therefore be allowed to make their own contracts and the ratepayers 'may be trusted to call the guardians to account, sooner or later' – and what if there were weak drugs for a while? 'Who will suffer – the people will only die a nationalist death'.[59] Augustine Birrell, who succeeded to the Chief Secretary position in January 1907, had a more realistic view: he told the House of Commons in May of that year that

> The Local Government Board of any country had difficult duties to perform and it could not always be popular if it performed those duties properly. No public department could do its duty properly if it did not aim at the popularity which followed after long years of good work rather than the popularity which was sought after by making easy the path of everybody with whom it was brought into contact.[60]

Speaking again in the Commons a year later, in light of experience of his role as President of the LGB, he conveyed the impression that there were no real difficulties in the board's relationship with local councils at that stage: the system had worked extremely well in almost all areas and stated: 'I know of nothing in Ireland to equal revelations made in municipal affairs in this country; allowing for personal preference and for other influences which work in all bodies ... Irish business has been marvellously well done by men who – one would have thought until these heavy duties were imposed upon them – had very little fitness or experience for it.'[61]

Concessions to Local Demands

While the general approach of Robinson's board in the early years was to ensure that the new councils operated strictly in accordance with the letter of the law, he and the Chief Secretary were not unwilling to consider amending or supplementing the 1898 Act in response to some of the demands made by councillors and local officials. In little more than a year after the commencement of the act, Robinson, with Vanston, the board's legal adviser, and John Atkinson, the attorney general, was working with Balfour and subsequently with Wyndham, to produce legislation that would allow for changes for which a case had been made at grass-roots level.[62] In all, five amending local government bills were brought forward and enacted between June 1900 and December 1902. While much of the content consisted of relatively minor technical amendments, there were also some significant concessions. For example, an act passed in August 1900 cleared the way for the introduction of direct labour on road works as requested by a number of county councils, instead of the contract system which had operated throughout the grand jury era.[63] Another act passed in 1902 provided statutory recognition for the General Council of County Councils and allowed councils to pay a subscription of up to £10 a year towards the organisation's funds, and to meet the expenses of not more than two delegates at two meetings each year.[64] There had been fears at an early stage about this new organisation because the promoter, Sir Thomas Esmonde MP, had announced that he was going to create 'a People's Parliament in Dublin'[65] and because of a concern that the council might develop into something like Arthur Griffith's proposed 'Council of Three Hundred', but these fears did not prevail.[66] The risk that the council would be completely dominated by nationalist members was averted when all thirty-nine of the county and county borough councils, including those controlled by unionists in the north, were represented in the early years when, according to Robinson, he had induced the chairmen of the northern councils to attend. This happy situation came to an end in 1904 when the adoption by the General Council of a resolution allowing for discussion of Home Rule and other political issues led to the withdrawal of four of the northern county councils and of Belfast Corporation.[67] As Robinson recalled it years later, they found 'the anti-English atmosphere of the council too strong for them'.[68]

Suffering a Hammering in Print and in Parliament

Reports of disputes and court cases involving the board in the local and national press made it possible for journals such as *The Leader* to consistently promote the view that the LGB was an organisation which had been found guilty of a series of blunders and high-handed actions, accusing it of wasting public money and constantly wrangling with the elected local councils, worrying, snubbing and belittling them as far as possible, interfering in a petty, spiteful and waspish manner in matters of no importance, making it 'absurd, ridiculous and old-maidish'.[69] By 1908, the journal was complaining that the board's lack of sympathy for the problems of local councils had become even more evident – the most junior official was now to be regarded as 'a superior person whose dictum is not to be questioned, whose word is law and whose sympathy or friendliness is not to be expected for any nationalist elected public body'.[70] Dubois, also writing in 1908, described the board as a foreign power, bureaucratic, arbitrary narrow-minded and anti-national, filled with a passion for directing and complicating everything and acting with despotic and irresponsible arrogance, thus making its rule as intolerable to the unionists of Ulster as it was to nationalists.[71] Some months earlier, the Catholic Defence Society's pamphlet, *Light on the Local Government Board,* had described the organisation in broadly similar terms, as 'at once bureaucratic and autocratic'.

Michael Wheatley's study of the Irish Party and provincial Ireland in the 1910–16 period rightly noted that 'the smallest dispute with a government body could trigger a press tirade', even from the most conciliatory of local newspapers.[72] As these newspapers were a vital link with their constituencies for London-based Irish MPs, their reports of disputes involving the LGB provided 'ammunition to form questions' as well as a continuous stream of material for use in speeches critical of the board.[73] As Robinson recalled it, board decisions were the daily subject of numerous questions in the Commons, and the board had always to be on the *qui vive.*[74] In addition to sharing in criticism of what Redmond described as the 'monstrous, inefficient, irresponsible and costly' system of boards which governed Ireland,[75] the LGB probably attracted more regular and severe criticism in the Commons between 1898 and 1911 than any of the many other boards and departments which made up the Irish administration. As Catherine Shannon saw it, members of the Irish Party never lost an opportunity of 'using their oratorical abilities to cast the board as a domineering and constantly interfering appendage of Dublin Castle'.[76]

Relatively minor disputes between the board and individual local councils provided a new starting point for critical speeches at Westminster from 1899 onwards. In the debate on the board's estimates in June 1899, it was already being accused of tyranny and meddlesome interference in local management. Councils were 'snowed under' by rules and orders; and the will of the people was being thwarted by the extent to which sanction was required in respect of relatively unimportant matters. The following May, when the estimates for 1900–01 came up for debate, Irish members resumed their attack on the board.[77] They largely relied on its actions in relation to the qualifications, conditions and salaries of some grades of staff to justify their indictment of a dictatorial organisation, which was actuated by 'the spirit of constantly desiring to dictate, interfere and meddle' and whose circulars were noted for their 'autocratic insolence'. In an August 1901 debate, mandatory qualifications for particular posts were attacked on the basis that they would debar nationalists and the poorer classes from obtaining appointments, and the 'new faddist idea' of insisting on trained nurses at workhouse hospitals was ridiculed.[78] Looking back on it, however, Robinson felt that the Irish members were good fellows on the whole, and while they had to attack the LGB with apparent ferocity and 'give it the usual hammering' in order to placate the local authorities, with a few exceptions, they were never personally offensive to him.[79] Criticism made in the course of the various debates at Westminster was, in fact, generally directed at the board as a corporate entity: 'A horde of carrion quartered on them in Ireland' according to Laurence Ginnell MP, in 1907.[80] Individual members of the board, apart from Bagwell, were rarely condemned. On one occasion, Robinson was criticised as a man who had been 'born and bred in the Castle', which was of course true only in the metaphorical sense. On another occasion, Joe Devlin, the West Belfast MP, one of Robinson's most severe critics, told the House of Commons that 'any recommendations by Sir Henry Robinson are repugnant to the Irish people'. But Robinson also had his defenders in Commons' debates – and not always on the government benches. One of the nationalist MPs for Dublin city and a regular critic of the board, William Field, arguing for more co-operation between the board and local councils, spoke in August 1901 of his many interviews with Robinson at which he found him to be 'a most cultured, patient, and efficient official', whose 'opinion he had frequently managed to change'.[81] Robinson, for his part, described Field as 'a great friend of mine' and as for his attacks on the board, recalled what was said of Ben Gunn in *Treasure Island* (1883): 'Nobody minds Ben Gunn, dead or alive.'[82] As late as 1910, John O'Dowd, another nationalist MP who was severely critical of the activities of the board, was careful to distinguish between what he saw as a defective system and the men who constituted the board. He had no fault to find with Robinson or Micks, whom he knew to be gentlemen of high standing.[83]

In the context of the Home Rule debates, simplistic comparisons of the operating cost of the LGB and of its counterparts in Britain were used in Parliament to support the argument that the government of Ireland was the costliest and most extravagant in the world, and that the only class that profited from this was 'a horde of officials'.[84] The reality of the situation was, of course, conveniently disregarded, with no account being taken of the fact, pointed out by Birrell in the House of Commons in 1908, that a large proportion of the expenses of the Irish board arose from functions such as the administration of the dispensary system and the Labourers Acts, which had no parallel in England.[85] Although criticism of the board as a body unfit to supervise democratically elected local councils continued into the second decade of the century, it occurred less frequently after 1908. This mirrored developments in the national newspapers, who reported fewer disputes and confrontations between the board and local councils in those years. This may have been a reflection of the fact that the system had settled down after the triennial elections of 1902 and 1905, and an indication of the improved relationship at national level between the new liberal government and the Irish Party. Indeed, Redmond's advice to one of his colleagues in the 1910 Commons debate on the board's estimates illustrated a new approach: instead of indulging in what Robinson would have called 'the usual hammering' of the board and roaming over the whole question of its conduct, it would be more useful for Ireland if they confined themselves to the most urgent point and attempted to reach some practical conclusions.[86] It is also significant in this context that there was no repetition of the effort made early in 1900 by a group of nationalist MPs who had brought in a bill, voted down on 14 February, which would drastically alter the balance of power by establishing a Board of Control, which would assist the LGB in implementing the 1898 Act.[87] The proposed seven-man board was to consist of four persons appointed by the chairmen of county councils, one appointed by the lord mayors/mayors of county boroughs, and two members of the LGB itself, and would have power to hear appeals from local councils against orders made by the board.

A Great, Stupendous and Even Rash Experiment Worked Remarkably Well

In the absence of the board's own files, which were destroyed in the Custom House fire of May 1921, it is difficult to reach firm conclusions about the extent to which Henry Robinson's own views and directions influenced the board's relationship with the new county and district councils (and indirectly with parliamentarians) in the early years. His letters to Gerald Balfour suggest that he set out to avoid open confrontation and, while some of the rules and orders made by the board certainly involved an excessive level of regulation, he also attached importance to the provision of advice to the new councils rather than continuous dictation. The Attorney General, John Atkinson MP, praised him in a 1901 debate for his desire to make local government a success, and for his work in nursing and restraining the inexperienced local bodies so that they might be able to go steadily and cautiously forward.[88] Wyndham, who was never very close to Robinson, spoke of him as a distinguished Irishman who deserved respect for the energy and devotion with which he had applied himself to the implementation of the 1898 Act and for the consideration and courtesy with which he had conducted the business.[89] Some years later, James Campbell MP (later Lord Chancellor Baron Glenavy) praised him as 'an officer whose whole desire was to discharge his duties efficiently and with due regard to every interest concerned in Ireland'.[90]

Interventions by some of the board's auditors and inspectors were occasionally insensitive and undoubtedly suggested that a rigid hard-line approach was being pursued. In the absence of the original files, however, it is impossible to determine whether the men concerned (and particularly the auditors) were 'following orders' and operating in accordance with the culture of the organisation, or whether they were acting entirely independently (as they were legally entitled to do). An incident recalled in the Seanad in 1930 by Laurence O'Neill, Lord Mayor of Dublin from 1917 to 1924, suggests that the latter may often have been the case: O'Neill, who had many interviews with Robinson on housing and other civic matters, recalled that on one occasion, when he had 'the temerity to twit him' on a ridiculous order made by a senior official of the board, Robinson's reply was 'Damn these fellows, they are always getting me into no end of trouble but, blast them, I must stand behind them.'[91]

What Birrell described in 1908 as a great, stupendous and even rash experiment – entrusting difficult work to people who had strong national feelings and political prejudices and who had no experience of the kind before – had worked remarkably well in the previous ten years.[92] R. B. McDowell concluded that, in those years, relations between the LGB and the local authorities 'seem to have been remarkably harmonious' notwithstanding a 'trace of paternalism'.[93] If that conclusion is accepted – and there are strong grounds for doing so – then, in the view of Virginia Crossman, much of the credit is due to Henry Robinson, who 'sought with some success to maintain a working relationship with local authorities in the face of growing hostility from Sinn Féin councils seeking to throw off the restraints of British control'.[94]

NOTES

1   Robinson to Balfour, 4 Oct. 1899, TNA, PRO 30/60/15.
2   Robinson to Balfour, 26 Dec. 1899, NAS, Balfour Papers, GD 433/2/114/12.
3   Robinson to Balfour, 19 Mar. 1900, NAS, Balfour Papers, GD 433/2/114/13.
4   Robinson to Balfour, 16 July 1899, TNA, PRO 30/60/15.
5   Robinson to Balfour, 19 Feb. 1899, TNA, PRO 30/60/15.
6   Robinson to Balfour, 30 Apr. 1899, TNA, PRO 30/60/15.
7   Robinson to Balfour, 14 June 1899, TNA, PRO 30/60/15.
8   William L. Feingold, *The Revolt of the Tenantry* (Boston, 1984), p.181.
9   Virginia Crossman, *Politics, Pauperism and Power in Late Nineteenth-Century Ireland* (Manchester, 2006), p. 48.
10   Local Government Board Memorandum, 2 Apr. 1892, NAI, CSORP 1892/4813.
11   NAI, CSORP 1890/7728.
12   Sir Henry Robinson, *Memories: Wise and Otherwise* (London, 1923), pp.131–32.

13   Sir Henry Robinson, *Further Memories of Irish Life* (London, 1924), p.185.

14   R. B. McDowell, 'Administration and the public services, 1870–1921' in *NHI* VI, p.593.

15   Letter of 30 Sept. 1920 quoted in T. J. McArdle, BMH, WS 501, 19 Feb. 1951, p.32.

16   Robinson to Balfour, 16 July 1899, TNA, PRO 30/60/15.

17   *The Leader*, 1, no. 2, 8 Sept. 1900, p.18.

18   Crossman, *Politics, Pauperism and Power*, pp.20, 30, 51–2 and 221.

19   Christine Bellamy, *Administering Central–Local Relations 1871–1919* (Manchester, 1988), p.139.

20   Robinson to Balfour, 14 Dec. 1899, NAS, Balfour Papers, GD 433/2/114/11.

21   *Hansard* IV, 53, 21 Feb. 1898, 1227.

22   Robinson to Balfour, 6 Mar. 1899, TNA, PRO 30/60/15.

23   Robinson to Balfour, 16 July 1899, TNA, PRO 30/60/15.

24   *Report of Departmental Committee of Inquiry into Department of Agriculture and Technical Instruction (Ireland)*, HC 1907 [Cd. 3572].

25   McDowell, 'Administration and the public services', p.593.

26   Philip Bull, 'The UIL and the Reunion of the Irish Parliamentary Party', *IHS*, xxvi, No. 101 (May 1988), p.62.

27   *Irish Times*, 16 Dec. 1898.

28   W. T. Cosgrave, BMH, WS 449, 14 Nov. 1950.

29   Robinson, *Further Memories*, p.185–88.

30   *Hansard* IV, 174, 7 May 1907, 83.

31   Sir Horace Plunkett, *Ireland in the New Century* (London, 1904), p.247.

32   Robinson, *Further Memories*, pp.185–88.

33   *Royal Commission on Local Taxation, Minutes of Evidence, Vol. V,* HC 1900 [Cd. 383], evidence of Sir Henry A. Robinson, 18 Oct. 1899.

34   *AR*, 1899–1900, pp.ii, xiii.

35   *AR*, 1900–01, pp.i-ii.

36   *AR* 1901–02, p.ii.

37   *Dáil Debates*, Vol. 7, No. 16, 29 May 1924, 1601, P. J. McGoldrick TD; McGoldrick did not say when or where the statement was made.

38   Robinson to Balfour, 11 July 1899, TNA, PRO 30/60/15.

39   *Irish Times*, 25 Mar. 1901.

40   *Irish Times*, 16 May 1901.

41   Robinson to Bryce, 6 Apr. 1906, NLI, James Bryce Papers, MS 11,012 (4).

42   R (Wexford County Council) v. The Local Government Board for Ireland (Webster's Case), [1902] IR 2 (348).

43   Robinson to Balfour, 4 Oct. 1899, TNA, PRO 30/60/15.

44   *Hansard* IV, 187, 30 Mar. 1908, 124–25.

45   J. A. Glynn, 'Irish Local Government' in Basil Williams (ed.), *Home Rule Problems* (London, 1911), pp.49–56.

46   L. Paul Dubois, *Contemporary Ireland* (Dublin, 1908), p.194.

47   Harold Spender, *Home Rule* (London, 1912), p.26.

48   *Irish Times*, 16 Dec. 1898.

49   Eunan O' Halpin, *The Decline of the Union* (Dublin, 1987), p.16.

50   Patrick Maume, *The Long Gestation: Irish Nationalist Life 1891–1918* (Dublin, 1999), p.30.

51   J.J. Lee, 'Centralisation and Community', in *Ireland: Towards a Sense of Place* (Cork, 1985), p.84; Joseph Lee, *The Modernisation of Irish Society 1848–1918* (Dublin, 1973), p.128.

52   Arthur Griffith, *The Resurrection of Hungary* (Dublin, 1905), p.154.

53   Catherine Barbara Shannon, *Local Government in Ireland: The Politics and Administration* (MA Thesis UCD, Autumn 1963), pp. 273–75.

54   *Irish Builder*, 1 July 1899, p.73.

55   Wyndham to Arthur Balfour, BL, Balfour Papers, Add MS 49804, f 219–221.

56   *Irish Times*, 4 Jan. 1902.

57   *Irish Times*, 13 Jan. 1906.

58   *Irish Times*, 11 Sept. 1906.

59   MacDonnell to Bryce, 4 Feb. 1906, NLI, James Bryce Papers, MS 11,012 (2).

60   *Hansard* IV, 173, 2 May 1907, 1147–1148.

61   *Hansard* IV, 187, 30 Mar. 1908, 160–161.

62   TNA, PRO 30/60/19.

63   Local Government (Ireland) (No. 2) Act 1900, 63 & 64 VIct., c. 41, 6 Aug. 1900.

64   Local Government (Ireland) Act 1902, 2 Edw. 7, ch. 38, 18 Dec. 1902.

65   Plunkett to T. P. Gill, 17 Apr. 1899, NLI, Gill Papers, MS 13494(6).

66   Wyndham, in a conversation with his cousin, Wilfrid Scawen Blunt, in May 1902, viewed with equanimity the possibility that the 1898 act might indirectly lead to 'a sort of Home Rule … it might come to a union of the local councils under one general council at Dublin which would practically settle all Irish affairs' – Wilfrid Scawen Blunt, *My Diaries* (2 vols) (London, 1919–20), p. 438.

67   *Irish Times*, 21 Oct. 1904.

68   Committee on Ireland, Memorandum by the Right Hon. Sir Henry Robinson, Bart. on the Powers of the Council of Ireland, 17 Feb. 1920, TNA, CAB 27/69.

69   *The Leader*, x, No. 5, 25 Mar. 1905, pp.71–73.

70   *The Leader*, xvi, No. 1, 22 Feb. 1908, p.13.

71   L. Paul Dubois, *Contemporary Ireland* (Dublin, 1908), p.195.

72   Michael Wheatley, *Nationalism and the Irish Party: Provincial Ireland 1910–16* (Oxford, 2005), p.88.

73   James McConnel, *The Irish Parliamentary Party and the Third Home Rule Crisis* (Dublin, 2013), p.39.

74   Robinson, *Memories*, pp.131–32.

75   *Hansard* IV, 169, 12 Feb. 1907, 92–94.

76   Shannon, *Local Government in* Ireland, p.278.

77   *Hansard* IV, 83, 24 May 1900, 1127–1219.

78   *Hansard* IV, 99, 8 Aug. 1901, 83–139; 9 Aug. 1901, 311–50.

79   Robinson, *Memories*, pp.282–83.

80   *Hansard*, IV, 173, 2 May 1907, 1140.

81   *Hansard* IV, 99, 8 Aug. 1901, 126–27.

82   Robinson, *Memories*, p.146.

83   *Hansard* V, 18, 7 July 1910, 1804–08.

84 Jeremiah MacVeigh MP, *Home Rule in a Nutshell: A Pocket Book for Speakers and Electors* (4ᵗʰ edn, 1912).

85 *Hansard* IV, 186, 26 Mar. 1908, 1679–1681.

86 *Hansard* V, 18, 7 July 1910, 1810–1811.

87 Local Government (Ireland) Act 1898 Amendment Bill (Bill 18), 2 Feb. 1900.

88 *Hansard* IV, 99, 9 Aug. 1901, 341.

89 *Hansard* IV, 91, 26 Mar. 1901, 1418–19.

90 *Hansard* V, 173, 2 May 1907, 1159.

91 *Seanad debates*, vol.13, no. 22, 28 May 1930, 1288–89.

92 *Hansard* IV, 187, 30 Mar. 1908, 161–162.

93 McDowell, 'Administration and the public services', p.594.

94 Virginia Crossman, *Henry Augustus Robinson, DIB*, vol. 8, pp.536–7.

CHAPTER V

A Focus on Ensuring Efficient Administration Rather than Improving Local Services?

'No Kind of Preference for One State of Society over Another'

After the dramatic structural changes implemented in 1899, it might have been expected that the emphasis in the following years would be on the development of local services rather than further structural change. But did Robinson and his colleagues initiate new or improved services in those years and press chief secretaries to legislate and secure funds to implement them? Had Robinson strategies of his own for developing services or was he happy simply to adopt English initiatives and otherwise respond to events? Was he an effective adviser on policies relating to various services or can he be criticised – as the Under-Secretary and his staff were in 1920 – for acting only as glorified clerks? As Ruth Barrington suggested in her 1987 study, *Health, Medicine, and Politics*, was it indeed true that he had few ideas of his own for reforming the system?[1] And finally, was he to blame for the extent to which Irish health and welfare legislation was permissive and not as well developed as in Britain, or was this the fault of the government or of local councillors, supported by their MPs?

Answers to questions such as the foregoing are not easily found as the files and other records of the LGB were destroyed in the Custom House fire. The surviving Chief Secretary's Office registered papers at the National Archives of Ireland are no real substitute, and many of the British Treasury files, which would have included detailed submissions and reports about the board's services and activities, have not survived at the British National Archives. Apart from his comments and early reports on the Poor Relief System, Robinson himself left no real record of how he viewed local services or the possible need for action to remedy deficiencies. His two volumes of memoirs are largely silent on such issues. Beatrice Webb, who got to know him well when they were both members of the Poor Law Commission (1906–09) subsequently wrote that 'during our long motor rides together, I have discovered no kind of preference for one state of society over another'.[2] And, when asked what kind of society he desired to see if he had power to bring it about, he told her that he had lived all his life at concert pitch and 'never really thought of all these questions in which you are interested'. What had instead concerned him during his career was 'keeping my successive chief secretaries out of trouble' – a concern which, as F. S. L. Lyons saw it, might have been shared by under-secretaries as a class in those days.[3]

According to Christine Bellamy's study the culture and organisation of the English LGB was not well adapted to the development of services. It also had 'few political, limited organisational and almost no financial resources with which to dominate either the process of policy formulation or its administration'.[4] It has been suggested in another study that the deficiencies of the English board were notorious while John Burns MP was its full-time president from 1905–14; the board was considered the Cinderella of Whitehall, and did not attract high-quality civil servants. That study also maintained that Burns allowed the organisation to be left behind in the rush of social legislation between 1907 and 1910, and that it continued to be a conservative organisation during his presidency, enmeshed in red tape and hostile to the reform of the poor law.[5] While Robinson was not the political head of his board as was Burns, and while the status of the English board suffered by comparison with powerful Whitehall neighbours like the Treasury and the Home and Foreign Offices, it is still reasonable to consider whether the LGB in Dublin was better or worse under his management than its English counterpart is alleged to have been. Did Robinson and his colleagues focus on ensuring efficient administration (as their nineteenth-century predecessors are said by Virginia Crossman to have done) rather than initiating and promoting the improvement and development of public services?[6]

There is no comprehensive modern study of the LGB, although there are valuable studies of particular services, including health[7] and housing[8], and various studies by Virginia Crossman. Mary Daly's *The Buffer State* begins by reviewing the operations of the LGB, but relates in the main to organisational and service developments after the dissolution of the board in 1922.[9] There is, therefore, no single existing source which can be drawn on to help to provide answers to the questions mentioned above. Daly's study did lead to the conclusion that reports from inspectors and auditors concentrated on detail, rather than on policy, and that the board's powers over unsatisfactory local authorities were more reactive than proactive. This conclusion is supported by Birrell's statement in the debate in the House of Commons on the report of the 1913–14 departmental committee on Dublin housing, which was highly critical of the performance of the city corporation:

> ... As president of the Local Government Board for Ireland ... my responsibility for a great corporation such as that of Dublin is very small. The authority which I possess is of a kind which is called affirmative. I cannot initiate anything; I really cannot act with any degree of authority at all except on a complaint, and the complaints which have been made from time to time as regards the Dublin Corporation have not been great or numerous and the powers I have therefore been able to exercise are very small.[10]

If Birrell believed that it was not open to him as Chief Secretary to initiate anything, Robinson can hardly be criticised if there appeared to be a failure to follow up recommendations made in various reports and an overall impression of inertia. Whether the Chief Secretary's attitude reflected the advice of Robinson and other senior officials, or whether those officials made any real effort to convince him that a more interventionist approach should be adopted in particular cases, is of course another matter.

In modern terminology, the LGB after 1898 combined the functions and duties of at least four of today's government departments: local government/environment, transport, health, and social protection, just as its successor, the Department of Local Government and Public Health, did until 1947. Under Robinson's stewardship, the role and functions of the board expanded significantly in the first decades of the century as a result of new legislation – in fact, the 1909 report of the Poor Law Commission recorded that twenty-two new acts affecting the board had been passed since 1898.[11] The liberal government, which came into office at the end of 1905, enacted substantial legislation in the fields of health and welfare. Two of their major initiatives – the introduction of old age pensions in 1909 and the national health insurance system in 1911 – required the simultaneous implementation by the LGB of services which were intended from the outset to apply throughout the entire United Kingdom. Other public health and welfare legislation involved the application to Ireland of services which had already been in operation in England for some years, while major developments (such as the improvements made in 1906 in the procedural and funding arrangements for the provision of labourers' cottages) followed sustained pressure by local councils and by the Irish Party. Finally, some new legislation and financial arrangements – notably the Housing of the Working Classes (Ireland) Act 1908 – were at least in part the product of private members bills introduced by Irish Party members. It is simply not possible, with the limited availability of relevant primary sources, to reach definite judgments about Robinson's personal contribution to the development of these or other services from 1898 onwards. An attempt, however, is made in the following paragraphs to draw conclusions from the material which has survived and to make some deductions from the actions of his board in relation to a number of major issues.

Reforming the Poor Law

Robinson's experience of the administration of the Poor Law and of the operation of relief schemes in western areas in the twenty years before his promotion to the Vice-Presidency left him with definite attitudes towards the often exaggerated reports of distress in these areas. Although he had worked with Gerald Balfour to devise section 13 of the 1898 Act, which placed primary responsibility for dealing with distress on the local councils, he found that demands for action at national level continued to be a regular feature of the following years. In 1906, for example, when there were alarming reports about the appearance of blight in the West, Robinson, unlike Under-Secretary MacDonnell, was quite relaxed about the reports and warned the Chief Secretary that a visit to the area could raise false hopes and lead to accusations of 'callous Saxon brutality' if special grants did not follow. Although he warned that the reports could turn out to relate to a bogus famine, he instructed his inspectors to continue discreet inquiries in the affected areas. Most notably, he undertook personally to visit those districts 'where we have had most trouble in past years'.[12] Some months later, when Chief Secretary Bryce was called on by John Dillon to make a full statement in the House of Commons on the subject, his reply was clearly influenced by the briefing he had received from Robinson. He referred to the demoralising results that followed special measures when these were not absolutely necessary. He also stressed the primary responsibility of the county councils and the guardians to initiate the procedure laid down in the 1898 Act if the circumstances warranted this.[13] At the same time, Robinson took the reports of almost complete crop failure in the Belmullet area seriously enough to warrant a personal tour of inspection, after which he reported to Bryce that for the present there was no talk of distress in Belmullet where the people were in a ferment of excitement about a speculative proposal for a railway to a new port at Blacksod. Local officials and priests whom he interviewed (including the priest whose parish was the poorest in the union and who was 'a great distress agitator') saw no immediate prospect of any exceptional distress, and potatoes in the pits, which had been opened specially for his inspection, were apparently sound. Nevertheless, he accepted that the board would have to be prepared to come to the rescue at short notice if circumstances changed.[14] Subsequently, he allocated the bulk of the money available under the Unemployed Workmen Act 1905 to newly-formed distress committees in western areas, even though the act had been intended primarily to deal with urban unemployment.[15] This brought him into conflict with the Treasury because, as Sir George Murray, the powerful joint permanent secretary put it, 'Connemara peasants' were not 'workmen' and were not 'unemployed' within the meaning of the act.[16]

On the more general question of Poor Law Reform, the limited terms of reference of the Vice-Regal Commission appointed by the Lord Lieutenant in 1903 were almost certainly influenced by Robinson. Taken together with the fact that two of the commission's three members were already members of the LGB, there was nothing to suggest that a fundamental reform of the system was envisaged. The commission was simply asked to report on what administrative and financial measures were desirable to secure a more economical system without impairing efficiency. Despite this, their 1906 report recommended radical changes, having found that after almost seventy years, the Poor Law was no longer operating in the way that was originally intended: a different and more popular system appeared to have taken root, under which relief payments were no longer the sole support of the destitute, but merely an item in the receipts of poor persons.[17] Accepting this as a *fait accompli*, the commission recommended that some of the remaining restrictions on the granting of outdoor relief should be removed. They also proposed that the existing mixed workhouse system should be abolished, with the different classes of persons found amongst the workhouse populations being catered for in future in different categories of hospitals and institutions served by a new medical service, which would incorporate the existing dispensary service. Given that the recommendations as a whole had the united support of all classes and creeds of the people, according to John Redmond, one might ask whether the failure to implement them with reasonable expedition can be attributed to inactivity on the part of Robinson and his colleagues.[18] This, however, was not the case because, as Birrell explained in the House of Commons in April 1908, he had been forced to make a choice between different subjects when it came to allocating parliamentary time for Irish affairs. For better or worse he had opted to give priority to the bill which established the National University.[19] A Royal Commission on the Poor Laws, with a mandate extending to the UK as a whole, sat from 1906 to 1909, which further delayed action on the Irish report.

Robinson himself was one of eighteen men and women appointed by the government to form the 1906 Commission, having failed to evade the assignment by attempting to have the retired Under-Secretary, Sir David Harrel, appointed instead.[20] He admitted that he had little knowledge of English conditions himself but, with the only other Irish member, Denis Kelly, the Catholic Bishop of Ross, he attended the commission's meetings in London nearly every fortnight primarily to monitor whatever reforms were being proposed for England, and ensure they would be adapted to make them suitable for Irish conditions.[21] He resented the heavy demands this made on his time, complaining angrily on one occasion in 1908 that a meeting had been 'profitless' and that he had been 'called all the way from Ireland to discuss a silly memorandum and we have come to no conclusions'.[22] On the other hand, when the commission held a number of sessions in Ireland, he revelled in the task of escorting members on a tour of the West. For Beatrice Webb, this was an enjoyable Irish holiday at the Treasury's expense and a most delightful rest, but she was shocked by the extent of the misery and squalor in which the people of the area lived. She believed at one stage that Robinson was attracted to the radical scheme she had planned to submit as a minority report, but she failed to convince him to support her. Instead, the commission conveniently left it to Robinson and Bishop Kelly to draft a report on Ireland and, not surprisingly, this endorsed the recommendation of the Vice-Regal Commission that the general mixed workhouses – many of which were then nearly empty – were unsuited to the condition of Ireland and were 'foreign to the sentiment of the country'. Instead, the counties and county boroughs should replace the unions and guardians as the areas of administration for health and welfare services, and local public-assistance committees should be established to deal with applications for relief from within each union. Robinson and the bishop severely criticised the proposals of some of their colleagues, who maintained that decisions on these applications should be entrusted to salaried officers. They did not believe that intelligent men would be willing, as committee members, to spend their time investigating applications if they were powerless to ensure that relief was given. Because the number of paid officials in Ireland was already a heavy tax on the ratepayers, they also deprecated the proposal 'to flood the country with a new class of paid officer' even if these persons of 'the superior order of intelligence' would keep the committees straight and correct their blunders in the matter of outdoor relief.[23]

The report drafted by Robinson and Bishop Kelly did not endorse the recommendation of the Vice-Regal Commission for a unified health service operating outside the poor law framework in place of the extensive dispensary system over which the LGB presided. Unlike anything which operated in the rest of the UK, this system was based on some 1,000 dispensaries staffed by 800 medical officers and more than 600 midwives. In 1911, when he was closely involved in the preparation of the National Insurance Bill, Robinson had another opportunity for arguing for the continuation of the dispensary system. Working with William J. Braithwaite, the brilliant young Treasury Assistant-Secretary, who was primarily responsible to Lloyd George for developing the scheme, Robinson was called to London on more than one occasion to discuss the Irish clauses of the bill, which, according to Braithwaite, were both long and troublesome. At the end of April 1911, having wrestled with the Irish difficulties at a meeting in London, both men were summoned to Brighton to meet Lloyd George, who was staying there for the weekend. They finally agreed the scheme with him, just days before the bill was to be introduced in the House of Commons. Robinson considered the bill to be 'a most extraordinarily able one'. While Braithwaite saw this as Irish blarney, it is clear from his memoirs – written over twenty-five years later, but not published until 1957 – that Robinson made a great impression on him.[24] The Irish clauses, for which Robinson was primarily responsible, allowed for the continuation of the dispensary service, with the new insurance scheme grafted on to it. This, according to Ruth Barrington, involved the option of least possible change because, as Robinson saw it, there was no need to reorganise medical relief in Ireland.[25] When the bill was published, the scheme was criticised for widely different reasons by a coalition of interests: the medical profession, the county councils and the catholic hierarchy. After debating the issue for months, the Irish Party demanded the exclusion of medical benefit (given the existence of the dispensary service) and the bill was amended accordingly. Two years later, after a committee set up to review the issue had reported on it, Robinson again opposed the idea of a state medical service, although his medical commissioner, Dr T. J. Stafford, had supported it.[26]

Old Age Pensions

Robinson welcomed the introduction of the centrally-financed old age pension system in 1909 as the payment of pensions to small-holders would spare the infliction on the Chief Secretary – and on himself – of the 'perennial famines' which had been so great a source of embarrassment and because the pensions removed forever the menace of destitution arising from the failure of the potato crop.[27] Ten years earlier, however, when a scheme of old age pensions had been under consideration by the Conservative government, Robinson was far from enthusiastic about the idea – and prepared a long 'strictly private and personal' memorandum for Chief Secretary Balfour, strongly arguing that it could be a hazardous experiment to extend to a purely agricultural country a new scheme which was thought to be suitable for the manufacturing and artisan population of England.[28] The proposed scheme, he suggested, would effectively place outdoor relief within the reach of the small-holders who represented about four-fifths of the poorer classes. There was no need for this, however, as the resources of these small-holders did not necessarily diminish when they reached sixty-five years of age: in many cases they were better off at that stage because they had a son or daughter assisting them in tilling the holding and often had children in America who sent money home every Christmas. While 'no one could feel confident how anything will turn out in this country of surprises', he suggested that if the scheme were applied without restriction in Ireland, the entire population of small-holders from Donegal to West Cork would consider themselves entitled to pensions. Proof of age could not be obtained in the case of persons born before 1863, census returns could not be relied on as a basis for costing the scheme, there would probably be abuse 'among a class of people who have brought scheming for the purposes of obtaining state and charitable aid to a pitch of perfection', and people would be unsettled and distracted from their ordinary pursuits. In addition, the clergy would promote the scheme because they would see it as a means of ensuring that Christmas and Easter offerings of reasonable amount were promptly paid. In fact, Robinson claimed that 'there are many who see in the application of the old age system to the congested districts nothing beyond a proposal to largely endow the Catholic clergy from public funds'. The only sensible course, in his view, was to apply the quarter-acre clause or an analogous provision so as to deprive aged small-holders of pensions which they did not need. Pensions should only be provided, he suggested, for the classes who were dependent on earnings from their labour to sustain them.

When Lloyd George, as Chancellor, decided in 1908 to lift 'the shadow of the workhouse from the homes of the poor' by introducing old age pensions, Robinson was consulted by a Treasury committee that had been given the task of devising implementation arrangements. It was too late at that stage to object in principle to the scheme, but he restated his views on the difficulty of obtaining proof of age in Ireland, suggesting that every man or woman over sixty would claim the pension and would regard the age limit as 'a mere irritating restriction'. He was challenged on this point by another Irish-born official, Joseph P. Crowley, who accused him of casting aspersions on his countrymen and asked indignantly if he meant to convey that an Irishman would tell a lie for the sake of five shillings. Robinson had no hesitation in replying that plenty of them would, after which it was decided that census returns would be accepted as evidence in the absence of a record of birth. Failing this, Crowley's suggestion that a clergyman's certificate would be deemed to be sufficient evidence was accepted.[29]

When the Old Age Pensions Act became law in August 1908, providing pensions of 5s a week to men and women over seventy years of age whose weekly means were less than £21 a year, the LGB became the central authority for the administration of the system in Ireland. It also fell to the board to put in place all necessary arrangements for the commencement of the system. Notwithstanding his original personal reservations about the scheme and the relatively short lead time, Robinson arranged what must, in retrospect, be regarded as a remarkably efficient and successful drive to allow pension payments to be made to eligible persons from 1 January 1909. Excise officers around the country were appointed to act as pension officers and to investigate claims for pensions. The duty of determining these claims was assigned to local committees set up for this purpose, and appeals were to be decided by the LGB itself. Detailed instructions were issued, explaining the steps to be taken to set up committees and subcommittees, 448 of which were soon in operation. Forms were devised and printed in huge quantities with 700,000 of them dispatched to post offices, committees and subcommittees around the country in early October. Augmented by temporary employees, the board's staff worked up to 11 p.m. on weekdays as well as on Sundays, and some even attended the offices on Christmas Day 1908 to cope with the workload. In what was described at the time as a 'striking tribute to the organisational resources and efficient administration of the staff', 127,000 applicants had been recommended for pension by early December.[30] By 31 March 1909, almost 262,000 claims had been made – far more than had been anticipated on the basis of the 1901 census figures[31] and the indications were that pension payments in Ireland would cost three times the Treasury estimate.[32] Appeals to the LGB were soon running at a rate of around 200 each week. There was constant litigation, questions in Parliament almost on a daily basis, and difficulties arising from the fact that local solicitors were 'throwing dust in the eyes of the board' where it was in their client's interests to obscure relevant evidence. In 1915, when the board took the view that it could no longer continue to deal with the intake of appeals without a system of local inspection, Robinson accused the Treasury of failing to appreciate the heavy burden of work involved. He explained that he personally had to deal with many of the more difficult cases, working early and late and even on Sundays at his home. Although the Treasury discounted this 'rather alarmist description' of the work, they eventually sanctioned the board's proposal to engage four temporary assistant inspectors, although they saw a risk that those appointed on this basis would be 'making friends with the Mammon of Unrighteousness by dealing with doubtful cases in a popular and patriotic manner'.[33] In the event, Robinson's eldest son, Christopher, was one of those appointed to fill the new posts while another son, Adrian, was appointed to one of the posts on a temporary basis.

Personal and Public Health Services

By 1898, an impressive body of Irish public health legislation had been enacted, but the gap between reality and the statute book was wide: elected representatives had little concern for public health issues, and intervention by the LGB was liable to be resented and resisted. Much of the legislation was adoptive largely because of opposition from parliamentarians, leaving individual local authorities free to decide whether particular acts should be brought into operation in their areas. As late as 1919, Sir Edward Carson was complaining in the House of Commons that Ireland was 'miles behind' England as regards public health: there were only a few city or county medical officers of health, most of the part-time dispensary medical officers were badly paid and did not hold public health qualifications, and the permissive character of public health legislation resulted in a sad farce in provincial and rural areas where things were 'still in an antediluvian state of chaos'.[34] In the same debate, the attorney general for Ireland concluded that 'we want more health and less politics', and hoped that the public bodies concerned would use their powers to address the terrible state of public health in Ireland.[35]

Robinson cannot be blamed for the situation of which Carson complained. The reluctance of local councils to implement legislation in the health and welfare fields, even when pressed by the board, was often supported by nationalist MPs, partly because of the view, held by Redmond among others, that measures of social reform suited to English needs were not necessarily suitable for Ireland, where circumstances and national resources were very different. In the House of Commons in 1911, he complained that English measures had been 'very often imposed, or bestowed, if you like, upon Ireland without any adequate consideration', and he went so far as to tell Lloyd George 'that might be said with some truth even of your most beneficent old age pension scheme' – presumably fearing that the escalating cost of that scheme would become an insupportable burden for an independent Irish administration as happened in 1924 when the government imposed the infamous cut of one shilling a week in the pension. As late as 1919, local councils, with rare exceptions, were still lamentably apathetic in failing to recognise their responsibilities as guardians of the public health and few of them shared the board's concern for the welfare of lunatics and for the good management and maintenance of asylums.[36] The board frequently alluded in their annual reports to the unsuitability of workhouses for the significant numbers of 'lunatics, idiots and epileptics' who were still accommodated in these institutions. They urged the local councils to transfer the chronic and harmless lunatics to auxiliary asylums with the aid of the available capitation grants but asylum management continued to be preoccupied with financial matters rather than treatment and living conditions, and the board's position was often criticised and even mocked. For example, Tim Healy MP, in a typically embellished and overstated intervention in the House of Commons in 1901, complained that the board had shown such great zeal for lunatics that it was a mistake for any man to be sane in Ireland where – in contrast to the labourer living in an insanitary house – the insane man 'was lodged in a palace ... got electric light and four meals a day, and port wine, and he had a magnificent garden to roam in and 300 inspectors to come and feel his pulse'.[37] More than ten years later, when the board's concern for standards at workhouses was still not matched at local level, Robinson was hoping to get Treasury sanction to employ one or two female doctors to carry out workhouse inspections. Although he could see no reason for paying female medical inspectors less than their male colleagues, he did manage to employ the board's first female medical inspector, Dr Florence J. Dillon, in 1914 with unexpected results: when her critical report was read out to the Letterkenny guardians, one of them suggested that instead of carrying out all of the improvements that the inspector desired, it would be cheaper to send the workhouse inmates to a hotel.[38]

It was not, however, simply 'the incapacity or ignorance of boards of guardians' and other local councillors that frustrated LGB plans for the development of health services at local level, as Arthur Samuels KC, later to become the attorney general, argued in a 1915 debate concerning the enforcement of the Vaccination Acts.[39] In that instance, there were well-organised pressure groups,[40] as well as conscientious objectors and others like George Bernard Shaw, who argued that it was sanitation alone which would save the nation from another epidemic such as that which had occurred at the time of the Franco–Prussian war.[41] The fight against tuberculosis was another service in which the efforts and plans of the board were adversely affected, not just by the indifference of many local councils, but also by interference from an unexpected quarter. In 1908, because of general hostility to compulsion in the case of services of this kind, and local reluctance to commit additional funds to these services, pressure from nationalist MPs succeeded in making the notification of certain forms of TB compulsory only in areas where the local council so decided. Similarly, little progress was made in the provision of hospitals and dispensaries for the treatment of those suffering from TB. By 1912, when the situation was reviewed by a departmental committee on which Ireland was represented by the LGB medical commissioner, the provision available was 'extremely small'.[42] The LGB quickly set about implementing the committee's recommendations and invited county councils to prepare schemes for providing a TB service in their areas, with the aid of the state grants that were available. However, before any action could be taken by the board to allocate grants on a systematic basis, Lady Aberdeen, wife of the lord lieutenant, sought and obtained approval to a grant of £25,000 for the erection of a sanatorium at Peamount, County Dublin, to which patients from all parts of Ireland could be referred. When issues arose a few years later about the treatment of Donegal patients at Peamount, Robinson explained to the Under-Secretary that the LGB had foreseen that 'the Donegal peasants' would hate to have to leave their friends and homes for treatment. Efforts to persuade the county council to join with Fermanagh in building a sanatorium convenient to both counties were frustrated by Lady Aberdeen, who had entertained the Council Chairman at the Vice-Regal Lodge and succeeded in convincing the council that Donegal patients should be sent to Peamount. Kerry and Mayo County Councils, according to Robinson, had also 'practically deprived their consumptives of sanatorium treatment by expecting them to go to Dublin'.[43]

Roads

Like several of his senior public service colleagues, Robinson developed an interest in motoring soon after petrol-engined motorcars came to Ireland in 1896. He enjoyed driving, and by all accounts was a good driver, but he also employed a chauffeur from 1902 onwards. He became a member of the Irish Automobile Club in 1906 (from 1918, the RIAC), but five years before that he was one of twenty-seven motorists who responded to an invitation from the RDS to parade their vehicles during the annual cattle show at Ballsbridge in April 1901. According to *The Motor News*, a vast concourse of people thronged the arena. Robinson's new French-built De Dion Voiturette, with his seventeen-year-old son Christopher (Kit) at the helm, was described as a neat little car and wonderfully managed, with a new exhaust valve, which got rid of the noise that had previously proved so annoying.[44] Later that year he was a passenger in Sir Hickman Bacon's white 12 hp Panhard, one of sixteen vehicles participating in the IAC Motor Tour of Ireland, starting from the Shelbourne Hotel in Dublin and going on to Waterford, Kerry, Clare, Connemara and Mayo.[45] Bacon and Robinson separated from the other motorists and followed their own route in County Mayo, taking in Newport and Achill, relying, no doubt, on Robinson's personal knowledge of the area's roads.[46] Robinson regarded Ireland as a paradise for motorists because, while the roads were not as good as those in England, this was offset by the fact that the RIC were not active in enforcing the speed limits (which were applied and administered by his own board) while motorists in England were, as he saw it, harassed by rigorous enforcement of these limits.[47] In the small world of Dublin, personal relationships between members of the RIAC and men like Robinson were therefore invaluable in curbing some of the unrealistic speed limits and other regulations sought by local councils in defence of their equine lifestyle.[48] These relationships also facilitated arrangements for the holding of the international Gordon Bennett Motor Race in Ireland in July 1903. The race was held in Ireland when no suitable course could be agreed in Britain: a figure-of-eight-course based on Athy, County Kildare, was chosen, and special legislation was enacted to allow county councils, subject to the direction of the LGB, to close the relevant road sections and to exempt participants from speed limits. Robinson accompanied Selwyn Francis Edge, the Australian-born British businessman who had won the 1902 race, on an inspection of the course in April. Both men expressed satisfaction with the course itself and the road work which had been undertaken.[49]

Robinson's influence can again be detected in the unexpected willingness of the authorities to concede so readily to the demand from some county councils to permit the introduction of direct labour on roads even though it was evident that at least some of the councils were influenced more by the need to provide employment for rural labourers than by considerations of efficiency and effectiveness, or by the motorists' lobby for better roads. For over a century, grand jury law had required all road work to be carried out on a contract basis and the 1898 Act had confirmed this traditional bias in favour of contracting. Nevertheless, after a number of councils had pressed to be permitted to have work carried out by their county surveyors, using labourers and other directly employed staff, the board arranged to have the law amended in 1900 to permit this. Acceptance of direct labour at a time when 'opinions are divided as to which system is the better and more economical', and when there was 'no general desire on the part of county councils to embark on large schemes of this kind',[50] was remarkable. This must surely have been strongly influenced by Robinson, who had been personally impressed by an August 1899 report prepared by John Ouseley Moynan, the county surveyor for Tipperary North Riding, which he forwarded to Gerald Balfour 'as a very good way of dealing with the direct labour question'.[51] By 1906, the board was reporting that the new system continued to give satisfaction,[52] and in 1908, when the number of councils using the system had increased to thirteen, they noted a claim that the decrease in pauperism in one County Clare union was attributable to employment on the roads.[53]

Rural and Urban Housing

In the fifteen years before Robinson assumed the Vice-Presidency, the building of 15,544 cottages by boards of guardians in rural areas had been authorised by the LGB under the Labourers Acts, and 12,340 had thus far been completed.[54] The new rural district councils built up activity to a significant extent from 1899 onwards, and the board responded by obtaining Treasury sanction for the appointment of additional inspectors to speed up the processing of the numerous schemes submitted to it. As a result, the number of cottages provided had increased to 20,600 by March 1906. In contacts with Chief Secretary Bryce early that year, one of the most urgent demands made by Redmond was for a new Labourers Bill to be enacted to provide for further progress in relation to the cottages. The government's intention to bring forward such a bill was signalled in the King's speech in February. In the meantime, Redmond had asked the party's financial and local government expert, and one of his own closest confidants, John J. Clancy KC MP, to send Under-Secretary MacDonnell a draft of a suitable bill. The latter asked Robinson to prepare his own ideas on what the bill might contain.[55] Thereafter, although MacDonnell sent Robinson's suggestions to Bryce,[56] he commented critically on his proposals for financing an expansion of activity and, notwithstanding the political pressure for the bill, he went so far as to suggest to Bryce that he might see his way to giving it a lower priority in the parliamentary programme.[57] In this case, as Redmond told Dillon, MacDonnell (unlike Robinson) was 'giving further evidence that he is inclined to utterly disregard popular opinion and the views of the representatives of Ireland'.[58] The bill introduced by Bryce on 28 May incorporated Robinson's suggestions and was warmly welcomed by both nationalists and unionists.[59] Redmond described it in 1910 as 'one of the best and most beneficent bills that Ireland has ever obtained',[60] and notwithstanding his reservations about the role of the LGB and his personal animosity towards Robinson, Dillon went even further, claiming that after five years' experience of its operation, no act had ever done more for the country.[61]

The 1906 Act shortened and reduced the cost of the procedure for bringing building schemes to construction stage. It did so by making it possible for the board's inspectors and the board itself, on appeal, to make final decisions. A huge acceleration in the submission of schemes followed, with schemes for building a total of 22,377 cottages being received by the board in the first nine months. Anticipating this large build-up of activity, Robinson personally took charge of the initial implementation arrangements: he told Bryce that having contemplated how best the board might manage the administration of the act, he was planning to constitute a new department 'on a practical working basis which, to all intents and purposes, will be what the Irish Party are pressing for'. He also proposed to seek a personal interview with Sir George Murray at the Treasury to obtain sanction for the extra staff, which would allow the new system to go into operation like clockwork.[62] He planned to assign responsibility at board level to Micks (when he did not exercise it himself), to create an additional post of Assistant Secretary to head the new department and to recruit a team of inspectors to carry on the work. When he shrewdly decided to promote one of his principal clerks – Michael O'Sullivan, a Kerryman and a Catholic, who had been closely involved with housing administration since 1883 – to fill the new senior post, MacDonnell again interfered, telling Bryce that while O'Sullivan was probably a good man in his own way, he was 'of the departmental clerk type, not suited in my opinion for executive work'.[63] In the event, Robinson's staffing proposals were accepted and O'Sullivan was appointed to the new post in November at a salary of £800 a year. He served until his death in 1919 when an *Irish Times* obituary (11 March) noted that 'his ability and never-failing courtesy were generally recognized' by the various public bodies who came into contact with him. In addition to O'Sullivan's appointment, the clerical staff were reorganised and strengthened, and a team of temporary inspectors was recruited to hold the local inquiries which were necessary before the schemes could be authorised to go ahead. All of this resulted, some years later, in a grudging tribute from J. J. Clancy MP to the board's administration of the act: while legislation relating to Ireland was rarely administered properly, according to Clancy, the 1906 Act had been 'worked in a more or less sympathetic spirit' by the LGB and procedures had in practice been shortened and cheapened as planned.[64] By 1914, when wartime restrictions on capital expenditure brought the programme to a virtual halt, almost 44,000 cottages had been built, more than 30,000 of them since 1898.[65]

Although a Royal Commission reported in 1885 that a 'miserable condition of things' existed in relation to workers' housing in many Irish towns,[66] urban housing did not carry the same political weight as rural housing in the later years of the nineteenth century.[67] In 1911, large numbers were still living in the run-down, unsanitary and seriously overcrowded tenement dwellings that had existed in Dublin for years. The population had grown to more than 400,000, while limited male employment prospects and low wages in the unskilled casual sector meant that thousands could only afford the rents of tenements. With little or no financial assistance from the government before 1908, and the high cost of acquiring central-city property, the city corporation had re-housed less than 1,500 families in the twenty years since the restatement of their housing powers in 1890. There was little evidence until 1913 of urgency or of public concern with regard to the slums, or of political commitment to resolving the problem.[68] Matters came to a head in September of that year when, with the city engulfed in strikes and lockouts, two tenement houses collapsed in Church Street, killing seven people. The case for establishing either a Royal Commission or a Vice-Regal Commission to consider the housing problem was pressed on Chief Secretary Birrell by various influential deputations, but he argued that a commission would involve large expenditure and a great loss of time. While he stated that he held no brief for the LGB, he believed that a committee made up of men who already knew a great deal about the subject would be well able to present the information which was needed to make the case for the right kind of action.[69] The *Irish Times* rejected this view, arguing that, while the board was 'one of the best equipped and most efficient departments in Ireland', an inquiry at which the corporation would be more or less on trial would not be independent if carried out by officials who were 'acclimatised' to their methods.[70] *The Leader* saw the proposed committee as a farce and 'a mere pretence of facing the situation' designed by Henry Robinson to mark time until the burden could be thrown on the Home Rule Parliament.[71] The corporation itself passed a motion declaring that the proposed committee would not command public confidence but Birrell adhered to the original plan and the committee was duly established on 3 November.[72] Even then, criticism did not cease: the four-man group, according to *The Leader*, was made up of officials chosen to suit Sir Henry's game, including J. F. (Jack) MacCabe, son of a former member of the board, who was employed as an LGB inspector, but was described as 'a Cawtholic Unionist' and known to his friends as 'Adrian's tutor' (Adrian being the son of Sir Henry) and Samuel Watt, a former private secretary of Robinson's whose name 'is not unfamiliar to the wire-pullers of Trinity College'.[73]

Notwithstanding the advance criticism, most observers were forced to agree that the committee went about its assignment impartially, energetically and competently, taking evidence from seventy-six witnesses at public hearings in the City Hall between 18 November and 23 December, and allowing the entire proceedings to be reported extensively in the newspapers. A comprehensive report was completed in just over three months, vindicating the LGB's view that a departmental inquiry was the most efficient way of proceeding. In the House of Commons on 16 April, the Irish Party spokesman, J. J. Clancy, had to admit that the contrast between the action of the committee and that of a royal commission was rather striking – if the task had been given to a commission, the work would scarcely have been commenced at that time.[74] The published report was unusual, if not unique at the time, in that it included a collection of photographs of the slums taken by John Cooke of the National Society for the Prevention of Cruelty to Children (NSPCC) and presented to the inquiry in November 1913.[75] It provided a concise overview of existing housing and living conditions, and put forward a programme involving tenement reconstruction, and the building of some 14,000 new suburban houses. However, the report has been said to have been 'too honest for its own good', in that it was critical of the corporation's use of the legal powers available to it to improve standards in tenement dwellings.[76] There was particular criticism of the city's 83-year-old medical officer, Sir Charles Cameron, who had dispensed, in some cases, with the requirements of the corporation's bye-laws relating to unfit tenement dwellings, some of which were owned by councillors.

When the report was debated at Westminster in April 1914, Birrell accepted that 'a lamentable state of things' existed. However, in restating the opposition to subsidies which he had expressed as far back as 1908, he was not prepared to say that the public must supply the money to build 'nice, clean, charming residences', where men who were earning as little as 15 shillings a week could live with their wives and children, while the rent was provided out of the pockets of other people. He agreed that something must be done, but building houses, which from the beginning would have to be subsidised from central or local taxation, was something that required more consideration than he could be expected to give it at that time. He hoped that rebuilding and reconstruction of the tenements could soon begin to cater for 'well-to-do artisans and clerks', but as to where the many thousands of their present inhabitants were to go, he offered no specific proposals.[77] In effect, as Murray Fraser put it, Birrell continued to sit on the fence in an effort not to compromise his personal dislike of state subsidy, while appearing to go along with Irish demands to implement the committee's proposals. Robinson, on the other hand, personally supported the findings of the inquiry, notwithstanding the scale of the recommended building programme and the enormous cost. In light of the report, his board advised the Treasury in November that no barrier should be placed in the way of advancing money to the corporation for housing schemes estimated to cost almost £370,000 that the board had already approved.[78] However, having been told that there was no abnormal unemployment in Dublin at that stage, the Treasury sanctioned loans of only £75,000 in the early months of 1915, notwithstanding representations by Redmond and other MPs.[79] With the wartime restrictions on borrowing, which had then come into force, the board was obliged in October 1915 to tell the corporation that they could not count on any further advances from the State for housing or other domestic reforms 'until the allied armies carry the war to a successful conclusion'.

Strong on Management and Administration of the Law, but ...?

Under Robinson's stewardship, the LGB was entitled to be regarded as efficient by the standards of the day, being undoubtedly strong on management and their administration of the law. While neither Robinson nor his board may have been the prime mover in the case of much of the legislation enacted during his Vice-Presidency, he certainly deserved credit for having set about implementation of that legislation promptly and effectively. His personal contribution to the financial and procedural clauses of the 1906 Act relating to labourers housing were significant, as was his recognition of the importance attached by the Irish Party and the government to the efficient administration of the programme. It would probably have been convenient for him to advise the Chief Secretary to concede the demand for the establishment of a Royal Commission on Dublin housing, which arose from many quarters in the autumn of 1913 (in that way postponing the need for decisions for several years and until, perhaps, a Home Rule government had come into office.) Instead he supported a short sharp exercise by a committee of his own officials and which, but for the outbreak of war in 1914, would probably have led to the start of a major programme to rid Dublin of its notorious slums. While there was little he could have done to offset the preference of local councillors and Irish MPs for adoptive health and welfare legislation, he could perhaps have done more to advance the reform of the poor relief/workhouse system on which there was fairly general agreement by 1910. However, in this – as in other cases where substantial and complex legislation would have been required – he and the Chief Secretary had to contend with the pressure from other departments, and indeed ministers, for an allocation of parliamentary time for their own priorities. He may not have been an enthusiastic supporter of the old age pensions system (except to the extent that it reduced demands on the poor relief system), but his oversight of the implementation of the system was above reproach.

If, as Robinson told Beatrice Webb, what had concerned him during his career was keeping his successive chief secretaries out of trouble, he must be considered to have been generally successful in achieving this.[80] His knowledge of rural and urban Ireland was not matched by any of the other senior officials in the Dublin administration, and the inspectors' reports, local council minutes, letters and local press reports, which were fed into the Custom House on a daily basis, meant that he had his ear to the ground in the metaphorical sense. He knew when to make a stand on a point of principle, but he was also adept at recognising situations where flexibility was called for and at raising a red flag when possible dangers were looming. In February 1916, for example, writing to the Under-Secretary about what was then being described as a proposed 'mother and child' scheme, he warned that

> … Infant life protection is a thing which the RC clergy are feverishly anxious to keep in their own hands, or the hands of their chosen people. We must be careful not to alarm them about it. I don't want the LGB to be dragged into a hostile struggle with the RC clergy over their business – and I am convinced we must rely largely on the help of the RC clergy if we are to make any mothercraft scheme a success.[81]

If advice of this kind had been available – or had been heeded – by a Minister for Health some thirty-five years later, when another mother and child scheme was being formulated, the political history of the 1950s might have been very different.

NOTES

1   Ruth Barrington, *Health, Medicine & Politics in Ireland 1900–1970* (Dublin, 1987), p.19.

2   Beatrice Webb, *Our Partnership* (eds Barbara Drake and Margaret I. Cole) (London, 1948), p.408.

3   F. S. L. Lyons, *Ireland Since the Famine* (London, 1971), pp.72–73; Redmond, not unlike Robinson, never articulated a comprehensive social vision of his desired Home Rule Ireland – Dermot Meleady, *John Redmond, The National Leader* (Sallins, 2014), p.4.

4   Christine Bellamy, *Administering Central–Local Relations, 1871–1919: The Local Government Board in its Fiscal and Cultural Context* (Manchester, 1988), p.155.

5   John Turner, 'Experts and Interests: David Lloyd George and the Dilemmas of the Expanding State, 1906–19', in Roy MacLeod (ed.), *Government and Expertise* (Cambridge, 1988), pp.216–17.

6   Virginia Crossman, *Politics, Pauperism and Power in Late Nineteenth-Century Ireland* (Manchester, 2006), p.26.

7   Ruth Barrington, *Health, Medicine & Politics*.

8   Murray Fraser, *John Bull's Other Homes: State Housing and British Policy in Ireland, 1883–1922* (Liverpool, 1996).

9   Mary E. Daly, *The Buffer State: The Historical Roots of the Department of the Environment* (Dublin, 1997), p.35.

10   *Hansard* V, 61, 16 Apr. 1914, 388–390.

11   *Royal Commission on the Poor Laws and Relief of Distress: Report on Ireland* (HC 1909 [Cd. 4630]), para. 123.

12   Robinson to Bryce, 4 Aug. 1906, NLI, James Bryce Papers, MS 11,013(4); MacDonnell to Bryce, 6 Aug. 1906 and Robinson to Bryce, 11 Aug. 1906, *ibid.*

13   *Hansard* IV, 5 Dec. 1906, 941–45.

14   Robinson to Bryce, 11 Jan. 1907, NLI, James Bryce Papers, MS 11,015.

15   *AR*, 1906–07.

16   G. C. Peden, *The Treasury and British Public Policy, 1906–1959* (Oxford, 2000), p.64.

17   *Report of the Vice-Regal Commission on Poor Law Reform in Ireland* (Vol. I), HC 1906, Cd. 3202.

18   John E. Redmond, *Some Arguments for Home Rule* (Dublin, 1908), pp.73–79.

19   *Hansard* IV, 187, 3 Apr. 1908, 840.

20   Robinson to Gerald Balfour, 27 Aug. 1905, NAS, Balfour Papers, GD 433/2/273/27.

21   Sir Henry Robinson, *Memories: Wise and Otherwise* (London, 1923), p.212.

22   Webb, *Our Partnership*, pp.404–405.

23   *Royal Commission on the Poor Laws and Relief of Distress: Report on Ireland*, HC 1909 [Cd. 4630], p.87.

24   William J. Braithwaite (ed. Henry N. Bunbury), *Lloyd George's Ambulance Wagon* (London, 1957), pp.148, 150–52.

25   Ruth Barrington, *Health, Medicine & Politics*, pp.40–41, 48.

26   *Report of Committee Appointed to Consider Extension of Medical Benefit under the National Insurance Act to Ireland*, HC 1913 (Cd. 6963).

27   Robinson, *Memories*, pp.206–207.
28   Old Age Pension Scheme, memorandum dated 22 Nov. 1899, initialed HAR, TNA, Balfour papers, PRO 30/60/28; the memorandum is erroneously attributed to Gerald Balfour in *David R. C. Hudson, The Ireland That We Made* (Ohio, 2003) p.130.
29   Robinson, *Memories*, pp.208–209.
30   *Irish Times*, 13 Jan. 1909.
31   *Return as to Old Age Pensions in Ireland for each Financial Year since the Passing of the Old Age Pensions Act 1908*, HC 1913 (3).
32   *Irish Times*, 14 May 1909.
33   TNA,T1/11223, Treasury files 11926 and 14686.
34   *Hansard* V, 112, 26 Feb. 1919, 1850–52.
35   *Hansard* V, 112, 26 Feb. 1919, 1860–62.
36   *Irish Times*, 26 Feb. 1919, letter from Dr D. Edgar Flinn.
37   *Hansard* IV, 89, 8 Aug. 1901, 104.
38   *Irish Times*, 2 May 1914.
39   *Irish Times*, 23 Jan. 1915.
40   *AR*, 911–12,
41   *Irish Times*, 14 Jan. 1916.
42   *Interim Report of the Departmental Committee on Tuberculosis*, HC 1912–13 [Cd. 6164].
43   Robinson to Nathan, 3 Mar. 1915, Oxford, Bodleian Library, MS Nathan 460, f. 178–79.
44   *The Motor News* II, No. 5, May 1901, pp.111–114.
45   Sir Hickman Bacon, a wealthy Lincolnshire landowner, was an early motoring enthusiast and also the owner of an important collection of British watercolours, including a large number by J. M. W. Turner.
46   Bob Montgomery, *An Irish Roadside Camera* (Dublin, 1997), p.52.
47   Robinson, *Further Memories*, p.160.
48   Cornelius F. Smith, *The History of the Royal Irish Automobile Club, 1901–1991* (Dublin, 1994), p.93.
49   *Kildare Observer*, 18 Apr. 1903.
50   *AR*, 1900–01 and 1901–02.
51   Robinson to Balfour, 23 Nov. 1899, NAS, Balfour Papers, GD 433/2/114/9.
52   *AR*, 1905–06.
53   *AR*, 1907–08.
54   *AR*, 1896–97.
55   MacDonnell to Bryce, 8 Jan. 1906, NLI, James Bryce Papers, Ms 11,012(1).
56   MacDonnell to Bryce, 10 Mar. 1906, NLI, James Bryce Papers, Ms 11,012(3).
57   MacDonnell to Bryce, 4, 10 and 16 Apr. 1906, NLI James Bryce Papers, MS 11,012 (4); MacDonnell to Bryce, 16 Apr. 1906, Oxford, Bodleian Library, MS Bryce 215, f. 37–39.
58   Redmond to Dillon, 3 Apr. 1906, NLI, Redmond papers, MS 15,182/10; Redmond to Edward Blake MP, 13 Nov. 1906, MS 15,170/3.
59   *Hansard* V, 158, 28 May 1906, 107–116.
60   *Hansard* V, 18, 7 July 1910, 1810–11.
61   *Hansard* V, 26, 31 May 1911, 1174.

62 Robinson to Bryce, 11 Aug. 1906, NLI, James Bryce Papers MS 11,013(4).

63 MacDonnell to Bryce, 20 Oct. 1906, NLI, James Bryce Papers MS 11,014(2).

64 *Hansard* VI, 18, 7 July 1910, 1797.

65 *AR*, 1913–14, pp.xlvi-xlviii.

66 *Third Report of H. M. Commissioners for Inquiring into the Housing of the Working Classes, Ireland*, HC 1884–85 [c. 4547].

67 Murray Fraser, *John Bull's Other Homes*, pp.92, 93.

68 Mary E. Daly, *Dublin – The Deposed Capital: A Social and Economic History, 1860–1914* (1984), pp.318–19.

69 *Irish Times*, 1 Nov. 1913.

70 *Irish Times*, 8 and 18 Nov. 1913.

71 *The Leader*, vol. xxvii, no. 13, 8 Nov. 1913, pp.297–98.

72 *Irish Times*, 11 Nov. 1913.

73 *The Leader*, vol. xxvii, no. 13, 8 Nov. 1913, pp.297–98.

74 *Hansard* V, 61, 16 Apr. 1914, 343–44.

75 *Report of the Departmental Committee Appointed by the Local Government Board for Ireland to Inquire into the Housing Conditions of the Working Classes in the City of Dublin*, HC 1914 [Cd. 7273].

76 Pádraig Yeates, *A City in Wartime: Dublin 1914–18* (Dublin, 2011), p.11.

77 *Hansard* V, 61, 16 Apr. 1914, 388–395.

78 Murray Fraser, *John Bull's Other Homes*, pp.112–114; NAI, CSORP 1913/24059; 1914/5006.

79 LGB to Treasury, 17 Nov. 1914 and subsequent correspondence, TNA, T1/11785.

80 Webb, *Our Partnership*, p.408.

81 Robinson to Nathan, 11 Feb. 1916, Oxford, Bodleian Library, MS Nathan 460, f. 229–230.

CHAPTER VI

Was the LGB the Fountainhead of Corruption in Ireland?

Robinson had gained unrivalled experience during his service as a member of the LGB from 1891 onwards, and as Vice-President, he was given a pre-eminent decision-making position by the 1898 act. He was the only member who served the board continuously from 1898 until the end of March 1922, and was clearly its dominant personality. While still a commissioner, he told the chief secretary in 1897 that 'there is an actual board sitting every day'[1] and his evidence to the Royal Commission on the civil service in 1913 confirmed that daily meetings were still the norm. Minute books for 1916 and 1921, which have survived, record these meetings, but while decisions made on relatively trivial matters are noted, much of the business was covered by a single sentence: 'Directions were given by the Vice-President and the commissioners on the papers laid before them this day.'[2] On paper, the work was distributed among the three full-time members, but Robinson told the Royal Commission that 'it really is not a board' because the final decision could only be made by himself, and matters were never put to a vote: 'We never differ. We talk the whole thing out and decide.'[3] In these circumstances, Robinson clearly had a major impact on the organisation and staffing of the LGB – for better or worse – in its final twenty-five years. That was certainly how the Catholic Defence Society viewed matters in 1907. It criticised the board as an autocratic institution, whose powers were entirely wielded by one man who, for good measure, was 'a protestant of anti-popular opinions and a pronounced party man, surrounded officially by a solid masonic ring'.[4] More than ten years later, Arthur Griffith went further when he alleged that the board was 'the fountainhead of corruption in Ireland'.[5]

Notwithstanding the reforms which had been implemented from the 1870s onwards, 39 per cent of more than 1,600 'principal positions' in the Irish administration were still filled by direct nomination in 1911, and another 48 per cent were filled after a qualifying examination, leaving only 13 per cent filled after open competitive examinations – and the situation was little different in 1920.[6] Thus, a department head, in making recommendations on the appointment and promotion of key staff, could bring about a profound change in the character of his office – one that could last even after his retirement. This chapter considers whether Robinson was responsible for a change of this kind in the LGB, or whether he simply inherited and operated systems and procedures which predated his appointment.

Growth in Staff Numbers

The huge increase in staff numbers over which Robinson presided is the first and most obvious point to note in considering his impact on the organisation. In 1897–98, the authorised establishment amounted to a total of eighty-four civil servants, excluding the three members of the board, an increase of no more than eight on the total ten years earlier.[7] With its wider responsibilities under the 1898 act for the organisation of local government, and for overseeing the operations of the new county and district councils, the volume of work increased dramatically. According to the annual report for 1898–99, some idea of the increased workload could be gained from the fact that the number of letters sent out in a typical week had trebled since 1897.[8] The Royal Commission on the Poor Laws reported ten years later that the number of papers dealt with annually by the board had increased since 1898 from about 70,000 to approximately double that number.[9] Figures of this kind were regularly used at the time to assess workloads in various departments but they were, of course, only a crude measure because, as Robinson pointed out, a paper with a single reference number often dealt with a large number of points and, as the extra work was entirely new, the board had to lay down a principle for future guidance in every new case.

In the short term, the work of implementing the 1898 act was assigned to a special staff unit, for which the Treasury sanctioned the employment of a corps of temporary clerical staff. These positions were exempted from the normal recruitment arrangements, leaving Robinson and his colleagues free to appoint whomsoever they chose.[10] To cope with the additional work on an ongoing basis, Robinson succeeded in significantly increasing the board's staff numbers in the years after 1898 when 'a very satisfactory arrangement', which he had made with the Treasury, gave him a considerable amount of discretion 'within certain limits' in the recruitment of extra staff.[11] Thus, with the absorption of many of the temporary clerks into the permanent establishment, and the creation of other new posts, staff numbers had grown to 181 by 1906, more than twice the 1897 figure. By 1911, the total provided for in the published estimates had increased still further to 234. But even these numbers did not disclose the full picture as the estimates regularly included lump-sum provisions for temporary clerks and for copying and typing services – these allowed for the engagement of at least forty additional junior staff in any year without examination or competition of any kind. Strong views 'as to the undesirability of temporary clerical labour of this kind except to meet a passing temporary emergency' were expressed by the Royal Commission on the civil service in 1914. It suggested that safeguards were especially necessary in Ireland where 'this temporary clerical employment is an outstanding and a demoralizing feature in departmental administration'.[12] Provisions in the estimates also allowed for the engagement of up to five additional assistant engineering inspectors or architects, again without competition. In a return presented to Parliament, inclusion of the temporary staff numbers caused the total staff at 31 March 1911 to be shown as 274, instead of the estimates figure of 234. The LGB had by then become the largest Dublin-based bureaucracy, and by comparison with other large departments, a greater proportion of its staff (40 per cent) had salaries of £160 a year or more.[13]

Andrew Gailey's study of the 1890s and early 1900s suggests that the Treasury was generally unsympathetic towards submissions from Irish departments and exercised petty and oppressive control over relatively small matters.[14] Robinson's memoirs include similar criticism of the attitude towards Ireland of the permanent officials of the Treasury,[15] but the 'satisfactory arrangement' on staffing, which he made with them in 1898–99, was not the only example of a favourable response to his submissions. He often travelled to London on official business and was well known to senior officials so that, when necessary, he was able to call on them directly to promote his staffing and other claims. In the event, he succeeded in maintaining the board's staff complement at a relatively high level, even during the war years, and in 1922 the number stood at almost 300, more than three times what it had been at the beginning of the century. It is clear from Treasury files that his good relationship with the Treasury Remembrancer, Maurice Headlam, also helped from 1912 onwards to obtain sanction in many cases for staffing proposals. When files were referred to him from London, Headlam occasionally engaged with Robinson, suggesting compromise solutions which, if agreed, he would then recommend to London. Headlam considered Robinson to be outstanding among the heads of Dublin departments, both in ability and in knowledge of Ireland and its problems, and his attitude to staffing proposals obviously reflected this.[16]

'New Lodgings' for the Board

With the virtual doubling of its staff numbers, the Custom House headquarters of the LGB became seriously overcrowded. However, when the Public Offices Site (Dublin) Bill was presented to the House of Commons in March 1902, there was no mention of the need to provide for the LGB. Instead, the objective was stated in general terms to be the compulsory acquisition of a block of thirteen houses at Upper Merrion Street as a site for a proposed Royal College of Science and other offices and buildings for the public service.[17] In the Commons,[18] Irish members protested that the site chosen was in the most expensive residential area of the city and that the houses that were to be demolished were 'some of the noblest old houses remaining in Dublin'. The debate took a new twist when Austen Chamberlain, Financial Secretary to the Treasury, disclosed that the new college was to be built in the area occupied by the back-gardens and stables, and that the houses themselves were to be refurbished internally to provide offices for DATI (which already occupied some of them) and for the LGB, all of whose staff were to transfer from the Custom House. Chamberlain suggested that while Irish members might disapprove of the policy of the LGB, they should not punish the board's clerks by forcing them to continue working under conditions inimical to their health, but this was not enough to convince the Irish members that they should support the scheme. 'Not a shilling for the Local Government Board' was Tim Healy's blunt response: the board already occupied one of the most glorious buildings in Dublin and for as long as Irish labourers were forced to live under insanitary conditions, he would not be a party to providing funds to erect 'a new arsenal of ascendancy' for Robinson and his colleagues. John Dillon and others protested that additional offices could be acquired at far less cost in Gardiner Street (not far from Dillon's home in North Great Georges Street) or elsewhere on the north side of the city, and that the new College of Science should not be hidden away behind 'the board's new lodgings'.

Despite the objections in Parliament and reservations expressed by Dublin Corporation and others, the bill became law in August 1903. In a change of plan, however, it was the OPW, rather than the LGB, which moved from the Custom House in 1905 to occupy temporarily the houses at Upper Merrion Street. After completion of the College of Science in 1911, the OPW, in a further change of plan, moved to the premises formerly occupied by the college at St Stephen's Green. The Merrion Street houses were then demolished and work began on the two-block complex now known as Government Buildings, the intention being that the north block (nearest Leinster House) would house the LGB, while the south block would accommodate DATI.[19] Wartime restrictions on capital expenditure and shortages of steel and other building materials delayed construction work, but good progress was again being made at the end of 1920 when Robinson met the Under-Secretary to discuss the allocation of offices in the complex.[20] In the event, the buildings were not completed until 1922. Neither Robinson nor his board, nor the department which succeeded it, was allowed to take over the accommodation planned for them, even though their existing headquarters at the Custom House had been burned down in May 1921. Instead, the north block was pressed into use as the offices of the President of the Executive Council and of the Department of Finance, and the room designed for Robinson as Vice-President came to be used as the Council Chamber and later as the Cabinet Room.

Administrative and Clerical Positions

After the 1870s, recruiting practices and clerical/administrative staff structures in the civil service in Ireland were essentially the same as they were in Britain. By the turn of the century, educational developments had allowed Irish catholics and nationalists to enter the lower and intermediate clerical grades in growing numbers. These people constituted the majority of the LGB staff at that stage, filling positions as second division clerks, abstractors or boy clerks. Those who sat the annual open competitions conducted by the civil service commissioners for these grades were allowed to indicate a preference for service in a particular location. When Englishmen were appointed to posts in Dublin they often sought exchanges with Irish officials serving in England so that both could return to posts nearer their homes. Promotion on merit within was possible, and promotion to higher (first) division posts was also allowed for, but only in exceptional circumstances. In 1899, twenty-five men were serving as second division clerks in the LGB, of whom four had been promoted, ostensibly on merit, to fill supervisory and higher grade posts, but still within the second division.[21] Promotions of this kind were made at the discretion of the board and were regularly a source of complaint, with allegations of favouritism or discrimination being made. In 1907, for example, *The Leader* drew attention to the fact that an Englishman had been 'shovelled' into a higher grade second division vacancy over the heads of five 'mere Irish papists', all of whom had served longer than he and some of whom held university degrees. Around the same time, the only Englishman remaining in the lower grade of the second division was also promoted.[22] By 1915, the number of assistant clerk positions had increased to forty-four, there were forty-four second division clerks and the number of higher grade (staff officer) posts had been increased to twelve.[23]

One of the most significant and enduring features of the LGB organisation under Robinson's management – and one for which he personally took credit – was the fact that, within a few years of his appointment, the office was employing a significant number of higher (first) division clerks – the grade intended to be filled on the basis of the annual examination of university degree standard conducted by the civil service commissioners.[24] In December 1899, when the board had seven higher division posts, Robinson made formal proposals to the Treasury seeking to have all of the important branches headed by first division men, as in England. 'This question so vitally affects future local government administration in Ireland', he told Gerald Balfour at the time in a hand-written letter marked 'private', that he thought it necessary to submit to him 'certain considerations bearing upon this matter that cannot very well be put in an official minute'.[25] Up to 1894, he went on, the office had always been an upper division one, but as a result of reorganisation by the Treasury, some of the important work was now in the charge of lower division men, recruited as school leavers, and the whole work of the office would eventually get into their hands. Now, he continued –

> ... while the Irish Lower Division includes some good men, and while they would no doubt be well suited to the work of such offices as Customs, Inland Revenue, Education, etc. they are particularly unsuited to the work of the administrative branches of our department. They are men of a very much lower class than the English lower division clerks belong to – generally they are the sons of small farmers and tradesmen and catholics with strong nationalist and anti-English sympathies.

Out of the lower division clerks in this office we have only two or three at most who are protestants, and considering how the judgment of local authorities in Ireland is apt to be warped by political and religious considerations, it seems especially necessary that the central authority should not be manned exclusively by a class liable to be influenced by the same ideas; and when we remember that one of the inherent beliefs in the national mind is that the British Treasury takes every opportunity of swindling Ireland out of millions, the Treasury's own interests would be in the direction of giving us a proper proportion of upper division clerks.

Robinson had been warned confidentially by Sir Thomas Esmonde MP, Chairman of the General Council of County Councils, that unless the board kept the tightest possible supervision over the councils, county government would rapidly go to the bad, and while he felt that Esmonde's approach was perhaps too sweeping, there was a good deal of truth in it. He concluded, therefore, in his letter to Balfour that 'considering that our administration of the multifarious acts relating to local government has to be carried on in the light of a fiercely hostile public opinion, hampered by religion and political pitfalls, it seems only fair and reasonable that our senior branches should be recruited from men of education and ability and paid at the same rate as those in the English board.' He asked Balfour to make personal representations to the Treasury in support of the board's proposals, and less than two weeks later he was able to tell him that 'whatever you said to the Treasury has had its effect for I think it pretty clear that they will make us an upper division office again'.[26] The formal sanction which followed allowed the board to have sixteen higher division posts in addition to the secretary, against the total of seven less than a year earlier. Four of the sixteen were to be graded as senior clerks with maximum salaries of £700 a year, and four of the others with basic salary maxima of £500 were to be paid allowances of £100 a year for acting as deputies to the senior clerks, or for other higher duties.[27] The board then became the largest employer in Ireland of higher division clerks, with twice as many as were employed in the Chief Secretary's office, and with only one other Irish office (the Public Record Office) employing a first division clerk in 1913.[28]

Robinson's view that the more senior positions in the LGB could be better filled by higher division men was similar to that of Under-Secretaries MacDonnell and Dougherty, who believed that the top positions in the Chief Secretary's Office should be filled from the first division.[29] Robinson's view was also vindicated by the 1914 report of the Royal

Commission on the civil service: 'Want of officers recruited by the class 1 examination is the great defect of office organization in Ireland.' The report found that it was essential to have 'a reasonable complement of the best educated men' on the staff of the LGB.[30] Unlike Robinson, T. P. Gill, the catholic and nationalist secretary of DATI, considered that all higher positions in public departments should be filled by internal promotion of men who had entered through the lower clerical grades. He attached more importance to 'rearing and breeding than to subsequent education', but this approach was firmly rejected by the Royal Commission because Gill had not 'allowed due weight to the permanent and solid advantages of the best education in the management of the weighty affairs of his department'.[31] Robinson's evidence to the commission in February 1913 was effectively a restatement of the views he had expressed to Balfour in 1899. He spoke of the need to employ the best educated men and he told the commission that, because politics and religion found their way into many local government matters in Ireland, and because local government had been placed in the hands of people who had no experience of it, he was anxious to leaven his staff – who until his appointment as Vice-President were nearly all Irishmen and in second division clerkships – with a few Englishmen and Scotchmen who would be ignorant of the political questions and might look upon things in a new and fresh light:

> It really turned out to be a great advantage to us to have in our upper division a few strangers who looked upon our political dissensions with a certain amount of indifference; I have seen the characteristics of the three, English, Irish and Scotch and, working together, they make a really perfect combination. The Englishmen we have had from the upper division examination have been stolid, sensible, highly competent persons. The Scotchman is a rock of common-sense, accurate, and cautious. The Irishman is brilliant, resourceful, and quick, but he is rather impulsive and wants the steadiness of the English and Scotch. An office with all three nationalities represented is perfectly equipped.[32]

This evidence has been quoted and commented on by several historians over the years. O'Halpin, for example, who saw Robinson as a highly partisan civil servant, suggested that it was partly in order to block the eventual progression of the ablest of the second division clerks to higher posts that he made the LGB a class 1 office, 'thus securing in its higher reaches a preponderance of politically reliable English and Scottish graduates impervious to Irish nationalist sentiment'.[33] More recently,

Robinson has been accused of running 'a frankly sectarian department' disguised as a mix of English, Scottish and Irish.[34] But to what extent was the policy of relying heavily on first division men, with some from England and Scotland, implemented in practice?

In 1913, the LGB had nineteen higher division officers, including the secretary, an assistant secretary, eleven others who were either graded as senior clerks or were receiving allowances for higher duties, and six who were described as junior clerks. Nine of the nineteen were graduates who had entered the civil service by the class 1 examination and ten had been promoted from the second division.[35] There were two Scots, six English and eleven Irish, while the religious breakdown was six catholics against thirteen others. Fourteen of the men serving in 1913 had been appointed since 1898, and if these are considered separately, a better assessment of the impact of Robinson's policy can be made. The fourteen included two young graduates who had taken up positions with the board following the August 1899 examinations (Codling, an Englishman, and Diamond, a Scot) and three Irish-born graduates (Watt, Harris and Stephens), who had originally been appointed to first division positions in other departments but transferred to the board between 1901 and 1909. The remaining nine appointees to first division posts (six of the nine were Irish and four of them catholics) had been selected and promoted from among the second division clerks already serving with the board.[36] Overall, the net effect over the years 1898 to 1913 was to increase the number of Scottish-born officials in the first division from one to two, and to increase the number of Englishmen from two to six, bringing to eight (or just over 40 per cent) the number of non-Irish first division men and bringing the number of non-catholics in these positions to thirteen, or almost 70 per cent.

The consistent refusal of the Treasury to concede that salaries for higher division posts in the LGB should be the same as those paid for comparable posts in England (even though the higher English scale applied in the Chief Secretary's Office) clearly affected Robinson's prospects of recruiting more of the young English, Scottish or other graduates about whom he spoke so highly in his evidence to the Royal Commission. However, notwithstanding his admiration for these young men, Robinson told the commission that some second division clerks could also be extraordinarily good – and this may explain why the number of men promoted from the second to the first division within the LGB accounted for almost one-third of all such promotions in the entire UK civil service between 1899 and 1903.[37] The high proportion of available positions filled by promotion was viewed with disfavour by the Royal Commission because it could lower the educational standard of the class.[38] There was also, of course, the question of whether all of these promotions were made strictly on a merit basis without regard to political, religious or other extraneous considerations. While the specific approval of the Treasury and the civil service commissioners was required in each case, the LGB itself had absolute discretion in initiating the procedure and in selecting persons for promotion, and its judgment of an individual's suitability was unlikely to be challenged by officials in London. Objective assessments of suitability can hardly explain why only four of the nine men promoted from the second division between 1899 and 1913 were catholics – even though the vast majority of those serving in that division were catholics.[39]

Discrimination on Religious Grounds

In the 1890s, the religious composition of the LGB staff was 'really indefensible and ought to be exposed', according to Edward Ennis, a barrister and former reporter on the *Freeman's Journal*, who was then serving as registrar of the court of chancery.[40] The claim that catholics were being discriminated against continued to flare up at intervals during Robinson's management of the board. In September 1898, the *Freeman's Journal* drew attention to the fact that only six of the twenty-two men employed as inspectors and auditors were catholics. The *Journal* also derided a statement by Balfour in the House of Commons two years earlier when he claimed that it was difficult to find suitable catholics to fill senior positions because of the absence of a catholic university education.[41] When Tim Healy complained in the Commons in May 1900 that the board's offices were 'stuffed full of ascendancy men', that less than 15 per cent of the permanent staff were catholics, and that not more than four of thirty-four temporary clerks were catholics, Balfour asserted that religious opinions did not influence appointments, and that catholics were not under any disadvantage. However, while 'the religion of those who are taken into the service of the state is not officially known', he was still able to insist that at least half of the temporary staff were catholics.[42]

The board's staffing did not attract derogatory comment in *The Leader* – the popular, influential and militantly pro-catholic and Irish-Ireland periodical founded and edited by D. P. Moran – when it first began to publish analyses of the staffing of major public bodies and railway companies, with trenchant criticism of the small proportion of catholic employees and their even smaller share of higher posts. There was criticism of various activities of the board, especially during 1905, but the staff structure itself escaped Moran's criticism until 1907 when the Catholic Defence Society circulated *Light on the Local Government Board*

– a pamphlet documenting the board's staffing situation in great detail and alleging glaring discrimination in its employment policies. This was grist to the mill for Moran, who reprinted the findings and embellished them with his own critical comments on how the non-catholics (the 'saved', as he usually referred to them) managed to acquire most of the nominated positions and a high proportion of the promotions, at the expense of the catholic 'idolaters'.[43] In a subsequent issue, he berated the *Irish Independent* for having published a 'cooked' version of the pamphlet, omitting passages which contained the more critical comment, including its description of Henry Robinson as 'a protestant of anti-popular opinions and a pronounced party man'.[44] In 1913, when *The Leader* began another round of assessments of the staffing policies of public departments, it turned its attention to the LGB in its edition of 15 February, but did not name names or provide individual salary details as it had done in its treatment of other departments. Overall, the journal's conclusion at that stage was that fifty-four of the eighty-one most senior and best-paid LGB officials were protestants, while there were just twenty-seven catholics or 'idolaters' in these positions. After the publication of *Light on the Local Government Board*, Jeremiah MacVeagh, MP for South Down, asked the Chief Secretary what steps he proposed to take to eliminate 'the evil of religious ascendancy' whereby – as shown in the pamphlet – only thirteen of the forty-seven nominated officials employed by the board were catholics and had average salaries lower than the average for the thirty-four others who were believed to be mainly Episcopalians. Birrell's predictable reply was that the board had no record of the religious persuasion of its staff and that fitness for a particular post, and not religious denomination, was the test applied in making appointments.[45] In early May, however, replies to further questions by MacVeagh disclosed that Birrell had no difficulty in providing a breakdown of the teams of resident magistrates, senior police officers and others on the basis of religious affiliation, all of which must have helped to add weight to allegations concerning the deliberate withholding by Robinson of information on the religious affiliations of his staff.[46]

Political Patronage

The fact that many of the better-paid posts in the LGB were filled by nomination, or by nomination with limited competition, left the way open for political patronage and jobbery to thrive. There is ample evidence that Gerald Balfour regularly intervened when inspector and auditor appointments were being made by the LGB, as did one of his liberal successors, Augustine Birrell. On paper at any rate, Irish Party members were precluded from attempting to advance the claims of supporters or acquaintances to public positions. This was due to a resolution that Redmond arranged in 1906 to be passed stating that 'it is inconsistent and improper for any member of the party to use influence, direct or indirect, to obtain paid government situations, or appointments, or promotions of any kind whatsoever, for any person'. The resolution (or pledge) was adopted annually from then on.[47] Redmond regularly stated publicly that he had never sought a position for a friend, but not everyone was convinced of this and not everyone was satisfied that other members of the party observed the rule. The destruction of LGB records in 1921 rules out any possibility of establishing definitively whether MPs or others made representations to Robinson in support of the appointment of particular individuals, but in his memoirs, he claimed that when the liberals held office, nationalist MPs, especially the more recent ones and those associated with the AOH (but not 'the old nationalists' like Redmond, Dillon, Esmonde and Healy) 'worked like blacks for their friends'. Those who wrote to him personally in favour of particular candidates usually adopted a face-saving formula acknowledging the existence of the pledge but going on to say that if it were not for the pledge the writer would be quite unable to resist recommending the candidate in question.[48]

While historians have tended to endorse the view that Irish Party members generally observed the policy of abstaining from the use of influence, recent studies have thrown up examples of efforts by MPs to help family members, friends or supporters to secure positions at national or local level. Accepting that these add up to 'fairly slim pickings', a study by James McConnell draws attention to the view that the use of political patronage was justified, and in the national interest, to help catholics who had previously been denied a fair share of some categories of civil service jobs.[49] *The Leader*, which was no friend of the Party, had in fact demanded in 1908 that nationalist Ireland should 'take what it can get', and that MPs should pursue patronage openly.[50] Thus, while jobbery and place-hunting were widely deplored in public, and while relatively few MPs were guilty of jobbing on their own behalf, or of place-hunting for family members and personal friends, it was not uncommon for them to lobby for appointments for their constituents and political supporters who sought help in negotiating the glass ceiling that many still saw as preventing catholics and nationalists from securing career advancement. Lobbying of this kind was often privately condoned as advancing the greening of Dublin Castle.[51] The Dillon Papers at TCD, the Nathan Papers at the Bodleian Library and the Bryce/MacDonnell correspondence at the NLI all disclose instances in which proposed appointments were the subject of soundings with Dillon while the liberals were in office. Birrell subsequently consulted with nationalist leaders about appointments to such an extent that G. A. Birmingham, writing in 1913, saw these politicians as the Irish branch of the Liberal Party in everything but name, with power to influence policies and the exercise of patronage.[52] Robinson recorded that Devlin, parliamentary leader of the AOH, 'fought for and obtained an almost complete ascendancy over the Irish government during the liberal administration, in patronage and other matters', whereas Sinn Féin pushed sectarian differences into the background – they were 'sincere and self-sacrificing, even if misguided'.[53] William O'Brien was another who was very critical of the Irish Party's efforts at place-seeking for catholics,[54] as was Nancy Wyse Power, a prominent Dublin Sinn Féin/Cumann na mBan leader, who denounced those party members who used the years of waiting for the enactment of the Home Rule Bill to advance their followers. As she saw it, practically everyone was benefiting in one way or another from the party's access to Castle patronage because 'as adherents of the government', the party was in a position to secure various positions for their nominees, including positions as LGB inspectors.[55]

In 1991, the late Lawrence McBride concluded that the Irish administration was completely transformed at the higher levels between 1892 and 1922 because of the nature of the direct appointments made by members of the executive. His claim – accepted by some other historians – was that a greening process was taking place at the higher levels during that period, leading to a situation in which the whole administration in 1921, from top to bottom, was largely controlled by nationalists and catholics instead of by a unionist and protestant elite. More recently, this claim has been challenged by Fergus Campbell in a study of the 1,200 or so most powerful people who effectively ruled Ireland between 1879 and 1914 (including administrators and civil servants who held positions of power). Based on his review of data for the period 1891 to 1911, Campbell argues that there are grounds for revising McBride's hypothesis and for re-examining his conclusions – and his findings in this respect are entirely consistent with the situation in the LGB, where catholics and nationalists were still heavily under-represented in higher-level positions in 1911. For McBride, Birrell's term as Chief Secretary (beginning in 1907) was the key period in the greening of the civil service, but Campbell's analysis relating to the years up to 1911 shows that the process had a long way to go at that stage, leaving the majority of top civil servant posts still held by protestants.[56] He found that the proportion of catholics in the top ranks had increased slightly from 33 per cent to 37 per cent between 1891 and

1911, giving some support for the greening hypothesis, but not supporting the assertion that a systematic greening process was underway, or that a complete transformation was being effected.

Nepotism

Nepotism had flourished within the LGB – and elsewhere within the higher ranks of the Irish public service – since the 1870s, and continued to do so in the LGB while Robinson was Vice-President. He persuaded his own eldest son, Christopher, to join the army on the understanding that if at the end of ten years he was not happy to continue, he would give him a post in the civil service. When Christopher resigned his commission, his father had no difficulty in arranging an appointment for him as a temporary assistant inspector in the board's old age pensions department and some years later, through his father's influence with Birrell, Christopher succeeded in gaining appointment at an unusually early age as a resident magistrate. Just before that, Robinson had appointed Birrell's stepson, Alfred Browning Stanley Tennyson, the eldest grandson of the poet laureate, to another post of temporary assistant inspector under the Old Age Pensions Act. When Laurence Ginnell MP questioned that appointment in the House of Commons in 1913, Birrell objected that the question was not 'a fair way of dealing with a young man even though he may happen to have the misfortune of being a relative of mine', and he went on to make the rather implausible claim that his stepson had been appointed by Robinson 'without any operation or movement on my part'.[57] Not long after that, when Birrell agreed to the appointment of Robinson's youngest son, Adrian, then a law student, as another temporary assistant inspector, Robinson, in thanking him, wrote that it would be a splendid thing for Adrian to have work to do when not engaged in his studies, because there were long intervals between law lectures and it was very bad for a young man with an active mind to have so much leisure.[58]

Family connections also played a large part in other sections of the LGB organisation. For example, A. E. Quekett, the board's legal assistant from 1900 until his death in December 1911, was succeeded by his son, Arthur Scott Quekett, and Thomas Macready, who had been the board's solicitor for some forty years, was succeeded in 1916 by his son, James. In what he admitted was an act of 'shameless nepotism', W. E. Wylie, then a junior counsel, who had been called to the bar only in 1906, was given a brief by Robinson in 1909 after his uncle, J. W. Drury, the board's inspector of audits, had asked that he should be given a chance in a particular case. Wylie's performance on that occasion, in the absence of his two seniors, so impressed Robinson, who was himself in court, that he subsequently gave him 'every brief the LGB had as long as I was at the bar either as junior or senior'. This was the beginning of a stellar career, leading to his appointment as legal adviser to the Irish government in 1919 and his appointment as a high court judge in 1920.[59] In the board's medical service, while Dr Edward Coey Bigger was medical commissioner, his son, Dr Joseph Warwick Bigger (afterwards a professor at TCD and a senator) was appointed as temporary bacteriologist and pathologist (a position for which he was well qualified) while Dr John D. MacCormack, son of a serving medical inspector, was appointed to a similar position on his discharge from the RAMC (Royal Army Medical Corps) in 1919. Jack McCabe, a graduate engineer and son of a former medical commissioner, was appointed temporary inspector in 1905 and permanent inspector in 1910, while in the audit service, A. C. Ellis was appointed in January 1912 to a vacancy which arose from the retirement of his father, W. E. Ellis.

Inspectors and Auditors

The most serious criticism of LGB staffing practices arose from the fact that inspectors and auditors, who were better paid than other categories of staff, were appointed on the basis of blatant political patronage, a practice which was regularly condemned by nationalist MPs. In 1901, for example, D. D. Sheehan, MP for Mid-Cork, described the inspectorate as a repository for half-pay army officers and militia colonels who knew nothing of legal technicalities and could not be relied on to act impartially. In the same Westminster debate, John Cullinan of South Tipperary spoke of the inspectors as lawyers without briefs, doctors without practice, orangemen, army pensioners, or sons of unionist representatives of Ulster.[60] The inspectors were central to the board's operations; each of them was required, twice a year, to provide a report on each union in his district and to hold formal sworn inquiries at which he could summon witnesses and enforce the production of documents. His chief function, however, as stated in 1908 by Edmund Bourke, the senior inspector, was 'to act as the local agent of the board, to keep them posted on all matters ... that should be brought under their notice and ... to endeavour to get local authorities to carry out the board's regulations and views when any conflict of opinion between them and the central authority happens to arise'.[61] Robinson put it less formally in 1920: the inspector's work involved 'attending meetings and haranguing boards of guardians' as well as holding sworn inquiries, surprise visits to local offices, examining institutions' books and accounts, and representing the board at various local committee meetings.[62]

There were no prescribed qualifications or age limits for the general inspectors, a fact which was noted by George A. Birmingham, who wrote that an inspector was not asked to convince anyone that he could inspect anything but 'we give him his £500 to £700 a year if we feel reasonably sure that he is not actually blind'.[63] Gerald Balfour, however, was able to tell the Commons in May 1898 that five of the eight men then serving in permanent inspector posts had given evidence of their fitness for the position when they were temporarily in the service of the board prior to their permanent appointment. In many cases, this temporary service would have involved acting as paid vice-guardian in one of the unions or dealing with relief works.[64] Wyndham told the House of Commons in June 1903 that in filling vacancies in the inspectorate, the LGB 'invariably proceeds upon the principle of selecting persons who, in the board's opinion, are the most competent and best qualified',[65] but Robinson and his colleagues were not, in practice, always free agents in this matter. For example, Balfour was directly responsible for the appointment to a succession of positions of Edward Aremberg Saunderson, second son of the leader of the Ulster unionists, Colonel E. J. Saunderson MP, culminating in his appointment to a permanent inspector position at the end of March 1900.[66] A vacancy in June 1903 was filled by a catholic, Charles Hugh O'Conor, who had been given a temporary auditor position in 1899 after Balfour had asked Robinson to give him a trial. He was a younger son of the O'Conor Don, a substantial County Roscommon landowner and former MP who had been elected to the first county council in 1899 – one of a small number of landlords who won council seats at those elections – and controversially carried the 'Standard of Ireland' at the coronation of Edward VII in 1902. In 1906, when the number of inspectors in various grades had increased to twenty-five, the board acknowledged in a report to Parliament that all of them had been appointed without competitive or other examination and that it was not their practice to require inspectors to undergo a literary examination before appointment.[67]

A new situation arose after Birrell became Chief Secretary in 1907, when a number of appointments to the inspector grade were obviously dictated by him at the behest of, or following consultation with, Irish Party leaders. A sub-editor with the *Freeman's Journal*, Maurice J. Cosgrave, was appointed to a temporary position in 1907 (before becoming a permanent auditor in 1908) as was John Gerald MacSweeney, who had worked on the *Freeman* for a few years before his appointment as editor of the *Weekly Freeman*. As the *Freeman* had been the semi-official organ of the Irish Party since the age of Parnell, there were obvious grounds for suspicion that the party must have had a hand in the appointment of its staff to public positions. However, any suggestion that these appointments were designed to influence its policy was hotly rejected by the *Freeman's* owners. They denied any advance knowledge of the appointments, insisted that they could not control the departure of staff to other positions and, turning the argument on its head, argued that the government's actions were intended to weaken the paper by removing men of experience and training from its service and prejudicing the journal in the eyes of the public.[68] Arthur Griffith, who had been among its critics for years, considered that the *Freeman* and its supporters had finally sold out to the government, but when unionist MPs raised questions in the Commons about the appointment of men such as Cosgrave and MacSweeney, they received little satisfaction.[69] Asked about the previous occupations and qualifications of the two men, Birrell simply referred to an earlier reply to the effect that, while qualifications had not been formally prescribed, the fitness of the applicants had been carefully considered. Asked in 1910 to explain MacSweeney's promotion, as part of a series of eight appointment in various departments of men who had connections with the *Freeman*, Birrell shamelessly denied any knowledge 'of their past connection (if any) with the journal' and, for good measure, added 'the fact, if it be a fact, that such connection at any time existed had no influence whatever upon their appointments'.[70]

By 1913, the practice of appointing permanent inspectors only from the ranks of the temporary inspectors had become the norm, enabling Robinson to tell the Royal Commission on the civil service that the appointment of inspectors was no longer made 'from outside', and that the appointments were not 'pure patronage'. He went on to make a virtue of the system: if a man appointed from outside proved to be a bad bargain, the board were saddled with him and could not get rid of him, whereas a man employed as a temporary inspector could be let go, if unsuitable, or kept on if found to have the makings of a valuable official. He made no effort, however, to explain how those appointed initially as temporary inspectors were selected – nor was he challenged on this point. He did imply that in some cases pressure had been put on the Chief Secretary 'to put a man in', and claimed that he would not make an appointment himself without the Chief Secretary's concurrence – a claim which the available evidence appears to support.[71] The royal commissioners were concerned to see how even an *appearance* of patronage might be eliminated from civil service appointments, and were obviously not impressed by Robinson's evidence. Having recalled him for further questioning, they pressed him strongly on the possibility of establishing an independent competitive interview system, but he robustly defended the *status quo*. He could not conceive of any form of examination which would provide men who knew the country and the land, understood the minds of the guardians and of the people, knew the condition of agriculture in different districts, and could cope with crises and emergencies. Besides, as the board and its officials were looked on as 'nominees and instruments of a sort of alien government' and were often met by resistance at local level, men of 'imperturbable good temper and of great tact', rather than men of many attainments, were needed in order to be successful in influencing guardians.

The case made by Robinson for continuing the existing system of selection and appointment was broadly similar to the stance adopted by Lloyd George in 1911 when he argued that the best inspectors for service under the Insurance Commissioners would not be found by resort to the civil service commissioners. Instead, those making the appointments should have a free choice, and medical men and others could not be humiliated by being brought before the commissioners as if they were applicants for second division clerkships.[72] However, the example Robinson chose to illustrate his point can hardly have impressed the commissioners: he cited the case of 'one of the best inspectors we ever had' (Colonel T. Y. L. Kirkwood, who had retired in 1908), who could not write English or spell but whose 'judgment was so sound, and his diagnosis so unerring, and his influence with guardians so amazing, that he was worth his weight in gold'. In addition to his inspector post, Kirkwood was a colonel in the Roscommon militia, a substantial landowner and a successful race-horse breeder, one of whose horses won the Grand National in 1881, while another won the Ascot Gold Cup twice: in 1907 and in 1908.[73] Robinson admitted at a later stage that he had frequently been pressed by chief secretaries to lay down some educational qualification for the general inspectors and found it very difficult to get them to understand 'that it was not a man with a college degree who was wanted, but one with a thorough knowledge of Irish life, and with some practical experience of local administration ... his spelling was a matter of very secondary importance'.[74] Inevitably, the royal commissioners recommended that inspectors should in future be appointed on the basis of competitive examinations[75] but, like so many of the other recommendations of this and other commissions of that era, no action was taken to give effect to them during the war years and the revolutionary years which followed.

Like the general inspectors, the board's medical inspectors were appointed on the basis of patronage. They attracted much less criticism because they were required by law to have not less than seven years' experience after qualification, and were almost invariably drawn from the corps of up to 1,000 doctors who were serving as dispensary or workhouse medical officers. The positions were eagerly sought after, and canvassing of the Chief Secretary and of board members was the norm. When a vacancy was imminent in May 1898, Redmond made representations to Balfour in favour of Dr Joseph Smyth, a catholic dispensary medical officer at Naas whose 'fitness would be recognized by all sections and parties', and whose appointment would help to promote respect for the board. However Robinson told Balfour that while Smyth seemed to be a man of 'ability of a certain kind', it would be a great risk to appoint him 'as he is full of incoherent ideas and fads', and was excitable and unreasonable at interview.[76] That particular vacancy was filled by the appointment of Surgeon-Colonel Dr David Edgar Flinn (also a catholic), a distinguished clinician, lecturer and writer on medical subjects, who had been employed intermittently by the board as a temporary medical inspector in the 1890s. A few months later, when 'poor Clements' – a medical inspector based in Galway since 1888 – was ill and had little chance of being able to return to work, Robinson reminded Balfour that he was pledged to give the next medical inspector vacancy to Sir James Acheson MacCullagh, a medical officer in Derry, and a unionist member of the corporation. When the Treasury sanctioned additional appointments in 1900, the file was referred again to Balfour, who directed the appointment to a permanent post of Edward Coey Bigger, a superintendent medical officer and former alderman of Belfast corporation. Having met Bigger a week later, Robinson concluded that he was a 'good-hearted northerner and just the sort of man we need'.

Although some restrictions also applied in relation to appointments as auditors, Robinson and the Chief Secretary had a relatively free hand in making appointments. Correspondence between the two men gives a good indication of how the system worked. When the question of appointing a retired officer, Major G. M. Eccles of the Sligo Artillery, was raised by Balfour in August 1898, Robinson expressed reservations: Eccles had no special qualifications and while he was intelligent and energetic, and had acted as a temporary inspector and as vice-guardian, he was not the kind of man who would make a strong auditor. Robinson had definite views on the need for an effective audit system and reminded the Chief Secretary that the audit was 'the sheet anchor of your Local Government Bill on which you rely to prevent abuse'. He suggested, therefore, that it might be better to choose a lawyer or competent accountant. At the time, four former military men were serving as auditors and 'although they gave us no trouble, none of them exercised the same influence over local authorities as the shrewd lynx-eyed trained businessmen' who filled other auditor positions. 'What would you think', he asked, 'of appointing a grand jury secretary, or would you like a man from our office, and what would you think of Connolly, Sir David Harrel's secretary who seems just the sort of pertinacious self-opinionated sort of man who would keep the local bodies in splendid order'.[77] Finally, the name of a Mr Ormsby of Ballinamore, County Mayo was on the list – he was a clerk with many years of accountancy training and experience in the office of the Treasury Remembrancer at the Castle, and as additional qualifications, he was a Mayo landlord, an expert on grand jury law and knew the people well. 'There's your man', Robinson's letter concluded, but Balfour was obviously not impressed.[78] Neither Ormsby nor any of the other men suggested by Robinson was appointed in 1898. Instead, Richard Bourke (junior) was appointed after Balfour had persuaded the Civil Service Commissioners that Bourke's age (he was almost 50) should not preclude his appointment to a permanent and pensionable post. Robinson was happy enough to make the appointment as Bourke 'had a good commercial training in some China merchant's office', was a good hand at figures and had every necessary qualification. It probably helped that the new auditor's father had been an inspector with the board until 1886, and that his brother Edmund was then one of the board's longest serving inspectors and would later become a member of the board.[79]

Robinson explained to the Royal Commission in 1913 exactly how the selection procedure then operated. Auditor vacancies were not advertised, he said, because interested persons generally knew when a vacancy was likely to arise but, he went on: 'We would never dream of appointing a man we had not seen', and insisted that a very careful inquiry was made as to a man's merits. The critical stage in the process effectively involved canvassing: 'A man who wants the post would try and get an introduction to the president [the chief secretary] and then he would interview all the members of the board down to the secretary, and he would see everybody who he thinks is likely to recognize his merits.' A person selected following these interviews was appointed directly to the assistant auditor grade after examinations had been dispensed with because 'they did not work very successfully … the candidate crammed for a fortnight or so and passed' and the whole process only caused delay.[80] In an age when exemptions from the rule requiring competitive examinations were relatively few, the members of the Royal Commission were not impressed by Robinson's evidence. Their 1914 report recommended that the system should be replaced by new arrangements of the kind which they had recommended for professional appointments generally, but these recommendations, published only a few months before the outbreak of war, were never acted on.[81]

By the end of 1918, when the audit service comprised a total of twenty-one men, the board believed that the starting salary for the entry grade was not attracting suitable candidates, and the political situation was adding to the difficulties. Robinson personally pressed the case for higher salaries, arguing that few officials had more responsible or important work, that a good auditor would let nothing pass and 'braces up the local authorities to a sound and careful administration'.[82] At the salary on offer, he believed that candidates 'found it impossible to maintain the position of officials of their status', while Devlin, the board's assistant secretary, put much the same point more colourfully in his submission to the Treasury. 'It is said,' he told them, that he 'who drives fat oxen should himself be fat – and although the auditor cannot hope to attain the sleek financial rotundity of a town clerk or city treasurer, it is felt that his emaciation in the matter of salary calls for treatment'. Eventually, in June 1919, the Treasury agreed to amalgamate the second and third classes of auditors in a new grade, with a salary scale rising to £600 a year.[83]

Employment of Women

Up to one-third of the sixty women who were employed in Irish government offices in 1914 worked in the LGB as typists and clerks. This number increased during the war as women replaced enlisted men.[84] In 1919, when the board was seeking sanction to employ still more women, they were advised that 'an ordinary good woman clerk' could be obtained at 30s or 31/6d a week, but the board secretary argued that lady typists with decent shorthand qualifications were needed and pointed to the fact that 'Sir Henry keeps two and sometimes three going, outside the ordinary office work.'[85] It seems that Robinson had no difficulties of principle relating to the employment of women at the Custom House. He was happy that the board's lady typists mixed with the male clerks in the old age pensions office, although at the time, women in most departments were accommodated separately. He noted that the women were, of course, treated with greater respect than the boy clerks had been and they got on very well with one another. When it was put to him that Under-Secretary Dougherty had declared that public opinion would not tolerate lady clerks working in the same room with boy clerks, his humorous response to the Royal Commission was that 'I hope public opinion will not penetrate into our old age pensions department.' Despite this statement, he still had mixed views about the practicality of employing women. On the one hand, they did their work just as well as men, and it was useful to have a staff of ladies in connection with OAP work because very often 'if there is an old woman, and there is doubt about her age, we send one of the pension staff to see her'. On the other hand, there could be difficulties because 'when you train your lady, and when she has become very useful and efficient, she will marry and retire ... you never can be certain of keeping her, and besides ladies working in the office are knocked up much more easily than men – there are casual absences, and more complaints of headache and so forth. Also, when faced with very great pressure of work, they are inclined to lose their heads and not get on so quickly ... they get disheartened'.[86]

Robinson was happy to employ women in professional as well as in clerical positions and the LGB was, in fact, among the first of the government departments to do so. In 1902, in anticipation of legislation which widened the powers of boards of guardians in relation to the boarding-out of children, the board obtained sanction from the Treasury to the employment on a temporary basis of a lady inspector who would carry out 'a wise and effective inspection' of these children in their new homes. Mrs Marie Louise Dickie was appointed to the new post at a salary of £200 a year (less than one-third of the rate paid to the board's general and medical inspectors at the time),[87] but controversy soon followed when guardians around the country strongly protested against the appointment to a post which involved dealing with children who were predominantly from catholic families of a person whom they understood to be an English protestant lady – Mrs Dickie was actually a native of Dublin and a member of the Church of Ireland.[88] In due course, the controversy was resolved by the appointment of a second inspector, Miss Aneenee FitzGerald-Kenney, of Ballyglass, County Mayo, who, according to Robinson, turned out to be a very smart lady. He told Nathan in 1916 that what she lacked in efficiency 'she makes up in gush'; she knew her job thoroughly 'though a little too drastic in her methods, which have formed the subject of an Abbey play *The Shulers Child*, which was clever and dramatic', and which Nathan should make a point of seeing next time it was performed.[89] When Mrs Dickie resigned in 1912 to take up an appointment as one of the Irish commissioners under the National Insurance Act 1911, it seems highly unlikely that Robinson was responsible for the choice of her successor – Dr Florence Dillon LRCPI LRSCI, a sister of James C. R. Lardner, nationalist MP for Monaghan North and wife of William Blake Dillon, a grand-nephew of the Young Irelander and a cousin of John Dillon MP. Although the Treasury agreed later in 1912 that the two boarded-out children inspector posts should become established ones, Mrs Dillon, as a married women, was precluded by the regulations from filling the post, but was allowed to continue instead as a temporary medical inspector, even though Robinson doubted whether a lady inspector could be assigned to hold inquiries because 'you have a noisy turbulent people sometimes, with sharp solicitors, and it is not the sort of task that you would like to set a lady to'.[90]

Was Robinson's LGB really the Fountainhead of Corruption in Ireland?

Judged by the standards of the early twentieth century, the LGB was an efficient and effective organisation, and proved itself to be capable of taking on new responsibilities and carrying them out satisfactorily. To the extent that some appointments were made on the basis of patronage, improper use of influence or involved discrimination on religious grounds, there was undoubtedly a case for Griffith's corruption allegations – but was Robinson alone the culprit? His political masters, the successive chief secretaries, and at least for some years, Irish Party members, enthusiastically worked the system which allowed individuals to be appointed to well-paid permanent positions as inspectors and auditors on the basis of nomination alone, with less than fair shares of these posts being awarded to catholics and nationalists. While Robinson was happy to participate in and to defend this system, it would be wrong to blame him personally for its continuation. His strategy of attracting English and Scottish graduates to man elite first division posts and of promoting selected second division men to these posts brought the number of non-Irishmen serving in these positions to 40 per cent of the total, and the number of non-catholics to almost 70 per cent. It is difficult to avoid concluding that this involved discrimination on religious and other grounds for which he must carry a large share of the blame. In the junior clerical grades, the introduction of competitive examinations for permanent positions substantially increased nationalist and catholic representation – whether Robinson and other senior managers liked it or not. However, the disproportionate success of non-catholics in gaining temporary clerical positions and in achieving promotion within the second division grades can only be explained by Robinson's willingness effectively to participate in the protestant-dominated networks which continued, during his term of office, to influence advancement in business and in some of the professions, as well as in the civil service. As one small point in his favour, however, it should be recorded that representatives of the board's assistant clerks told the Royal Commission on the civil service in 1913 that they had been treated 'considerately' by the LGB, and that their case for better salaries and better promotion prospects had Robinson's sympathy and support.[91]

NOTES

1   Robinson to Balfour, 3 Nov. 1897, TNA, PRO 30/60/21.
2   LGB minute books for 1916 and 1921 held by The Department of the Environment and Local Government.
3   Robinson's evidence, 18 Feb. 1913 in *Second Appendix to Fourth Report of the Royal Commission on the Civil Service*, HC 1914 [Cd. 7340], para. 199, 206 (hereafter, Robinson *Evidence*).
4   Catholic Defence Society, *Light on the Local Government Board* (Dublin, 1907).
5   Arthur Griffith, *Nationality*, 16 Mar. 1918.
6   G. F. H. Berkeley, 'The Present System of Government in Ireland' in J. H. Morgan (ed.) *Home Rule Problems* (London, 1911), p.47; *Sixty-fifth report of H.M. Civil Service Commissioners*, 1921, Cmd. 1477.
7   *Estimates for Civil Services, 1887–88 and 1897–98.*
8   *AR*, 1898–99, 19.
9   *Royal Commission on the Poor Laws and Relief of Distress, Report on Ireland*, HC 1909 [Cd. 4630], para. 123.
10 Robinson to Balfour, 19 Aug. 1898, TNA, PRO 30/60/15.
11 Robinson to Bryce, 11 Aug. 1906, NLI, James Bryce Papers, MS 11,013(4).
12 *Fourth Report of the Royal Commission on the Civil Service*, HC 1914 [7338], para. 70 (hereafter, *Fourth Report*).
13 *Return showing as regards public civil departments in Scotland and Ireland … the number of established and unestablished officials employed on the 31st day of March 1911 etc*, HC 1912–13 (104).
14 Andrew Gailey, *Ireland and the Death of Kindness* (Cork, 1987), pp.79–88.
15 Sir Henry Robinson, *Memories: Wise and Otherwise* (London, 1923), pp.94–95.
16 Maurice Headlam, *Irish Reminiscences* (London, 1947), pp.31, 35–6, 58.
17 Public Offices Site (Dublin) Bill, 1902 (Bill 113), 6 Mar. 1902.
18 *Hansard* IV, 108, 28 May 1902, 797–826.
19 Frederick O' Dwyer, 'The Architecture of the Board of Works 1831–1923', in *Public Works: The Architecture of the Office of Public Works, 1831–1987* (Dublin, 1987).
20 Treasury Ireland letter of 18 Nov. 1920, TNA, T.158/1.
21 *Estimates for Civil Services, 1899–1900.*
22 *The Leader*, xiv, No. 19, 29 June 1907, 291–92.
23 *Estimates for Civil Services, 1915–16.*
24 Robinson *Evidence*, para. 199.
25 Robinson to Balfour, 14 Dec. 1899, NAS, Balfour Papers, GD 433/2/114/11,
26 Robinson to Balfour 26 Dec. 1899, NAS, Balfour Papers, GD 433/2/114/12.
27 *Estimates for Civil Services, 1900–01.*
28 Robinson *Evidence*, para. 208; Memorandum as to the Organisation and Staff of the Chief Secretary's Office and Other Departments Concerned with the Irish Government (Dublin, 1913), NLI 350 c 9.
29 Leon Ó Broin, *No Man's Man* (Dublin, 1982), p.8.
30 *Fourth Report*, para. 76, 80.
31 *Fourth Report*, para. 80.
32 Robinson *Evidence*, para. 201.

33   Eunan O'Halpin, 'The Politics of Governance in the Four Countries of the United Kingdom, 1912–1922' in S. J. Connolly (ed.), *Kingdoms United? Great Britain and Ireland Since 1500* (Dublin, 1999), p.245.

34   Martin Maguire, *The Civil Service and the Revolution in Ireland, 1912–38* (Manchester, 2008), p.20.

35   *Fourth Report*, para. 80; Robinson *Evidence*, para.200.

36   Returns prepared for the Treasury in April and September 1913, TNA, T 1/11625; Robinson *Evidence*, para.201.

37   Robinson *Evidence*, para. 200–201; *Appendix I to the First Report of the Royal Commission on the Civil Service*, HC 1912–13 (Cd. 6210).

38   *Fourth Report*, para. 80.

39   Information in this and previous paragraphs about nationality and religion is derived from the census of 1901 and 1911.

40   Ennis to Dillon, 2 May 1895, TCD, John Dillon Papers, MS 6800/111; Ennis to Dillon, 17 July 1898, MS 6800/116.

41   *Freeman's Journal*, 27 Sept. 1898; *Hansard* IV, 43, 24 July 1896, 653.

42   *Hansard* IV, 83, 24 May 1900, 1201–02, 1212–13.

43   *The Leader*, xiii, No. 21, 12 Jan. 1907, p.333.

44   *The Leader*, xiii, No. 22, 19 Jan. 1907, pp.350–51.

45   *Hansard* IV, 172, 10 Apr. 1907, 228–29.

46   *Hansard* IV, 173, 3 May 1907, 1166–1170.

47   *Freeman's Journal*, 15 Feb. 1906.

48   Robinson, *Memories*, p.284.

49   James McConnel, 'Jobbing with Tory and Liberal: Irish Nationalist MPs and the Politics of Patronage 1880–1914', *Past and Present*, 188 (2005), pp.105–131.

50   *The Leader*, xvi, 4 Apr. 1908, 97.

51   James McConnel, *The Irish Parliamentary Party and the Third Home Rule Crisis* (Dublin, 2013), pp.72–73.

52   George A Birmingham, *Irishmen All* (London, 1913), 15.

53   Sir Henry Robinson, *Further Memories of Irish Life* (London, 1924), pp.145–46.

54   Lawrence W. McBride, *The Greening of Dublin Castle* (Washington, 1991), p.167.

55   Nancy Wyse-Power, BMH, WS 541, 5 Jan. 1951.

56   Fergus Campbell, *The Irish Establishment 1879–1914* (Oxford, 2009), pp.72–75.

57   *Hansard* V, 48, 13 Feb. 1913, 1170–71.

58   Robinson to Birrell, 22 Feb. 1914, Oxford, Bodleian Library, MS. Eng. c. 7034, f. 39–40.

59   Memoirs of W. E. Wylie, photocopy of typescript, NLI, León Ó Broin Papers, Acc. No. 6710, Box 1.

60   *Hansard* IV, 99, 8 Aug. 1901, 97–98; 91, 26 Mar. 1901, 1404.

61   *Royal Commission on the Poor Laws and Relief of Distress, Minutes of Evidence, Appendix Vol. X*, Edmund Bourke, 25 Apr. 1908.

62   Robinson to Waterfield, 23 Dec. 1920, TNA, T. 158/2.

63   George A. Birmingham, *The Lighter Side of Irish Life* (London, 1911), pp.96–97.

64   *Hansard* IV, 57, 3 May 1898, 173–74.

65   *Hansard* IV, 124, 22 June 1903, 81.

66 Robinson to Balfour, 9 Aug. 1898, NAS, Balfour Papers, GD 433/2/114/9; Balfour to Col. Saunderson, 16 May 1899, PRONI, Saunderson Papers; Robinson to Balfour, 19 Aug. and 25 Sept. 1898; 3 May 1899; 31 Mar. 1900, TNA, PRO 30/60/15.

67 *Return up to the 31ˢᵗ day of Dec. 1904 showing the number of Inspectors etc … appointed by the Local Government Board for Ireland,* HC 1905 (100); *A return of all the inspectors now in the service of the Local Government Board etc,* HC 1906 (297).

68 *Irish Times,* 28 Dec. 1907.

69 *Nationality,* 26 June 1915.

70 *Hansard* V, 19, 28 July 1910, 2328–30.

71 Robinson *Evidence,* para. 203.

72 *Hansard* V, 31, 14 Nov. 1911, 282–83.

73 Robinson, *Evidence,* para. 408–410.

74 Robinson, *Further Memories,* p.190.

75 *Fourth Report,* para. 76.

76 Redmond to Balfour, 26 Apr. 1898 and Robinson to Dowdall (private secretary), 29 Apr. 1898, TNA, PRO 30/60/15.

77 Robinson to Balfour, 6 Aug. 1898, NAS, Balfour Papers, GD 433/2/114/5.

78 Robinson to Balfour, 10 Aug. 1898, NAS, Balfour Papers, GD 433/2/114/7.

79 Robinson to Balfour, 9 Aug. 1898, NAS, Balfour Papers, GD 433/2/114/9.

80 Robinson *Evidence,* para. 204–05.

81 *Fourth Report,* para. 80.

82 Robinson to Headlam. 29 Jan. 1919, TNA, T1/12562.

83 Treasury files 14989, 30815 and 49525, TNA, T1/12562.

84 R. B. McDowell, *The Irish Administration 1801–1914* (London, 1964) p. 35; *Return … of all salaried officials in the various Government Departments in Ireland,* HC 1911 (326), 28 Nov. 1911; HC 1913 (42), 31 Mar. 1913.

85 Headlam to LGB, 12 Mar. 1919 and Barlas to Headlam, 13 Mar. 1919, TNA, T 1/12290.

86 Robinson *Evidence,* para. 189, 204 and 206.

87 *AR* 1902–03, p.v.

88 See Marie Louise Dickie by Brendan O Donoghue, a new entry added to the DIB online, December 2014.

89 Aneenee was a sister of James Fitzgerald-Kenney SC, later Cumann na nGaedhael TD for Mayo and Minister for Justice 1927–32; Robinson to Nathan, 24 Mar. 1916, Oxford, Bodleian Library, MS Nathan 460, f. 231–32.

90 Robinson *evidence,* para. 204.

91 *Second Appendix to Fourth Report of the Royal Commission on the Civil Service,* HC 1914 [Cd. 7340], Duffy evidence, pp.209, 211.

CHAPTER VII

'We Never Were Subordinate, Except To Parliament'

On his appointment as Vice-President, Robinson became one of the most senior civil servants employed in the complex array of departments, boards and offices which made up the Irish government. Ultimate control of the Dublin offices of the revenue departments, the Post Office, the OPW and some others rested with their parent departments and ministers in London. Other departments were controlled from Dublin Castle by the Chief Secretary and the Under-Secretary, while organisations like the LGB were managed by statutory boards, of which the Chief Secretary was President. R. B. McDowell's survey of the situation as it was in 1914 listed forty departments and offices, but figures of up to fifty were also cited at the time for the number of separate boards, departments and offices which were concerned in one way or another with the administration of Ireland.[1] Indeed, a popular saying was that Ireland had as many boards as would make her coffin. A survey in the *Nationalist* in 1906 listed sixty-seven departments, which were said to constitute the civil administration of Ireland,[2] while Chief Secretary Birrell, in a Commons debate in May 1907, mentioned that a list of forty-five organisations had been supplied to him.[3] Less than a year later, however, when he had more experience of the situation, Birrell dismissed the argument that the number of organisations was either excessive or was creating problems: he regretted that he had been led astray in the earlier debate by enumerating 'a great number of perfectly trumpery boards which exist in Dublin – about which far too much fuss has been made for they will be found existing in other places besides Dublin'.[4] Nevertheless, the administration as a whole has rightly been portrayed as 'a mess, with limitless opportunities for misunderstanding and collision' between different organisations,[5] and, with only a relatively small number of these organisations under its immediate direction, the Chief Secretary's Office has been well described as a bureaucratic and constitutional enigma.[6] Within this intricate web of bureaucracy, it was a matter of supreme importance for Robinson to maintain the independence of the LGB – and of course his own status – even in the face of what his son described as 'attempts by our English masters to control it'.[7]

Administrative Reorganisation Schemes

The stand-alone position of the LGB had been challenged a number of times in the years before Robinson's appointment as Vice-President. Joseph Chamberlain, then a member of Gladstone's second ministry, failed in 1885 to get agreement on a scheme for an elected central board, which would have subsumed the LGB.[8] Six years later, Arthur Balfour's powerful Under-Secretary, Colonel Sir Joseph West Ridgeway, proposed 'the abolition of that chaotic anachronism – administration by semi-independent boards, whereby three men do the work of one'. Following this proposal, Balfour took limited action towards strengthening the role of Dublin Castle at the expense of the LGB.[9] He directed that files and papers should be submitted to Ridgeway, leaving it to him to decide when it was necessary to refer them to the Chief Secretary. The result, according to Barry O'Brien's *Dublin Castle and the Irish People* (1909), was that the Under-Secretary was allowed for a time to dominate the LGB but, according to Robinson, the new procedure was not a palatable one as in his view it prevented the board from dealing with their President, except through a man whom they regarded as an *ex-officio* junior member of the board with no relevant experience.[10] The procedure became so troublesome 'that in the end we hardly sent him any papers at all', but sought a personal interview whenever a decision by him was essential.[11] John Morley, who succeeded Balfour in 1892, 'got rid of Ridgeway's interference with outside departments' and next got rid of Ridgeway himself, as Robinson was happy to record,[12] but Sir David Harrel, who then became Under-Secretary, was again critical of the fact that 'forty-six government departments are brought into requisition in carrying out the administration of public affairs'.[13] Harrel argued that administration by boards like the LGB could be 'cumbrous in ... action and prejudicial to departmental discipline and efficiency', but his proposals were not acted on by Morley or by Gerald Balfour, who succeeded him.

When George Wyndham became Chief Secretary, he reminded Arthur Balfour, then prime minister, that while Ridgeway had drawn the strings tighter together and made the LGB, at least, work through him, it was because Robinson made difficulties that Harrel abandoned that practice.[14] Initially, Wyndham's practice was to consult Harrel on policy matters arising in relation to the LGB and other boards, and he tried to draw the boards closer 'by the modest device of getting their chiefs to lunch or dine with me', with Harrel acting as his premier in an informal cabinet.[15] Sir Antony MacDonnell, who replaced Harrel, attempted to take matters further by submitting to the Treasury a scheme for placing the LGB and other organisations under the control of the Chief Secretary's Office, with a new secretariat branch reporting to himself as Under-Secretary.[16] However, the Chancellor, Austen Chamberlain, would not agree 'to the subordination of all the semi-independent boards, not to the Chief Secretary, but to a staff of clerks working in his office in Dublin Castle'. Wyndham and MacDonnell reluctantly backed down at that stage, a retreat which, no doubt, was viewed with some satisfaction by Robinson, who disliked MacDonnell's attempt to establish himself as the Chief Secretary's chief of staff.[17]

MacDonnell's retreat was only a tactical one, and not long afterwards his declared aim of securing 'the co-ordination, direction and control of boards and other administrative agencies',[18] led him to contribute to the devolution scheme, which was published in the name of Lord Dunraven's Irish Reform Association in September 1904.[19] The scheme proposed the establishment of an Irish Financial Council, with twelve indirectly elected and twelve nominated members. The council would prepare and submit to Parliament all estimates of expenditure for Irish departments (including the LGB) and would be competent to supervise and control every item of departmental expenditure. In addition, the scheme envisaged that the responsibility to the Irish government of 'the numerous boards and departments, now operating with much irresponsibility, should be made clear and complete', and that Parliament should be allowed to refer certain legislation and other Irish business, including provisional orders made by the LGB, to what was described as a new 'Statutory Body' composed of Irish representative peers and MPs. Robinson and his colleagues knew nothing about the scheme before its publication, and it came to them like a bolt from the blue. As Robinson saw it, it was not practical politics, and he believed that there could not have been a more inopportune time for reopening the question of Home Rule, because the northern MPs had become a powerful influence with the government.[20] However, when it emerged that MacDonnell had been involved in the preparation of the scheme, unionists were infuriated, while nationalists generally considered it to be no substitute for Home Rule. The whole episode led to Wyndham's resignation in March 1905 – sacrificed, as Catherine Shannon described it, to Ulster Unionist paranoia.[21] Nearly twenty years later, with the benefit of hindsight, Robinson saw possible merit in Dunraven's scheme: 'One may speculate now', he wrote in 1923, whether the scheme 'if it had won through, might not have saved Ireland from the tribulations of six years of anarchy'.[22]

MacDonnell's ideas on coordination and devolution were anathema to Walter Long, who replaced Wyndham. The liberal, James Bryce, however, who came next to the Chief Secretary position in December 1905, spoke with approval at an election meeting in Aberdeen the following January of 'the remarkable new departure' represented by the devolution scheme, and regretted that its progress had been arrested by 'the demand of the landlords and the Orange section'.[23] It was no surprise, therefore, that one of his main priorities during his term of office of little more than a year was to advance and refine proposals for what MacDonnell began to describe as a 'scheme of reform of Irish government'.[24] By early February, he was able to send Bryce the *Outline of Irish Constitutional Reform,* which provided for an executive council of thirty members (twenty-one of them elected by delegates from county and county borough councils) to advise and assist the government of Ireland and to 'coordinate and bring under a reasonable measure of popular control all the departments of government now working in Ireland'.[25] There were to be six committees of the council, including a local government committee chaired by the Vice-President of the LGB.[26] During the following months, MacDonnell worked up 'the scheme', as he described it in his frequent letters to Bryce, consulting with Dunraven and the Treasury (but not with the LGB) and revising it to take account of points raised by Bryce and some of his cabinet colleagues. In October, Bryce presented the proposals to Redmond and Dillon, who rejected them out of hand.[27] A memorandum signed by both men and by T. P. O'Connor, which was submitted to the cabinet in December, indicated that they could not support any scheme which did not provide that the Irish MPs should form the council.[28] A few days later, a letter from Dillon to John Morley, then Secretary of State for India, blamed MacDonnell rather than Bryce for the lack of progress: he was 'a gentleman ... who moves on an Indian atmosphere quite aloof from the facts of the situation ... and who has indoctrinated Bryce'.[29]

Notwithstanding the impact his scheme would have had on the LGB, MacDonnell had not informed Robinson about it. Even when collecting essential financial data from departments, he was careful not to disclose what he was doing, and told Bryce that he had provided no explanation to departmental heads as to the reasons for his requests.[30] In November, when reports were already appearing in the press about the scheme, Robinson told Walter Long that he knew 'nothing about it beyond what is known to everyone' and that he felt 'very dismal' about it:

> I have more experience of government by locally elected bodies in Ireland than anyone else, and I know what it means if it is not hedged round with safeguards – tyranny and jobbery – nothing else. We tied them down very securely in our Local Government Act, and it is lucky we did. But this idea of electing a Central Council to control the public departments is sheer madness, it will cripple the government of the country and cause the direst embarrassment and trouble to the government both in and out of the House of Commons. And as for the idea of relying on a majority of government nominees on the Council! What use will that be when the government will have to nominate those that the Irish Party approve of – I wonder what sort of nominees Lord Dudley would give us? Really, I think Home Rule would be preferable. However, my idea is that when the government understand the criticisms, they will ride for a fall, and aim for getting it thrown out by the Lords so as to have another *casus belli* to go to the country against them.[31]

A letter from Robinson to Bryce was very different: it contained no comments of any kind on the principles of the scheme, and dealt only with the need to provide statutory protection for officials like himself against arbitrary retirement or unfair treatment by a new regime:

> I am generally regarded in this country as responsible for any unpopular acts of yours and your predecessors ... and I shall most certainly be given very short shrift by any elected council ... I have always managed to keep out of politics ... but the Irish Party seem to consider that those who are not entirely with them are against them, and I would defy any man to hold my position and do his best for all his chiefs without incurring the enmity of political parties in Ireland. I do not think that, individually, any of the Irish politicians I am known to would do me an injury if they could avoid it, but collectively, a national elected council would feel that to allow a non-catholic official, who had been instrumental in carrying out the hated English government policy under seventeen chief secretaries, to remain at the head of the most important public department in

Ireland, would be utterly inconsistent with the principles of the new regime, especially while there were so many of their own supporters ready to fill the office.[32]

Robinson went on to tell Bryce that, without statutory backing, political assurances that the heads of departments would not be interfered with by the proposed council would be of no value as he was sure that his position would be made untenable, or that his resignation would be insisted on, by the council. Compulsory retirement on a pension of two-thirds of his pay would not be an acceptable solution in his case: it would be a cruel wrong to turn him out for purely political reasons, or to force him to suffer any pecuniary loss whatever – he was contracted to serve until age sixty-five, was then only forty-nine, had heavy insurance to pay, and three boys to educate. However, whatever assurance he subsequently received from Bryce took a load off his mind.[33]

The Irish Council Bill 1907

The King's speech in February 1907 committed the Liberal government to the introduction of 'measures for further associating the people of Ireland with the management of their domestic affairs, and for otherwise improving the system of government in its administrative and financial aspects'.[34] With Redmond making it clear that nothing short of the concession to Ireland of a parliament with executive responsibility would settle the question,[35] and the Conservatives repeating their opposition to anything resembling Home Rule, it was not surprising that Birrell, who had taken up the Chief Secretary position at the end of January, was 'ill-disposed to take up the business' at the point where Bryce had left it. MacDonnell soon found that there was a serious difference of opinion between Birrell and himself and, subsequently, there were clashes between the two men about matters of detail and of principle.[36] As Birrell described it 'we looked at the same problem from opposite ends: I may have attached too much importance to the House of Commons. He ignored it completely'.[37] When, eventually, a final set of proposals was agreed, Birrell introduced the Irish Council Bill on 7 May, providing for a council of eighty-two elected and twenty-four nominated members, which would have control over the administration, funding and staffing of eight departments, including the LGB.[38] There were to be four committees, one of them a local government committee, each with a salaried chairman, and there was provision for the constitution at a later stage of new government departments to replace existing organisations such as the LGB.

If enacted, the bill would have dramatically and immediately reduced Robinson's status and freedom of action. In Arthur Balfour's words, senior officials – no longer permanent – would be responsible to a committee, then to a semi-elected assembly, which would be responsible to a lord lieutenant, who in turn would be responsible to the cabinet and to the House of Commons.[39] The complete replacement of the LGB by one of the new departments would almost certainly have been a priority for the new council, bearing in mind the criticisms of the board which had been expressed by nationalist politicians in the previous few years. It could also safely be assumed that members of the board would have opted to retire, or been forced by the council to retire, under the enhanced pension arrangements for which the bill provided because, as Walter Long put it in the Commons, they and other civil servants were to be handed over to 'those who have never concealed their hostility towards them'.[40] Robinson and his colleagues did not have to worry about this prospect for very long as a convention of the UIL, obsessed as its members were with the principle of full legislative independence, rejected the scheme out of hand on 21 May, even though there was support among some nationalists, including P. H. Pearse and Eoin MacNeill, for the measure, which would have given Irishmen a real degree of control over their own affairs. Redmond – although for years he had made a point of referring in public speeches to the 'monstrous, inefficient, irresponsible and costly' system of government in Ireland – opted to go along with the majority of his party and failed to grasp the opportunity to begin to overhaul the system. This decision left Bryce, in his new position as ambassador in Washington, despondent: 'So it is all over', he told his friend, Alice Stopford Green, the historian and nationalist, 'and all Sir Antony's labours and mine go for nothing'. The cabinet quickly agreed that the bill should be dropped, and despite sporadic efforts by MacDonnell in the following years to revive interest in it, the OPW Chairman, Sir Philip Hanson, was able to tell Wyndham in 1910 that 'really no one cares what Antony's scheme of devolution is'.[41]

Problems with the Lord Lieutenant

The lord lieutenant had no power to supervise or interfere with the business of the LGB and any attempt to do so was effectively and promptly rebuffed by Robinson. The 3rd Earl of Dudley, who became lord lieutenant in 1902, created problems when he began to seek comments and explanations from the LGB on newspaper reports relating to its activities. This practice ceased when Robinson, tongue in cheek, pointed to the need to obtain instructions from Wyndham as President of the board in so important a matter as a challenge to the board's action, and sent a file with masses of papers to Wyndham, who had no time or inclination to become involved.[42] In 1905, Robinson strongly objected to Dudley's demand that the board's reports to parliamentary committees on private bills should be submitted for his approval. The board, he insisted, could only take instructions from the Chief Secretary, and he would be placed in a most embarrassing position if he were required to depart from the latter's instructions on any point.[43] Walter Long, who was then Chief Secretary, had no difficulty in recording his full support for Robinson and ruling that the procedure which had been proposed by the lord lieutenant was calculated to embarrass the LGB, impede the local authorities, and inconvenience the chairmen of committees.[44] Overall, Robinson's attitude to Dudley was somewhat inconsistent. His memoirs record his admiration of the lord lieutenant's ability as a sportsman. He also praised his 'real, good, entertaining company', his exceptional hospitality and his successful efforts to persuade King Edward to visit Ireland in 1903 when Robinson, along with Horace Plunkett, was commissioned to plan the royal party's visit to the West and to accompany them on their tour.[45] However, the memoirs also record that Dudley had developed strong nationalist leanings, which explains why Robinson was pleased to be able to report to Long in December 1905 that the lord lieutenant's farewell reception was remarkable due to the absence of 'people of position and loyalists and supporters of the government'. He was personally unable to screw himself up to going because Dudley had made utter fools of the loyal people in Ireland, had done irreparable harm through his speeches, and had chosen for his confidants people like Gill, secretary of DATI, and Walter Callan, his private secretary, who was the son of a one-time prominent nationalist MP.[46]

More serious problems for Robinson were created when the Earl of Aberdeen began a second term as lord lieutenant in December 1905. At an early stage, Aberdeen and his Countess, Ishbel, came to the conclusion that the promotion of social work and the improvement of public health were objects of supreme importance and Lady Aberdeen's philanthropic and other activities in pursuit of these objectives soon brought her and her husband into direct conflict with Robinson. When he refused to authorise a grant for a non-statutory unemployed committee formed by the Aberdeens, Ishbel sought and obtained a letter from Queen Alexandra, which emphatically stated her 'earnest and particular desire' that £500 should be made available to the committee, and regretted extremely that there should have been so much delay in relieving the pressing necessities of the unemployed. Robinson stood his ground, however, notwithstanding this royal intervention, and refused to authorise the payment, leaving it to Chief Secretary Bryce to resolve the matter.[47]

Differences and disagreements between Robinson and Lady Aberdeen's Women's National Health Association (WNHA) became especially acute, and a matter of public knowledge in the implementation of the government's programme for the treatment and eradication of TB. Without reference to the LGB, Lady Aberdeen sought and obtained a grant of £25,000 for the erection of a sanatorium at Peamount, County Dublin, to which patients from different areas could be referred. She dismissed Robinson's protests about the grant: these were based, she alleged, on the premise that it was wrong for the state to be 'handing over a considerable money grant to an association composed of irresponsible women', and she claimed that 'every possible discouragement and hindrance' was afterwards placed in her way, causing 'perpetual friction'.[48] However, she conveniently ignored the fact that before the Peamount scheme was initiated, an official committee had recommended that the establishment of publicly-funded sanatoria should be organised in accordance with schemes made by county and county borough councils, and that the LGB had planned to allocate the available funds on a systematic basis in accordance with these recommendations.[49] Robinson's attitude to the Peamount scheme was supported by an unusual coalition of interests. There were strong local protests, based on fears that disease would be spread in the area, culminating in an attempt by some fifty local men in July 1912 to demolish some of the completed pavilions.[50] The *Irish Times* objected to 'the exercise of large government functions [and] the spending of large public funds' by Lady Aberdeen's association.[51] The unionist MP for Armagh North, William Moore, suggested that WNHA was a 'so-called philanthropic association ... run chiefly on political lines by the wife of the lord lieutenant'.[52] Arthur Griffith's newspaper, *Sinn Féin*, which had always been critical of the Aberdeens, declared that Dublin never had need of Peamount, and that Lady Aberdeen had invented the TB scare as part of a plot to kill Irish exports.[53]

Lady Aberdeen's involvement in issues relating to town planning and housing, and her practice of leading deputations from a variety of organisations on controversial issues to the Chief Secretary, or to Robinson and his colleagues at the Custom House, cannot have helped her relationship with the LGB. The real breaking point, however, arose in relation to appointments to the staff of the board. Having already been accused in 1912 by the *Irish Times* [54] (and by others) of securing appointments and promotions in the public service for people who were associated with the causes she had espoused, Lady Aberdeen attempted, with the aid of her husband, to have two LGB medical inspector vacancies filled by doctors favoured by her, instead of by men who had already been selected by Robinson in consultation with Birrell. Robinson refused to appoint her favourites and, from this time on, he wrote later, 'the Aberdeens' dislike and mistrust of me became … a perfect obsession with them'. He believed that Aberdeen had gone so far as to suggest to Birrell that Robinson might be transferred to a colonial governorship.[55] Robinson, however, continued in office at the Custom House long after Aberdeen had been replaced in 1915.

Relations with the Chief Secretary

Because of his parliamentary and cabinet duties in London, the Chief Secretary could not spend long periods in Dublin, especially when Parliament was sitting and because of his responsibilities for security and for Irish affairs generally, he could not devote as much time and attention to his role as President of the LGB as could his colleague who headed the English board. In fact, chief secretaries rarely attended meetings of the LGB and, taken together with the wide powers held by Robinson as Vice-President, this might suggest (as some of its critics were quick to do) that the LGB was virtually an independent republic, or even a kind of dictatorship – but this was not the case. There was always a clear recognition that the Chief Secretary, as President of the board, and its spokesman in Parliament, was entitled to be kept informed of major developments, to be consulted on major issues (including senior appointments) and to give directions on policy issues. Matters of importance were referred in writing to the Chief Secretary by Robinson for decision, and the two men met at the Castle when he was in Dublin. Soon after his appointment, Robinson told Balfour that at any time, on receipt of a wire from him, he could come over to London and 'tell you how everything stands and what we are doing'.[56] Subsequently, Robinson went to London once a month to discuss matters with the Chief Secretary at the Irish Office, with the overall Dublin–London journey via Holyhead, by sea and rail, taking no more than nine hours in 1914.[57]

The relationship between Robinson and the men who held office as Chief Secretary varied. A Chief Secretary who was not a member of the cabinet could spend more time in Ireland, and give more attention to the board's business than would otherwise be the case. Given that Robinson's unionist sympathies were well known, a liberal Chief Secretary might not be expected to have as good a relationship with him as would a member of the Conservative/Unionist Party. Other factors that affected the relationship were the personality of the Chief Secretary himself, his previous experience (if any) of dealing with Irish issues, or local government and public health matters, the amount of time he was willing to devote to his ministerial duties generally, and the extent to which he had to involve himself in major political and security or other issues during his term of office. In the last analysis, however, as James Bryce told Alice Stopford Green in 1907, 'no English minister going straight to Ireland can possibly know things for himself, so much depends on his advisers'.[58] Thus, Robinson, with his long experience of Irish administration and undoubted mastery of his brief, gained the confidence of almost all of the chief secretaries he served, and came to be relied on by many of them for advice, even on matters well outside his own area of responsibility. He was able to boast in 1918 that he had 'served twenty chief secretaries and earned the good will of them all'.[59]

Robinson had a particularly close relationship with Gerald Balfour, who was responsible for his promotion to the Vice-Presidency. Because he was not a member of the cabinet during his term as Chief Secretary, Balfour was able to be more actively involved in the business of the board than most of his predecessors – in fact, he insisted in Parliament in 1898 that his presidency had not merely been a nominal one, and he repudiated any suggestion that he had no control over the board's actions.[60] He went further in 1899, telling the House of Commons that he had personally examined into, and ultimately approved, every important decision of principle made by the board: 'The final decision in every case has been sanctioned by me and I take the full responsibility.'[61] This unprecedented level of involvement did not upset Robinson: in fact, the large number of handwritten letters which he addressed to Balfour between 1895 and 1900, most of them marked 'private' or 'personal', suggests that there was a very friendly personal and working relationship between the two men, a relationship based on mutual trust and confidence.[62] Through these informal letters, Balfour, when he was not in Dublin, was kept closely in touch with the business of the board, and consulted on a wide range of issues. His opinions and advice on particular problems were regularly sought, and he was informed of progress at local level in relation to matters such as rate collection, the declaration of main roads, and appointments to senior positions in local councils. Letters from Robinson sometimes mentioned health issues affecting members or staff of the board, and the deaths of officials, and often included accounts of incidents at local level which he found amusing. There were also occasional comments of a party-political nature – for example, in February 1899, when he told Balfour that he had heard of great rejoicing in Mayo 'at the way you wiped the floor [in the House of Commons] with Dillon and Davitt [then MPs for

Mayo East and South, respectively] ... how these men can have the face – after inciting the people in the West to do everything that leads to disquiet and trouble – to get up in the House and pose as people with the interests of the country at heart is hard to conceive'.[63] Robinson's letters also strayed on occasion into wider political issues: on 26 December 1899, for example, in thanking Balfour for his sympathy on the death of his brother at the battle of Magersfontein in South Africa on 11 December, he went on to congratulate the Chief Secretary on a major speech that he had delivered in Glasgow after the disastrous battle of Colenso, and in which he criticised disloyal speeches in Ireland 'which had driven the last nail into the coffin of Home Rule'. The speech, according to Robinson, was 'very fully reported over here, and heartened the people up wonderfully, and after it we heard no more of the hysterics about losing South Africa, which were becoming very prevalent just then'.[64]

Robinson was concerned in July 1899 that while Balfour had acquired a knowledge of local government in Ireland better than anybody else, the board might not obtain the same support and guidance from any successor. As Vice-President, he would then find himself in a situation in which he would have to direct and work the whole local government of the country himself, as had been the case during the terms of office of most of the previous chief secretaries.[65] As it happened, Robinson's fears were well-founded: little over a year later he was having to deal with a Chief Secretary who spoke so 'long and earnestly, but at the same time so incomprehensively' about very ordinary local government matters that he used to think that he had got an attack of migraine to which he had been subject in the past.[66] Overall, the term of office of little more than four years of Balfour's successor, George Wyndham, was not a happy period for Robinson: in fact, according to Beatrice Webb, who knew him well, Robinson detested Wyndham.[67] In his own memoirs, Robinson described his new chief as 'a tempestuous sort of genius, in the sense that he was flashing about the Irish atmosphere like summer lightning, with inspirations and brilliant ideas about current problems, which fairly took one's breath away'. In their business meetings, Robinson found it difficult to understand Wyndham's wishes and instructions, or to conceive how his schemes could be carried into practical effect. The Chief Secretary in turn could be impatient with his senior officials,[68] and was unimpressed by most of those he encountered in Dublin, apart from Robinson and a few others.[69]

Official life became much more agreeable when Walter Long replaced Wyndham in March 1905. Long had served at the English LGB as parliamentary secretary from 1886 to 1892, and as president from 1900 to 1905. He had been heavily involved in the drafting and enactment of the Local Government Act 1888, which introduced county councils in England and Wales. He had been opposition front-bench spokesman when the bill that created urban, rural district and parish councils in England and Wales was put before the Commons. He is likely to have been aware of Robinson's reputation and activities as a member of the Irish LGB from 1891 onwards, and he may well have been in touch with him on official matters before taking up office in Ireland. Apart from this, Long, who had Irish ascendancy connections, had paid numerous visits to Ireland to visit family and friends, and had wide contacts among Irish unionists. From the beginning, he had a high opinion of Robinson, who in turn recorded that 'the advantage to us of having his advice ... was inestimable'.[70] The personal relationship between the two men was strengthened in the course of several tours of Ireland 'of the most delightful description', on which Long was generally driven by Robinson in his own car. Long's *Memories* (1923) describe Robinson as an expert motorist who possessed a very excellent car, which was known as *The Fast Lady* and he was a perfect companion who knew every inch of the country, every place of interest that was passed, and all the leading people; he was, in addition, 'a thorough Irishman, with an inexhaustible fund of anecdote and a very remarkable knowledge of his country, its people, their needs, peculiarities, their virtues and vices'.[71] The two men's travels were often reported in the newspapers. In April 1905, for example, the *Irish Times* reported a visit to Wicklow and Arklow harbours; a visit to Belmullet and Achill later that month; a visit to Kerry, Galway and Leitrim in June; and a twelve-day tour in September from Dublin to Waterford, Lismore, Killarney, Connemara, Mayo, Donegal, Derry and Belfast.[72] There was also a visit by the two men to Castle Saunderson, County Cavan – the home of the ailing Col. E. J. Saunderson, the unionist leader, whom Long consulted regularly on matters of policy and patronage. The fact that he chose Robinson to drive him on such an occasion says much for the relationship which had developed between the two men.[73] While visiting Belmullet in April, Long told a deputation of his good fortune to be accompanied by Robinson who 'has at heart the welfare of Ireland' and who had suggested modes by which the isolation of the local community might be remedied. In September, he went further, telling a deputation in Coleraine that Robinson was 'one of the most distinguished permanent officials of the Irish government ... whose labours ... were well known to them all and who deserved their gratitude'.[74] Long's tours with Robinson appear to have been quite informal affairs, generally without army, police or other escorts, and provided opportunities for local groups, sometimes accompanied by their priests, to meet the two men outside their hotels and to raise issues of local concern with them.

After Long had left the Chief Secretary's office in December 1905, Robinson wrote to him to wish him and his wife a speedy return to Ireland, and added the rather improbable comment that this would be 'a toast in many an Irish household on Christmas Day'.[75] In the following ten years, while he played a central role in Parliament and in the country campaigning to promote and orchestrate opposition to any moves by the liberals towards Home Rule, Long maintained and developed his relationship with Robinson. Although only fragments of his correspondence during those years seem to have survived, it is clear from what is available that Robinson was one of a number of Irish civil servants who continued to correspond privately with him on Irish affairs when, as civil servants, they would have been expected to abstain from involvement in matters of political controversy and from contact on such matters with opposition figures. In Parliament, Long expressed his admiration of Robinson when opportunity offered – for example, in a Commons debate in 1909, in which he argued for the setting up of a new tribunal to deal with issues arising in connection with compulsory acquisition under a new Land Bill, he suggested that Robinson was an official who might be selected 'with universal approbation', if it were decided to have such a tribunal. He was 'a man of exceptional experience in connection with … the general government of Ireland, against whom there never has been the smallest suggestion by anybody, either nationalist or unionist, and a man whose services to Ireland have been of the highest possible character.'[76]

James Bryce, classical scholar, historian and supporter of Home Rule, who succeeded Long, was the first liberal Chief Secretary with whom Robinson had to deal and he appeared to find himself in difficulty from an early stage. Bryce was heavily influenced by Antony MacDonnell whom he held in high regard, having never met anyone 'with a more sincere devotion to Ireland or a higher sense of public duty.'[77] On the other hand, Robinson had not been five minutes in Bryce's company before discovering that he was suspect, but, he told Long, that was something which did not really concern him: 'If he prefers not to be advised by me on local government matters, it relieves me of such responsibility'.[78] Robinson believed that MacDonnell, or possibly Irish Party members, had warned Bryce that he was tarred with the unionist brush, and was not to be trusted, having been appointed by the Balfours as commissioner in 1891, and as Vice-President in 1898.[79] He continued his normal practice of addressing his submissions on various matters direct to Bryce, but there is evidence in surviving papers that Bryce diverted some of these to MacDonnell for comment or advice. While that advice regularly differed from that offered by Robinson, it appears that whatever initial suspicion Bryce may have had quickly evaporated. Although Beatrice Webb recorded that Robinson 'found Bryce a bore',[80] Robinson's own memoirs describe him as a very likeable and interesting man, being pleasant and easy to work with, and record that he tried to do everything he could to meet his wishes and to make his responsibility for local government a light one.[81] Together, the two men succeeded in having the important Labourers (Ireland) Act 1906 enacted and implemented, providing additional funds for the construction of cottages in rural areas, and introducing simplified new procedures to speed up the processing of applications by local councils for approval of new schemes.

The fact that Bryce broadly supported 'the scheme' being worked up by MacDonnell in 1906 for the establishment of an executive council, which would have had a drastic effect on the independence and operating procedures of the LGB, seems not to have affected the relationship between Robinson and the Chief Secretary. Perhaps this was because he believed, like Redmond, that Bryce was 'absolutely under the domination' of MacDonnell, and that as many people said of him, he meant well.[82] When he learned at the end of 1906 that Bryce was to become British ambassador in Washington, his reaction was surprising: expressing his sincere regret that their official relations were to end, his letter to Bryce asserted that he had never had 'any chief who has given me more kindly or generous support, or one whose loss I more deeply deplore'. Remarkably, also, in view of the criticisms he had expressed to Long about the Irish Council Scheme to which Bryce had devoted so much time and effort, Robinson went on to tell him that his 'departure at this juncture is just about the worst thing that could possibly happen to the country, and will make reform of administration doubly difficult to carry'. His reasoning, apparently, was that 'the unionists, however much they may attack you, believed in their heart of hearts that while so strong a constitutionalist piloted the ship, the soundings would be pretty carefully taken'.[83]

With his reputation as an essayist and literary critic, his mandate to win back the confidence of the leaders of the Irish Party which Bryce had lost, and his policy of paving the way for Home Rule which, as Robinson saw it, involved governing Ireland in the interim as far as possible according to Irish ideas, Robinson might not have been expected to find himself at ease with Bryce's successor, Augustine Birrell.[84] His unionist pedigree and close relationship with earlier conservative chief secretaries must have been well known to Birrell but, although the new Chief Secretary came to distrust several of the senior officials at the Irish departments,

Robinson, according to the Treasury Remembrancer, Maurice Headlam, was 'almost the only non-political Irishman' to succeed in 'establishing intimate personal relations' with him, something which came as a surprise to observers generally.[85] Birrell relied on him for information and advice on a range of issues and, in turn, won Robinson's confidence and respect. He had been in office for only a few months when he told the House of Commons in May 1907 that Robinson was 'one of the most devoted servants that Ireland could hope to have under any form of government' and even though he had first met him only a few months earlier, his interest in Ireland had struck him forcibly. He went on to say that he was quite sure that nationalist MPs, 'if they could enjoy the privilege of knowing and conversing with Sir Henry Robinson, [would] share the opinion, which he now unhesitatingly expressed, of that distinguished public servant'.[86] A few days later, he referred again in the House of Commons to Robinson as 'the exceedingly able Vice-President',[87] and at the end of June, when appealing for support for the Evicted Tenants Bill, he cited Robinson as his informant when describing the depressing state of affairs in the west of Ireland: rain was falling piteously, the turf lay rotting, the seaweed was as wet as the day it came out of the sea and the outlook was dismal and gloomy.[88]

As one of the earliest car owners in Ireland, a feature of Robinson's relationship with Long and the chief secretaries who followed him was their reliance on him to conduct them on tours of the West and other regions around the country. In *Further Memories* (1924),[89] he records that he circled Ireland many times with chief secretaries, generally following coastal routes, sometimes driving one of his own cars and sometimes being driven by Lynch, his chauffer. Generally, there was no army, police or other escort, but occasionally a hired car followed with the luggage. Sometimes , family members of the Chief Secretary were included in the touring party, and occasionally one of Robinson's sons, Christopher, was involved. As the latter recalled it, Robinson used to take the Chief Secretary 'into the depths of the wildest parts of Ireland, into the homes and cottages of the people, and thus give the minister an intimate and real knowledge of Irish conditions'.[90] Robinson was surprised at first that Birrell went with him on official tours 'regardless of what nationalist opinion might be, as I was aware that there was great jealousy over it and that he was in more than one quarter advised to beware of the LGB'. He speculated, however, that Birrell may have found it useful to avail of the knowledge of the country and its people, which he had gained over many years.[91] Birrell, in fact, made good use in various debates at Westminster of knowledge acquired on tours with Robinson. For example, in debating a Labourers Bill in

1911, he was able to comment on the varying quality of the designs of newly built cottages, and to insist on the inclusion of a provision allowing the LGB to direct the demolition of older dwellings to prevent them being used once again for human habitation as he had observed in some areas.[92]

Birrell disliked Dublin Castle and the Chief Secretary's lodge – he took every opportunity on his rare visits to Ireland to get out of Dublin and into the countryside with Robinson or, less frequently, with some other civil servant. While many of the projects and schemes viewed on these occasions were the work of the CDB, it was Robinson who was his regular guide and companion and, according to Treasury Remembrancer, Maurice Headlam, Robinson was 'practically a minister' during Birrell's regime.[93] The two men visited Killarney in April 1908,[94] while Birrell and his wife travelled via Waterford to Kerry in May 1909, again accompanied by Robinson.[95] Visits to Connemara and Mayo (some of them with Birrell's wife and son) were reported in November 1910, June 1911 and February 1916, including on some occasions a voyage along the coast or to the western islands in the CDB steamer *Granuaile*.[96] A trip to Cashel, Cork, and on to the west was reported in May 1912, during which the party called on Denis Kelly, the Catholic Bishop of Ross, in Skibbereen, and the pair were in Kerry again in May 1913, in Wicklow in October (viewing coastal erosion near the town) and in Donegal in June 1914.[97] The party frequently stayed at the Great Northern Hotel at Bundoran, the Midland Great Western Railway Company's hotel at Mallaranny (Mulrany), County Mayo, or at Robinson's favourite hotel at Recess, County Galway, which had been acquired by the Railway Company in 1895, and expensively refurbished. G. C. Duggan, who worked at Dublin Castle between 1911 and 1914, never once saw Birrell at the Castle in those years: 'London was his home ... we fed him weekly with a summary of what we regarded as important files dealt with in the office ... yet Birrell did see something of Ireland in 1914 ... the all-powerful Sir Henry Robinson ... lured him away on a journey to Connemara along with the under-secretary.'[98] Similarly, Headlam noted that on his occasional visits to Ireland, Birrell 'usually retired with Sir Henry to the comfortable hotel at Recess in Galway and considered Irish problems from there.'[99] As D. P. Moran's *Leader* saw it in 1914, Birrell 'comes over and a plausible Unionist jobocrat takes him round in a motor car, then he goes back to London'.[100] Andrew Magill, who served as private secretary to a number of chief secretaries, described Robinson as the *fides achates* (true friend) of Birrell and other chief secretaries, and the man who had always acted as *cicerone* (guide) on their tours.[101] Oliver St John Gogarty, who knew Robinson well and who owned a house at Renvyle within about twenty miles of the hotel in Recess, noted that he would whisk chief secretaries to the hotel in his well-kept automobile, saving them from a boring visit to Dublin Castle and many possible deputations and other vexations. [102] He also recalled how well the local RIC had been trained to salute men in positions of responsibility – 'or in the company of Sir Henry, which was much the same thing'. [103]

Relations with the Under-Secretaries

In the absence in London of the Chief Secretary, day-to-day business at Dublin Castle was handled for much of the year by the Under-Secretary – in theory at any rate an apolitical civil servant whose tenure of office would not be directly affected by changes of government. The Under-Secretary was the most senior and best-paid civil servant in the country, with a salary of £2,000 a year in the 1910s, the key figure in the permanent government and – nominally at any rate – the principal adviser of the Chief Secretary on policy matters. While he was an *ex-officio* member of the LGB, he rarely attended meetings of the board and it was stated officially in 1913 that 'he takes no part in its proceedings'. [104] Robinson insisted on maintaining his practice of dealing directly with the Chief Secretary as president of the board, instead of submitting files through the Under-Secretary, and he was careful to address his formal written submissions to the Chief Secretary as 'President'. For him, the Under-Secretary's function in relation to the LGB was simply to act as one of the commissioners (if he chose to do so) and not to exercise any supervisory or advisory functions in relation to the board or its business.

When Robinson became Vice-President, Sir David Harrel had been Under-Secretary for more than five years, having previously served as an RIC officer, as resident magistrate in Mayo, and as Chief Commissioner of the Dublin Metropolitan Police. Never, according to Robinson, was the Under-Secretary post more ably filled than by Harrel who was 'one of the wisest men of our time'. There is no evidence of any conflict between the two men, or any evidence of interference by Harrel in the business of the LGB. [105] Harrel resigned in November 1902 because, according to Robinson, [106] he had an unsatisfactory working relationship with George Wyndham. [107] This is consistent with the view of Andrew Magill, who recalled that Wyndham had insisted on getting rid of Harrel because, although he was shrewd and able, he was 'too much of the old school'. [108] Against this, however, Harrel himself recorded that by the spring of 1902 he was 'feeling tired and much in want of a long rest' after forty years of public service, but had been dissuaded by Wyndham from resigning. [109] Moreover, Wyndham told Arthur Balfour in August of his 'deep and even poignant regret' that Harrel was about to retire on health grounds, and that he had been assured that his decision to leave his post was motivated neither by disapproval of government policy nor by unwillingness to serve under a relatively young Chief Secretary.[110]

Had Gerald Balfour continued as Chief Secretary for another few years, it is very likely that Robinson would have been promoted to replace Harrel: he was held in high regard by Balfour and he was well known to the Prime Minister, Balfour's brother, Arthur, during whose term as Chief Secretary he had first been appointed as a member of the LGB. Robinson himself was aware that he was seen as 'first favourite' when Harrel's resignation was anticipated, and it was in fact widely speculated at the time that he would be transferred to the top post at Dublin Castle because he was then the senior head of a department in Ireland and was generally believed, in official circles, to have made a success of implementing the 1898 act. He was also personally aware that 'some influential people' were urging his appointment but, he wrote later, he also 'knew Wyndham sufficiently to be sure that he would do nothing so prosaic as to appoint as Under-Secretary a man who everyone guessed would be appointed'. Wyndham, in fact, wrote to Robinson in October, on the eve of the announcement of the appointment of Sir Antony Patrick MacDonnell as Under-Secretary, virtually apologising for the fact that he was being passed over. Recognising that he might have had a legitimate aspiration to the post, Wyndham told him that he could not then be spared from his post at the LGB. However, by adding that youth is on your side – Robinson was then 45 years old – he appeared to hold out hope of promotion at a future date and, by way of immediate compensation, added that he had asked the lord lieutenant to submit Robinson's name for appointment to the Privy Council – an unusual appointment at the time for a serving Irish civil servant.[111] In a wider context, Wyndham told Robinson that his motivation for passing him over for promotion was that he had need of a person in Dublin as his chief of staff to assist him in his work with the Treasury on 'correlating the financial aspects of the different departments of the Irish government'. MacDonnell, with his years of experience of governing four Indian provinces, seemed well suited to this task. In his letter to Robinson, however, Wyndham was economical with the truth, having already advised the Prime Minister of quite different reasons for failing to appoint him. He had in fact discussed four possible successors with Harrel some months before the latter's resignation, and had briefed the Prime Minister on the outcome in August. Sir West Ridgeway, who had previously held the post, was rejected because there would be grave objections to bringing back a man after ten years, while Walter Lawrence, private secretary to the viceroy of India, was ruled out because Wyndham believed instinctively that he would not succeed in Ireland. He went on to tell the Prime Minister that Robinson lacked the necessary amount of initiative and drive, that his selection 'would give umbrage to others in the service here', and that he could not be spared from the LGB.[112] But who were those others about whom Wyndham was so concerned? Sir James Brown Dougherty, who had been Assistant Under-Secretary since 1895, and had just been knighted, would probably have considered himself entitled to the promotion, but it is difficult to identify other senior civil servants who would have had a stronger claim than Robinson for advancement. Wyndham and Harrel, however, seem to have been determined not to give the position to him: even if MacDonnell were not available, Wyndham told the Prime Minister that Harrel could then only recommend the recall of Ridgeway – and he saw grave objection to that.[113] Although Balfour had real concerns about the wisdom of MacDonnell's appointment, and warned Wyndham to move cautiously, the Chief Secretary was willing to take the risk because, he told Balfour, he needed to have someone of sufficient experience to pull the office together and to correlate it with the different boards. Besides, although the LGB was 'running the new Local Government Act well', the expansion of housing and other activities was raising policy and local taxation issues, which called for attention.[114]

Having agreed that his new Under-Secretary should be placed 'in a position to master the administrative and financial conditions of all the boards', it was entirely logical for Wyndham to ask Robinson to give MacDonnell all the necessary facilities for educating himself on the working of the LGB.[115] MacDonnell spent the month after his appointment visiting the various branches of the Irish administration and acquainting himself with his new colleagues.[116] Within a few weeks, however, he discovered that his coordination ideas were not well received by Robinson at the Custom House: 'I was struck with the gulf which exists between this board [the LGB] and Dublin Castle', he told his wife on 18 November, adding that 'the feud of Hindu and Mahometan is not more bitter, nor so enduring and persistent'.[117] He then persuaded Wyndham to write personally to Robinson, explaining that he wished certain LGB files and papers to be submitted to him through the Under-Secretary but this initiative was easily rebuffed by Robinson. He took the line that if he were prevented from having direct communication with his 'official chief', he would 'have to send a vanload of papers every day to the Castle' so that the issues could be discussed by MacDonnell with the Chief Secretary. Robinson was told by Wyndham to use his own discretion in giving effect to the direction – and then, in his own words, 'following the dictates of experience, I took no more notice of it'.[118] However, unknown to Robinson, it appears that MacDonnell may have surreptitiously achieved his objective, at least in part, because Wyndham had also directed that all departmental correspondence intended for himself should be addressed to him at the Castle, rather than at the Irish Office in London. This arrangement allowed MacDonnell, rather than one of the private secretaries, to open and read letters and submissions 'and then have an opportunity of noting my views without coming into prominence'.[119]

According to Andrew Magill, who became his private secretary in June 1904, MacDonnell had a reputation 'for having left a trail of broken men behind him' and because of resentment at his autocratic ways, he constantly found difficulties in his way, put there by other departments.[120] Robinson's relationship with MacDonnell was a difficult one, and although he was afterwards to claim that he had not wanted the Under-Secretary position in 1902 as he considered his existing position to be 'more independent and in many ways preferable', it must have given him some satisfaction to be able to record that 'things might have been easier for Wyndham' if he, rather than MacDonnell, had been appointed. Wyndham 'would have been spared a good deal of vexation' and the devolution crisis of 1904–05, 'which led to his undoing' would never have occurred.[121]

There were many who expected that MacDonnell would be removed when Walter Long replaced Wyndham in 1905. Rumours that Robinson was to succeed him were reported in several London and Dublin newspapers.[122] However, while he told the cabinet that Robinson was an official 'of long standing, of great ability and of fearless character',[123] Long advised his colleagues that although MacDonnell had been 'allowed an undue latitude', he was 'averse from removing a permanent head unless the case is very strong'.[124] He continued to resist pressure from Irish loyalists to get rid of MacDonnell, but in the months that followed he rarely accepted MacDonnell's advice.[125] And Robinson, even though he believed that 'the prospect of Sir A. with an absolutely free hand is causing dismay', told Walter Long after the event that 'it would have been a very bad thing for the unionists if you had dismissed Antony before giving him a fair chance of carrying out your orders'.[126]

MacDonnell's star rose again when James Bryce became Chief Secretary. An ineffective administrator, Bryce allowed MacDonnell to interfere to an unprecedented extent in the affairs of the LGB. He regularly included comments and suggestions about local government matters in his frequent letters to Bryce, and his advice on particular topics was sometimes directly in conflict with that offered by Robinson. He disagreed with Robinson's proposals regarding the financing of increased activity under the Labourers Acts and notwithstanding the political pressure from Redmond for a Labourers Bill, he even suggested to Bryce that he might see his way to substituting 'the scheme' for it in the parliamentary programme.[127] In this and in other cases MacDonnell – unlike Robinson – was insensitive to the likely party-political impact of his recommendations and proposals: as Redmond saw it, he was in fact every day 'giving further evidence that he is inclined to utterly disregard popular opinion and the views of the representatives of Ireland'.[128] In some cases, MacDonnell advocated giving local councils more freedom than was permitted by the rules and regulations of the LGB – even if that meant they were to make mistakes – and on at least one occasion he took issue with important staffing proposals that Robinson had decided to implement. All of this contributed to a less than harmonious relationship between the two men. In that respect, Robinson was no different to many others – as Lord Aberdeen said, in favour of a possible new appointee to another post, 'he would get on with Sir Antony – and of what other man could this be safely predicted?'[129]

Birrell had a difficult relationship with MacDonnell and was in office for only a few months when he told Bryce that his main antagonist had been 'our excellent friend and "colleague" (woe's me!), Sir A. M., late of Bengal' who was obstinate, irritating and exhausting.[130] MacDonnell told Birrell on 1 July 1907 that he wished to resign,[131] and even though the Chief Secretary requested him to continue in office, he paid less and less attention to his views, believing him to be a man who ignored the House of Commons, and one who suffered from delusions concerning what was feasible.[132] According to Robinson, MacDonnell's administration had been a complete failure. He told Beatrice Webb in May 1908 that the Under-Secretary was a broken man who had intended to reform each department on Indian lines, but was perplexed and baffled to find himself face-to-face with the very different circumstances of Ireland and with democratic institutions which he began by ignoring but which effectively frustrated his schemes.[133]

Speculation about the filling of MacDonnell's position had been rampant for a year before his retirement at the end of July 1908, and at least six men – all of them Irish and each with important supporters – were said to be in the running at different times.[134] Writing from London in June 1907, Horace Plunkett told T. P. Gill that he had heard that Sir Antony's successor was to be William Bailey[135] – a barrister who had been a member of the Estates Commission since 1903 and who was regarded by Robinson as 'a pleasant but pushing little official ... who had always made himself useful to every Under-Secretary'.[136] It was rumoured in November that Birrell would give the post to Robinson if he had a free hand, but that nationalist opinion would prevent him from doing so, leaving. This would leave the way open for Sir James Brown Dougherty, the Assistant Under-Secretary, who hoped that the 'embarrassment surrounding the question of filling the position will enable him to slip in at the last minute'.[137] Another who was mentioned as a possible successor was Edward Ennis, a catholic barrister and former reporter and leader-writer with the *Freeman's Journal*, who had been registrar of the Court of Chancery since 1895.[138] He was regarded within the Chief Secretary's Office as a strong contender and had attempted in 1895 to secure the post of Assistant Under-Secretary, claiming that because he was a catholic, he would be more or less agreeable to the Church.[139] Beatrice Webb confided to her diary on 3 May 1908 that Robinson was thinking a good deal about who was to succeed; he felt that Dougherty who was 'an old man with one year to run' would probably be appointed, but who would be next?[140] In the event, Birrell's admiration for Robinson was not enough to induce him into taking the risk of appointing him. He told the House of Commons on 4 May that MacDonnell was to be replaced by Dougherty at the end of July.[141] A native of Garvagh, County Derry, Dougherty studied for a career in the Presbyterian Church and was active in Church affairs until June 1895 when, according to Robinson, he had been 'dragged out of the obscurity of the Presbyterian ministry … to everyone's surprise' by the liberal Chief Secretary, John Morley, to become Assistant Under-Secretary. Since then, because of his lack of administrative experience and general helplessness, he had been 'a silent and comparatively unknown figure, with little influence with the government of the day'. As Robinson saw it, the appointment was simply a case of Buggin's turn,[142] but according to Dougherty's friend and second cousin, Rev. J. B. Armour, Presbyterian minister at Ballymoney, Birrell had a decided respect for him.[143] His appointment as Under-Secretary, little more than a year before he was due to retire at age 65, was criticised by unionists and advanced nationalists alike, but his continuation in office after he had reached retirement age was sanctioned by the Treasury. They deployed the statutory formula that he possessed 'peculiar qualifications which would be difficult to replace by a fresh appointment'.[144]

Any disappointment Robinson may have felt at Dougherty's appointment must have been offset by the knowledge that, after thirteen years in a position which was inferior to the Vice-Presidency of the LGB, the new Under-Secretary was never likely to challenge his management of the board, or to attempt to upset his close relationship with Birrell. This, indeed, was how it turned out: Dougherty told the committee on Irish finance in 1911 that 'formerly all the business of the Local Government

Board passed through the Chief Secretary's Office, but now the Vice-President goes to the Chief Secretary and transacts his business with him'.[145] Two years later, he told the Royal Commission on the civil service that his sole function in connection with the LGB was 'signing the annual report of proceedings, of which I know nothing', and because the Vice-President transacted the business of the board directly with the Chief Secretary, 'we in the Chief Secretary's Office know nothing about it'.[146] Robinson told the same commission that, although the board was required by the Treasury to submit applications relating to financial and staffing matters through the Chief Secretary's Office, this was a waste of time as that particular office had no administrative control over the actions of the board. A cursory review of surviving Treasury files confirms that, even in LGB staffing matters, the Chief Secretary's Office at this period effectively functioned as a post office, forwarding the board's submissions to the Treasury for consideration – but generally without comment. Ten years earlier, T. L. Heath, of the Treasury, had actually advised the chancellor that the office at Dublin Castle appeared to be nothing more than a post office.[147] G. C. Duggan's memoir corroborates this: documents, he says, were merely copied and sent on with a covering letter 'for consideration' or, occasionally, 'for favourable consideration', and nothing more.[148]

'Never Subordinate, Except to Parliament'

In 1923, when looking back over his twenty-four years as Vice-President, Robinson wrote that he had not cared what winds prevailed at Dublin Castle so long as his board was left alone.[149] When asked by a member of the Royal Commission on the civil service in 1913 if the LGB was practically a parallel department to that of the Under-Secretary, he neatly avoided answering the question directly by asserting that 'we never were subordinate, except to Parliament'.[150] Throughout his career, he made it his business to ensure in various ways that there continued to be substance in this proud boast. He took a jaundiced view of various proposals for the coordination of the activities of the various boards and other agencies operating in Dublin and did not co-operate in any of them, and he managed to repel occasional attempts by the lord lieutenant of the day to interfere in the business of the board. He did his best to frustrate efforts by some of the under-secretaries to bring the activities of the LGB under their supervision and to interfere in LGB affairs. He was still able in 1913 to assert that Dublin Castle had no administrative control over the board and had 'nothing whatever to do with it'.[151] He was happy to work closely with successive chief secretaries of different political persuasions, recognising their status as President of the board, and had no difficulty in carrying out each man's wishes and directions while developing remarkably close personal relations with several of them. Finally, while he occasionally visited the offices of the English Local Government Board in London, he was able to arrange that the LGB (like its Scottish counterpart) continued to operate in 'watertight departments' as the president of the English board, Herbert Samuel, stated in 1914, and as the Haldane Committee noted in 1918.[152]

NOTES

1   R. B. McDowell, *The Irish Administration, 1801–1914* (London, 1964), appendices II and III.

2   *Nationalist*, 11 Jan. 1906.

3   *Hansard* IV, 174, 7 May 1907, 83–84.

4   *Hansard* IV, 187, 30 Mar. 1908, 157.

5   David Fitzpatrick, 'Ireland and the Empire' in Andrew Porter (ed.), *The Oxford History of the British Empire, Vol. III, The Nineteenth Century* (Oxford, 1999), p.496.

6   Kieran Flanagan, 'The Chief Secretary's Office, 1853–1914: A Bureaucratic Enigma', *IHS* xxiv No. 94 (Nov. 1984).

7   Sir Christopher Lynch-Robinson, *The Last of the Irish R.M.s* (London, 1951), p.18.

8   Memorandum dated 25 Apr. 1885 by Joseph Chamberlain, reprinted in C. H. D. Howard, 'Documents relating to the Irish "central board" scheme 1884–5', *IHS* viii, No. 31 (Mar. 1953), pp.255–57.

9   Letter from West Ridgeway, 7 Oct. 1904 to *The Times*, reprinted in the *Irish Times*, 12 Oct. 1904.

10   R. Barry O'Brien, *Dublin Castle and the Irish People* (Dublin, 1909), pp.139–140.

11   Sir Henry Robinson, *Memories: Wise and Otherwise* (London, 1923), pp.97–98.

12   Ibid. p.100.

13   Departments connected with the Government of Ireland, memorandum dated 7 May 1895 by Sir David Harrel, TNA, PRO 30/60/15; Sir David Harrel, *Recollections and Reflections* (TCD, typescript, for private circulation, 1926), pp.158–160.

14   Wyndham to Balfour, 14 Sept. 1902, J. W. Mackail and Guy Wyndham (eds), *Life and Letters of George Wyndham* (London, 1925), pp.757–759.

15   Wyndham to Lord Lansdowne, 12 Sept. 1902, Wyndham, *Life and Letters*, pp.755–6.

16   MacDonnell to the Treasury, 21 Sept. 1903, Government letters viii, B/6/20, cited in Andrew Gailey, *Ireland and the Death of Kindness* (Cork, 1987), p.203.

17   Note by Wyndham of a meeting with the Chancellor, quoted in letter of 9 Oct. 1906 to Chamberlain, BL, Balfour Papers, Add.49806; Chamberlain–Wyndham correspondence, Oct. 1903 to Dec. 1903, quoted in Gailey, *Kindness*, pp.204–05.

18   MacDonnell to Wyndham, 22 Sept. 1902, Wyndham, *Life and Letters*, pp.760–61.

19   *Irish Times*, 1 Oct. 1904; a letter from MacDonnell to Alice S. Green, 1 Sept. 1904 (NLI, MS 15,089) suggests that he was in fact the principal author of the scheme.

20   Robinson, *Memories*, p.161–2.

21   Catherine B. Shannon, 'Lord Randolph Churchill and Ireland: The Road To and From The Orange Card, 1886–1893', in Robert McNamara (ed.), *The Churchills and Ireland 1660–1965* (Dublin, 2012), p.120.

22   Robinson, *Memories*, p.161.

23   *Irish Times*, 13 Jan. 1906.

24   Note (undated, but probably Jan. 1906) by Redmond of a discussion with MacDonnell, NLI, Redmond Papers MS 15,174/1.

25   MacDonnell to Bryce, 3 Feb. 1906, NLI James Bryce Papers, MS 11,012(2).

26   Outline of Irish Constitutional Reform, 14 Feb. 1906, Oxford, Bodleian Library, MacDonnell Papers, MS. Eng. hist. c. 369, f. 1–14.

27   Bryce to Dillon, 11 Oct. 1906, Oxford, Bodleian Library, MS Bryce 215, f. 64; MacDonnell to Bryce, 17 Oct. 1906, NLI, James Bryce Papers, MS 11,014(2).

28   Memorandum on the Constitution of the Proposed New Administrative Body To Be Set Up in Ireland, Dec. 1906 (copy), NLI, James Bryce Papers, MS 11,014(4).

29   Dillon to Morley, 19 Dec. 1906 (copy), NLI, James Bryce Papers, MS 11,014(4).

30   MacDonnell to Bryce, 30 July 1906, NLI, James Bryce Papers, MS 11,013(3).

31   Robinson to Long (no date but probably Nov. 1906), WRO, Long Papers, WRO 947/126/10.

32   Robinson to Bryce, 30 Nov. 1906, NLI, James Bryce Papers, MS 11,014(3).

33   Robinson to Bryce, Dec. 1906, NLI, James Bryce Papers, MS 11,014(3).

34   *Hansard* IV, 169, 12 Feb. 1907, 1–3.

35   *Hansard* IV, 169, 12 Feb. 1907, 89–90.

36   A. C. Hepburn, 'The Irish Council Bill and the Fall of Sir Antony MacDonnell, 1906–07', *IHS*, xvii, No. 68 (Sept. 1971), pp.470–498.

37   Birrell to Bryce, 17 June 1907, Oxford, Bodleian Library, MS Bryce 215, f. 147.

38   Irish Council Bill, Bill No. 182, 7 Mar. 1907; *Hansard* IV, 174, 7 May 1907, 78–196.

39   *Hansard* IV, 174, 7 May 1907, 106.

40   *Hansard* IV, 174, 7 May 1907, 184–86.

41   Sir Philip Hanson to My Dear Chief, 4 Nov. 1910, (photocopy), NLI, MS 24,948 (ii).

42   Robinson, *Memories*, pp.146–47.

43   Robinson to Long, 31 Mar. and 17 Apr. 1905, WRO, Long Papers, WRO 947/78.

44   Memorandum initialled W.H.L. 8 Dec. 1905, WRO, Long Papers, WRO 947/78.

45   Robinson, *Memories*, pp.149–150.

46   Robinson to Long, 23 Dec. 1905, BL, Long Papers, Add. MS 62409.

47   Aberdeen to Bryce, 3 and 8 Sept. 1906, NLI, James Bryce Papers, MS 11,014(1); Robinson to Bryce, 29 Aug. 1906, NLI, James Bryce Papers, MS 11,013(4).

48   Ishbel, Marchioness of Aberdeen and Temair, *The Musings of a Scottish Granny* (London, 1936), pp.156–57; *More Cracks with 'We Twa'* (London, 1929), pp.164–65.

49   *Interim Report of the Departmental Committee on Tuberculosis*, HC 1912–13 [Cd. 6164].

50   *Irish Times*, 23 July 1912.

51   *Irish Times*, 3 Sept. 1912.

52   *Hansard* V, 39, 13 June 1912, 1029–30.

53   *Sinn Féin*, 22 Mar. 1914.

54   *Irish Times*, 3 Sept. 1912.

55   Robinson, *Memories*, pp.226–8.

56 Robinson to Balfour, 4 Aug. 1898, NAS, Balfour Papers, GD 433/2/114/4.

57 *Second Appendix to Fourth Report of the Royal Commission on the Civil Service*, HC 1914 [Cd. 7340], para. 199, 204, 206; D. B. McNeill, *Irish passenger steamship services* (vol.2) (Newton Abbot, 1971), pp.13–14.

58 Bryce to A. S. Green, 5 Aug. 1907, NLI, A. S. Green Papers MS 15,070 (3).

59 Robinson to Long, 2 July 1918, WRO, Long Papers, WRO 947/332.

60 *Hansard* IV, 55, 21 Mar. 1898, 511–12.

61 *Hansard* IV, 73, 30 June 1899, 1225.

62 TNA, PRO 30/60/15 contains sixty letters of this kind; others are in the Balfour Papers at the British Library and in the National Archives of Scotland.

63 Robinson to Balfour, 19 Feb. 1899, TNA, PRO 30/60/15.

64 Robinson to Balfour, 26 Dec. 1899, NAS, Balfour Papers, GD 433/2/114/12.

65 Robinson to Balfour, 16 July 1899, TNA, PRO 30/60/15.

66 Robinson, *Memories*, pp.138–39.

67 Beatrice Webb, *Our Partnership* (London, 1948), p.408.

68 Robinson, *Memories*, pp.138–39, 141.

69 Gailey, *Kindness*, p.173.

70 Robinson, *Memories*, pp.172, 182.

71 Walter Long, *Memories* (London, 1923), pp.163–65.

72 *Irish Times*, 22, 27 and 28 April, 14 June, 16, 19, 22 and 23 Sept. 1905; Robinson's notes on the tour were included by Long in an Appendix to his *Memories*.

73 *Irish Times*, 23 Oct. 1905; Robinson, *Memories*, p.172.

74 *Irish Times*, 22 Sept. 1905.

75 Robinson to Long, 23 Dec 1905, BL, Long Papers, Add 62409, f. 114.

76 *Hansard* V, 13, 24 Nov. 1909, 227–28.

77 Bryce to A. S. Green, 5 and 6 May 1907, NLI, A. S. Green Papers, MS 15,070 (3).

78 Robinson to Long, 23 Dec 1905, BL, Long Papers, Add 62409, f. 114.

79 Robinson, *Memories*, p.185.

80 Webb, *Our Partnership*, p.408.

81 Robinson, *Memories*, pp.185, 187.

82 Redmond to Dillon, 3 Apr. 1906, NLI, Redmond papers, MS 15,182/10; Redmond to Edward Blake MP, 13 Nov. 1906, NLI Redmond Papers, MS 15170/3.

83 Robinson to Bryce, 22 Dec. 1906, NLI, Bryce Papers, MS 11,014 (4).

84 Robinson, *Memories*, p.189.

85 Maurice Headlam, *Irish Reminiscences* (London, 1947), p.58.

86 *Hansard* IV, 173, 2 May 1907, 1147.

87 *Hansard* IV, 174, 7 May 1907, 85.

88 *Hansard* IV, 177, 27 June 1907, 131–32.

89 Sir Henry Robinson, *Further Memories of Irish Life* (London, 1924), p.166.

90 Lynch-Robinson, *The Last of the Irish R.M.s*, p.120.

91 Robinson, *Memories*, p.193.

92 *Hansard* V, 26, 31 May 1911, 1166–69.

93 Minute of 4 Dec. 1919 on Treasury file 48935, TNA T1/12410.

94 *Irish Independent*, 21 Apr. 1908.

95 *Irish Times*, 29 May 1909.

96 *Irish Times*, 1 Nov. 1910, 9 and 12 June 1911, 12 Feb. 1916.

97   *Irish Times*, 24 May 1912 and 6 June 1914; *Irish Independent*, 14 May 1913; *Freeman's Journal*, 22 Oct. 1913; *Skibbereen Eagle*, 25 May 1912.
98   G. C. Duggan, 'A World that Passed Away', *Irish Times*, 4 Aug. 1964.
99   Headlam, *Irish Reminiscences*, p.58.
100 *The Leader*, 1 Aug. 1914.
101 Memoirs of Andrew Philip Magill, Oxford, Bodleian Library, MS. Eng. C. 2803, f. 273–280.
102 Oliver St John Gogarty, *Tumbling in the Hay* (London, 1939), pp.120–21).
103 Oliver St John Gogarty, *As I Was Going Down Sackville Street* (London, 1937), p.255.
104 Memorandum as to the organisation and staff of the Chief Secretary's Office and other departments concerned with the Irish Government (Dublin, 1913), NLI 350 c 9.
105 Robinson, *Memories*, pp.100–101, 141.
106 Robinson, *Memories*, p.141.
107 *The Times* (29 Oct 1912) spoke of surprise at Harrel's removal and hinted that the two men may have differed about the enforcement of the Crimes Act.
108 Magill, *Memoirs*, f. 92.
109 Harrel, *Recollections and Reflections*, p.161.
110 Wyndham to Balfour, 25 Aug. 1902, BL, Balfour Papers, Add. 49804, f. 22.
111 Robinson, *Memories*, pp.141–142.
112 Wyndham to A. J. Balfour, 25 Aug. 1902, BL, Balfour Papers, Add 49804, f. 22.
113 Wyndham to A. J. Balfour, 27 Aug. 1902, BL, Balfour Papers, Add. 49804, f. 30.
114 Wyndham to A. J. Balfour, 13 Sept. 1902, Wyndham, *Life and Letters*, pp.757–9; BL, Balfour Papers Add. 49804, f. 36.
115 Wyndham to Harrel, 22 Oct. 1902, Wyndham, *Life and Letters*, p.451.
116 M. L. Brillman, 'A Crucial Administrative Interlude: Sir Antony MacDonnell's Return to Ireland, 1902–04', *New Hibernia Review*, 9, No. 2 (Summer 2005), p.75.
117 MacDonnell to his wife, 18 Nov. 1902, Oxford, Bodleian Library, MacDonnell Papers, MSS Eng. Hist., c. 220.
118 Robinson, *Memories*, pp.141–42, 144–46.
119 MacDonnell to Bryce, 23 Dec. 1905, NLI, James Bryce Papers, MS 11,011.
120 Magill, *Memoirs*, f. 159.
121 Robinson, *Memories*, p.142.
122 *Irish Times*, 15 Mar. 1905, drawing on a report in the *Daily Express*, *Evening Mail* and *Irish Independent*, 14 March 1905.
123 Confidential memorandum regarding Sir Antony MacDonnell, W.H.L., 28 Apr. 1905, BL, Long Papers, Add. 49776, f. 56.
124 Memorandum submitted to the Cabinet regarding Sir A.P. MacDonnell by W.H. Long, 31 Mar. 1905, TNA, CAB 37/75
125 Long, *Memories*, pp.146–49.
126 Robinson to Long, undated 1905, WRO, Long Papers, WRO 947/114; 16 Sept. 1906, WRO 947/126/10.
127 MacDonnell to Bryce, 4 and 10 Apr. 1906, NLI James Bryce Papers, MS 11,012 (4).
128 Redmond to Dillon, 3 Apr. 1906, NLI, Redmond papers, MS 15,182/10; Redmond to Edward Blake MP, 13 Nov. 1906, NLI, MS 15170/3.

129 Aberdeen to Bryce, 16 Dec. 1906, NLI, James Bryce papers, MS 11,014(4).

130 Birrell to Bryce, 17 June 1907, Oxford, Bodleian Library, MS Bryce 215, f. 147.

131 MacDonnell to Ponsonby, 31 July 1907, BL, Campbell-Bannerman Papers, Add 41240 f. 29.

132 Birrell to Bryce, 17 June 1907, Oxford, Bodleian Library, MS Bryce 215, f. 147.

133 Webb, *Our Partnership*, pp.408–09.

134 Lawrence W. McBride, *The Greening of Dublin Castle* (Washington, 1991), pp.143–44.

135 Plunkett to Gill, 9 June 1907, NLI, Gill Papers, MS 13,496 (7).

136 Robinson, *Memories*, p.246.

137 Taylor to Long, 6 Nov 1907, BL, Long Papers, Add. 62412, f. 29.

138 Taylor to Micks, 28 July 1907, NLI MS 28,814.

139 Ennis to Dillon, 2 May 1895, TCD, John Dillon Papers, MS 6800/111.

140 Webb, *Our Partnership*, pp.408–09.

141 *Hansard* IV, 187, 4 May 1908, 1628; *Irish Times*, 25 July, 1908.

142 Robinson, *Memories*, pp.219–220.

143 J.B. Armour to an unidentified correspondent, Nov. 1907, PRONI, Armour papers, D1792/A/2/23.

144 *Copy of Treasury Minute ... stating the circumstances under which certain civil servants have been retained ... after the age of 65, HC 1912–13 (98)*.

145 *Committee on Irish Finance, Minutes of Evidence*, HC 1913 [Cd. 6799], 36.

146 *Second Appendix to Fourth Report of Royal Commission on the Civil Service*, HC 1914 [Cd. 7340], para. 82.

147 Memorandum dated 27 Oct 1903, UL Birmingham, ACP AC/22/2/5, quoted in Gailey, *Kindness*, p.204.

148 G.C. Duggan, Extract from draft of an unpublished book entitled 'The Life of a Civil Servant', typescript, p.13, NLI, Leon Ó Broin Papers, MS 31,689.

149 Robinson, *Memories*, p.265.

150 *Second Appendix to Fourth Report of Royal Commission on the Civil Service*, HC 1914 [Cd. 7340], para.206–7.

151 Ibid.

152 *Hansard* V, 63, 18 June 1914, 1345; *Report of Machinery of Government Committee*, HC 1918 [Cd.9230].

PART II

ACTIVITIES OTHERWISE:
THE OTHER ROBINSON

Throughout the first decade of the twentieth century, Henry Robinson's prominence within the Irish administration was becoming increasingly evident. His success in implementing the 1898 Act was unquestionable and, notwithstanding routine and regular sniping from nationalist politicians, the working relationship he established with the thousands of new local councillors was better than might have been expected. At national level, he maintained the independence of the LGB, and while working closely with five successive chief secretaries, he managed to fend off occasional attempts by lords lieutenant and Dublin Castle officials to interfere in its business. He successfully managed the introduction of old age pensions and arranged for the efficient implementation of an expanded programme of labourers housing. In the process, he built up the LGB into the largest and most powerful bureaucracy operating in Dublin.

There was never any doubt about Robinson's unionist status and his views on political issues, but he does not emerge as an adviser to ministers on these issues until 1912, after which a new and very different Robinson comes alive in the papers of British political figures and in cabinet and other official papers. He was drawn into the 1912–14 Home Rule controversy, particularly the issue of defining a north–south border, and his unofficial advisory role continued throughout the revolutionary period. His advice was sought at the time of the 1918 Conscription Crisis, and he was marginally involved with some of the ineffectual reform measures promoted during the chaotic regime of Lord French. As one of a few within the administration who appreciated that there were different factions within Sinn Féin, he argued after the 1918 general election that de Valera and the more moderate internees should be released in the hope that productive negotiations might follow. Although relations with his Local Government Board were broken off by most local councils following the 1920 local elections, he attempted – even before the Truce and the Treaty – to persuade the government to restore local councils to a sound financial position by reversing the withholding of State grants and by terminating the imposition on them of heavy liabilities in respect of criminal injuries awards.

Accepting that some form of Home Rule was inescapable, but concerned to avert any solution which involved partition, he made an unsuccessful last-minute effort in 1920 to persuade the cabinet that a Council of Ireland with substantial functions should be provided for in the Government of Ireland Act to mitigate the effects of partition. Two months before a Truce was actually agreed by the cabinet, he was one of the small number of officials who expressed support for a cessation of violence. However, for him the Treaty went too far – he saw it as a British surrender to the forces of disorder. He continued to head the LGB until it was absorbed into the new Department of Local Government on 1 April 1922. After a raid on his house in County Dublin in August he went to live in the south of England, where he died in October 1927.

CHAPTER VIII

Home Rule: 'You Will Find that The Ulstermen's Minimum Will Be Six Entire Counties, and No Option'

'A Plan to Set Up ... a System of Full Self-Government in Regard to Purely Irish Affairs'

While he loved Ireland, Henry Robinson never made any secret of the fact that he was a unionist by conviction who could never see Ireland as anything but part of the British Empire.[1] Given the fears he had expressed to Bryce in 1906 about the fate which would await him if the modest changes then proposed in the administration of Ireland were to become law, he must have welcomed the decision of the Liberal government to concentrate on issues such as the University Question and land reform after 1907. He and the other senior staff of the LGB can hardly have been too pleased, however, when the government had to face up to the problem of securing the votes of the Irish Party at Westminster by committing itself to introducing a measure of Home Rule after the next general election. The commitment was confirmed when Asquith announced on 10 December 1909, as he opened the election campaign, that the absolute House of Lords veto was to be removed, making it possible to proceed with a plan to 'set up in Ireland a system of full self-government in regard to purely Irish affairs'.[2] This marked the beginning of a new and very different period in Irish political history – a period in which the seeds of change in British–Irish relations were sown.[3] Coincidentally, the years from 1910 onwards also saw the emergence of Henry Robinson as an adviser to British ministers on political matters far outside his official responsibilities.

While the first 1910 election left the Irish Party holding the balance of power in the House of Commons, serious work on the drafting of a Home Rule Bill had to await the debates on the powers of the Lords, the December 1910 election and the enactment of the Parliament Act in August 1911. As a result, the third Home Rule Bill did not begin to take concrete shape until the first few months of 1912 when Birrell worked out the detailed provisions of the bill in London with Redmond, Dillon, Asquith and some of his cabinet colleagues.[4] Robinson's contribution, if any, to the evolution of the scheme provided for in the bill is not documented in surviving papers, and notwithstanding his objective of writing 'something of all the happenings which ... made my intimate association with twenty chief secretaries so full of interest',[5] his two volumes of memoirs, extending to more than 600 pages, make no reference to any involvement as an unofficial adviser on political and strategic issues in the years 1910 to 1912 or, indeed, in later years. The unpublished memoir, written by George Chester Duggan, a senior official in the Chief Secretary's Office at the time, confirms that the bill was 'hatched out in London', but he surmised that the contents would have been intimated by Birrell to the Under-Secretary and the law officers in Dublin.[6] Given the particularly close relationship that had developed since 1907 between Robinson and Birrell and the long hours they had spent together on the roads of Ireland and in west of Ireland hotels before 1912, it would be surprising if Robinson, too, were not given an opportunity to present his views on the Home Rule issue. Indeed, a letter from Robinson to Birrell in late January 1912 suggests that the two men did discuss at least some of the issues: he told Birrell that Denis Kelly, the Catholic Bishop of Ross, had called to the Custom House the previous day and was very anxious to have a word with him before publication of the bill, and 'when I see you, I will tell you what is in his mind'.[7]

Robinson was one of a substantial number of English and Irish civil servants who gave evidence to an expert committee chaired by Sir Henry Primrose which reported to the cabinet in October 1911 on the difficult issue of the financial and taxation arrangements which should apply when a separate Irish administration was established.[8] Within the cabinet, only Birrell favoured the scheme proposed by the committee, which would have given Ireland a considerable degree of control over expenditure and taxation, including customs and excise, but it was quickly rejected.[9] Robinson's personal position on the issue cannot be established at this stage: witnesses before the committee had been assured that their evidence would be treated as confidential, and while the government eventually agreed in 1913 to publish the evidence of those who consented to this, Robinson – for reasons which were never explained – adamantly refused to give his consent, notwithstanding a memorial signed by the majority of the members of the House of Commons.[10] He was, in fact, the only witness who took up what the *Irish Independent* described as 'the peculiar attitude' of not allowing his evidence to be placed before the public: 'We fail to see why ... [he] should have regarded his utterances and opinions, if he expressed any, as too sacrosanct to be given publicity.'[11] It seems likely that his reluctance to have his evidence published stemmed from personal dissatisfaction with the financial provisions of the Home Rule Bill: he told Birrell in 1914 that there were 'genuine financial objections' to the bill and that it would be desirable to make concessions towards satisfying these.[12]

'Let Them Screech and Yell Till They Were Tired'

At the beginning of 1912, when Ulster unionists, led by Sir Edward Carson, had already demonstrated the strength of their opposition to Home Rule, and while Birrell and his colleagues were finalising the text of the bill which was expected to be introduced within a matter of months, major controversy developed in Belfast arising from the announcement that Winston Churchill, First Lord of the Admiralty, along with John Redmond and Joe Devlin, nationalist MP for West Belfast, were to address a meeting in the city on 8 February. The meeting was being arranged by the Ulster Liberal Association under the chairmanship of Lord William Pirrie, Chairman of Harland & Wolff, who had come out in favour of Home Rule as early as 1902, but the plan to hold the meeting in the Ulster Hall created a storm of protest. This was the location where Churchill's father had made his militant anti-Home Rule speech in February 1886, and its use for a Home Rule rally was seen as a deliberate challenge by the Ulster Unionist Council (UUC), who resolved to take steps to prevent the meeting being held. Plans were subsequently made to have the hall occupied by Orangemen on the eve of the proposed meeting and to pack up to 70,000 supporters into the adjoining streets. Extra troops and police were sent to Belfast to deal with any violence that might occur but, in view of the risk of serious disorder, Churchill wrote to the Marquess of Londonderry (chairman of the UUC) on 25 January, insisting on his right to speak in public in Belfast, but advising him that the meeting would be held at another venue 'least likely to cause ill-feeling to the Orange Party'.[13]

Reports on the situation in Belfast, and on possible developments there, were received by Birrell from both the RIC and the military, and were supplemented by Robinson whose sympathies lay with the southern unionists, and who had no time for the methods and rhetoric of the northerners. He was pleased when the immediate crisis in Belfast had been averted because 'the spectacle of the First Lord of the Admiralty at the head of an army of police and soldiers trying to evict 2,000 religious fanatics from their sacred temple would not have been very edifying'. However, he was critical of both sides in a letter of 26 January to Birrell.[14] He was 'not in the least surprised at the arrogance of the Orange leaders', but was astounded by the stupidity of the local Liberal leaders who had arranged the meeting: they had turned the lime-light full blaze on the Belfast Orangemen whereas 'the sound policy was to have ignored them and to have let them screech and yell till they were tired'. He went on:

> The real trouble is this: the catholics are really well under the control of Devlin and their priests who can keep them in their homes and out of the way. But the unionist leaders have no control over the protestants although they <u>pretend</u> they have, and while Londonderry and Carson would like to content themselves with the point they have scored by Winston C.'s abandonment of the Ulster Hall, they won't be able to prevent the Ulster protestants demonstrating in force, more especially as T. W. Russell and John Redmond in today's [newspaper] are declaiming that the Orangemen are not serious and it is all bluff and stupid bellowing. This is the one thing needful to keep up the bad blood and I cannot understand what there is to be gained by it.[15]

'Religion is a Total Failure in this Country'

Robinson feared that Churchill could still be in serious danger, even if the meeting in Belfast were held at a venue other than the Ulster Hall and he hoped that something could be done to postpone his visit to Belfast until the excitement had died down. At the same time, he recognised the difficulty in this: it would be a 'great score for the Orangemen', but not much more so than if Churchill had to hold his demonstration 'protected by soldiers and machine guns'.[16] While he was writing to Birrell about this situation, one of his inspectors, Eddie Saunderson, son of the late unionist leader, Col. E. J. Saunderson, was on his way to County Down where he was to spend a weekend in what Birrell might have considered to be the enemy camp – Mount Stewart. This was the home of the Marquess of Londonderry and his wife, Theresa, who was leader of the Ulster Women's Unionist Council, and a close friend and confidante of Carson and a lady who was privy to information from others in the very top echelons of unionism, including Walter Long. Saunderson had been offered an appointment as the Conservative Party's chief agent in 1906, but opted to continue his civil service career while completely and consistently ignoring the rules which prohibited formal party political activity; as Alvin Jackson put it, he exchanged 'low-grade gossip and confidences at Tory dinner parties and at weekend retreats'.[17] It seems clear that he was the 'anonymous, but seemingly very accurate, Dublin informer', referred to by Diane Urquhart in her study of Lady Londonderry,[18] and that he effectively acted on a continuing basis as a kind of double-agent.[19] On 1 February, a few days after his return to Dublin, he was able to pass on to the Marchioness information which he had got from 'my chief' – obviously Robinson – who was probably an unsuspecting and unintentional participant in this amateur espionage work; the information was that Birrell was 'very much upset by the turn things have taken' [in Belfast], that 'they are going to fill Belfast with infantry and cavalry' in advance of Churchill's meeting and that there were growing dissentions in the cabinet on the Home Rule issue generally.[20] He had already reported that the parliamentary draftsman was 'nearly off his head' trying to draw up the Home Rule Bill with the cabinet committee – 'a motley gang who appear to be suffering from a sort of political DT' – fighting over every section. When Saunderson wrote again to Theresa on 7 February he was 'anxious to find out any news there might be' in exchange for what he knew 'as all incidents in the campaign are worth noting at the War Office of Ulster', but he had very little news on that occasion:

> Except that both the sittings of the cabinet on Home Rule were entirely taken up trying to crack the Ulster nut, and as far as I can gather, with little success, except that they have now raked up a scheme devised by Gladstone in '93, which never became public property and that is to place the five counties in Ulster that have a preponderance of unionists under the English Home Office. This is a subtle scheme worthy of the serpents. I think it cannot be too much rubbed in now that nothing will cause Ulster to desert the rest of Ireland.[21]

Saunderson had told Lady Londonderry in his letter of 1 February that he had 'made my chief write to Birrell that they could not send too many [troops]', but the letter that Robinson actually despatched to the Chief

Secretary was far more measured in its assessment of the situation: he advised that all would be quiet on the day of Churchill's meeting – the country orange lodges were well in hand and not a man would be sent to Belfast on the day unless some new situation supervened. There still remained a real possibility that there could be trouble: if Devlin were to 'bring out his crowd in order to demonstrate their strength ... there will be counter-demonstrations from the Queen's Island men'. In addition, the Ulster Unionist Council were desperately afraid for the peace of the city between 6.00 p.m. and 8.00 p.m. on 8 February:

> The factory girls, who are of all religions working together, turn out at this time and they are met by their young men, mostly a rather bad lot, and as religious rancour is tuned up to a high pitch, and the excitement as to what has happened will be at boiling point, a very harmless remark from one girl to another such as 'Go along ye papist bitch', which would ordinarily pass unnoticed, would set them at one another, their young men would join in, and word would be sent to the forces of both sides that protestant and catholic were killing each other.

Robinson agreed with Saunderson that there would be no trouble to speak of on 8 February, but the atmosphere was electric, and he warned Birrell that it would be well to be prepared for any eventuality. He also relayed some news which Saunderson had brought from Mount Stewart: £50,000 had been subscribed or promised to the Ulster Fund, and the bulk of this was to be spent on sending Presbyterian lecturers to England to preach against Home Rule. He also mentioned a more ominous development, that nearly five tons of nuts and bolts had disappeared from Harland & Woolff's yard, as well as from Workman and Clark's yards, and that the number of revolvers that were in the hands of the people was enormous. He ended by contributing his own views on those he described as the 'Orange fanatics' and on the 'grossly insulting and provocative terms' of recent Presbyterian speeches about the catholics. He did not believe in 'Ulster's so called loyalty: what is at the root of it all is a firm determination not to be under the rule of a Roman Catholic Parliament.' Obviously well aware also that the tactics of the UUC had been strongly supported in Ulster by all sections of the Church of Ireland,[22] he went on to advise that 'they won't be torn away from their protestant parliament', that's the whole thing, he told Birrell, concluding sadly that 'religion is a total failure in this country'.[23] Birrell wrote to Churchill on 28 January, complaining about the lack of warning before arrangements were made for the meeting in

Belfast, and suggested that if he and his advisers had been consulted, they could have prevented 'all this agitation and trouble'. He had been told by the Belfast police (just as Robinson had told him) that the excitement was still intense, having been judiciously worked up, and that it could not be assumed that the altered plans for the meeting would reduce it. The moral is, he told Churchill: 'Leave Ireland alone in future.'[24] Churchill's meeting went ahead on 8 February at the Celtic Park Football Grounds – a nationalist area of west Belfast, and while hostile crowds gathered in the city centre and surrounded Churchill's car, the police and the thousands of additional troops sent from Dublin managed to ensure that there was no serious disorder. The crisis in Belfast was over – but not for long.

In Dublin, by contrast, there was no fear of disorder when elaborate arrangements were being made for a major demonstration that was to take place on 31 March in order to highlight the strength of the demand for Home Rule. Although the *Irish Times* reported that the crowds were not as great as had been expected, the whole affair seemed to have taken on something of a carnival atmosphere, with about seventy special trains bringing thousands of people from all parts of the country. The demonstration included a procession which began at the Mansion House, with numerous marching bands leading speakers to four large platforms, each 'strikingly decorated and festooned' in different parts of Sackville Street.[25] Robinson joined Maurice Headlam, the newly-appointed Treasury Remembrancer, and some of his own senior civil service colleagues to form a large party for lunch at the Imperial Hotel in Sackville Street. After their lunch, they sat in the sun on the hotel balcony watching the procession and the speeches made by John Redmond, Eoin MacNeill and Patrick Pearse. The party on the balcony, according to Headlam, 'seemed strongly unionist but not as a rule contemptuous'.[26] Robinson, who struck Headlam on this first meeting as a most intelligent man, gave it as his opinion that the farmers were frightened at the approach of Home Rule because of doubts about the continuation of land purchase arrangements. They also, according to Robinson, feared that without Irish members at Westminster, the importation of Canadian cattle would be allowed, thus ruining the Irish export trade.

Robinson's belief in January 1912 that the Orange leaders should have been ignored was soon proven to be entirely wide of the mark. Within the administration, he was of course not alone in adopting this view, or in completely underestimating the strength of the opposition in Ulster to Home Rule. The former Under-Secretary, Sir David Harrel, himself a northern protestant, told the cabinet in February that he did not think platform speeches in Ulster would materialise into deliberate and armed resistance to authority and he advised them that resistance would be kept 'within the bounds of political warfare'.[27] Sir J. B. Dougherty, the northern Presbyterian who had been Under-Secretary since 1908, was also of the same view at that stage. Even as late as August 1913 he still held that the Ulster unionists were engaged in a gigantic game of bluff.[28] Only a month after that, Joe Devlin assured ministers that the danger of civil war was 'grotesquely exaggerated',[29] and T. P. O'Connor MP, campaigning throughout Britain on behalf of the Irish Party, also attempted during 1913 to persuade his listeners that the unionist threat was an empty one.[30] However, a very different view of the temper of the working-men in the north who opposed Home Rule was held by others, including Sir Horace Plunkett who, as far back as 1904, had argued that no one should be under any illusion as to the account these men would give of themselves 'if called on to defend the cause of protestantism, liberty, and imperial unity as they understand it'.[31]

On 9 April 1912, Andrew Bonar Law, the new Conservative Party leader, addressed a large demonstration at Balmoral, near Belfast, and pledged the support of his party for Ulster resistance to Home Rule. In July, at a Blenheim Palace rally, he expressed his support for resistance in much stronger language, and in September, tens of thousands of unionists throughout Ulster signed the Solemn League and Covenant – pledging to resist Home Rule 'using all means which may be found necessary'. Throughout this period, Saunderson was keeping in touch with the situation on the ground in Ulster ('making my work fit in with some of Carson's reviews') and continued to meet and correspond with Lady Londonderry, urging her to put pressure on her associates to ratchet up the Anti-Home-Rule campaign. He was also sending her suggestions for publicity postcards and passing on scraps of information which he had picked up either from Robinson or from other sources in Dublin. On 6 June, having reported that Birrell was not as happy as he had been about the situation in Ulster, he hoped to find out more, as the Chief Secretary was to travel to Dublin a few days later and was to dine with 'my chief'. In December, he was again urging Theresa to 'stir up the Ulster people' – and 'no one can stir them up as well as you can' – because he had heard on absolutely reliable authority that the government were changing their view on the question of whether Ulster's opposition was really serious.[32]

Although the Home Rule Bill introduced in the House of Commons in April 1912 provided only for a limited measure of self-government for Ireland, it would have brought an end to the operations of the LGB as such. Under the bill, the making of laws relating to the services for which the board was responsible (except old age pensions) would be a matter for a new bi-cameral Irish Parliament. Moreover, unlike the 1886 and 1893 bills, the 1912 bill expressly provided that the administration of each of the Irish services would become the responsibility of one of a number of new departments operating under ministers who would be members of one or other of the houses of that parliament. While it is not clear whether Robinson and his senior colleagues had been consulted about these provisions, satisfactory terms to protect the interests of the staff of the LGB (and existing civil servants generally) were provided for. Staff were to continue in office, with the same tenure, terms and conditions as they already held, and with generous provision for compensation for removal from office, or for retirement within five years where duties had materially been altered. These terms had been negotiated by a widely representative General Committee of Civil Servants, chaired by A. R. Barlas, the LGB Secretary.[33] Following further representations and personal contact between Barlas and the parliamentary draftsman, amendments introduced at committee stage in the Commons provided for even better terms.[34] Barlas had been one of the LGB representatives on a large committee that had worked in 1893 to protect the position of civil servants in the event that the Home Rule Bill of that year became law.[35] On that occasion, Robinson's predecessor as Vice- President had led a delegation of high-ranking civil servants to meet Chief Secretary Morley to press for amendments to the bill, but in 1911–12, Robinson left it to Barlas and others to take the initiative.

Exclusion of Counties – or 'Home Rule within Home Rule'?

By the beginning of 1914, the Home Rule controversy had been raging for over two years and the bill had completed two circuits of the House of Commons and the House of Lords, as required by the Parliament Act. Before the introduction of the bill, and on a number of occasions in the following years, individual members of the cabinet had proposed that temporary exclusion or other special treatment should be provided for Ulster and had engaged in secret soundings and talks with Bonar Law, with Carson, and with leaders of the Irish Party. However, there was no public indication until the beginning of 1914 that the government as a whole – dependent as it was on the support in Parliament of Redmond and his party – had any intention of amending the bill to meet the opposition of the Ulster unionists and their supporters. Under the procedure provided for in the Parliament Act, the second reading was expected to be moved in the House of Commons for the third time when Parliament resumed in mid-February. As the government could count on sufficient support to carry the bill, it would then simply be a matter of submitting it to the King for signature with the expectation that it would quickly become law and be brought into operation no later than July 1915. However, London and Dublin newspapers were already carrying reports of concessions expected to be made to the Ulster unionists to meet their objections to the bill. There was speculation that a generous measure of administrative autonomy would be provided for the north, assuring effective control over all important local services and safeguards regarding appointments, while there was also speculation that the four north-eastern counties were to be excluded entirely from the Home Rule scheme. Birrell himself had believed from as far back as August 1911 that the Ulstermen were not bluffing: he told Churchill that their 'yells are genuine' and had suggested that temporary Ulster exclusion on a county-by-county option basis could be provided for – the first Liberal minister to suggest such a compromise, according to Patricia Jalland.[36] Nevertheless, and notwithstanding his private belief that a unitary solution was impossible, he adhered to the strategy of delaying a compromise. Throughout 1912 and 1913 he consistently maintained his public commitment to going on with the scheme provided for in the bill, without adulteration.[37] When exclusion of the four north-eastern counties was formally proposed by a rebel liberal back-bencher by way of committee stage amendment in the Commons in June 1912, Birrell spoke about the need for a very great deal of evidence from Ulster itself before such an approach could be considered.[38] However, in concluding the debate on the third reading of the bill in the following January, he left open the possibility of some compromise on the details, challenging the unionist opposition to make their proposals and to work with the government in finding a solution.[39] Then, in offering an assurance that 'we at any rate will be perfectly ready to consider any proposals you wish to make', he asked them to apply their minds to questions such as 'are you going to have your own Local Government Board' – in effect floating an idea that Asquith put forward in a confidential note to Carson in December 1913, and which came to be discussed as one of the elements of a Home-Rule-within-Home-Rule solution.[40]

In 1913 Birrell was receiving conflicting advice from Dublin on the Ulster issue. Harrel's view of the strength and danger of the northern opposition had completely changed in the course of 1912, and he was now advocating the exclusion of Ulster, notwithstanding the administrative complications, in order to improve the prospects for Home Rule in the rest of Ireland.[41] On the other hand, Dougherty – as late as August 1913 – was still expressing derisory views about unionist plans for resistance, while noting in a private letter to one of his friends that Birrell was a bit anxious about things and 'takes this gasconade more seriously than I am disposed to do'.[42] In November, after there had been 'some conversations under the seal of confidence between leading men', [i.e. between Asquith and Bonar Law][43] the options were again discussed by the cabinet and there appeared to be a majority in favour of temporary exclusion. However, despite the fact that he had just arranged for the submission to the cabinet of two memoranda, setting out details of the formidable strength of the Ulster Volunteers and of the arms and ammunition imported by them and their supporters,[44] Birrell still strongly opposed the principle of exclusion and, having submitted a letter of resignation, had to be forced by Asquith to carry on.[45]

Whether Birrell consulted Robinson as well as Dougherty and Harrel, or even kept him informed, as the cabinet debated temporary exclusion and other possible solutions to the northern dilemma between 1912 and 1914, can only be a matter of conjecture at this stage. Given the relationship that had developed between the two men since 1907, it seems reasonable to assume that he would have done so. The earliest relevant letter from Robinson which survives among Birrell's papers at the Bodleian Library certainly suggests that the two men had already been in contact on the issue, and on the options. In this private letter, hand-written in haste at his home in Dublin on Sunday 22 February 1914, a few days before the Cabinet deputed Birrell and Lloyd George to advise Redmond and Dillon of their intention to consider temporary exclusion of the four north-eastern counties, Robinson offered the firm view that exclusion was, tactically, an unsound proposition.[46] He put forward his own version of what the Foreign Secretary, Sir Edward Grey, had described in an October 1913 speech, as a 'Home-Rule-within-Home-Rule' solution:

> My belief is that if the Ulstermen accept exclusion, they will do so in the hope of being able to spill you on the working details, and they will succeed if you attempt to hitch them on to England, or to set up a separate executive for Ulster with a full set of departments. It would be much better to leave your Dublin departments as they are now, carrying out the government of the whole of Ireland, but with a chief secretary for Ulster, with a small department of his own in London and an office in Belfast.[47]

If this solution were adopted, Robinson went on, Dublin departments would work to, and take direction from, the new Ulster Chief Secretary on all matters affecting Ulster, and county court judges, resident magistrates and LGB inspectors for the north would be appointed by him, as well as a deputy inspector general of the RIC who would have control of the Ulster police. Moreover, private bills and provisional orders relating to Ulster counties could be submitted either to Westminster or to the Dublin Parliament, at the option of the proposers, leading to a situation in which Derry business would probably gravitate to Dublin, while Antrim business would go to London. 'All this may sound very grotesque', Robinson concluded, but 'I have thought it out and believe it could be worked and every difficulty surmounted'.[48] His scheme may to some extent have been motivated by self-interest, and by his hope of preserving intact the substantial LGB organisation which he had built up since 1898. It also reflected the desire to avoid – or minimise the effects of – partition, which was to be consistently and strongly expressed by him until 1922. His proposal was, nevertheless, a shrewd one, which had much to recommend it – by giving Ulster control over sensitive matters, it could be held out as an arrangement which would allay the fear of 'oppressive administration', which Carson had been articulating. If a proposal of this kind had been incorporated in the bill as originally introduced, Patricia Jalland has suggested that it would have been accepted by Redmond and Dillon, and would have undermined the most persuasive aspect of the unionist case.[49] However, the proposal came much too late, for the cabinet had already moved away from Home-Rule-within-Home-Rule solutions and decided in principle on 4 March to propose that any Ulster county should be allowed to opt for temporary exclusion from the jurisdiction of the proposed Parliament.

Defining a Border

Before March 1914, the public debate on exclusion, as well as the secret discussions between party leaders, had centred on the question of whether four, six or nine *complete* counties should be considered to make up, temporarily or permanently, a possible excluded area. On 5 March, however, when a press leak allowed the *Daily News* to prematurely publish the cabinet decision about temporary exclusion on a county-option basis, Robinson sent Birrell 'as you suggested' a scheme showing how an excluded area might be defined by reference to a grouping of rural districts rather than counties.[50] The scheme was based on 1911 census statistics of the catholic and non-catholic populations of the different rural districts in nine-county Ulster. The accompanying copy of a printed map of these rural districts (see Map 1 on page 177) was marked up by Robinson to show districts with catholic majorities shaded green and non-catholic districts in red. This implied, of course, that the traditional

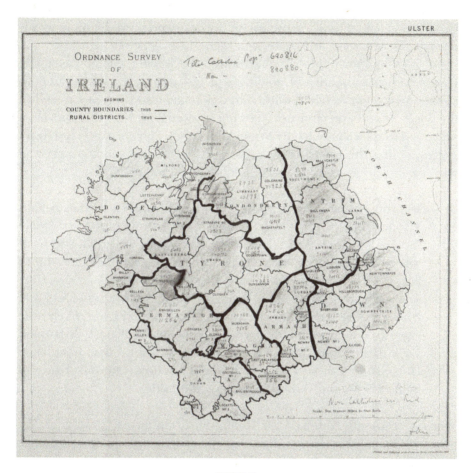

MAP 1

Map of rural districts sent by Henry Robinson to Chief Secretary Birrell on 5 March 1914 showing how a northern excluded area might be defined by reference to rural district boundaries; districts with catholic majorities were shaded green and non-catholic districts red *(The Bodleian Library, University of Oxford, Birrell Papers, MSS. Eng. c. 7034, f. 60)*. A full colour version of this map appears in the plate section between pages 240 and 241 as Plate 10.

equations of protestant = unionist and catholic = nationalist continued to apply. In a commentary on the map, Robinson pointed out that 'the rural districts where protestants predominate are a nice compact little block – Omagh is the chief outlying protestant district – and if you let those evenly divided districts such as Magherafelt come in or stay out by a vote, you could get a combination of administrative areas which could be managed'. Commenting on the idea of holding a plebiscite on exclusion, county by county, *throughout the whole* of Ireland, which had also been mentioned in the *Daily News* report and not knowing, presumably, that this had been suggested to the cabinet by the Prime Minister on 25 February,[51] Robinson suggested that the report 'may be all rot', but he was still concerned to warn against the risks inherent in holding an all-Ireland vote:

> You run a great danger of losing Cork and Dublin as well as Belfast. The nationalists will not be voting upon a straight issue of Home Rule or no Home Rule. The point actually put to Dublin and Cork will be 'with the four rich northern counties excluded, are you in favour of being under a so-called Home Rule Parliament or not'. The Larkinites, a numerous body in Dublin, are so furious with the Irish Party at having deserted them that they will very likely vote against coming under their control. Possibly William O'Brien and Cork might hold that the present state of things was better than Home Rule without Ulster; so it would not do to run the chance of Belfast, Cork and Dublin all being left outside.

Whether through contact with Robinson or otherwise, Walter Long, who was then in opposition, had some knowledge of the government's excluded area proposals and had serious reservations about them. He told Carson on 6 March that he 'knew for a fact that a messenger was sent from the cabinet the other day to the Irish Office for a map which they have there, giving the total population of the Ulster counties divided into protestants and catholics'. However, he believed that holding a plebiscite in each county would be an impossible proposal, and if counties side-by-side were to be under different forms of government, there would be such hopeless confusion that anything less than the six counties would not be practicable.[52] The government adhered to the decision concerning county-option which they had made on 4 March, although it is reasonable to conclude from Asquith's remarks in the House of Commons on 9 March that they may have considered Robinson's rural district scheme: Asquith told the House that they had considered whether the county was the best area for taking the poll, but had come to the view that, even though the county was not altogether satisfactory, 'any other alternative, such as the rural districts, would be less convenient in itself and less trustworthy in its results'.[53] He saw no major difficulty in administering a group of northern counties separately from the proposed Parliament and departments in Dublin, suggesting in particular that local government could be dealt with by the creation of 'an administrative board'. Failing agreement on any other approach, Asquith was forced to tell the House of Commons that the only practical way forward was to introduce an amending bill which would allow any of the Ulster counties or county boroughs to opt out for six years. It was clear from an early stage that this approach would not satisfy the unionists, and while the House of Commons continued to debate the original bill, desultory efforts were made by Asquith outside the House to settle the problem. Robinson was not impressed, however, by what he knew of some of these initiatives: having seen a newspaper report on 6 May that the Prime Minister was to seek the opinions of 'various leaders of thought in Ireland', including Lord MacDonnell, his old adversary, and Sir Horace Plunkett (who, to his mind, was like a red rag to Ulster people at that stage), his reaction, as conveyed to Birrell, was 'God help us! Has it come to this?'[54]

In parallel with the Prime Minister's consultations, further consideration was also being given – at least by Birrell – to the possible size and shape of an excluded area. On 6 May, the day after Asquith had met Bonar Law and Carson to discuss possible solutions, Robinson sent Birrell, at his urgent request, maps 'giving you my idea of the excluded area'[55] and two days later, Bonar Law was told privately that Birrell had begun the task of plotting a boundary between the excluded area and the rest of Ireland.[56] Robinson's scheme, he told Birrell, was not the Ulstermen's 'irreducible minimum, but on the other hand it goes rather further to meet them than you would quite like'. It was based 'on the location of the two sects as far as practicable, but there were geographical, administrative, financial and other considerations, such as rail and road communications'. The approach, however, was not altogether a scientific and objective one, in that it took account of 'the degree of obstreperousness of the rival sectarian factions on the border line'. Although there was no time to explain the scheme fully, Robinson assured Birrell that he 'could stand cross-examination pretty fairly on it'.

It is difficult to determine at this stage whether Robinson's second scheme was based on rural districts, poor law unions or a combination of the two. The map, which survives among Birrell's papers at the Bodleian Library (see Map 2 on page 180), is a relatively small-scale printed map of Ireland, showing county and union boundaries with a note in Robinson's

MAP 2

Map sent on 6 May 1914 by Henry Robinson to Chief Secretary Birrell, at his urgent request, giving him 'a rough idea' of an area (defined by reference to poor law union boundaries and coloured yellow) which might be excluded from Home Rule arrangements; this is likely to have been 'the Irish Office map' referred to by John Redmond in his note on the Buckingham Palace Conference of July 1914 *(The Bodleian Library, University of Oxford, Birrell Papers, MSS. Eng. c. 7034, f. 71)*. A full colour version of this map appears in the plate section between pages 240 and 241 as Plate 11.

handwriting showing the 'proposed excluded area coloured yellow'. This map, Robinson told Birrell, was 'only to give you a rough idea of the part I would exclude', but a larger-scale map of Ulster to which he referred is not included in the papers available at the Bodleian. The map that survives shows *union* boundaries but a tabular statement, which seems to have accompanied it, as well as Robinson's covering letter, suggests that this second scheme may have been based more on *rural districts* than unions. The map and tabular statement imply an excluded area, comprising the complete counties of Antrim, Londonderry and Tyrone; the county boroughs of Belfast and Londonderry; parts of the counties of Armagh, Down and Fermanagh, excluding two rural districts in each case (Newry No. 2 and Crossmaglen, Newry No. 1 and Kilkeel, and Clones No. 2 and Beleek); and bringing in two Donegal rural districts (Londonderry No. 2 and Strabane No. 2). As compared with a straightforward six-county scheme, all of this involved net reductions of just over 50,000 in the catholic population, and almost 31,000 in the non-catholic population, producing totals for the excluded area of 379,013 catholics and 799,573 non-catholics. Relying presumably on information received from Robinson, Edward Saunderson, who was still acting as Lady Londonderry's secret agent in Dublin, was able to report to her on 26 May that a map had been 'prepared and sent over to the cabinet, setting forth the rural districts in Ulster, which are predominantly protestant and that the map 'brings in a good slice of Donegal and excludes bits of Armagh and Fermanagh'.[57]

In hastily written notes on some of the details of his scheme, Robinson drew attention to the fact that he had omitted Crossmaglen and Newry No. 2 rural districts in County Armagh from the excluded area 'because Crossmaglen nationalists are about the warmest lot I know – we had hideous trouble with them in the bad times and they are largely in excess of the protestants in their corner of County Armagh'. He expected that Armagh unionists would be furious at the omission of Newry No. 2, but the nationalists were in a majority there and, besides, any alternative approach would be 'politically and administratively most troublesome'. On the other hand, he favoured leaving the County Fermanagh districts of Enniskillen and Lisnaskea in the excluded area, although they then had an aggregate catholic majority of 3,000; the protestant stake, as represented by rateable valuation was 'enormously preponderating', but 'there has been more money spent on armament and drilling here than in any part of the county, and these Enniskillen and Lisnaskea protestant farmers are the most blood-thirsty set of ruffians I know, and there would be no peace or settlement along the whole border line if these people were left out [of the excluded area]. They would stir up the Cavan and

Monaghan people and be an endless source of trouble to the [southern] Irish Parliament'.

Robinson's concern for a possible future southern parliament is worth noting. He did not seem to be concerned with the fact that a contrary argument could just as easily be made – that the catholic/nationalist majorities in Tyrone and Fermanagh would create problems for any future northern administration which would obviously be anathema to them. Dealing with the controversial areas in the north-west about which he had been 'much exercised in my mind', he suggested that the Strabane No. 2 and Londonderry No. 2 rural districts, where 'the sectarian populations were almost evenly balanced with a slight R.C. majority', should move from County Donegal to the excluded area because of the balance of convenience and advantage. He did admit that this was 'a line-ball case and one which might be used with advantage' in any subsequent negotiations. While it could be argued that Derry City with its catholic and nationalist majority should be omitted from the excluded area, he was unable to offer any good reason for not omitting it, except that it would be administratively impossible to separate 'the maiden city' from its parent county.

Having gone to the trouble of working out the detail of an excluded area scheme, Robinson assured Birrell that he had been thinking out the executive machinery which would be needed if the area were defined as he had suggested, and that he could see pretty clearly what needed to be done. In the last analysis, however, he held out no hope that any such scheme would satisfy the unionists: 'I expect you will find that the Ulstermen's minimum will be six entire counties, and no option.' He was, of course, proved to be correct in this. Schemes based on rural districts or poor law unions appeared to have been rejected when Asquith told the House of Commons on 25 May that the amending bill, which was to be introduced in the House of Lords, would embody county option as he had announced it on 9 March.[58] But although that bill was introduced on 23 June (and amended by the Lords on 8 July to provide for permanent exclusion of all Ulster), Asquith and Carson were still in touch in May and June about maps of a possible excluded area which 'cuts county boundaries'.[59] It seems reasonable to suggest that Robinson's maps were taken into account in this exercise when, as Asquith described it, 'there were comings and goings of negotiators, and long discussions of ministers', both before and after the introduction of the bill.[60] The maps would also have been significant when proposals were made to Redmond on 30 June by Lord Murray of Elibank, a former liberal chief whip, for an excluded area of 'roughly five counties',[61] and when Murray was authorised to make broadly similar proposals to Bonar Law and Carson at meetings on 1 and 15 July. These involved the omission of areas of south Armagh, south Fermanagh and south Down from the excluded area and the addition of a strip of Donegal.[62] After the last of these meetings, Asquith told Venetia Stanley (the young woman whom he adored and to whom he wrote almost daily from 1912 onwards) that Murray, who 'had been in confabulation with Carson', had called on him with 'a large supply of maps'. He also told Venetia that he had asked Murray to find out if Carson and his friends would treat if he made an offer based on an excluded area of Antrim, Derry and Down (excluding the catholic parts of the south), Armagh, again excluding the catholic south, North Fermanagh and with the possibility of a split Tyrone.[63]

Toiling around Muddy Byways

Robinson's maps – or copies of them – are likely to have been among those on the table at the Buckingham Palace conference in late July, when King George V made a last effort to facilitate a resolution of the border issue. According to Denis Gwynn's *History of Partition* (1950), which draws heavily on memoranda prepared contemporaneously by Redmond,[64] detailed maps showing the distribution of nationalists and unionists, presumably catholics and protestants, by poor law unions were in the hands of every member of the conference, one handed in by the nationalist side and another which had been prepared by the Irish Office. The nationalists' map seems likely to have been similar to the one which survives among Redmond's Papers in NLI – a printed map of Ireland showing county and union boundaries, with unions in Ulster coloured green to show those with catholic majorities, yellow to show those with protestant majorities and blue to show those 'with no majority' (see Map 3, page 184). A copy of the same printed map of Ireland, but showing a proposed excluded area shaded yellow, had been sent by Robinson to Birrell on 6 May (see Map 2, page 180). It is tempting to speculate that this may have been 'the Irish Office map' referred to by Redmond.

Before the conference, Redmond had been informed that the question of deciding on the area to be excluded on the basis of popular voting in poor law unions had been rejected by the cabinet for technical reasons (i.e. because the electors registered to vote at union level included women, who were still not entitled to vote at parliamentary elections). However, his note on the proceedings on the second day of the conference records that Asquith suggested that consideration should again be given to a division of Ulster on the basis of poor law unions.[65] Asquith then produced a map,

MAP 3

A map of Ireland similar to map 2 but showing unions in Ulster coloured green for those with catholic majorities, yellow for those with protestant majorities and blue for those 'with no majority'. This map, which survives among John Redmond's papers, is likely to have been the map presented by the nationalists at the Buckingham Palace Conference in July 1914 *(National Library of Ireland, John Redmond Papers, MS 15, 266).* A full colour version of this map appears in the plate section between pages 240 and 241 as Plate 12.

showing the religious persuasion of the population in each union – but, the note continues, it became quite apparent that no such arrangement would meet with the approval of the two sides. Asquith himself told Venetia Stanley that he and Lloyd George worked hard at the conference 'to get rid of the county areas altogether and proceed on poor law unions, which afford a good basis of give and take [but] both Irish lots' would have none of it.[66] Charles Hobhouse, then postmaster general, noted in his diary for the following day that the Prime Minister had given a similar report to the cabinet: he and Lloyd George had suggested 'division and concession in the debatable counties by poor law unions, as these gave truer geographical and religious boundaries'.[67] Bonar Law and Redmond separately recorded that any such scheme was ruled out completely as it would involve a system of swapping districts in different parts of Ulster, which was universally agreed to be an impossible thing.[68] James Lowther, Speaker of the House of Commons, who chaired the conference, recalled that while maps 'showing the boundaries of parishes, poor law unions, baronies, and every conceivable local government unit' in the counties of Tyrone and Fermanagh were examined, the difficulty of separating the protestant and catholic populations appeared insuperable, with large pockets of catholics in the midst of a protestant community and vice versa'.[69] For Asquith, the last day of the conference was a black-letter day for, having spent another hour and a half discussing maps and figures, the parties were 'always getting back to that most damnable creation of the perverted ingenuity of man – the County of Tyrone', which neither side would agree to divide.[70] The last word is best left to Churchill, who recorded that the cabinet meeting on 24 July again discussed the boundaries of Fermanagh and Tyrone, and the 'disposition of clusters of humble parishes' but, as he put it, 'while the cabinet toiled around the muddy byways of those counties in search of an exit from the deadlock, news of the Austro-Hungarian ultimatum to Serbia brought an end to the exercise and left the parishes of Fermanagh and Tyrone', in Churchill's memorable phrase, 'to fade back into the mists and squalls of Ireland'.[71]

Robinson's approach to the problem of determining a north–south border was in sharp contrast to that of the Boundary Commission, which sat between October 1924 and December 1925 and which, under article XII of the Treaty, was required to determine the north–south boundary 'in accordance with the wishes of the inhabitants, so far as may be compatible with economic and geographic conditions'.[72] Robinson's initial ideas in March 1914 were based on rural districts, while his subsequent proposals were again based on administrative areas – primarily poor law unions. It seems from the notes made by Redmond and Asquith that the Buckingham Palace conference concentrated exclusively on these relatively large areas. The Boundary Commission, however (or more accurately, its chairman) decided that, for the purpose of determining the wishes of the inhabitants, it should work on the basis of 'the smallest area which can fairly be entitled ... to be considered separately and with regard to which separate data are available'. It expressly rejected the use of poor law unions (which had been supported by the government of the Free State as a basis for plebiscites). This was because, as pointed out in a memorandum prepared by the Chairman, the union was not the smallest administrative area in the north, and there was no evidence of a general correspondence between the unions and market areas as there had been, at least in theory, when the unions were established in the late 1830s.[73] It found that the smallest areas, in respect of which separate data was available, were the district electoral divisions, only about half of which, in the border counties, had populations of more than 1,000, and that data could be obtained, if necessary, for the numbers of catholics and protestants in each of the townlands which made up these divisions. Thus, Robinson's broad-brush approach and, his treatment of each rural district as an indivisible unit so as to provide 'a combination of administrative areas which could be managed'[74] was set aside on the grounds that this could mean treating administrative considerations as a new factor superior to the wishes of some inhabitants. This decision of the commission was, of course, to have major implications, particularly for the nationalist populations of Tyrone and Fermanagh, in the decades that followed.

'You will have a Real Good Chance of Home Rule by Consent After the War'

What may have been the last of Robinson's letters to Birrell on the Home Rule issue was written on 18 August. This was two weeks after the outbreak of the First World War, and at a time when private discussions between the government and Conservative Party leaders on the fate of the Home Rule Bill were in progress in London. 'Could you not bring in a bill delaying the presentation of it [the original bill] to the King till after the war?', was his suggestion, adding that a delay would not cause the National Volunteers to rise up, because catholic hatred and terror of the Germans was 'something incredible', based on reports that were already circulating about the burning of villages and the conduct of German soldiers in Belgium, which was worse than that of savages. He went on to suggest that the situation would be very different after the war:

I really believe, and most rational protestants believe, that the trials, which protestants and catholics will have to go through shoulder to shoulder, the help they will have to give [one] another in relief arrangements, their comradeship for purposes of defence, will do so much to destroy the hatreds and allay the fears which are keeping them now apart, that you will have a real good chance of Home Rule by consent after the war, or if not, at all events, Home Rule to be settled on a business-like practical working spirit and not in a spirit of mutual hatred and distrust.... After the war you will have a golden opportunity of a real settlement of the eternal Irish question.[75]

While Robinson was writing to Birrell, Asquith was writing to Venetia Stanley about the options available for dealing with the Home Rule issue. Coincidentally, or otherwise, he stated his personal preference for the course advocated by Robinson – he felt that 'hanging up the Bill' rather than placing it on the statute book with a suspensory clause would be fairest to both parties, although he accepted that Redmond was likely to jib at this.[76] Preoccupied with reports from France and Belgium of military reverses and by defeatist reports from Sir John French, who was in command of the British Expeditionary Force, he was wishing by the end of August that 'we could submerge the whole lot of them [the Irish] and their island for, say ten years, under the waves of the Atlantic'.[77] By 9 September, however, after a meeting with Redmond and Dillon, he had reluctantly concluded that the bill would have to be enacted, but with its operation suspended until after the war, and that course was decided on in spite of Conservative Party protests.[78] In welcoming the Suspensory Bill which Asquith introduced in the House of Commons on 15 September, Redmond's comments on the likely post-war situation were remarkably similar to the views that Robinson had expressed to Birrell a few weeks earlier:

Catholic nationalist Irishmen and protestant unionist Irishmen from the North of Ireland will be fighting side by side on the battlefields on the continent, and shedding their blood side by side; and at home in Ireland, catholic nationalists and protestant Ulstermen will, I hope and believe, be found drilling shoulder to shoulder for the defence of the shores of their own country. The result of all that must inevitably be to assuage bitterness, and to mollify the hatred and misunderstanding which have kept them apart, and I do not think I am too sanguine when I express my belief that when the time has arrived ... we may have been able ... to come to an agreement amongst ourselves whereby we can suggest to the government an Amending Bill, which they can easily accept and ratify ...[79]

The Home Rule Bill was passed into law on 18 September 1914 and the Suspensory Act, which became law at the same time, provided that no steps should be taken to put the act into operation for twelve months or, if the war was not then ended, until such later date as might be fixed by order in council.[80] Controversy over an Irish settlement was then swept into the background and, as Asquith recorded it, 'for four years the mind and heart of the nation were concentrated on the gravest and most perilous task which has ever confronted a free people'.[81] But, while Patrick Buckland has suggested that the post-war situation foreseen by Robinson and Redmond might have become a reality if the atmosphere of 1914–16 had been allowed to continue – with southern unionist opinion broadly accepting Home Rule – subsequent events destroyed any prospect that the issue would be less difficult to resolve after the war than it had previously been.[82] By 1916, all was 'changed utterly', as W. B. Yeats saw it, and the unfortunate Birrell, instead of being able to seize Robinson's golden opportunity to settle the eternal Irish question, found 'ten of the best years of his life wasted'.[83]

NOTES

1   Christopher Lynch-Robinson, *The Last of the Irish R.M.s* (London, 1951), pp.166, 174.
2   *Irish Times*, 11 Dec. 1909.
3   Ronan Fanning, *Fatal Path* (London, 2013), p.30.
4   Patricia Jalland, *The Liberals and Ireland: The Ulster Question in British Politics to 1914* (Brighton, 1980), pp. 41–44.
5   Sir Henry Robinson, *Memories: Wise and Otherwise* (London, 1923), p.xi.
6   G. C. Duggan, draft of unpublished book *The Life of a Civil Servant*, NLI, Leon Ó Broin Papers, MS. 31,689.
7   Robinson to Birrell, 26 Jan. 1912, TNA, CO 906/18/1.
8   *Report of the Committee on Irish Finance*, HC 1912–13 [Cd. 6153]; *Minutes of Evidence etc*, HC 1913 [6799]; Patricia Jalland, 'Irish Home Rule Finance: A Neglected Dimension of the Irish Question, 1910–14', *IHS* xxiii, No. 91 (May 1983), pp.233–253.
9   John Kendle, *Ireland and the Federal Solution* (Montreal, 1989), p.141.
10   *Hansard* V, 52, 28 Apr. 1913, 804–05.
11   *Irish Independent*, 17 May 1913.
12   Robinson to Birrell, 5 Mar. 1914, Oxford, Bodleian Library, Birrell Papers, MS. Eng. c. 7034, f. 55–59.
13   *Irish Times*, 26 Jan. 1912.
14   Robinson to Birrell, 26 Jan. 1912, TNA, CO 906/18/1.

15 Redmond had dismissed 'orange bellowings' as 'insolent bluff' (*Roscommon Messenger*, 27 Jan. 1912).

16 Robinson to Birrell, 26 Jan. 1912, TNA, CO 906/18/1.

17 Alvin Jackson, *Colonel Edward Saunderson* (Oxford, 1995), p.235.

18 Diane Urquhart, 'Pillar of Unionism: The Politics of Theresa, Sixth Marchioness of Londonderry', in *From the United Irishmen to Twentieth-Century Unionism: A Festschrift for A.T.Q. Stewart* (Dublin, 2004), p.114.

19 Diane Urquhart offers this as a possibility in *The Ladies of Londonderry* (London, 2007), p.239, note 195.

20 Saunderson to Lady Londonderry, 1 Feb. 1912, PRONI D 2846/1/7/46.

21 Saunderson to Lady Londonderry, 7 Feb. 1912, PRONI D 2846/1/7/47.

22 Andrew Scholes, *The Church of Ireland and the Third Home Rule Bill* (Dublin, 2009), pp.53–57.

23 Robinson to Birrell [no date but probably late January 1912], TNA, CO 906/18/1.

24 Birrell to Churchill, 28 Jan. 1912, TNA, CO 906/18/1.

25 *Irish Times*, 29 Mar. and 1 Apr. 1912.

26 Maurice Headlam, *Irish Reminiscences* (London, 1947), pp.30–31.

27 Sir David Harrel, Memo. for the use of the cabinet, Feb. 1912, Oxford, Bodleian Library, Asquith Papers 38, cited in Timothy Bowman, *Carson's Army* (Manchester, 2007), p.34; Pauric Travers, *Settlements and Divisions Ireland 1870–1922* (Dublin, 1988), p.129.

28 Letter of 15 Aug. 1913 from Dougherty to Armour, PRONI, Armour Papers, D 1792/A/1/1/17.

29 *Irish News*, 25 Sept. 1913.

30 Erica S. Doherty, 'Ulster Will Not Fight', in Gabriel Doherty (ed.), *The Home Rule Crisis, 1912–14* (Cork, 2014, pp.102–117.

31 Horace Plunkett, *Ireland in the New Century* (London, 1904), p.86–87.

32 Saunderson to Lady Londonderry, 10 Mar., 6 June and 10 Dec. 1912 and 10 Aug. 1913, Durham County Record Office, Londonderry Papers, D/Lo/C 672.

33 Martin Maguire, *The Civil Service and the Revolution in Ireland, 1912–38* (Manchester, 2008), pp.9–17.

34 Irish Civil Service Provisions under the Government of Ireland Bill 1912, TNA, TS 18/235.

35 Supplementary statement on behalf of the permanent civil servants of the Crown serving in Ireland, with suggested amendments of the Government of Ireland Bill, 1893, NLI, Ir. 3511 c. 11.

36 Jalland, *The Liberals and Ireland*, pp.58–59.

37 Fanning, *Fatal Path*, pp.90–91, 351–52.

38 *Hansard* V, 39, 11 Jun. 1912, 774.

39 *Hansard* V, 46, 16 Jan. 1913, 2404.

40 Asquith to Carson, 23 Dec. 1913 and enclosed note, reproduced in Ian Colvin, *The Life of Lord Carson II* (London, 1934), pp.264–67.

41 Jalland, *The Liberals and Ireland*, pp.110 and 135.

42 Letter of 15 Aug. 1913 from Dougherty to Armour, PRONI, Armour Papers, D 1792/A/1/1/17.

43 H. H. Asquith, *Memories and Reflections I* (London, 1928), p.205.

44 Further Notes on the Movement in Ulster, Nov. 1913, TNA, CAB 37/117/83; Further Notes from Ulster, Dec. 1913, CAB/37/117/85.

45 Jalland, *The Liberals and Ireland*, pp.170, 174–75.

46 Edward David (ed.), *Inside Asquith's Cabinet: From the Diaries of Charles Hobhouse* (London, 1977), pp. 161–62.

47 *Glasgow Herald*, 28 Oct. 1913.

48 Robinson to Birrell, 22 Feb. 1914, Oxford, Bodleian Library, Birrell Papers, MS. Eng. c. 7034, f. 39–40; a typed version of part of the letter (at f. 41) may have been produced for circulation to cabinet colleagues.

49 Jalland, *The Liberals and Ireland*, pp.69–70.

50 Robinson to Birrell, 5 Mar. 1914, Oxford, Bodleian Library, Birrell Papers, MS. Eng. c. 7034, f. 55–59.

51 David, *Hobhouse Diaries*, p.162.

52 Long to Carson, 6 Mar. 1914 reproduced in Colvin, *Carson*, pp.290–291.

53 *Hansard* V, 59, 9 Mar.1914, 914.

54 Robinson to Birrell, 6 May 1914, Oxford, Bodleian Library, Birrell Papers, MS. Eng. c. 7034, f. 67–70.

55 Ibid.

56 Alvin Jackson, *Home Rule: An Irish History, 1800–2000* (London, 2003), p.137.

57 Saunderson to Lady Londonderry, 26 May 1914, quoted in Colvin, *Carson*, pp.399–400.

58 *Hansard* V, 63, 25 May 1914, 80.

59 Colvin, *Carson*, pp.398–99, 407, 410; H. H. Asquith, *Letters to Venetia Stanley* (Oxford, 1982), letters 78 and 79, 11 and 14 June 1914.

60 Asquith, *Memories* II, pp.2–4.

61 Redmond memorandum, printed in Denis Gwynn, *The History of Partition* (Dublin, 1950), pp.105–106.

62 R.J.Q. Adams, *Bonar Law* (London, 1999), p.163.

63 Asquith, *Stanley Letters*, letter 97 of 15 July 1914.

64 Gwynn, *The History of Partition*, pp.12, 116–125.

65 Typescript memoranda, 'Home Rule Conference', dictated by John Redmond, 21–24 July 1914, NLI, MS 15,257/3.

66 Asquith, *Stanley letters*, letter 102, 22 July 1914.

67 David, *Hobhouse Diaries*, p.175.

68 Redmond papers, NLI, MS 15,257/3; Memorandum prepared by Bonar Law on 22 July 1914, cited in John D. Fair, *British Interparty Conferences* (Oxford, 1980), p.179.

69 James William Lowther, Viscount Ullswater, *A Speaker's Commentaries* (vol. II) (London, 1925), pp.162–4.

70 Asquith, *Stanley Letters*, letters 102 and 103, 22 and 24 July 1914.

71 Winston S. Churchill, *The World Crisis 1911–1918* (new edn) (London, 1938), p.155.

72 Geoffrey Hand (ed.), *Report of the Irish Boundary Commission 1925* (Shannon, 1969).

73 *Boundary Commission Report*, Annex to Chapter III, Part I, Chairman's Memorandum on Article XII.

74   Robinson to Birrell, 5 Mar. 1914, Oxford, Bodleian Library, Birrell Papers, MS. Eng. c. 7034, f. 55–59.

75   Robinson to Birrell, 18 Aug. 1914, Oxford, Bodleian Library, Birrell Papers, MS. Eng. c. 7034, f. 140–144.

76   Asquith, *Stanley Letters*, letter 124, 18 Aug. 1914.

77   Asquith, *Memories* II, p.29.

78   Asquith, *Stanley Letters*, letter 148, 9 Sept. 1914.

79   *Hansard* V, 66, 15 Sept. 1914, 907–908.

80   The Suspensory Act 1914, 4 & 5 Geo. 5, ch.88, 18 Sept. 1914.

81   Asquith, *Memories* I, p.185.

82   Patrick Buckland, *Irish Unionism One: The Anglo-Irish and the New Ireland, 1885–1922* (Dublin, 1972), p.38.

83   Robinson, *Memories*, p.241.

CHAPTER IX

Booting Out a Weak and Incompetent Lot

'Old Dougherty' is Finally Replaced – But Not by Robinson

The development of the Home Rule/Ulster crisis underlined the weaknesses within the Irish executive as well as the lack of reliable information and assessments on the Ulster unionists' plans and intentions.[1] 'Old Dougherty', as Asquith referred to him, had been an inactive and easy-going Under-Secretary since 1908, and although he seems to have made no real contribution to the evolution of policy, he was allowed to continue in office long after normal retirement age. Arthur Norway, who came to Dublin to head the Irish Postal Service in 1912, found that Dougherty was 'a man of supine temperament and narrow, if capable, ideas, to whom one would not look for quick and resolute action on the sudden appearance of a public danger'.[2] His tenure was marked by caution and inaction, according to G. C. Duggan, who worked under him at the Castle from 1911 to 1914.[3] By contrast to this inactivity, the various submissions and suggestions which Robinson volunteered to Birrell in the 1912–14 period, even if they were not all acted on, were noteworthy. The indications are that he may have been the only official within the Dublin administration who attempted to make any contribution to strategic policy formation during that difficult period.

As far back as December 1909, when Dougherty reached the age of 65, one of the LGB inspectors told John Dillon that it was being stated in official circles that Birrell had decided to appoint Robinson as Under-Secretary.[4] The grant of a service extension to Dougherty, however, brought that speculation to an end. In August 1910, when Dougherty was awarded a KCB 'altogether unexpectedly', he believed that it was Birrell who had put him forward for the honour and he received yet another distinction – a KCVO – in July 1911, apparently in recognition of the successful organisation of the royal family's visit to Ireland.[5] With his two years of extended service due to expire in November 1911, Birrell asked him early that year to continue because, his friend, J. B. Armour, believed, 'they have nobody to put in his place' and because he had acted as mediator between Lord Lieutenant Aberdeen and Birrell.[6] Some months later, however, Armour was worried that severe criticism of Dougherty in the *Northern Whig* might be part of a campaign to get him to resign as it was being said that 'the government intended to appoint Sir Henry Robinson, an incorrigible tory, as his successor'.[7] In 1912, a few months after the Home Rule Bill had been introduced at Westminster, there was fresh speculation that Robinson might be about to replace Dougherty. The *Irish Independent* carried a report in July that Dougherty's resignation was imminent and suggested that his successor would be either Robinson or Max Sullivan Green, who had worked briefly as an LGB inspector in 1907 and was at the time serving as private secretary to Lord Lieutenant Aberdeen.[8] The report drew an instant response from Sarah Cecilia ('Celia') Harrison, the well-known painter and social campaigner who had been elected as the first woman member of Dublin Corporation six months earlier. In a letter to the editor of the *Independent*, Harrison argued that Robinson's presence in a high official position would be a difficulty, and a danger, in the new Ireland, although he was a distinguished personality and a man of brilliant powers who had served British ministers faithfully and well. He was, however, a past master in the application of the 'divide and conquer' principle and 'the brilliant incarnation of English (mis)government in Ireland'. While he deserved recognition and reward, this should take the form of an English peerage rather than promotion to Dublin Castle.[9]

In the event, Dougherty continued in office until October 1914, when he retired, aged 70. This was shortly after the publication of the report of the Royal Commission on the Howth Gun Running, which found him to be 'free from blame' for the incidents which led to the deaths of three civilians at Bachelors Walk on 26 July, when the military opened fire on a crowd.[10] However, his fate had been sealed several months before that verdict was reached: following what Asquith described as 'a real rough and tumble' adjournment debate on the incident in the Commons on 27 July, during which Dougherty had been criticised by several members,[11] the Prime Minister confided to Venetia Stanley the following day that:

The state of things in Dublin is still far from agreeable and I am tempted to regret that I didn't take the 'clean cut' six months ago, and insist upon the booting out of Aberdeen, Dougherty, Ross, Chamberlain and the whole crew. A weaker and more incompetent lot were never in charge of a leaky ship in stormy weather, and poor Birrell's occasional and fitful appearances at the wheel do not greatly improve matters.[12]

Later that day, Asquith had a meeting at Westminster with Redmond, Dillon, Lloyd George and Birrell at which he pointed out how the Commons debate 'had illustrated the need of overhauling Dublin Castle and especially of replacing old Dougherty ... by a younger man'. Having canvassed various names, Lt Col Sir Matthew Nathan 'found the most favour', and Asquith decided to sound him out immediately as to his willingness to take up the position.[13] By early August, a formal decision to appoint Nathan had been made.[14]

'A Fresh Mind and No Party or Sectarian Prejudices'

Nathan took up duty as Under-Secretary on 12 October 1914. He had served for almost twenty years in the army, followed by nine years as a colonial governor, two years as secretary of the Post Office and three years as Chairman of the Board of Inland Revenue. The value of this experience was acknowledged in an *Irish Times* editorial but the journal asked, not unreasonably, why an Irishman had not been appointed to supervise the implementation of the Home Rule legislation and to introduce a new system of administration.[15] Robinson found Nathan to be a hard worker who viewed Irish departments and Irish officials with a fine Semitic scorn and a kind of patient tolerance, but did not take any of the heads of departments into his confidence.[16] Nevertheless, he came to have a high regard for Nathan, and when a bitterly critical leader in the *Irish Independent* suggested that the country was to be ruled and despoiled by the Under-Secretary, and that his appointment had shown an extraordinary contempt for the people of Ireland,[17] he was prompted to write 'I blush for my country after reading the *Independent* leader about you. What must you think of us?'[18]

It was Nathan's practice after an interview with an official or other individual to commit to writing his recollection of everything that had passed at the meeting. This practice is reflected in the survival among his papers of three bound volumes comprising a total of some 1,000 typescript pages of brief – generally one-page – memoranda of these interviews.[19] It is clear from these papers that Robinson was a regular caller at Nathan's office in the Castle, sometimes on his own initiative and sometimes at Nathan's request, and that their discussions ranged over individual items of LGB business, as well as the board's dealings with the Treasury, issues arising between the board and other public departments and offices in Dublin, and the state of the country generally. But while Nathan's approach was a more interventionist one than that of his immediate predecessor, there is nothing to suggest that this gave rise to any friction between the two men or that Nathan attempted to over-rule actions or decisions of the board, or to interpose his authority between Robinson and Birrell. In submitting the text of the board's annual report for 1914–15 to Nathan (who was, at least nominally, a member of the board), Robinson rather pointedly told him that Birrell had already read it all but he would still be very proud if the Under-Secretary 'could see his way to give us the moral support of your signature to this record of our year's work'. Nathan complied immediately, although he made it clear that he was not to be taken as tied to the board's views on certain points.[20]

Robinson took the unusual step of inviting Nathan to attend a meeting of the LGB to discuss particular issues in May 1915, and on another occasion Nathan himself suggested that he would be willing to attend a meeting to discuss an issue which the two men agreed was an important and sensitive one.[21] More than once, Nathan appears to have taken action to resolve disputes between the LGB and other public departments. In April 1915, for example, when his intervention appeared to succeed in resolving a dispute between the board and the National Health Insurance Commissioners, Robinson told him that he was a magician: 'I had given up Glynn [chairman of the commission] in despair as a bad job. I found him so peevish and unreasonable; but your *via media*, which he seems to have accepted, should put an end to all differences between his department and mine for all time and I hope he will now shake hands.'[22] Later that month, in congratulating Nathan on the outcome of another of his initiatives, he told him that his success was due to the fact that he had 'come with a fresh mind and no party or sectarian prejudices'.[23]

Some of Robinson's letters advising Nathan on the handling of various issues are quite amusing, and suggest that the two men were at ease with one another – even if at times the letters illustrate the rather cynical and sardonic attitude adopted by Robinson and his sometimes derisive attitude to women. In November 1914, only two weeks after he had taken up duty, Nathan decided to chair the first meeting of a women's employment advisory committee. He was warned by Robinson that his position 'will be akin to that of a super-dreadnought, surrounded by submarines: you may expect an explosion whichever way you turn'. Robinson therefore suggested that Nathan should merely state the functions of the committee and advise the members that any points on which they required further information should be addressed to the LGB, which was to provide a secretary for the committee.[24] Before Nathan met another deputation of women in March 1916, Robinson told him that he hadn't the remotest idea what these good ladies wanted and the only thing he could suggest was that he 'should sit tight and hear what they have to say and don't believe everything or promise anything until you have verified it'. One of the women, he warned, 'was a rather clever and attractive lady, and she knows it. It is my firm conviction that her chief reason for her visit to you is that she intends you to know it also'. He would need to be careful of another of the women who was 'a tartar, a real fighting suffragette' who would 'chuck an inkpot at you as soon as look at you'. And, for good measure, Nathan, who never married, was warned that among Irish ladies generally 'there is a most perfect and outspoken unanimity as to your personal charm and sterling worth. Hence, these interviews and deputations will grow and grow and increase until some Dark Rosaleen ultimately annexes you for her very own'.[25]

The End of the Aberdeens

Robinson was pleased when, six months after Dougherty's retirement, Lord Lieutenant Aberdeen and Lady Aberdeen were finally forced by Birrell and Asquith to leave Dublin after a term of office of more than nine years. He recorded with obvious pleasure that their final departure from the city in February 1915 was not marked by any crowd in the streets or by any demonstration whatever.[26] His dislike of the Aberdeens arose not from their support of a Home Rule policy – something which caused them to be distrusted, snubbed and even ridiculed by most unionists as well as by nationalists – but from their regular and inappropriate interference in the business of the LGB. In his memoirs, he described them as 'an earnest, kindly, well-intentioned couple' and was willing to admit that many of Lady Aberdeen's schemes were 'generally excellent', that her intentions 'were of the very highest' and that her work for public health reform was meritorious. But, because he believed that she loved power and patronage and wanted to direct and dominate the LGB, his overall assessment of her was a critical one:

> She had too many irons in the fire and attempted too much, and in her desire for power, influence and patronage, she interfered with

public departments in matters for which she had no responsibility, and in a manner which led to much unpleasantness. She was surrounded with advisers who gave way to her in everything, and never liked the risk of offending her by warning her of financial and administrative dangers in her schemes. Those who did not yield at once to her proposals were taboo, and I was unfortunate enough to be one of these, and had constant disputes with her ... I never ceased to regret that she was not better advised.[27]

Robinson was not alone in his dislike of Lady Aberdeen's activities. She and her husband irritated Birrell to such an extent that communication between them practically ceased and 'a state of armed neutrality was maintained'.[28] He told Asquith during the Dublin Lockout in 1913 that the Aberdeens 'won't be left out of anything for a moment. It is a capital disaster their being here at this crucial time'.[29] As Robinson recalled it, Birrell found Lady Aberdeen to be 'rather exhausting', the constant friction between the LGB and her Women's National Health Association bored him, and he realised that the board could not be subordinated to her 'voluntary and irresponsible' organisation. A bitterly critical editorial in the *Irish Times* in September 1912 complained that, from the point of view of local government, the Aberdeens' influence had 'a demoralising influence', had injuriously affected some important public services and had interrupted the traditional conduct of official life. Her Association had become a vast power in the land and its influence had pervaded every government department and threatened to disorganise more than one of them.[30] A biography by her daughter Marjorie conceded that Lady Aberdeen 'should have taken care to keep on the right side' of someone as powerful as Robinson, on whose good graces depended the smooth working of her schemes.[31] A more recent biographer, however, is more critical of Robinson, concluding that some of her work was met by:

official obstructiveness – a combination of bureaucracy and personal animosity, especially from Sir Henry Robinson ... [who] regarded her as an interfering amateur, and she regarded him as an obstructive bureaucrat. He was not a man to be steamrolled, even by someone as imperious as Ishbel and it was not, apparently, in her nature to use flattery or coaxing or even straightforward diplomacy.[32]

Clashes between the two were recalled by a senior English civil servant, Sir Arthur Salter:

Her ample form firmly seated at one side of the table and at the other Sir Henry Robinson, sharp-witted, lean, wiry; opposite in build, alike in determination … they reminded him of a torpedo destroyer in action against a battleship; or in a more abstract metaphor, of the possible fate of any object – say Birrell – placed at the point of impact between the immovable mass and the irresistible force.[33]

Baron Wimborne 'Must Not Dance on my Platform'

For months before the eventual departure of the Aberdeens, Birrell had been anxious to find an Irish peer who could be appointed as lord lieutenant – someone with a historic name who lived on his Irish estates and had not taken any strong line in politics. Birrell accepted Robinson's suggestion that the qualifications of Mervyn Wingfield, 8th Viscount Powerscourt, seemed to fit these requirements like a glove. Robinson wrote privately to Powerscourt in October 1914, mentioning that he had suggested him to Birrell as a possible lord lieutenant, and having been authorised by Birrell to 'draw him discreetly', he met him at the Kildare Street Club, and put it to him that he might allow his name to go forward. Powerscourt, however, declined on the grounds that he could not afford the expense involved.[34] Lord Wimborne was then selected to replace Aberdeen, but when he arrived to take up duty in February 1915, there was already some concern that he might be disposed to interfere to an unacceptable extent in the business of government as the Aberdeens had done.[35] This led Birrell, Nathan and Robinson to conspire together to keep him occupied in innocuous activity. 'He must not dance on my platform', Birrell told Nathan on 21 February, adding that Robinson had already been introduced to the new man 'and I can see [that he] initiates a campaign of his own … a tour is always Sir Henry's recipe and very agreeable it is too'.[36] Birrell agreed that a tour for Wimborne should be arranged, but felt that Robinson 'need not appear in this first crusade' but might make arrangements for a visit by Wimborne to Belfast 'as he alone can do through the machinery of the LGB'.[37] He felt that it would be a pity not to have Robinson with Wimborne in the West but, if he were to join the tour, Max Green or some well-known nationalist 'of social girth' should be there too.[38] When a tour was decided on in early March, Robinson suggested to Birrell that it might not be politic that he himself should take part, presumably because, with Home Rule already on the statute book, someone as closely associated in the public mind with the established regime as he was might not be seen to be an acceptable guide for the new lord lieutenant. Birrell agreed with this, but requested that Robinson should assist Nathan in preparing 'the kind of tour which will combine instructive interest and promote good feeling'. Then, as Robinson put it to Nathan, having made all the arrangements regarding the itinerary and hospitality, 'I should retire gracefully to my shell and leave you to tour around with or without an entourage of officials, which may appear to you as likely to give a sunburstry atmosphere to the procession as foreshadowing the dawn of Home Rule.'[39] In April, when another tour was suggested, Robinson told Nathan that as the lord lieutenant would be a long time in Ireland 'it is not necessary to give him too large a dose of hospitals and institutions at the start'. He had therefore selected a few that were not too far from Dublin, including the Central Reception Unit for Belgian refugees at Dunshaughlin Workhouse.[40]

Birrell – the Reluctant Survivor

The replacement of Dougherty and Aberdeen between October 1914 and February 1915 meant that Birrell, as Chief Secretary, was the only major figure who remained in place in the Irish administration, even though he had pressed Asquith on a number of occasions to replace him. Contemporary accounts agree that Birrell spent less time than ever in Ireland from 1912 onwards while his wife, Eleanor (widow of Lionel Tennyson, elder son of the Poet Laureate), to whom he was devoted, suffered from an inoperable brain tumour, which led to insanity and to her eventual death in March 1915. Robinson was happy to continue his association with Birrell as he considered him to be an ideal Chief Secretary who – if judged on the basis of his legislative work between 1907 and 1912 – would rank higher than any of his predecessors, except perhaps Gerald Balfour, having secured the enactment of no fewer than fifty-six 'important' acts of Parliament.[41] And, unlike one of his ministerial colleagues who considered Birrell an incompetent administrator whose sole concern in dealing with public matters was whether or not the Irish Party would accept them, Robinson admired how his chief managed the relationship with the party.[42] In particular, he considered Birrell's success in having the Land Act 1909 enacted to be a magnificent achievement: no unionist government would have dared to bring in a measure of the kind, and for a liberal minister to do so was a feat of statesmanship, which could only be realised by those who understood the forces and the strength of feeling working against him.[43] He appreciated the speed at which Birrell came to conclusions and dealt with papers submitted to him, and the fact that he always defended the LGB in the House of Commons 'through thick and thin'.

Writing about Birrell in his memoirs, Robinson recorded that 'the further he got away from Dublin Castle the more his spirits rose' and he was happier at Recess than anywhere else.[44] In his own memoir, *Things Past Redress* (published posthumously in 1937), Birrell wrote about the pleasure he derived from his many western tours: 'I always found it hard to refuse any opportunity that presented itself of jumping into a motor-car, with my wife by my side, and rushing across Ireland under the skilful and instructive guidance of our friend, Sir Henry Robinson, who knew every road in the whole country.'[45] He told Nathan in February 1915 that a tour of Ireland with Sir Henry was very agreeable: 'My wife and I and Sir Henry have been in every county in Ireland and our motors have carried us over higher passes and along rougher roads than ever could be conceived.' A month later, shortly after the death of his wife, he was planning a short visit to Dublin, after which he intended to 'disappear to the country with Sir Henry Robinson'.[46] Years later, after both his wife and Robinson had died, Birrell still treasured memories of his visits to the West. He wrote to his former private secretary, Andrew Magill, that: 'I often in my dreams visit Connemara and the mountains of Kerry but never Dublin Castle or the Lodge', and 'I should like to see Achill Sound again, but I do not suppose I ever shall. I should feel dull without my wife and Sir Henry Robinson to drive the motor. To recapture former experiences is impossible.'[47]

The Informal Conference on Irish Transfer Orders

In January 1915 Nathan decided to set about making preparations for the coming into operation of the Home Rule Act, even though, in light of the Suspensory Act and the stalemate on the Western Front, planning for the implementation of new governmental arrangements did not then seem to be a matter of great urgency. Initially, with the assistance of his private secretary, Gaston Pierre Kurten, a 26-year-old Londoner whom he had brought with him from the Board of Inland Revenue, he secretly began work on the preparation of memoranda setting out in detail the functions of the existing Irish departments, boards and offices, and proposing how these functions might be organised and administered in due course by the departments which were to be set up by the lord lieutenant under the 1914 Act.[48] Then, beginning on 17 February, and with the approval of the Prime Minister,[49] he held a series of five meetings with the Irish Party leaders in an effort to reach agreement on the number of departments and their titles, the functions and duties to be assigned to each of them, and the legal steps required to give effect to the new arrangements. Portrayed somewhat extravagantly in Kurten's detailed minutes of the meetings as the *Informal Conference on Irish Transfer Orders in Council*, the discussions proceeded on the basis of papers and suggestions submitted by Nathan.[50] At the first meeting held in Dillon's house at North Great Georges Street, Dublin, and attended only by Dillon, Redmond and Nathan, it was agreed 'in view of the necessity of keeping the proceedings of the conference strictly secret', that representatives of departments and offices should not be asked to attend future meetings but that their opinions should be obtained 'by formulating questions to them'. Two of the subsequent meetings were also held at Dillon's house, although one breakfast meeting in March and one other meeting were held at Nathan's lodge in the Phoenix Park in order, as he put it, 'to break through the evil tradition of nationalists not going there'.[51] In the months which followed, the Irish Party's financial and economic expert, J. J. Clancy MP, was allowed to attend the meetings at the request of Redmond and Dillon, and the parliamentary draftsman, Francis Greer, travelled from London to attend some of them also. Greer also began work on the drafting of the orders in council and the adaptation of enactments orders which would be necessary, although he complained of the difficulty of carrying out this work without broaching the subject with the departments concerned but which he had been precluded from doing.

At an early stage, Nathan advised Birrell of his proposals for new departments and reported that 'it was amusing how Redmond had admitted – with perfect truth as well as candour – his entire ignorance of Irish government'.[52] In response, Birrell remarked in a letter of 21 February that 'the dead secrets of the Castle, when unfolded to the founders of the Land League, will seem very flat', but felt it was 'a great thing to get people to discuss even the machinery of civil government'. He stressed, however, that the work should proceed informally on the basis of 'casual conversations between interested parties', and that the results should be kept in as few hands as possible because 'if it gets about that a secret committee is in weekly session to arrange for Home Rule, there will be a silly rumpus'. He was worried in particular about the participation of Clancy – 'the most soporific talker I ever slept under' – who was quite unfit, in his view, to be trusted with the custody of secret documents and was known to have left such documents on a London omnibus on a previous occasion.[53] Nathan took this warning seriously, telling Dillon a few days later that he would not send copies of documents to Clancy 'in view of the facilities for their disposal afforded by the Dublin Tramways'.[54] Birrell seemed to be having second thoughts about the whole exercise when he wrote again to Nathan on 23 February – only two days after his earlier letter – saying that while he hoped the work of 'constitution making' would prosper, he was nervous about it and wondered if it might be seen to be contrary to the spirit of the Suspensory Act. And, writing yet again five days later, he remarked on 'the charms of constitution making', but he had other worries: he wished that he saw 'a dozen good administrators' for the new departments, but recognised that this was probably an unreasonable demand.[55]

The 'imaginary conversations' as Nathan described them in one of his letters to Birrell continued for some months, but the Irish Party representatives contributed very little to the evolution of a final scheme. [56] There was some initial disagreement about the most appropriate grouping of functions relating to trade, industry, agriculture, land and public works, but in March agreement was reached on Nathan's original scheme which involved a Prime Minister's department and seven others, one of which was to be a Department of Local Affairs and Public Health. Taking over responsibility for all of the functions of the LGB except those relating to old age pensions (responsibility for which was to remain at Westminster), and with a title which was designed to reflect the growing importance of the health functions of the board, the new minister and his department were also to have overall responsibility for the Registrar General's Office, the Inspectors of Lunatic Asylums, the Central Lunatic Asylum, Hospitals and Charities, and Charitable Donations and Bequests. The LGB itself was not to be abolished as it was felt that this would have disastrous results. Instead, the legal view was that the board should simply be attached to the new department as one of its branches or divisions and placed under the control of the new minister who would become president of the board in place of the chief secretary.

While Nathan's proposals regarding the new local affairs department had been agreed in a discussion with Robinson on 20 February, he told the third meeting of the conference on 5 March that he then proposed to consult the heads of all of the various departments and offices about the adaptation of enactments that would be necessary to fit the existing organisations into the draft scheme. [57] He called for a detailed memorandum from the LGB on the proposals on 12 June, but it seems from the collections of Brennan and Dillon papers, which survive in the NLI and TCD, that no such memorandum was ever submitted and that, unlike his counterparts in the CDB and OPW, whose comments on Nathan's memoranda led to their revision and expansion, Robinson personally took no real interest in the project. At the end of December, he told Nathan that, after their original discussion on the subject, he had put the matter into the hands of the board's legal assistant who had told him that he had gone through all the acts and orders and was ready to discuss the matter with Nathan. In response, Nathan suggested on 4

January that the best course would be for the legal assistant to see Greer, the draftsman, who would explain to him what was required: 'namely, an examination of all enactments affecting the board's powers and duties, a note on the effect which the act will have upon the execution of these powers and duties and on the constitution of the board, and a draft order making the necessary adaptations.'[58] Whether the issue was ever pursued in this way or otherwise is not clear.

When the fifth meeting of the conference was held on 10 September 1915, sufficient progress had been made to allow for consideration of the draft of a public notice and detailed explanatory notes about the proposed new departments and their functions. Although it was planned to discuss a memorandum on a proposed Department of Justice and its satellites at the next meeting, it seems – for reasons which are not clear – that no further meetings were held. It was obvious of course that an early end to the war was not then in prospect, and the suspense period of twelve months provided for in the 1914 Act had been extended to eighteen months by order in Council on 14 September 1915. Asquith's Liberal government had been replaced in May by a coalition, some of whose members (and particularly the new Attorney General, Edward Carson) would not support the commencement of the 1914 Act in its existing form. Although Birrell had retained his position as Chief Secretary, he had become increasingly ineffective and his initial nervousness about the compatibility of the exercise with the Suspensory Act had probably intensified. While his letter to Robinson in January 1916 suggests that Nathan was still anxious to complete the exercise, it may be that he was subsequently instructed that working only with nationalist representatives was inappropriate, or a waste of time because the project on which he had embarked related only to the establishment of a parliament and governmental machinery for a thirty-two county Ireland, with no special provision, as had been pledged by Asquith in September 1914, to meet what he described as 'the fair scruples and objections of the Ulster minority'.[59] The view that there was an element of unreality about the whole exercise had been bluntly expressed months before that by Maurice Headlam, the Treasury Remembrancer, who was a reluctant participant in the project after he was consulted by Nathan about the possible structure of a new Department of Finance.[60]

John Dillon attended all five of the meetings of the 'Informal Conference' between January and September 1915, and carefully preserved Nathan's letters to him about the work, as well as the documents prepared for each meeting by Nathan and Kurten. His biographer, F. S. L. Lyons, commented that the work 'has a pathetic ring about it in retrospect' and 'even then it must have seemed a trifle premature'.[61] The exercise was undoubtedly premature, but the scheme on which broad agreement was reached in 1915 does seem to have influenced the arrangements provided for in 1922 and again in 1924 when, for the first time, the Ministers and Secretaries Act set out in legislative form the titles and functions of the ministers and departments that were to operate in the Irish Free State. The major responsibilities, which were to be combined with existing LGB functions to form the new department proposed in 1915 (registration of births, marriages and deaths, lunatic asylums and the Central Mental Hospital) were included among the successor department's functions in 1922 and 1924. Interestingly, too, new departmental titles, which had been devised in 1915 (including Justice and Posts and Telegraphs) were again provided for in 1924 (but not in 1922)[62]. In the case of the LGB, the title of the 1924 department included 'Public Health', as in most of the 1915 documents, although the Dáil Department, which operated from 1919 to 1922, and the first Free State Department of 1922–24 did not. A possible explanation for this was the involvement in 1923–24, and also in 1915, of Joseph Brennan, who succeeded Kurten as Nathan's private secretary in October 1915 and to whom Nathan had given his personal papers relating to the confidential 1915 exercise when he departed Dublin Castle on 5 May 1916.[63] Brennan retained these files in his personal possession for many years (along with those of Kurten)[64] and could have drawn on them when, as secretary of the Department of Finance, he worked with C. J. Gregg in framing the 1924 Act.

NOTES

1   Eunan O'Halpin, *The Decline of the Union: British Government in Ireland 1892–1920* (Dublin, 1987), p.100.
2   A. H. Norway, 'Irish Experiences in War' in Keith Jeffery (ed.), *The Sinn Fein Rebellion as They Saw it* (Dublin, 1999), p.92.
3   G. C. Duggan, 'A world that Passed Away', *Irish Times*, 4 Aug. 1964.
4   J. G. MacSweeney to Dillon, 2 Dec. 1909, TCD, John Dillon Papers, MS 6800/127j.
5   Dougherty to J. B. Armour, 27 Aug. 1910, PRONI, Armour papers, D 1792/A/1/1/16.
6   J. B. Armour to W. S. Armour, 16 Mar. 1911, PRONI, Armour papers, D 1792/A/3/2/12.
7   J. B. Armour to W. S. Armour, Sept. 1911, PRONI, Armour papers, D 1792/A/3/2/3.
8   *Irish Independent*, 26 July 1912.
9   *Irish Independent*, 27 July 1912.
10 *Report of the Royal Commission into the circumstances connected with the landing of arms at Howth on July 26 1914*, HC 1914 (Cd. 7631).
11 *Hansard* V, 65, 27 July 1914, 1022–1066.

12   Ross and Chamberlain were the heads of the DMP and RIC, respectively.

13   H. H. Asquith, *Letters to Venetia Stanley* (Oxford, 1982), letters Nos. 107 and 108, 28 July 1914.

14   Robinson to Nathan, 26 Apr. 1915, Oxford, Bodleian Library, MS Nathan 460, f. 192–93.

15   *Irish Times*, 5 Oct. 1914.

16   Sir Henry Robinson, *Memories: Wise and Otherwise* (London, 1923), p.223

17   *Irish Independent*, 16 Dec. 1915.

18   Robinson to Nathan, Dec. 1915, Oxford, Bodleian Library, MS Nathan 460, f. 216–17.

19   Memoranda of Interviews, Ireland, Oxford, Bodleian Library, MS Nathan 467, 468, 469.

20   Robinson to Nathan, 20 and 21 July 1915, Oxford, Bodleian Library, MS Nathan 460, f. 199, 201–202.

21   Memorandum of interview with Robinson, 18 May 1915, Oxford, Bodleian Library, MS Nathan 468, f. 84–86; Nathan to Robinson, 20 Feb. 1916, Oxford, Bodleian Library, MS Nathan 466, f. 324–25.

22   Robinson to Nathan, 8 Apr. 1915, Oxford, Bodleian Library, MS Nathan 460, f. 188–89.

23   Robinson to Nathan, 26 Apr. 1915, Oxford, Bodleian Library, MS Nathan 460, f. 192–93.

24   Robinson to Nathan, 4 Nov 1914, Oxford, Bodleian Library, MS Nathan 460, f. 156.

25   Robinson to Nathan, 24 Mar. 1916, Oxford, Bodleian Library, MS Nathan 460, f. 231–32.

26   Robinson, *Memories*, p.228.

27   Robinson, *Memories*, pp.224–26; 199–200.

28   Patricia Jalland, 'A Liberal Chief Secretary and the Irish Question: Augustine Birrell, 1907–1914', *The Historical Journal*, 19, 2 (1976), p.422.

29   Oxford, Bodleian Library, Asquith Papers, MS 38, f. 236, cited in Pádraig Yeates, *A City in Wartime: Dublin 1914–18* (Dublin, 2011), p.34.

30   *Irish Times*, 3 September 1912.

31   Marjorie Pentland, *A Bonnie Fechter* (London, 1952), pp.167–68.

32   Maureen Keane, *Ishbel: Lady Aberdeen in Ireland* (Dublin, 1999), pp.148, 151.

33   Sir Arthur Salter, assistant secretary, National Insurance Commission, quoted in Pentland, *A Bonnie Fechter*, p.170.

34   Robinson, *Memories*, pp.229–230; letter of 29 Oct. 1914 from Robinson to Powerscourt, referred to in NLI Special List 352 but not now to be found per NLI Collection List 124, Appendix I.

35   It appears from the Asquith–Stanley letters that Wimborne was being considered for the appointment in mid-October but that his appointment was not decided on until mid-November and announced in early January (Letters nos. 184, 206 and 233).

36   Birrell to Nathan, 21 Feb. 1915, Oxford, Bodleian Library, MS Nathan 449, f. 126–27.

37   Max Sullivan Green, an engineer, was an inspector with the LGB before his appointment as private secretary to Aberdeen in 1907; he became chairman

of the General Prisons Board in 1912 and married John Redmond's youngest daughter in 1913.

38   Birrell to Nathan, 21 Feb. 1915, Oxford, Bodleian Library, MS Nathan 449, f. 126–27.

39   Robinson to Nathan, 1 Mar. 1915, Oxford, Bodleian Library, MS Nathan 460, f. 176–77.

40   Robinson to Nathan, 19 Apr. 1915, Oxford, Bodleian Library, MS Nathan 460, f. 190.

41   Robinson, *Memories*, pp.193–96.

42   Edward David (ed.), *Inside Asquith's Cabinet: From the Diaries of Charles Hobhouse* (London, 1977), p.72.

43   Liverpool University Library, Birrell Papers, MSS 10.3, cited in Leon Ó Broin, *The Chief Secretary* (Connecticut, 1970), pp.20–21.

44   Robinson, *Memories*, pp.199, 200.

45   Augustine Birrell, *Things Past Redress* (1937), pp.208–09.

46   Birrell to Nathan, 21 Feb. 1915, Oxford, Bodleian Library, MS Nathan 449, f. 126–27; 25 Mar. 1915, idem. f. 144–45.

47   Charles W. Magill (ed.), *From Dublin Castle to Stormont: the Memoirs of Andrew Philip Magill, 1913–25* (Cork, 2003), p.8.

48   Leon Ó Broin, *No Man's Man* (Dublin, 1982), pp.34–36; NLI, Joseph Brennan Papers, MSS 26,149(1), 26,149(2), 26,167, 26,173(1), 26,173(2), 26,174, 26,175; TCD, John Dillon Papers, MS 6801/156–198.

49   Nathan diary 1915 (MS Nathan 50) cited in Leon Ó Broin, *Dublin Castle and the 1916 Rising* (revised edition) (London, 1970), p.45.

50   Minutes of Informal Conference on Irish Transfer Orders in Council, 1915, NLI, Joseph Brennan Papers, MS 31,700 (7); John Dillon Papers, TCD, MS 6801/156–198.

51   Nathan to Birrell, 3 Mar. 1915, Oxford, Bodleian Library, MSS. Eng. c. 7033, f. 57–62.

52   Nathan to Birrell, 18 Feb. 1915, Oxford, Bodleian Library, MS Nathan, 462.

53   Birrell to Nathan, 21 Feb. 1915, Oxford, Bodleian Library, MS Nathan, 449, f. 126–27.

54   Nathan to Dillon, 25 Feb. 1915, TCD, John Dillon Papers, MS 6801/163.

55   Birrell to Nathan, 23 Feb. 1915, Oxford, Bodleian Library, MS Nathan, 449, f. 128–29; 28 Feb. 1915, f. 134–37.

56   Nathan to Birrell, 3 Mar.1915, Oxford, Bodleian Library, MSS. Eng. c. 7033, f. 57–62.

57   Memorandum of an interview with Robinson, 20 Feb.1915, Oxford, Bodleian Library, MS Nathan, 467, f. 157.

58   Robinson to Nathan, 31 Dec. 1915 and Nathan to Robinson, 4 Jan.1916, NLI, Joseph Brennan Papers, MS 26,155.

59   Asquith, Herbert Henry (Earl of Oxford and Asquith), *Memories and Reflections, 1852–1927* (vol. 2) (London, 1928), p.189.

60   Headlam to Nathan, 1 Apr. 1915, NLI MS 26,175.

61   F. S. L. Lyons, *John Dillon: A Biography* (Chicago, 1968), p.363.

62 In the Dáil debate on the 1924 Act, Cosgrave explained that 'Justice' was being substituted for 'Home Affairs' at the request of the department as the former title was 'very wide in description and indefinite in its interpretation' (Dáil Debates 5, 16 Nov. 1923, 917).

63 A note by Brennan to this effect is included in one of the folders of the papers held in NLI, MS 26,149(2).

64 Kurten moved to the Department of Recruiting for Ireland in October 1915 but left Ireland in January 1916 to enlist in the army; he was an acting major in the Royal Artillery and had been mentioned in dispatches when he was killed in action in France on 24 April 1918.

CHAPTER X

The World War:
The War To Unite Us All?

When Archduke Franz Ferdinand and his wife were assassinated in Sarajevo on 28 June 1914, a major war was not an inevitable outcome, nor was it clear that British involvement would be unavoidable if war broke out on the continent. However, after Germany had rejected an ultimatum to withdraw from Belgium, Britain declared war on 4 August. Sir Edward Grey, the foreign secretary, had remarked pessimistically to a friend at his office a few days earlier that 'the lamps are going out all over Europe; we shall not see them lit again in our lifetime' but the sense of doom encapsulated in this famous remark was not shared by Henry Robinson, or by many others in Ireland. Robinson, in fact, told Birrell at the time that he, and most rational protestants, believed that wartime experience would do much to destroy the hatreds and fears which were keeping protestants and catholics apart.[1] This assessment of 'a war to unite us all' and of the impact of the common sacrifice on likely post-war developments on the political front was shared by John Redmond, Tom Kettle, John Henry Bernard, Church of Ireland Archbishop of Dublin and many others – but it proved to be wildly over-optimistic.

By causing the implementation of the Government of Ireland Act to be deferred, the First World War effectively extended the independent existence of the LGB for more than seven years, including the turbulent 1919–22 period. Apart from this, it had a range of impacts on the board and its services. By forcing action on foot of the report of the Royal Commission on the civil service to be deferred, it allowed the board's recruitment and personnel practices to continue virtually unchanged for another six years, although clerical vacancies arising from enlistment or otherwise could be filled only by temporary appointees, many of them women. Because the enormous cost of the war forced the government to clamp down on capital projects which were deemed to be inessential, and to attempt retrenchment in other programmes, some important services for which the board was responsible were badly affected – but for the war, a government response might have been expected to the report by LGB inspectors on Dublin housing, which was published in February 1914, and implementation of some or all of the 1909 recommendations of the Royal Commission on the poor laws, involving the separation of poor relief, health and social services could hardly have been further delayed. In effect, traditional LGB services were more or less frozen at 1914 levels until the application to Ireland of the post-war reconstruction programme came to be considered in 1919 – and by then a very different Ireland had emerged.

Recruiting for the New Army

Recruiting for what was being described as the 'New Army' began almost immediately after the declaration of war. Over 30,000 reservists were quickly called up in Ireland to join the 20,000 Irishmen who were already serving in the forces. On 7 August, Lord Kitchener, Secretary of State for War, called for 100,000 men to enlist. Advertisements declaiming that 'Your King and Country Needs You' began to appear in the press in the following days, and public recruiting meetings were soon being held throughout the country. Almost 90,000 men had enlisted in Ireland by January 1916,[2] by mid-April the number had risen to almost 100,000,[3] and despite further enlistment in the following months, which brought the number who had joined since the outbreak of the war to more than 130,000, Parliament was told in November that more than 161,000 men of military age were still available in Ireland for military service.[4]

The LGB had no responsibility for recruitment, but several of the board's senior officials became involved on a personal basis. The medical commissioner, Sir Thomas Stafford, whose eldest son, Captain Edward Stafford King-Harman, was killed near Ypres in November 1914 while serving with the Irish Guards, was prominently associated with the campaign in 1915, particularly in County Roscommon, where the large Rockingham estate had been inherited by his son. In Dublin, Charles O'Conor, a brother of O'Conor Don and one of the board's most senior inspectors, was an active member of the City and County Recruiting Committee, and addressed public meetings as part of the committee's campaign. Speaking at what an *Irish Times* headline described as a 'Patriotic Meeting' at Dundrum on 25 April 1915, he declared that 'the fate of the

Irish nation was as much at stake in this struggle as was that of any of the belligerents'. He went on to argue that it was not inconsistent with the Irish people's ideas of nationality to recognise their duty to the Empire, the destinies of which were at stake – 'if the Empire were to sink … Ireland would also sink beyond recall … if the Germans came … farmers and others would be deprived of their lands and other possessions and their nationality would be gone also.'[5] Harry Murphy, a temporary inspector, was among the other LGB staff members who became publicly associated with the recruiting effort; addressing an open-air recruiting meeting in Athlone in September 1915, he won loud applause for his criticism of 'runaways' who were attempting to travel to America to avoid enlistment or possible conscription and who should never again be allowed to land in the county.[6] Ernest Aston, another temporary inspector, was also prominently associated with the campaign.[7]

Henry Robinson did not become personally involved in the recruiting effort, but attempted behind the scenes to influence matters. Andrew Magill, then Private Secretary to the Chief Secretary, recalled Robinson advising him at one stage that recruiting posters showing the horrors of the war at the front and the brutalities of the Germans were having the opposite effect to what was hoped for. Robinson's reasoning – probably based on his long experience of feelings in the west of Ireland in cases of failure to recover the bodies of fishermen lost at sea – was that 'the women are all saying they don't mind their sons and brothers being killed at home, where they can bury them and weep over them, but they won't let them go to the front where they will be blown to bits and not a scrap left to mourn over'.[8] Robinson's own memoirs restated his view that recruiting was rather badly handled: in particular, he believed that the war pictures, cinema films and posters were simply terrifying, showing wounded soldiers left alone on the battlefield or big shells exploding in the midst of troops as they went over the top, whereas pictures of laughing young soldiers sitting outside a café, with girls on their knees and brimming goblets of porter on the table beside them, might have attracted more recruits. At the same time, he was realistic enough to accept that however well the recruiting campaign was managed, it would not blind people to the meaning of the casualty lists, and would not influence those who 'found sanctuary in the avowal of Sinn Féin principles'.[9]

National Registration and Conscription Schemes

Unlike its counterpart in England, the LGB continued until the end of the war to have no official role in the various recruitment campaigns. It had no significant functions under the National Registration Act, which became law in July 1915,[10] and the decision in January 1916 to exempt Ireland from conscription meant that Robinson and his colleagues again escaped the additional work which their English counterparts had to undertake. Under the 1915 Act, local authorities in England and Wales were required to compile and maintain registers of all males and females between the ages of 15 and 65 in their areas, containing personal information on each individual and details of their occupations and skills. Birrell argued in the House of Commons that circumstances in Ireland were very different – unlike industrialised England, most of the male population were living 'in the depths of the country', many of them were small farmers and agricultural labourers, and sufficient information on available manpower could be compiled from existing sources quickly and inexpensively.[11] Nothing has emerged to suggest that Robinson dissented from this view, but he was sure to have been consulted by Nathan before the latter told Birrell that he doubted whether Irish county and county borough councils would assist in implementing the registration scheme.[12] Some senior officials in other departments were among those who were deeply disappointed that Ireland was to be 'singled out as usual for special treatment'[13] and as a compromise, the act allowed for its application by order of the lord lieutenant to specified areas. It was applied in July to the county boroughs of Belfast and Derry and to the counties of Antrim and Down and was extended in early August to Armagh and Derry at the request of the county councils.[14] Robinson's only function, however, was to sanction the amount of the administrative expenses which could be paid out by the local councils in these areas, from funds provided by the government.

Like the National Registration Scheme, the first measure of compulsion to join the forces, which became law in January 1916, did not apply to Ireland – although the Ulster unionists argued strongly that it should – and so Robinson was spared the task of setting up an elaborate system of local tribunals on the lines of the system which was introduced in England to deal with claims for exemptions. In defending the exclusion of Ireland, Birrell told the House of Commons that, having heard his views on the subject, the government had come to the wise and prudent conclusion that Ireland should not be included. He went on to tell the House that account should be taken of Irish history and of the state of mind and feeling of a great number of the Irish people. On a practical level, he suggested that it would be impossible in Ireland to fashion local tribunals of the kind on which the success of the scheme in England was to depend – indeed he shuddered to think of what would happen if the enforcement of conscription was left to individual county councils. Finally, he argued that Ireland had already done wonderfully well in contributing 95,000 enlisted men, and advised the House not to risk all for the sake of a few, and for the sake of a dangerous uniformity.[15]

Enlistment by LGB Staff

In February 1915, Robinson was advised of an appeal by the Committee on Imperial Defence to employers throughout the UK to contribute to the recruitment effort by employing only women or men who were ineligible for military service and there was a suggestion that government departments and local authorities should set an example in this respect. He immediately told Nathan that the board would 'be glad to fall in with the idea of holding out no offers of employment to able-bodied young men who won't take their part in the defence of the country'.[16] In June, after the War Office had directly called on civil servants to enlist, the heads of the Irish departments issued a circular to every man of military age on their staff urging them to join up.[17] While another circular was sent to each man in November, inviting them to sign a form of undertaking to enlist when called on to do so, the response was still not particularly satisfactory from the authorities' point of view.[18] It might be assumed that Robinson would personally have put pressure on family, acquaintances and staff in the Custom House to enlist – just as Under-Secretary Nathan urged staff at the Castle, including his own private secretary, Joseph Brennan, to do when issuing the November circular – but if he did so he met with little success.[19]

Robinson's 30-year-old eldest son, Christopher, who had been employed as a temporary inspector by the board in 1911–12, and had been serving as a resident magistrate in Donegal since then, did not enlist, even though he had held a commission in the Royal Fusiliers from 1904 to 1911. This may be explained by the fact that he was suffering in 1914 from malaria contracted during his service in Jamaica as aide-de-camp to Lord Olivier, and had a very painful form of neuritis in his neck in 1915.[20] His second son, Bryan, was commissioned as a second lieutenant in the Royal Army Service Corps in January 1916 while his third son, Adrian, an assistant inspector with the board since May 1914, was recorded in the 1914–15 annual report as one of those who had enlisted, but he was serving again with the board, and in a higher grade, in August 1915. Of the twenty most senior administrative and clerical staff in the Custom House, only five were less than 40 years of age in 1914, and only two of them, both higher division clerks, enlisted. In all, fifteen members of the board's staff were reported to have joined the forces by March 1915.[21] These included Alfred Tennyson, Birrell's step-son, who was then a general inspector, and another of the inspectors, Jack MacCabe, son of the former medical commissioner, Sir Frederick MacCabe. There were seven recruits from the administrative and clerical staff and five from the subordinate establishment, presumably messengers and fire-lighters. In 1915–16, additional enlistment was recorded (two inspectors and four clerical staff), bringing the total to twenty-one. These were joined by at least twelve sons, sons-in-law or brothers of some of the more senior staff members, including the two sons of the medical commissioner, Sir Thomas Stafford; two sons of the chief engineering inspector, Dr Peter Cowan; and a son of the board's secretary, Alexander Barlas.

Overall, the percentage of Irish male civil servants of military age who enlisted was less than half the comparable figures for England and Scotland. A return prepared in the Chief Secretary's Office (but not, apparently published) showed that a total of 1,197 staff of Irish public departments had joined the forces by 30 November 1915, but this figure is misleading to the extent that it includes 562 officers and men of the RIC, 46 DMP constables, and 45 prison officers and warders.[22] The total of twenty shown for the LGB was well below the figures for DATI, CDB, OPW and other agencies. In relative terms, the figure was significantly below the figures for the English and Scottish Local Government Boards, where almost sixty per cent of the eligible staff had enlisted by 1 April 1916.[23] In October that year the Chief Secretary was asked in the House of Commons what efforts were being made by the LGB and other Irish departments to 'comb out' of the civil service all of those fit for military service, whether local authorities were being pressed to do likewise, and whether they had been requested not to employ men of military age. Chief Secretary Duke's unimpressive reply was that he was 'making enquiries about the matter'.[24] Shortly afterwards, when further questions were put down, Duke replied that while no compulsory process was applicable, encouragement to enlist was offered in all departments subject to the exigencies of the public service, but he refused to provide a return of men of military age who were still employed.[25] Whatever action may subsequently have been taken had little effect, at least in so far as the LGB was concerned. A return submitted to Parliament in June 1918 showed that, since the outbreak of hostilities, almost 48.5 per cent of the total number of men employed in 1914 by government departments in England, Wales and Scotland had been released for service with the forces, whereas if a similar proportion of the men employed by the LGB in 1914 had enlisted, the number would have come to more than one hundred, five times the number who actually did so.[26] It was presumably figures like these which led the *Irish Times* to complain in June 1918 that something more than verbal pressure should be applied to the many hundreds of young men of military age who 'for more than three years have been in shelter under the gigantic umbrella of the Irish civil service'.[27]

Frank Sparrow, killed at the Somme in August 1916 while serving as a lieutenant in the Royal Engineers, appears to have been the only member of the board's staff who died like tens of thousands of other Irishmen on active service; a qualified architect, he had been an assistant inspector since 1907. In addition to Stafford's loss of his son and heir, the board's chief engineering inspector, Dr Peter Cowan, lost two of his sons, both captains in the Royal Flying Corps, in 1916 and 1917, a blow from which he was said to have never fully recovered. Other staff members who lost sons or close relatives included Dr Thomas Browne, a medical inspector, who lost both a son and a son-in-law; William Ellis, an auditor, whose son, an engineering graduate of TCD, was killed in action at Suvla Bay in October 1915; F. A. S. King, a temporary architect, whose son was lost in the battlecruiser *Indefatigable* at Jutland in June 1916; Arthur Scott Quekett, the board's assistant legal adviser, whose brother was killed at Ypres in July 1917; and Ernest Leach, then Robinson's private secretary, whose 20-year-old son, a captain in the Royal Irish Rifles, was killed in action on 2 January 1917.

Enlistment by Local Councils' Staff

Robinson and his board did what they could to encourage and facilitate enlistment by employees of local councils. In September 1914, councils were authorised to make allowances – usually half-pay – to the dependants of employees who joined the army or navy, and to employ substitutes – but only on a temporary basis – so that places would be available for enlisted men returning after the war.[28] In February 1915, Robinson told Nathan that he had no objection to the issue of a circular advising county councils to fill vacancies only by the employment of women or men who were ineligible for military service, but he believed that it would have very little effect.[29] Later in the year, and bearing in mind that a significant proportion of the dispensary medical officers had volunteered to join the Royal Army Medical Corps, he directed that sanction would be refused for permanent appointments as dispensary doctors of men who might be eligible to serve in the forces so as to ensure that men who had joined the army and navy would have opportunities of competing for positions of this kind in their own localities after the war.[30] Initially, the board's legal adviser took the view that refusal to sanction permanent appointments was *ultra vires*, but Robinson was pleased to be able to tell Nathan in January 1916 that the legal adviser had changed his opinion, and that it was now open to them to disapprove permanent appointments on the sole ground that the doctor concerned was urgently required for military service.[31] Later on, when they observed that most of the men being appointed to temporary positions were of military age and apparently eligible for service in the RAMC, the board took matters further by refusing sanction to a large number of these appointments. The board adhered strictly to this policy even when, in the course of the great flu epidemic of 1918–19, boards of guardians were urgently demanding a relaxation so as to enable them to provide medical assistance for those affected.[32]

Civil Service Retrenchment

Restrictions on civil service employment were in operation from the early stages of the war, and although Robinson had promised the Treasury that he would not fill any vacancies without their special sanction, he was still having difficulty with them in settling the estimates for 1915–16: 'They are full of weird suggestions' he told Nathan in January 1915, explaining that they wanted the board to employ as inspectors land surveyors for whom OPW had no work. This was a step 'which would turn us into a laughing stock and weaken our administration'.[33] In February, after he had accepted that the board should not make offers of clerical jobs to young men of military age, he was pleased to be able to report that in place of such men, the board had 'a heap of women employed already as clerks and typists'.[34] Later that year, he reported that the organisation was under severe pressure because of the numbers released for military service, and because special units had to be created to administer wartime services. All of this meant that additional temporary clerical staff – mainly women – had to be engaged, and extensive overtime had to be worked.[35]

Because of the heavy demands on the Exchequer which were created by the war, the drive to secure economies in current expenditure was taken a stage further when the Committee on Retrenchment in the Public Expenditure was set up by the Treasury to advise on what savings could be secured in civil departments. In a first report submitted in September 1915, the committee made a number of suggestions, including a reduction in expenditure on road maintenance, less pressure by central departments on local authorities to undertake new work, and a ban on the filling of vacancies except in special cases.[36] When the Treasury followed up by asking departments to postpone all items of new expenditure and to restrict all recurrent expenditure as far as possible,[37] Robinson sought directions from Nathan as to whether this meant that the board's estimates for 1916–17 should provide only for expenditure which was absolutely obligatory, or whether the board should make sufficient provision to ensure that services would not become less efficient than they were.[38] This issue was overtaken in November when it was decided that the retrenchment committee would meet under Birrell's chairmanship to deal with Irish services, in preparation for which all departments were asked to submit memoranda showing what economies had already been achieved and those that might be possible in future. After Nathan had told Birrell that Robinson 'ought to be able, I should think, to make some reduction in staff',[39] Robinson duly prepared lengthy memoranda, reviewing in detail the organisation and functions of the board and stressing the additional work which had fallen on it because of the war.[40] His conclusion was that the board's estimated expenditure of £126,566 in 1915–16 could be reduced by no more than about £4,000 in the following year – a saving to be achieved mainly by dispensing with the services of three temporary inspectors and two architects who had been engaged for work under the Labourers Acts which had been largely suspended.

The retrenchment committee held three meetings to review expenditure on Irish services, at one of which Robinson was called to give evidence. Having been advised of the steps already taken to secure economies, the committee concluded in early December that further savings were possible but, as these could only be achieved by legislation which was likely to prove contentious, they decided to leave it to the Irish government and the Treasury to deal with the question in the context of the estimates.[41] Headlam, the Treasury Remembrancer who participated in the work of the committee, attributed its failure to recommend savings to the influence of John Redmond, who had argued that savings could only be made by a properly constituted Irish government and who had refused to allow Irish Party participation in the work of the committee, notwithstanding the party's repeated claims that the cost of the Irish administration was excessive.[42] The final report of the committee concluded in February 1916 that, while they were at liberty to examine the Irish estimates again, 'no useful result would be obtained'.[43] There were a number of general recommendations of some relevance to the LGB (including the curtailment of inspection work and a reduction in the demand for statistical and other returns from local authorities), but the net result of the exercise was that the board emerged virtually unscathed from the drive for wartime economies. Birrell's reply to a parliamentary question in March 1916 bore this out: the suspension of borrowing for housing and public health purposes had resulted in a 'large retrenchment' of £4,738 a year, arising from a reduction of staff – five professional staff members and nine clerks, but eleven important Acts of Parliament had thrown heavy additional duties on the board since 1905, requiring an increase in staff numbers since that year.[44]

Restrictions on Capital Expenditure

Action to reduce capital expenditure below the normal level was ruled out in the early stages of the war because of the widely-held view that serious unemployment and distress might arise in some areas. In the early months of 1915, however, when proposals to restrict borrowing by local authorities for public health purposes were under consideration by the government, Robinson urged that restrictions should 'be pressed to the very uttermost limits consistent with the avoidance of outbreaks of disease', not just because the financial situation made such a policy necessary, but also because he was conscious, as Foy and Barton put it, that 'Dublin was strangely detached from the conflict, hardly burdened by the disciplines of total war.'[45] He therefore advised Sir Basil Blackett at the Treasury that something should be done to change this:

> Over here in Ireland, the people have not really had the war brought home to them; the difference in atmosphere in Ireland and England is amazing – I have been through England lately and the glow of the khaki is touching everything like the dawn of the morning sun. But in Ireland, you hardly see any difference – no one seems to be pulling in their horns where public expenditure is concerned and the fact of these huge separation allowances in a country such as this where wages run from 12s. to 18s. a week have created the impression that the resources of England are unfathomable, and that if anyone presses hard enough, with all the money that is being scattered about in the war, they will be able to get loans for anything. Therefore, anything you can do to dispel this impression and let it be seen that the Nation must economize will have a very salutary effect.[46]

Matters moved quickly after that. The Treasury asked Robinson to arrange for the issue of a suitable circular to local councils in Ireland, which of course he was happy to do. The circular issued on 4 May announced severe restrictions affecting housing and other local services: new works were not to be undertaken except where they were of pressing necessity for public health reasons. Where schemes had already been commenced, arrangements were to be made with contractors, where possible, to postpone further work.[47] Robinson strongly supported the enforcement of these restrictions and felt that the best way to make local authorities confine their borrowings to essential purposes was to force them to borrow expensively in the open market. He was able to tell the Treasury in July that the board had 'to all intents and purposes, shut down inexorably' on housing loans, and were very glad to do so as Ireland hardly realised the seriousness of the situation. The only way to put a stop to anti-recruiting blackguardism was to make the people feel the inconvenience of the war.[48] In the same vein, he wrote in December that many of the urban authorities were 'packed with Sinn Féiners who are openly anti-British and who declare that the war is no concern of theirs ... it is a very good object lesson to let them see how they are affected by the war'.[49]

Borrowing restrictions were rigidly enforced by the board throughout 1915, even where the schemes involved were relatively inexpensive ones and were already in progress. In September, for example, sanction for further loan instalments for Mullahoran RDC in County Longford was refused, forcing the council to instruct their contractor not to proceed with the remaining six cottages in a partially completed scheme. The hard line adopted by the board was questioned even by Birrell's private secretary, Andrew Magill, who wondered how he could tell the people of Athy that a loan was being refused for a thirty-seven-house scheme, which was claimed to be essential for reasons of public health. But the LGB were not for turning: Magill was told that Athy was 'no worse off now than ever it was'. Besides, there were very few towns in Ireland that would not be able to make as good a case as Athy had made for replacing existing insanitary houses. Their need was no greater than in many other cases, and so the scheme would have to be postponed until more favourable conditions arrived.[50]

Some councils attempted to secure exemption from the borrowing restrictions by pointing to the fact that, in addition to the need for new houses to replace the wretched hovels in which people were then living, unemployment was rampant in the building trades in their areas. Deploying arguments of this kind, John Redmond appealed personally to Robinson in August 1915 to release a further instalment of a loan for a scheme of 180 houses, which had been commenced in his Waterford city constituency, but he was told by Robinson that 'with £3 millions a day going out for the war, money is simply not to be got for these domestic reforms', for which applications were pouring in. But there were other considerations too: because prices for materials of all kinds in the building trade had increased, Robinson's strong view was that it would be ruinous for the ratepayers to proceed with building schemes on the basis of inflated wartime prices, leading to rents that could not be afforded by the working classes and/or heavy deficits, which would have to be borne by the rates. He therefore appealed to Redmond to use his great influence in Waterford to make the city corporation understand that it would be a serious mistake to commence a new phase of building in these circumstances. However, Redmond was unwilling to accept this and took up the matter directly with Edwin Montagu, Financial Secretary to the Treasury, after which senior officials at the Treasury, in consultation with Robinson, prepared a succession of drafts of a letter for issue to Redmond, taking the line that the borrowing restrictions would have to be enforced – but Montagu was unwilling to issue any of them. For his part, Robinson told the Treasury that he had no difficulty in accepting responsibility for the refusal to sanction the loan instalment, and did not have 'the very smallest objection to fighting Redmond and the whole Waterford Corporation over it, as I am clear we should not give the loan. If Waterford gets it, what are we to say to Belfast, Derry, Dublin and the other cities?' Anticipating defeat, however, he advised that if the loan instalment had to be conceded, it would be better that the whole thing should be seen as an amazing instance of the unfairness of the LGB, because the board would never dream of letting it be known that the Treasury had yielded to Redmond and overruled them. Eventually, Montagu, as a political concession, directed the release of an instalment of £5,000 to finance continuation of the Waterford scheme for another year. While Robinson was forced to concede defeat, he could not resist a parting shot at the corporation: 'They are the stupidest people in the world to build now – the prices they will pay for timber, wood, cement, slates etc will bring the cost of the houses up to an absurd figure ... however, Devil mend them!'.[51]

Dublin Housing

Only a few months after the Waterford episode, a more serious, more public and more embarrassing overturning of a board decision occurred. Dublin Corporation were still smarting under what they considered to be the unfair criticism levelled at their housing administration in the report which LGB officials had completed in February 1914. Notwithstanding the enormous cost of implementing the report's recommendations that 14,000 new housing units and as many as 13,000 modernised inner-city apartments were required, Robinson personally stood firmly behind the findings of his officials.[52] The Treasury was therefore advised in November

1914 that, as a start, no barrier should be placed in the way of advancing money to the corporation for housing schemes estimated to cost almost £370,000, which the board had already approved. However, having been told that there was no abnormal unemployment in Dublin at that stage, the Treasury allowed loans of only £75,000 to be sanctioned, notwithstanding representations by Redmond and other MPs. With the restrictions on borrowing, which had then come into force, the board was obliged in October 1915 to tell the corporation that they could not count on any further advances from the State for housing or other domestic reforms 'until the allied armies carry the war to a successful conclusion'.[53]

Robinson personally attracted strong criticism following a notification to the corporation that it could not benefit under special housing acts which had been applied to Ireland in August 1914.[54] The Treasury had ruled that funds provided under these acts could be drawn down only in areas where there was widespread and acute distress in the building trade as a result of the war. Because the corporation's case for funding was based solely on the need for housing, the board believed that it would be a waste of time pursuing the matter without evidence that distress was 'existent and insistent', and without official figures showing a wholly unprecedented amount of unemployment in the building trade.[55] Within a few weeks of the act being passed, Robinson – without the knowledge of the corporation and on his own initiative – had made a strong case to the Treasury for an alternative approach, arguing that £350,000 of the £4 million available under the acts should be earmarked for Ireland, and that if the interest on that sum were allowed to be used to augment the subsidy on loan charges already available to the corporation, up to 6,000 additional houses could be provided. Birrell had followed up with a personal letter to the Treasury supporting this ingenious scheme, but the officials in London were not impressed. They ruled that Robinson's proposals were both naïve and inadmissible, and skated lightly over the fact that the 1914 act was passed to relieve wartime distress and unemployment, and not to finance a general housing scheme.[56] Unaware of Robinson's efforts to bend the act to help finance Dublin housing schemes, a special meeting of the city council in October 1915 condemned the failure of the board to secure the required funding, one councillor describing their conduct as 'deceit and jugglery'. The meeting went on to pass a resolution proposed by W. T. Cosgrave, who declared that the report on Dublin housing had been 'utilised for the purpose of slandering the administration of the metropolis'; that the initiation of the 1913 inquiry was not actuated by honourable motives; and that the LGB had forfeited whatever confidence it should have commanded.[57] The large attendance at a meeting organised by the Dublin United Trades Council in early December joined in the criticism of what the chairman described as the extraordinary conduct of the board and its failure to respond to the appalling housing conditions documented in the report of their own inspectors – according to the Rev John Flanagan it was simply the Irish branch of the Treasury whose business it was to find ways to avoid spending any money in Ireland.[58] Four years later, Cosgrave was still complaining that not a single penny of the £4 million was ever spent on housing in Ireland, which lead him to conclude that the 1914 act was passed simply 'to popularise the war in Ireland'.[59]

As Murray Fraser rightly notes, much of the resulting Irish acrimony was directed towards Robinson, although the real source of intransigence lay in the Treasury and the government, but Robinson was quite happy to stand over the decisions which had been notified to the corporation.[60] He told the Treasury that he had 'no feeling ... one way or another' about the press reports of the various public meetings, but he was shocked to find that J. J. Clancy MP, having made a personal approach to the Chancellor of the Exchequer, was told that the Treasury's failure to approve loans for Dublin was due to the fact that no loans had been recommended to them by the LGB. To make matters worse from Robinson's point of view, the Chancellor replied in similar terms to a parliamentary question from another of the Dublin MPs, William Field.[61] When the city treasurer showed him Clancy's letter from the Treasury and asked 'with a note of triumph in his voice' if the board was now prepared to recommend the loans, Robinson was forced, as he put it in one of the naval metaphors he loved to use, to 'haul down my flag' and congratulate the corporation on the persuasive power of their member. Privately, however, he was furious, and protested to the permanent secretary of the Treasury that what had happened appeared to support the contention of the citizens that the government was quite ready to lend money but were hampered by the obstructive tactics of the LGB, adding that it was very hard for the board to force the policy of retrenchment on the local authorities when ministers made promises in individual cases without first hearing what the board had to say. To smooth his feelings, the Chancellor's private secretary explained to Robinson that the whole matter had been due to misunderstandings and conveyed the Chancellor's personal appreciation of the manner in which he was carrying out his difficult and unpopular duties.[62] The Chancellor himself explained the true position in the House of Commons on 15 December, and the immediate issue was brought to a conclusion when loans were sanctioned to meet commitments entered into before the borrowing restrictions were imposed.[63] The whole episode, however, reflected unfairly on Robinson and cannot have enhanced the councillors' already poor impression of him, and of his board's approach to the city's housing problem.

The wartime restrictions on borrowing and capital expenditure continued to be enforced with very limited exceptions until 1919–20, delaying indefinitely the full implementation of the Dublin housing programme which both the board and the corporation agreed was an urgent necessity. Henry Duke had been in office as Chief Secretary for only a few weeks when Robinson reported to him on 21 August 1916 that he had told the Lord Mayor that 'you wanted his confidential help and advice as to what you could do about housing' whereat his 'heart warmed to you as he expressed it'.[64] Nothing was done, however, until April 1917 when, after the corporation had flirted with the idea of raising a housing loan of $1.5 million in the United States at a very high interest rate, Duke sought and obtained the agreement of Bonar Law, then Chancellor of the Exchequer, to provide loans to allow work to begin on four Dublin schemes costing £285,000, all of which had been approved by the LGB before the war. Duke and Robinson personally visited the different housing sites in April and a few days later Duke told the Lord Mayor to agree details of a building programme with Robinson, adding that 'nobody has pressed this necessity upon me more constantly than he'.[65] Matters moved quickly after that: Robinson told Duke and the Treasury on 17 April that the corporation would be able to spend £100,000 on five approved schemes in 1917–18 and noted that they were most anxious to proceed so as to relieve unemployment in the building trades. He added that by relieving distress in the city, the immediate commencement of work would remove a great deal of unrest. Bonar Law approved the necessary loans on 19 April,[66] and Duke immediately advised the Lord Mayor of this, telling him to arrange the details with Robinson who was 'fully informed as to the views of the government'.[67]

In order to plan ahead for the longer term, Robinson suggested to Duke a few months later that he might direct the board's chief engineering inspector, Dr Peter Cowan, 'whose mind is saturated with ideas of Dublin improvement schemes' to report on how a complete scheme for housing the working people in Dublin who were living in insanitary dwellings could be carried out on a phased basis. Duke gladly accepted 'this helpful proposal', and on 24 July, in a letter drafted personally for him by Robinson, he notified one of the Dublin nationalist MPs of Cowan's special assignment.[68] The report which Cowan completed in January 1918, but which was not published until August, concluded that 'there is a great emergency now and it must be met by emergency measures'. He advised that an expenditure of almost £9 million should be undertaken to build at least 16,500 new houses on greenfield sites served by cheap and rapid transit, and to reconstruct some 3,800 of the better-class tenement houses to cater for another 13,000 families. He concluded with the rather extraordinary statement that 'the rebellion of 1916, with its terrible results in loss of life, vast material waste, the re-birth of dying antagonisms, the creation of new enmities and the setting back of the clock in many most vital movements might possibly have been prevented if the people in Dublin had been better housed'.[69] More extraordinary still, perhaps, was the fact that W. T. Cosgrave, as the Dáil Minister for Local Government, opted to quote this very paragraph from Cowan's report in a letter to Arthur Griffith in August 1919 about the need for action on Dublin housing. He added, however, that if Cowan had been of the same opinion about the Rising when holding various housing inquiries 'he kept his views to himself'.[70]

Wartime Services

The scale of the LGB's existing organisation, the multi-purpose nature of its role and its links with local authorities around the country fitted it particularly well to take on some new wartime services:

- Employment Schemes: Although the anticipated wartime unemployment never arose, limited funds were made available by the LGB to assist distress committees and local councils to provide employment in areas where distress was both 'existent and insistent'. Ernest Aston, a Dublin consulting engineer, was appointed as a temporary inspector and commissioned to prepare a report which would make the case for continuing relief efforts. His lengthy report of March 1915 provided a valuable assessment of the employment situation for both men and women in the various industrial sectors in the major urban centres.[71] However, the Treasury was opposed to the provision of further relief, especially in Dublin 'where there is a strong predisposition to State pauperization' and where 'all the weaklings in Ireland collect'. As far as they were concerned, unemployed labourers could join the army, obtain employment in England or Scotland, or go back to the land, and so the LGB was advised that no further grants from public funds would be forthcoming to cater for wartime distress.[72]
- Belgian Refugees: Robinson and his board were given general responsibility for the welfare of the Belgian refugees who began to arrive in Ireland soon after the outbreak of war. A central committee was served by members of the board's staff and efforts were made

to organise temporary housing accommodation at workhouses and elsewhere.[73] From an early stage, Robinson was complaining to Nathan that difficulties were arising because of 'undesirable' refugee families and 'obstreperous Belgians', and demanded that 'we must have some place of our own to which we could send undesirables'.[74] However, there were competing demands from the military for workhouse accommodation for German prisoners of war,[75] and for this reason some refugees had to be placed in relatively remote locations such as Balla, County Mayo, where a refugee settlement was inspected by Birrell and Robinson in February 1916.[76] In all, 2,300 Belgian refugees had been catered for before repatriation commenced soon after the end of the war.[77]

- Petrol Rationing: Given his own interest and involvement in motoring from its earliest days, it was not surprising that Robinson agreed in 1917 to act as chairman of a petrol rationing committee, supported by temporary women clerks and a large number of other LGB clerks and typists, some of whom were working overtime after normal office hours.[78] With the increased availability of supplies, the operation was wound up in 1919.[79]

- Allotments: With a view to increasing the supply of food, the LGB was instructed at the beginning of 1917 to introduce schemes for the provision of allotments by local councils in both urban and rural areas. Councils were authorised to borrow money to acquire land for allotments of up to one-eighth of an acre in urban areas and up to an acre in rural areas, and the rural district councils were authorised to provide seed potatoes, manure and implements on credit to smallholders and tenants of labourers' cottages. Robinson did his best to restrict the scope of these schemes in view of the general prosperity among those engaged in agriculture, and he resisted agitation for the use by urban authorities of compulsory powers to acquire land, believing that the agitation was 'based on a desire to get hold of some of the demesnes of the manor houses, which are to be found near every town'. By the end of March 1918, the total area under cultivation was approximately 2,000 acres, and the number of individual allotments was about 17,500. Urban allotment schemes were continued until the end of the war, and in view of their popularity, statutory provision for their operation on a permanent basis was made in 1926.[80]

- Food Rationing: In May 1917, when the War Cabinet was concerned that shortages of essential foodstuffs might arise, it considered proposals for the establishment, by local councils throughout the UK, of arrangements through which a rationing system could be operated should the need arise.[81] A conference in Dublin Castle agreed in May that the co-operation of local councils in Ireland could not be relied on if rationing became necessary, and while it would be extremely difficult to find a competent person to supervise the operation of an alternative system, all were agreed that if Robinson would take up the duty it would be admirably done.[82] In August, when it was decided to control bread prices through a licensing system, the chief secretary was again advised that it would not be practicable in rural Ireland to entrust this task to the local councils. Duke, who was clearly annoyed by this, told the under-secretary that it was a matter of grave concern that the LGB should deem it inadvisable to enlist the services of local councils outside the county boroughs in the business of food control. The contrast between the arrangements made in England and Scotland and the 'arbitrary and artificial methods to which we seem to be driven with regard to the same problem in Ireland will, I fear, furnish the text for criticism upon the shortcomings of Irish administration and the want of practical contact and co-operation between the executive and the people of Ireland.' While he appreciated the 'undoubted subjection of many of the local representative bodies to influences outside their own membership, which are notoriously hostile to the government', and while he attached great weight to the judgment of Robinson in the matter, Duke made 'a new and emphatic request' that the issue should be reviewed in light of the policy considerations he had stressed.[83] In the end, however, Robinson's view on the prospects of obtaining co-operation by local councils prevailed, and he declined the suggestion that he should become personally involved in overseeing a rationing system – possibly the only occasion on which he refused to undertake an official assignment of any kind. The task of advising the UK Food Controller on Irish requirements and implementing his statutory orders in Ireland had then to be assigned to a national committee under the chairmanship of Frederick S. Wrench, a land commissioner.[84]

Conclusion

The war, which was expected by some people to have ended by Christmas 1914, dragged on for nearly four years after that. Despite this, it had relatively little impact on the organisation of the LGB, partly because reductions in the workload arising in some sections were offset by the need to allocate staff to provide new services. On 1 August 1914, staff numbers totalled 255, whereas in November 1918 there were 243 on the payroll. Vacancies arising from enlistment or otherwise had been filled by temporary appointments, many of whom were women, but in March 1919, normal arrangements for filling vacancies in the authorised establishment were resumed. The board quickly took full advantage of this relaxation of control – by August 1921 it had appointed no less than forty-three ex-servicemen to permanent and temporary positions, some of them for work connected with the sailors and soldiers housing programme.[85]

The embargo on capital expenditure, which Robinson enthusiastically supported, and the other restrictions on public expenditure drastically curtailed improvements in services between 1914 and 1918. There were some limited developments in relation to such matters as maternal, child welfare and school meal services, but the most significant consequences of the war for the board were the deferral of action on housing in Dublin and other urban areas, and the further postponement of action to reform the poor relief system. When it became possible in 1919 for the cabinet to turn its attention again to matters such as these, and to contemplate additional spending, the changed political circumstances in Ireland effectively precluded the long-overdue reforms.

NOTES

1   Robinson to Birrell, 18 Aug. 1914, Oxford, Bodleian Library, MSS Eng. c. 7034, f. 140–144.

2   *Report on Recruiting in Ireland*, HC 1914–16 [Cd. 8186].

3   *Royal Commission on the Rebellion in Ireland: Minutes of Evidence and Appendix of Documents*, HC 1916 [Cd. 8311], table of statistics submitted by Sir Matthew Nathan, p.124.

4   *Statement giving particulars regarding Men of Military Age in Ireland*, HC 1916 [Cd. 8390]; Estimates prepared in the chief secretary's office, NLI, Joseph Brennan Papers, MS 26,168.

5   *Irish Times*, 14 June 1915.

6   *Irish Times*, 8 Nov. 1915.

7   Memorandum of interview, 17 June 1915, Oxford, Bodleian Library, MS Nathan 468, f. 164.

8   Charles W. Magill (ed.), *From Dublin Castle to Stormont: The Memoirs of Andrew Philip Magill, 1913–1925* (Cork, 2003), p.51.

9   Sir Henry Robinson, *Memories: Wise and Otherwise* (London, 1923), pp.232–33.

10 National Registration Act, 1915, 5 & 6 Geo. 5, c. 60, 15 July 1915.

11 *Hansard* V, 73, 8 July 1915, 577–584.

12 Nathan to Birrell, 8 July 1915, Oxford, Bodleian Library, MSS Eng. c. 7033, f. 157–164.

13 Copy of letter of 2 July 1915 from Frederick Wrench to Walter Long, PRONI, Carson Papers, D 1597/A/13/6.

14 Letter of 21 Aug. 1915 from Nathan, published in the *Irish Times*, 2 Sept. 1915.

15   *Hansard* V, 77, 11 Jan. 1916, 1560–68.

16   Robinson to Nathan, 9 Feb. 1915, NLI, Joseph Brennan Papers, MS 26,168.

17   Leon Ó Broin, *No Man's Man* (1982), p.39.

18   Copy of circular of 25 Nov. 1915 sent by Nathan to Brennan, NLI, Joseph Brennan Papers, MS 26,130.

19   Letters of 28 Nov. and 7 Dec. 1915 to Joseph Brennan from his father, NLI, Joseph Brennan Papers, MS 26,006; Leon Ó Broin, *No Man's Man* (1982), pp.39–40.

20   Nathan to Birrell, 3 Nov. 1914, Oxford, Bodleian Library, MSS. Eng. c. 7033, f. 8–17; Robinson to Nathan, 2 Nov. 1914, MS. Nathan 460, f. 154–55; C. H. Robinson to Nathan, 19 June 1915, MS. Nathan 460, f. 150.

21   *AR*, 1914–15, p.lxx.

22   Irish Public Departments: return of numbers of staff who have joined the armed forces to 30 Nov. 1915, NLI, Joseph Brennan Papers, MS 26,168.

23   *Return showing the number of persons employed in the various government departments in Great Britain at the outbreak of War and on 1 April 1916; the number who have joined the forces; and the number of military age remaining on the same date*, HC 1916 (78).

24   *Hansard* V, 86, 26 Oct. 1916, 1272.

25   *Hansard* V, 87, 16 Nov. 1916, 946–47; 88, 31 Dec. 1916, 1590–91.

26   *Return showing the Number of Persons Employed in the various Government Departments at the outbreak of War and at the present Time, the Number who have joined the Forces etc*, HC 1918 (76).

27   *Irish Times*, 4 June 1918.

28   Circular of 9 Sept. 1914, *AR*, 1914–15, p.39.

29   Robinson to Nathan, 9 Feb. 1915, NLI, Joseph Brennan Papers, MS 26,168.

30   *AR*, 1915–16, p. xxiii; *Irish Times*, 18 Dec. 1915.

31   Memorandum of Nathan–Robinson interview, 25 Jan. 1916, Oxford, Bodleian Library, MS Nathan 469, f. 211–212.

32   Caitriona Foley, *The Last Irish Plague: The Great Flu Epidemic In Ireland 1918–19* (Dublin, 2011), p.106.

33   Robinson to Nathan, 29 Jan. 1915, Oxford, Bodleian Library, MS Nathan 460, f. 168–69.

34   Robinson to Nathan, 9 Feb. 1915, Oxford, Bodleian Library, MS Nathan 460, f. 172–73.

35   Memorandum prepared by Robinson, 22 Nov. 1915, Oxford, Bodleian Library, MS Nathan 475, f. 147–151.

36   *First report of the Committee on Retrenchment in the Public Expenditure*, HC 1914–16 [Cd. 8139].

37   Treasury circular of 1 Oct. 1915, Oxford, Bodleian Library, MS Nathan, f. 475.

38   Note of Nathan–Robinson interview, 25 Oct. 1915, NLI, Joseph Brennan Papers, MS 26,160/2.

39   Nathan to Birrell, 22 Nov. 1915, Oxford, Bodleian Library, MSS. Eng. c. 7033, f. 230–34.

40   Memoranda dated 22 and 26 Nov. 1915, Oxford, Bodleian Library, MS Nathan, 475, f. 147–151, 153–55.

41 *Second Report of the Committee on Retrenchment in the Public Expenditure*, HC 1914–16 [Cd. 8139].

42 Maurice Headlam, *Irish Reminiscences* (London, 1947), pp.69–70; *Irish Independent*, 4 Dec. 1915.

43 *Final report of the Committee on Retrenchment in the Public Expenditure*, HC 1916 [Cd. 8200].

44 *Hansard* V, 80, 15 Mar. 1916, 2093–2095.

45 Michael T. Foy & Brian Barton, *The Easter Rising* (2011 edition) (Stroud, 2011), p. 213.

46 Robinson to Blackett, 22 Mar. 1915, TNA, T 1/11914.

47 *AR* 1915–16, pp.xlvii–xlix.

48 Robinson to Heath, 22 July 1915, TNA, T 1/11808/17813,

49 Robinson to Treasury, 8 Dec. 1915, TNA, T 1/11914.

50 Magill to Leach 14 May 1915 and Leach to Magill, 19 May 1915, NLI, Joseph Brennan Papers, MS 26,175.

51 Robinson–Treasury–Redmond correspondence, Aug.-Sept. 1915, TNA, T 1/11914; Redmond–Robinson correspondence, Aug.-Sept. 1915, NLI, Redmond papers, MS 15,261/6, 15,261/7.

52 Murray Fraser, *John Bull's Other Homes: State Housing and British Policy in Ireland, 1883–1922* (Liverpool, 1996), pp.112–114.

53 LGB to Treasury, 17 Nov. 1914 and subsequent correspondence, TNA, T 1/11785.

54 Housing (No. 2) Act 1914, 4 & 5 Geo. 5, c. 52, 10 Aug. 1914; Housing (No.2) (Amendment) Act 1914, 4 & 5 Geo. 5, c. 71, 28 Aug. 1914.

55 Memorandum of 27 Oct. 1915 from LGB to Birrell, NLI, Joseph Brennan Papers, MS 26,165.

56 Robinson to Treasury, 8 Sept. 1914, Birrell to Montagu, 22 Sept. 1914, and subsequent correspondence, TNA, T 1/11668.

57 *Irish Times*, 26 Oct. 1915.

58 *Irish Times*, 8 Dec. 1915.

59 Cosgrave to Griffith, 28 Aug. 1919, UCDA, de Valera MSS, vol.2, P 150, Item 1400.

60 Murray Fraser, *John Bull's Other Homes*, pp.149–150.

61 *Hansard* V, 76, 8 Dec. 1915, 1409.

62 Robinson to Treasury, 8 and 9 Dec. 1915 and Treasury to Robinson, 15 Dec. 1915, TNA, T 1/11914.

63 *Hansard* V, 76, 15 Dec. 1915, 2065.

64 Robinson to Duke, 21 Aug. 1916, Oxford, Bodleian Library, MSS, Dep. c.714, f. 81, cited in Murray Fraser, *John Bull's Other Homes*, p.157.

65 *Irish Times*, 12 and 14 Apr. 1917.

66 Duke–Bonar Law – Duke and other correspondence, Apr. 1917, TNA, T 1/12396, annex to Treasury file 13447/17.

67 Letter of 19 Apr. 1917 from Duke to Lord Mayor O'Neill, NLI, Laurence O'Neill Letters, MS 35,294/1.

68 Robinson to Magill, 16 July 1917 and subsequent notes and correspondence, NAI, CSORP 1921/2381.

69 P. C. Cowan, *Report on Dublin Housing* (Dublin, 1918), p.31.

70 Cosgrave to Griffith, 28 Aug. 1919, UCDA, de Valera MSS, vol.2, P 150, Item 1400.

71 E. A. Aston, Special report upon the administration of the National Relief Fund in Ireland to 28 Feb. 1915, TNA, T 1/11781.

72 Correspondence 12 Mar. to 1 Apr. 1915, TNA, T 1/11881.

73 Minute Book of the Belgian Refugees Committee, UCDA, P 105.

74 Robinson to Nathan, 6 Jan. 1915, Oxford, Bodleian Library, MS Nathan 460, f. 166–67.

75 Robinson to Nathan, 13 Nov. 1914, Oxford, Bodleian Library, MS Nathan 460, f. 160–61.

76 *Irish Times*, 8 Feb. 1916.

77 *AR*, 1918–19.

78 *Irish Times*, 18 July, 20 Aug. 1917.

79 *Fourth Interim report, Committee appointed to enquire into the organisation and staffing of government offices*, HC 1919 [Cmd. 61]; Committee on Staffs, sub-committee reports, No.3, Dublin, TNA, T.1/12286.

80 *AR*, 1917–18, pp.xxiv–xxvi; Acquisition of Land (Allotments) Act, 1926, No. 8 of 1926, 6 Mar. 1926.

81 Memorandum (G. 149) by Food Controller for submission to War Cabinet, 28 May 1917, NLI, Joseph Brennan Papers, MS 26,131.

82 Minutes of a conference held at Dublin Castle on 4 May 1917, NLI, Joseph Brennan Papers, MS 26,131.

83 Confidential minute, 8 Aug. 1917, H.E. Duke to the under-secretary, NLI, Joseph Brennan Papers, MS 26,131.

84 *Irish Times*, 3 Sept. 1917.

85 Assistant Under-Secretary Papers, PRONI, AUS 3/32; Barlas to chief secretary's office, 20 Aug. 1921, NAI, CSORP 1921/3504.

CHAPTER XI

The Easter Rising: Was There A Living Soul … Who was Prepared for What was to Follow?

If Henry Robinson had been Under-Secretary from 1914 onwards, 'many of the troubles, and possibly the rebellion of 1916, would have been avoided'. This was the view – not altogether an unreasonable one – expressed by Maurice Headlam, the English civil servant, who was Treasury Remembrancer at Dublin Castle from 1912 to 1920, in his *Irish Reminiscences* published over thirty years after the Easter Rising. Headlam believed that if Robinson had been Under-Secretary, Birrell might have been persuaded to pay some attention to the warnings of the police and to take measures in time to avert the Rising. He felt that Robinson was one of only two men in Ireland who knew the country sufficiently well to be able to show the cabinet how to deal with the Sinn Féin mentality. He had no doubt that Robinson, with his greater knowledge of Ireland, and his more active and ingenious brain, would have succeeded, somehow, in persuading the Chief Secretary to take the precautions which might have prevented the rebellion. Alternatively, if Birrell had refused to take action, Robinson would not have hesitated to resign 'if there had been no other way of overcoming Mr Birrell's inertia, and to make his reasons, and the danger, public'.[1] Headlam's comments were made with the advantage of hindsight, and clearly took account of the finding by the Royal Commission on the Rebellion that Nathan as Under-Secretary 'did not sufficiently impress upon the Chief Secretary during the latter's prolonged absences from Dublin the necessity for more active measures to remedy the situation'. But the view that the Rising – or serious armed conflict in some form and at some date – would not have occurred if Robinson had been in office at Dublin Castle from 1914 onwards is not credible. It is certainly reasonable to suggest that events in Ireland in that period would have been quite different if he, rather than Nathan, had been Under-Secretary – but the likelihood is that instead of averting a crisis, he would have brought matters to a head long before April 1916.

Highly Improbable that the Sinn Féiners would Take On the Army

Some months before the Rising, Nathan discussed the security situation with Robinson, who recalled that the Under-Secretary was becoming very uneasy at the information reaching him of the growing strength of Sinn Féin, who were 'openly drilling and marching with dummy guns all over the place'. Nathan asked Robinson to send a private note to all of the board's inspectors, asking whether they had any information as to 'the seriousness or otherwise of this menace'.[2] Strictly speaking, both the political and security situations were not matters of official concern to Robinson or his inspectors. However, the use of the inspectors on analogous occasions to provide snapshots for the authorities on developments in different parts of the country was a practice which had been resorted to at different times since the 1870s. Unfortunately, the reports provided by the individual inspectors in 1915–16 do not appear to have survived, but Nathan's papers include the covering letters with which Robinson forwarded reports from some of them in December 1915.[3] He had not asked the inspectors in the West for their views as he 'understood the Sinn Féiners are not of much account there', but he supplied reports from the other inspectors, including those based in Belfast and Waterford, and promised that reports from other areas, including Cork and Kerry, would follow. The report from inspector Alfred Delany, a former *Irish Times* journalist, and 'an RC and a nationalist (only electro-plated)', was very interesting, according to Robinson. A report from Charles O' Conor, one of his most senior inspectors, relating to the situation in Dublin 'takes a more alarmist view than the facts would warrant', and the report on the Belfast district by Francis McCarthy, who had been Robinson's private secretary at one stage, attracted no comment except the explanation that McCarthy – an RC and a Jesuit – had been a sterling nationalist, 'but the political squabbles in Belfast put him off and now he takes only an academic view of the Irish question'.

Seven years after the event, Robinson's recollection was that the inspectors, while reporting the numerical strength of the Sinn Féin movement in their areas, 'did not attach much gravity to it, as they said it was highly improbable that the Sinn Féiners would take on the British army, and even if they did, they would be knocked out within a week'. The general opinion at the time, Robinson believed, was much the same.[4] On the other hand, judging by a letter which he sent in early 1916 to Major General Oliver Nugent, one of his former motoring companions who was then commanding the 36th Ulster Division in France, he seems to have had some concern for the developing situation. Writing on 3 February, Wilfrid Spender, then serving as a staff officer with the division, was able to tell his wife that Nugent had just heard from Robinson that 'Redmond and his party are entirely discredited, and that their following have lost all interest in them now.' The Sinn Féiners, according to this account of Robinson's letter, were 'very much on the upgrade and are getting very large funds thro' America from Germany, and with the tolerance which is accorded them, are becoming more and more above themselves and openly pro-German. There seems to be a chance of a bust-up there'.[5] If this was an accurate representation of Robinson's views at the time, they were remarkably similar to the opinions expressed by one of his senior civil service colleagues, William Bailey, the estates commissioner, when he told Carson in a private and confidential letter in August 1915 that the situation was 'much more grave than the executive thinks', and that the government was constantly climbing down. He was amazed that only a few days earlier, thousands of men carrying rifles had been facilitated by the police in marching triumphantly through the streets at O'Donovan Rossa's funeral, even though they were Sinn Féiners and were largely pro-German.[6]

Liberty Hall, facing the Custom House, was the headquarters of the Irish Transport and General Workers Union (ITGWU) and of James Connolly's Irish Citizen Army and, according to the *Irish Times*, was 'the centre of social anarchy in Ireland, the brain of every riot and disturbance'.[7] Robinson's own office windows faced the building, and he must have noted that it was a hive of activity in the weeks before the Rising. 'We serve neither King nor Kaiser, but Ireland' had been emblazoned across the face of the building for more than a year. Aside from this, armed men could be seen on guard at the entrance, the green flag of the Irish Republic had been raised over the building on Sunday 16 April in the presence of a large crowd, munitions were being stockpiled in the building, meetings were being held there daily, and the Proclamation was printed there.[8] But, as preparations for the Rising were made by the men and women of the

Citizen Army, Robinson and his civil servants at the Custom House, like most others in Dublin, would have had no reason to suspect that dramatic developments were imminent. He had directed that the offices were to be closed on Good Friday, 21 April 'as on Sundays' and that Saturday 22 April as well as 24 and 25 April – the Monday and Tuesday of Easter Week – could be observed as office holidays, subject to arrangements being made to transact any urgent business on the Tuesday.[9] Thus, the offices were closed when the Rising began, with only the resident caretakers and their families remaining in occupation of the building. They most likely watched in amazement as parties of Volunteers and Citizen Army members formed up in Beresford Place and set off just before noon on Easter Monday to occupy the GPO and the City Hall. Many of the office staff had probably left the city for the weekend, taking short holidays elsewhere, and as Robinson put it, outside 'the Sinn Féiners themselves ... there was [not] a living soul in Ireland who was prepared for what was to follow'.[10] He himself travelled to Mallaranny, Co. Mayo, where Birrell was to join him on the Tuesday of Easter week, effectively disappearing to the country with Robinson, as he had described his plans in a letter to Nathan in advance of a similar visit to the West a year earlier.[11]

Robinson planned to be back in Dublin in time to attend the production at the Abbey Theatre of a new three-act play *The Spancel of Death* (or '*Booraugh Waash*'). In the weeks before Easter, he had found time to correspond with the author, Thomas Henry Nally, a civil servant at Dublin Castle, about the play, which centred on real events involving alleged witchcraft and superstition in County Mayo in the eighteenth century and related to early members of Robinson's wife's family, the Lynch-Blosses. Having been given an opportunity to read the script, he told Nally that the play was 'the most powerful and dramatic thing' he had ever read. It held him spellbound and the dialogue was so natural that he could almost hear the people speaking. He believed that if properly staged, the play would 'create a great sensation' and he was looking forward to the production.[12] However, while the theatre was booked out for the opening on the Tuesday of Easter week, the performance was cancelled because of the Rising and it seems that the play was, subsequently, never to be professionally produced.[13]

Rebel Staff Activity

Responding in April 1912 to a question about an alleged disloyal address by a civil servant at a nationalist meeting in Dublin, Birrell told the House of Commons that there was 'a well-known though unwritten rule that civil servants must refrain from taking an active part in politics',[14] but this rule was regularly ignored. By November 1914, when Nathan had just taken up duty as Under-Secretary, he noted that a good number of the lower officials in the civil service were members of Sinn Féin, and remarked some time later that 'for some reason which I am unable to fathom, a large proportion of the people treasonable to England ... are to be found in the lower ranks of the government service'.[15] Arthur Hamilton Norway, secretary of the Irish Post Office – by far the largest public sector employer at the time – recorded in his memoir that for months before the Rising he was receiving police and army reports of disloyalty or seditious activity – some of them based solely on suspicion – among the 17,000 staff for which he was responsible.[16] In February 1915, Nathan told Charles Hobhouse, the Postmaster General, that many of the minor civil service officials were imbued with Sinn Féinism but he reported at the same time to Birrell's private secretary that the number of officials against whom 'steps could be taken on the basis of our present information does not amount to more than a dozen'.[17] Half of these were said to be in the Post Office, and none were LGB employees.[18]

Whether the LGB or Robinson personally may have received police or army reports relating to any of the board's staff is not known, but all the indications are that only a tiny minority of the staff had any involvement in political or revolutionary activity before 1916. Indeed, as a clerk in the Dublin office of the National Health Insurance Commission subsequently wrote, there can have been no more than a handful of civil servants who had any inkling of what was brewing for Easter, with the result that the week burst upon them with shattering surprise.[19] Immediately after the Rising, a circular issued by Nathan asked heads of departments to arrange for each Dublin-based civil servant to make a full statement of his movements and occupations on each day between 22 April and 1 May, and to forward the statement to him, with any comments.[20] According to one OPW official who described the process in his diary, 'we had to state all our doings and where we slept each night'.[21] Unfortunately, the file containing the statements made by LGB staff members and submitted to the Chief Secretary's office on 4 July cannot be found in NAI, although statements submitted by other departments have survived there.[22] In mid-June, heads of departments were advised that it was a matter for them in the first instance to consider the cases of any of their officials who were suspected of complicity in the rebellion and, where there were grounds for serious suspicion, to suspend those involved.[23] Departments were then to send reports on each suspended official to the Chief Secretary's Office, which would submit them for review to a committee under Mr Justice

Sankey, which was already dealing with cases arising in England under the Defence of the Realm Regulations. By July, long lists of officials who were believed to have connections with Sinn Féin, including considerable numbers employed by the local authorities, were provided by the RIC county inspectors, leading the LGB secretary to ask the Castle for directions as to what steps the board was to take in relation to the persons concerned.[24] None of the lists included men or women employed directly by the board but, having established that Richard Hayes, dispensary doctor at Lusk, County Dublin, had been convicted by court martial of having taken part in the battle of Ashbourne on 26 April, Robinson signed an order dismissing him from the service on 19 May.[25]

More than 3,500 men and women were arrested and detained or deported after the Rising, but only two members of the LGB staff – James P. Kenny, an assistant clerk, and James J. McElligott, a higher division clerk – were among these. McElligott's case was taken up by M. J. Flavin, MP for North Kerry, who asked in the House of Commons on 22 May why a young man with 'an unimpeachable character' and no direct or indirect action with the rebellion had been arrested and was being detained at Stafford Gaol without charge. The official response was simply that the case was being investigated.[26] As the Sankey committee already had too much work on their hands, two commissioners, Sir Guy Fleetwood-Wilson and Sir William Byrne, both English civil servants, were appointed by the Home Secretary at the end of July to review the cases of forty-two civil servants who, like Kenny and McElligott, had been suspended, and to advise how they should be dealt with. Having interviewed Robinson, Barlas, the LGB secretary, and the two LGB suspects in Dublin, the commissioners recommended on 16 August that they should both be dismissed along with twenty-one others from other departments. Kenny was still in custody at that stage but McElligott, like more than half of those arrested, had been released within a few weeks.[27]

Kenny, aged about 17, was a member of the Rathfarnham Company of the Volunteers and had served in the GPO during Easter week. After imprisonment in England, he was released in July 1917.[28] McElligott was a 23-year-old graduate, with an honours degree in classics from UCD, who had joined the LGB in November 1913 but was not particularly happy there. He told his friend, Joseph Brennan (then serving in a first division post in the Chief Secretary's Office) that the LGB was an office where a protestant freemason clique looked askance at papists, the worst offender being Barlas.[29] According to Michael Knightly, a native of Tralee and a Dublin journalist, who chanced to have tea with McElligott while they were both serving in the GPO (McElligott on the roof and Knightly at a ground floor window), McElligott had no illusions about the outcome of the Rising. When Knightly suggested pessimistically to him that all of them in the GPO would be wiped out, McElligott's response was 'what matter, it will keep up the old spirit'.[30]

Eunan O'Halpin's study of the Chief Secretary's Office Registered Papers suggests that when Robinson was faced with the Wilson–Byrne recommendation that McElligott should be dismissed, he set aside his political principles in trying to save the career of his promising first class clerk.[31] He argued that McElligott should simply be transferred to work in England, pointing out that he had severed his connections with the Irish Volunteers in 1915 when warned that these would affect his career, and had taken part in the Rising only under compulsion. He had reported for work on Tuesday 25 April but had found the offices of the LGB locked. On his way home he met the professor of constitutional law at Trinity College, and was talking to him in Abbey Street when a group of his former Volunteer associates came along and forced him at gunpoint to join them. According to O'Halpin, this strange tale was checked by the DMP, who confirmed with the Trinity witness that it was true – but McElligott does not seem to have been the innocent abroad which Robinson made him out to be. In fact, he provided a very different version of his 1916 activity in the application for a Military Service Pension which he made in September 1953, some months after he had resigned his position as secretary of the Department of Finance to succeed Brennan as governor of the Central Bank. His application (and the award of a small pension which he assigned for the benefit of a widowed sister-in-law) was based on claims that he had been a member of the Volunteers since the establishment of the organisation in 1913, that he had been a member of B Company of the Second Battalion of the Dublin Brigade (based mainly in Jacob's Factory), that having been cut off from his colleagues he joined up in the GPO, served there until the surrender, was arrested and detained in Richmond Barracks and then deported to Stafford Gaol, from which he was released at the end of May. He stated also that he had been engaged to some extent in Volunteer activity in subsequent years and that his involvement in the 'Chequers Incident' in 1921 had led to a brief imprisonment in Aylesbury and a subsequent requirement to report regularly to Scotland Yard.[32]

When invited in mid-August to comment on the Wilson–Byrne report, Robinson urged that it should be given wide circulation (the only head of department to support publication) and suggested – as some of his colleagues did – that the officers who were to be dismissed were entitled to know the grounds which influenced the commissioners in their recommendations.[33] As a result, Duke and Home Secretary Samuel asked the commissioners to provide a supplementary report, setting out the nature of the offences found to have been committed in each case, but the commissioners refused to do so. Robinson then forced the Chief Secretary's Office to seek the advice of the attorney general for Ireland on whether the men concerned could legally be dismissed without cause shown. Having been told that the Lord Lieutenant had this power, Robinson suggested that he – rather than the LGB – should act without delay so that the board, which was 'very short-handed', could engage new men before the winter work set in, and so that the two men, who had been kept waiting for a very long time, should be free to look for employment elsewhere. However, after the Home Office had objected to what they saw as an attempt to transfer responsibility for the dismissals from Robinson to the King, he and other heads of departments were directed by the Lord Lieutenant on 5 October to take the necessary steps to remove the men from office and was advised that the Lord Lieutenant considered that they '*may* be paid their salaries up to the date of dismissal'. Robinson conceded defeat at that stage, at least in relation to the dismissals, by arranging to have a curiously worded addendum included in the LGB minutes for 11 October: 'In accordance with the decision of His Majesty's Government, the undermentioned clerks [Kenny and McElligott], who were assigned by the Civil Service Commissioners to the Department of the Local Government Board for Ireland, are hereby dismissed from the employment of the Board.'[34]

While departments generally implemented the Lord Lieutenant's instructions without question, Robinson created new difficulties by challenging the suggestion that salaries should be paid to men who had been suspended and were absent from duty since 24 April. In a personal submission to Duke on 10 October, he suggested that, as accounting officer, he should either have Treasury sanction or explicit directions from the Chief Secretary, as President of the board, before paying six months' salary arrears to men 'who were prevented from discharging their duties … owing to having taken up arms in open rebellion against the Crown'. He argued that it would be 'especially difficult to justify payment of their salaries during the week they were actually in arms and engaged in slaying the soldiers and police'. While the Treasury agreed with Robinson, the attorney general adhered to the view that because of the delay, the men had an equitable claim to their salaries for the period of suspension, and Sir Edward O'Farrell, who was acting as under-secretary at the time, pointedly drew attention to the fact that there was nothing in the Wilson–Byrne report to justify Robinson's reference to 'slaying the soldiers and police'. Duke acted on the legal advice and instructed Robinson that the men were to be paid as originally suggested, and that ended the matter. However, one is forced to ask why Robinson initiated a skirmish about salary payments with the Lord Lieutenant and the Castle that he must have known he could not win and which appeared to be inconsistent with his earlier support for McElligott and his reluctance to dismiss him. Was it simply a further effort to demonstrate disagreement with dismissals for which no specific case had been adduced? Was it because of his annoyance at being forced to implement dismissals, which he felt should have been made by the Lord Lieutenant? Or, could it have been influenced by his contempt for O'Farrell, whom he regarded as 'a spent fish',[35] and was rumoured at the time to be favoured for appointment to the under-secretary post for which Robinson himself was being recommended by Walter Long?

The *Irish Times* was able to report on 21 October that two clerks had been discharged from the LGB as a result of the inquiry into the part alleged to have been taken by civil servants in relation to the rebellion.[36] McElligott, who had been notified of his dismissal ten days earlier, subsequently asked the board to inform him of the exact reasons for his dismissal, but was simply told, in a letter drafted by Duke himself, that it was based on the report of the Wilson–Byrne committee, even though this had not been published in any shape or form. In November, McElligott wrote several letters to the Chief Secretary's Office, seeking his reinstatement, but the dismissal stood despite a submission from the Catholic Bishop of Limerick, Edward O' Dwyer, suggesting that the charges against him were unfounded.[37] In the following year, when Robinson was asked to supply material for reply to parliamentary questions which challenged the procedure of the Wilson–Byrne committee, and asked for the specific grounds of dismissal in the case of each official, his less than helpful reply suggests that he was still unhappy about the outcome: 'It does not appear from any papers in the board's possession on what evidence, or on what specific grounds' the decision to dismiss Kenny and McElligott was made by the government.[38] The reply given by Duke in the House of Commons confirmed that no specific grounds had been relied on, but that 'in each case, the ground of dismissal was unfitness for the service of the Crown'.[39]

As Private Secretary to the acting Under-Secretary, Joseph Brennan had been heavily involved in making arrangements for the review which led to McElligott's dismissal, but the friendship between the two men survived and they corresponded regularly in the following years. In March 1919, McElligott wrote that 'it is hard luck that I should be condemned to live on the wrong side of St George's Channel' as a result of the rebellion, while in January 1920 he was attempting to help Brennan overcome the 'low tricks of the government orange gang in Dublin' which, the latter complained, had deprived him of a promotion to which he felt entitled.[40] 'Mac', as he signed himself, who was then editor of *The Statist* in London, arranged, at that stage, an offer to Brennan of a position on the journal worth £500 a year (which he did not take up),[41] while Ernest Blythe, as the Dáil's Director of Trade and Commerce, proposed in September 1920 that McElligott should be appointed as secretary of a proposed National Economic Council, only to find that his colleagues in the ministry preferred Erskine Childers for the position.[42] In due course, after Brennan had joined the new Department of Finance in 1922, he was able to arrange for McElligott's return to the civil service as an assistant secretary in that department, where he succeeded Brennan as secretary in 1927.[43]

In addition to James Kenny and J. J. McElligott, Thomas J. McArdle, who had joined the LGB as a second division clerk in November 1901 at the age of 19, was also a casualty of the Wilson–Byrne committee, although indirectly so. The committee recommended that civil servants throughout the UK should be obliged to take an Oath of Allegiance to the Crown. Nothing was done about this, however, until July 1918, when a new Chief Secretary wrote to the Prime Minister that he hoped that 'something has been done about the Oath of Allegiance to be taken by local bodies. It is regarded here as most important'.[44] After the War Cabinet had considered the issue, Bonar Law told the House of Commons that an Oath of Allegiance was to be introduced for those entering the civil service.[45] When consulted, James MacMahon, who had just been appointed as Under-Secretary, raised no objection to extending this requirement to all existing Irish civil servants. He did point out, however, quite sensibly, that this would serve no useful purpose as a civil servant who was disloyal at heart would not hesitate to take the oath, and would hold himself morally free from its obligations on the grounds that taking it was compulsory – just as several civil servants who had been required to sign undertakings to keep themselves free of disloyal associations had taken an active part in the 1916 rebellion, and just as de Valera and his supporters were to do in August 1927.[46] In August 1918, a regulation was eventually made under the Defence of the Realm Acts, requiring persons who were established civil servants on 2 August, or who were to be appointed after that date, to take the Oath of Allegiance before 1 November. The regulation was condemned by the Irish Trade Union Congress and by civil service organisations, but only a small number of civil servants refused to comply.[47] McArdle was the sole LGB official among these, and he was dismissed by

Robinson on 31 October 1918. He was subsequently employed by the Dáil Department of Local Government, was assimilated to the staff of the Free State's Department of Local Government in July 1922 and, like McElligott, subsequently had a successful career in the civil service of the new state. He became secretary of his department in November 1946, before serving briefly as secretary of the new Department of Health until his retirement in 1947.

Staff Activities – Official Side

On the official side, the number of LGB staff who were directly involved in the events of Easter week was very small. Most attention focussed on Major George A. Harris, a higher division clerk, who was adjutant of the Officers Training Corps (OTC) at Trinity College and OC of the 1st (Dublin) Battalion of the Associated Volunteer Corps (the Georgius Rex or, as they were known, The Gorgeous Wrecks). Founded at Trinity in 1910, the OTC had been expanded on the outbreak of the war to provide facilities for military training for men of the professional and business classes. Under Captain E. H. Alton, a classical scholar, fellow of the college and later provost, the corps took an active part in the defence of the college on the Monday of Easter week. They held it until regular troops from the Curragh moved in on Tuesday, allowing them to fire on the GPO with machine guns and with 18-pound field guns. Harris was not involved in the initial action at Trinity because of his leadership on Easter Monday of a volunteer corps training exercise at Ticknock in the Dublin Mountains. In a report written on 17 May for General Sir John Maxwell, Harris recorded that the Lord Chancellor, who had driven to Ticknock in his motor car, advised him at about 3.00 p.m. that the rebellion had broken out and that he should bring the corps back to their headquarters at Beggars' Bush Barracks. With up to 100 men who carried drill-purpose rifles, but no ammunition or bayonets, Harris started back on horseback 'taking all the usual military precautions', and left his second-in-command, F. H. Browning (a 48-year-old barrister who was examiner of titles at the Land Registry) to collect the remaining men and follow on as soon as possible. Having marched across Ball's Bridge, and along Shelbourne Road, the column led by Harris came under heavy fire from the railway as it turned into Haddington Road. About eighty men succeeded in getting safely into the barracks, but one man was hit and subsequently died. Browning and his smaller party were not so fortunate: unaware that houses near Mount Street Bridge were occupied by the rebels, they attempted to reach the barracks via Northumberland Road. They came under heavy fire, without warning or challenge of any kind, as the official report put it, and which they were unable to return. He and three of his men were killed, nine others were wounded, and the majority had to take shelter in neighbouring houses until they were able to make their way to their homes under cover of darkness.

Harris and his men remained at Beggars' Bush for some days. One of them was killed and another wounded by rebel fire later in the week. Although he was relieved of overall command by a more senior officer, Harris was responsible on the Wednesday morning for organising a continuous barrage of rifle fire against the windows of the houses in Northumberland Road from the sand-bagged windows of the barracks.[48] He appears to have continued to serve at Beggars' Bush for the rest of the week, rather than joining the garrison at Trinity, which included W. E. Wylie KC who acted for the LGB in many of their court cases from 1909 onwards, and was a 2nd lieutenant in the OTC.[49] Wylie was appointed the following week to act as prosecutor at the courts-martial of leaders of the Rising. General Maxwell subsequently told the Under-Secretary that the accounts he had received of the behaviour and gallant conduct of the OTC filled him with admiration, and that their assistance at a critical time was of very great value.[50] Accompanied by Harris, and in the presence of Prime Minister Asquith, Maxwell reviewed a parade of some 1,000 members of the corps at College Park on 13 May and personally thanked them for what they had done.[51] In August, Harris and the other officers were each presented with inscribed swords by a committee of local property owners in recognition of their services during the Rising.[52]

The Aftermath of the Rising

Having heard rumours of a rising in Dublin, Robinson drove back from Mayo by a circuitous route to his home at Foxrock, but there was no question of reporting for duty at the Custom House.[53] Although the building was not among those occupied by the rebels, it was 'in the hands of the military authority' from 26 April to 2 May, according to the board's minute book, 'martial law having been proclaimed in Dublin in consequence of armed insurrection'.[54] A substantial British force had taken possession of the building and its grounds by nightfall on Easter Monday.[55] On the following morning, the soldiers fired on Ernest Kavanagh, an accomplished cartoonist with *The Irish Worker* and a clerk at Liberty Hall and shot him dead on the steps of the building to which he was seeking entry.[56] On the Wednesday, the armed yacht H.M.S. *Helga* moored opposite the Custom House and began a bombardment of

Liberty Hall,[57] while the building was also shelled from the quay near Tara Street.[58] After the building had been partially destroyed, troops charged across Beresford Place from the Custom House, only to find that the building had been unoccupied. Later, snipers and machine-gunners on the Custom House roof and in the dome swept Beresford Place, Lower Abbey Street and some of the rebel positions in O'Connell Street. The building and its grounds were also used throughout Easter Week to house innocent civilians detained by British soldiers as well as men, women and children who fled from their houses on Eden Quay. At the end of the week, captured Volunteers, including those led by W. J. Brennan-Whitmore and Frank Thornton, who had been manning positions in North Earl Street and O'Connell Street close to the GPO, were held in one of the building's enclosed courtyards, before being transferred to Richmond Barracks on the following Monday.[59]

Although access to their headquarters was denied to LGB staff for more than a week after the Rising, Robinson was appointed in the meantime by the Lord Lieutenant to chair a food supply committee because no food had come into Dublin since Easter Saturday and supplies of bread, milk and meat were running short.[60] Meeting throughout the week at Dublin Castle, to which he drove daily from Foxrock ('a creepy business driving through deserted streets' and occasionally encountering gunfire),[61] he and his committee arranged for cattle and sheep to the value of about £4,000 to be purchased and slaughtered at the corporation's abattoir, from where the meat was sold to local butchers at normal prices. Other supplies of groceries and foodstuffs were brought in from the country by rail, depots were set up throughout the city where shopkeepers could obtain supplies, and other supplies were distributed by military transport.[62] By the weekend, the distribution of food direct to necessitous cases was being carried out in conjunction with the Society of St Vincent de Paul, which established thirty-one depots throughout the city.[63] This arrangement was commented on favourably at the time by Professor George O'Neill S.J., who noted also that the whole operation had been 'organized by the government with a promptitude quite unexampled on their part'.[64] From 8 May, when the critical period was deemed to have passed, the function was handed over to the guardians of the North and South Dublin Unions, but a team of seven LGB officials continued to be directly involved for some time in organising the processing of over 10,000 applications for food tickets, which could be redeemed at centres throughout the city. When detailed reports on the first week's work were presented on 18 May, the guardians offered Robinson and his staff their special thanks for the able manner in which relief had been administered.[65]

16. The grave of Sir Henry Robinson and his wife at Parkstone Cemetery, Poole, Dorset. (*Courtesy of Mary Millar*)

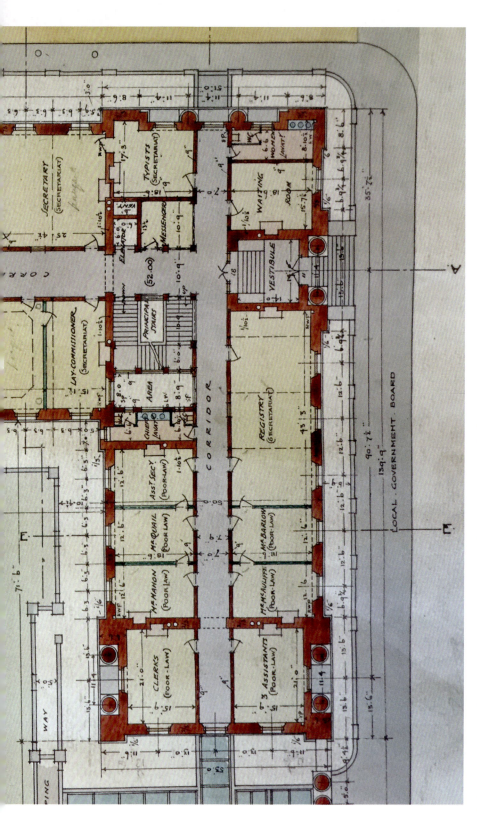

15. Drawing, c.1915, of the proposed ground floor of the North Block of Government Buildings, Dublin, showing the room designed for Robinson as Vice-President of the LGB, but subsequently used as the Cabinet Room. (*Irish Architectural Archive*)

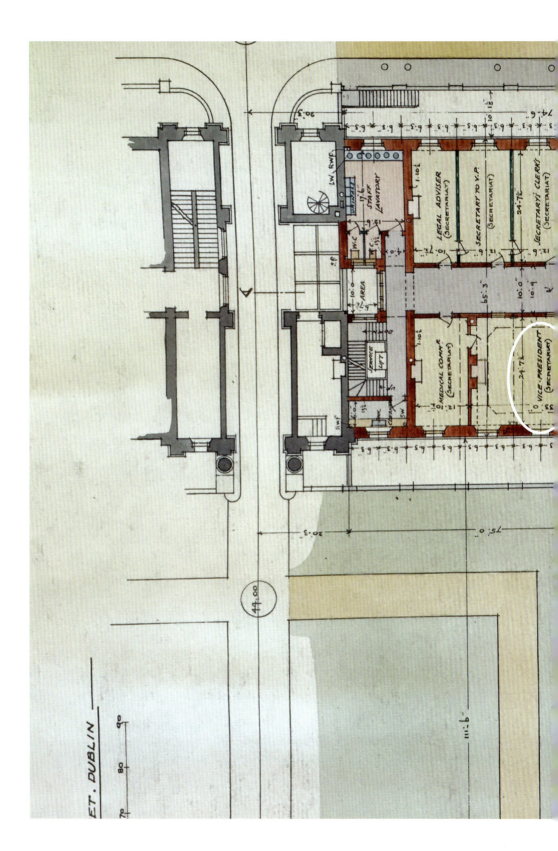

ET. DUBLIN

13. Sir Henry Robinson leaving Dublin Castle on 16 January 1922, after the 'surrender' of the government to Sinn Féin. (*British Pathe*)

14. Lisnacarrig, Brighton Road, Foxrock, Co. Dublin, home of Sir Henry Robinson until 1923. (*Irish Times*, sale advertisement)

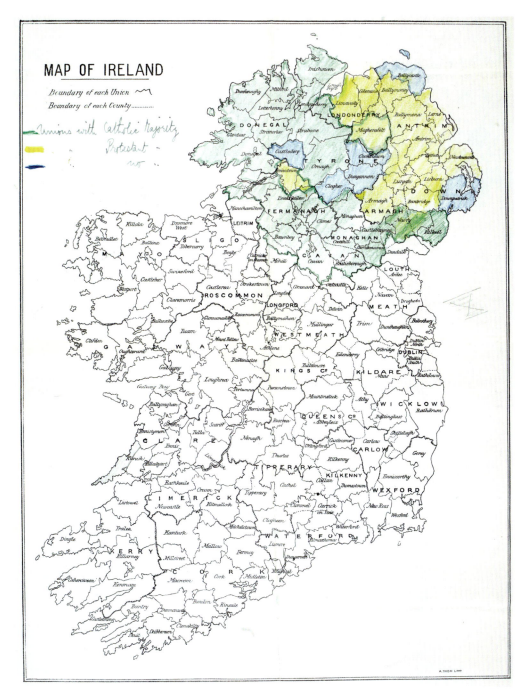

MAP OF IRELAND

Boundary of each Union ⌒
Boundary of each County...........

Unions with Catholic Majority
"   "   Protestant   "
"   "   no   "

12. A map of Ireland similar to map 2 but showing unions in Ulster coloured green for those with catholic majorities, yellow for those with protestant majorities and blue for those 'with no majority'. This map, which survives among John Redmond's papers, is likely to have been the map presented by the nationalists at the Buckingham Palace Conference in July 1914 *(National Library of Ireland, John Redmond Papers, MS 15,266).* See also page 184.

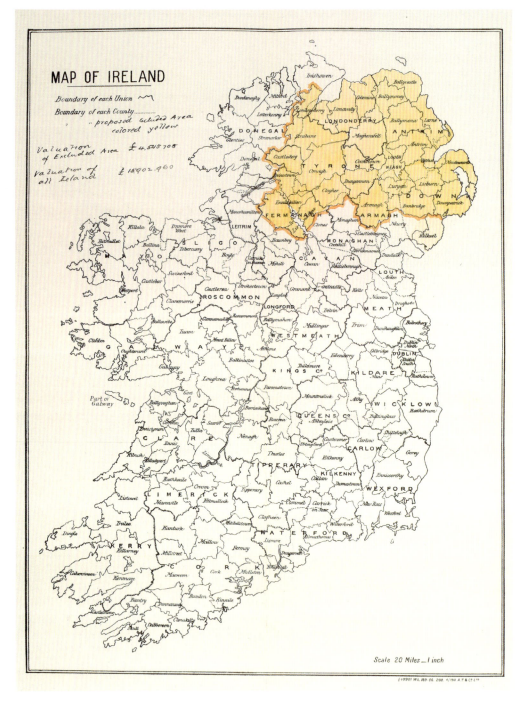

11. Map sent on 6 May 1914 by Henry Robinson to Chief Secretary Birrell, at his urgent request, giving him 'a rough idea' of an area (defined by reference to poor law union boundaries and coloured yellow) which might be excluded from Home Rule arrangements; this is likely to have been 'the Irish Office map' referred to by John Redmond in his note on the Buckingham Palace Conference of July 1914 *(The Bodleian Library, University of Oxford, Birrell Papers, MSS. Eng. c. 7034, f. 71)*. See also page 180.

10. Map of rural districts sent by Henry Robinson to Chief Secretary Birrell on 5 March 1914 showing how a northern excluded area might be defined by reference to rural district boundaries; districts with catholic majorities were shaded green and non-catholic districts red *(The Bodleian Library, University of Oxford, Birrell Papers, MSS. Eng. c. 7034, f. 60)*. See also page 177.

8. The Custom House on fire, May 1921. (*Old Ireland in Pictures*, issued by Wilson Hartnell & Co. Dublin, July 1922)

9. The ruins of the Custom House after the fire of May 1921, showing what remained of the dome with the statue of Commerce which stood above it. (*Old Ireland in Pictures*, issued by Wilson Hartnell & Co. Dublin, July 1922)

6. Robinson driving Chief Secretary Augustine Birrell and Mrs Birrell on a tour of the West, c. 1910. (*Memories: Wise and Otherwise*)

7. Robinson's favourite hotel at Recess, Co. Galway, which he regularly visited with Chief Secretaries (and with King Edward VII and his Queen in 1903); the hotel was destroyed by fire in October 1922 and never rebuilt. (*National Library of Ireland, Lawrence collection, CAB 07355*)

4. On tour with King Edward VII in the West in July 1903 – waiting for the King to emerge from the Weaver's House in Leenane, Co. Galway. (*Memories: Wise and Otherwise*)

5. Robinson and Chief Secretary, Walter Long, in discussion with a parish priest during a tour of the West in 1905. (*Memories: Wise and Otherwise*)

2. The De Dion Voiturette of Sir Henry Robinson, driven by his 17-year-old son, Christopher (right), in a parade of motor cars at the RDS, Dublin, in April 1901. (RIAC, Guinness Seagrave Archive)

3. Sir Henry Robinson (on the right) as a passenger in the white 12 hp Panhard of Sir Hickman Bacon, at Pontoon Bridge, Co. Mayo, during the IAC Motor Tour of Ireland, August 1901. (RIAC, Guinness Seagrave Archive)

1. Grave of Sir Henry Robinson (senior) (d. 1893) and his wife, Eva, in Mount Jerome Cemetery, Dublin. (Author photo)

Destroyed Property Committee

In the weeks after the Rising, Robinson became heavily involved in efforts to arrange for the restoration or replacement of buildings which had been damaged in central Dublin. There were more than 200 such buildings, according to the chief fire officer, Captain Purcell, whose initial estimate of the cost of the damage to buildings and their contents – mainly in the Sackville Street area – was £2.5 million.[66] While reports of executions of the leaders of the Rising were still appearing daily in the newspapers, the restoration and/or replacement of the damaged buildings was already a matter of concern to the Dublin Chamber of Commerce and the Dublin Fire and Property Losses Association, formed by William Martin Murphy, who were looking to the government to meet the cost.[67] As practically all of the property damage had been caused by the military, and as the standard insurance policies did not cover what had occurred, the acting Under-Secretary lost no time in proposing to the Prime Minister that the government should step in and provide a limited scheme of compensation. Asquith approved the proposals and they were publicly announced on 16 May.[68] In effect, the government was to assume, on an *ex-gratia* basis, the same liability for losses caused by the destruction of buildings and their contents as would have fallen on the insurance companies if the losses had been covered by the fire risk policies in force at the time. Thousands of claims were subsequently reviewed by a three-man committee, chaired by Sir William Goulding, whose work, aided by a large staff of expert assessors, went on into the first half of 1917.

The government's proposals were reasonably satisfactory from the point of view of the property owners, but Robinson was drawn into the business when Dublin Corporation and the Royal Institute of the Architects of Ireland took the view that rebuilding should not be allowed to go ahead, especially in Sackville Street, on a piecemeal, unplanned basis. They argued that some of those who were to receive compensation might not rebuild at all, which would be a calamity for the city. They also advised that unworthy replacement buildings should not be allowed to rise from the ashes, and that there was now a glorious opportunity to carry out street widening and improvement works in North Earl Street and Henry Street. For these reasons, the corporation sought special legislation which would give them power to prepare an improvement scheme to which all new buildings would have to conform and which would provide for government grants or long loans to finance the additional costs which would arise under a scheme of this kind. Robinson was deputed by the acting Under-Secretary to meet representatives of the corporation on 24 May to discuss their proposals, and although he told them that any legislation would have to be promoted as a private bill, he gave them a rough draft of a bill, which would authorise them to borrow to finance the extra cost of rebuilding to the standard demanded by an improvement scheme. In a subsequent report which was forwarded to Asquith's office, Robinson stressed the strong feeling that if the government did not agree to authorise the necessary funding, the only alternative was 'to allow the city to remain in ashes as a monument of ten years of liberal government'. Chalmers, the acting Under-Secretary, like Robinson, was adamant that a private bill would have to be promoted, but was not at all clear that borrowing from the Exchequer should be allowed. He believed that 'heads are swollen' in the corporation and that they were 'in dread of the interested criticisms of the hungry architects of Dublin' whose aim, he told Asquith, was 'to saddle the corporation with the cost of the tune they may call'.[69]

The corporation pressed their case when they met the acting Chief Secretary, who was accompanied by Robinson on 5 June, but Exchequer grants were again ruled out and the possibility of government loans was deferred until after the war.[70] A subsequent request to the Treasury to authorise such a loan was rejected by the chancellor, his officials having advised that 'making Sackville Street architecturally finer' could only be regarded as a luxury and that the corporation should not be encouraged to embark on 'grandiose schemes of beautification' at the expense of the British taxpayer.[71] The corporation, however, persisted, and having met Asquith in London in early July, were told that if they agreed a scheme with Robinson, he would contact the chancellor about it.[72] Robinson was asked at the same time to press on with the preparation of the estimate of cost required by Asquith,[73] and having discussed modified proposals and costings with the corporation, submitted a generally favourable report on 17 July.[74] He was subsequently in touch with the corporation and with the parliamentary draftsman to settle the details of a bill, and was able to report that 'the maddest part' of the original scheme had disappeared and that shortage of materials – particular iron girders – would rule out significant expenditure on rebuilding in the short term. The chancellor then agreed in principle that a government loan of up to £750,000 would be made available. This cleared the way for the introduction in the House of Commons of the Dublin Reconstruction (Emergency Provisions) Bill on 3 August.

After the second stage debate was opened on 17 August by Chief Secretary Duke, who had taken up duty only a fortnight earlier, the bill attracted serious criticism.[75] Duke stressed that the bill had been agreed between the corporation and the LGB, which, he understood 'has not been a very lenient critic of the doings of local authorities in Ireland' and could not be accused of any undue sympathy with local aspirations. However, he had discovered that property owners were objecting to the wide powers which the board was to be given to make final decisions on improvement schemes, and to deal with appeals from decisions about the suitability of particular building proposals. As a result, further debate on the bill was deferred and negotiations between the parties went on for some months. Raymond Unwin, town-planning adviser to the English LGB, was involved at different stages, as was Robinson, who, according to the nationalist Lord Mayor, James Gallagher, had 'proved a good friend' to the corporation.[76] When the bill came back before the Commons in December it was heavily amended, reducing significantly the LGB's role and providing that disputes concerning the reasonableness of requirements imposed by the corporation in particular cases would be settled by arbitration, with the Lord Lieutenant as final arbitrator.[77] When consulted about the proposed amendments, Robinson commented that while they were based on expediency, they were better than might have been expected when such conflicting interests had to be mollified. However, he viewed the substitution of the Lord Lieutenant for the LGB as a retrograde step and one which conflicted with the trend in recent legislation. In addition, he suggested mischievously that it looked like an admission by the Chief Secretary – as President of the LGB – that he would be less impartial than the Lord Lieutenant: 'We must only hope that it passes unnoticed and that no one presses him to explain the reason for the apparent doubt as to his own integrity.'[78] In the event, the amendment did not attract comment and the bill became law in December.[79]

Although it had been decided in principle in June that compensation would not be paid from public funds in respect of deaths or injuries to civilians in the course of the rebellion,[80] Chief Secretary Duke, only a few weeks after his appointment, submitted formal proposals for a compensation scheme, pointing out that since the principle of paying compensation had been admitted in the case of property losses, compensation could not reasonably be withheld in the case of persons killed or injured on the same occasion.[81] Following Treasury approval, a Rebellion Victims Committee was formally established by the Lord Lieutenant on 11 October[82] to investigate and report on applications for compensation by persons who had suffered personal injuries without misconduct or default on their part, and by the dependants of innocent persons who had been killed or injured. Neither Robinson personally nor the LGB had any responsibility for the operation of the committee, although Charles O'Conor, the inspector who had been prominently associated with the relief of distress in the immediate aftermath of the Rising, was one of its members. In all, 550 applications were submitted to the committee, 304 involving personal injury and 246 in respect of deceased persons.[83] An initial list of awards to persons whose sole wage-earners were killed was published in the following February,[84] but the work was not completed until June 1917.

The LGB minutes for the months immediately after the Rising make no reference to any of the exceptional activities in which Robinson and other staff members were involved. Instead, the minutes continue to record the routine business transacted by the board at its daily meetings at 1.00 p.m. and even note that the customary office holiday was observed on 22 June, the anniversary of the coronation of King George V. Apart from a reference on 11 October to the dismissal of Kenny and McElligott from the board's service, there is nothing in the minute book to suggest that the Rising had, or was to have, any effect on the operations of the board.

The Lloyd George Settlement Scheme

A period of intense political activity followed the Rising. Prime Minister Asquith himself travelled to Dublin overnight on 11 May and spent a week in Ireland consulting with officials and others, including Robinson. He also visited a number of the prisoners. On 17 May, when he attended a meeting of the Privy Council at Dublin Castle, at which he was sworn as a member, Asquith would have had another opportunity of meeting Robinson and other officials but, writing from Dublin that same day to Redmond about 'the desperate character of the situation' and the distress in the city, Dillon told him that he had not 'the slightest faith in Asquith's inquiry, which appears so far to have been strictly limited to the military and a mere circle of officials, Sir H. Robinson, Horace Plunkett, etc.'[85] In his memoirs, Robinson was even more dismissive of Asquith's efforts and made little of his meeting with him after a dinner hosted by Wimborne at the Vice-Regal Lodge. He felt that Asquith's meetings were 'a mere piece of window-dressing and that the wearied Prime Minister did not want to be bothered with Irish officials' ideas ... I could see that he was very tired and the only thing he spoke to me about was the impending doom of Roger Casement and its probable effect on Irish opinion. The rest of our time together was spent in stifling our yawns and in a perfunctory discussion on climate, the crops, and other casual topics'.[86]

Asquith's discussions convinced him that not only was there a need to create a government responsible to the Irish people at the earliest possible moment, but that there was a possibility of negotiating a settlement which would be acceptable to all parties. He therefore put it to the Cabinet that it was their duty to do everything in their power 'to force a general settlement'. His memorandum, however, made no specific reference to the views of any of the officials he had met, with the single exception of the Attorney General, James Campbell, whose advice had been that the time to act was now or never.[87] After Lloyd George had declined an invitation to take up the chief secretary position, he agreed to Asquith's request that he should work with the parties in Ireland in an attempt to find a basis for a settlement and, after discussions with Carson and Redmond, he came up with a scheme involving the immediate implementation of the 1914 Act subject to the exclusion of six Ulster counties.[88] This was accepted by Carson and the Ulster unionists on 12 June (on the understanding that exclusion was, in effect, to be permanent) and by a nationalist conference in Belfast on 23 June, at which exclusion was understood to be a temporary expedient. The southern unionists, who were implacably opposed to any Home Rule settlement in the wake of the Rising, were outraged by the Lloyd George Scheme and mounted a major campaign against it in London with the aid of their supporters in the Cabinet. At home, Major Somerset Saunderson, brother of the LGB inspector, was prominent in the movement on behalf of the unionists of Cavan, Monaghan and Donegal, and in defiance of Carson.[89]

By 1916, when Walter Long had come to play an influential part in Irish affairs, Robinson was one of his most trusted sources of information on the situation in Ireland. He had returned to office as president of the English Local Government Board in the coalition government formed in May 1915, and with Lord Lansdowne, unionist leader in the House of Lords and minister without portfolio in that government, he campaigned relentlessly in June and July to undermine the Lloyd George Scheme, although their party leader, Bonar Law, had accepted it.[90] Long threatened to resign on several occasions during this period and strongly argued the southern unionist case.[91] Matters were brought to a head when Lansdowne told the House of Lords on 11 July that the exclusion of Ulster must be permanent in any settlement scheme. A week later, when an amending bill to give effect to the settlement had already been drafted, a memorandum submitted by Long to the Cabinet suggested that they should not come to a conclusion on the bill until they had reports from Robinson and Attorney General Campbell. Long's memorandum told the Cabinet that all sorts of questions arose from the proposed exclusion of the northern counties, and these could only be answered by 'those who were thoroughly familiar with Irish government in all its details'. Questions that occurred to him included the effect on the national education system, the local government and poor law acts, the effects on finance, customs, the post office and cable stations and the position of civil servants in Ireland.[92] While Long was undoubtedly correct in implying that a simple bill to permit Home Rule to be implemented outside of Ulster would have created administrative chaos, John Kendle's study of Long's involvement in Irish affairs wisely suggests that the memorandum probably astonished the liberal members of the Cabinet, given that both Campbell and Robinson were known to be ardent supporters of the union.[93] It may well be that the proposal to await reports from Robinson and the attorney general was more of a delaying tactic than anything else, because the more crucial question, Long concluded – and the real objection to going ahead with an amending bill – was that it would divert the attention of the government and Parliament from the war to complicated and extremely controversial proposals relating to Ireland.

Robinson was obviously in full sympathy with the views of Long and of the southern unionists. He shared their sense of betrayal and desertion by Bonar Law and Carson who, for the first time, had formally committed themselves to a scheme which would create a formal division between northern and southern unionism. On 18 July, the date of Long's submission to the Cabinet, Robinson wrote to assure him in relation to 'this mischievous settlement' that:

> Among the unionists who have watched day by day with breathless suspense your splendid fight against it and who have been hoping and praying that you might succeed, there is not one of them so far as I can find out who is not thanking God that when you found out you were overborne, you did not resign, and that you are still there in the Cabinet to be reckoned with when any proposal to sacrifice the loyal people of the country comes up.

> The truth is the unionists have had a bad shock over the way Bonar Law, Carson etc. have chucked them and you are the only man who in their eyes upholds the honour and promises of the Tory party, and if you were to let yourself be elbowed out of the Cabinet their case would be utterly lost. This I can assure you is the universal opinion.

> One other point. Let no one persuade you that, if this wretched compromise fails, there will be trouble in the country. There will indeed be trouble of the worst kind if it passes, but there will be a feeling of relief and thanksgiving among all parties over the four

corners of the land if it fails – and if we are given a decent chief secretary who will take the advice of experienced people instead of nationalist politicians alone, things will carry on till after the war without any real trouble.[94]

The amending bill, with a provision, insisted on by Lansdowne and Long, for a more permanent exclusion of the six counties, was dropped following Redmond's withdrawal of support for it in the House of Commons on 24 July. Robinson was delighted by the outcome. His last word on the subject was contained in a letter to Long on 27 July:

It is quite extraordinary how little excitement has been caused over here by the collapse of the Partition Bill. The newspapers are bickering at one another over it, but so far as the man in the street is concerned, one only hears a single opinion, namely, profound satisfaction that this bone of contention is in the ash pit. I see in the London Correspondent's column that deep resentment over here is felt against Lord Lansdowne. I hear the very reverse, even from the strongest RCs and nationalists. I believe it has strengthened his authority and influence in the eyes of the people.

What everyone seems to want now is to be let alone till after the war and not to have anybody's experiments and panaceas forced on the country – no new scheme can be proposed now that will not produce a fresh outburst of wrangling and strife, and if the government will only give us a fair and courageous chief secretary who will back up the police and RMs and who will not try and discriminate between individuals who defy the law, they will be adopting the course which will lead to the minimum of trouble.

The Nationalist Party, will no doubt, try and rehabilitate themselves by being as troublesome in and out of the House as possible, and the Boards of Guardians will pass resolutions of the usual 'sun bursting' description, and cattle driving will no doubt be attempted. But the people are not really in it. They are tired of the whole business. But in any case we have been through it all before over and over again, and this kind of thing is only serious under a milk and water administration like the Aberdeens.

The Sinn Féiners and the IRB and AOH are the dangerous elements and they are at present waiting to see how the cat is going to jump, and if the Castle has another attack of nerves, this lot will certainly make things unpleasant, but they haven't the pluck or the stamina to stand out against a resolute Government for long.[95]

A New Administration – But Still No Place for Robinson

Having arrived in Dublin on 27 April, the Thursday of Easter week, to assess the situation, Birrell returned to London after a few days and resigned on 3 May. Nathan left for London on 2 May and his resignation was also accepted on 3 May. Working with Nathan between 1914 and 1916 had been a happy experience for Robinson, and although he found Nathan 'to be terribly upset at not having seen the eventuality of the rebellion'; he was disappointed that the government accepted his resignation so quickly and 'did not imagine that they would let him go at such a juncture'.[96] For some months, the positions vacated by Birrell and Nathan were filled on a temporary basis: the Home Secretary, Herbert Samuel, carried out the duties of the Chief Secretary while Sir Robert Chalmers, joint Permanent Secretary at the Treasury, was appointed to act temporarily as Under-Secretary. A three-man Royal Commission, which was set up to inquire into the causes of the rebellion, reported at the end of June and was highly critical of both Birrell and Nathan.[97] Robinson was not listed among the witnesses, but as one of the most senior and longest-serving civil servants in Ireland he was probably one of the persons 'who kindly discussed with us the subjects into which we had to inquire'. The fact that he and Lord Hardinge of Penshurst, who chaired the commission, were closely connected by marriage adds to the likelihood that this was so.

Although the Hardinge Commission described the Irish system of government as 'anomalous in quiet times and almost unworkable in times of crisis', Asquith decided aafter the collapse of the Lloyd George Settlement Scheme that the simplest and least objectionable plan would be to restore the traditional governance arrangements. Accordingly, Wimborne, who was seen by Robinson as 'an impetuous man with an active mind' who much resented the fact that he had no real power, was reinstated as Lord Lieutenant and the office of Chief Secretary was filled by the appointment of Henry Edward Duke, a unionist MP, who was given a seat in Cabinet.[98] A successful lawyer and a newcomer to ministerial office, Duke took up duty on 3 August and was sworn in at the Castle a week later. He had no previous experience or knowledge of Irish affairs but, according to Robinson, was hard-working and conscientious and 'put himself to more trouble to obtain useless information than anyone I have ever met'.[99] It was to take nearly another three months to appoint a successor to Nathan. Leon Ó Broin suggests that Chalmers, as temporary Under-Secretary, fought with Robinson almost immediately after meeting him and treated others rudely or with contempt.[100] However, although Robinson noted his 'brusque off-handedness',[101] he seems to have worked harmoniously with him in dealing with some of the fallout from the Rising, particularly the working out of the scheme of compensation for property losses in Dublin. In June, Chalmers complained to Maurice Bonham-Carter, Asquith's son-in-law and private secretary, about having to work 'in this dog-hole of a Castle',[102] and told Robinson that he had been forced to take the post; besides, according to Robinson, 'he had no interest whatever in the Irish question ... and his one idea appeared to be to get back to London as soon as ever he could'.[103]

Walter Long had continued and developed his relationship with Robinson since leaving the Chief Secretary's Office at the end of 1905. He was probably the most powerful single voice on Irish affairs in British governing circles in 1916 when he told Robinson, even before Duke's appointment was publicly announced, that he would ensure that the new man knew all about him and would advise him to get into close touch with Robinson without delay. At the same time, he suggested to Robinson that he had 'always been too modest in dealing with the chief secretary of the day' and that he should make a point of seeing Duke immediately he arrived in Ireland.[104] He followed up by advising Duke on 8 August that he should lose no time in relieving Chalmers and replacing him with Robinson: 'I do not think he [Chalmers] at all cares for his present job and I don't wonder at it. He knows it is only temporary and therefore he cannot be expected to take the same interest in his work and he also knows that he is wanted very badly at the Treasury.' Irishmen of all politics, creeds and classes, Long went on, properly resented the appointment of Englishmen to the post of Under-Secretary and it was an insult to Ireland to suggest that there was no Irishman resident in the country who was capable of filling it. He urged Duke, therefore, to appoint Robinson for a six-month period after which 'if he did well and the opposition of the nationalists, which really would only be for show purposes, died down, and if you and he found that you worked pleasantly together, you could appoint him permanently'. He went on:

> There is nobody who knows Ireland, her peculiar difficulties and complications and her people and the peculiarities of Irish government as well as Sir Henry Robinson. Of course the Irish would make a fuss because he is a unionist but believe me, there would be

no reality in this, it would be all 'blank cartridges' and he is really very popular with all parties and classes in Ireland. I am quite sure it would be an inestimable advantage to have him at your right hand for the first six months whatever you might do afterwards.[105]

Long took his case also to Wimborne, telling him that what the post required was a capable, loyal and experienced Irish civil servant. Robinson had 'most of the necessary gifts' and the right training and experience and was 'so obviously the right man that to appoint anybody else would mean passing him over and his age [he was then almost 60] removes any possible difficulty as to the future'.[106] There was, he acknowledged, an 'alleged weakness' (not detailed in the correspondence but probably the critical views of some nationalists) but even if this were so, Long believed that it would not matter because, as Wimborne and Duke meant to govern, the new under-secretary would have to carry out their orders. He wrote again to Duke on 31 August suggesting that Robinson's appointment was 'vital in this most critical period of Irish history' and warning that it would be 'a death-blow to all our hopes' if he selected T. P. Gill of DATI, for whom Redmond was believed to be canvassing – another proof, as Long saw it, of Redmond's faulty judgment as to what was best in his own interests.[107] Ignoring the fact that Birrell had told him that Gill was 'a scribbler and a humbug who has already had too much pudding',[108] Nathan was another who hoped that Gill would be appointed. In September, in one of his numerous letters to the 26-year-old Dorothy Stopford, he told of his hope that Gill would be selected: 'His characteristics are all the exact opposite of mine so that he ought to succeed.'[109]

Duke's response on 1 September cannot have pleased Long, who prided himself on his knowledge of Irish affairs. Sensibly enough, Duke told him that his inclination was to defer making an appointment until he had seen more of the needs of the situation, and while he was sure that Robinson was an excellent administrator and that his claims could not be ignored, he already held a post in which his abilities were available and valuable, and he was not sure that 'his removal into an area of controversy would be the best thing'.[110] Long made a last effort on 5 September to have Robinson appointed. He suggested that the government of Ireland should not be entirely in the hands of Englishmen and that Robinson could be allowed to continue to supervise LGB work, while being appointed temporarily as Under-Secretary for a trial six-month period, as Sir David Harrel had been in 1893, but Duke was not impressed.[111] In the meantime, Wimborne, who had been keeping Asquith informed of developments, told him that Robinson was an attractive candidate 'but being a Kildare

Street unionist, his appointment would emphasize "the unionist rule" of which the parliamentary party are making a grievance'.[112] Wimborne went on to tell Asquith that while Chalmers had held out well, his absence on leave at the beginning of September facilitated a trial in his place of Sir Edward O'Farrell, a catholic and a nationalist, who had been Assistant Under-Secretary since 1908. Chalmers had strongly recommended O'Farrell and, according to Wimborne, felt that he 'possessed more personality than was allowed to appear under Nathan'. However, Nathan's own private assessment of the 60-year-old O'Farrell was that, while he met the requirements in that he was a catholic and an Irishman, it was not in him at that stage to take responsibility, so he doubted if he would accept the post if it were offered to him.[113]

While this correspondence was in progress, there was inevitable speculation in the press about the outcome. The *Irish Independent* reported confidently on 21 August that Robinson was to succeed Chalmers, prompting one of his most severe critics, Celia Harrison, to write to the editor of the *Freeman's Journal*, restating the opposition to Robinson's appointment which she had first expressed in 1912. This time she protested in the strongest possible manner against the appointment of a man 'who had used his gifted and resourceful mind … to oppose and delay every reform for the benefit of the people of Ireland' and whose board had 'earned the well-merited mistrust and contempt of all members of local authorities irrespective of political parties'.[114] In early September, there were rumours that the new under-secretary was to be Robinson, Gill or O'Farrell. The latter was sufficiently confident that the choice would fall on him that he told Joseph Brennan of his plans for reorganising the work and staffing of the Chief Secretary's Office.[115] This confidence must surely have been misplaced as, according to O'Halpin's verdict, which seems to be fully justified, O'Farrell was a hopeless civil servant, without energy or ideas, who contributed nothing either to policy or administration during his years at the Castle. [116] In October there were again press reports that Robinson was to become Under-Secretary and that Charles O'Conor, the senior LGB inspector, was to succeed him at the Custom House. The Tralee board of guardians went so far as to pass a resolution congratulating Robinson on his new appointment, noting that he 'had earned the respect and admiration of the people of Ireland' during his long career with the LGB, and praising the cordial relations which had existed with the board during his years as Vice-President.[117] A similar resolution was passed unanimously by the Rathdown board of guardians, after the proposer had expressed his confidence that Robinson would act in the post without fear, favour or bias.[118]

When Chalmers finally resigned in October to return to his post in London, the *Irish Times,* quoting the parliamentary correspondent of the *Daily Chronicle,* reported that his successor would probably be Sir Henry Robinson.[119] Instead, however, the position was filled on 23 October by Sir William Patrick Byrne, a 57-year-old English catholic civil servant who had served at the Home Office for over thirty years and who had been one of the commissioners appointed to review the cases of the Irish civil servants who were suspended for alleged complicity in the Rising. Robinson must have been disappointed at his failure to secure the appointment but confined himself, in his memoirs, to noting that Byrne's appointment 'was not greeted with any enthusiasm'; while he was popular among officials, he 'had come into the Irish maelstrom too late in life to be of much help to anyone ... and he did not appear to be on very cordial terms with his chief'.[120] Disappointment at his failure to be appointed as Under-Secretary did not lead to a break in Robinson's relationship with Long, who continued to take a close interest in developments in Ireland and to rely on Robinson for updates on the situation. In January 1917, for example, when he was complaining to his party leader, Bonar Law, about the release just before Christmas of the remaining untried prisoners, he wrote that 'the release of some of the worst Sinn Féiners is deplorable, and for what use? No recruits and according to [the] last paper from Robinson more soldiers required to keep Ireland quiet'.

Duke Was an Able Man but Was 'Uninformed as to the Root of the Irish Trouble'

From the outset, a certain tension must have pervaded the relationship between Robinson and his new Chief Secretary, knowing, as he must have done, that Duke had turned down Walter Long's representations in favour of his appointment as Under-Secretary. In his memoirs, he had little good to say about Duke.[121] He saw him as an able man but he had no special qualifications for governing Ireland, and people could not discern what reason the government may have had for appointing him. He was 'uninformed and blind as regards the root of the Irish trouble' and afraid to take any initiative; there was little room in him for the 'imagination so essential for anyone dealing with Irish affairs'; and he never realised that it was 'the very act of giving the country to such as he – wise, superior and English in thought – which made the Irish people so fractious and difficult to govern'.

Over the years, Robinson's personal influence on chief secretaries was sometimes remarked upon and criticised by nationalist MPs, so that only a few days after Duke's arrival, he was surprised to be asked to arrange a tour for him. He surmised that someone in London must have advised the new Chief Secretary to visit the poorer districts with him, whereas he felt that officials at the Castle would have warned Duke to take someone who was in the confidence of the nationalists. A week-long tour of the West was duly arranged in September, but, although any business conducted was totally unrelated to the responsibilities of the LGB, Robinson had no option but to accompany Duke.[122] He recalled later that instead of taking people and things as they came, as his predecessors had done, Duke went straight to the police barracks on his arrival in Galway, initiated long discussions with the senior officers about the state of their districts and resumed these discussions that night in the hotel at Recess.[123] This concentration on political and security issues obviously did not impress Robinson, who was pleased that when the party travelled on to Mulrany, he had arranged for Micks of the CDB to meet Duke 'and take him off my hands'. The *Condition of Ireland* report, which Duke subsequently submitted to the Cabinet, makes it clear that his objective in undertaking the tour was to assist him in assessing the political situation.[124] Among other things, he was able to tell the Cabinet that the relationship between 'the extremists' and the general population had been altered following the 'recent rebellion' and that, as one RIC inspector put it to him, the Volunteers were now being admired instead of being disliked or laughed at.

Magill, his private secretary, recorded that when Duke proposed another tour in 1917, this time to Donegal, Robinson was reluctant to become involved because he did not care for Duke as a travelling companion, believing that 'he was much too serious and too anxious to learn about the country and the people'.[125] Robinson's aversion to touring with Duke may also have had something to do with the growing criticism of his personal influence on chief secretaries by nationalist MPs, one of whom (Patrick White) told Duke in the House of Commons in April that he was overpowered by the mass of officialdom, which weighed down every chief secretary. Aside from this, it was his first duty as a new Chief Secretary 'to go around the country in a perambulator pushed by Sir Henry Robinson', from whom he takes all his advice and his first lessons on the country and, in the course of a tour of the West, thinks that he learns more than by listening to the people's representatives in the Commons.[126] For this or for other reasons, Robinson tried to evade his traditional task on this occasion by suggesting that Magill should advise Duke that it would be madness for him to risk being hung up in some remote village in Donegal because of lack of petrol. However, when the private secretary diplomatically suggested that Duke understood that Robinson would be far too busy to be able to absent himself from his office for ten days, any difficulties about petrol supplies were quickly resolved by Robinson (as chairman of the wartime Petrol Control Committee) who also quickly provided maps and tips about roads and hotels.

Unlike his predecessors, Robinson found that Duke resented criticism by his officials of any of his proposals relating to LGB business, and because he had little experience of poor law administration the board, seldom troubled him with papers on the subject.[127] On the other hand, it is clear that Duke came to value Robinson's advice on wider political issues and told the War Cabinet in April 1918 that he had found his judgment to be trustworthy in all his experience of him.[128] His term as Chief Secretary, which ended in May 1918 when Viscount French was appointed as Lord Lieutenant and quasi-military governor, was seen by Robinson as, in a sense, the end of an era – our last glimpse, as he put it in exaggerated terms in his memoirs, of life in Ireland when people could 'pursue their avocations without dread of the pestilence that walketh in darkness and the arrow that flieth by day' – quoting psalm ninety-one, which had become popularly known as the 'soldiers' psalm' during the war.[129]

NOTES

1   Maurice Headlam, *Irish Reminiscences* (London, 1947), pp.12, 60–61.

2   Sir Henry Robinson, *Memories: Wise and Otherwise* (London, 1923), pp.233–34

3   Robinson to Nathan, 11, 13 and 20 Dec. 1915, Oxford, Bodleian Library, MS Nathan 460, f. 212–19.

4   Robinson, *Memories*, pp.233–34.

5   Margaret Baguley (ed.), *World War I and the Question of Ulster: The Correspondence of Lilian and Wilfrid Spender* (Dublin, 2009), p.41.

6   Letter of 5 Aug. 1915 to Carson from W. F. Bailey, PRONI, Carson Papers, D 1507/A/13/15.

7   *Irish Times Weekly*, 29 Apr. 1916.

8   Robinson's son, Christopher, wrote that the first copy of the proclamation to be run off the presses in Liberty Hall was specially kept for his father as a souvenir and duly sent to him with a suitable inscription by a man in the rebel camp who liked and respected him; as reproduced in Christopher's book, the copy is inscribed 'presented ... by an old friend, 3.5.16' (Sir Christopher Lynch-Robinson, *The Last of the Irish R.M.s* (London, 1951), pp.120, 139).

9   Department of the Environment and Local Government, Secretary's Office, LGB Minute Book 1916, entry for 14 April.

10 Robinson, *Memories*, p.235.

11 Birrell to Nathan, 25 Mar. 1915, Oxford, Bodleian Library, MS Nathan 449, f. 144–45.

12   Robinson to Nally, 2 and 6 Apr. 1916, NLI, T. H. Nally papers, MSS 36, 213–36,217, List No 104.

13   Poster advertising the first production of *The Spancel of Death*, a play in three acts by T. H. Nally on Tuesday, 25 Apr. 1916 and following evenings, Abbey Theatre archive.

14   *Hansard* V, 36, 11 Apr. 1912, 1389.

15   Leon Ó Broin, *Dublin Castle & The 1916 Rising* (London, 1966), pp. 32–33.

16   Keith Jeffery (ed.), *The Sinn Fein Rebellion As They Saw It: Irish Experiences in War* by Arthur Hamilton Norway (Dublin, 1999), pp.104–08.

17   Edward David (ed.), *Inside Asquith's Cabinet: From the Diaries of Charles Hobhouse* (London, 1977), p.220.

18   Nathan to Magill, 24 Feb. 1915, Oxford, Bodleian Library, MS. Eng. c. 7033, f. 51.

19   M. J. Gallagher, 'The Fateful Week' (section of an unpublished manuscript), *Administration*, vol. 14. No. 2 (Summer 1966), pp.171–185.

20   Circular of 1 May 1916, NAI, CSORP 1916/7690.

21   J. R. Clark, diary entry for 4 May 1916, UCDA P 169.

22   Statements made by Dublin staff of the National Health Insurance Commission are held at TNA (CO 904/25/2) but there appears to be no similar file of LGB staff statements there.

23   Circular of 14 June 1916, TNA, T 1/12042; also at NLI, Joseph Brennan Papers, MS 26,194.

24   TNA, CO 904/26/2, civil servants in sympathy with Sinn Féin.

25   Department of the Environment and Local Government, Secretary's Office, LGB Minute Book, 1916, entry for 19 May; *Drogheda Independent*, 27 May 1916.

26   *Hansard* V, 82, 22 May 1916, 1797–1798.

27   Report on the cases of Irish civil servants suspended in connection with the recent rebellion, 16 Aug. 1916, TNA, CO 904/25/1 and HO 144/1463/319502; copy in NLI, Joseph Brennan Papers, MS 26,185; the report was never published officially but is reproduced in Keith Jeffery, *The GPO and the Easter Rising* (Dublin, 2006), pp.189–200.

28   James Kenny, BMH, WS 141, 31 Aug. 1948.

29   Diary of Joseph Brennan for 1913, quoted in Leon Ó Broin, *No Man's Man* (Dublin, 1982), pp.21–22.

30   Michael Knightly, BMH, WS 833, 27 Apr. 1953.

31   CSORP 1917/ 11801, quoted in Eunan O'Halpin, *The Decline of the Union: British Government in Ireland 1892–1920* (Dublin, 1987), pp.127–28.

32   BMH, Military Service Pensions collection, MSP 34REF63503.

33   Letter of 23 Aug. 1916 and later correspondence, Wilson Byrne Committee file, TNA, CO 904/25/1 (Part 1).

34   Department of the Environment and Local Government, Secretary's Office, LGB Minute Book, 1916, entry for 11 October.

35   Robinson to Long, 14 Mar. 1918, WRO, Long Papers, WRO 947/332.

36   *Irish Times*, 21 Oct. 1916.

37   Letter of 6 Nov. from Bishop O Dwyer (20141), and letters of 6 and 13 Nov. from McElligott (20142 and 20881), NAI, CSORP Register for 1916; the letters themselves cannot be found in NAI.

38   Letter of 19 July 1917, Wilson Byrne Committee file, TNA, CO 904/25/1 (Part 2).

39   *Hansard* V, 96, 19 July 1917, 560; 20 July 1917, 762.

40   McElligott to Brennan, 8 Mar. 1919, NLI, Joseph Brennan Papers, MS 26,009.

41   Letters of 16 and 19 Jan. 1920, 'Mac' to Brennan, NLI, Joseph Brennan Papers, MS 26,185.

42   NAI, DE 2/40.

43   McElligott to Brennan, Oct. and Nov. 1922, NLI, Joseph Brennan Papers, MS 26,012.

44   Shortt to Lloyd George, 4 July 1918, Parliamentary Archives, Lloyd George Papers, LG/F/45/6/6.

45   *Hansard* V, 108, 22 July 1918, 1444–45.

46   Telegram to Watt, Irish Office, 23 July 1918, TNA, CO 904/25/3.

47   *Irish Times*, 4 Nov. 1918.

48   Capt. E. Gerrard, BMH, WS 348, 5 Feb. 1950.

49   'Inside Trinity College by One of the Garrison' in *Blackwood's Magazine*, July 1916, republished in Roger McHugh (ed.), *Dublin 1916* (London, 1966), pp.158–174.

50   TNA, T 1/11985.

51   *Irish Times*, 14 and 15 May 1916.

52   *Irish Times*, 7 Aug. 1916.

53   Robinson, *Memories*, pp.235–38.

54   Department of the Environment and Local Government, Secretary's Office, LGB Minute Book 1916, entries for 26 Apr.–2 May.

55   A postcard published by Eason & Sons in the *Irish Rebellion* series showed 'soldiers bivouacking' in the Custom House grounds opposite Liberty Hall (Emmet Dalton papers, NLI, MS 46,687/2).

56   Frank Robins, BMH, WS 585, 10 Sept. 1951; James Curry, *Artist of the Revolution: The Cartoons of Ernest Kavanagh (1884–1916)*, (Cork, 2012), pp.29–33.

57   The ship's bridge log (reproduced in Pat Sweeney, *Liffey Ships & Shipbuilding* (Cork, 2010), pp.81–82) records that 24 rounds were fired at Liberty Hall from the ship's 12-pound gun beginning at 8.00am on 26 April.

58   Frank Robins, BMH, WS 585, 10 Sept. 1951.

59   Frank Thornton BMH, WS 510, 18 May 1951; W. J. Brennan-Whitmore, *Dublin Burning: The Easter Rising from Behind the Barricades* (Dublin, 2013), pp.138–149.

60   James Stephens, *The Insurrection in Dublin* (3rd ed., Dublin, 1966), pp.55, 57; Mons. M Curran, BMH, WS 687, June 1952.

61   Robinson, *Memories*, p.240.

62   Robinson, *Memories*, pp.138–242; *Irish Times*, 3 and 4 May 1916.

63   *Irish Times*, 2 May 1916.

64   Letter by Professor George O'Neill S.J., written in April and May 1916, *The Clongownian*, Aug. 1965, reprinted in Roger McHugh (ed.), *Dublin 1916* (London, 1966), pp.183–188.

65   *Irish Times*, 18 May 1916.

66   *Irish Times Weekly*, 1 May 1916.

67   Letters of 6 and 9 May 1916 to under-secretary Chalmers, NLI, Joseph Brennan Papers, MS 26,186; Thomas Morrissey S.J., *William Martin Murphy* (1997), pp.62–63.

68   Chalmers to Asquith, 9 and 11 May and Asquith to Chalmers, 13 May 1916, NLI, Joseph Brennan Papers, MS 26,186.

69   Robinson to Chalmers, 24 May 1916 and Chalmers to Bonham Carter, 24 May 1916, NLI, Joseph Brennan Papers, MS 26,186.

70   Minutes of meeting 5 June 1916, chief secretary's office file relating to the Dublin Reconstruction Bill, NLI, Joseph Brennan Papers, MS 26,187.

71   TNA, T 1/12038.

72   Samuel to Chalmers, 13 July 1916, NLI, Joseph Brennan Papers, MS 26,187; *Irish Times*, 25 July 1916.

73   Brennan to Robinson, 14 July 1916, NLI, Joseph Brennan Papers, MS 26,187.

74   Robinson to Chalmers, 17 July 1916, NLI, Joseph Brennan Papers, MS 26,187.

75   *Hansard* V, 85, 17 Aug. 1916, 2098–2162.

76   *Irish Times*, 20 Nov. 1916.

77   *Hansard* V, 88, 4 Dec. 1916, 769–772.

78   Robinson to Greer, 27 Nov. 1916, TNA, T 1/12038.

79   Dublin Reconstruction (Emergency Provisions) Act 1916, 6 & 7 Geo. 5, c. 66, 22 Dec. 1916.

80   Home Secretary to Chalmers, 15 June 1916, NLI, Joseph Brennan Papers, MS 26,008; Treasury minute 17356/16 of 15 July 1916, TNA, T 1/11985.

81   Minutes of 30 Aug. and 16 Sept. 1916, TNA, T 1/11985.

82   Warrant of appointment dated 11 Oct. 1916, TNA, T 1/11985; copy in NLI, Joseph Brennan Papers, MS 26,175.

83   Report of the committee dated 30 July 1917, NLI, Joseph Brennan Papers, MS 26,175.

84   *Irish Times*, 9 Feb. 1917.

85   Dillon to Redmond, 17 May 1916, TCD, John Dillon papers, cited in F. S. L. Lyons, *John Dillon* (Chicago, 1968), p.384.

86   Robinson, *Memories*, pp.258–59.

87   Asquith's Memoranda on Ireland, 19 and 21 May 1916, TNA, CAB 37/148/18; John D. Fair, *British Interparty Conferences* (Oxford, 1980), Appendix V, pp.294–98.

88   Note of meeting with Lloyd George, 25 May 1916, Trevor Wilson (ed.), *The Political Diaries of C. P. Scott 1911–1928* (London, 1970), p.205.

89   Alvin Jackson, *Colonel Edward Saunderson* (Oxford, 1995), pp.228–231.

90   R. J. Q. Adams, *Bonar Law* (London, 1999), pp.14–19.

91   *Irish Times*, 5 July 1916.

92   Memorandum, 'Government of Ireland Amendment Bill', by W. H. L., 18 July 1916, TNA, CAB 37/151/42.

93   John Kendle, *Walter Long, Ireland and the Union, 1905–1920* (Montreal, 1992), pp.128–29.

94   Robinson to Long, 18 July 1916, WRO, Long Papers, WRO 947/331.

95   Robinson to Long, 27 July 1916, WRO, Long Papers, WRO 947/331.

96   Robinson, *Memories*, p.241.

97   *Report of the Royal Commission on the Rebellion in Ireland*, HC 1916 (Cd. 8279); Minutes of Evidence etc, HC 1916 (Cd. 8311).

98   Robinson, *Memories*, p.230.

99 Robinson, *Memories*, pp.245–47.

100 Leon Ó Broin, *No Man's Man*, p.53, presumably relying on the diary of Joseph Brennan, private secretary to both Nathan and Chalmers.

101 Robinson, *Memories*, p.256.

102 Chalmers to Bonham-Carter, 5 June 1916, Oxford, Bodleian Library, MSS Asquith 37, f. 37.

103 Robinson, *Memories*, pp.245–46.

104 Long to Robinson, 30 July 1916, WRO, Long Papers, WRO 947/331.

105 Long to Duke, 8 Aug. 1916, WRO, Long Papers, WRO 947/208.

106 Long to Wimborne, 10 Aug. and 7 Sept. 1916, WRO, Long Papers, WRO 947/394.

107 Long to Duke, 31 Aug. 1916, WRO, Long Papers, WRO 947/208.

108 Birrell to Nathan, 1914, Oxford, Bodleian Library, MS Nathan 449, f. 58.

109 Nathan to Dorothy Stopford, 25 Sept. 1916, NLI, Stopford-Price Papers, MS 15,341 (1).

110 Duke to Long, 1 Sept. 1916, WRO, Long Papers, WRO 947/208.

111 Long to Duke, 5 Sept. 1916, WRO, Long Papers, WRO 947/208.

112 Wimborne to Asquith, 3 Sept. 1916, Oxford, Bodleian Library, MSS Asquith 37, f. 119–122.

113 Nathan to Dorothy Stopford, 23 Oct. 1916, NLI, Stopford-Price Papers, MS 15,341 (1).

114 *Freeman's Journal*, 24 Aug. 1916.

115 O'Farrell to Brennan, 3 Sept. 1916, NLI, Joseph Brennan Papers, MS 26,008.

116 Eunan O'Halpin, *The Decline of the Union: British Government in Ireland 1892–1920* (Dublin, 1987), p.94.

117 *Irish Times*, 19 Oct. 1916; *Irish Independent*, 11 and 16 Oct. 1916.

118 *Irish Times*, 12 Oct. 1916.

119 *Irish Times*, 14 Oct. 1916.

120 Robinson, *Memories*, p.257.

121 Robinson, *Memories*, pp.244–7.

122 *Irish Times*, 11 Sept. 1916.

123 Robinson, *Memories*, pp.247–250.

124 Confidential memorandum on the Condition of Ireland, initialled H. E. D., 26 Sept. 1916, TNA, CAB 37/156/1.

125 Memoirs of Andrew Philip Magill, Oxford, Bodleian Library, MS. Eng. C. 2803, f. 273–280.

126 *Hansard* V, 92, 18 Apr. 1917, 1772.

127 Robinson, *Memories*, p.251.

128 Memorandum G.T. 4364 for the War Cabinet, Feeling in Ulster, 27 Apr. 1918, TNA, CAB 24/49.

129 Robinson, *Memories*, pp.259–260.

CHAPTER XII

'Sheer Madness' To Attempt Conscription

Sinn Féiners hoping to Sweep Everything Outside of Ulster

Robinson had suggested to Walter Long in July 1916 that when the war was over, there would be such a slump and such financial upheaval in Ireland that the nationalists would be afraid to take over Home Rule and face the situation by themselves: 'After the golden promises the actual realisation at such a time would be like a nightmare to the people.'[1] This wishful thinking was soon dispelled and in February 1917, little more than six months later, he was forced to adopt a very different position. By then he would have been aware of the work which had been initiated throughout the country, following the release of the remaining untried internees in December 1916, to reorganise both the Volunteers and the political wing of the separatist movement. He would also certainly have noted the vigorous and reasonably cohesive campaign which led to the election of Count Plunkett as Sinn Féin's first MP at a North Roscommon by-election on 3 February – a result which, ironically, had to be formally announced by the high sheriff of the county, Sir Thomas Stafford, who had just retired from his position as LGB medical commissioner.[2] Having already warned Chief Secretary Duke that if local elections were to take place in June 1917 as scheduled 'there would be a desperate trial of strength' between nationalists and Sinn Féiners, Robinson sent him a further minute on 12 February drawing attention to fresh information that 'the Sinn Féiners are mobilizing all their strength for this event and hope to sweep everything outside of Ulster'.[3] Duke quickly submitted this minute to the War Cabinet and asked them to consider the further postponement of the elections because of Robinson's 'very urgent representation' – and this was readily agreed to. While Robinson, whose board had overall responsibility for the electoral system, would have been expected to press for a decision on whether the making of arrangements for elections should go ahead, his submissions to Duke went far beyond this. Not for the first time, he was trespassing on a policy area which was more properly the preserve of the Under-Secretary, Sir William Byrne, for whom he had little respect, and once again, his advice was relied on in relation to a matter of policy outside his own area of responsibility.

A Striking and Perhaps a Brilliant Failure

With the postponement of the local elections and the continuing deferral of a general election, the main event on the Irish political stage in 1917 was the Convention, whose meetings began at Trinity College, Dublin in July. Designed to produce an agreed scheme of Irish self-government as had been achieved in the Union of South Africa, the Convention, to quote R. B. McDowell, was 'one of the most striking failures in Irish history', and perhaps even a brilliant failure.[4] The largest group of Convention members (46 out of the total of 101) was made up of representatives of the local authorities – thirty-two chairmen of county councils, the lord mayors and mayors of the six county boroughs, and eight representatives of the urban councils and towns. Robinson was given the task of arranging meetings at provincial level towards the end of June, at which two representatives of each of the urban councils and boards of town commissioners could meet to elect two of their number to represent the group at the Convention.[5] He personally issued invitations to the various chairmen and attended the meetings himself, having been requested by the Chief Secretary to do so and 'to afford any assistance that may be desired'.[6] Apart from this, neither Robinson nor any of the others directly associated with the LGB were involved in the Convention, although some nationalists could not resist describing the initiative as a sham and 'the latest British farce ... under the guidance of that adept English manager, Sir Henry Robinson'.[7]

Local government issues do not seem to have arisen in any substantive form in the course of the Convention's deliberations. Towards the end of its life, however, in February 1918, the Prime Minister wrote to its Chairman, Sir Horace Plunkett, setting out suggestions for a solution which included consideration of the possibility of making provision for immediately dealing with the 'vital problem' of housing, which had been raised with him by the labour representatives.[8] Despite compromises by the representatives of the southern unionists and by some of the nationalists, it was apparent by the end of March 1918 that the Convention would fail; the eventual failure was due to the attitude of the more extreme nationalists and the refusal of the Ulster unionists to agree to any scheme which would win the support of a substantial majority, as required by Lloyd George, if it were to be given effect by legislation at Westminster. The issue of making provision for a new housing programme was then deferred for at least another year.

Everything is Very Much Changed at the Castle

There were reports in the *Irish Times* in February and March 1918 that Walter Long, who was then colonial secretary, was thinking of accepting the chief secretary post in place of Duke, rumours of whose imminent resignation had appeared in the press.[9] Having seen these reports, Robinson took it on himself in mid-March to advise Long of the situation in Ireland before he made up his mind. On the political front, the year had begun in unspectacular fashion: the war was dragging on; the Convention was continuing its work; after its four by-election victories in 1917, Sinn Féin was continuing to grow in confidence and in strength; and drilling, political agitation and local disturbances in some areas were resulting in small numbers of prosecutions for relatively minor offences. Overall, as Robinson saw it, there were no great difficulties facing the government in Ireland at the beginning of 1918, although there were 'trivial annoyances, and petty troubles and miserable little disputes' to be dealt with.[10] These problems would presumably have included the agrarian troubles being fermented by Sinn Féin in the west and south, and the organised cattle driving in some of the grazing districts under pretence of clearance of land for tillage, about which Duke reported to the War Cabinet on 19 February.[11] However, 'everything is very much changed at the Castle since you were here', Robinson told Long in a letter of 14 March, 'the whole staff (perhaps except Taylor) have become cowed, inefficient and lacking in resource [and] I believe you would be driven mad by their slowness of action and comprehension'. He went on to provide highly critical – but generally valid and defensible – assessments of the entire top echelon of the administration, all of whom had been replaced within a few months:

- the Attorney General, Sir James O'Connor, was a very third-rate lawyer, swayed by every village politician [he was promoted to the bench in April 1918];
- the Solicitor General, Arthur Warren Samuels KC MP, though honest, was a nervous old woman [he became Attorney General in April 1918];

- the Lord Chancellor since 1913, Sir Ignatius O'Brien, spent his time packing the bench with appalling selections of magistrates and was absolutely discredited [he was replaced in June 1918];
- Sir William Byrne, the Under-Secretary, was a decent, loyal soul but was utterly at sea [he resigned in July 1918];
- Sir Edward O' Farrell, the 62-year-old assistant Under-Secretary was a spent fish [he was replaced in June 1918]; and
- Lord Lieutenant Wimborne [replaced in May 1918] was jealous of the Chief Secretary's powers and would be a thorn in Long's side if he replaced Duke.

Although Robinson personally would have been glad to see Long back in Dublin as local government under his direction and advice had been 'supremely easy', he strongly advised Long against returning to the chief secretary post which he had held for nine months in 1905. He would be 'disgusted with the smallness of it all' and would regret leaving the Colonial Office at a time of crisis in the Empire. Besides, the difficulties to be faced in Ireland at that stage – when no one could have foreseen the conscription crisis which was to erupt only two weeks later – did not demand statesmanship of a high order and a minister of first rank but 'some plucky young minister with a soul of his own and his own mark to make' and who, by fair play and the maintenance of the law, would restore order and prosperity as rapidly as Arthur Balfour had done in 1887, or as speedily as Long himself had done in 1905. In addition, he suggested that if Wimborne could be got rid of, Lord Decies would make an admirable lord lieutenant – an Anglo–Irish former army officer who was then an Irish representative peer and had been acting as press censor since 1916, Decies was said by Robinson to be rich, extraordinarily popular with all classes and the press, and a bluff, honest, straightforward fellow. He admitted that he personally knew Decies only slightly and he cannot have known that Decies differed from his own assessment of the state of the country. Decies believed that the country was as bad as it could be and that the Cabinet were living in a fool's paradise. However, the two men's opinions on what should be done were very similar: a letter from Decies to Sir Edward Carson, which was submitted to the War Cabinet, suggested that there was need to completely replace the existing administration with a new Lord Lieutenant who knew something of the country and a chief secretary who would rule in a fair and just manner, not be afraid of responsibility and live most of his time in Ireland. In addition, a clean sweep should be made of the officials at the Castle who were 'out of date and not in touch or sympathy with the people'.[12]

Robinson's final warning to Long on 14 March was clearly influenced by the split, which was already developing, between those southern unionists led by Viscount Midleton who were willing at the Convention to work for a settlement, and the 'die-hard' group, which included his former LGB colleague, Richard Bagwell, for whom the question of the union was not susceptible to compromise.[13] If Long were to return to Ireland, 'many of your old supporters, who haven't sense enough to see that some form of Home Rule or other is sooner or later inevitable, would be crying out that you had deserted them if you didn't pin your faith to a policy that was dust and ashes ten years ago'. Long's reply to this unsolicited advice has not been traced, but it seems likely that he was already familiar with Robinson's views on the inadequacy of the existing regime at Dublin Castle – he had in fact told the Prime Minister in a letter on 4 March that he was 'convinced it is necessary to change the Irish government from top to bottom' although for reasons of a purely domestic character, he found it impossible himself to accept the offer of the chief secretary post 'with full powers of government'.[14] He made specific proposals to Lloyd George in that letter for filling the office of lord lieutenant (Londonderry was favoured with Decies as second choice) with Macpherson as Chief Secretary and with himself as a kind of over-lord but, surprisingly, he did not put forward Robinson's name for appointment as under-secretary as he had done two years earlier, and as he was again to do a few months later. Instead, it was General Joseph Byrne, Inspector-General of the RIC, whose promotion he favoured, as he was 'a very determined, capable man, and has acquired a really great position in Ireland'.[15]

The Conscription Crisis that Nobody had Anticipated

A few weeks after Robinson's comforting assessment of the state of affairs in Ireland, the situation changed dramatically when the conscription crisis broke. In 1916, when compulsory military service was introduced in Britain, it was not applied to Ireland for reasons of principle as well as sound practical reasons advanced by Birrell.[16] Duke had again advised the Prime Minister in January 1917 that conscription should not be imposed unless the Home Rule issue was also dealt with.[17] The exemption for Ireland was not seriously challenged after that and as late as January 1918 the Minister of National Service told the House of Commons that the reasons which led to the exclusion of Ireland had lost none of their cogency. He said that the decision was based on expediency, and it would be folly to do otherwise, because of the difficulty and delay that would be involved in putting in place the tribunal machinery, which would be required at county and district council level, to operate a conscription system.[18] However, after a major German offensive had begun on 21 March, the serious situation of the British Fifth Army in France led to a hasty review of military manpower, which resulted in the submission to the War Cabinet by the Prime Minister of plans for raising an additional 555,000 men for the army, of whom 150,000 were to come from Ireland.

The initial Lloyd George proposals, which were to be coupled with a vague promise of Home Rule, were discussed at a number of meetings of the War Cabinet in late March. At these meetings, the reservations of the head of the RIC, the commander of the army in Ireland, Lord Lieutenant Wimborne, Chief Secretary Duke, the Attorney General, Lord Chief Justice Campbell and Sir Edward Carson about conscription were effectively over-ruled.[19] When a draft military service bill, with provision for extending conscription, was discussed at a meeting of the War Cabinet presided over by Bonar Law on 3 April, Robinson as well as Wimborne and Duke was in attendance. The committee which had prepared the draft bill advised that if conscription were introduced, local tribunals based on county and district councils (which were used to administer the scheme in England) could not be relied on in Ireland,[20] but had been told by Duke that it should be possible to staff tribunals largely with officials of the LGB and of the Board (sic) of Agriculture, together with members of the military and police forces. It might be thought that Robinson's attendance at the meeting arose from the need to give further consideration to this administrative issue and to other questions of implementation, but it is clear from the Cabinet minutes that his role was not the limited one that would have been appropriate to his civil service position. Instead, he was called on to advise and assist in considering the wider policy issue and in assessing the possible impact of conscription.[21] The meeting had already come to the view that the best course would be to introduce conscription and Home Rule together, effectively making impositions on both nationalists and unionists, when Robinson was invited to comment. Different classes would be differently affected, he said, according to the minutes:

> The young shopmen in towns would give trouble, while farmers' sons in the country would probably try to escape service. From the labour ranks he did not think that many men would be got, by reason of the increased number employed on additional tillage. On the whole, he thought that they would not be disappointed in getting a fair supply of men. Questioned about the possibility of outrages and anarchy resulting, Sir Henry said that that depended

entirely on the way the matter was put to the people. If they were convinced that it was going to be carried through, they would accept the position. It depended on the administration: if this were faulty and weak, the people would fight to the death against it, but if they saw that the administration was determined, they would accept.

If conscription was started and resolutely carried through, Sinn Féin would die at once. The farmers were not supporters of Sinn Féin, but had to appear at markets as if they were, because otherwise no one would deal with them. The farmers hated Sinn Féin and wanted to be quit of it. If Sinn Féin was defeated, opposition to conscription would certainly collapse. There would be a hard fight at first, but it would not last long, if it was thought the measure was meant. They had to remember the great effect of the large amount of money which was pouring into Ireland in respect of separation allowances and compensation.[22]

Like Bonar Law, who was concerned about the danger of an explosion in Ulster if the two projects were taken together, Robinson feared that there could be trouble in the province, which would affect the supply of materials required for the war. He believed that there would be great unrest, especially among the women linen-workers who were employed in the production of fabric for aeroplane wings, and he was afraid that output would be reduced. However, in response to Arthur Balfour's concern about the effects of a possible strike at the shipyards, he offered the view that an actual strike would not take place: output would certainly be reduced, but because the men were making so much money, he did not think that they would go so far as to down tools.

Duke did not accept Robinson's assessment of the situation and continued to advise the Cabinet that the enforcement of conscription would be disastrous, that instant rebellion would be the inevitable result and that 'we might almost as well recruit Germans'.[23] In deference to this view, the Cabinet decided to incorporate a compromise provision in the legislation which, instead of directly applying conscription, would allow it to be extended by Order in Council at a later stage. In addition, to get around the perceived objections to establishing a different system of local tribunals in Ireland, it was decided to include a provision allowing existing tribunals in Britain to be remodelled so as to bring them into line with whatever system might possibly be operated in Ireland.[24] The Home Secretary, Sir George Cave, later told the House of Commons that both local and appeal tribunals in Ireland would be nominated by the LGB or appointed on their recommendation – a remarkable decision according to the *Irish Times,* which assumed (incorrectly) that the majority of the administrators of the act in Ireland were to be local councillors – some of the very people who were organising resistance to it.[25] The revised bill was introduced by Lloyd George in the Commons on 9 April, with a promise to introduce also a measure of self-government for Ireland,[26] and was heavily criticised by nationalist MPs. Duke was forced to admit in the House on 12 April that he had not readily acquiesced in what was for him a painful conclusion.[27] Four days later he told Lloyd George that he could not continue as Chief Secretary as he still believed that bringing the bill into operation would lead to disaster.[28]

Sheer Madness to Attempt either Home Rule or Conscription

Robinson's initial assessment of the likely results of a decision to apply conscription conflicted not only with that of his immediate chief, Duke, but also with that of almost all other Irish officials and officeholders. His assessment was undoubtedly skewed by his view that Ireland had been prospering until then while sacrifices were being made in England. His assessment coincided closely with the advice subsequently tendered by his admirer, Walter Long, who had been absent from Cabinet meetings for some weeks because of illness, but who told Bonar Law on 4 April that the responsible officials in Ireland should strike boldly and quickly to introduce conscription and face the consequences, and the row which would follow would soon come to an end.[29] Long told Lloyd George a few days later that the Irish would talk, shout and perhaps get up a fight or two, but if the government sat tight and made no concessions, there would soon be up to 300,000 fine fighting Irishmen in the ranks.[30]

The Military Service Act received the Royal Assent on 18 April, but the events of the following few weeks, including the one-day general strike on 23 April, which united virtually all sections of the community in Ireland (including the Catholic Bishops) in opposition to conscription, soon demonstrated that the opinions expressed by Robinson and Long were not soundly based. By 13 April, Duke was panicking, advising the Cabinet that 'a very grave situation is arising in Ireland'. He warned on 18 April that no moves to introduce conscription should be initiated without close and careful consultation with the heads of the RIC and the DMP.[31] Robinson, for his part, quickly realised that he had misread the situation: he told Long on 25 April that resolutions of local councils protesting against conscription with or without Home Rule were 'showering down upon us like snowflakes', adding that 'the country is now in such a highly nervous hysterical state, and religious and political antagonisms are wrought to such a white heat by this joining of the forces of the RC church and the Sinn Féin, that it is sheer madness to attempt either Home Rule or conscription with things as they are'.[32] In a note written the following day, he told Duke that the situation had entirely changed, forcing him to withdraw the opinion offered to the Cabinet three weeks earlier that Ulster opposition to Home Rule 'would not be intractable, long-lived, or a serious danger':

> The linking up of the RC Hierarchy with the Sinn Féin rebels and their joint refusal to allow the Irish catholics to help win the war by agreeing to conscription has had such an effect on the protestants of the North and of Belfast that they seem to have gone mad.
>
> They are beside themselves at the idea of being placed under such a Parliament – a Popish and Rebel Parliament as they call it – and I truly believe that as matters stand the introduction of a Home Rule Parliament would be accompanied by serious religious riots in the North which would react on the protestants of the South, and that ship-building and munitions work in Belfast would be to a very serious extent shut down.
>
> Over here, the consensus of opinion seems to be to let things cool down, and drop both conscription and Home Rule till after the war.

Duke – who had consistently opposed conscription – immediately circulated Robinson's note to the War Cabinet and advised them in a short memorandum that, having found Sir Henry's judgment to be so trustworthy in all his experience of him, he was much impressed by his observations that the recent occurrences had entirely altered the mind of Ulster with regard to self-government.[33] Two weeks later, Long told the Cabinet, in words which closely paralleled what he had been told by Robinson, that the evidence from Ireland led to the conclusion that it would be folly (Robinson had suggested 'sheer madness') to attempt to implement either Home Rule or conscription at that stage.[34] Soon afterwards, he advised in a further submission, that to attempt conscription would most certainly be met with violent opposition.[35] Although any question of enforcing conscription in the short term was then abandoned, Robinson – who was quite sure that 'funk of bullets was at the bottom of all the high-flown romantic talk of the anti-conscriptionists'[36] – offered some advice to Long on how any formal announcement might be tailored:

It would be a great sedative in the present state of unrest if some responsible minister ... announced that care would be taken, in the event of conscription, that there should be no steps taken which would be prejudicial to agriculture and food production and that the labour necessary for increased tillage and harvest would not be interfered with. It is these small farmers and ignorant labourers who are most in terror over conscription: they are sleeping out at night and hiding in the hills. Now if they all knew that farming was still to carry on and that only the able-bodied men in shops and offices were to join up, half the outcry would die down. In fact, the agricultural population would be rather pleased than otherwise if they knew that these town youths were to be taken. There is no love between town and country in Ireland. [37]

Long took this advice seriously and advised the administration in Dublin that there should be early announcements to the effect that wholesale taking of men was not contemplated and that there would be proper consideration for food production and other essential industries.[38] A proclamation was quickly issued announcing that steps were to be taken to facilitate and encourage voluntary enlistment ... in the hope that, without resort to compulsion, the contribution of Ireland ... may be brought up to its proper strength, and made to correspond to the contributions of other parts of the Empire.[39] When detailed proposals for the campaign were announced on 4 June, it was made clear – just as Robinson had advised two weeks earlier – that there was no intention that enlistment should disturb farming interests or food production, that not many of the rural population were expected to be available for military service, and that the government were looking almost entirely to the large number of young men in the towns to make up the required numbers.[40]

Rebuilding the Relationship with the Catholic Bishops

Although he still had no official involvement in the conscription or recruitment issues, Robinson's advice and assistance were enlisted when Lord French, soon after his arrival in Ireland in early May, was considering with Walter Long how the government's relationship with the Irish catholic hierarchy might be restored. The War Cabinet had decided against consulting Cardinal Logue in advance of any public announcement about conscription, but ministers were subsequently furious about the fact that in throwing their weight behind the opposition, the Catholic Bishops had for the first time directly supported resistance to legislation passed by the Imperial Parliament, whose right to legislate for Ireland they had recognised until then.[41] Walter Long told the War Cabinet in May that 'the hierarchy have taken the field against the government' and their action was seen by Lloyd George as a direct challenge to the supremacy of Parliament.[42] The ancient rivalry between the English and Irish catholic hierarchies had been fuelled during the years 1915–17 by resentment of the attempts of the Cardinal Archbishop of Westminster, Francis Bourne, to position himself as the overall authority in the recruitment and appointment of the large number of catholic chaplains required by the army.[43] Ministers still seemed to think, however, that Bourne might be willing and able to help in rebuilding their relationship with the Irish Bishops. Walter Long therefore wrote to Bourne on 11 May seeking his advice, counsel and assistance.[44] He subsequently met the cardinal and endeavoured to get him to use his influence with the Irish hierarchy. Bourne could not see his way to becoming involved directly but agreed to meet 'the head of the Catholic University in Cork', Sir Bertram Windle, with whom he was friendly. Windle, an English-born catholic who had been president of UCC since 1904, was concerned in April 1918 that nothing had been done to collar the 'hordes of shirkers' who had fled to Ireland to escape conscription, but he believed at that stage that it was madness to attempt to enforce conscription in the country.[45]

The Under-Secretary, Sir William Byrne, was a catholic and there were several other catholics in senior official positions in Dublin, but it was Robinson who was called on for advice regarding the suggestion that Windle or another intermediary should be sent to meet Cardinal Bourne. Robinson's first reaction was that Bishop Denis Kelly of Ross, with whom he had co-authored the Irish section of the report of the Poor Law Commission in 1909, would be a better man and a better intermediary than Windle.[46] When the cardinal agreed to meet either man or both it was left to Robinson to decide what would be best. As he explained it to Long on 13 May, he would have liked to have sent Bishop Kelly, who was 'a wise, moderate man and can diagnose the trend of popular feeling and can give a better opinion as to the way out of difficulties better than any man I know'.[47] But he was aware of the strained relationship between the Irish bishops and Bourne and so, he explained that he did not like to send Bishop Kelly 'in view of the anger and distrust of all the hierarchy now towards Cardinal Bourne. In fact, if it was known that you had taken counsel with the cardinal it would be in itself enough to prejudice an impartial consideration of your bill [the promised Home Rule bill, presumably] by the hierarchy'. He therefore told Long that he had sent Charles O'Conor, his senior inspector, who was a catholic and a personal friend of Windle, to Cork to 'find him and send him over and [to] wire you from Cork when to expect him'.[48] In a letter to his friend and biographer, Sr Monica Taylor, Windle told her that having received a very urgent call to London from a government office, he had crossed to London on 16 May, did his business there next morning (without giving any indication of what that business was) and crossed the other way on the following night without meeting Bourne.[49] His diary records that he met Long at the Colonial Office on 17 May and that he had a very interesting talk with him about what was to be done in Ireland,[50] but, in view of Robinson's advice, it had been agreed by then between French and Long that any further action should be postponed.[51]

The Aftermath of the Crisis

After the government had backed down on the proposal to introduce conscription and decided to rely instead on a new recruiting campaign to secure the enlistment of 50,000 volunteers, the newly appointed Lord Lieutenant, Field Marshal French, after conversations with Robinson on the subject of grants of land to ex-soldiers, decided that if something could be said publicly about this it would be of great help in the campaign.[52] He followed up by announcing that steps were being taken to ensure as far as possible that land would be made available for men who had fought for their country and, although the proposal was described by critics as an unworthy bribe, a bill was introduced in the House of Commons on 31 July to give effect to it. After criticism by Irish members during a debate on 22 October, the bill was withdrawn.[53] It had already become clear at that stage that recruitment was falling far short of the target, but moves to revert to a conscription policy were halted when it became apparent that the war would soon come to an end.

Apart from its wider effects in building up opposition to British rule in Ireland, Robinson believed that the attempt to introduce conscription had resulted in the Catholic Bishops finding themselves in a 'very ugly fix over their joining up with Sinn Féin' in the anti-conscription campaign. He told Long that:

> They are terribly afraid of the IRB who have become very strong during the past five years and who are now the militant group of the Sinn Féin and who are the link with Germany. If the Irish Party had kept in with the group, they and the clergy would have been able to hold their own against the secret societies and to have dominated them. But now there is this split: the Sinn Féin have the cash and

the hierarchy are mixed up in a combination a section of which –
the IRB – will wipe out the church's influence if it can by terrorism
whenever the church opposes them or shrinks from the extreme
steps they advocate.[54]

As in other cases, Robinson's view on the issue was overstated – but, in light
of the events of the following three years, not entirely wide of the mark.

NOTES

1   WRO, Long Papers, WRO 947/331, Robinson to Long, 27 July 1916.
2   Michael Laffan, *The Resurrection of Ireland* (Cambridge, 1999), pp.77–84.
3   Irish Local Elections, Memorandum for the War Cabinet GT 20, minutes by Mr
     Duke and Sir H. Robinson, Feb. 1917, TNA, CAB/24/6.
4   R. B. McDowell, *The Irish Convention 1917–18* (London, 1970), p.vii.
5   *Irish Times*, 15 June 1917.
6   Copy of Robinson's letter of 13 June to the chairman of Listowel UDC, NLI, MS
     44,607.
7   Letter from Patrick White MP, *Meath Chronicle*, 7 July 1917.
8   Copy of letter of 25 Feb. 1918 from D. Lloyd George to Sir Horace Plunkett,
     NLI, MS 18,545.
9   *Irish Times*, 28 Feb., 13 and 14 Mar. 1918.
10   Robinson to Long, 14 Mar. 1918, WRO, Long Papers, WRO 947/332.
11   State of Ireland – Irish Policy, Memorandum GT 3668 for War Cabinet by the
     Chief Secretary for Ireland, 19 Feb. 1918, TNA, CAB 24/42.
12   Memorandum GT 3667 for the War Cabinet, copy of a letter from Lord Decies
     to Sir Edward Carson, 19 Feb. 1918, TNA, CAB 24/42.
13   *Irish Times*, 18 Mar. 1918.
14   Letters of 1 and 4 Mar. 1918 from Long to Lloyd George, Parliamentary Archives,
     Lloyd George Papers, LG/F/32/5/9, LG/F/32/5/10.
15   Copy of letter of 4 Mar. 1918 from Long to Lloyd George, Parliamentary Archives,
     Bonar Law Papers, BL/83/2/21.
16   Nathan privately recorded in 1918 that he too had advised against conscription
     – letter of 29 Apr. 1918 to Dorothy Stopford, NLI, MS 15,341 (1).
17   Duke to Lloyd George, 30 Jan. 1917, Parliamentary Archives, Lloyd George
     Papers, LG/F/37/4/10.
18   *Hansard* V, 101, 17 Jan. 1918, 579–80.
19   War Cabinet Minutes, 372, 25 Mar. 1918; 374, 27 Mar. 1918; 375, 27 Mar. 1918;
     376, 28 Mar. 1918, TNA, CAB 23/5.
20   In England and Wales, the Local Government Board had overall responsibility for
     implementing the conscription scheme; to deal with applications for exemptions
     and conscientious objectors, local councils were required to set up tribunals
     (on which councillors generally formed a majority) and appeal tribunals were
     established at county level.

21   War Cabinet Minutes, 381a, 3 Apr. 1918, TNA, CAB 23/14; although the *War Memoirs of David Lloyd George* (London, 1938), pp.1597–1601, discuss the advice received from various officials, no mention is made of Robinson, perhaps because Lloyd George did not attend the meeting of 3 April.

22   According to Peter Hart (*The IRA at War, 1916–23* (Oxford, 2000), pp.114–116), shop assistants and clerks were disproportionately over-represented in the Volunteers and may have formed up to one fifth of the active members.

23   War Cabinet Minutes, 375 27 Mar. 1918, TNA, CAB 23/5; idem 383, 5 Apr. 1918, TNA, CAB 23/6.

24   War Cabinet Minutes, 384, 6 Apr. 1918, TNA, CAB 23/6

25   *Hansard* V, 105, 15 Apr. 1918, 103–104; *Irish Times*, 6 Apr. 1918.

26   Military Service (No 2) Bill, 1918, Bill no. 16.

27   *Hansard* V, 104, 12 Apr. 1918, 1912–15.

28   D. G. Boyce and Cameron Hazlehurst, 'The Unknown Chief Secretary: H. E. Duke and Ireland', IHS xx, 79 (Mar. 1977), pp.308–09.

29   Long to Bonar Law, 4 Apr. 1918, Parliamentary Archives, Bonar Law Papers, BL/83/2/2.

30   Long to Lloyd George, 10 Apr. 1918, Parliamentary Archives, Lloyd George Papers, LG/ F/32/5/20.

31   Memoranda by the chief secretary for Ireland: Grave Crisis in Ireland, G.T. 4218, 13 Apr. 1918; Organisation of Irish resistance to conscription, G.T. 4272, 18 Apr. 1918, TNA, CAB 24/48.

32   Robinson to Long, 25 Apr. 1918, WRO, Long Papers, WRO 947/332.

33   Memorandum G.T. 4364 for the War Cabinet, 'Feeling in Ulster', 27 Apr. 1918, TNA, CAB 24/49.

34   War Cabinet Minutes, 408A, 10 May 1918, TNA, CAB 23/14.

35   Memorandum for the War Cabinet, Ireland, G.T. 4889, W.H.L., 29 May 1918, TNA, CAB 24/52,

36   IWM, French Diary, 14 May 1918.

37   Robinson to Long, 14 May 1918, WRO, Long Papers, WRO 947/332.

38   Long to Robinson, 16 May 1918, WRO, Long Papers, WRO 947/332; Long to French, 17 May 1918, IWM, French Papers, JDPF 8/3.

39   *Irish Times*, 18 May 1918.

40   *Irish Times*, 4 June 1918.

41   War Cabinet Minutes, 377, 29 Mar. 1918, TNA, CAB 23/5.

42   Memorandum for the War Cabinet, Ireland, G.T. 4889, W.H.L., 29 May 1918, TNA, CAB 24/52; War Cabinet Minutes, 453, 29 July 1918, TNA, CAB 23/7.

43   John Privilege, *Michael Logue and the Catholic Church in Ireland, 1879–1925* (Manchester, 2009), pp.101–108.

44   Copy of letter of 11 May, WRO, Long Papers, WRO 947/161.

45   IWM, French Diary, 14 May 1918; Ann Keogh and Dermot Keogh, *Bertram Windle, the Honan Bequest and the Modernisation of University College Cork, 1904–1919* (Cork, 2010), pp.153–54, 202–205.

46   IWM, French Diary, 14 May 1918.

47   Robinson to Long, 13 May 1918, WRO, Long Papers, WRO 947/332.

48   Robinson to Long, 14 May 1918, WRO, Long Papers, WRO 947/332.

49   Letter of 9 June 1918 to Sister Monica Taylor, in Monica Taylor, *Sir Bertram Windle, A Memoir* (London, 1932), pp.270–271.
50   Windle Diary, 17 May, quoted in Keogh, *Windle*, p.210.
51   IWM, French Diary, 15 and 16 May, 1918.
52   French to Long, 28 May 1918, IWM, French Papers, JDPF 8/3.
53   *Hansard* V, 110, 22 Oct., 1918, 668–735; 18 Nov. 1918, 3315; a subsequent scheme to provide housing for sailors and soldiers which was operated by the LGB from late 1919 to 1922 is discussed in chapter XIV.
54   Robinson to Long, 13 May 1918, WRO, Long Papers, WRO 947/332.

CHAPTER XIII

'A Fair and Square Fight ... As To Who is Going to Govern the Country'

A Quasi-Military Government

In early May 1918 Lord Lieutenant Wimborne was replaced by Field-Marshal Lord French, who understood that he was to be head of a quasi-military government.[1] Robinson was pleased at the appointment and soon after French was sworn in at Dublin Castle on 11 May in the presence of Robinson and the other members of the Privy Council, the two men began a series of discussions on a wide range of matters, most of which had nothing to do with Robinson's official responsibilities.[2] In a long talk with French on 14 May, Robinson got the impression that the establishment of Home Rule was the viceroy's ultimate hope, and that he wanted to clear away all obstacles that stood in the way of achieving this.[3] French's diary confirms that discussions on that occasion ranged over 'many interesting things' including the Catholic bishops' participation in the anti-conscription campaign, the competence – or lack of it – of Sir Ignatius O'Brien, the Lord Chancellor, and the possibility of appointing Lord Chief Justice Campbell in his place, an appointment which was made one month later. Robinson also briefed French on the reaction of the people to his arrival and on the attitude of Dublin Corporation to the new administration.[4]

Coinciding with the appointment of French, Edward Shortt, a Liberal MP with no previous ministerial experience, became Chief Secretary and, like French, a member of the Cabinet. However, French soon made it clear to Shortt that his wishes and decisions were to prevail and that he was to be *de facto* as well as *de jure* governor of Ireland.[5] Robinson was not impressed by Shortt, who struck him as 'a capable but obstinate man, too much bound to preconceived opinions and too apt to regard blind obstinacy as representing strength'.[6] He did eventually come to admire Shortt's iron constitution and his ability to consume large quantities of whiskey and poteen without ill-effects when being entertained by parish priests during their tours together of the West. Shortt had only been a few weeks in Ireland when he travelled in Robinson's car to Connemara and demonstrated an 'amazing power of carrying his drink', which Robinson saw as a priceless asset for a chief secretary on tour. The objective on that occasion, as Robinson recalled some years later, was to see what could be done for the survivors (sic) of the *Pretty Polly* fishing boat, which had been blown up by a German submarine on 31 May – presumably he intended to refer to the *dependants* of the fishermen, as contemporary press reports indicate that the seven-man crew had all perished.[7]

At his own request, Walter Long was assigned by Lloyd George to liaise between the new French–Shortt administration and the government at Westminster. He suggested that he should, in addition, act as virtual over-lord of the administration because he believed that 'it would be very wrong that the War Cabinet should be called upon to give any portion of their time and thoughts to these domestic questions'.[8] Long was a major influence on French; the two men were birds of a feather according to Richard Holmes' biography of French, *The Little Field-Marshal* (1981) and their friendship 'survived even the trials of Ireland',[9] allowing them to dominate Irish policy at a time when the Cabinet was preoccupied with more pressing matters. Initially, the new administration did not consider the appointment of a new under-secretary to be a priority: while French recorded in his diary a few days after his arrival in Ireland that Robinson seemed to be a very sound man who understood the situation, he noted on the same day that Shortt was averse to making any change at that stage because he had formed a favourable opinion of Sir William Byrne, who had been Under-Secretary since October 1916.[10] Two days later, he told Long that there was some 'difference of opinion as regards the under-secretary and that a decision must be postponed for a time'.[11] Robinson, as usual, had no difficulty in reaching a conclusion in such matters: Byrne, he had already told Long, was 'a decent, loyal soul, but was utterly at sea'.[12]

As far back as December 1917, press reports were suggesting that Byrne was to be replaced by Robinson,[13] and rumours to this effect were again circulating six months later, prompting the usual letter of protest from Celia Harrison, this time describing him as an official who 'represents all the worst influences at work in the public life of Ireland'.[14] At the beginning of July 1918, when Byrne's relationship with French was already deteriorating to such an extent that he wished to return to his former position as chairman of the Board of Control for Lunacy in London, Long attempted to have Robinson appointed to replace him. He told Shortt at a meeting in London that Robinson was the senior official in the Irish service, that he had done 'most conspicuous work for Ireland and for the Empire', that 'his claims upon us are of the strongest possible kind' and that 'if it was necessary ... to pass him over, the opportunity should be taken to see him before any public announcement was made and generally explain the situation'.[15] His high opinion of Robinson was bolstered by some of his correspondents, including the aptly-named Fr John Flattery, a County Mayo parish priest, who told him that Robinson's appointment would be a real blessing to the country as no more competent man could be found with a record of success in dealing with Irish affairs over a long period.[16] Robinson's promotion to head the team at Dublin Castle was also recommended by his former colleague, Sir Thomas Stafford, who was well known to French after he had acquired a small country house at Drumdoe, County Roscommon, which was close to the large Stafford King-Harman estate at Rockingham, which was effectively controlled by Stafford after the death of his wife in 1916. In a letter to French, Stafford argued that 'knowledge of the country, brains and firmness, combined with a little bit of human sympathy' were required for the government of the country at the time – and few people (other than Robinson) possessing this rare combination were to be found.[17] For whatever reasons, Shortt did not agree to Robinson's appointment. He instead told the Prime Minister on 4 July that he had decided to appoint James MacMahon, secretary of the Irish Post Office since 1916, who had impressed him greatly.[18] Long felt pretty sure that Shortt's action was due to 'some of his own department [who] have been getting at him' due to 'a long-standing and deplorable jealousy between the under-secretary's office and the Local Government Board' – all combined to condemn any proposal to appoint an outsider but 'when it is sought to find an Irishman, each department proceeds to oppose the selection of anybody except from their own men'.[19]

'Against Stupidity, the Gods Fight in Vain'

A northerner and a catholic, MacMahon was a career civil servant who, in 1914, had been passed over for promotion to head the Post Office when

Arthur Hamilton Norway was brought from England to fill the position. He had been promoted in 1916, however, when Norway returned to England. When unofficial reports that MacMahon was to be appointed as Under-Secretary appeared in a Dublin newspaper on 2 July, Robinson was clearly incensed – not just because he had been passed over again, but because of his contempt for what he saw as a futile and stupid attempt to win favour with the Catholic bishops and nationalists.[20] He immediately dashed off a strongly-worded letter to Walter Long, criticising the appointment:

> One would have thought that by this time the Irish government might have learned the futility of endeavouring to govern this country by favour of the RC hierarchy and the Ancient Order of Hibernians.

> Birrell tried it and it ended in the Rebellion. Duke resumed the attempt and brought us perilously near Rebellion a second time, and now for a third time, Shortt – blind to these lessons – plays to the gallery by appointing an under-secretary over the heads of all the Irish civil servants senior to him for no other reason than that he is completely in the hands of the Catholic bishops and Devlin and his AOH.

> It is such a hopelessly vain display of weakness just now because the Sinn Féin party are the only people who count in the country at present and they will not be placated by the *Freeman's Journal* control of the under-secretaryship, and the only effect of it will be the government will be surrounded with an atmosphere of intrigue and clerical and Devlinite influence, which will discredit them in the eyes of all loyal people and will demoralize the police all over the country.

> I can assure you I have no disappointment at being passed over. I have served twenty chief secretaries and earned the goodwill of them all and I know too much of the pitfalls of Irish administration to be a safe person – from the nationalist point of view – to be allowed to work beside the chief secretary at the Castle, so I never imagined Shortt would face the *Freeman* protests which would inevitably follow my appointment. But there are plenty of other officials who are not the slaves of any party in Ireland from whom he might have made a selection if it was necessary to remove Byrne.

But against stupidity, the Gods fight in vain. This appointment will be regarded all over the country as an exhibition of sheer funk and the Sinn Féiners will take heart from it, as well they may. I know perfectly well that you had nothing to do with it.[21]

Long replied immediately, indicating that his first knowledge of the appointment had come from the newspapers (which would be very surprising if it proved to be true), but he challenged Robinson's comments on Shortt's motives and noted that he himself had been assured that MacMahon was an imperialist, intensely loyal, and not under the thumb of anybody.[22] He went on to assure Robinson that both French and Shortt had the highest opinion of him, of his knowledge of Ireland, and his judgment, and that both of them would attach the greatest importance to any advice he might offer them. However, he recognised that –

This is rather adding insult to injury for as you know I have never made any secret of the fact that in my judgment you ought to have been appointed long ago. Whether now you would care for it, or whether it would be suitable, I really don't know. I imagine that a man wants to be young to tackle a thankless and almost impossible job like that of the under-secretary. You will have had many disappointments to endure and they have never prevented you from rendering fine service to your country.

Clearly concerned by Robinson's reaction, Long also wrote to French, telling him that he had received some very severe criticism of MacMahon's appointment because it was said 'that he is entirely in the hands of the hierarchy, Mr Devlin and the AOH' – a paraphrase of what Robinson had told him. While he acknowledged that others in whom he had absolute confidence told him that the appointment was the best that had been made for a very long time, he warned French that there were reliable people who believed that MacMahon was not a free agent and that it would be desirable 'to watch how things go'.[23] In further letters to French, Long conceded that MacMahon was suitable for the office given his ability, probity and imperialism. He suggested that any criticism by the protestant minority based on MacMahon's catholicism and nationalism should be ignored if he was a capable and straight man who would carry out government policy. However, he profoundly regretted that the appointment had been made without first informing Robinson and explaining the position to him. And, because Robinson now felt that he had been passed over for an outsider without even a word of explanation or sympathy, Long urged French, even at that stage, to do what he could to lessen any feeling of bitterness he might entertain.[24]

In retrospect, Robinson believed that MacMahon had been appointed on the advice of Lord Granard and much to his own dismay he was taken from the Post Office, where he was popular, and plunged into a vortex of trouble in a department in Dublin Castle that was a severe trial to him, but it was impossible for him as a loyal civil servant to refuse.[25] Only three months after MacMahon's appointment, French provided Lloyd George with an even more critical assessment of him than he had received from Robinson: 'He is a rigid catholic and in close touch with the hierarchy,' he told the Prime Minister in October, and was 'simply the mouthpiece for the most rabid of the Irish priests'.[26] Similarly, French's private secretary, who originally thought that Robinson had allowed his personal feelings to get the better of his judgment in criticising the MacMahon appointment, also changed his mind.[27] He told Long in January 1919 that he had been having a 'steady war with the dirty elements in the Castle' and that MacMahon was doing everything he could to defeat efforts to keep French properly informed.[28] MacMahon was pushed aside early in 1919 after Shortt had been replaced by Ian Macpherson, and Sir John James Taylor, the hard-line Assistant Under-Secretary, was allowed to dominate. Taylor had worked in the Chief Secretary's Office since the 1880s; he had been Long's principal private secretary during his term as Chief Secretary in 1905 and had been promoted to the assistant under-secretary position in 1918, following representations by Long. French was obviously complicit in the demotion of MacMahon in 1919, even though he told Bonar Law in April 1920 that it was Macpherson who had been responsible.[29] He then, after Robinson had told him that he was strongly in favour of re-instating MacMahon, told Bonar Law that he was adopting this course.[30]

Sir Henry Robinson's Young Men ... Undergraduates of the Custom House

Having failed, not for the first time, to have Robinson appointed as Under-Secretary, and having campaigned more successfully to have Taylor promoted to the Assistant Under-Secretary position, Long combined with Robinson to arrange the appointment of two LGB officials, both strong unionists, to other influential positions in the new administration. Despite this, he made the rather extraordinary statement that 'I do not want it to be thought that I am trying to influence the Irish government in regard to appointments – it would be a great mistake if it were thought that I can get things done.'[31] The new appointments were:

Samuel Watt, in a move which was quite irregular in civil service terms, was transferred from the Custom House to become Shortt's private secretary. A 42-year-old presbyterian native of Newry and a graduate of TCD, Watt had joined the LGB in 1901 as a higher division clerk and had been Robinson's private secretary for some years. His new appointment was resented by Joseph Brennan, then a higher division clerk at the chief secretary's office, who had expected to be promoted to the post, which carried an allowance of £300 a year; Brennan was told that because of his experience he would have to be retained in the finance division but he saw this as 'a faked excuse' to get the job for a candidate favoured by Sir Henry Robinson.[32] When a proposal was made to the Treasury at a later stage to create a permanent post for Watt at the Castle, Brennan and his two higher division colleagues in the office protested that it would be a grave injustice if Watt were promoted over their heads but – as G. C. Duggan who worked at the Castle at the time saw it – 'it was apparent that the recommendation of Sir Henry Robinson, backed by Sir John Taylor, had greater weight than any views held by the under-secretary'.[33]

Edward (Eddy) Saunderson, an LGB inspector, then 50 years old, joined the staff at the Vice-Regal Lodge in 1918 on foot of Long's determination to have one of his favourites in a position of influence there and, as he told French, 'to act as a link between us'.[34] Long's determination to advance Saunderson's career arose also from his association with Eddy's late father, Colonel E. J. Saunderson, unionist MP for Armagh North, Orangeman, bigoted protestant and leader of the Irish Unionist Alliance until his death in October 1906. Saunderson moved from the Custom House to take up a new position as assistant private secretary in July, and he became principal private secretary to French on 1 November.

Although he was by no means an objective observer, Wimborne's critical comment in the House of Lords in June 1918 on the reconstruction of the executive in Dublin was still significant. Noting that the ramifications of the change in the administration extended into offices both great and small, including simple private secretaries, he remarked that this was somewhat unfortunate because it had the effect of removing all, or nearly all of those, 'who professed sympathy with the cause of Irish nationality and most of those ... who profess the catholic faith'.[35] In time, newspapers criticised the appointment and the performance of Watt and Saunderson, referring to them as 'Sir Henry Robinson's young men' and as 'undergraduates of the Custom House'.[36] Robinson, however, insisted that he was not responsible for the appointments, which he claimed 'were wrongfully attributed by the nationalist press to my desire to infuse an Orange atmosphere into Dublin Castle ... My part in the matter was confined to giving these two gentlemen the recommendations asked for and agreeing to their being seconded to the particular services'.[37]

According to his friend, Andrew Magill, Watt was under great strain as private secretary, having been coupled with 'the very reactionary policy of Dublin Castle' and of Sir John Taylor.[38] He was described in what *The Times* called 'a vehement leading article' in the *Freeman's Journal* in February 1920 as 'chief light to the uninformed ignorance' of Chief Secretary Macpherson, and the person responsible for an Education Bill, which proposed to make inroads on the rights of local authorities.[39] He was replaced in May 1920 when a new Chief Secretary, Hamar Greenwood, brought Cornelius Gregg from the Inland Revenue in London as his private secretary. Like Watt, Saunderson also attracted criticism and was said to be 'in charge of the vice-regal intellect and will'.[40] He wrote frequently to Long, dealing with a great variety of subjects, keeping him up-to-date on developments in Dublin, commenting on the performance of the administration in general and criticising the conduct of individuals within it. Long's papers at the Wiltshire and Swindon Record Office include no less than eighty-two letters to and from Saunderson between April 1918 and June 1920.[41] These letters give the impression that Saunderson saw himself conducting a one-man crusade against others in the administration and bear out the view that, with or without the knowledge and consent of French, he had come to play a far more significant and influential role than befitted a mere private secretary. Alvin Jackson, in fact, sees him as, occasionally, the most important individual influence on the government of Ireland in 1919–20, at times effectively deputising for French, sustaining the cause of die-hard loyalism and promoting uncompromising protestantism.[42]

Sinn Féin's Preparations for a General Election

In mid-February 1918, Chief Secretary Duke had warned the War Cabinet that there was already a grave chance that the members elected for a majority of the Irish constituencies at the next general election would be 'avowed advocates of Irish independence ... [who] will command attention on quasi-constitutional grounds in a way which has not been possible for any Irish revolutionary party in modern times'.[43] From mid-summer 1918 onwards, Sinn Féin began preparing for the long-awaited opportunity to secure the election of a parliament dominated by its own members.[44] In August, Robinson reported to French that the activity of the militant section of the organisation had considerably lessened during the previous month, mainly because the whole of the organisation's energies had been taken up with franchise work in preparation for the next elections. This work focused in particular on ensuring revision of the electoral registers to include the large numbers of their likely supporters who would be entitled for the first time to vote under the legislation enacted earlier that year. This is a matter of life and death to Sinn Féin, he went on, because –

> If on the new register, they can get a majority on the county and district councils, there will be no occasion to continue the drilling, raiding, and vicious propaganda, which is so perilous and uncertain in its results, and leads to such uncomfortable consequences when they are up against a viceroy like Lord French, but which is unfortunately necessary as things now stand in order to capture the imagination of the people and secure their adhesion to the Sinn Féin movement.

> If their franchise work is successful, and the Irish members are wiped out at the next election and the whole of the county government, representing an annual expenditure of £4,828,501, falls into Sinn Féin hands, the country people will find it the easiest and safest course, and the one best calculated to secure their own interests, to support Sinn Féin and secure their protection, and the risky violent propaganda, which at present is followed by loss of liberty and broken heads, will die out.

While there was still a great danger posed by the small IRB faction who were financed from America and were anxious 'to goad on the Sinn Féin [party] to bombing and every kind of outrage, which will let the Gaels in America think they are getting value for their money', Robinson's conclusion was that Sinn Féinism was then in a 'soberer, quieter and more thoughtful mood'. It was, however, gaining in numbers and influence, not just because of the successful defeat of conscription, but also because of the people's utter disgust at the Irish Party's servility to the Asquith government in return for the patronage they had been allowed to exercise for twelve years. The people also felt resentment in border areas at the 'tyranny and truculence' of the AOH.[45] When Lord French submitted the next of his regular 'State of Ireland' reports to the War Cabinet at the end of August 1918, he included not just the general thrust of Robinson's report, but also some of his language, including the references to the whole of the energies of the Sinn Féin organisation being taken up with franchise work, the organisation's hope of being able to wipe out the Irish Party at the next election, and the prospect that county government would come completely under their control.[46] The influence of Robinson can similarly be detected in other reports in the 'State of Ireland' series submitted by French in the following two years.

Official Preparations for the General Election

Although Sinn Féin had begun working in mid-1918 to ensure that their supporters were included in the new electoral register, neither the organisation (nor the first Dáil after 1919) exercised any power over the registration process itself or other electoral arrangements. It therefore continued to be the responsibility of Robinson and his staff to plan and oversee the machinery for an election which, although they did not know it at the time, was to mark the beginning of the end of the board's supremacy. Legislation enacted in February 1918 had considerably extended the right to vote by removing almost all of the former property qualifications for men over 21-years-of-age and by enfranchising women over 30-years-of-age, subject to property qualifications. The net result was to increase the Irish electorate from about 700,000 to almost two million, creating a whole generation of voters who had never voted before. The LGB had overall responsibility for the registration of the new electorate and for devising new schemes of polling districts and polling places, but the board's influence on electoral arrangements – and the likely results – was much more significant and controversial because of Robinson's personal involvement in the revision of the constituencies.

The Home Rule Act, which had been on the statute book since 1914, set out new constituencies for elections to the Westminster Parliament, as well as to the proposed Irish Parliament. The view was taken initially that the revision of Westminster constituencies, which was under way in 1917–18, should not therefore extend to the existing constituencies in Ireland. This view, however, could not be maintained in light of the wide divergence that had arisen since the 1884 revision in the ratio between seats, population and electorate in different constituencies. Belfast city, in particular, was seriously under-represented, with only four seats, while seven southern constituencies with a smaller aggregate population had fourteen. The East Belfast constituency alone had more than ten times the population of the Kilkenny city constituency, for which W. T. Cosgrave had been elected at an August 1917 by-election. Thus, no one can have been surprised when Ulster unionist members argued during the committee stage debate on the Representation of the People Bill in October 1917 that the Irish constituencies and the distribution of seats between them should be revised.[47] The government conceded, notwithstanding strong objections from Redmond and Dillon, and ten days later a commission was established, with instructions to quickly devise a new scheme so that enactment of the bill as a whole would not be delayed. James Lowther, the Speaker of the House of Commons, an assistant secretary of the English local government board, and Robinson were appointed as members of the commission. This was a somewhat peculiar arrangement according to the *Irish Independent*, given that officials are always inclined to do what may be pleasing to those who happen to be in power and given the need to prevent any suspicion of gerrymandering.[48] As the only member with local knowledge and contacts, it can be safely assumed that Robinson must have played a leading role in shaping the final report, which was completed with remarkable speed and presented on 27 November.[49]

Draft proposals had been published by the commission towards the middle of November. Seven LGB inspectors and auditors were appointed by Robinson to be assistant boundary commissioners, and to conduct local inquiries in cases where the proposals involved substantial changes. In Belfast, where nine seats were planned, the inquiry conducted by J. W. Drury, inspector of audits, was described by nationalist representatives as 'a manoeuvre for unionist party ends' and having made the case that the draft scheme would allow them to win only one seat (as transpired to be the case) they withdrew. In Tyrone, where a reduction from four to three seats was proposed, it was alleged that changes made on foot of unionist submissions were designed solely to ensure a unionist majority in south Tyrone.[50] Tim Healy was of the view that the scheme which emerged was devised by Robinson alone – which was probably true – and that the boundary revisions proposed in the case of the northern counties were designed by him to maximise the number of seats unionists might win. He alleged that Robinson had played into the hands of the Orange extremists in redrawing the boundaries and that he was in constant conference with the Ulster Tories on the matter. A joke of one of them, he wrote, was that a Tyrone tory slept in Robinson's office while the revision work was in progress.[51]

The Boundary Commission's report was controversial: it proposed to eliminate the separate constituency of Waterford City, which had been represented by John Redmond since 1891. It allowed Dublin University (then represented by Sir Edward Carson) to stand as a separate constituency while the two universities created in 1908 were not to be represented.

Also, it was alleged that the new arrangement of constituencies proposed in Dublin and in some of the northern counties had been devised to suit the unionists. When the issue was debated acrimoniously over four days in the House of Commons in December 1917,[52] Healy questioned why Irish voters 'were left to the mercy of Sir Henry Robinson' who, although the most expert civil servant in Ireland, was also the 'leading official tory' in the country, and the representative of a 'department of odium and contempt'.[53] In response, Chief Secretary Duke argued unconvincingly that there were objective grounds for the various boundary adjustments, and insisted that while he had no idea whether Robinson was a liberal or a tory, he had found him to be 'not only one of the ablest and most upright, but one of the most popular and trusted, public officials in Ireland'.[54] After further debate, agreement was reached on a compromise put forward by Bonar Law under which a speaker's conference, comprising two nationalist and two unionist MPs, was convened to consider the commission's recommendations. As a result, the legislation enacted in February 1918 allowed Waterford city to retain its separate seat, created two additional university seats (although this added to the over-representation of Ireland as a whole) and made some minor boundary revisions affecting the County Down constituencies.[55] Healy believed that the original scheme framed by Robinson was so unjust that Bonar Law had been forced to concede that it should be reconsidered but that Robinson, having reconsidered it, 'decided that it was perfect'. Healy told his brother on 18 January that 'nothing is to be changed in the redistribution of seats in Ulster from the recommendations of Sir Henry Robinson ... the Speaker's arrangements will result in leaving the Carsonites in a permanent majority of three in Ulster'.[56] In the event, unionists won twenty-three of the twenty-eight seats in the six counties that were later to become Northern Ireland, leaving nationalists with only one seat in Armagh, Belfast and Fermanagh, and two in Tyrone.

Only a few months after the revision of the Westminster constituencies was completed, Robinson's pre-eminent position in electoral matters was recognised again. Duke requested him to prepare, within six days, a scheme of constituencies and electoral arrangements which could be incorporated in the Home Rule Bill which it had originally been intended to introduce in parallel with conscription legislation in April 1918. When Robinson protested that this was a task more suitable for a commission, Duke told him that there was no time for this and that, in any case, he was sure that Robinson's 'intimate knowledge of the configuration of the country and location of population' would enable him to do the job himself. In mid-June, when Robinson had completed the necessary maps and schedule, the idea of going ahead with either a Home Rule Bill or a Conscription Bill had been dropped.[57]

'A Fair and Square Fight ... as to Who is Going to Govern the Country'

The long-deferred general election was announced in the House of Commons on 15 November, a few days after the First World War ended. By 17 December, even before the votes at the election held three days earlier had been counted, Robinson had come to the conclusion, based on what he had heard from all parts of the country in the previous few days, that Sinn Féin had triumphed. In a letter addressed that day to Saunderson at the Vice-Regal Lodge – but obviously intended for the information of Lord French – he reported that 'the marvellous organization and the success of the Sinn Féiners, and the voting of Cardinal Logue and Archbishop Walsh for Sinn Féin, has made such an impression that the Nationalist Party is now without any following except the middle class: solicitors, shopkeepers and the like'.[58] Saunderson passed a copy of Robinson's letter to Walter Long, who in turn quickly had it typed and circulated at the end of December for the information of the War Cabinet, describing it as 'a report which I have received from a confidential but an absolutely reliable source'.[59] Robinson's letter went on:

> I have watched the rise and fall of every political party in Ireland for the last forty years, and I think the present movement is much the most difficult and dangerous of any the Government have had to deal with and for this reason.

> Their Leaders are brave and fanatical and do not fear imprisonment or death; they are not to be influenced by private negotiations with Bishops and Priests, or captured by getting the patronage of appointments, which has been the favourite instrument of the Irish Government since 1905. Neither do they care a straw for the Press.

> It is a fair and square fight between the Irish Government and the Sinn Féin as to who is going to govern the country.

Long must be assumed to have accepted and endorsed these views by submitting Robinson's letter to the Cabinet, but the words themselves cannot be attributed to him as has previously been done. In 1975, for example, Charles Townshend quoted them as a 'striking analysis' by Long of the confrontation which had now begun,[60] while in 1991 Lawrence W. McBride, repeating Townshend's mistake, described the text as Long's reflections on his forty years of experience in Irish affairs.[61]

Robinson's assessment of the strength of Sinn Féin was, of course, an accurate one, while his further comments on the situation facing the Sinn Féin leaders, whose *Manifesto to the Irish People*[62] had committed them to abstention from Westminster, were also perceptive, if not altogether accurate:

> The main difficulty they have is this. While the leaders are prepared to organise and fight anything, whether it be compulsory levy of taxation, the repudiation of the land purchase annuities, the suspension and regulation of traffic etc, the rank and file are dead against any extreme measures which will bring them up against Lord French.

> This is the Sinn Féiners' great trouble. Because if they cannot do something bold to capture the imagination of their Irish and American following and to enable them to keep their grip till the county and district elections in June (when they will have the administration of £3,000,000 a year if they win these elections) they will lose caste and then the handful of official nationalists in the House of Commons may make such play in the lime-light, that as a last resort the Sinn Féin may have to take the oath and go to Westminster also, and once they do that, all idea of a Republic or a kind of government they want, or a Sinn Féin created government at home, is gone for ever.

> It is a desperately critical time for them, this first six months, unless Lord French can be got rid of by some means or other.[63]

French himself advised the War Cabinet on 16 December that the newly elected MPs were likely to refuse for some time to attend Westminster and might cause trouble by trying to set up a bogus parliament in Dublin. Despite this, he was confident that firm government would prevail.[64] In a letter to the King two days later, he told him that Sinn Féin were fully determined not to take their seats at Westminster, but were planning to establish a kind of mock parliament in Dublin and – drawing on the report he had just received from Robinson – he advised the King of the serious risk that, after the next local elections, Sinn Féin would have in their hands the use of up to three million pounds of government money, and the likelihood that the leaders would have to take some drastic action to retain their hold over their followers.[65]

'A Solemn Act of Defiance of the British Empire'

It cannot have come as a great surprise to the authorities in Dublin that Sinn Féin won 73 of the 105 seats at the December general election. This overwhelming victory made it possible for the party to implement the policy of abandoning Westminster, which had been advocated by Arthur Griffith fifteen years earlier, assuming responsibility for the administration of Irish affairs, and behaving as if British rule did not exist. Following a Christmas holiday in England, French arrived in Kingstown on the mail boat early on the morning of 8 January and soon began a meeting with Robinson, at which he 'learnt a great deal of the state of affairs'. They discussed the election results and the action likely to be taken by the Sinn Féin leaders. Robinson reiterated how impressed he had been by the performance of the party's candidates. The two men also debated whether the catholic hierarchy might influence the future course of action, but according to Robinson, the priests and the bishops had 'lost their powers over the people' – a view which French accepted, even though Under-Secretary MacMahon disagreed. There was some discussion also about the possibility of a general strike, but Robinson thought this to be unlikely 'as the last one-day conscription strike was most unpopular with all classes'.[66] French had further meetings with Robinson on 11 and 14 January when discussions again centred on major political and strategic issues.

Both French and Long and, to a lesser extent, Robinson, had underestimated the strength, determination and organisation of Sinn Féin. Robinson's speculation about the willingness of the movement and its allies to countenance extreme measures, and about their ability to capture the imagination of their supporters, was answered – if not altogether by design – by the events of 21 January. On that day, the first shots in the War of Independence were fired in County Tipperary, resulting in the deaths of two RIC men, while the twenty-seven Sinn Féin MPs, who were not in jail or on the run, met in Dublin's Mansion House to set up an Irish Parliament and to declare a republic – 'a solemn act of defiance of the British Empire' according to the *Irish Times* 'by a body of young men who have … not a particle of experience on the conduct of public affairs'.[67] French told Long on 22 January that he was sure that the Sinn Féin MPs would 'soon go bag and baggage over to Westminster' and Long agreed, bearing in mind that the newly-elected members could not draw salaries in Dublin.[68] French appeared not to be particularly concerned about the events in the Mansion House – although George Moore, who had attended the meeting, told him that the proceedings were perfectly orderly and that those present 'represented the general feeling of the country', he told Long on 23 January that 'the Mansion House Parliament' had been a ludicrous farce.[69] At the end of January, he told Ian Macpherson, the new Chief Secretary, that 'no one ever seems to speak about the parliament now at all'[70] and as late as 15 May, his State of Ireland report told the War Cabinet that most of the proceedings of the Dáil were conducted in Irish and had 'failed to awaken any enthusiasm in the country'.[71] In January, he had actually been more concerned about the situation in Belfast than he was about the Dáil proceedings: gas, electricity and other services had been suspended in the city due to strikes by 120,000 workers in support of a demand for a forty-four hour week.[72] Robinson had sent the LGB medical commissioner to the city to review what might need to be done to ensure that serious risks to public health would not arise, but he told Macpherson at the end of January that he was not as yet seriously perturbed about public health issues. However, Robinson had another and more serious concern: aware that the strikers were holding large meetings and marches almost daily and had the support of Joe Devlin, he advised the Chief Secretary to 'keep Carson out of Belfast, if you can ... if Carson comes over now, it may mean that there will be rival crowds – and, in Belfast, rival crowds are always a danger'.[73]

Releasing the German Plot Internees

Before the December election, French and Shortt had jointly advised the War Cabinet that it would be highly dangerous to allow the majority of the German Plot prisoners to be at large in Ireland.[74] These Sinn Féin leaders – over seventy of them – had been arrested overnight and deported following the publication on 18 May of a proclamation by French, announcing the need for drastic measures to put down and disrupt the so-called plot.[75] Robinson had quickly sought informal reports from his inspectors throughout the country as to the general impression left upon the people by the announcement of the plot and the arrests, and forwarded these reports to French on 30 May with some comments of his own. The arrests, he believed, had taken Sinn Féin supporters by surprise, and if convincing evidence was forthcoming, the separatist movement would never recover.[76] But no such evidence was, of course, produced. Robinson was forced to tell French at a later stage that the arrests had unintended consequences because of the militancy of the men who rose to prominence in the absence of the more moderate internees.

Six months later, he was to develop this point in further correspondence with French.

In January 1919, before the meeting of the first Dáil, a report in the *Irish Times* suggested that Shortt was about to make proposals to the Prime Minister about the release of the prisoners, nearly thirty of whom had been successful at the election.[77] Shortt had submitted a memorandum to the War Cabinet on 27 December – but without consulting French – proposing that for legal and other reasons, the prisoners should be quietly released before agitation inside and outside the prisons built up.[78] Walter Long, however, submitted a counter-memorandum urging that the Cabinet should await a full report from French and suggested that some of the prisoners, if released, would be an immediate cause of grave public danger.[79] After a day of public protests throughout the country on 5 January, and having seen the *Irish Times* report about Shortt's proposals, Robinson immediately wrote to French's private secretary, expressing the hope that the Cabinet had a complete understanding of the issues involved.[80] Surface indications, he went on, 'give a most misleading impression of the situation and it is scarcely possible for anyone who does not realise what Sinn Féin is aiming at, and know of the conflicting elements within the movement, to form a sound judgment as to how the country may be affected by whatever decision the government may take in the matter'. He freely acknowledged that there were obvious arguments in favour of keeping the prisoners interned – the recent outrages, the police reports on the disturbed state of the country and the risk that the release of the leaders would be regarded as a sign of weakness, which would embolden the rank and file and lead to further and even more nefarious acts – but in spite of the risks, he came down strongly in favour of the opposite view:

> It may be urged that these methods to which Sinn Féinism has of late shown a tendency to degenerate are entirely contrary to the policy and interests of the Sinn Féin leaders. In their absence, Sinn Féinism is getting out of hand and is being locally controlled by the irresponsible hooligan minority, who are in the movement for what they can get out of it and as an outlet for their criminal instincts; they are being made the tools of the Irish Republican Brotherhood who have strong financial backing in America and if they get a secure hold on the country by terrorism and intimidation, Sinn Féin will be extinguished and nothing will be left in its place but scattered societies out for murder, looting of country houses and revolution. If the Sinn Féin leaders are unable to stem this tide of anarchy, the

bulk of their followers will be alarmed and they will lose the support of the decentest section of their supporters who were carried off their feet by the wave of enthusiasm for Sinn Féin ideals.

The aim of the real Sinn Féin party now is concentrated on securing the seats on the county and district councils at the June elections – and I look forward to their doing so without misgiving as I believe they will in many ways be more honest administrators than many of the present boards. It is essential for their candidature that they should not, in the meantime, embroil the country in disturbances and violence, which would give the government a valid reason for suppressing the whole movement, putting the country under military law and imposing heavy penalties for malicious injuries upon the ratepayers.

De Valera and his so called ministry, in spite of their rebellion, their German alliance and their clap-trap oratory, are courageous and patriotic according to their lights, and they are running a movement, which they honestly, though perhaps foolishly, believe will in the end secure a sympathetic national government for Ireland. They alone can put an end to these cold-blooded murders of police and no one can doubt that it is in their interest to do so.

But as they are out of the country and unable to use their personal influence, the town hooligans and the sons of labourers and those who care nothing of Sinn Féin ideals are speculating openly on what they think is, or should be, the plan of campaign, and the well-to-do people are being privately advised to send their plate and valuables to the bank and to remove their women-folk, and there is a restless and nervous feeling about which can only be quelled if the Sinn Féin leaders resume control and make it clear to their followers that, by all their braggadocio and outrage, they are taking the straight and certain way to smashing up the whole movement.[81]

For all of these reasons, Robinson's advice to French was that if the interned prisoners (who included de Valera, Griffith and Cosgrave) were not to be brought to trial, the wisest course would be to release them and give them a chance to persuade their more militant colleagues who had avoided capture (including presumably Collins, Boland and Brugha) to abandon murder and intimidation. He repeated this advice at his meetings with French on his return to Ireland in early January, and it was endorsed by Lord Chancellor Campbell.[82] Robinson was well ahead of his time in recognising that de Valera, in relative terms, was a moderate and that he and his close associates alone could put an end to murders and violence. This was not generally accepted by the British authorities until the end of 1920, and not until May 1921 was Chief Secretary Greenwood prepared to recognise, in a letter to Craig, that de Valera 'was the one man who can deliver the goods'.[83]

Analysis of events subsequent to Robinson's January letter suggests that his advice on the prisoners issue was decisive or, at least, as William Murphy has concluded, that French came under the influence of Robinson on the issue.[84] French, who had previously been resolutely opposed to any releases, pressed the War Cabinet strongly by telegram on 4 February to agree to the immediate release of the prisoners (especially those who had been elected to Parliament), but the Cabinet were unwilling to agree to this until they were advised of the reasons for his *volte face*.[85] Even Walter Long, who was French's greatest supporter at Cabinet level, continued strongly to oppose the release, which would be a 'great and grave danger' in his view, and added that he had heard nothing from any source in Ireland to suggest that de Valera and his prisoner colleagues would be likely to lead the people along the right path. A telegram from French to the Cabinet office on 5 February explained that 'during the last month, the reliable information I have got makes me sure that the influence of these leaders is far more likely to lead their followers towards a less unfavourable attitude than the influence under which they now act'. He went further in a memorandum submitted a few days later, discussing the different factions within Sinn Féin and suggesting that the murder of police constables, such as had occurred at Soloheadbeg, 'was but the natural effect of the withdrawal of de Valera from his position of responsibility', and the assumption of that responsibility by reckless men. The time had arrived, he concluded when the prisoners should be released, adding that he was supported in this view 'by leading men both in and out of the government' – a group which obviously included Robinson.[86] When the issue came before the War Cabinet again on 4 March, French's recommendation, which was supported by Macpherson, was accepted, and the Chief Secretary was authorised gradually to release the prisoners, although by then de Valera had escaped from Lincoln Jail.[87] In retrospect, there is much to be said for the view, expressed by Brian Feeney in his history of Sinn Féin, that the arrests in May 1918 backfired by removing from the scene the moderate leadership of the republican movement, leaving the way open for the more hard-line and less political leaders to become the real driving-force in the separatist movement.[88]

The significance of Robinson's intervention in the debate on the release of the prisoners is that he was ready, before Macpherson, French, Long and other members of the Cabinet and the Dublin administration were, to make a distinction between the different elements of the separatist/ nationalist movement and to recognise the danger that Sinn Féin, as a successful political party – but without a mandate for war – was in danger of being swept aside by those who favoured a physical force approach. As Alvin Jackson put it, he had a much better grasp of the morphology of the Sinn Féin movement than most others in the Dublin administration.[89] He differed in particular from the civil servants and advisers at Dublin Castle who were heavily criticised by Sir Warren Fisher in his confidential report to the Prime Minister in May 1920 for failing to recognise that Sinn Féin – which had been declared to be an illegal organisation – represented the great majority of Irishmen and for using the label Sinn Féin to cover 'murderers and criminals on the one hand and everyone whose political persuasion it dislikes on the other'.[90] Sinn Féin, Fisher insisted 'is a political party, however much people may dislike it' and it was not synonymous with outrage. If this same advice, when it was offered by Robinson in January 1919 – almost eighteen months earlier – had been accepted and acted on, would the history of the following years have been very different?

NOTES

1   IWM, French Diary, 5 May 1918.

2   *Irish Times*, 13 May 1918.

3   Sir Henry Robinson, *Memories: Wise and Otherwise* (London, 1923), pp.261–62.

4   IWM, French Diary, 14 and 15 May 1918.

5   French to Shortt, 26 Sept.1918, IWM, French Papers, JDPF 8/2.

6   Robinson, *Memories*, p.264.

7   Robinson, *Memories*, pp.269–271; *Irish Times*, 13 and 15 June 1918.

8   Copy of letter of 4 Mar. 1918, Long to Lloyd George, Parliamentary Archives, Bonar Law Papers, BL/83/2/21.

9   Richard Holmes, *The Little Field-Marshal* (London, 1981), p.340.

10   IWM, French Diary, 14 May 1918.

11   IWM French Diary, 16 May 1918.

12   Robinson to Long, 14 Mar. 1918, WRO, Long Papers, WRO 947/332.

13   *Cork Examiner*, 10 Dec. 1917.

14   *Freeman's Journal*, 7 June 1918, 12 June 1918.

15   Long to French, 9 July 1918, IWM, French Papers, JDPF 8/3.

16 Flattery to Long, 10 June 1918, WRO, Long Papers, WRO 947/224.

17 Stafford to Saunderson (private secretary), 15 May 1918, WRO, Long Papers, WRO 947/358.

18 Shortt to Lloyd George, 4 July 1918, Lloyd George Papers, Parliamentary Archives, LG/F/45/6/6.

19 Long to French 9 July 1918, IWM, French Papers, JDPF 8/3; Long to French (no date), IWM, French papers, JDPF 8/3.

20 *Irish Times*, 2 July 1918.

21 Robinson to Long, 2 July 1918, WRO, Long Papers, WRO 947/332.

22 Long to Robinson, 3 July 1918, WRO, Long Papers, WRO 947/332.

23 Long to French, 3 July 1918, WRO, Long Papers, WRO 947/229; IWM, French Papers, JDPF 8/3.

24 Long to French, 4, 9 and 18 July 1918, IWM, French Papers, JDPF 8/3.

25 Robinson, *Memories*, pp.264–65.

26 French to Lloyd George, 12 Oct. 1918, IWM, French Papers, JDPF 8/1B.

27 Saunderson to Long, 8 July 1918, WRO, Long Papers, WRO 947/347.

28 Saunderson to Long, 28 Jan. 1919, WRO, Long Papers, WRO 947/347.

29 IWM, French Diary, 15 Apr. 1920.

30 French to Bonar Law, 18 Apr. 1920, Parliamentary Archives, Bonar Law Papers, BL/103/2/11.

31 Long to Robinson, 14 June 1918, WRO, Long Papers, WRO 947/332.

32 Manuscript note by Brennan, NLI, Joseph Brennan Papers, MS 26,164.

33 G. C. Duggan, extract from draft of an unpublished book entitled *The Life of a Civil Servant*, p.15, NLI, Leon Ó Broin Papers, MS 31,689.

34 Long to French, 16 June 1918, IWM, French Papers, JDPF 8/1C.

35 *Hansard* V, 30, 20 June 1918, 304–306.

36 *Freeman's Journal*, 3 Feb. and 29 April 1920.

37 Robinson, *Memories*, p.265.

38 *Irish Independent*, 24 May 1920; Memoirs of Andrew Philip Magill, Oxford, Bodleian Library, MS. Eng. c. 2803, f. 331.

39 *Freeman's Journal*, 2 Feb. 1920; *The Times*, 4 Feb. 1920.

40 Ibid.

41 WRO, Long Papers, WRO 947/347 and WRO 947/348.

42 Alvin Jackson, *Colonel Edward Saunderson* (Oxford, 1995), pp.236–38.

43 State of Ireland – Irish policy, Memorandum for the War Cabinet by the Chief Secretary for Ireland, GT 3668, 19 Feb. 1918, TNA, CAB 24/42.

44 Michael Laffan, *The Resurrection of Ireland* (Cambridge, 1999), p.152 et seq.

45 Report from Sir H. Robinson, 2 Aug. 1918, IWM, French Papers, JDPF 8/1D.

46 Report by Lord French on the State of Ireland, 30 Aug. 1918, G.T. 5570, TNA, CAB 24/62.

47 *Hansard* V, 98, 17 Oct. 1917, 95–122.

48 *Irish Independent*, 30 Oct. 1917.

49 *Report of the Boundary Commission (Ireland)*, HC 1917–18, [Cd. 8830].

50 *Irish Independent*, 4 Dec. 1917, letter from W. T. O' Doherty, P. P., Omagh.

51 T. M. Healy, *Letters and Leaders of My Day*, vol. II (London, 1928), pp.587, 590.

52 *Hansard* V, 100, 4, 5, 6 and 7 Dec. 1917.

53 *Hansard* V, 100, 4 Dec. 1917, 325.

54 *Hansard* V, 100, 4 Dec. 1917, 336.

55 *Conference on the redistribution of seats in Ireland: letter from Mr Speaker to the Prime Minister, HC 1917–18,* [Cd. 8919]; the new constituencies were provided for by the Redistribution of Seats (Ireland) Act, 1918, 7 & 8 Geo. V, c. 65, 6 Feb. 1918.

56 Letter of 18 Jan. 1918, T. M. Healy, *Letters and Leaders of My Day*, vol. II (London, 1928), p.590.

57 Robinson to Long, 13 June 1918, WRO, Long Papers, WRO 947/332.

58 Robinson to Saunderson, 17 Dec. 1918 (typescript), WRO, Long Papers, WRO 947/347; the original manuscript letter is held at IWM, French Papers, JDPF 8/1B.

59 Memorandum for the War Cabinet, W.H.L. 31.12.18, G.T. 6574, TNA, CAB 24/72.

60 Charles Townshend, *The British Campaign in Ireland 1919–1921* (Oxford, 1975), pp.1, 14; Townshend also quotes extracts from the memorandum in *Political Violence in Ireland* (Oxford, 1983), pp.325–26 and in *Ireland: The 20th Century* (London, 1999), p.86; an extract from the memorandum is also quoted in Murray Fraser, *John Bull's Other Homes* (Liverpool, 1996), p.243, and attributed erroneously to Long.

61 Lawrence W. McBride, *The Greening of Dublin Castle* (Washington, 1991), p.259.

62 Dorothy Macardle, *The Irish Republic* (London, 1937), p.955.

63 Under the law as it stood, local elections were due to be held in June 1919 but were postponed to 1920.

64 The State of Ireland, Report by Lord French, 16 Dec. 1918, G.T. 6540, TNA, CAB 24/72.

65 French to the King, 18 Dec. 1918, IWM, French Papers, JDPF 8/3.

66 IWM, French Diary, 8 Jan. 1919, IWM.

67 *Irish Times*, 25 Jan. 1919.

68 French to Long, 22 Jan. 1919, IWM, French Papers, JDPF 8/1A.

69 IWM, French Diary, 21 Jan. 1919; French to Long, 23 Jan. 1919, IWM, French Papers, JDPF 8/2.

70 French to Macpherson, 31 Jan. 1919, Oxford, Bodleian Library, MS. Eng. hist. c. 490, f. 86.

71 The State of Ireland: Report by Lord French to the War Cabinet, 15 May 1919, G.T. 7277, TNA, CAB 24/79.

72 *Irish Times*, 27 Jan. 1919.

73 Robinson to Macpherson, 31 Jan. 1919, Oxford, Bodleian Library, MS. Eng. hist. c. 490, f. 87–88.

74 Release of Interned Candidates: Joint Memorandum by Lord Lieutenant and Chief Secretary, 15 Nov. 1918, G.T. 6298, TNA, CAB 24/69.

75 *Irish Times*, 18 May 1918.

76 Robinson to French, 30 May 1918, IWM, French Papers, JDPF 8/1D.

77 *Irish Times*, 6 Jan. 1919.

78 Memorandum submitted to the War Cabinet by the Chief Secretary for Ireland, 27 Dec. 1918, G.T. 6560, TNA, CAB 24/72.

79   Memorandum for the War Cabinet, W. H. L., 30 Dec. 1918, G.T. 6571, TNA, CAB 24/72.

80   Robinson to Saunderson, 6 Jan. 1919, IWM, French Papers, JDPF 8/1D.

81   The elections due to be held in June 1919 were postponed to 1920.

82   IWM, French Diary, 8 Jan. 1919.

83   John Bowman, *De Valera and the Ulster Question 1917–1973* (Oxford, 1982), pp.43–44.

84   William Murphy, *Political Imprisonment and the Irish, 1912–1921* (Oxford, 2014), pp.127–28.

85   War Cabinet Minutes, 526, 4 Feb. 1919; 527, 5 Feb. 1919, TNA, CAB 23/9.

86   Memorandum G.T. 6749, 5 Feb.1919, TNA, CAB 24/74; Memorandum by Lord French, Release of Sinn Féin Prisoners, 7 Feb.1919, G.T. 6912, TNA, CAB 24/76.

87   War Cabinet Minutes, 541, 4 Mar. 1919, TNA, CAB 23/9.

88   Brian Feeney, *Sinn Féin: A Hundred Turbulent Years* (Dublin, 2002), pp.100, 102.

89   Alvin Jackson, *Saunderson*, pp.240–41.

90   Confidential report by Sir Warren Fisher, 15 May 1920, TNA, HO 317/50.

CHAPTER XIV

Supporting the Chaotic Administration of Lord French

The Scheme of a Provisional Irish Administration

In March 1918, before consideration of the report of the Irish Convention had been eclipsed by the conscription controversy, Robinson held the view that some form of Home Rule was inevitable sooner or later.[1] Perhaps because of this, and with the prospect of continuing delay in holding a general election, he unofficially put forward some ideas for an interim administration to Captain Stephen Gwynn, whom he considered to be a 'most brilliant Irishman'.[2] Gwynn was the most senior protestant in the Irish Party, had been MP for Galway city since 1906, had served with the army in France until 1917, and had been a member of the Convention. He told his party colleague, John P. Hayden, editor of the *Westmeath Examiner* and MP for Roscommon South, on 4 May that Robinson had suggested 'the scheme of a provisional Irish administration – necessitated by the impossibility of getting a satisfactory Irish parliament before October'.[3] Gwynn himself believed that the Home Rule question could only be competently dealt with *after* a general election, and agreed with Robinson's view that this pointed to the need for the immediate creation of a provisional coalition government to carry on until then. He therefore fleshed out Robinson's scheme so as to provide for a government which, broadly speaking, would take over the functions of the Chief Secretary, and whose work would be subject to review by an Irish assembly which, he thought, could be the

Convention, which was already known in Ireland, the members knew each other, and it was 'essentially coalition in atmosphere and tradition and Ulster had accepted it'. Gwynn suggested that the new administration might be headed by Horace Plunkett and be composed of nine men, seven of whom had been members of the Convention, with either Devlin or himself holding the local government portfolio. He believed that arrangements on these lines could be set up by a short bill, that Ulster would agree to participate, and that there should be a guarantee that conscription would not be enforced while the administration was in place.

Gwynn discussed the scheme with Dillon, who had become party leader after the death of Redmond some weeks earlier, but Dillon was not close to Gwynn politically and 'would not hear of such a thing ... he regards a settlement before the close of the war as impossible'. Gwynn then went on to suggest to Hayden that 'you and I would have to take the lead' if a coherent Irish Party policy were to be adopted. But he also thought that he could form a coalition administration himself because he believed that the Ulster unionists liked him, and violently disliked Plunkett – and in naming himself rather than Plunkett he told Hayden that this was Robinson's very strong opinion. He noted also that having served in France, the soldiering helped.

Whatever about Robinson's modest original idea, Gwynn's more detailed scheme was unrealistic and hopelessly optimistic. Dillon, however, agreed to have it copied to 'men in touch with the government' – presumably including Robinson, on whose original suggestions the whole edifice was constructed, and Horace Plunkett, whom Gwynn knew well. It may be no more than coincidence that proposals which Plunkett then put forward in a series of three articles, published in the *Irish Times* and subsequently in a short pamphlet,[4] were broadly similar to the Robinson–Gwynn scheme. Gwynn naively believed the situation at the time was so fluid that any suggestion might be jumped at, but there was little prospect that a scheme of the kind that either he or Robinson had in mind would be adopted at that stage.

French Had Yet to Learn the ABC of Irish Affairs

French was more than 65-years-of-age when he became Lord Lieutenant in May 1918. Although his branch of the family had lived in England since the eighteenth century, he always considered himself to be an Irishman and believed that he had a special understanding of the country. However, apart from a few years in the 1870s when his cavalry regiment was based in Ireland, he had never lived in the country, and his army experience, including his undistinguished command of the British Expeditionary Force in France between August 1914 and December 1915, did nothing to equip him for his new role. He was a man of strong prejudices and of limited intellect, whose qualifications for high command were meagre.[5] His appointment as Lord Lieutenant was a disastrous one. He was out of his depth, with no experience whatsoever of public administration. Even Walter Long, his strongest supporter, admitted to Robinson in June 1918 that he had 'yet to learn the ABC of Irish affairs'.[6] Similarly, his private secretary, Eddy Saunderson, although well connected in northern unionist circles, was ill-equipped for his new role as *de facto* chief adviser. Saunderson's previous service as an inspector with the LGB had not involved any responsibility for broad policy matters or any official dealings with the Castle administration, the security services, or government departments in London. As a result, the French administration turned out to be chaotic and inconsistent, strangled by administrative incompetence and demonstrating what has fairly been described as a 'general comic-opera air'.[7] Confusion was compounded by the viceroy's efforts to overturn the traditional balance of power between himself and the Chief Secretary; the lack of co-ordination between the Vice-Regal lodge and the Castle; and the apparent failure or inability of MacMahon and other senior officials at the Castle to influence events.

Although he must have found it a frustrating and rather futile experience as the months passed, any bitterness Robinson may have felt at having been passed over in favour of MacMahon for the under-secretary position did not prevent him from responding to requests from French and Saunderson for advice on organisational and administrative matters. French's diary records Robinson's regular visits to the Vice-Regal Lodge, offering opinions on the state of the country, information on reaction to government decisions, and comments on a variety of other matters – in short, the kind of political and strategic intelligence which, according to Paul McMahon's study of British intelligence in Ireland in the years after 1916, was not often provided by the official system.[8] Thus, while Walter Long was probably the greatest single influence on French during his years in Dublin, Robinson must also be seen to have had a significant influence on him. He does not, however, deserve to be included in the hard-line clique formed by the combination of his protégés Watt and Saunderson, with Sir James Taylor, who worked throughout 1918 and 1919 to convince French, Long and Macpherson that the Castle was full of spies and informers and men who could not be trusted.[9] As Sir Warren Fisher saw it in 1921, that group 'convinced themselves that the only cure for the (then) sporadic and infrequent exhibitions of force in Ireland was the total excommunication of Sinn Féin as such with bell, book and candle'. They completely misread the situation, drawing no distinction between the relatively small physical-force faction and Sinn Féin the political party.[10] As is clear from his advice to French on the prisoners issue in early 1919, Robinson did not subscribe to the policy which attracted this criticism from Fisher, and there is no evidence that he played any part in any of the disreputable activities engaged in by Taylor and his associates.

Special Assignments for Robinson

In addition to being called on for advice on administrative matters, Robinson was asked by French from time to time to undertake other assignments well outside his own area of responsibility. In December 1918, for example, after a dangerous state of affairs had arisen in Belfast where the linen manufacturers who had been producing enormous amounts of cloth for aeroplane wings were planning to lay off staff, French asked him to visit the city and interview all the leading men concerned. Robinson reported that the inflammatory political situation that already existed in the city might involve the whole country in a religious war unless it was properly handled. The danger of a vast mob of mill-hands, he advised, with unemployment moneys to spend, and no work to do, ranging about the city at any time would be a serious source of danger – but just then, when political feeling was at boiling point in the midst of the general election campaign, the danger would be increased one hundred fold.[11] French believed that Robinson's report stated the case very well, and he forwarded copies to Churchill (then Minister of Munitions) and to the Prime Minister, begging them to adopt Robinson's suggestions because he was 'a man of great ability, tact and judgment, and well versed in all that pertains to the trade of Ireland'.[12] Edward Carson, who supported the linen manufacturers, subsequently told Chief Secretary Macpherson that French and Robinson had shown great activity in the matter, for which he was much indebted.[13]

Another assignment undertaken by Robinson arose from the high-profile visit to Ireland of the three-man American Commission on Irish Independence in May 1919. On that occasion, Robinson used his LGB inspectors to conduct a survey of the state of the country, enabling him to send a private and confidential summary report to French on 14 May. The country was in a really bad state, he reported, and he joined in the criticism of the visit which was already being expressed at political level and in sections of the British press.[14] The visit had an appalling result in the disparagement of the executive and in restoring the prestige of

Sinn Féin. Until the Irish-American delegates were launched upon the country, supporters among traders, farmers and shopkeepers had begun to see Sinn Féin as a lost and hopeless cause with its burlesque parliament and its hopeless collapse before the military, and people were beginning to ask 'what good is to come of all this?' But the visit had seriously alarmed people who supported peace and good government in the country and had caused the extremists who had swallowed all the promises of the delegates to look upon a republic as something like a *fait accompli*. Just now, he concluded, 'the general feeling is that as matters stand, the political barometer is decidedly stormy and falling, but there are many signs of a break in the horizon'.[15]

The Advisory Council

On taking up duty, French noticed what he described as an extraordinary lack of any method of co-ordination by which the Viceroy, the Chief Secretary and the heads of departments could exercise authority and reach decisions which would represent their united will and opinion.[16] He therefore set up an executive council, which met more or less weekly, comprising himself as President and with the Chief Secretary and Commander-in-Chief as members.[17] He later established a military council also chaired by himself. Robinson was not a member of either of these councils and seems not to have had any involvement in any of their business, but he was drawn into some of the work of another French initiative – the ill-fated Advisory Council – which arose from Long's suggestion that the viceroy should interest himself in economic development schemes as well as in administrative reform. Long believed that Arthur Balfour had been the most successful and most popular of the chief secretaries – a view which did not chime with the nickname 'Bloody Balfour' – because in addition to repressing crime and disorder, he had dealt with neglected development issues and introduced valuable reforms.[18] In July, after Lloyd George had apparently agreed that he would get French 'to try and form an Irish cabinet to prepare the way for Home Rule',[19] French told Long that he had been trying to arrange for the appointment of a few additional members to the Privy Council who would 'form a kind of special committee of the council to meet every two or three weeks in Dublin and assist us with their advice, etc'.[20] In September, he was able to tell the Prime Minister that he had arranged to set up the Viceroy's Advisory Council. 'I am to preside over it', he explained, 'and it is composed of seven members. They are all men of influence and power, taken from all parts of Ireland ... they should periodically report on the state of feeling in their respective areas ... and projects of reform or otherwise should be submitted to them for their opinion ... and probably they would be of great value in many other ways'.[21] A few days later, he told the King that he hoped through the council 'to be able to keep in touch with the condition of affairs and the feeling of the people'.[22]

While Robinson saw the members of the Advisory Council 'as men of mark representing different parts of the country',[23] the reality was quite different: in fact, to quote Eunan O'Halpin, 'a less representative collection of Irishmen it would have been hard to find'. [24] Most of the Council belonged to the landed classes and were members of the Kildare Street Club, according to *The Times*.[25] As well as Sir Thomas Stafford (Robinson's colleague as LGB medical commissioner from 1898 until the end of 1916), they included the Marquess of Londonderry, a prominent unionist, and two other peers: the Earl of Dunraven, whose 1904 devolution proposals had led to the downfall of George Wyndham, and the Earl of Granard. Other members included Walter Kavanagh of Carlow, holder of the MacMurrough Kavanagh title who had been a nationalist MP until 1910 and a member of the Convention; Sir Stanley Harrington, a prominent Cork industrialist and company director; and Frank Brooke, a personal friend of French, who was agent of the Fitzwilliam estate in County Wicklow and Chairman of the board of the Dublin & South Eastern Railway Company.

When news of the appointment of the council leaked out towards the end of November,[26] confusion and disagreement at official level about its role and functions were reflected in the initial press reports, causing French to complain to the Prime Minister that the *Freeman's Journal* had started 'a virulent assault' on the council.[27] Questions were raised as to whether the council was to act solely as an advisory and consultative body or whether it was to be a body with statutory authority to assist the government. French attempted, through his private secretary, to clarify the situation,[28] but his efforts were not enough to prevent a well-informed correspondent of *The Times* from writing critically on 13 December about the muddle and the curious and unfortunate crisis which had arisen.[29] The letter suggested that French and his Chief Secretary seemed to be in 'acute disagreement' – which was in fact the case. The Advisory Council was criticised by nationalists as an unrepresentative and incompetent body, Dublin Corporation declared it to be a body in which they could have no confidence and one of its members blamed Robinson and Saunderson, among others, for having persuaded French to establish it.[30] For his part, Robinson lamented the fact that 'the Transport Union crowd, who are Sinn Féin to a man, [are] all joining in this anti-Advisory Committee campaign, by which they have some hope that Lord French may be discredited and given some other command by the Government'.[31]

Gas and Water Home Rule

At its first meeting, the Advisory Council considered a memorandum from Walter Long suggesting that the council might be turned into 'a sort of Irish cabinet, openly sharing in the government and therefore in responsibility'.[32] When Robinson's advice on this proposal was sought, his reply of 12 November offered a realistic appraisal of the situation. He pointed out that ideas of this kind were not new, and had always been rejected … because there was no hope that 'Home Rule on the Instalment System' or 'Gas and Water Home Rule' as it was called, would satisfy a people, even temporarily, who wanted an Irish parliament with an executive responsible to it, and wanted it at once. He suggested, however, that if the government wished to bring the Castle administration more into touch with local and national requirements, a lord lieutenant's council could serve as a temporary stop-gap measure pending the general election. In putting forward a rough idea of how such a council might operate, he proposed that it could be empowered to deal finally with private bill legislation, leaving the promoters of bills emanating from Ulster free to suffer the extra cost and delays involved in having them processed at Westminster. In addition, the council could be given power to pass 'measures of a non-contentious character which were urgently demanded to enable schemes for the development of the resources and industries of the country to be carried through, or other domestic reforms such as public health, reclamation and drainage, for which there was a unanimous demand'. The council could also do useful preliminary work by sifting and eliciting public opinion on other measures which affected different interests but were too important to be dealt with except by Parliament.

As Robinson saw it, there would be plenty of work – legislative and administrative – for a council of the kind he had in mind; practically all the administrative work carried out by the Chief Secretary as President of the LGB and of DATI, and all of his patronage work, could be carried out by the Lord Lieutenant after consultation with the council. The government of the country would then be in the hands of the Lord Lieutenant, leaving the Chief Secretary to act merely as the link between the Imperial Parliament and Ireland. He would carry all Irish measures approved by the council through Parliament and would be the representative of the Lord Lieutenant there, explaining any of his acts which were questioned or criticised. Robinson believed that the constitution of the council would need very careful consideration, but his own view was that there should certainly be representatives of commercial, banking and railway interests, with heads of government departments and, significantly, members of Parliament.[33]

When Robinson's proposals were copied to Long he objected strongly to the inclusion of elected politicians in the membership of the proposed council. He told French on 21 November that the proposals 'carry us further than it is either intended or desirable that we should go in present circumstances'. His letter, however, was a confusing one: he accepted that if it were proposed to revert to the plan of trying to substitute something of a minor character for Home Rule, the scheme outlined in the memorandum could possibly be adopted, but it was his understanding that the intention was simply to set up a statutory body to advise the Irish Government and possibly to discharge certain executive functions. He suggested, therefore, that a short bill should be prepared to allow such a body to be established – 'a sort of cabinet for the Irish Government rather than a legislative body of any kind'[34] – while at the same time he told the War Cabinet that the proposal to set up an advisory council with statutory authority to assist the Irish government would be 'most helpful … as the government in Ireland had always been isolated from contact with the Irish people'.[35] A confusing situation then developed: Long seems to have prepared a memorandum for the Cabinet elaborating his approach while Chief Secretary Shortt argued that a proposal to give statutory power to a purely nominated body would not be successful or desirable unless it was composed of men elected to Parliament or to the county councils. French continued to advise the War Cabinet that 'the present form of Castle Government is quite unsuited to the requirements of the country, and it would be advisable to consider carefully whether any advisory, administrative, or executive body should be temporarily brought into being which would enable the Irish government to keep in closer touch with the general feeling of the people, pending the arrival of the time when the state of Ireland will admit of the establishment of some form of self-government'.[36] The issue had not been considered by the War Cabinet again before Shortt's tenure as Chief Secretary ended in early January with his transfer to the Home Office and his replacement by Ian Macpherson.

Concentrating Power in the Lord Lieutenant

When Saunderson, on behalf of French, turned again to Robinson for advice in light of Long's critical reaction to his November proposals, Robinson was understandably confused: 'I am afraid I don't quite catch on to what is in your mind as to how far this reorganisation of the executive is to go', he told him on 10 December.[37] He pointed out that he had already sketched out proposals showing how private bills and non-contentious legislation might be delegated as a transitory measure to a partly elected and partly nominated body under the Lord Lieutenant, which would be 'a sort of half-way house between Birrell's Irish Council Bill of 1907 and the present system of government'. But, in a reply which hinted that he was irritated and exasperated, if not angry, at the further demands being made of him, he declared that if the aim was to put an end to 'the divided authority and responsibility such as for the last twelve years has rendered Dublin Castle a by-word of weakness, indecision and corruption', the remedy under the law as it stood was to concentrate all authority in the Lord Lieutenant by adopting Earl Spencer's regime of 1883 – 'the only possible one during the very bad times we had following the Phoenix Park murders'. Ignoring the fact that Spencer's administration, in the view of John Redmond, had been more universally despised and detested than any other, forcing the Lord Lieutenant to travel in the south like the Czar with a military and police escort, Robinson went on to explain that he had seen a good deal of the inside working of Spencer's administration, during which his own father had been Vice-President of the LGB.[38] 'The viceroy practically initiated and directed the whole government of the country, and his chief and under-secretary were not permitted to give any decision in his name, or to do any final act, or make any appointment in his name without his express sanction.' A committee of advisers sifted the papers for the Lord Lieutenant while the Chief Secretary was merely 'his chief councillor and took his policy from him and voiced his wishes in Parliament'.[39] Robinson offered to discuss his experience of the Spencer regime and explain how it worked with French whenever it suited[40] and it was, presumably, by way of follow up, that he called to the Vice-Regal Lodge on 11 January after French had returned from holiday in England. At that meeting, as French described it in his diary, Robinson made valuable suggestions as to the conduct of official business so as to bring the viceroy more in touch with all that was being done and enable him to exercise proper control over government measures and procedure.[41] The diary entry went on to record that French was arranging with the Under-Secretary to adopt Robinson's suggestions. There is no evidence, however, that working methods and procedures were reorganised in the months that followed; neither is there any evidence that the new Chief Secretary, Ian Macpherson, who had a lunch meeting with French and Robinson at the Vice-Regal Lodge on 20 January – his first day in Dublin – was willing to be subservient to French as Trevelyan had been in Spencer's day.[42]

Turning War Factories into Peace Factories in Ireland

Robinson was involved again when Sir Thomas Stafford took the initiative of proposing that, in parallel with the post-war reconstruction committee which was sitting in London, a sub-committee of the Advisory Council should be established to 'turn war factories into peace factories in Ireland'. A report completed on 20 November 1918 by Stafford and Frank Brooke 'with the advantage of the experience' of Robinson, among others, was described by French as a most enlightening document. It concluded that there was a need for transitional measures to cater for up to 120,000 civil and military personnel who would need alternative employment on the cessation of hostilities, but suggested that the resumption of construction work by local councils and others would ease the situation considerably. For the longer term, there was an urgent need to launch 'a bold, attractive reconstruction programme, which will give the people something wherewith to occupy their minds to the exclusion of the vague revolutionary doctrines' which were being preached by others. To put such a programme in place, there should be a twelve-man executive committee, made up of the best business intellects drawn from various parts of the country with full power to act and without waiting for preliminary steps to be taken by the local authorities.[43] French agreed with these proposals, but Chief Secretary Shortt felt that the scheme would be unworkable and cumbersome. He also believed that the Treasury would never agree to confer powers over expenditure on such a committee and would simply throw the whole thing back. The net result of the exercise was that Robinson and the LGB were asked to look into the question of what road work schemes would be available to provide employment for demobbed soldiers.

Stafford's sub-committee proposal seems to have been the only initiative of any significance undertaken by the Advisory Council, which was not very active in 1919, and began to fall apart in 1920. One of its members, Frank Brooke, told Long that he feared for his life in July 1920.[44] He was in fact shot dead by the IRA at his office at Westland Row railway station at the end of the month. Stafford, who had come to believe that repression by itself would be much more likely to do harm than good and that dominion government would be the best solution,[45] publicly resigned from the council a week later, explaining in a letter to French, which was published in the *Irish Times,* that the refusal of the Prime Minister to take the only step 'which gives us a chance of peace in Ireland – the firm and immediate offer of a form of dominion government – renders it impossible for me to remain any longer a member of your Advisory Council ... My remaining [as a member] places me in the invidious position of seeming to approve of a policy with regard to the government of Ireland with which I have no sympathy'.[46] French was not surprised by the resignation and accepted that 'the so-called Viceroy's Advisory Council [has] gone into complete abeyance by reason of the dislike displayed towards that body by certain people'.[47]

More Development and Reorganisation Schemes

The chaotic French–Shortt administration generated a variety of other schemes in 1918–19 for development projects in the field of industry, agriculture, fisheries and transport, and for the resettlement of the thousands of Irish ex-servicemen who might not receive the same patriotic welcome which their counterparts would receive elsewhere in the UK.[48] Most of these schemes failed to attract the support of both the Chief Secretary and the Lord Lieutenant, and they involved over-lapping and inconsistency to a large extent. Robinson had little or no connection with the drafting or promoting of any of them, although in one case, Captain Stephen Gwynn MP, who had been heavily involved in the recruitment drive, proposed that Robinson should be chairman of a new commission with a large budget that would create thousands of jobs in road-building, foreshore reclamation, etc. for discharged soldiers.[49] This and other such schemes were never adopted; instead, the Chief Secretary was authorised to announce in February 1919 that a reconstruction grant of £250,000 was being made available for approved works of public utility involving the employment of demobilised men.[50] However, rather than establishing a new organisation, the grant was to be administered by a committee chaired by the Chief Secretary himself, with schemes being carried out through existing agencies such as the LGB, the CDB and the OPW.[51]

The only resettlement scheme which actually reached implementation stage during the French administration was the scheme to provide a decent standard of housing for returning sailors and soldiers which Robinson prompted him to propose in 1918. Legislation enacted in December 1919 assigned a central role in this scheme to the LGB, which was authorised to arrange for the provision of houses and cottages for ex-servicemen, with or without plots or gardens of up to two acres, and relying generally on OPW to handle construction.[52] Robinson was personally determined to advance the work as rapidly as possible, believing that the whole *fons et origo* of the act was that the local councils, both urban and rural, had openly refused to allocate any houses for men whom they considered to have disgraced themselves by fighting England's battles.[53] He was allowed to set up a separate branch of the LGB to deal with the work and to engage additional temporary inspectors (most of them with senior military rank), as well as temporary clerks, draftsmen and typists, and to redeploy staff from other branches, building up to a total of about thirty-five in mid-1921.[54] By the end of March 1920, the board had already received applications for housing from 7,702 ex-servicemen, and there was no slow-down in activity in 1920–21.[55] Officials at the Castle were shocked and annoyed when Robinson advised them in September 1921 that, instead of paying attention to political developments in the form of the July Truce and the progress towards negotiations for a treaty, they had built up large commitments by approving almost 3,500 applications for houses.[56] Robinson wanted the programme to continue with a limit of up to 6,000 on the number of houses to be built,[57] but the decision eventually arrived at was that a limit of 3,700 should apply.[58] By March 1922, when the government of Northern Ireland was already in place and a provisional government was about to take over in the south, relatively few of the authorised houses had been completed. This created a real dilemma for the officials at the Castle, who were attempting to implement an orderly transfer of power and functions to the new governments.

The transitional difficulties were compounded by the fact that a scheme of 247 houses at Killester in north Dublin – the only housing scheme ever undertaken directly by the LGB – had been promoted by Robinson to provide employment, as well as homes, for ex-servicemen who, in his view, might otherwise be 'forced into the ranks of the republican army, who are doing all they possibly can to recruit them at the present time'.[59] Although the Under-Secretary continued to have doubts about the wisdom of employing direct labour, he allowed Robinson to continue on foot of an assurance that a satisfactory result could be achieved within a cost limit of no more than about £900 per house.[60] However, when a statement of the financial position was supplied to Dublin Castle in mid-March 1922, the work was far from completion, and the cost per house appeared to be working out at far more than the agreed limit.[61] It fell to the new provisional government to devise arrangements with the Colonial Office to have the houses at Killester, as well as the many other schemes throughout the thirty-two counties, completed and tenanted. This is dealt with in Chapter XVIII.

Reforming the Castle, May 1920

The Hardinge Report of June 1916 found that the Irish system of government was 'anomalous in quiet times and almost unworkable in times of crisis'.[62] Lord Wimborne told Asquith a few months later that the administration was 'deplorably loose-jointed ... nearly all the old public officials have an acquired propensity to act independently in their own discretion, which is fatal to clear policy or concerted action'.[63] Nothing was done, however, to change the system in the following two years, with the result that when French became Lord Lieutenant in May 1918, he was soon complaining of the need for administrative reform. At the end of November he advised the Cabinet that there was need for careful inquiry into the practical efficiency of the 'Castle Rule', which then obtained, but he made no specific proposals for reform.[64] After General Sir Nevil Macready arrived in Ireland in April 1920 to take up the position of Commander-in-Chief of the army, he was 'astonished at the chaos that prevailed' at the Castle and (as he recorded it later in his *Annals*) he talked the matter over with several officials who were in the confidence of the Lord Lieutenant and obtained his permission to write to London to ask that a small committee of experts should be sent to overhaul the various departments in the Castle. He had found many of the departments to be out of touch, with officials practically confined within the castle walls. He wrote to Lloyd George on these lines, suggesting that the civil administration needed to be put on a more business-like footing.[65]

What is probably a more accurate account of the events which led to the review of the Castle administration in 1920 is provided in the diary of Lord French which recorded that he had a conference on 15 April with Robinson and Wylie, at which Macready was present. Wylie criticised very strongly the manner in which business was conducted at the Castle, and Robinson agreed with this and went on to suggest 'the appointment of a committee to investigate and report upon the whole system of Castle Government' – and the diary entry concludes with the note that 'we are taking steps to carry this out'.[66] It seems, therefore, that the suggestion for a review committee originated with Robinson rather than Macready. The letter, which French sent to Bonar Law the following day, confirms that Macready's letter to London was written on French's specific instructions:

> I have asked Macready to write to London to secure if possible two or three experts in departmental organisation to come over here as soon as possible to thoroughly investigate the conditions of affairs in the Castle and to report thereon. I would associate with them someone in Ireland. I feel convinced that until the machinery of the Castle has been placed on a sound basis it would be useless to hope for efficient, effective working of the Castle machine.

I hope you will support me in this, and that the committee may be enabled to get to work as soon as possible. I feel certain that the mere fact of its being known that the Castle administration is being overhauled will have an excellent effect throughout the country – and indeed in its present state it seems useless to expect efficient working.[67]

Matters moved quickly after that. Bonar Law suggested that Sir Warren Fisher, secretary of the Treasury and head of the civil service, would probably be the best man to chair the proposed committee.[68] In welcoming this, French repeated his view that 'government administration in Ireland is ... just as bad as it is possible for it to be' and complained that he had frequently brought this to the notice of the two Chief Secretaries who had served in Ireland since his appointment.[69] When it emerged that others who might have been appointed to serve on the committee of investigation were not available, Fisher agreed to undertake the task himself, bringing with him an assistant secretary of the Treasury (R. E. Harwood) and the second secretary of the Ministry of Pensions (Alfred Cope).[70] Fisher and his team arrived in Ireland on 6 May and the report which they presented to Lloyd George, Bonar Law and Chamberlain on 12 May, was scathing in its assessment:[71]

The Castle administration does not administer. On the mechanical side, it can never have been good and is now quite obsolete; in the infinitely more important sphere (a) of informing and advising the Irish government in relation to policy and (b) of practical capacity in the application of policy it simply has no existence.

The prevailing conception of the post of under-secretary – who should be the principal permanent adviser of the Irish government in civil affairs – appears to be that he is a routine clerk ... no one in the Chief Secretary's Office, from the under-secretary downwards, regards himself as responsible even for decisions on departmental papers, let alone for a share in the solution of difficulties in the realm either of policy or of execution ... Mr MacMahon is not devoid of brains, but lacks initiative, force, and driving power ... he has had no experience of running a big show or of shaping policy.

The review confirmed that the Chief Secretary's Office appeared to have 'become, to a large extent, merely a transmitting body, which passes on important administrative matters to other departments, and both on its advisory and its executive sides it fails to fulfil its function as the chief governmental organ of the country'.[72] Fisher's confidential supplementary report of 15 May 1920 went further, stating that the government of Ireland, with the notable exception of General Macready, 'strikes one as almost woodenly stupid and quite devoid of imagination. It listens solely to the ascendancy party ... and never seemed to think of the utility of keeping in close touch with opinions of all kinds'.[73] After Chief Secretary Greenwood had indicated that he agreed with the report, a high-powered team of ten English officials was quickly assembled and sent to Dublin to take over and reform the Castle.[74] The team was led by Sir John Anderson, Chairman of the Board of Inland Revenue, who took office as a second Under-Secretary, effectively relegating MacMahon to what has been described as 'an ornamental role'.[75] Other members included Alfred (Andy) Cope as Assistant Under-Secretary, Alexander P. Waterfield, who took charge of personnel and financial matters, and Mark Sturgis, whose diary provides a vivid account of the team's official and other activities until their departure in 1922, detailing the officials they met, their recreational activities, the hospitality they received and the events they attended.[76]

Working with Sir John Anderson

As well as implying in his memoirs that the idea of appointing a committee to overhaul the administration at the Castle was his own idea, Macready boasted in his *Annals* that the conclusions of the group 'tallied exactly' with the impressions he had formed when listening to the discussions at the Vice-Regal Lodge on his arrival in Ireland.[77] Robinson, on the other hand, made no effort in his memoirs to claim any of the credit for having initiated the process which led to the reorganisation – in fact the memoirs fail to make any mention of the enquiry conducted by Fisher, even though it seems more than likely that he would have been interviewed by Fisher and his team. The reorganisation itself probably left him with mixed feelings: he must have been pleased that MacMahon, whose appointment two years earlier he had heavily criticised, was being pushed aside, although he cannot have been very happy at the effective transfer of power from Irish to English civil servants. He devoted a short chapter in his memoirs to a discussion of the *outcome* of the enquiry, describing how 'some of the brightest ornaments of the English civil service and the army were dispatched to Ireland in the hope that they would be able to cope with the growing seriousness of the position'.[78] And, while he told Anderson that Waterfield's 'virility sometimes runs away with him when possibilities of achieving economies present themselves',[79] he had no difficulty in working with Anderson himself, recognising that he 'was beyond all doubt a really great administrator':

> Once in a blue moon the open competitive examination for the civil service brings to light a man of his exceptional type whom no power on earth can prevent from sprinting like a flash to the top of the ladder. I doubt very much, however, whether in the whole history of the British civil service any of these supermen ever had a heavier responsibility thrown upon him than Anderson had in taking on the part of chief of staff to the English in Ireland at this critical period. It was only a few like myself who obtained passing glimpses of what was going on behind the scenes who could realize the forces he was up against, what between his own parliamentary chiefs and the press and the public, while always before his eyes was the daily bulletin of disheartening crime and the hopeless outlook for the future. But he stood it with courage and infinite patience; he saw passing events, appalling as they were, in their true proportion to the whole problem, and he never appeared to be unduly cast down or uplifted over the day's work ... he was captain of the ship in more than name, and his final word on any subject went, and when the vessel was having a bad time among the shoals and breakers, he was always to be found on the bridge with his hand on the engine-room telegraph.[80]

Notwithstanding his deep-seated and historic aversion to the personnel of the Chief Secretary's Office, surviving official correspondence between Robinson and Anderson suggests that there was a friendly, good-humoured rapport between the two men, and that they worked harmoniously together in dealing with major issues such as the local councils' withdrawal of recognition from the LGB, the financing of criminal injuries awards and preparations for partition. In addition, the diaries of Mark Sturgis suggest that Robinson continued throughout 1920 and 1921 to provide unsolicited – and at times perhaps unwanted – advice and information to Anderson and his team on the political and military situation.[81] When Anderson's service in Ireland ended, he went on to have a glittering career in the civil service and in politics in England. He rose to become Chancellor of the Exchequer and one of the most important ministers in Churchill's Wartime Cabinet. He was elevated to the peerage as Viscount Waverly in 1952.[82] During his period of less than two years in Dublin he completely transformed the organisation, staffing and operation of Dublin

Castle, ensured that the primacy of the Chief Secretary was restored and provided coherent advice to the Chief Secretary and the Cabinet which, unfortunately, was not always accepted. Indirectly, also, his appointment brought an end to the situation in which Robinson had been placed, where he was heavily relied on for advice on organisational and administrative matters completely outside his area of responsibility.

NOTES

1   Robinson to Long, 14 Mar. 1918, WRO, Long Papers, WRO 947/332.
2   Sir Henry Robinson, *Memories: Wise and Otherwise* (London, 1923), p.269.
3   Gwynn to Hayden, 4 May 1918 and attached memorandum, NLI, MS 8380.
4   *Irish Times*, 9, 10 and 13 July 1918; Horace Plunkett, *Home Rule and Conscription* (Dublin 1918).
5   Max Hastings, *Catastrophe: Europe Goes to War 1914* (London, 2014), p.132.
6   Long to Robinson, 14 June 1918, WRO, Long Papers, WRO 947/332.
7   Patrick Maume, 'Sir John Denton Pinkstone French', *DIB*, Vol. 3, pp.1100–1104.
8   Paul McMahon, *British Spies and Irish Rebels: British Intelligence and Ireland, 1916–1945* (Woodbridge, 2008), pp.13, 52.
9   Leon Ó Broin, *W. E. Wylie and the Irish Revolution 1916–1921* (Dublin, 1989), p.44.
10 Fisher to Lloyd George and Austen Chamberlain, 18 Nov. 1921, Chamberlain Papers, AC 23/2/16, quoted in Eunan O'Halpin, *Head of the Civil Service: A Study of Sir Warren Fisher* (London, 1989), pp.84–85.
11 Robinson's report to French, 7 Dec. 1918, IWM, French Papers, JDPF 8/3.
12 French to Churchill, 7 Dec. 1918, IWM, French Papers, JDPF 8/1B; French to Long, 7 Dec. 1918, IWM, French Papers, JDPF 8/3.
13 Macpherson to French, 24 Jan. 1919, IWM, French Papers, JDPF 8/2.
14 F. M. Carroll (ed.), *The American Commission on Irish Independence 1919* (Dublin, 1985), pp.13–15.
15 Private and confidential report from Robinson, 14 May 1919, IWM, French Papers, JDPF 8/1D.
16 Speech by French, 10 Oct. 1918 at first meeting of the Advisory Council, IWM, French Papers, JDPF 8/5.
17 Minutes of the council's meetings until August 1919 are included in the French Papers, IWM, JDPF 8/6; references to meetings later in 1919 appear in French's Diary, 1919–20, NLI, MS. 2269.
18 Long to French, 4 July 1918, IWM, French papers, JDPF 8/3.
19 Lt Col Maurice Hankey, secretary to the War Cabinet, diary entry for 9 May 1918, quoted in Stephen Roskill, *Hankey: Man of Secrets*, vol. 1, 1877–1918 (London, 1970), p.544.
20 French to Long, 17 July 1918, IWM, French Papers, JDPF 8/1B.
21 French to Lloyd George, 7 Sept. 1918, IWM, French Papers, JDPF 8/1C.
22 French to the King, 10 Sept. 1918, IWM, French Papers, JDPF 3; the King to French, 15 Sept. 1918, IWM, French Papers, JDPF 3.
23 Robinson, *Memories*, pp.265–66.

24 Eunan O'Halpin, *The Decline of the Union: British Government in Ireland 1892–1920* (Dublin, 1987), p.171.

25 *The Times*, 13 Dec. 1918.

26 *Irish Times*, 29 Nov. 1918.

27 French to Lloyd George, 30 Nov. 1918, IWM, French Papers, JDPF 8/1A.

28 *Irish Times*, 9 Dec. 1918, letter from Edward A. Saunderson, private secretary.

29 *The Times*, 13 Dec. 1918.

30 *Irish Times*, 7 Jan. 1919.

31 Robinson to Saunderson, 17 Dec. 1918, WRO, Long Papers, WRO 947/347; also IWM, French Papers, JDPF 8/1B.

32 Minutes of the first meeting of the Advisory Council, IWM, French Papers, JDPF 8/5.

33 Robinson to Saunderson, 12 Nov. 1918, IWM, French Papers, JDPF 8/1B.

34 Long to French, 21 Nov. 1918, IWM, French Papers, JDPF 8/1B.

35 War Cabinet Minutes 505, 21 Nov. 1918, TNA, CAB 23/8.

36 The State of Ireland: Report by Lord French, 16 Dec. 1918, G.T. 6540, TNA, CAB 24/72.

37 Robinson to Saunderson, 10 Dec. 1918, IWM, French Papers, JDPF 8/1B.

38 *Hansard* III, 293, 24 Oct.1884, 208.

39 For a recent review of Spencer's 1882–85 administration see James H. Murphy, *Ireland's Czar: Gladstonian Government and the Lord Lieutenancies of the Red Earl Spencer* (Dublin, 2014).

40 Robinson to Saunderson, 10 Dec. 1918, IWM, French Papers, JDPF 8/1B.

41 French Diary 11 Jan. 1919, IWM.

42 French Diary, 20 Jan. 1919, IWM.

43 Minutes of the meeting of the Advisory Council, 7 Nov. 1918, IWM, French Papers, JDPF 8/5.

44 Brooke to Long, 1 and 2 July 1920, WRO, Long Papers, WRO 947/164.

45 Memorandum dated 4 Aug. 1920 sent to French, IWM, French Papers JDPF 8/1B.

46 *Irish Times*, 11 Aug.1920.

47 French to Stafford, 17 Aug. 1920, IWM, French Papers, JDPF 8/1B.

48 Memorandum on demobilisation and resettlement in Ireland, 19 Dec. 1919, GT 6527, TNA, CAB 24/72.

49 Gwynn to Long, 19 Nov. 1918, WRO, Long Papers, WRO 947/245.

50 *Irish Times*, 19 and 25 Feb. 1919.

51 *Hansard* V, 113, 5 Mar. 1919, 415.

52 *Hansard* V, 121, 18 Nov. 1919, 853–58; Irish Land (Provision for Sailors and Soldiers) Act 1919, 9 & 10 Geo. 5, ch. 82, 23 Dec. 1919.

53 Robinson to Waterfield, 20 Oct. 1920, TNA, T 160/214.

54 *AR*, 1919–20, p.xcii; Department of the Environment and Local Government, Secretary's Office Papers, Folder No. 4.

55 *AR*, 1919–20, p.lxxix.

56 Robinson to under-secretary, 1 Sept. 1921, TNA, T.160/214; also NAI, CSORP 1921/3434; Waterfield to Anderson, 15 Oct. 1921, TNA, T.160/214

57 Robinson to chief secretary, 21 Oct. 1921, TNA, T.160/214.

58 Anderson to Waterfield, 16 Nov. 1921, TNA, T.160/214.

59 Robinson to Anderson, 26 Jan. 1921, TNA, CO 904/26.

60 Anderson to Robinson, 17 Feb. 1921, TNA, CO 904/26; 25 February 1921, TNA, T.158/2.

61 Waterfield to Robinson, 4 and 6 April 1922, TNA, T.158/8.

62 *Report of the Royal Commission on the Rebellion in Ireland*, HC 1916 [Cd. 8279].

63 Wimborne to Asquith, 3 Sept. 1916, Oxford, Bodleian Library, MSS Asquith 37, f. 119–122.

64 The State of Ireland: Report by Lord French, 26 Nov. 1918, G.T. 6391, TNA, CAB 24/70.

65 General C. N. F. Macready, *Annals of an Active Life* (New York, 1925) (vol. 2), pp.446–49

66 French Diary 15 Apr. 1920, IWM.

67 French to Bonar Law, 16 Apr. 1920, Parliamentary Archives, Bonar Law papers, BL/103/2/9.

68 Bonar Law to French, 17 Apr. 1920, Parliamentary Archives, Bonar Law papers, BL/103/2/10; Bonar Law to Greenwood, 17 Apr. 1920 Bonar, BL/102/5/3.

69 French to Bonar Law, 18 Apr. 1920, Parliamentary Archives, Bonar Law papers, BL/103/2/11.

70 Bonar Law to French, 23 Apr. 1920, Parliamentary Archives, Bonar Law papers, BL/103/2/11.

71 Confidential report of 12 May 1920 entitled 'Dublin Castle' by Sir Warren Fisher, TNA, HO 317/50; copy also in Parliamentary Archives, Lloyd George papers, LG/F/31/1/32.

72 Report to Sir Warren Fisher by A. W. Cope and R. E. Harwood, 12 May 1920, TNA, HO 317/50.

73 TNA, HO 317/50; copy also in Parliamentary Archives, Lloyd George papers, LG/F/31/1/33.

74 Bonar Law to Greenwood, 14 May 1920 and Greenwood to Bonar Law, 16 May 1920, Parliamentary Archives, Bonar Law papers, BL/103/3/8 and BL/103/3/9.

75 Charles Townshend, *The Republic: The Fight for Irish Independence, 1918–1923* (London, 2013), p.138.

76 Michael Hopkinson, *The Last Days of Dublin Castle: The Mark Sturgis Diaries* (Dublin, 1999).

77 Macready, *Annals*, p.457.

78 Robinson, *Memories*, pp.292–94.

79 Robinson to Anderson, 23 July 1921, TNA, T.160/214.

80 Robinson, *Memories*, pp.292–293.

81 Hopkinson, *The Mark Sturgis Diaries*.

82 John W. Wheeler-Bennett, *John Anderson Viscount Waverly* (New York, 1962).

CHAPTER XV

The Sinn Féin Takeover of Local Government and the Government's Response

PR: 'To Prevent the Rebels Sweeping the Country'

Irish local elections were postponed until mid-1919 by wartime legislation relating to the United Kingdom as a whole. Early in 1919, however, when wartime conditions no longer prevailed, it was decided to postpone the elections for a further year and to introduce a new code of electoral law which would prevent Sinn Féin from gaining control of all councils outside of Ulster, replicating the party's success at the December 1918 general election. In July 1918, Walter Long (probably relying on information from Robinson) had advised the War Cabinet that if municipal elections were held in Ireland, Sinn Féiners would capture 90 per cent of the seats outside Ulster.[1] Lord French provided similar advice in August: paraphrasing part of a report he had received from Robinson, he told the Cabinet that if successful at the general election, Sinn Féin anticipated that 'the whole of the county government ... and the essential centres of administrative work throughout Ireland' would come under their control.[2] In analysing the outcome of the general election, Robinson had again drawn attention to the likelihood that continuing support for Sinn Féin would give them control over the local authorities,[3] while French, taking his line once more from Robinson, told the King that the most serious element in the problem raised by the election was the danger that the local councils would become 'absolutely Sinn Féin' at the next local elections.[4]

Although the introduction of proportional representation (PR) had been rejected in England in the debates leading to the enactment of the Representation of the People Act 1918, the circumstances prevailing in Ireland at the beginning of 1919 were thought by the government to justify the application of the system at Irish local elections. In his memoirs, Robinson summed it up as: 'to give a chance to minorities and to prevent the rebels sweeping the country'.[5] The use of PR at Irish elections had been considered as early as 1906 when James Bryce, in attempting to make the Irish Council proposals more acceptable, flirted briefly with the idea of providing for elections on a PR system and took advice on the subject from Baron Courtney of Penrith, a liberal politician who had been an advocate of the system since the 1870s.[6] Courtney lectured on the system in Dublin in 1911, leading to the foundation of the Proportional Representation Society of Ireland of which Arthur Griffith was a founder-member. Ernest Aston, a Dublin consulting engineer, journalist and author, and from time to time a temporary LGB inspector, was secretary of the society, which had attempted to have PR included in the Home Rule Bill in 1912. Amendments carried during the debates on the bill provided for PR elections on the single transferable vote system in the larger parliamentary constituencies.[7] The same system was introduced, following local agreement, at a Sligo borough election in January 1919.

In debating the Local Government (Ireland) Bill, 1919, which provided for PR at Irish local elections, the attorney general for Ireland, Arthur Samuels K. C., told the House of Commons on 24 March that 'almost everywhere it is politics, and politics alone, that have succeeded in winning local government elections' in Ireland. Since 1878, he went on, the machine has captured the whole representation on local authorities and businessmen, professional men and others who by training, capacity, or commercial standing, ought to be involved in directing county affairs were practically excluded because of political feelings or dogma. Noting that it was the declared object of Sinn Féin to make local government absolutely impossible, he concluded that it could not be left to the party to use local councils to break down British rule as was done in Hungary.[8] In support of the proposals, Samuels referred to the backing the scheme had received in Ireland and quoted an extract from a letter he had just received from 'a person in the very highest position in Ireland, who has, perhaps, the best possible opportunity of any man in the country for knowing what the state of feeling is'. Samuels' correspondent had written that he had 'never known any bill which has received such wide support from all sections of the press and the people as this one; indeed, men of all classes, politics and religions are convinced of the urgent necessity of the measure'. Pressed by Edward Carson, who opposed the bill, Samuels was forced to disclose that his correspondent was none other than Sir Henry Robinson, who somewhat inconsistently had told Lord French a few months earlier that he looked forward without misgiving to the winning of seats on the county and district councils by Sinn Féin 'as I believe they will in many ways be more honest administrators than many of the present boards'.[9] Later in the debate, as if to corroborate Robinson's view on PR, Samuels noted that Arthur Griffith – 'the intellectual originator of Sinn Féin, its most able protagonist, a most brilliant writer, a man of great ability, and a most dangerous opponent' – was a prominent member of the Proportional Representation Society. The few nationalists remaining at Westminster supported the bill, as did Sir Maurice Dockrell, describing himself as the sole representative in the House of Commons of some 350,000 southern unionists. Outside the House, Sinn Féin recognised that the introduction of PR was designed to prevent them from completely capturing local government but welcomed it as a just system and decided to meet it head-on.[10] On the other hand, Ulster unionists bitterly opposed the system. They argued that as it had already been rejected in England it should not be experimented with in Ireland. Ignoring the outcome of the Sligo borough election of 1919, they also contended that the system would do nothing to improve the position of minorities in the south and west.[11] Carson was particularly trenchant in his criticism, describing the bill as a most wretched, miserable one which nobody wanted, and one which he regarded with the greatest contempt.[12]

According to the *Irish Times*, Sinn Féin's orators and newspapers had been proclaiming in the early weeks of January 1919 that they proposed 'to capture the machinery of local government and in that way to bring the country's entire administration to a standstill'.[13] In response to this threat to create local anarchy, the government included in the PR bill a provision under which the LGB's power to appoint a person to discharge the duties of a board of guardians would extend also to any county or district council which the board was satisfied had failed to perform all or any of their statutory duties. The nationalist members who remained in the House criticised the proposal to give such a monstrous and obnoxious power to 'a number of old hoary reactionaries' as Joe Devlin described the members of the LGB. Captain Redmond saw it as an attempt by the bureaucracy to bolster up Robinson's 'almost omnipotent' board, which had already done so much harm to the country. Even Carson objected to the idea that a county council could be abolished 'on the *ipse dixit*' of the board – he asked what becomes of local government in Ireland if it was necessary to introduce such a clause. While Samuels himself seemed determined to press on, the government backed down at committee stage – hoping perhaps that the introduction of PR would be enough to prevent the domination of local councils by Sinn Féin.

When PR reached the statute book in June 1919, Robinson and his colleagues were required to divide the various counties, boroughs, urban and rural districts and towns into completely new sets of electoral areas and to settle the distribution of seats between these areas, each having at least three seats.[14] It was left to Carson to vehemently oppose this provision in the House of Commons on the grounds that leaving these decisions to the supreme judgment of the LGB – which would be 'able to gerrymander matters to suit whatever policy they have in view' – involved delegating a far greater power than anything granted before, and was an outrage on the procedure of the House. In practice, the process proved to be controversial in some cases, particularly in Derry city and County Tyrone, where the board's proposals were challenged unsuccessfully in the King's Bench Division of the High Court. After the event, Sinn Féin complained that the electoral arrangements had given the advantage, where possible, to their opponents.[15]

First Dáil: Marking Time in 1919–20

While the authorities were making plans to prevent a Sinn Féin takeover of local government, the first Dáil was also turning its attention to local government. At its first meeting on 19 January 1919, it adopted a declaration of independence, which ordained that 'the elected representatives of the Irish people alone have power to make laws binding on the people of Ireland, and that the Irish Parliament is the only parliament to which that people will give its allegiance'. In addition, the Dáil adopted a democratic programme which, although it did not mention local government directly, contained commitments on child welfare, the abolition of the poor law, and the care of the aged and the sick, all of which foreshadowed action in areas that were central to the existence of the LGB. The second ministry approved by the Dáil on 2 April included a Secretary for Local Government– W. T. Cosgrave,[16] who had just been released from gaol where he had been interned since April 1918 as a result of the alleged German plot; he had been a Sinn Féin member of Dublin Corporation since 1909 and was one of only 10 per cent of Dáil members who had previously taken any part in local government.[17] However, Cosgrave's department simply marked time throughout 1919 and had not initiated any specific programme of action of its own by year-end. As late as April 1920, when James Kavanagh, who had been the Sinn Féin accountant, took up the position of secretary and accountant to the department on the invitation of Kevin O'Higgins, the staff consisted only of himself, a typist and a messenger, working under the direction of O'Higgins, who had been appointed as substitute minister on 9 April when Cosgrave was in gaol.[18]

At local authority level it was business as usual in most cases throughout 1919: notwithstanding the Rising, the subsequent executions, the success of Sinn Féin candidates at the general election and the establishment of the Dáil, relations with the LGB generally followed the traditional pattern and the Dáil department made no effort to change this. Most of the councillors who held office at the beginning of the year were those who had been elected in June 1914 in the case of the county and rural district councils, and in January 1915 in the case of the municipal authorities. Many of them outside Ulster would have been supporters of the Irish Party rather than Sinn Féin, and quite a number of them – even in the south and west – had supported the war effort by agreeing to the investment of balances from their current accounts in the War Loan, as well as borrowing more than £1.1 million for that purpose in 1916–17.[19] While the relatively small number of councillors who stood for election as representatives of Sinn Féin in 1914–15 had been joined as supporters of the party by many others before 1919, the party did not hold a majority of the seats in any of the major councils at that stage.[20] Nevertheless, some councils began to challenge the LGB on routine day-to-day issues. Mullingar RDC, in electing a chairman in January, agreed to a proposal that they should conduct the business as they thought best because 'it was not the law as laid down by the Local Government Board that they were there to observe'.[21] Later that month, a meeting of the Dublin board of guardians decided to appoint a medical officer for a south city district in defiance of a direction from the board – classed as dictation by one member – that no such posts should be filled until the young medical officers who had been serving temporarily in the army were available to compete.[22] While there was a belief in official circles that even the 'more moderate Sinn Féiners are preparing to organize passive resistance to the government and to clog the wheels of local administration', the official approach throughout the year was to allow matters to take their course and to await developments.[23] For example, after Robinson told Lord French in January that poor law guardians and district councils in Kerry were refusing to carry on under the present government, French and his executive council decided to take no action for a short time 'in order to cause dislocation and inconvenience locally, as a punishment'.[24]

The Post-War Reconstruction Programme

Overall British policy on Ireland remained undefined and confused throughout most of 1919, partly because the Cabinet were still unable or unwilling to give the issue their full attention, and partly because of the hopelessly incompetent administration headed by French and the inept staffing at the Castle. However, although Macpherson, who had become chief secretary in January, told Lloyd George in mid-April that the state of the country was never worse than it was then, it was still thought necessary to apply to Ireland some of the initiatives being taken in pursuance of the policy of 'making Britain a fit country for heroes to live in'.[25] A new urban housing programme, which formed part of this policy, created a dilemma for the Dáil by forcing it to demonstrate that it too was concerned about the housing problem, leading to a situation in which Cosgrave's department and the LGB appeared to be working on parallel lines. In March, after urban authorities had been notified by the LGB of new subsidy arrangements and asked urgently to formulate building schemes, the Dáil agreed a motion from Cosgrave calling on Sinn Féin *cumainn* throughout the country to tabulate housing requirements and to present their findings to the local authorities with a view to putting the necessary machinery in motion.[26] A Dáil committee reported in August, having examined the provisions of the Housing (Ireland) Bill, that there was no better machinery available. They recommended that local authorities should proceed 'full steam ahead' to avail of the facilities it provided.[27]

For their part, Robinson and his colleagues pressed ahead energetically: a programme of planning, land acquisition and other work led by the board built up rapidly and by the end of March 1920, nearly 42,000 houses had been authorised to go to construction stage. However, the programme ground to a halt later that year, partly because of what the board's annual report described as 'action on political grounds' and partly because of local councils' dissatisfaction with the subsidy rates.[28] At different stages in 1919, throughout 1920, and even in 1921, Robinson personally pressed the chief secretary and the Treasury to agree to more favourable subsidy terms, making a special case for Dublin, the one city in the UK where, he pointed out, the condition of working-class housing was most insanitary and deplorable.[29] Murray Fraser, in his detailed study of state housing policy in Ireland up to 1922, points to several other contributions made by Robinson to 'sort out the problems caused by ill-considered decisions made at Westminster' at a time when there was virtually no real representation of Ireland in the House of Commons. He noted particularly the significance of the decision, inspired by Robinson, to set up a separate committee of the LGB, led by Peter Cowan, the chief engineering inspector, to promote the housing programme and to assign other high-calibre staff to serve in the board's housing department, all of which had begun to bear fruit until developments at political level in the autumn of 1920 supervened.[30]

Other elements of the government's post-war reconstruction programme, which had implications for both the LGB and the local authorities, included the establishment in August 1919 of a new Ministry of Transport, with a branch in Dublin which took over the powers and duties of the LGB relating to roads, road vehicles and the regulation of traffic.[31] On the other hand, the establishment of a Ministry of Health to take over all of the powers of the English Local Government Board was not followed by the establishment of a similar ministry in Ireland, or by any diminution of the powers and functions of the LGB. Instead, the law was amended to provide that the chief secretary would be the Minister of Health for Ireland, and an Irish Public Health Council was set up to give advice and assistance to the chief secretary in that capacity. When it was initially suggested that Robinson would become Chairman of the new council, Joe Devlin claimed that the organisation would be nothing more than 'a gang of bureaucrats' who had neglected public health issues for years.[32] In the event, the LGB medical commissioner was appointed as full-time Chairman, leaving his successor, the junior commissioner, and Robinson to fill three additional *ex-officio* places. Thus, the LGB, instead of going out of existence as its English counterpart had done, was to maintain its dominant role in health as well as local government matters, until 1922.

Municipal Elections, January 1920

Elections to fill the 1,735 seats on 127 municipal authorities throughout Ireland were held on 15 January 1920, after a lapse of six years. The elections provided an opportunity for Sinn Féin to seek confirmation of the mandate the party had achieved at the general election of December 1918. However because PR was to be used and because of competition from the Labour Party, which had not contested that election, it was clear that Sinn Féin candidates would not win as great a proportion of the seats. Doubts about the outcome also existed because of fears that many voters would not fully understand PR, although the LGB had arranged for lectures to be delivered on the system, to conduct practical demonstrations for local staff, and to organise a programme of education for the public. Sinn Féin had been proclaimed and suppressed by a proclamation published on 25 November 1919,[33] and its election manifesto itself was deemed, under the Defence of the Realm Regulations, to be a seditious document likely to cause disaffection.[34] While the manifesto contained commitments on housing, health and 'progress, purity and efficiency' in local administration generally, the national issue was the paramount one: the appeal to the electors was 'to ensure that the public representatives shall be only such as are willing to stand by the properly elected Government of Ireland'.[35] Other parties, reform candidates and nationalists adopted different strategies, campaigning on issues such as public housing and local employment. On the eve of the elections, an *Irish Times* editorial made an eloquent – but largely unsuccessful – appeal to unionists in the south and west of the country, to 'sensible nationalists' and to public-spirited ratepayers to strain every nerve to prevent Sinn Féin candidates, who were pledged to ignore the authority of the government, from gaining the upper hand and wrecking the municipal system.[36]

On election day, over 331,000 people (almost 70 per cent of the electorate) voted in 259 separate electoral areas; there were no contests in 36 other areas.[37] An analysis of the results compiled by the Proportional Representation Bureau suggested that PR had indeed deprived Sinn Féin of the clean sweep achieved in December 1918. Overall, their candidates won just over 30 per cent of the seats, as against 20 per cent for unionists, 14 per cent for nationalists, 21.5 per cent for labour, and 14.5 per cent for others. However, only about 20 per cent of the unionist seats were won outside the six counties of Ulster, leaving Sinn Féin candidates with majorities in 72 of the 127 councils and sharing control with other nationalists in another 26.[38] Returns compiled by the Dáil Department presented the results in broadly similar terms but emphasised that unionists now controlled only 25 councils, all but two of them in the north. There was no reference in these returns to Labour candidates, but a letter from Cosgrave explained that in most areas outside the north, 80 per cent of the Labour councillors supported the republic, making it possible for Sinn Féin and Labour to have working arrangements in these areas.[39]

While the War Cabinet had rejected a suggestion that all candidates for public office should be required to declare allegiance to the Crown,[40] the Dáil department took care to ensure that their candidates were genuine supporters of the separatist cause.[41] It followed up by issuing a form of resolution of allegiance to each authority which had an effective republican majority, and a variant of the resolution was sent to other authorities. Overall, the response did not meet expectations although a policy of challenging the authority of the LGB was put into place in some areas.[42] For example, the Limerick guardians insisted, notwithstanding threats of mandamus proceedings by the LGB, on retaining as their clerk a man who was in gaol in Belfast,[43] while Cork Corporation, at their first meeting, passed a resolution pledging allegiance to the Dáil.[44] Three months later, Dublin Corporation members voted by thirty-eight to five to acknowledge the authority of the Dáil,[45] but they agreed in July to apply to the LGB for a loan of £98,000 to allow them to complete a number of housing schemes.[46] They also participated in a conference with the board on 13 August at which mutually acceptable courses of action in relation to other housing schemes were agreed.[47] Some authorities decided to take no action pending the outcome of the county council elections, and others decided to hedge their bets. Thurles UDC, for example, passed the standard resolution acknowledging the authority of the Dáil and undertaking to give effect to its decrees, but decided to continue to send their minutes to the LGB because, as one member was reported to have said, the council 'should not fall out with them, as the council will be applying for building loans and should try to get all they could out of them'.[48]

County and Rural District Council Elections

When elections for the county and rural district councils were held in early June, Labour contested very few seats, leaving the way open for Sinn Féin to emerge as the dominant party in most areas, with majorities in twenty-eight of the thirty-three county councils and in roughly 80 per cent of the 206 rural district councils. A circular letter dated 1 June from Kevin O'Higgins, writing as substitute Minister for Local Government, had instructed the new councils to adopt resolutions acknowledging the authority of the Dáil, pledging compliance with its decrees, directing that minutes of meetings should in future be sent to the Dáil department and not to the LGB, that no rate should be struck for malicious and criminal injuries, and that data required for income tax purposes should not be passed on to the inland revenue authorities.[49] In the following weeks, the provincial and national newspapers carried reports almost on a daily basis of the adoption of these resolutions.[50] There were regular reports also of letters from the board being greeted with laughter at council meetings, or burned or torn up in council chambers, and of directions from the board being openly flouted. Some councils directed that the republican flag was to be flown on all of their buildings, others made efforts to conduct some of their business through Irish, a number pledged that special consideration would be given to Irish speakers when making appointments and others stipulated that new appointees should take an Oath of Allegiance to the Dáil. Newspaper reports also told that LGB inspectors were not permitted to make visits to workhouses; that books and accounts were not to be submitted for audit 'by agents of the British Government' as the auditors were regularly described; and that all disputes involving the council were to be referred to the courts established by the Dáil. There were reports also of decisions that claims for compensation for criminal and malicious injuries should be ignored and should not be defended in the courts. The scope for decrees of this kind had been extended by legislation enacted in April 1919 to cover cases where magistrates, police, soldiers, sailors and civil servants were murdered, maimed or maliciously injured, whether in the execution of their duty or not.

In advance of the elections, the Dáil department had cautioned against any form of drastic action which might, in the short term, endanger the payment of government grants. On 29 June O'Higgins told the Dáil that the question of 'the attitude of republican councils to the English Local Government Board' had been considered by the ministry but that it had been decided to leave the question open for decision by the Dáil. In the subsequent discussion, he said that the question was whether to break with the LGB and immediately have a war, or whether it would be better to wait for some months until a uniform scheme would be ready and could be placed before the local councils. He favoured the latter course and therefore proposed the setting up of a commission of experts to report no later than 1 September on the possibility of carrying on local administration without financial aid from the government. This was agreed but not without some dissent.[51]

A Period of Phoney War

What might be termed a period of phoney war followed the June elections, with neither side committed to significant follow-up action. The Dáil was anxious to avoid outright confrontation with the LGB and to ensure that local councils would not go on passing 'foolish resolutions' or refuse to recognise the board on which they depended for up to 20 per cent of their current revenue and for loans for housing and other purposes. The LGB and the government were equally slow to react to the resolutions of allegiance that were being adopted by the new councils, so much so that they could almost be said to have adopted the approach of burying their heads in the sand. As Robinson explained it in his memoirs, the fact that the board was now effectively at war with the local authorities was 'rather ominous and disquieting' but –

> We made no countermove at first, hoping that, as the councils were still corresponding with us and could not legally borrow money

without our consent or make valid appointments, this attitude towards us was only a passing phase, which would end when Treasury advances were required for housing of the working classes, or feeding school children, or relief of unemployment. We therefore thought we would leave it at that for a while, in the hope that the hanging up of all these loans would convince the local authorities that there was nothing to be gained by refusing to allow the ratepayers the protection of an audit.[52]

In public, spokesmen for the government in June and July played for time, and in classic bureaucratic fashion, the attorney general for Ireland told the House of Commons on 21 June and again on 23 June that the LGB had 'received no official intimation' from any council on the subject, even though newspapers were carrying extensive reports of the adoption of resolutions acknowledging the authority of the Dáil.[53] Robinson was, of course, well aware of what was going on throughout the country and was seriously concerned about the turn of events. On 4 July he told Sir John Anderson, who had taken up duty as an additional Under-Secretary in late May, that:

We are up against real difficulties in connection with local government administration. The local authorities are declining to fulfil their duties according to regulations and acts of Parliament. The collectors are being required to pay rates to trustees for Sinn Féin and the officials are being ordered to disregard the LGB instructions and to refuse to send us returns. The payments are being made by men of straw who are not a mark for costs, and every conceivable kind of legal ruse has to be faced, and we have to make orders for dealing with these matters.[54]

Robinson did not spell out what form of orders he had in mind to deal with the crisis, but insisted that to advance the work, the board's legal assistant, Arthur Quekett, should return immediately from London where he had been working with the parliamentary draftsman on the Government of Ireland Bill which was going through Parliament. He explained that 'our chief legal adviser [68-year-old Sir George Vanston] is slow', and 'two heads are better than one in this emergency ... the man who is doing the orders in Quekett's absence thinks he is quite able to advise the board on the points of difficulty; I take an entirely opposite view'. However, despite his plea not to 'upset our apple cart', it was decided that Quekett was to continue his work in London.

When asked in the House of Commons on 8 July if it was proposed to continue to pay grants to those public bodies which were flying the republican flag on their premises, the attorney general stated for the first time that the future administration of these grants was under consideration.[55] This was not good enough for the *Irish Times*, which complained that the government's lack of action was allowing the country to drift into a republic.[56] Chief Secretary Greenwood took matters somewhat further on 15 July when he indicated in the House of Commons that legislation was proposed to allow grant monies to be used to pay decrees, which had been obtained for murders and injuries to property, and which should have been paid by what were already being described as 'recalcitrant local authorities'.[57] On the following day, anticipating that the government would be pressed to define their policy in response to a question put down for answer at Westminster by Edward Carson, Anderson asked Robinson to prepare urgently a memorandum for the chief secretary indicating the line he would recommend under the law as it stood, and how the law might be amended to deal with the situation.[58] Robinson's response has not been traced, and it is impossible, therefore, to say what strategy he may have proposed, but a separate submission from him to Greenwood on 16 July on the question of proposals for increased urban housing subsidy gives a good indication of his thinking. It is impossible, he advised, to ignore the political situation: the municipal authorities were asking for loans on favourable terms and for increased grants from a Government which they decline to recognise and pledge themselves to do all in their power to resist. The irony of the situation, he concluded, was demonstrated by a report in one of the day's newspapers, from which it appeared that an urban council, having ordered the water supply to be cut off from the military and police barracks, then proceeded to consider an application to the government for a large loan for housing purposes for the benefit of their district! [59]

No Grants for Recalcitrant Local Councils

Carson's parliamentary question brought matters to a head by forcing ministers to decide urgently, and to announce, how they planned to deal with the situation. In the reply to Carson, an assurance was given in the House of Commons on 19 July by Bonar Law, then Leader of the House, that before payments from the Exchequer were made to any council, the government would have to be satisfied that all the requirements of the law with respect to such payments had been complied with. In particular, he stated that the government would not permit any loan to be issued or any subsidy to be paid for housing, water supply, public health or other local services to any local authority which would not undertake to submit their accounts to audit and to abide by the statutory orders, rules and regulations of the LGB.[60] A few days later, after Robinson had been asked by the chief secretary's office to list the county and county borough councils who intended to disregard demands for the payment of compensation for criminal and malicious injuries, he passed on to Dublin Castle all the information the board had on the subject but added that 'you may take it that every county and county borough council outside those included in the area of the northern Parliament intends to disregard these demands'.[61]

The crisis in local government was discussed when Lloyd George and senior members of his Cabinet were given an up-to-date briefing on the Irish situation at a conference in London with Irish officials (not including Robinson) on 23 July. W. E. Wylie KC, who had considerable experience of representing the LGB in the courts before becoming law adviser to the Irish government in 1919, told the meeting that while the local authorities were prepared to function so far as their own local affairs were concerned, they would give no assistance in carrying out the instructions of the Irish government.[62] Anderson, who supported Wylie's assessment of the situation, submitted a note to the Cabinet a few days later stating his views: 'The local authorities, which over a wide sphere are the agents of the central government, are profoundly disaffected', and the local civil service 'composed entirely of Irishmen, while in a sense not disloyal, is politically alienated and, exposed as it is to various kinds of pressure and in many cases of intimidation, cannot be relied upon in the execution of a vigorous policy'.[63] However, instead of making any recommendation on how the local government situation might be dealt with, Anderson's note dealt with the wider policy issue and advised the Cabinet (more or less as Wylie had done) that they were facing a stark strategy choice: there were two alternative methods of proceeding – depending entirely on naked superior force, in effect a military dictatorship, or introducing Dominion Home Rule with protection for Ulster, in which case he believed that local authorities would continue to function with no discontinuity in administration.

Completely disregarding Anderson's advice on the wider issues, the Cabinet opted to pursue the local government policy which had been outlined by Bonar Law on 19 July, and to back it up by legislation. Robinson was warned that strict observance of that policy would be required and, as instructed by Anderson in a note dated 28 July, arranged for the issue of a circular to local councils on the subject of withholding loans and grants.[64]

The circular, issued on 29 July, incorporated the words used by Bonar Law in the House of Commons[65] and, unusually, a circular in broadly similar terms was issued to local councils by the joint Under-Secretary, James MacMahon, on 4 August.[66] The official response was taken a stage further when the draft of the Restoration of Order in Ireland Bill was submitted to the Cabinet on 30 July and enacted ten days later. The bill included a provision which was designed 'to enable recalcitrant local authorities to be dealt with by withholding public grants which otherwise would be payable' and to allow the monies involved to be used to pay awards of compensation for criminal injuries or other liabilities such as the salaries and pensions of dismissed local officers.

Was Robinson 'An Ardent Apostle of the New Doctrine'?

In an article published in *Blackwood's Magazine* roughly two years later under the *nom-de-plume* 'Periscope', George Chester Duggan, who was a principal officer in the finance section of the Chief Secretary's Office in 1920 and directly involved until November 1921 in the administration of the scheme of grant deductions, claimed that Robinson was the prime mover in introducing the scheme provided for in the Restoration of Order Act:

> One of the most ardent apostles of the new doctrine embodied in the Act was Sir Henry Robinson, the vice-president of the Local Government Board. It was he who mainly talked Sir John Anderson into the belief that the extension of the policy of the previous act would starve the county councils into submission and compel them to recognise the Imperial Government and not Dáil Éireann. He was infatuated with the child of his own creation. He had been chiefly responsible for putting the Local Government Act of 1898 into operation, and he believed that all power in Ireland rested in the hands of the County Councils, and that what they thought today Ireland would think tomorrow. He lived in a period which left out of calculation the spirit engendered by the Rebellion of 1916. He thought in terms of rates, of grants-in-aid and Exchequer subsidies, while his opponents were thinking of revolvers and Irish Republican bonds. He seems to have over-estimated the volume of government assistance to the Councils, and forgotten that a good deal of the expenditure was permissive and that with a falling income, retrenchment would solve much of the financial trouble.[67]

In his own memoirs, published less than a year after Duggan's article had appeared, Robinson reacted strongly to the 'most inane and erroneous' statement that Anderson had been influenced by him to take the step of announcing the withdrawal of grants, and had been persuaded by him that the threat would force the local authorities to 'give way and forswear allegiance to the Sinn Féin and come back into the fold'. Robinson wrote that 'neither Anderson nor I had any more to do with the policy of withholding the grants than the Man in the Moon'.[68] However, surviving papers suggest that Anderson – but not Robinson – was at least privy to some of the discussions on 15 July of a Cabinet committee relating to the matter.[69] On balance, it seems reasonable to accept that Robinson did not propose – and is unlikely to have supported – the decision to withdraw grants from local authorities. This view has been advanced by Mary Daly, who wrote that this pre-emptive strike was ordered by Bonar Law 'apparently against the advice' of Robinson[70] and is consistent with David Fitzpatrick's observation that 'Robinson, pragmatically dismissive of republican manifestos and determined to avoid anarchy, worked skilfully to postpone irrevocable conflict with the local councils.'[71] In retrospect, a wish not to be seen to be directly responsible for the new hard-line policy can be read into the reference in the LGB circular of 29 July to the fact that the government had given the board <u>explicit instructions</u> on the matter, and in the defence provided in the circular for the board's own orders which, it insisted, 'were not framed with a view to restricting the authority of the councils; their sole object and intention is to secure efficiency and uniformity in the system of administration and to safeguard the interests of the ratepayers throughout the country'.

Another indication of the attitude of Robinson and the other two permanent members of the LGB to the blanket withdrawal of grants may be deduced from the fact that, although they formed a significant block of the membership of the Irish Public Health Council, they did not dissent from the council's suggestion to the Chief Secretary in September 1920 that dangers to the health of the community would result if grants for health services were withheld. The council's request that these grants should be continued, even where local authorities refused to submit their accounts for audit, met an uncompromising response from Cornelius Gregg, then the Chief Secretary's Private Secretary. Gregg wrote that Greenwood fully realised 'the appalling misfortune which will befall the people of the areas where the beneficent services for the treatment of tuberculosis, child welfare and other vital public health purposes are suspended', but the LGB had no discretion to advance public money to authorities which were acting in defiance of the law. Instead of looking to the government to relax statutory requirements, the real appeal should be made to those local bodies who prefer to sacrifice the health and the lives of the children, the poor and the afflicted, rather than submit to reasonable legal requirements.[72] Robinson himself took a similar hard line at a later stage when the management committee of the Richmond Asylum were in financial difficulty because of the withdrawal of grants. He insisted that it was entirely the responsibility of the committee themselves to decide whether they would comply with the regulations, or whether they would prefer to close their institution and send the lunatics back to their relations.[73]

Managing the Grant-Withholding Operation

In 1918–19, government grants had financed about 20 per cent of the net revenue expenditure of local councils, and government loans financed the bulk of the capital expenditure on housing and other services. County councils were the major beneficiaries, with their share of the agricultural grant paid from the Local Taxation Account alone amounting to more than £727,000. Grants towards medical and related expenditure, including accommodation for the lunatic poor, came to £277,000, while grants for roads and other purposes totalled £248,000, bringing total grants to a figure of more than £1,252,000.[74] Notwithstanding the prospect that these substantial sums would be lost to them, many local authorities appeared initially to be indifferent to the steps announced by the government. Their reaction to the circular of 29 July was closely monitored by the board and reported to the Chief Secretary's office from where, at the end of September, Mark Sturgis sent various government agencies a summary of the known responses. Of the 160 authorities for which information was then available, 24 were said to be willing to comply with the circular's requirements, 8 had refused, and 96 had simply directed that the circular be marked 'read' and had taken no further action. A significant number of others had adjourned consideration of the matter, a few had referred the issue to the Dáil for guidance, but for eleven others there was to be no compromise and no difficulty in reaching a decision: the circular was either to be ignored, placed in the waste-paper basket, or burned.[75] Of the councils which remained loyal to the LGB, urban councils were the worst offenders, according to O'Higgins, who told the Dáil that most of these councils had passed resolutions of allegiance but very few were acting on them, even as late as January 1921.[76]

By way of follow-up to the July circulars, a regulation made on 13 August under the Restoration of Order Act decreed that the grants withheld from local councils were to be used, in the following order, to meet compensation awards for malicious injuries, the cost of providing government services towards which local contributions should have been paid, debts due to the government by local authorities, debts due to private individuals, and finally, the cost of operating reformatory schools. In November, the policy was refined, with priority now being given to compensation to crown employees for personal injuries; next after that came compensation for the property of these employees and for personal injuries to private individuals; this left compensation for injuries to crown property and various sums due to the government to rank last.[77] At that stage, the entire operation was in the hands of Waterfield, Cope and Duggan at Dublin Castle who were in touch regularly with LGB officials, demanding further reports on the position of individual local councils[78] and who gave directions as to what grants were to be withheld and to whom payments were to be made.[79] Separate orders were made in the name of the Lord Lieutenant authorising specific deductions from the grants payable to individual local councils and these began to be published in the *Dublin Gazette* in October 1920.[80] When the money available for transfer from the Local Taxation Account to meet the liabilities of some councils was exhausted, it was decided that the government contribution in lieu of rates would also be liable to be withheld, although Robinson had been assured in August that it was not the intention to withhold it even from defaulting local authorities.[81] By the beginning of 1921 a Local Liabilities Deposit Account, operated jointly by the Chief Secretary's Office and the Treasury, had been set up. The LGB and other departments were instructed periodically to transfer specific sums from various grant subheads to this account so that payments could continue to be made to meet decrees for criminal injuries and other liabilities of the recalcitrant authorities.[82] Orders made in February 1921 and May 1921 provided for the withholding of grants from long lists of local councils, and the process continued, notwithstanding the Truce, until December 1921.[83]

'A Clean Break ... With the Enemy Institution in the Custom House'

The possibility that grants and loans might be withheld had been recognised by the Dáil department at an early stage and had been referred to in reports submitted by O'Higgins to the ministry on 11 May and 2 June.[84] The July circular, however, injected a new urgency into the eighteen-month-long deliberations on what action should be taken by the Dáil. On 6 August Cosgrave submitted the interim report of the commission on local government,[85] which among other things insisted that there would be little use in having a Department of Local Government unless the general business of the local authorities were under its supervision.[86] A few days later, with the approval of the ministry, a circular was issued to all public bodies, advising them to make arrangements to close off their bank accounts and instead to appoint trustees who would accept control of their funds and oversee disbursements; these were said to be interim instructions, pending further communication about a complete severance with 'the English Institution in the Custom House'.[87] Then, at a private session of the Dáil on 17 September, Cosgrave opened a debate on the commission's final report, which recommended that as 'the natural and inevitable result of the proclamation of the republic', there should be a complete severance with the LGB. Instead, all local councils were to recognise the department as the agency to supervise and control them and, to compensate for the loss of grants, cuts in services were to be made to save £277,500 before the end of the financial year.[88] Dáil approval of the report; with some amendments, was communicated to all local authorities in a circular dated 30 September. The local authorities were then directed that all communication with the Custom House should cease as from 1 October. The supervision and authority of the department was to be accepted instead, but as the aim was 'to have no drastic change', all existing laws and regulations were to continue in force, subject to any amendments that might be made by the department. The circular described the stoppage of grants as 'a last despairing attempt to bribe the people of Ireland back to slavery', but it was seen as a problem that could be met and solved by the series of cuts in services and expenditure detailed in the circular.[89]

At the time of the 'clean break', the staff of the Dáil department consisted of the minister, the assistant minister, five other men, a typist and a messenger.[90] Having assumed the role of *de facto* central authority, and having agreed that the laws and regulations which had been administered by the LGB should remain in force, the department quickly decided to replicate the key elements of the supervisory system which had been operated by Robinson and his board for decades, and which had regularly been criticised by nationalists. The indoor staff, under James Kavanagh as secretary, was built up in subsequent months, beginning with the appointment in September of Tom McArdle, who had been dismissed from the LGB in October 1918 for refusing to take the Oath of Allegiance and had subsequently been employed by the Transport Union. In addition, Michael de Lacey joined the department on 10 October as officer in charge of the outdoor staff. Titled 'Chief of Inspections', he was responsible for building up and managing teams of inspectors and auditors.[91] To enable the department to undertake the work of controlling and supervising the local councils, four inspectors, nineteen auditors and ten clerks were said to be necessary at an annual cost on £23,000, but Collins, as Finance Minister, refused to provide more than £5,000 to cover expenses to the end of 1920.[92]

Resisting the Auditors

A major element of the clean break policy was the refusal by local councils to submit their accounts for audit. Reports of incidents involving individual auditors had been appearing regularly in the press from July 1920 onwards: armed men were reported to have raided the workhouse boardroom in Midleton in July and held up the auditor there;[93] another auditor who was inspecting the books at Mountmellick was forced to leave by a party of armed men in September; while yet another was refused access to the books of Skibbereen UDC in October.[94] The case which attracted most publicity was that of Dublin Corporation which, on the motion of Cosgrave, and in compliance with an instruction from his own department, decided on 1 November – the day on which Kevin Barry was hanged – to instruct its officials not to furnish the corporation's books and accounts to the British Local Government Board auditor.[95] A few days later, when the councillors discovered that the town clerk, Henry Campbell, and his assistant had ignored the instruction, holding it to be illegal, a further meeting of the Corporation decided to suspend both men, to abolish their positions, and to place them on pension.[96] Campbell, who had been a nationalist MP for Fermanagh before his election as town clerk in 1893, then resigned because of the 'illegalities, irregularities and indecencies' which had been perpetrated against him, but he was compensated with a substantial pension and a knighthood in the New Year. The dispute with the Dublin auditor was taken a stage further when the LGB obtained a conditional order of mandamus from the High Court directing the books to be produced and this was made absolute in December.[97] Similar orders directed to thirty-five other councils were subsequently granted on the application of the board and individual auditors, and the process continued into the early months of 1921.[98] This long series of court proceedings achieved no result, according to Robinson's memoirs. The action taken against about eighty authorities 'turned out a very costly proceeding and the delays were interminable' due to the difficulty in serving the mandamus orders on the officials and councillors concerned. By the time matters were ripe for applications to the courts, the Truce had been agreed, leading to the abandonment of the proceedings.[99] But while Robinson's memoirs blame the Chief Secretary's Office for this wasteful strategy, he seems to have overlooked the fact that he himself had insisted to Waterfield in September 1920 that the auditors were duty bound to apply to the courts and leave no stone unturned to fulfil their statutory obligations.[100] Not unreasonably, therefore, he was held to be at least partly to blame when Waterfield complained in August 1922 that he had run up legal bills of over £13,000 in two years, with a single Kings Counsel, 'presumably a friend of his', in pursuit of the mandamus orders.[101]

In December there were reports that to frustrate the enforcement of mandamus orders, the offices of a number of authorities (including Dublin and Cork Corporations) were raided – presumably by prior arrangement with the councillors – by armed men who took away the books and other documents that would have been required by the auditor. On the other hand, there were also reports towards the end of 1920, when negotiations with the government were being advocated by a variety of individuals and organisations, that some authorities had decided to conform to the requirements of the LGB because of the impact on their services of the loss of grants. Particular significance was attached to the outcome of a meeting of Galway County Council in early December at which the clerks of some of the county's Poor Law Unions advised that they were rapidly running out of funds and suggested that the question of refusing to submit accounts for audit should be reconsidered. The six councillors present passed a resolution expressing sorrow and grief at the violence on both sides and calling for delegates to be appointed to negotiate a truce. Both the county council and the urban councils followed up by voting to submit their books for audit.[102] A few days later Lloyd George drew the attention of his Cabinet to the county council's resolution, describing it as the 'first occasion on which a Sinn Féin county council had condemned the Sinn Féin policy of murder and outrage'. A subsequent meeting of the Cabinet approved a draft letter for issue by the Prime Minister stating that it had learned with satisfaction of the decision to submit the accounts for audit and assuring the local councils of the government's full support, provided they loyally carried out their obligations under the law.[103] Although the council's Vice-Chairman, Alice Cashel, who had not been present at the meeting, held that the resolution was not a valid one because a quorum had not been present, the episode was a valuable publicity coup for the authorities.[104]

Paying for Criminal Injuries

As the War of Independence intensified in the second half of 1920, the number of deaths and injuries suffered by soldiers and police climbed to a total of almost 1,600, with the result that the total amount of compensation awarded under the criminal and malicious injuries code, as extended in 1919, built up rapidly. By the end of December decrees totalling £2,260,696 had been made, mostly against counties and county boroughs in the south, and very little had been paid, leaving a balance of more than £2 million overhanging these councils. This liability was increasing by the day throughout the first half of 1921, as large numbers of claims arising from deaths, injuries and the destruction of residential, commercial and other premises were processed expeditiously through the courts. For example, the widows, children and other relatives of sixteen men killed by the IRA in the ambush at Kilmichael, County Cork, at the end of November 1920 had obtained decrees for sums of up to £4,000 in each case by mid-January 1921.[105] In this and many other cases, the local authorities concerned refused even to be represented in court to challenge the amounts being claimed, and all of them, except a few of the councils in Northern Ireland, continued to refuse to make any provision to pay the court awards.

To cater for this situation, the Criminal Injuries (Ireland) Bill 1920 was enacted at the end of December in order, as the attorney general for Ireland explained, to make court awards effective by compelling the county councils to pay them.[106] The act represented a new and more serious threat to the finances of councils because, in addition to providing that decrees were to be payable on demand out of any monies in the hands of their treasurers, it allowed the main source of their income – the local rates, which met about 80 per cent of current expenditure – to be diverted to meet court awards. This was to be achieved by authorising the High Court to make garnishee orders, under which the monies payable by any ratepayer to a particular council could be attached to satisfy a compensation award, even where this would mean that no funds would be available to finance local services. In Dublin city, where the withholding of grants of about £200,000 had already resulted in severe cutbacks in services, members of the Corporation reacted to the act by proposing in February that a blacklist should be published, giving the names and addresses of every person who secured a garnishee order, so that the citizens would know who was responsible for depriving them of essential services and causing staff to be laid off.[107]

Another possible response to the difficulties that were arising in different areas in December 1920 was considered by Robinson and

Anderson, arising from representations by the town clerk of Westport, who was concerned that, because of the failure to elect an urban council in the previous January, a rate could not be levied to meet a large criminal injuries award and to allow his own salary and that of the other staff to be paid. Robinson suggested to Anderson that it might be possible either to amend the Criminal Injuries Bill or to make regulations under the Restoration of Order Act to deal with the situation, but Anderson felt that it would not be prudent at that stage to seek any substantial amendment.[108] A few days later, arising from a visit to his office by the Dublin town clerk who had just been dismissed by the Corporation, Robinson told Anderson that the Corporation had got itself into a financial mess and that 'you could not get a majority ... who would be mentally capable of extricating the city from its difficulties and getting it re-established on a proper financial basis.' He suggested, therefore, that 'a clause providing that we might appoint commissioners where any local authority came to grief' might be considered again. A clause of this kind had been included in the Local Government Bill in 1919 but was withdrawn as the government did not have a majority in the committee. He went on to say that:

> I dislike the idea of pulling the nuts out of the fire for the Corporation and local bodies and think that the ratepayers should stew in their own juice if they elected useless representatives, but in the event of councils not being elected, or resigning in a body, the government might find it useful to have up their sleeves a power by which they could appoint commissioners to rehabilitate the local authorities.[109]

Anderson, in reply, told Robinson that the desirability of taking some general power to appoint commissioners to straighten out the affairs of a local authority that had got into hopeless difficulties had been considered earlier in the year by a Cabinet Committee but –

> the decision at the time went against the inclusion of any such provision mainly on the ground that it might afford a dangerously easy way of escaping for members of local authorities from the consequences of their own misguided action and might even lead to the adoption of a definite policy to bring local government everywhere into chaos and then throw on the central government the whole onus of putting things right. It may eventually prove necessary to do something of the kind, though I still contemplate the prospect with grave misgivings. In the martial law area, however,

it might be possible to do something of the sort and test its efficiency without establishing a general precedent, and if you like we will consider whether anything can be done on these lines if we can find a suitable locality to experiment on in the four counties. Perhaps we might talk the matter over next time we meet.[110]

Whether Anderson and Robinson ever met to consider taking the suggestion further does not emerge from surviving files. What can be said, however, is that it was left to the government of the Irish Free State in 1923 to enact legislation under which defaulting local authorities could be replaced by commissioners, prompting Birrell years later to comment wryly that he would have been forced to resign by a combination of unionists and nationalists if he had attempted this.[111]

Robinson's Proposals to Allow for a Programme of Peace, Reconciliation and Development

At a private Dáil session on 25 January 1921, Cosgrave (who had been absent from his post for several months before that) reported that 'all the councils were in fairly good financial positions',[112] but O'Higgins, who had privately been very critical of Cosgrave,[113] and had been substituting for him for much of the previous year, challenged this: 'The situation was not so rosy as pictured by the minister, it was very serious in many places.'[114] A circular issued by Cosgrave a few days later adopted the line that the many difficulties that local councils had to sustain were due to the persistent attempts of the British government to destroy local administration and in particular to the imposition of conditions other than those originally provided for before grants would be paid.[115] In March, at another private Dáil session, Cosgrave spoke of his concern about the additional difficulties that might follow the implementation of garnishee orders and later issued a circular in which he angrily attacked the criminal injuries legislation, citing for maximum effect its possible impact on health and welfare services, although these accounted for a relatively small percentage of grant-aided local expenditure.[116] The government's new approach, he went on, was a despicable and infamous war 'upon the sick and the helpless poor, upon the mother, the infant and the aged', a war which was in breach of the humanitarian principles and custom that had always applied in civilised warfare.[117] In light of these considerations, Cosgrave's April circular incorporated a strongly-worded and solemn warning to those who held decrees for criminal injuries, to those who had secured garnishee orders and to their solicitors, threatening that they would be 'proceeded against with all the forces that the people's government can command'. He insisted that just compensation for the injuries caused by Crown forces would have to be paid by the British government to the individuals concerned and promised that where injuries to persons and property had been caused 'by the necessary operations of the National Forces, the Home Government will see to it at the proper time that the loss is distributed over the nation as a whole'.

Cosgrave would, no doubt, have been amazed to know that two months before the issue of his solemn warning, and while the level of IRA violence was still escalating, Robinson was so concerned at the appalling burden which ratepayers would have to meet in future years in respect of compensation awards that he took the initiative in proposing a solution. Estimating that these awards would amount to roughly £6 million in total, he proposed that government funds should be made available to allow compensation to be paid to all of those who had suffered losses, *regardless of which of the combatants had caused the losses.* He acknowledged the argument 'that in strict equity, Ireland has no claim to relief from the Imperial Exchequer in respect of this debt, and that the Republican Army and the people who have supported it, and have done nothing to hinder its ravages, are morally responsible for the whole of the damage done by the Government Forces as well as by Members of Sinn Féin'. Nevertheless, and looking ahead to the elections which were to take place in mid-1921 under the Government of Ireland Act to the two new parliaments, he submitted to the Under-Secretary that a strong case could be made for an imperial contribution towards the awards, in the interests of the trade and industry of the country, to enhance the prospects of a successful administration of the act, to encourage businessmen to come forward as candidates at the elections, and 'to allow a new start with a programme of peace, reconciliation and development' without a millstone of debt, which in some local council areas would not be wiped out for generations. He argued that an exact precedent for such assistance had been provided by the government's admission of liability for the destruction of Dublin during the Rising, and he argued that account had also to be taken of the government's admission that 'in a few cases', such as at Balbriggan and Cork city, government forces 'got out of hand' after they had been 'maddened by the murder of their comrades, and destroyed property in the confusion and excitement of the reprisals'.[118] Robinson's proposals were qualified by a suggestion that if the people of southern Ireland failed under the 1920 Act to elect a working parliament, 'they must only be left to stew in their own juice and must bear the whole responsibility for the breakdown of any public services which may follow'. On the other hand – unlike Cosgrave – he was adamant that whatever relief the government might decide to give should not involve an attempt to determine the proportion of the damage to life and property caused by the Crown forces and the proportion caused by the IRA. In his usual pragmatic fashion, he suggested that with the vested interests involved and the 'convenient memories and great imaginative powers' of Irish witnesses when the issue at stake affects their pockets, any attempt at discrimination on this basis would be useless and would only give rise to a recrudescence of anger and its consequences.

In quickly forwarding Robinson's submission to the Chancellor of the Exchequer and the Chief Secretary, Anderson pointed out that he was 'an officer with very great experience of Irish politics and a thorough knowledge of Irish psychology', and therefore invited their special attention to his comments on the convenient memories and imaginative powers of Irish witnesses. He had no hesitation in endorsing the view that it would be impossible in practice and indefensible in policy and equity to distinguish compensation claims according to the authorship of the damage but, pending 'a final settlement with the Irish nation', which was to be ten months away, he proposed an interim scheme of repayable loans rather than *ex-gratia* compensation to provide relief both for public bodies and for individuals who had suffered.[119] These proposals, as well as Robinson's original submission, were put to the Cabinet by Greenwood in a memorandum dated 1 March 1921.[120] However a decision was deferred at a meeting on 22 March, and the issue was not taken up again by the Cabinet until after the Treaty.

'Have We Come Nearer to Freedom by Refusing to Recognise the Local Government Board?'

This was the rhetorical question posed by Dr Daniel Coholan, Catholic Bishop of Cork, in his Lenten pastoral of February 1921 – and historians have generally answered 'yes' to the question.[121] Commentators have also considered the Department of Local Government to be among the more successful of the departments established by the first Dáil in 1919, notwithstanding the almost complete lack of action by the department until mid-1920 and the absence for one reason or another of the minister, W. T. Cosgrave, for long periods before that. Inevitably, Henry Robinson has been identified with the events of June–July 1920, which precipitated the department's promotion of the 'clean break' between the local councils and the LGB, and lead to virtual bankruptcy for some councils and severe curtailment of services for some of the most vulnerable sections of the community. It is suggested, however, that Robinson's role during this period was an honourable one and that the strategy of withholding grants and loans from councils classified as 'recalcitrant' by Dublin Castle was neither proposed nor supported by him. He deserves credit also for having been the first to recognise early in 1921 – months before the Truce and after his own resignation from his substantive post had been accepted – the need for the government to step in and implement arrangements for compensation for criminal and malicious injuries which would not only relieve the ratepayers of a burden they were patently unable to bear but would compensate *all* of those who suffered losses during the conflict, which had gone on since 1919, regardless of which side had caused the losses. His stated objective at that stage was the commendable one of enhancing the prospects of a successful administration of the Government of Ireland Act 1920 in both parts of Ireland and of allowing whoever was to succeed him to make a new start with a programme of peace, reconciliation and development.

NOTES

1   War Cabinet Minutes 453, 29 July 1918, TNA, CAB 23/7.
2   The State of Ireland: Report by Lord French to the War Cabinet, G.T. 5570, 30 Aug. 1918, TNA, CAB 24/62.
3   Robinson to Saunderson, 17 Dec. 1918, WRO, Long Papers, WRO 947/347 (typescript); the original manuscript letter is held at IWM, French Papers, JDPF 8/1B.
4   French to the King, 18 Dec. 1918 and the King to French, 24 Dec. 1918, IWM, French Papers, JDPF 8/3.
5   Sir Henry Robinson, *Memories: Wise and Otherwise* (London, 1923), p.275.
6   James Bryce Papers, NLI, MSS 11,012(2), 11,012(3).
7   Cornelius O'Leary, *The Irish republic and its experiment with proportional representation* (Notre Dame, 1961), pp.1–7; *Irish Elections 1918–1977* (Dublin, 1979), pp.5–6.
8   *Hansard* V, 114, 24 Mar. 1919, 99–183.
9   Robinson to French, 6 Jan. 1919, IWM, French Papers, JDPF 8/1D.
10   *Irish Bulletin*, Vol. 2, No. 11, 19 May 1920; speech by de Valera in Dublin's Mansion House, 19 Apr. 1919.
11   *Hansard* V, 114, 24 Mar. 1919, 99–183.
12   *Hansard* V, 116, 27 May 1919, 1068.
13   *Irish Times*, 21 Jan. 1919.
14   Local Government (Ireland) Act 1919, 9 & 10 Geo. 5, c. 19, 3 June 1919.
15   *Irish Bulletin*, Vol. 2, No. 11, 19 May 1920.
16   Dáil Éireann, Minutes of Proceedings, 2 Apr. 1919.
17   J.L. McCracken, *Representative Government in Ireland: A Study of Dáil ireann, 1919–48* (London, 1958), p.31.

18   James Kavanagh, BMH, WS 889, 24 Sept. 1953; W. T. Cosgrave, BMH, WS 449, 14 Nov. 1950.

19   *AR*, 1916–17, p.vii.

20   Arthur Mitchell, *Revolutionary Government in Ireland* (Dublin, 1995), p.121.

21   *Irish Times*, 4 Jan. 1919.

22   *Irish Times*, 9 Jan. 1919.

23   The State of Ireland: Report by Lord French to the War Cabinet, G.T. 7277, 15 May 1919, TNA, CAB 24/79.

24   French Diary, 14 Jan. 1919, IWM.

25   Macpherson to Lloyd George, 14 Apr. 1919, Parliamentary Archives, Lloyd George Papers, LG/F/46/1/2.

26   Minutes of Proceedings, Fourth Session (Private), 19 June 1919, 130–131; T. J. McArdle, BMH, WS 501, 19 Feb. 1951, p.4.

27   NAI, DE/2/243; McArdle, WS 501, p.6.

28   *AR*, 1919–20.

29   Murray Fraser, *John Bull's Other Homes*, Liverpool (1996), pp.193–94, 225–26, 232–34; Robinson–Greenwood correspondence, CSORP 1921/2503; TNA, T.160/214, Robinson to chief secretary, 21 Oct. 1921.

30   Murray Fraser, *John Bull's Other Homes*, pp.209–210.

31   Order in Council of 23 Dec. 1919, *Dublin Gazette*, No. 21,754, 30 Dec. 1919, 1959; Ministry of Transport file S. 262, TNA, MT 45/199.

32   *Irish Times*, 27 Mar. 1919.

33   *Dublin Gazette*, 25 Nov. 1919.

34   Report of court proceedings involving the chairman of South County Dublin Sinn Féin Election Committee, *Irish Times*, 24 Jan. 1920.

35   Municipal Elections, January 1920, Sinn Féin Manifesto, NLI, Joseph Brennan Papers, MS 26,164; a broadly similar document (Elections 1920) was published in advance of the June elections, NLI, ILB 300.

36   *Irish Times*, 14 Jan. 1920.

37   *AR*, 1919–20, p.x.

38   *Irish Times*, 20 Jan. 1920; not all of those counted by the PR Bureau as successful labour candidates were actually party candidates – see Conor McCabe, 'The Irish Labour Party and the 1920 Local Elections', S*aothar* 35 (2010), pp.7–20.

39   Results of urban elections, returns compiled in the Department of Local Government and covering letter of 11 Mar. 1920 from Liam T. Mac Cosgair, NAI, DE 2/81.

40   Shortt to Lloyd George, 4 July 1918, Parliamentary Archives, Lloyd George Papers, LG/ F/ 45/6/6.

41   David, Fitzpatrick, *Politics and Irish Life 1913–1921* (2nd ed.) (Cork, 1998), p.154.

42   McArdle, BMH, WS 501, p.8.

43   *Irish Times*, 22 Jan. 1920.

44   Micheál Martin, *Freedom to Choose: Cork & Party Politics in Ireland 1918–1932* (Cork, 2009), pp.35–6.

45   *Irish Times*, 8 May 1920.

46   *Irish Times*, 17 July 1920.

47 Sheila Carden, *The Alderman: Alderman Tom Kelly (1868–1942) and Dublin Corporation* (Dublin, 2007), pp.180–181.
48 *Irish Times*, 19 May 1920.
49 NAI, DE 2/243.
50 See, for example, *Irish Times*, 16 June 1920; signed and in some cases sealed copies of many of the resolutions are included in the Austin Stack papers, NLI, MS 17,084 and some are also on file at NAI, DE/2/444.
51 Dáil Éireann, Minutes of Proceedings, 29 June 1920, 169, 185.
52 Robinson, *Memories*, p.307.
53 *Hansard* V, 130, 21 June 1920, 1769–70; 23 June, 2176.
54 Robinson to Anderson, 4 July 1920, NLI, Joseph Brennan Papers, MS 26,164.
55 *Hansard* V, 131, 8 July 1920, 1632.
56 *Irish Times*, 10 July 1920.
57 *Hansard* V, 131, 8 July 1920, 1632; 15 July 1929, 2569–70.
58 Anderson to Robinson, 16 July 1920, NLI, Joseph Brennan Papers, MS 26,164.
59 Robinson to Greenwood, 16 July 1920, NAI, CSORP 1921/2503.
60 *Hansard* V, 132, 19 July 1920, 48–49.
61 Cope to Robinson and Robinson to Cope, 21 and 22 July 1920, NAI, CSORP 1920/20971.
62 Notes of a Conference with the officers of the Irish Government, 23 July 1920, C.P. 1693, TNA, CAB 24/109; Conclusions of a Conference of Ministers, 23 July 1920, TNA, CAB 23/22.
63 Irish Situation: Note by Sir John Anderson, C.P. 1689, 25 July 1920, TNA, CAB 24/109.
64 Robinson, *Memories*, pp.308–09; Robinson to Anderson, 29 July 1920, NAI, CSORP 1920/20971.
65 *Irish Times*, 31 July 1920.
66 Circular letter dated 4 Aug. 1920, 'Withholding of grants from recalcitrant local authorities', TNA, T.160/54.
67 *Blackwood's Magazine*, Vol. 212, No. 1282 (Aug. 1922), p.161.
68 Robinson, *Memories*, p.308.
69 Note of a meeting in the chief secretary's room in Westminster on 15 July 1920, attended by Anderson to settle outstanding points on what was described as a criminal injuries bill (TNA, T.192/15).
70 Mary E. Daly, *The Buffer State* (Dublin, 1997), p. 52.
71 David Fitzpatrick, *The Two Irelands 1912–1939* (Oxford, 1998), p. 84.
72 *Irish Times*, 9 Oct. 1920.
73 Robinson to Anderson, 15 Dec. 1920, TNA, CO 904/26.
74 *Return showing total payments into and out of the Local Taxation (Ireland) Account for the Financial Year 1918–19*, HC 1920 (38).
75 Circular letter dated 28 Sept. 1920, 'Withholding of grants from recalcitrant local authorities', TNA, T.160/54.
76 Dáil Éireann, Minutes of Proceedings, Private Session, 25 Jan. 1921, 255.
77 Treasury Ireland letter of 15 November 1920, TNA, T.158/1.
78 CSO–LGB correspondence, Aug.–Dec. 1920, NAI, CSORP 1920/20971.
79 'Withholding of grants from recalcitrant local authorities', TNA, T.160/54.

80 *Dublin Gazette,* 1 Oct. 1920, 1399; 12 Oct. 1920, 1456.

81 Treasury Ireland letter of 27 Aug. 1920, TNA, T.158/1; Waterfield to Robinson, 4 Dec. 1920, TNA, T.158/1.

82 Treasury Ireland letters of 31 Jan. and 24 Mar. 1921, TNA, T.158/2.

83 *Dublin Gazette,* 4 Mar. 1921, p.323; 17 May 1921, p.763.

84 NAI, DE 2/243; McArdle, 501, p.33.

85 Dáil Éireann, Minutes of Proceedings, Private Session, 6 Aug. 1920, 203–205.

86 NAI, DE 2/243.

87 Circular of 10 Aug. 1920, Instructions re Funds of Public Bodies, NAI, DE 2/62.

88 Final Report of Commission of Enquiry into Local Government, 27 Aug. 1920; Dáil Éireann, Minutes of Proceedings, Private Session, 17 Sept. 1920, 218–223.

89 Circular dated 30 Sept. 1920 'to all public bodies in Ireland', NAI, DE/4/3/5.

90 McArdle, BMH, WS 501, pp.40–41.

91 Kavanagh, BMH, WS 889; McArdle, BMH, WS 501.

92 Dáil Éireann, Minutes of Proceedings, Private Session, 17 Sept. 1920, 222–23; a meeting of the ministry on 20 November 1920 eventually approved the employment of four auditors at salaries of £400 each (NAI, DE 2/61).

93 *Irish Times,* 28 July 1920.

94 *Irish Times,* 18 and 27 Sept.and 7 Oct. 1920.

95 *Irish Times,* 6 Nov. 1920.

96 *Irish Times,* 5 Nov. 1920.

97 *Irish Times,* 20 Nov. and 18 and 21 Dec. 1920.

98 *Irish Times,* 20 and 24 Nov. and 1 Dec. 1920; 3 Feb. 1921; *Freeman's Journal,* 18 Jan. 1921.

99 Robinson, *Memories,* p.309.

100 Robinson to Waterfield, 5 Sept. 1920, TNA, T.160/216.

101 Waterfield to Anderson, 4 Apr. 1922, TNA, T.158/8.

102 *Connacht Tribune,* 4 and 11 Dec. 1920.

103 Conclusions of a meeting of the Cabinet 66/20 of 6 Dec. 1920, TNA, CAB 23/23; conclusions of a meeting of the Cabinet 68/20 of 9 Dec. 1920, TNA, CAB 23/23.

104 Alice Cashel, BMH, WS 366, 6 Feb. 1950.

105 *Irish Times,* 12 and 17 Jan. 1921.

106 *Hansard* V, 134, 5 Nov. 1920, 737–38.

107 *Irish Times,* 22 Feb. 1921.

108 Robinson to Anderson, 3 Dec. 1920 and Anderson to Robinson, 4 Dec. 1920, TNA, CO 904/26.

109 Robinson to Anderson, 9 Dec. 1920, TNA, CO 904/26.

110 Anderson to Robinson, 14 Dec. 1920, TNA, CO 904/26.

111 Augustine Birrell, *Things Past Redress* (London, 1937), p.219.

112 Dáil Éireann, Minutes of Proceedings, Private Session, 25 Jan. 1921, 253.

113 Letters to his fiancée, Brigid Cole, June 1920 and subsequently, Kevin O'Higgins papers, UCDA, P197.

114 Dáil Éireann, Minutes of Proceedings, Private Session, 25 Jan. 1921, 255.

115 Local Government Department Circular No. 35, 30 Jan. 1921, forwarded by Robinson to Anderson, 15 Feb. 1921, TNA, CO 904/26.

116 Dáil Éireann, Minutes of Proceedings, Private Session, 11 Mar. 1921, 268–69.

117 *Irish Times*, 19 Apr. 1921; the complete text of the circular was included in a communication from Robinson which was submitted to the Cabinet on 16 Aug. 1921, C.P. 3230, TNA, CAB 24/127.

118 Robinson to Anderson, 5 Feb. 1921, TNA, T.160/214.

119 Anderson to Chancellor of Exchequer, 11 Feb. 1921, TNA, T.160/214.

120 Exchequer assistance towards payment of compensation for malicious damage in Ireland, Memorandum by the Chief Secretary for Ireland, C.P. 2637, 1 Mar. 1921, TNA, CAB 24/120.

121 *Irish Times*, 7 Feb. 1921.

CHAPTER XVI

'It was Difficult to Say Who Really was Safe in Those Days'

Were Robinson and his Colleagues at Personal Risk in 1920–21?

Repeated references in 1920–21 by O'Higgins and Cosgrave to 'the *English* Local Government Board' and to 'the enemy department', as well as Cosgrave's circular of March 1921 threatening action by all the forces that the people's government could command,[1] prompts the question of whether Robinson and others associated with the LGB and with the withholding of grants were at personal risk after the War of Independence had escalated in mid-1920 and after relations between the board and most local authorities were broken off.[2] It was clearly the policy of the Dáil at that stage to wreck the LGB itself, but there is no evidence that Robinson and other board members and headquarters officials, or even the inspectors and auditors who continued to travel around the country in the course of their duties, were at any stage in real danger from IRA violence. While the War of Independence may be said to have begun at Soloheadbeg on 21 January 1919, outbreaks of violence were sporadic and limited throughout the remainder of 1919. Twenty members of the police forces were killed as a result of political violence in that year, and RIC men and the military continued to be the main targets of the IRA in 1920, leading to 232 deaths by the end of the year.[3] Peter Hart notes that no unionist, Irish Party member or British politician was assassinated in 1919–21, although some attacks were attempted or planned.[4] The same was largely true of senior officials serving in Dublin: as Chester Duggan (a principal officer in the Chief Secretary's Office at the Castle) noted, attacks on public servants were relatively few, except where they were engaged in tracking down disaffection: 'The civil servant remained untouched though his master was an alien government, for his activities were either helpful to Sinn Féin, as for example, the postal service, or were harmless and futile, as for example, the Local Government Board and the Inland Revenue.'[5]

Alan Bell, an elderly resident magistrate and former RIC officer, was a prime example of the category of public servants who were at risk. After books and records had been seized in police raids on Sinn Féin headquarters in Harcourt Street, Dublin, in January and February 1920, Bell was assigned to work through these materials with a view to probing Dáil and Sinn Féin finances and tracking down the proceeds of the Dáil loan. Not wishing to live as a prisoner, he resisted the pleas of Lord French that he and his wife should live in Dublin Castle or at the Vice-Regal Lodge[6] and came and went every day on the Dalkey tram from his home in Monkstown to the Castle without an escort. He was taken off the tram at the Merrion Road – Simmonscourt Road junction in Ballsbridge by IRA men and shot dead on the morning of 26 March 1920. Around the same time, the services of two LGB auditors had been made available by Robinson to assist in examining and reporting on the account books and other papers which had been seized by the military and police from the offices of suppressed organisations, but, fortunately for them, their involvement in these activities did not apparently attract the attention that might have cost them their lives.[7]

Duggan himself never felt any fear of attack on his daily journeys between the Castle and his home in Dundrum,[8] although his colleague, Joseph Brennan, received a note sent by post in November 1920 asking 'As an Irishman and a Catholic, how long are you going to keep your rotten stinking job at the Castle? Be warned in time.'[9] Brennan's superior, Sir John Taylor, the Assistant Under-Secretary, who was primarily responsible for security matters in 1919–20, and was labelled by *Watchword of Labour* (the limited circulation newspaper published by the Irish Transport and General Workers Union) as 'Piggott's accomplice and castle cut-throat' moved into Dublin Castle with his family on police advice at the beginning of 1920 and ventured out only with an armed escort or in an armoured car.[10] Sir John Anderson and some of the ten other British civil servants who were sent to Dublin on loan in May 1920 initially lived at the Marine Hotel, Kingstown (Dun Laoghaire), and travelled by car or by train to their offices in the Castle each day – and this at a time when General Lucas was held by the IRA in the south and after Frank Brooke, a privy councillor and a member of Lord French's advisory committee, had been shot dead in his office in Westland Row Railway Station on 30 July. The Cabinet discussed the position of the British officials on 13 August, when fears were expressed that they might no longer be 'immune from the attacks of Sinn Féin', and although some ministers held the view that the danger was not so great, the Cabinet directed that the civil servants should reside in the Castle. They did so for the remainder of their assignment in Ireland and were paid special allowances to cover the element of risk involved, the increased responsibility and the conditions under which they worked.[11] Robinson was very annoyed about this and commented critically on it in his memoirs: it was galling, he wrote, that these English civil servants were given substantial salaries and special 'danger allowances' while Irish officials 'especially those of us who had to work in the open country unprotected and alone ... and the LGB officials who were prevented by violence and threats from fulfilling their duties ... received no similar consideration'.[12]

After Bell's assassination, Chief Secretary Macpherson had assured the House of Commons that every possible precaution was being taken to guard other officials who might be in danger.[13] Robinson, who commuted daily from his home in Foxrock to his offices in the city, would clearly have counted as one of these – he was one of the most senior and long-serving civil servants in the country, a privy councillor who signed proclamations from time to time declaring counties or parts of counties to be disturbed, and a confidant of the Lord Lieutenant and Chief Secretary. He would have been an obvious – and easy – target for the IRA if their activities were ever to extend beyond the military, police and resident magistrates. As he stated in his memoirs:

> It was difficult to say who really was safe in those days. As I was constantly being summoned to the Park Lodge to see Lord French or the Chief Secretary, and was in daily touch with the Castle, I certainly thought it quite probable that the Sinn Féiners would consider it a sound precaution to remove me on the grounds that I was in the confidence of Lord French and the Government. But as I had never been molested I assumed that they were well aware that my advice would not be asked in connection with military or police matters and that my business had to do only with local government administration and the relief of unemployment. I asked a legal friend who I knew was in touch with the militant Sinn Féin to find

out if they intended to wipe me out, and he subsequently told me that, so far as he could ascertain, he thought not, so long as I was not appointed under-secretary, but that circumstances changed very rapidly, and I should try to avoid the Castle and the Chief Secretary's Lodge.

This, however, was not possible, and one day the police found a notice posted on the door of the Custom House: 'Sir Henry Robinson, you are doomed. Prepare for death'. This was brought by the police to Colonel Edgeworth Johnstone, their Chief Commissioner, who thereafter insisted upon my being protected in the streets of Dublin. Wherever I went I was followed by two DMP men in mufti; splendid creatures they were, about six feet two in height, each of them so straight and well set up that no one could have suspected them of being anything but military or police.[14]

Much to his embarrassment, Robinson's protectors accompanied him on visits to Connemara where he was well known but he was able, after some time, to dispense with them entirely as he believed that they were 'a challenge rather than a protection'; besides, if it was decided that he should be removed, protection in the city during part of the day would have been of little use as he could easily have been shot at his Foxrock home or when driving in and out of the city. In effect, he believed, as Alan Bell did, that any ostentatious protection would defeat its own object; according to one of his sons, he loathed the police escort and 'used to stride along the streets of Dublin at the fearful pace which was his usual form of walking, with his unfortunate police shadow puffing along behind trying to keep up'.[15] But for the Truce, Robinson may well have found himself to be at real risk of assassination – Michael Collins had suggested in June 1921 that it was time to extend the range of IRA targets from the police and the army to officials of the central administration and to launch a regular, all round, well-thought-out onslaught on all the departments.[16] A few days earlier, Austin Stack, as Minister for Home Affairs, had submitted detailed proposals to his ministerial colleagues listing nine categories of public officials and office-holders who were to be 'declared enemies of the Republic' and against whom action should be taken. Dublin Castle officials were in the first category with active members of the Privy Council (who included Robinson) in the second. In the event, de Valera instructed that no action should be taken on these proposals while the negotiations which were to lead to the Truce were in progress.[17]

'Probably the Stupidest Thing the Sinn Féin Ever did'

Notwithstanding the deteriorating security situation, Robinson and his board colleagues continued to meet normally at the Custom House throughout the first months of 1921, although most of the business to be dealt with at their daily meetings related only to the sailors and soldiers housing scheme which was implemented directly by the board. There were the usual office closures on Ash Wednesday, at Easter and on 14 May, the day fixed for the celebration of His Majesty's birthday, as the board minutes described it, but only ten days later, the board's links with the Custom House were shattered for ever. Robinson had been warned 'from a source from which I had usually obtained sound advice' that a raid on the Custom House was more than probable at some stage; as a result, police guards had been placed on the building, but these were withdrawn after a few weeks, without a word of explanation.[18] The building had been the headquarters of the board since its establishment nearly fifty years earlier, and it housed a number of other public departments and offices. Apart from Dublin Castle, it was by far the most important centre of British administration in Ireland and was an obvious target for the IRA. Reports written by the head of the customs staff who occupied parts of the building[19] confirm Robinson's recollection of the security measures: it had been guarded day and night during Easter 1921 by some forty or forty-five fully armed auxiliary police, all doors except the main entrance facing Beresford Place were closed, and barbed wire entanglements were erected near all of the entrances. But the police guard, which had been provided at Robinson's request, was withdrawn without explanation after four or five days, and only one DMP constable was left to guard the building during office hours. Some weeks later, the barbed wire at a second door was removed to facilitate access by old age pension applicants to the LGB offices.

The intelligence services in England warned the Irish authorities in mid-May 1921 that a 'serious outbreak' in Dublin – probably involving an attack on the Castle – was imminent[20] but it was the unguarded Custom House which was selected for destruction, both to capture public attention at home and abroad and to disable the administration of a range of public services. Ironically, it was de Valera – who had on several occasions since 1919 been viewed by Robinson as one of the more moderate of the nationalist leaders – who suggested early in 1921 that the Dublin brigade of the IRA should aim at the destruction of Robinson's headquarters.[21] In an operation planned by the OC of the brigade, Oscar Traynor, over a number of months and without any inside assistance, the building was entered by some 120 Volunteers at lunchtime on 25 May, staff of the LGB and the other departments were rounded up, rooms were sprinkled with paraffin and set on fire, and large parts of the building were blazing fiercely within a short time. A gun-battle ensued when parties of Auxiliaries surrounded the building, resulting in the deaths of five of the Volunteers and the arrest of over one hundred others, some with bullet wounds. Four casualties were officially recorded on the British side.

With his usual good luck, as he put it himself, Robinson was not in his office at the Custom House when the building was attacked by the IRA: he had attended a short meeting of the board held at 12.30 p.m. that day (instead of the usual 1.00 p.m.) and had left the office before lunchtime to join some of his staff at the Royal Dublin Golf Links at Dollymount, where they were competing in a golf tournament for a silver cup, which he had presented some years before.[22] The author of the minutes of the board meeting confined himself to a terse statement of the facts: 'On this day, at about one o'clock p.m., the Custom House was invaded by armed men, members of the Irish Republican Army, who destroyed by fire the building wherein practically all the records of the board perished.'[23] However, wonderfully detailed handwritten reports on the fire and subsequent events were provided for his superiors in London by the collector of customs and excise, and other useful insider accounts were subsequently given by two members of the LGB staff, Pádraig Ó Cinnéide and Daniel McAleese.[24]

Of the staff working in the building, Francis (Frank) Davis, the 62-year-old resident caretaker/housekeeper, who had been employed by the customs service for thirty-eight years, was the first casualty; he was shot when trying to give the alarm and died later in the day from shock and haemorrhage, leaving a widow and three dependent children. Mahon Patrick Lawless, a temporary clerk employed by LGB, was also shot dead, having been mistaken for an attacker, and a small number of other civil servants, including two of the board's senior staff, were injured in the gunfire. Sir George Vanston, the board's elderly legal adviser, who was quite deaf, was fortunate not to have become another casualty – while fire raged in other parts of the building, he continued to work undisturbed in the first-floor room overlooking the quay, which he had occupied for twenty-one years. The fire did not penetrate the room as it had an arched stone roof and ceiling and only when he went into the corridor in search of a messenger was he discovered by a military officer to whom he was able eventually to identify himself.[25] One of Vanston's legal assistants, Charles W. Grant, was praised by Robinson for his great gallantry in going back into the building when 'the flames were at their height, accompanied by a few volunteers from the military ... [to] rescue all the orders and the most valuable documents and records in the possession of the board, which are quite indispensable to us'. The RIC District Inspector who attended the fire confirmed that Grant had shown 'great pluck and presence of mind' for over an hour in collecting records to be thrown through the windows onto the quay before he was advised to withdraw from the building because of the risk that the dome would collapse (which in fact it later did).[26]

Robinson and the heads of other affected departments attended a conference chaired by the Under-Secretary at Dublin Castle on the morning after the fire, following which temporary accommodation was arranged for all of them. As the new government buildings at Merrion Street to which the LGB was intended to transfer were not yet completed, the board was provided with offices at Jury's Hotel, 6–8 College Green, to replace the accommodation destroyed at the Custom House. The housing department, based at 29–30 Lower Fitzwilliam Street, the old age pensions staff at 198 Great Brunswick Street (now Pearse Street), and the public health staff working in offices at 33 St Stephen's Green were not, of course, affected. Thus, while the *Irish Times* noted that the ostensible object of the arson was to paralyse the whole system of local government by dispossessing the board of its offices and all its official memoranda and documents, Robinson insisted to the paper's reporter that the outrage would have no effect in suspending, even for a day, the operations of any single service directed by the board: 'The whole business is tragically futile', he went on, and while there would be some inconvenience and possible delay, the work of the board was continuing at alternative offices throughout the city.[27]

The destruction of the Custom House, described as one of the seats of an alien tyranny by the *Irish Bulletin* in its issue of 27 May,[28] at a time when the majority of local authorities outside Ulster had severed their links with the LGB and were not receiving any grants or loans from public funds, had little practical impact on the administration of local services in most areas. In normal circumstances, three-quarters of the board's staff were taken up by duties relating to the south and west of the country, but because of the action of local authorities in breaking off relations with the board, the position had practically been reversed by mid-1921, with three-quarters of the business and correspondence arising from the north. Many of the staff who had previously dealt with business arising in other areas had been redeployed to old age pensions work (which had fallen into arrears) and to the new section dealing with the scheme of housing for sailors and soldiers which Robinson was personally determined to advance as rapidly as possible.[29] While the Dáil was told that the action at the Custom House had 'finally eliminated the Local Government Board as a serious factor in the situation',[30] Robinson again dismissed the effects of the fire in his 1923 memoirs: he insisted that the burning of the building was 'probably the stupidest thing the Sinn Féin ever did', as the destruction of a building in which every Irishman took a just pride was 'nothing more than an inconvenience ... the office work went on in other buildings at 10 o'clock next morning; there was no deadlock in the work' and the Sinn Féin cause 'was not brought one step nearer its objective'.[31] The Chief Secretary had taken a somewhat similar line in reporting the 'incredible act of vandalism' to the Cabinet on 4 June: a certain amount of temporary inconvenience had been caused, he admitted, and important legal documents and records of permanent value to the Irish nation had been lost, but it was difficult 'to see what compensating benefit the authors of this crime imagine that they have gained for the injury thus inflicted upon the general body of the Irish people, and for despoiling the city of Dublin of a building which was universally regarded as one of the noblest monuments of late eighteenth-century architecture in the world'.[32]

The capture of so many Volunteers and the deaths of others was a severe setback to the Dublin Brigade of the IRA and led some of their leaders, such as Emmet Dalton, to welcome the agreement on a Truce a few weeks later.[33] A very different view of the effects of the fire was however advanced in later years by those who had planned and carried out the operation; Oscar Traynor wrote in 1948 that 'to it has been ascribed, rightly or wrongly, the ending of the war with the forces of occupation' because 'in a matter of about one month, Mr Lloyd George invited Mr de Valera to a conference' – and that eventually led to the Truce.[34] What Traynor did not know, however, was that after Lloyd George, at a Cabinet meeting on 2 June, had paid tribute to the behaviour of the Auxiliaries at the Custom House, the first reaction of his Cabinet to the spectacular attack on the building was to decide – not to sue for a truce – but to introduce martial law throughout the twenty-six counties on 14 July if the southern Parliament failed to function as planned.[35]

In commenting on the 'wanton and costly outrage', the *Irish Times* noted the loss of documents of a legal character and those relating to inland revenue, customs and excise and company registration, which were indispensable for official purposes. It also lamented that 'the loss in documents of historical, local and purely personal interest is irreparable'. Robinson agreed, and personally regretted the loss of archival material, especially the letters and other records dating from the establishment of the Poor Law System in 1838 that had been stored in the basement.[36]

LGB Casualties and Losses

On foot of her claim for compensation, Bertha Davis, widow of the Custom House caretaker, was awarded £1,500 for herself and £500 for each of her three children, together with an annual pension of £45.[37] William Geary, an acting principal clerk was injured during the attack by a bullet which shattered his right elbow; he was forced to spend four months in hospital and then to retire, following which his claim for compensation under the criminal injuries code led to an award of £1,800 plus £150 medical expenses.[38] Another of the board's senior staff, William H. Wilson, claimed £1,000 for gunshot injuries in his left arm and wrist, and a large number of other staff submitted claims ranging in amount from £10 to £50 for loss of property and personal effects. Robinson's claim of £25 represented his loss of some clothes, including a full morning dress-suit, while Edmund Bourke, who had retired from his commissioner position a month earlier, claimed £50 for the loss of 'a third class diplomatic levee dress uniform, complete with sword, case, etc'. In all, claims for compensation totalled almost £2 million by early June, including over £1.25 million claimed by OPW for the loss of the building itself, together with its furniture and fittings, and £100,000 claimed by the LGB for the loss of other furniture and chattels and the cost of reconstructing records which had been destroyed.[39] In order to substantiate the malicious injury claims, the board secretary asked each member of staff on 16 June to provide particulars of the rooms in which they had been working on the day of the fire, together with details of furniture and other contents, listing in particular items of high-class furniture and any other items which were of exceptional value. The individual responses, which were used to compile the return sent to OPW on 23 June, are sufficiently detailed to provide a vivid picture of the offices at lunchtime on the fateful day.[40]

Ernest Leach was the most senior LGB official at the Custom House at the time of the fire, and he became an indirect casualty of the attack on the building. A 62-year-old Englishman who had become assistant secretary of the board in January 1920, Leach – because of 'special services', which Robinson could not prudently specify in writing to the Chief Secretary at the time and the information which he gave on the occasion of the fire – incurred the displeasure of the IRA, was threatened with death, and was advised by the police in Dublin on 1 June to leave the country immediately. He sailed from Dun Laoghaire that night in disguise and travelled under a false name, but even in London he was advised by Scotland Yard that they had heard from two different sources that an IRA gang was lying in wait for him there. In the memoirs which he published in 1923, Robinson explained that Leach had been called on by the auxiliaries, when the staff and the attackers were paraded together after the fire, to identify the civil servants, leaving the raiders to be marched off as prisoners.[41] After his escape to London, Leach was obliged to sell his Dublin house and furniture at a heavy loss, his health broke down under the strain, his wife and family were outlawed and, according to Robinson, his life was utterly ruined as a result of his loyalty to the Crown. He was awarded a pension of £581 a year and a lump-sum payment of almost £2,000.[42]

Reconstruction and Restoration

The Custom House burned for five days in May 1921, after which little was left of the original interior of the building. A few of the rooms on the river front escaped with relatively minor damage, but Robinson's spacious first-floor office on the west front, facing Beresford Place, was destroyed. There were suggestions in the early 1920s that the entire site should be cleared in order to provide employment, but a rebuilding programme eventually got under way in 1925 and was completed in 1929 when the dome was reconstructed. While there was a great deal of internal reorganisation, the new office designed for Robinson's successor – the secretary of the department – was located in exactly the same part of the building where Robinson had operated for nearly twenty-five years. The even more spacious office planned for him in the north block of the new Government Buildings at Upper Merrion Street, completed in March 1922, became the Council Chamber where the new Executive Council met and has since continued in use as the Cabinet Room.

NOTES

1   *Irish Times*, 19 Apr. 1921; the text of the circular was included in a communication from Robinson which was submitted to the Cabinet on 16 Aug. 1921, C.P. 3230, TNA, CAB 24/127.
2   As a frequent traveller to London during the First World War, Robinson had endured the risk that one of the ships on which he travelled would be sunk by a German torpedo as was the RMS Leinster in October 1918 with great loss of life.
3   *Return of Serious Outrages in Ireland up to 1 January 1921*, Cmd. 1165.
4   Peter Hart, *Mick: The Real Michael Collins* (London, 2005), p.220.
5   George Chester Duggan (*Periscope*), 'The Last Days of Dublin Castle', *Blackwood's Magazine*, 1282 (Aug. 1922), vol. 212, pp.174–75.
6   Sir Henry Robinson, *Memories: Wise and Otherwise* (London, 1923), pp.300–301.
7   Correspondence between the LGB, Chief Secretary's Office and the Treasury, March 1920, TNA, T 1/12562.

8   George Chester Duggan, extract from draft of an unpublished book *The Life of a Civil Servant*, p.19, Leon Ó Broin Papers, NLI, MS 31,689.

9   Joseph Brennan Papers, NLI, MS 26,164.

10   Taylor to Long, 4 April 1920, WRO, Long Papers, WRO 947/369/1.

11   Conclusions of a meeting of the Cabinet, 13 Aug. 1920, TNA, CAB/23/22.

12   Robinson, *Memories*, p.294.

13   *Hansard* V, 127, 30 Mar. 1920, 1090–91.

14   Robinson, *Memories*, pp.303–307.

15   Sir Christopher Lynch-Robinson, *The Last of the Irish R.M.s* (London, 1951), p.168.

16   Collins to De Valera 27 June 1921, NAI, DE 2/296.

17   NAI, DE 2/296.

18   Robinson, *Memories*, pp.314–15.

19   Reports of 26 and 29 May and 16 June 1921, TNA, CUST 49/532.

20   Home Office, Directorate of Intelligence, Report on Revolutionary Organisations in the UK, C.P. 2952, 19 May 1921, TNA, CAB 24/123.

21   Oscar Traynor, 'The Burning of the Custom House', *Dublin's Fighting Story, 1916–21* (Tralee, 1948), p.163.

22   Robinson, *Memories*, pp.310–311; *The Leader* (vol. xxviii, no. 15, 23 May 1914), reporting the presentation in its usual sarcastic fashion, noted that Robinson 'wished to be brought into personal contact with the rank and file, but had ensured that neither he nor Birrell was paired with mere papists' in the 1914 golf competition.

23   Department of the Environment and Local Government, Local Government Board for Ireland Minute Book, 1921.

24   Reports of 26 and 29 May and 16 June 1921, TNA, CUST 49/532; 'Under Fire at the Custom House' by P. Ó C. (Pádraig Ó Cinnéide), *The Belvederian*, 1921; Daniel McAleese, BMH, WS 1411, 5 May 1956; Joseph Robins, *Custom House People* (Dublin 1993), pp.92–96; Sean O' Mahony, *The Burning of the Custom House in Dublin, 1921* (Dublin, 2000); Oscar Traynor, 'The Burning of the Custom House', *Dublin's Fighting Story 1916–21* (Tralee, 1948), pp.162–68; David Hogan, *The Four Glorious Years* (Dublin, 1953), pp.273–79.

25   Robinson, *Memories*, pp.313–14; note written on 19 June 1921 by Vanston, Department of the Environment and Local Government, Secretary's Office Papers, Folder No. 2.

26   Robinson to Waterfield, 17 Nov. 1921 and letter from D. I. Ryan to Robinson, 25 Oct. 1921, NAI, FIN 8/31.

27   *Irish Times*, 26 and 27 May 1921.

28   *Irish Bulletin*, vol. 4, no. 98, 27 May 1921; *Irish Times*, 28 May 1921.

29   Barlas to Treasury, 14 Dec. 1921, TNA, T.162/74.

30   *Irish Times*, 25 Oct. 1921, quoting the *Irish Bulletin's* account of a report submitted to the Dáil in August.

31   Robinson, *Memories*, p.310.

32   Survey of the State of Ireland for week ended 28 May, Chief Secretary for Ireland, C.P. 3019, 4 June 1921, TNA, CAB 24/125.

33   Sean Boyne, *Emmet Dalton* (Dublin, 2014), pp. 69–72.

34   Oscar Traynor, 'The Burning of the Custom House' in *Dublin's Fighting Story, 1916–21* (Tralee, 1948), pp.162–68.

35   Thomas Jones, *Whitehall Diary* (Vol. III), pp.72–74.

36   In 1985, when refurbishment works were being carried out at the Custom House, a collection of the original architectural drawings for the workhouses dating from the late 1830s were located in a previously inaccessible lower basement; the drawings, many of which had suffered water damage, are now held in the Irish Architectural Archive.

37   *Irish Times*, 4 Feb. 1922; according to a report in the *Freeman's Journal* on 4 June 1921, Mrs Davis had claimed £12,000 for the loss of her husband and personal property.

38   *Irish Times*, 27 Jan. 1922.

39   *Freeman's Journal*, 4 June 1921; Treasury direction of 1 June 1921, TNA, T.158/3.

40   Department of the Environment and Local Government, Secretary's Office Papers, Folder No. 2 contains the detailed information about furniture etc prepared by LGB staff members in June 1921.

41   Robinson, *Memories*, p. 313; this is consistent with the report presented to the cabinet by General Macready which stated that nearly 200 men and women who left the burning building with their hands up 'were carefully sorted out, being put up at once for identification by the Custom House officials' (C.P. 3003, 31 May 1921, TNA, CAB 24/125).

42   Robinson to Greenwood, 6 July 1921, TNA, T.192/60; Robinson, *Memories*, pp.315–16.

CHAPTER XVII

Drafting and Implementing The Government of Ireland Act

When serious consideration of the Irish situation was resumed by the government in the autumn of 1919, Robinson must have anticipated that the coming into operation of some measure of self-government could not be long delayed. While he had suggested in 1916 that when the First World War was over there would be such financial upheaval that nationalists would be afraid to take on Home Rule and face the situation in Ireland by themselves, that view would clearly have been modified in the light of events since then.[1] Thus, he made no effort to oppose progress towards Home Rule but, instead, made a real attempt to influence the form that new legislation should take. He was, in fact, one of the few officials – if not the only one – within the Dublin administration who became involved in this way and who sought to minimise the effects of the partitionist solution that was emerging.

Walter Long's Cabinet Committee on Ireland

In September 1919, with the Treaty of Versailles already signed and negotiations well under way to conclude a treaty with Turkey, a memorandum from Tom Jones, acting cabinet secretary, and Sir Gordon Hewart, the attorney general, drew the attention of the War Cabinet to the fact that the Government of Ireland Act 1914 would automatically come into operation on the date of the treaty with Turkey – the last of the 'enemy States'.[2] This forced Lloyd George and his Cabinet to consider what was to be done about Ireland bearing in mind that both he and his predecessor had given commitments to the Ulster unionists in the years since 1914 that they would not be forced into submission to a Dublin parliament. When the Cabinet sat to consider the Jones Memorandum on 25 September, they also had before them a memorandum submitted by Walter Long following a visit to Ireland, during which he had consulted with senior officials, including Robinson. Repeal of the 1914 Act was not 'within the range of practical politics', Long advised, but there was need for an early and definite statement of Irish policy which, he argued, should take the form of a declaration that on the adoption of a federal scheme for the UK as a whole, Ireland would receive such parliaments as might be thought necessary – one for Ulster and another for the three southern provinces.[3] The Cabinet agreed that simple repeal of the 1914 Act was not an option but decided that steps should be taken early in the next parliamentary session to prevent the act from coming into operation as it was not acceptable to any of the interests concerned.[4] At a further meeting on 7 October, Long was appointed to chair a cabinet committee which was asked to examine and report on possible policies and to advise on the approach which should be adopted.[5]

Long had told the War Cabinet in mid-1918 that he considered the exclusion of the six northern counties from a Home Rule settlement to be 'the worst settlement of all' and confirmed that his sympathies were with the southern unionists 'who were unable to protect themselves'.[6] In 1919, however, he was among the first to support the idea of establishing two separate entities in Ireland, each with its own parliament. This approach was endorsed by his committee in its third report dated 24 November. Subject to the retention by Westminster of responsibility for key functions such as foreign affairs, defence and external trade, two separate parliaments should be set up, together with a Council of Ireland, which would exercise whatever powers might be conferred on it by the parliaments. In addition, the committee suggested that in order to promote Irish unity, certain services 'which it is specially undesirable to divide' (including virtually all of those for which the Local Government Board was responsible) should be reserved for a year to the Westminster parliament 'in the hopes that within that time the Irish legislatures would have agreed either to transfer the services concerned to the control of the Council or to the control of an all-Ireland legislature constituted for the purpose'. Failing such agreement, the services would automatically be divided between the two parliaments.[7]

When the committee submitted a fourth and final report on 2 December, the idea of temporarily reserving some services had been dropped, following pressure from the Ulster unionists. So that the scheme 'should have more definiteness and finality about it', the services in question (local government and public health, housing, transportation, agriculture and technical instruction, old age pensions, unemployment insurance and employment exchanges) were to be administered from the outset by the two new parliaments, leaving it to them to agree on which services, if any, might be transferred to the Council of Ireland.[8] When Lloyd George outlined these revised proposals in the House of Commons on 22 December, he emphasised that it was still the wish of the government that 'every opportunity shall be given to Irishmen, if they desire it, to establish unity'. He also suggested that the Council of Ireland could serve not only as an invaluable link between the two parts of Ireland, but as an agency through which 'certain common services, which it is highly undesirable to divide' could be administered as a single service.[9] Given the events of the years since 1912 and the fact that Ulster unionists had never sought a parliament of their own but wished to remain as an integral part of the United Kingdom, it is difficult to imagine what reasonable grounds Lloyd George and his government might have had for believing that representatives of Ulster would be prepared, voluntarily, to operate a transfer provision of this kind and to share responsibility for the administration of services with a southern parliament, likely to be controlled by Sinn Féin. Walter Long saw a 'real weakness' in the proposals about the Council and, believing that another effort should be made to deal with the issue, submitted a memorandum to the Cabinet Committee on 1 January, arguing that for practical reasons all transport and diseases of animals functions should be assigned to it.[10]

'An End to all Hopes of a Parliament of Ireland'

Henry Robinson, who had been raised to the rank of baronet in the 1920 New Year honours and whose sympathies were always with the southern unionists, had opposed partition in 1914 and 1916. He held a realistic view of the likely outcome if the government's proposals in relation to the Council of Ireland were accepted and believed that they would do nothing to mitigate the effects of partition. However, he seems not to have had any opportunity to influence matters before the House of Commons announcement on 22 December. A few days before that, an obviously well-informed special correspondent of *The Times*, in one of a series of articles on the state of Ireland, wrote about the need for guidance for

Lord French and Macpherson, as strangers to Ireland, by men familiar with local conditions. The article went on to suggest that the Under-Secretary, Sir James MacMahon, was 'too modest and too moulded in the traditions of the civil service to force advice on them', whereas Sir Henry Robinson was a wise counsellor of unionist tradition and a man who 'by general admission, stands out, by his ability, from all other permanently employed servants of the crown in Ireland' but, the writer concluded, 'is he consulted?'[11] The validity of this anonymous assessment of the two men was demonstrated a few weeks later when Walter Long sought to have the final draft of the Government of Ireland Bill examined by people who were thoroughly conversant with the Irish problem and asked the Irish authorities to advise if there were other functions which could be assigned with advantage to the Council.[12]

After Ian Macpherson had been instructed by Downing Street 'to set my departments at work upon the details', he consulted MacMahon and Robinson about the bill in January 1920, but he instructed that it was not to be circulated to other departments. MacMahon was asked to submit a memorandum on the financial aspects as well as his general observations, and after making discreet enquiries, to embody his views in a memorandum, which could be submitted to the Cabinet Committee.[13] On 20 January he duly submitted a memorandum on financial matters which was prepared for him by Joseph Brennan,[14] but his brief comments on the general issue fell far short of what might have been expected from the most senior official in Dublin Castle and simply reflected his well-known nationalist sympathies and his admitted friendship with members of Sinn Féin:

> The Bill, as outlined in the Prime Minister's speech, has aroused no expression of approval from any people of political weight and influence in Ireland and there is a general feeling among all constitutional nationalists to whom I have spoken that the measure is simply unacceptable and therefore not to be discussed seriously. The absence of substantial financial advantages to overcome the disability of the objectionable partition proposals is regarded as an insuperable obstacle to acceptance of the measure by any of the nationalist elements.[15]

These comments were unlikely to have been welcomed in London, particularly because MacMahon made no effort to suggest what might be done to meet the difficulties he had outlined or to suggest alternatives. Robinson, on the other hand – and possibly with the encouragement of

Long who was in Dublin for a few days in January – took full advantage of the opportunity to make a last-ditch-effort to have the proposals amended and to avert a scheme which, as he saw it, would result in permanent partition. He prepared a lengthy memorandum arguing for the assignment of a list of twenty specified functions to the Council of Ireland, and this was submitted directly to the Cabinet on 20 January, evidence of the status he held at that stage in the eyes of ministers and of the significance attached to his views on political matters well outside his own civil service brief.[16]

Robinson's memorandum began by asserting that it was unlikely that a northern parliament would delegate any powers to a council sitting in Dublin and, if the powers of the council were to be as limited as was then proposed, it was doubtful whether northern delegates would even be elected to it, or bother to attend. But if they did attend at the start, history was likely to repeat itself. Recalling how the representatives of some of the northern county councils had been persuaded by the LGB to attend the General Council of County Councils on its formation in 1899 but had withdrawn in 1904 when political matters began to be discussed, he argued that northern delegates to a Council of Ireland would probably find the 'anti-English atmosphere' too strong for them, and withdraw after a few months in the absence of definite responsibilities to be fulfilled or patronage to be exercised. He went on:

> If the same thing should happen in the event of the Government of Ireland Bill becoming law, it would be an end to all hopes of a parliament of Ireland, which is the underlying principle of the whole Bill upon which all hope of a final settlement is based. To avert this danger, it is essential to vest in the Council of Ireland full powers over all matters relating to Ireland as a whole (except those specially reserved under the Bill) where sectarian considerations do not come in, but which affect the interests of the North indirectly, to such an extent that the northerners cannot afford to keep outside the council and must be brought into association with the southern delegates in order to ensure that the North participates in the services administered by the Council of Ireland.

The services that would be vested in the council under Robinson's proposals included some which he deemed to be 'of equal interest to the north and south' or which it would be impossible or unnecessary to split up. He included in this category the National Gallery, the National Library, the National Museum, the School of Art, the College of Science, the Botanic Gardens and the Geological Survey. For much the same reasons, and on the general principle that certain departments could be administered by the central authority without inconvenience or danger of political controversies, he suggested that the Commissioners for Charitable Donations and Bequests, the Public Trustee, the Registrar General, the Public Record Office, the Registry of Deeds, and the Office of Arms should all come within the responsibility of the council. His proposals also covered prisons, lunatic asylums, labour exchanges, sea fisheries, railways and canals, and diseases of animals, for all of which a reasonable case could be made. However, his remaining proposals involving the Congested Districts Board and the Dublin Metropolitan Police were difficult to defend: as matters stood, he conceded that no part of the congested districts was to be included in the area of the northern parliament, but he envisaged that congested parts of Donegal, Cavan and Monaghan might come under the control of that parliament in the future. In relation to the DMP, his rather flimsy and anachronistic argument was that the inhabitants of the north and the south were all equally concerned in the maintenance of law and order in the metropolis.

It is clear from their subsequent remarks in Parliament that a number of ministers must have had considerable sympathy for at least some of Robinson's proposals, but his was still a lone voice on the official side in early 1920 when there was no nationalist representation at Westminster. Inevitably, therefore, his proposals were rejected on 30 January by a subcommittee of the Cabinet Committee on Ireland which, in addition to advancing specific objections to some of the proposals, considered that an issue of principle was involved. Robinson's scheme 'might be regarded as an infringement of the pledge to Ulster … [and] the best way to induce the north and south to begin to co-operate was to place upon them the responsibility at the very outset of deciding whether these obviously unitary services should be divided, or whether they should not agree to transfer them immediately to the Council of Ireland'.[17]

The Bill in Parliament

When Macpherson opened the second stage debate on the Bill to provide for the better Government of Ireland in the House of Commons on 29 March, he acknowledged that 'as a matter of practical business it would, of course, be in the interests of administration and economy to transfer many Irish services' to the Council of Ireland, including the Local Government Board, but he asserted that to do so would violate the fundamental principle laid down by the Prime Minister in that it would place 'the six counties ... under a legislative body or parliament acting outside the six counties [and] this cannot be done without the assent of the six counties'.[18] As the three-day debate progressed, it became clear that Macpherson's hope that the council might become 'a real stepping stone on the way to Irish unity' was no more than what the southern unionist MP, Sir Maurice Dockrell, described as 'a beautiful dream'. The council would only be 'a fleshless and bloodless skeleton', according to Herbert Asquith, while for the Ulster unionists, Captain Charles Craig firmly declared at an early stage in the proceedings that there was not the slightest hope that the scheme provided for in the bill would lead to union within the lifetime of any man in the House.[19] Nevertheless, Lloyd George, in winding up the second stage debate, had not 'the faintest doubt' that it would be a mistake to divide responsibility for certain functions, including local government and – completely ignoring Robinson's more realistic appraisal of the situation – declared that he had no doubt at all that if representatives of both sides could 'discuss things in a fair and reasonable spirit, a great many of these powers will be handed over' to the council.[20]

As the bill was slowly passing through its remaining stages at Westminster, the escalating level of violence in Ireland was causing serious concern to members of the Cabinet, not all of whom were fully convinced that the arrangements proposed in the bill were satisfactory. Nevertheless, it was amended only to the extent that the Council of Ireland, rather than the two parliaments, was given responsibility for three of the services – railways, fisheries administration and diseases of animals – which had been included in Robinson's January scheme. However, even these relatively minor adjustments were attacked by Carson and Craig, proving – if proof were needed – that Robinson's assessment of the likely future conduct of the Ulster unionists and of the council's prospects of development was entirely accurate. Robinson was not personally involved as the bill was debated at Westminster, although Walter Long, who was primarily responsible for piloting the bill through the House of Commons, would have liked to have him present to support him during the debates because, he told Hamar Greenwood on 30 April, 'in my judgment he is by far the ablest and most reliable official that we have in Ireland'. Long was forced, however, to accept that it was essential for Greenwood, who had taken up duty in Dublin as Chief Secretary only two weeks earlier, to have Robinson's services available to him so he suggested that Robinson should find someone else who would be available in the House to advise on any pitfalls with which ministers might be confronted.[21] In the event, the task fell to Andrew Magill, who had served as private secretary to Birrell, Duke and briefly to Shortt.

Elections: North and South Together – or North First?

When the Government of Ireland Bill became law on 23 December 1920 it provided for two separate administrative areas, each with its own parliament, but no effort was made to establish what Robinson later described as 'an Ulster boundary rectified for sectarian purposes' by resorting to rural district and/or poor law union boundaries as had been proposed in 1914.[22] Instead, on the insistence of the Ulster unionists, an area of six complete counties – rather than a nine-county area – was prescribed because, in the words of Captain Craig MP, the unionist majority in a nine-county area would be reduced 'to such a level that no sane man would undertake to carry on a parliament with it ... we quite frankly admit that we cannot hold the nine counties ... it would be impossible for us to govern those [other] three counties'.[23] Although this basic political decision dictated where the north–south boundary was to be drawn, it had been necessary to provide, in the fifth schedule of the act, for some considerable grouping and regrouping of existing areas in order to define constituencies for the election of 46 members to the Westminster parliament, 128 to the new southern parliament and 52 to the northern parliament. It was Robinson who decided the detail of these electoral arrangements: 'Every alteration of a boundary for local government or parliamentary purposes has been made by me personally and the whole of the parliamentary areas in the act of 1920 are mine', he declared in December 1921.[24] However, the constituency arrangements in which he took obvious pride were later criticised as a shameless gerrymander.

Having devoted more than a year to the drafting and passage of the bill through Parliament, the Cabinet were naturally anxious to ensure that there would be minimum delay in bringing it into operation. Following some preliminary Cabinet discussion of the matter on 30 December,[25] Greenwood submitted a memorandum on 12 January dealing with the various issues on which decisions were needed and, in particular, raising the question of whether elections to the northern parliament might be held in advance of those in the south.[26] He submitted a progress report on 27 February in which he advised that the first and most important work to be completed was the adaptation of the existing electoral law to provide for the use of PR in the elections to the two Houses of Commons and the formulation of schemes for the election of senators.[27] This work, he reported, was being undertaken by the LGB, which had already held a conference of returning officers to instruct them in the method of counting votes under the PR system. Reporting on that conference to Anderson some days earlier, Robinson told him that the under-sheriffs who were to act as returning officers were 'rather glad for the sake of appearances to be disassociated from the Castle ... and to be able to bring their difficulties quietly and unobtrusively to my little gang of experts here' (i.e. at the Custom House), and while some of them in the south were disposed to show the white feather, 'I have harangued them as to their duties and as to the support they will get from the government and have left them in a much better temper.'[28] Greenwood's memorandum of 27 February advised the Cabinet that Robinson had again raised the question of whether the elections should be held and the parliaments established simultaneously in both parts of Ireland, or should the northern elections be held in advance. As reported to the Cabinet, Robinson's view (which Greenwood seemed to favour) was that much would be gained if the northern elections came first, with the parliament being summoned and formally opened in Belfast three months before the process began in the south. By that time, Robinson anticipated that conditions in the south would be more favourable than they were likely to be in the spring and early summer. Besides, 'the actual establishment of the parliament and government in the north will be indisputable proof that the Government of Ireland Act is a reality and the independence of Northern Ireland an established fact' – all of which would 'demonstrate, as nothing else would, to the whole world and to southern Ireland in particular, the fullness and importance of the powers that have been delegated by the act'. Whether Robinson realised it or not, this same view had been expressed in the House of Commons almost a year earlier by Bonar Law, who had argued that with the northern parliament working satisfactorily, there will be before the eyes of the southern nationalists 'the evidence that they can have the same self-government the moment they like it ... I do not believe when they see before them these powers working in the rest of Ireland, that they will refuse to accept the situation and take advantage of them'.[29]

Robinson's belief that more favourable conditions for elections would exist in the south later in 1921 was not based on a view of the security situation. Instead, his submission was that, by going ahead first with the northern elections, southerners would realise that there was no hope of preventing partition by holding out against the elections in the south. Secondly – more or less as Bonar Law had argued – the jealousy of the southerners would be stirred by their contemplation of 'the vast powers' of the northern parliament and by the patronage in its hands. Thirdly, the crisis in local government would be at its worst in late summer, with public services suspended and workmen unpaid, prompting the public to insist on the election of a parliament which would take action to prevent destitution, unemployment and the collapse of trade. And finally, by holding elections on different dates, military forces could be concentrated where elections were being held, instead of being spread thinly around the whole country. Robinson also believed (wrongly as it transpired) that Sinn Féin would not put forward any candidates, and would attempt to frustrate the elections by seizing the ballot boxes, burning the polling booths and intimidating 'partition candidates'.[30]

Looked at objectively in the light of the situation in the first quarter of 1921 – with almost 2,000 IRA men interned[31] and more police and military being killed and wounded than in any previous quarter[32] – it must have been difficult for ministers to see much merit in the arguments deployed by Robinson in his attempt to force the issue of postponement back onto the Cabinet agenda. He clearly underestimated the determination of the republican forces to press forward their demands and to resist the partitionist solution embodied in the 1920 Act. His submission to Greenwood must also be seen as an intervention on behalf of the southern unionists who, at a meeting of the Anti-Partition League in Dublin a few weeks later, confirmed that they strongly deprecated any attempt to bring the act into operation in the south in the conditions then prevailing.[33] In parallel submissions to Anderson, Robinson begged him to support his suggestion that the elections should be postponed because 'whether you are going to see a settlement of the Irish question this autumn mainly depends upon the Chief's answer to this suggestion'. He went on to say that 'if you delay the southern elections till the contagion of patronage has infected the southern blood, and until financial necessity is shown, you would have a good fighting chance of getting a decent lot to come forward'.[34] But Anderson greatly doubted whether postponement of the southern elections would have the desired effect – and Mark Sturgis, one of his staff at the Castle, was not impressed by the proposition that new candidates could be induced to come forward, even though Robinson told him that John Healy, editor of the *Irish Times*, to whom he had spoken about the idea, was enthusiastic. Sturgis told his diary on 21 January that:

> Robinson was in in the morning full of his idea that we must propagand the financial state of the country just before the election and get all the businessmen in a sort of panic enthusiasm to cry to Hell with politics, let us have a Business Government. I argued with him that this would be well enough but before you can have a Business Government you must have Business MPs and before you have Business MPs you must have Business candidates – and where were they? And will we get 'em?[35]

Notwithstanding his principal advisers' doubts, Greenwood opted to submit another memorandum to the Cabinet summarising Robinson's views, and the issue was considered on 3 March. However, having discussed various options, the Cabinet decided that the provisions of the act relating to the two parliaments should come into force on a single appointed day in early May.[36] But that was not the end of the matter because, while Craig continued to press for early elections in the north, the leader of the southern unionists, Lord Midleton, was allowed to attend a Cabinet meeting on 8 March at which he rehearsed the argument that the elections in the south should be deferred 'until the resistance of the rebels in large districts of the south and west, which had recently increased, had been overcome'.[37] General Macready was of the same view, arguing that holding elections in the south was 'little less than folly' unless a truce with Sinn Féin could first be arranged. He also warned of serious potential outrages if there were an attempt to hold these elections.[38] Some weeks earlier, Sir Warren Fisher, having spent six days in Dublin, bluntly told both Bonar Law and the Prime Minister that he could not see how, in the prevailing circumstances, the effort to assemble a southern parliament could be 'anything more than a fiasco at every stage': noting Greenwood's – and Robinson's – hopes that candidates 'of the proper colour' could be got to stand for election, he wrote that he was 'not quite sure how ... their election is to be ensured' unless by stationing 'Black and Tans in and about the polling booths'.[39]

The election issue was debated again by the Cabinet on 22 and 24 March, but the earlier decision was allowed to stand.[40] The discussions were being complicated at that stage by suggestions that the Sinn Féin leaders, or at least some of them, might be more amenable than they had been towards a settlement, and by reports that notwithstanding the continuing high level of violence, the IRA was facing defeat in some areas. The decision to bring the provisions of the act into operation on 3 May and to hold elections for the two parliaments later in May was announced in the House of Commons on 5 April.[41] Before that, Robinson had accepted defeat, telling Anderson on 26 March: 'All right – we must only do our damnedest to carry through both elections on the same day and shall spare no pains to make it a success.' He expected to have 'a desperate job in keeping up the hearts of the southern returning officers who are in an awful funk and who pinned all their hopes on the Ulster elections being held first'. Moreover, he complained bitterly to Anderson that in settling the dates and schedules for nominations and polling, he had been guided by legal men – Greer and Quekett, both based in London – who had no appreciation of the abnormal character of the elections and of the difficulties faced by those who had to conduct them.[42]

'A Temporary Cessation of Military Activity'

The desirability of announcing a truce to take effect during the period of the elections was discussed by the Cabinet on 24 March when it was agreed that consideration of the question would be resumed at a meeting after Easter.[43] As an input to that meeting, a handwritten note was sent to Lloyd George by Greenwood on 17 April, telling him that:

> Sir Henry Robinson, whom you saw in the Cabinet room three weeks ago ... reports that the S. Féiners are losing ground. That is my view. He and I agree that one must not judge this struggle and its present stage by murders only. Please do not make any pronouncement about truce or elections until we have a talk. There is no need to rush in these matters.[44]

When the Cabinet next met on 21 April, it agreed that the government should not, for the present, take the initiative in proposing a cessation of hostilities.[45] But just over a week later, Lloyd George instigated yet another review of the situation arising from concerns about (i) the security situation in the previous month when IRA activity had reached its peak, (ii) the obvious failure to restore law and order which the military advisers had confidently promised to achieve by May and (iii) the belief that if the elections went ahead, Sinn Féin would win the vast majority of the seats in the southern parliament. Greenwood found himself in great difficulty when asked to advise the Cabinet, noting that the attorney general, Denis Henry, was for going ahead with the elections, that Sir John Anderson, who had previously been against going ahead, was now, on balance, in favour, but that Robinson was still against, making him then the only official who continued to hold that line. Once again, although some ministers had serious reservations, the Cabinet decided that there was no option but to go ahead with both sets of elections: there was no guarantee that things would be any better in a few months, and if those elected in the south refused to work the act, that was their business.[46]

The Cabinet then resumed discussion of various proposals which had been made for a truce and at a meeting on 11 May they directed that Greenwood, who was in Ireland, should be telegraphed for his views and those of his principal civil and military advisers on the issue.[47] At a special meeting on the following evening, Lloyd George read out memoranda which had just come by telegraph, giving Greenwood's views and those of his advisers on what the Cabinet preferred to describe as 'a temporary cessation of military activity'. The official Cabinet conclusions note that there was 'an exhaustive review of the closely-balanced political and military considerations involved', and of the powerful reasons which were adduced both for and against, before it was decided by a majority that it would be a mistake to take the initiative in suspending military activities.[48] The official conclusions give no information on the positions adopted by different individuals, but the account of the two-hour-long discussion in the diary of Thomas Jones, then assistant secretary to the Cabinet, is more revealing.[49] Greenwood and General Macready, he records, were firmly against a truce, but Anderson 'was favourable to a cessation of hostilities'.

Anderson's memorandum of 11 May – clearly a rushed, handwritten one, of which a copy is preserved among the Lloyd George papers at the Parliamentary Archives – makes it clear that while he had opposed a truce when the question was mooted in December 1920, he believed that the position had entirely changed since then.[50] He reported that there was a growing desire for peace among the great mass of the people, and the whole country was thrilled by the recent meeting between Craig and de Valera, whose message – published in the last edition of the *Sunday Independent* – displayed statesmanship and generosity. In these circumstances, he felt very strongly that the time was ripe for a spontaneous declaration by the government to the effect that the Crown forces would, for a period of one month, 'confine themselves as far as possible within the limits of their ordinary peacetime activities'. He believed that there was an unrivalled opportunity for a *beau geste* of this kind and that it would be a thousand pities to let it slip. He stressed that he was greatly strengthened in his view 'by the knowledge that it is fully shared by Sir John Ross [a high court judge since 1896 who was soon to become lord chancellor] and Sir Henry Robinson, both of them men with an exceptionally wide knowledge of Ireland and by no means pacifist in their general outlook'. Although Jones recorded that Edwin Montagu, then secretary of state for India, hoped that the views of Anderson and Robinson would prevail, and although support for a truce was also expressed by Winston Churchill and a number of others, Greenwood felt that the best way of helping de Valera and Craig to settle the Irish question was by 'going straight and steadily on'.[51] The Cabinet majority supported this view and were unwilling to agree to the unilateral cessation of military activity which Robinson favoured. Ironically, at the time of the meeting, the IRA in Dublin were well advanced in their preparations for the assault – prompted by de Valera – on his department's headquarters at the Custom House, which they succeeded in destroying two weeks later.

The General Election

Polling day for constituencies in both parts of Ireland (if seats were contested) was to be 24 May, and the new parliaments were to meet on 7 June in Belfast and on 28 June in Dublin. Arrangements for the elections in both areas were made by the LGB, including the appointment and the remuneration of returning officers, the provision of stamping instruments, ballot boxes and voting compartments, and the organisation of briefing sessions at the Custom House for returning officers. The board's inspector of audits, J. W. Drury, who had become the in-house expert on PR, had retired in March but was retained for some months after that to supervise the planning and conduct of the elections. Robinson was also personally involved: Sturgis records that he was in the Castle on 16 April for a meeting about the elections, although he wondered if an unnecessary fuss was being made about polling booths, as not many seats were likely to be contested.[52] Months before the election date, the nationalist press was complaining that 'a shameless system of gerrymandering had been resorted to in order to increase the unionist representation'. On this occasion, the complaint related not to the actual boundaries of constituencies (except those in Belfast) but rather to the fact that, to maximise unionist representation, the counties of Fermanagh and Tyrone, with their catholic majorities, had been combined to form one large eight-member constituency, while Derry city and county had also been grouped to form a five-member constituency.[53] When the results were declared, the *Irish News* complained that constituencies had been 'scientifically and shamelessly gerrymandered', giving unionists an overall total of forty seats in the six counties against a combined total of twelve for their opponents.[54] It was difficult, however, to sustain this charge except in relation to Belfast where gerrymandering was 'more refined' than elsewhere, resulting in only one seat out of sixteen for nationalists who had won 23 per cent of the votes.[55]

There was a strong likelihood that the southern parliament would be controlled by Sinn Féin and would refuse to act in accordance with the 1920 Act. This led to some preliminary consideration in March 1921 of the establishment, as a last resort, of a form of Crown colony government with nominated members of the Privy Council and others taking the place of a government and parliament. When the Earl of Midleton pointed out to the Cabinet that 'the future usefulness in Irish government of those who might accept service' on such a council would be prejudiced, and that every man on the council would be a marked man,[56] it was suggested at a subsequent Cabinet meeting that if it were not found possible to utilise the services of public men, a council consisting of nominated soldiers or civil servants could be set up.[57] This idea was taken a stage further towards the end of May when it was decided to send military reinforcements to Ireland and to make preparations for the possible establishment of Crown colony government in the south and the application of a strict martial law regime in parts of the area.[58] The subsequent agreement on a truce suspended consideration of drastic measures like these, which would almost certainly have involved the appointment of Robinson as one of the members of such a government.

Preparing 'To Hand Over the Irish Civil Service in Good Working Order'

While Robinson was attempting in the early months of 1921 to influence decisions on the timing of elections to the new parliaments, his official position required him to become involved in the process of civil service reorganisation, which had been in progress since the summer of 1920, and in the designation of staff to serve each of the new governments. The British officials at Dublin Castle saw it as part of their duty to be ready, when the Government of Ireland Act came into operation, 'to hand over the Irish civil service in good working order, with staffs thoroughly overhauled and placed on a proper footing as regards pay, grading, number, and conditions of tenure and service'.[59] Robinson agreed in September 1920 that 'we must hand over the LGB as a going concern with its normal staff', but he delayed for more than a year the efforts made by Alexander P. Waterfield and his colleagues at the Castle to reach full agreement on the application to his organisation of a scheme which entailed the standardisation of grades carrying out clerical and administrative work, the regarding of individual staff members and the adjustment of salaries, all in accordance with a report of the National Whitley Council.[60] Waterfield experienced difficulty in several departments with regard to reaching agreement on the number of administrative, executive and clerical posts because, while some managers favoured reliance on a corps of administrative posts filled by graduate entrants, a majority of the staff preferred schemes based to a greater extent on executive posts as these schemes would open up prospects of advancement for a greater number of them.[61] At an early stage, Robinson nailed his colours to the mast, declaring that he personally had 'the strongest conviction – based upon past experience – which nothing will shake, that the administrative scheme is the one best suited for the class of work that comes before [the LGB]'.[62] However, following an inspection of the nature of the work being carried out at the Custom House, Robinson's draft scheme was rejected by Waterfield, who insisted in December 1920 that the LGB should be classed as an executive rather than an administrative organisation. This would involve having a substantial proportion of the work carried out by staff in the new junior executive (JEO) and higher executive officer (HEO) grades, with only six posts remaining in the principal (head of division) grades and with the entire elimination of five deputy principal posts held by men who had been promoted by Robinson to these positions.[63]

Robinson was furious that he had not been consulted before these conclusions were arrived at, and having managed since 1898, with the support of the Treasury, to increase the number of first division posts in his organisation to a level which exceeded that of any other department in Ireland, he told Waterfield that it was 'deplorable that a system built up by years of careful study and work should be swept away after a few hours' inquiry on the advice of two officials who have no knowledge of the past history of the department'. He repeated his 'profound conviction' that an executive scheme would be ruinous to the working of local government in Ireland[64] but, after the Treasury had trenchantly rejected his criticism of their procedure and conceded some adjustments, he conceded in April 1921 that 'we must get on as best we can with an executive establishment'.[65] In July, Waterfield was able to report to London that agreement had been reached with the heads of departments in practically every case, but after the Truce he was still troubled by the delay in finalising the LGB scheme. He urged Robinson at that stage to resolve the impasse because 'we are bound to do our best to straighten things out as far as we can for our credit as administrators and in the interests of the new government'.[66] Eventually an agreed LGB scheme was submitted to the Treasury and formal sanction to its retrospective implementation was conveyed at the end of September 1921.[67] The scheme provided for only five administrative-level posts in addition to the secretary and assistant secretary, with fourteen posts at HEO level, thirty-five at EO/higher clerical level, and eighty-eight posts at the lower clerical level, into which fifty-one assistant clerks had been assimilated.[68] This total of 144 was, of course, increased significantly by the addition of auditors, general, medical, and temporary inspectors, and the large numbers serving as messengers, cleaners and firelighters and other subordinate grades at the different offices occupied by the board.

Still unhappy about aspects of the scheme when it was approved in September 1921, Robinson continued until the very last minute to press the case for more favourable terms for the assimilation of particular groups of staff to posts within the new structure, forcing an exasperated Waterfield to tell him on 31 March 1922 – his last day in office – that he could not possibly strain a point to allow appointments of four newly-graded higher executive officers to be further backdated for salary purposes.[69] Waterfield was particularly concerned to avoid giving the provisional government any impression that individuals were being 'fixed up' before 1 April. For this reason he had already told Robinson that it would be better to do nothing about some promotions until the position had been discussed with the new ministers.[70] Throughout the reorganisation process, Robinson had also continued to press for better terms for favourites of his own. He succeeded in having the salary of his son, Adrian, advanced to the £700 maximum of the inspector grade before his transfer to a position in Belfast in 1921, and he managed to persuade the Treasury that there were special reasons for promoting Major George Harris, one of his former private secretaries, to be a principal clerk.[71] He failed, however, to have Charles W. Grant, the legal assistant who had distinguished himself on the occasion of the Custom House fire, placed on a higher salary scale. More significantly, he failed to prevent the winding up of the large staff unit which he had built up since 1919 to implement the urban housing programme. As late as January 1922 he was arguing that the unit should be allowed to continue because of the serious political importance attached by all sides to the urban housing issue and because the matter should be left for decision by the provisional government.[72] He was still smarting about his defeat by Waterfield and his colleagues on this and other staffing issues when he published his memoirs in 1923.[73] Waterfield and his staff, he claimed, had no experience of what the Irish civil servants had been through:

> All the public departments had already been cut to the bone in pursuance of Treasury circulars on war economies, and the civil servants who had spent the best part of their lives in the service of England, had hoped for some sympathy and protection from the British Treasury when matters came to be wound up, whereas, on the contrary, they now found themselves down and out, faced with the new peril of being at the mercy of soulless young Englishmen bent on further retrenchments at all hazards, who seemed to think the Irish civil servants had little to complain about if they were not thrown penniless into the street.

Planning for the Transfer of Services 'Without Breach of Continuity'

As far back as January 1921, Macpherson had been directed by the Cabinet to call on public departments to examine their positions under the 1920 Act and to report as soon as possible on the adjustments that would need to be made to enable the two new Irish governments to assume their functions.[74] All departments and offices were subsequently asked to provide material on which orders in council could be framed to give effect to the transfer of services 'in full working order and without breach of continuity'.[75] Departments and offices were also asked to prepare provisional lists of staff available for transfer to the two governments on the understanding that final decisions would rest with the civil service committee which was to be set up under the 1920 Act.[76] Robinson responded promptly to this request, sending Anderson draft schedules showing the allocation of the board's staff complement to serve two separate boards but naming the personnel concerned was, he said, a matter on which he would require a personal conference with the Chief Secretary and Anderson. He advised that, with the exception of a few inspectors and auditors, all of the staff were engaged in the administration of services in both north and south. He had instructed, however, that as from 1 April, all records and accounts were to be maintained separately for north and south and that all staff were to be provisionally allocated to the work in one or other of the new areas, without prejudice to whatever decisions would ultimately be made by the civil service committee.[77]

As he had often done on such occasions, Robinson did not confine himself to providing the information which had been requested but went on to raise issues of a more general nature.[78] Who, he asked, was going to meet the cost of moving 500 or more civil servants and their families and furniture to Belfast, all of which he calculated would cost up to £20,000? A more important point, however, was his belief that it was almost impossible at the time to find housing in Belfast and the surrounding districts, citing the example of one of the board's inspectors who had recently transferred to Belfast (this was his own son) who had failed to find any suitable vacant house. Because of this shortage, and because hotel accommodation in Belfast was insufficient and inferior, it would be absolutely impossible, he advised, to provide accommodation for the sudden influx of 500 civil servants and their families for many months or even years after the appointed day – but he offered a solution:

> The only way that I can see of getting out of this difficulty is to commence by adopting the Irish Office precedent – where there is a skeleton Ministry in London with a working staff in Dublin, and correspondence is carried on by special wire or telephone, with occasional visits from Heads of Departments backwards and forwards. To follow this precedent in the case of the Local Government Board, for instance, the Minister would have an office

in Belfast, with a private secretary and one of the permanent heads, and the Ulster portion of the Local Government Board staff should be given one section of this building [the Custom House in Dublin] or transferred to the offices of the Irish Council or other convenient place.

Given the political background and the fact that large numbers of applications for positions in the new northern administration were flowing in since early January to Sir James Craig, the Prime Minister designate, giving him 'a large number from which to select', Robinson's solution to a possible accommodation problem was never likely to have been countenanced by the northern unionists.[79] In any case, his concern about the additional demand for housing in Belfast was misplaced as the number of civil servants who transferred from Dublin to Belfast was far fewer that he had anticipated.

Northern Ireland began to emerge as a reality when the northern parliament met for the first time on 7 June. On the same day, a proclamation issued by the Lord Lieutenant specified the seven departments to be established in the north, appointed their ministers and parliamentary secretaries and listed the functions that were to be transferred to them at a later stage. One of the seven was to be a ministry of home affairs – in effect, a combined ministry of local government and justice – with responsibility for law and justice, prisons, reformatory and industrial schools, firearms and explosives, roads, road transport and bridges, health, local government and home affairs.[80] It was expressly stated that the functions of the ministry were to include those administered by the Local Government Board for Ireland and that a 'Local Government Board for Northern Ireland' was to be attached to the ministry. As a first step towards establishing the ministry, Craig personally got the approval of the Prime Minister and the Chief Secretary at the end of May for the appointment of Samuel Watt as its permanent secretary.[81] Although serving on loan since mid-1920 at the admiralty where Craig had been financial secretary, Watt had served in the LGB from 1901 to 1918, including a period spent as Robinson's private secretary. The fact that he was a native of County Down, a committed unionist, a protégé of Walter Long, and held hard-line views on security matters meant that his selection to head the new ministry must have been comforting for unionists. According to his friend, Andrew Magill, who came from Dublin as one of his assistant secretaries, Watt was of very frail physique but plunged into the herculean task of organising the new ministry with untrained and inadequate staff.[82] In Dublin, by contrast, the commencement of the 1920 Act, the uncontested general election and the abortive meeting of the parliament of Southern Ireland had no immediate effect. Until Transfer of Functions Orders were made late in 1921, Robinson and his colleagues continued to conduct LGB business for the whole of Ireland at the temporary offices provided for them after the Custom House fire and seem to have done little or nothing to facilitate the setting up of the new northern ministry.

NOTES

1   Robinson to Long, 27 July 1916, WRO, Long Papers, WRO 947/331.
2   Government of Ireland Act: Date of putting into operation, memorandum G.T. 8210, Sept 1919, TNA, CAB 24/89.
3   Situation in Ireland: memorandum G.T. 8215 by Mr Long, 24 Sept. 1919, TNA, CAB 24/89.
4   Minutes of a meeting of the War Cabinet no. 624, 25 Sept. 1919, TNA, CAB 23/12.
5   Ireland: Joint Memorandum by Lord French and Mr Macpherson G.T. 8227, 25 Sept. 1919, TNA, CAB 24/89; Minutes of a meeting of the War Cabinet no. 628, 7 Oct.1919, TNA CAB 23/12.
6   Minutes of a meeting of the War Cabinet no. 453, 29 July 1918, TNA, CAB 23/7.
7   Report and Proceedings of the Cabinet Committee on Ireland, Third Report, 24 Nov. 1919, TNA, CAB 24/68; Memorandum for the Cabinet on Third Report of the Committee, C.P. 190, 24 Nov. 1919, TNA, CAB 24/93.
8   Committee on Ireland, Fourth Report, C.P. 247, 2 Dec. 1919, TNA, CAB 24/94.
9   *Hansard* V, 123, 22 Dec. 1919, 1168–1223.
10   Committee on Ireland, Memorandum by Mr Long on Self Government for Ireland, C.I. 46, 1 Jan. 1920, TNA, CAB 27/69.
11   Reprinted in *Irish Times*, 16 Dec. 1919.
12   Committee on Ireland, Memorandum by Mr Long on Self Government for Ireland, C.I. 46, 1 Jan. 1920, TNA, CAB 27/69.
13   Macpherson to MacMahon, 12 Jan. 1920 and telegram of 16 Jan. 1920, NLI, Joseph Brennan Papers, MS 26,203(1).
14   When the memorandum attracted favourable comment in London, Brennan was told by MacMahon that 'the credit is yours and I shall see that you get it in proper time'.
15   MacMahon to Macpherson, 20 Jan. 1920, NLI, Joseph Brennan Papers, MS 26,203(1).
16   Committee on Ireland, Powers of the Council of Ireland, Memorandum by the Right Hon. Sir Henry Robinson, Bart., C.I. 48, 17 Jan. 1920, TNA, CAB 27/69.
17   Committee on Ireland, Report of the sub-committee, C.I. 55, 30 Jan. 1921, TNA, CAB 27/69.
18   *Hansard* V, 127, 29 Mar. 1920, 929–30.
19   *Hansard* V, 127, 30 Mar. 1920, 1112–14, 1167–68; 29 Mar. 1920, 984–85.
20   *Hansard* V, 127, 31 Mar. 1920, 1331.
21   Long to Greenwood, 30 Apr. 1920, WRO, Long Papers, WRO 947/240.

22 Robinson to Captain A. F. Hemming, private secretary to Greenwood (no date but probably late Dec. 1921), TNA, HO 317/60.

23 *Hansard* V, 127, 29 Mar. 1920, 991.

24 Robinson to Hemming, TNA, HO 317/60.

25 Conclusions of a meeting of the Cabinet no. 81 (20) of 30 Dec. 1920, TNA, CAB 23/23.

26 Home Rule Act, Memorandum C.P 2444 by the Chief Secretary for Ireland, 12 Jan. 1921, TNA, CAB 24/118; Conclusions of a meeting of the Cabinet no. 2 (21) of 14 Jan. 1921, TNA, CAB 23/24.

27 Government of Ireland Act: Memorandum by the Chief Secretary for Ireland, C.P. 2641, TNA, CAB 24/120.

28 Robinson to Anderson 16 and 25 Feb. 1921, TNA, CO 904/26.

29 *Hansard* V, 127, 30 Mar. 1920, 1132–33.

30 Robinson to Greenwood, 16 Feb. 1921, TNA, CO 904/26.

31 Charles Townshend, *The British Campaign in Ireland 1919–1921* (Oxford, 1975), p.223.

32 *Hansard* V, 140, 4 Apr. 1921, 15–16.

33 *Irish Times*, 5 Mar. 1921.

34 Robinson to Anderson, 16 and 19 Feb. 1921 and Anderson to Robinson, 17 Feb. 1921, TNA, CO 904/26.

35 Michael Hopkinson (ed.), *The Last Days of Dublin Castle: The Diaries of Mark Sturgis* (Dublin, 1999), Vol. III, p.114.

36 Conclusions of a meeting of the Cabinet no. 10 (21), 3 Mar. 1921, TNA, CAB 23/24.

37 Conclusions of a meeting of the Cabinet no. 12 (21), 8 Mar. 1921, TNA, CAB 23/24.

38 Letter of 21 Mar. 1921 to Miss Stephenson and enclosed copy of submission of 19 March to chief secretary,

39 Note on visit to Ireland by Sir Warren Fisher, 11 Feb. 1921, Parliamentary Archives, Bonar Law Papers, BL/103/1.

40 Conclusions of a meeting of the Cabinet no. 14 (21), 22 Mar. 1921, TNA, CAB 23/24; Conclusions of a meeting of the cabinet no. 15 (21), 24 Mar. 1921, TNA, CAB 23/24.

41 *Hansard* V, 140, 5 Apr. 1921, 91–92.

42 Robinson to Anderson, 26 Mar.1921 (two letters), TNA, CO 904/26.

43 Conclusions of a meeting of the cabinet no. 15 (21), 24 Mar. 1921, TNA, CAB 23/24.

44 Greenwood to the Prime Minister, 17 Apr. 1921, Parliamentary Archives, Lloyd George Papers, LG/F/19/3/15.

45 Conclusions of a meeting of the Cabinet no. 27 (21), 21 Apr. 1921, TNA, CAB 23/25.

46 Keith Middlemas (ed.), *Thomas Jones Whitehall Diary* (Vol. III) (London, 1971), pp.55–63.

47 Conclusions of a meeting of the Cabinet no. 8 (21), 11 May 1921, TNA, CAB 23/25: Secret Cypher Telegram to the Chief Secretary, Parliamentary Archives, Lloyd George Papers, LG/F/19/4/9.

48 Conclusions of a meeting of the Cabinet no. 9 (21), 12 May 1921, TNA, CAB 23/25.

49   Jones, *Whitehall Diary*, pp.63–70.

50   Anderson to Chief Secretary, 11 May, 1921, Parliamentary Archives, Lloyd George Papers, LG/F/19/4/10.

51   Greenwood to the Prime Minister, 11 and 12 May 1921, Parliamentary Archives, Lloyd George Papers, LG/F/19/4/10.

52   Hopkinson, *The Last Days of Dublin Castle*, vol. iv, 16 Apr. 1921.

53   *Irish Independent*, 4 Mar. 1921.

54   *Irish News*, 28 May 1921.

55   Michael Laffan, *The Resurrection of Ireland* (Cambridge, 1999), p.340; *Irish Independent*, 28 May 1921.

56   Conclusions of meeting of the Cabinet no. 10 (21), 3 Mar. 1921, TNA, CAB 23/24; Jones, *Whitehall Diary*, 54.

57   Conclusions of meeting of the Cabinet no. 14 (21), 22 Mar. 1921, TNA, CAB 23/24.

58   Conclusions of meeting of the Cabinet no. 41 (21), 24 May 1921, TNA, CAB 23/25.

59   Memorandum prepared by Waterfield for the Provisional Government, 23 Jan. 1922, TNA, T.162/85.

60   Robinson to Waterfield, 5 Sept. 1920, TNA, T.160/216.

61   Note of conference on 13 Oct. 1920 at Dublin Castle, TNA, T.158/1.

62   Robinson to Anderson, 31 Aug. 1920, NAI, FIN 8/15.

63   Waterfield to Robinson, 28 Dec. 1920, TNA, T.158/2; NAI FIN 8/15.

64   Robinson to Waterfield, 5 Mar. 1921, NAI, FIN 8/15.

65   Gilbert to Robinson, 6 Apr. 1921, and Robinson to Waterfield, 17 May 1921, FIN 8/15.

66   Waterfield to Treasury, 6 July 1921, TNA, T.162/95; Waterfield to Robinson, 26 Aug. 1921, TNA, T.158/4.

67   Waterfield to under-secretary, 22 Sept. 1921, NAI, FIN 8/29.

68   Information supplied under circular T.I. 1347/21, TNA, T.162/95.

69   Robinson to Waterfield 30 Mar. 1922 and Waterfield to Robinson, 31 Mar. 1922, NAI, FIN 8/34.

70   Letters of 14 and 19 Jan. 17 and 24 Feb. 1922, TNA, T.158/7.

71   Waterfield to under-secretary, 27 Oct. 1921, T.158/5; Harris transferred to Northern Ireland in 1921 and became secretary of the Department of Home Affairs in 1927; Adrian Robinson became secretary in 1939.

72   Waterfield to Robinson, 7, 16 and 22 Dec. 1921 and 9 Jan. 1922, TNA, T.158/6; Barlas to under-secretary, 18 Jan 1922, NAI, CSORP 3065/7.

73   Sir Henry Robinson, *Memories: Wise and Otherwise* (London, 1923), pp.292–4.

74   Conclusions of a meeting of the Cabinet no. 2(21), 14 Jan. 1921, TNA, CAB 23/24.

75   Government of Ireland Act: Memorandum by the Chief Secretary for Ireland, C.P. 2641,TNA, CAB 24/120.

76   Circular letter No. 2429 of 20 Jan. 1921, TNA, 488584.

77   Local Government Board, Ireland: Government of Ireland Act, 1920: Sub-division of work and records, notice to office staffs initialled H.A.R., 3 Mar. 1921, TNA, 488584.

78   Copies of reports by departments in response to CSO circulars of 20 and 26 Jan. 1921, Robinson to Anderson, 24 Jan. 1921, TNA, file 488584.

79   Craig to Long, 10 Jan. 1921, WRO, Long Papers, WRO 947/369/2.

80   *Dublin Gazette*, 7 June 1921, pp.849–51.

81   Notes of conference held in the Prime Minister's Room at the House of Commons, 30 May 1921, TNA, CAB 23/25; Ramsey to Craig, 15 June 1921, TNA, T.162/74.

82   Memoirs of Andrew Philip Magill, Oxford, Bodleian Library, MS. Eng. c. 2803, f. 331.

CHAPTER XVIII

'The Surrender of the Government to Sinn Féin'

The Truce

As Robinson portrayed it in his memoirs, the Truce, which came into operation on 11 July 1921, was accompanied by 'the humiliation of the government' and he lamented the fact that the Black and Tans had been called off 'at the psychological moment when they had established a reign of terror of their own which bid fair to take all the heart out of the Sinn Féin'.[1] Others, like his contemporary, Sir John Ross, the last Lord Chancellor, believed that the revolutionary party 'were almost at their last cartridge' and that another three weeks would have finished the business.[2] This view is supported by the British army's official record, compiled in 1922, which claimed that 'the rebel organisation ... was in a precarious condition' at the end of June and noted that eighteen army battalions had arrived for service in Ireland at about that time.[3] Whether Robinson and Ross were correct in the view that the Crown forces were close to victory in July 1921 and that the IRA were facing defeat (or that a stalemate had been reached) is an issue on which there is still no full agreement among historians of the period. But whatever the final verdict on that issue may be, the view expressed by the two men more than a year *after the event* is difficult – if not impossible – to reconcile with the fact that in April 1921, they had endorsed Sir John Anderson's confidential advice to the Cabinet that the time was ripe for a unilateral declaration that British military activity would temporarily cease.[4]

Reports made to the government generally commented favourably on observance of the military aspects of the Truce although the cessation of hostilities provided an opportunity for the IRA to import additional arms and to strengthen its organisation. In August, with no real progress being made in the correspondence between Lloyd George and de Valera concerning a basis for formal negotiations, consideration was being given by the authorities to the situation that would arise if the Truce broke down. On 16 August a coded warning of the possibility of an imminent resumption of hostilities was issued to the army in Ireland,[5] and Tom Jones recorded in his diary for the following day that 'there is talk of proceeding by martial law and a plan of campaign is being worked out in detail'.[6] Colonel Sir Wilfred Spender, who had become secretary of the Northern Ireland Cabinet, also believed in August that a martial law government was to be set up in the south, consisting of Macready, Tudor Anderson, and perhaps Robinson.[7] But, he warned, this would be 'a pretty form of government, all intriguing against each other as Dublin is at present'. Macready, he believed, was attempting to get rid of Tudor, and Anderson and Robinson 'are cat and dog', so it would be a hopeless mess.[8] Whatever about the Macready–Tudor relationship, Spender's assessment of the association between Anderson and Robinson was quite wrong because surviving official correspondence between the two men does not suggest that they had any difficulty in working togethe. In the event, Robinson never had the responsibility or the opportunity of becoming *de jure* a part of the government of Ireland: Crown colony government continued to be ruled out as an option and even in October, when the absence of a government or parliament in the south was delaying full implementation of the 1920 act in the north, Greenwood sensibly took the view that its introduction at that stage would prejudice the negotiations for a conference with representatives of the south.[9] Later that month, the secretary of state for war submitted proposals to the Cabinet on the steps that would need to be taken urgently 'in the event of the present conference failing to reach an agreement and hostilities recommencing'. These steps however related to purely military matters rather than wider governance issues which might have involved Robinson.[10]

'A Condition Approaching Chaos has Been Brought About'

After the Truce, when the Dáil and its agencies were able to come into the open, Cosgrave's Department of Local Government was free to intensify its activity, to strengthen its control over local councils, and to attempt to introduce reforms.[11] It appears, however, that Cosgrave's ambition was limited at that stage: on 21 August in what Dr Kathleen Lynn who was chair of the housing committee of Rathmines Urban Council, considered to be an 'eminently unsatisfactory letter', he told her, that his department was still only concerned with the administration of councils who had adhered to the Dáil and that the administration of others (like Rathmines) did not 'form the subject of our direction'.[12] At a public working session of the Dáil in August, he reviewed events on the local government front since 1918, and his report was generally well received when it was debated in private session on 22 August.[13] As he recalled it nearly thirty years later, local administration throughout the country was 'in fairly good shape' at the time,[14] but the reality, as O'Higgins had reported to the Dáil in January, was that the situation 'was very serious in many places'.[15] Mary Daly's study of the period correctly suggests that the latter was the more accurate assessment and that the local government system was actually on the verge of collapse in some counties by July 1921.[16]

On the official side, an Irish Office survey of the situation at the end of April (based apparently on a memorandum from Robinson which does not seem to have survived) noted that 'in the sphere of local government … by a policy of deliberate obstruction carried on through the Sinn Féin local councils, a condition approaching chaos has been brought about in callous disregard of the interests of the general community. Of constructive policy there is none'.[17] Robinson's subsequent and even more gloomy statement of the situation at the time of the Truce was also closer to reality than was Cosgrave's:

> Local government administration in particular had been blocked and the measures for the relief of the sick, the destitute, the children and the unemployed had been suspended. Some staff were left without pay, outdoor relief was suspended and no alternative measures had taken their place, as the Dáil Éireann Local Government Board, which had been created had not as yet money to finance new services in place of the old, which had been wrecked. The county and district officers, the doctors and relieving officers had been left without pay, and the sick without treatment, as the accommodation in the workhouse buildings had been reduced to an extent which made hospital relief almost inaccessible to the people in many parts of the country. The poor were not paid their outdoor relief in full, the workhouse wards were closed to the infirm and grants for feeding school children, for tuberculosis treatment and maternity benefits were all at an end.

And so, as Robinson recalled it in 1923, 'when the Truce came there were great hopes that it would mean a resumption of the old beneficent measures for the welfare of the people and the distribution of the usual Treasury grants, if not by the old Local Government Board, at all events by a board with the same powers but a different personnel'.[18] However, any hope that the Truce would lead to a restoration of normal relations between the LGB and local councils was quickly dashed.

At the beginning of April 1921, 319 councils out of a total of 516 were officially recorded as refusing to recognise the LGB, while the attitude of another 53 was stated to be doubtful.[19] In response to enquiries by Greenwood, Robinson sent him three separate reports summarising the situation after the Truce. These were circulated by Greenwood to the Cabinet in August in order to show clearly 'the nature of the difficulties that will have to be faced before it will be possible to return to normal conditions of local government'.[20] At that stage, all 27 county councils and the 4 county borough councils in the south were refusing to recognise the board, but the position in relation to the rural district and urban councils in the south was not as clear-cut: 136 of the rural districts refused recognition, while 27 recognised the board (some of them classed as doubtful) and the 65 urban councils in the south were divided almost equally in their allegiance. One of the reports which Robinson addressed to 'My dear Chief' in August, regretted that there had been no change for the better since the Truce:

> I threw out a feeler to some of the councils whose officers are still loyal to us, and one and all have taken the same view that no rapprochement would be permitted pending Sinn Féin announcement of the terms of peace, and, judging from the attitude and public utterances of local authorities at present, it seems doubtful whether, even if peace is achieved, the local authorities will recognise the existing law and comply with their statutory obligations unless the government make it part of the conditions of peace that they should do so.
>
> Of late the Dáil Éireann local government officials have become more truculent and dictatorial than ever. Without any foresight as to the ultimate consequences, they are bullying the councils into closing workhouses and infirmaries and transferring inmates from one place to another. Dáil Éireann inspectors go round giving directions to local authorities and any refusal on the part of boards of guardians to obey even the most short-sighted orders, they are told, will be regarded as a want of confidence in Dáil Éireann. These schemes must involve a failure to provide hospital treatment

to many people, but, unfortunately, the case of the sick and destitute seems to have become quite a secondary consideration.

…

Free medical assistance to the poor is in some districts a thing of the past. The dispensary doctors have received no salaries for months and naturally will not attend 'red ticket cases' without a fee. Road workmen are kept out of their wages and although rates have been increased to cover the loss of the local taxation grants, many of the persons collecting them are not legally appointed collectors, and the rates are therefore coming in slowly and some councils are in perpetual financial straits.

The manner in which officers who desire to fulfil their statutory obligations – foreseeing the after-effects of the present negation of the law – is most deplorable. Their salaries and fees are withheld, and every effort is made to worry them into vacating their positions.

…

The real truth is that the local Sinn Féin terrorists are so elated at the sway they have established and at the power of life, death and destruction which they wield that they have become utterly reckless as to the results of anything they may decide upon, and I believe that de Valera and Co. will have no easy task before them when he has to endeavour to bring them into line for the re-establishment of legitimate administration.

George Chester Duggan's account of the period after the Truce is consistent with Robinson's: local authorities, he noted, openly flouted the LGB and 'carried out, by direction of the Dáil minister, schemes of public health and poor law amalgamation, which Sir Henry Robinson and chief secretaries had for years regarded as necessary but never had the courage to carry through owing to local opposition'. The Dáil's methods were different, according to Duggan: if interested guardians or councillors demurred at accepting a scheme 'an order couched in no uncertain terms followed, and left no option but to obey'.[21] Even government schemes, which had originally been welcomed by local councils, continued to be at a standstill. Regarding urban housing, for example, Robinson reported on 16 July that 'the local authorities would have been content to go on with their schemes while negotiations were proceeding ... had it not been that they were ordered by Dáil Éireann to hold no communication whatsoever with the LGB'.[22]

Reducing the Impact of the Criminal Injuries Awards

The proposals made originally by Robinson in February 1921 for dealing with the burden which ratepayers would have to meet to finance criminal injury awards had been broadly endorsed by Anderson (see chapter XV) and submitted to the Cabinet by Greenwood in a memorandum dated 1 March, but the issue was put back for further consideration.[23] A decision was again deferred by the Cabinet in June, even though Greenwood advised that the matter had then become very urgent.[24] In August, when the grants withheld from some county councils had all been used up to pay compensation awards in their areas, the Cabinet authorised the diversion of the surplus of £700,000 standing to the credit of some of the other councils to pay these awards, but the wider questions which had been raised by Robinson six months earlier continued to be ignored.[25] Still concerned about the impact on ratepayers of the court awards and the difficulty which would be created for local councils by garnishee orders, he raised the issue again with the chief secretary that month, notwithstanding the continuing determination of so many of the local councils to completely disregard his board. At that stage he told Greenwood that people had been warned that if they attempted to apply for, or to enforce, garnishee orders, they and their solicitors would be shot, but the county councils feared that when peace came, the orders 'will come down upon them like snowflakes'. He pointed out – quite correctly – that compensation awards in many cases were entirely out of proportion to the damage done, as the local authorities had not always defended the claims which had been made. He also argued that when peace was established, there must be some enquiry in order to find a basis for revising the awards and for deciding how the amount which would fall upon the ratepayers, beyond their ability to pay, should be dealt with. This was a task, he told Greenwood, which he would personally be much interested in, and which he would be glad to undertake if necessary.[26] Not surprisingly, however, his offer to become involved was not taken up at that stage and the question of how to deal with the awards was still unresolved at the time of the Treaty.

At the beginning of 1922, the total amount of the compensation awarded to private individuals in the south in respect of injuries to person and property came to more than £7.667 million.[27] The withholding of grants to local councils had continued on Anderson's instructions throughout

1921, and solicitors and barristers continued to apply for garnishee orders in respect of unpaid awards, forcing the Dáil department in December to repeat its warning that any attempt to enforce these orders would be 'resisted and punished by the elected government of the people'.[28] In early January a British Cabinet sub-committee recognised that one of the most pressing issues that would have to be discussed with the Irish leaders on approval of the Treaty was the compensation question. The sub-committee suggested that as part of a 'comprehensive policy of oblivion', fair compensation to be determined by a specially constituted commission should be paid in respect of injuries covered by the Criminal Injuries Acts, including losses sustained through the destruction of property by order of the military authorities under martial law.[29] Agreement to proceed on these general lines was reached between the two governments on 24 January, with the proviso that each government should deal with, and be responsible for, payment of compensation in respect of personal injuries to its own supporters, and that the British government would reimburse an agreed proportion of the total cost of awards for property damage arising out of incidents from 1 January 1919 onwards, 'including advances made out of intercepted grants'.[30]

On the British side, the government then moved quickly, arranging to have a sum of £215,000 voted by Parliament on 22 February to meet the more pressing cases of compensation to Crown employees. Two days later, Winston Churchill moved a supplementary estimate in the House of Commons for a sum of £1.130 million, which was to be paid to the provisional government before 31 March.[31] In doing so, he explained that the objective was 'to liberate' the grants to local councils which had been 'intercepted' since 1920 and without which local services, especially roads, had fallen into a lamentable condition. The funds were also intended to allow the provisional government to assist councils in resuming their normal functions and to reduce unemployment. In effect, this generous action as Cosgrave saw it reversed the policy pursued since 1920 because, as Churchill put it, the government then accepted that however justifiable the interception of the grants may have been as a hostile measure in the conflict that had just been terminated, local funds were not a proper source from which the cost of injury to persons and property should be defrayed.[32] By agreement between the two governments, a commission was subsequently established to hear and determine all claims for damage to property caused between 19 January 1919 and the date of the Truce. The commission was specifically asked to review the excessive awards about which Robinson had been particularly concerned, and to determine what compensation would be 'fair and reasonable' in these cases in lieu of the amounts awarded by court decrees – but his offer personally to assist in the exercise was not accepted.[33]

'The British Surrender to the Forces of Disorder'

When the Treaty was signed on 6 December, the reactions of southern unionists varied – relief, shocked surprise, pessimistic acquiescence, and determination to make the best of a *fait accompli* were all expressed.[34] Robinson was appalled: he had consistently advocated strong government action as the only means of restoring stability in Ireland and, recounting his reaction to the Treaty, he wrote in 1926 that, like many others, he had visualised only a peace to be achieved by compelling the rebels to lay down their arms:

> I had never at any time thought or known that the government contemplated a different form of peace, namely the British surrender to the forces of disorder and this announcement, coming as it did just when the rebels were believed to be on the point of collapse owing to lack of ammunition, money and supplies, came to me like a bolt from the blue, for I knew how my service to the British in Ireland was regarded by the rebels, and I had a very unpleasant notion of what would probably be my lot when the government cleared out of the country with their police and military and left me and other Irish loyalists at the mercy of the rebels.[35]

While he didn't 'see eye to eye with Ulster on most things', Robinson felt bound to say in a letter to Greenwood's private secretary that the unionists of that province 'had been done down over this d......d boundaries business', and he questioned whether the provision in the Treaty for a boundary commission could be regarded as 'keeping faith with Ulster'. What funks me, he went on, from a personal point of view is that the government might also regard it as keeping faith with the pensioned civil servants and judges to refuse to guarantee their pensions and to leave it to the southern government to give or withhold these pensions according to their financial position. Nevertheless, while the debate was still continuing in the Dáil ('the popular impression seems to be that Griffith will win by four or five majority' – the actual majority later turned out to be seven), he submitted a suggestion to Greenwood in late December which he hoped 'might lessen the impasse' on the vexed question of boundaries.[36] Unfortunately, the document containing this suggestion does not seem to have survived, but it may well have involved some reworking of the schemes he had submitted to Birrell in 1914. In any case, he was not sanguine about the prospects for a boundary commission: noting that Chamberlain had said that he had got a commission to which neither side could object,[37] he supposed – sardonically – that the Archangel Gabriel was to be chairman and that the commissioners were to be two atheists because he could not 'conceive any commission otherwise constituted which would fulfil the bill' in a country where, as he had told Birrell ten years earlier, 'religion is a total failure'.[38] He went on:

> I know what I am talking about re these boundaries as every alteration of a boundary for local government or parliamentary purposes has been made by me personally and the whole of the parliamentary areas in the act of 1920 are mine, and I can assure you that you can have no conception of the consequential difficulties following on an Ulster boundary rectified for sectarian purposes. Thank God I'm not on the commission.

Writing little more than a year after the Treaty, he lamented the sacrifice of brave young lives, which might have been saved if the government had made their offer of peace immediately after they found they could not support the Black and Tans against the radical outcry, adding the astonishing and bizarre comment that these were 'a light-hearted, reckless set of men who carried out humorous stunts'. He was bitterly critical of Lloyd George for his statement (apparently at Leeds in mid-August 1922) that the act of his life in which he took the greatest pride was the Treaty, which 'leaves the country at the mercy of armed marauders who spare neither man, woman, nor child, who lay waste the country, burn and pillage the houses of the loyalists, rape their women, and shoot unarmed, defenceless men at sight'. In another overblown and immoderate passage – influenced, no doubt, by his own experience in August 1922 when his house was attacked by armed men – he repeated his criticism of the withdrawal of military and police protection from law-abiding Irish people which left them at the mercy of the blood-thirsty Irregulars. The Government in his view ought to have left sufficient police and military in the country to protect the loyal and law-abiding people until it was clear that the Free State government could do so.[39]

'The Formal Abdication of the Irish Government to Michael Collins'

The seven-man provisional government, which was established following the approval of the Treaty on 7 January 1922, included W. T. Cosgrave as Minister for Local Government and head of the department that he had administered since 1919. A meeting of the government in Dublin's Mansion House at 11 a.m. on 16 January elected Michael Collins as chairman and made arrangements for a visit to Dublin Castle at 1.40 p.m. 'for the purpose of taking over the various Departments of State'.[40] The subsequent ceremony at the Castle presided over by Lord Lieutenant FitzAlan marked the first stage in the transfer of power to the new government. This was the day which, according to the *Irish Times*, 'would be written in history as the day on which the old regime ceased to exist',[41] but Robinson saw it differently: it was the day fixed for the surrender of the Government to Sinn Féin; co-incidentally or otherwise, the minutes of a second meeting of the provisional government held a few hours after the Castle ceremony recorded the event in broadly similar terms: the government had 'received the surrender of Dublin Castle at 1.45 p.m.'.[42]

Having received a telephone message to attend the Castle 'to be introduced to the victors', Robinson found the heads of the Irish departments 'sitting on one side of the under-secretary's room, and the Sinn Féin leaders sitting opposite, glowering at each other'. Instead of joining the glad throng, he waited in the corridor until FitzAlan had made 'the formal abdication of the Irish government to Michael Collins' and 'being the senior in the service, was called in first and was marched round and introduced to each one [of the ministers designate] in turn'. What struck him forcibly was 'the extreme youth of most of the new men; they seemed scarcely out of their teens and all looked pale and anxious', their 'grave and anxious faces' possibly foreshadowing the troubles and responsibilities which they were undertaking. But Michael Collins was 'cordiality itself, and there was none of the top-dog attitude about him at all events'. People had asked whether the civil servants would be expected to shake hands with men whose hands were stained with outrage and crime, but 'if the civil servants had any doubt on the subject themselves they were speedily dispelled by Michael Collins who grasped their hands with his iron grip and shook them warmly with the greatest bonhomie'.[43]

According to the *Irish Times*, the meeting between Robinson and Cosgrave at the Castle was, perhaps, the most interesting incident on the day:

> The conflict between these two during the past eighteen months has been particularly keen. Both have been directing the local government of southern and western Ireland, and it is not too much to say that the policy of one has been for the most part the direct opposite of the other's. That the two departments will now

have to shape their future under one head and one policy is, of course, inevitable, and no doubt, they will at once set up an effective liaison, which will prevent overlapping or the issuing of conflicting instructions.[44]

Unfortunately, neither man has left any account of that meeting, and while some tentative liaison or other arrangements may have been discussed, Cosgrave told the Dáil on 1 March that he had not met Robinson since the event at the Castle on 16 January.[45] However, he subsequently told Collins that Robinson 'had been of very great assistance to us since the taking-over; as far back as February last, he gave £1,200 for the relief of distress in the West'.[46]

In London, the Cabinet had been advised on 10 December that the LGB was one of the departments which 'the Irish are most anxious to control for themselves at once',[47] but the timing of transfers of services had been left over by the Treaty for subsequent decision and, until April, there was no suitable legislative basis for transfers. As a result, control over the existing departments generally remained loose until then, with day-to-day administration for the most part being left in the hands of the civil servants.[48] For all practical purposes, the LGB and the Dáil department continued on their separate paths during the spring of 1922, as they had done during the previous autumn and winter. Robinson had been concerned about the situation which would face a new southern Irish government in the local government field after a possible settlement. Believing that it would take a long time to bring order out of the chaos which had been created in the previous two years and to re-establish the local authorities on a satisfactory financial basis, he had urged Greenwood in August 1921 that 'if there is to be peace and a transfer of administration to a southern parliament, and if the government is to be handed over as a going concern, it should be one of the conditions of peace that the LGB is to be supported and not obstructed by Dáil Éireann in restoring financial order and in making the final transitory arrangements'.[49] Although this suggestion was submitted to the Cabinet, it was not taken up and there is no evidence that there was any contact between the LGB and the personnel of Cosgrave's Dáil department either before the Treaty or in the following few weeks, or that any advance plans had been made on either side to smooth the transition.

James MacMahon, the joint Under-Secretary, wrote to Alexander Barlas, the board secretary, on 16 January, indicating that on the occasion of the installation of the provisional government earlier that day, it had been arranged that, 'pending consultation with British Ministers with a view to the taking of necessary steps for the transfer of the powers and machinery of existing departments, their work should be continued, without prejudice to the status quo'.[50] In addition to this specific direction, Robinson and the staff of the LGB, in common with Irish civil servants generally, were governed by the terms of a proclamation issued by the provisional government on 16 January, in which they took control of public services, prohibited any alterations in the status, rights or salaries, or the transfer or dismissal, of any existing official, and directed officials in all existing departments and boards to continue to carry out their functions unless and until otherwise directed.[51] Two days later, another official statement repeated the direction that existing departments were to continue to perform their normal functions, but added that 'for the better regulation and control of these services', members of the government had been appointed to direct their activities and to be responsible for their efficient conduct and maintenance.[52] This marked the first formal assignment to Cosgrave – or Liam T. MacCosgair as he was then officially referred to – of responsibility for the LGB, and he followed up on 21 January with a visit to the head office of the board – still temporarily located in Jury's Hotel – where he was reported to have spent some time in discussions with Barlas and Charles Hugh O'Conor, a commissioner since April 1921.[53]

'Living Under Dual Government'

On 26 January, the *Irish Times* political correspondent was impatiently complaining that 'we are living under dual government' – two sets of departments were operating with 'a certain amount of overlapping, which is not only unnecessary, but wasteful, and to some extent, annoying'.[54] The writer appeared to exempt local government from this general criticism, asserting that 'Mr Cosgrave has taken over most of the functions which were discharged by Sir Henry Robinson's department', but there was no basis for this statement at that stage, and neither co-ordination arrangements nor any clear demarcation lines had been established. Newspaper reports suggest that individual local authorities were still in direct contact about financial and other issues with officers of the Dáil department, and the department's inspectors were openly conducting local inquiries with the same degree of formality that had applied to their counterparts in the LGB. This led to confusion in some cases, for example, when Dr Joseph Boyd-Barrett, one of the department's medical inspectors, held a sworn enquiry at Dun Laoghaire in early March, the *Irish Times* was not clear about his status and opted to describe him as the 'Local Government Board (Dáil Éireann) inspector'.[55] Statutory public notices relating to inquiries, arbitration hearings and such matters continued to be published in the newspapers throughout February and early March 1922 in the name of the Local Government Board for Ireland and signed by the board's solicitor, James Macredy, and by R. E. Beckerson 'for Secretary'. A more remarkable item was a formal order of a fairly routine nature made in the name of the board on 14 March and carrying Robinson's signature, but which was published in the new state's official journal, *Iris Oifigiúil*.[56]

The staff of the Dáil department numbered seventy-nine at the time of the Treaty – thirty-six office staff and forty-one inspectors and auditors, roughly half of whom had been recruited after the Truce.[57] Believing that they were effectively to take over the LGB, they drafted a memorial for submission by Lorcan Robins, as Assistant Minister, to the government in mid-February, protesting that there was 'no unity of ideas or co-relation of work' between the staffs of the two organisations, and that the staff of the LGB 'are doing official acts, which in the eyes of the outside public we are responsible for'. The memorial demanded that the existing LGB board members and Barlas, its secretary, should be superannuated and that a new board drawn from the senior people in the department should be appointed with T. J. (Tom) McArdle as secretary.[58] It also sought to have the best men among the Dáil staff promoted to section-head positions in the new department and, as an alternative, demanded – quite unrealistically – that all LGB officials (except those dealing with old age pensions and a few other matters) should be placed on indefinite leave because they were 'useless and a menace under present conditions' and because 120 officials could do the work that the 275 officials in the existing 'incubus' were then being paid to do. Finally, it pronounced their unwillingness to join the LGB staff at their temporary offices in Jury's Hotel, as this might create the impression that they were being taken over by the LGB.[59] Cosgrave was not prepared to accede to these demands, but as a compromise suggested that Robins might visit Jury's on a daily basis to oversee the work and to approve all outgoing correspondence. Robins refused to undertake this assignment because of the extra work involved and because the LGB staff would question his authority.

At a meeting on 27 January the provisional government had approved a proposal from Cosgrave for the administration of the LGB 'by associating in its control certain members of his department'.[60] Presumably based on leaks from that meeting, reports began to appear in the newspapers about the future of the LGB. The *Freeman's Journal* reported on 1 February that 'three new commissioners of local government' were to be appointed, replacing the Chief Secretary, the Under-Secretary and Henry Robinson who was stated (erroneously) to have just retired.[61] One of the new men was to be a political appointee – probably Cosgrave – who would take the place of the Chief Secretary as President of the board, the second vacancy would be filled by a medical commissioner and the third seat would probably be filled by Lorcan Robins, the TD who had been unofficially appointed as Assistant Minister for local government on 11 January.[62] The report went on to say that Barlas, who had completed thirty years' service, was shortly to retire and that the name chiefly mentioned as his replacement was McArdle.[63] Two days later the *Irish Times* carried a somewhat similar report stating that 'steps are being taken to set up a new local government executive for Ireland with as little delay as possible and the Local Government Board, as it existed under the Dublin Castle *régime*, will be taken over on Monday next'. Robinson was to retire almost immediately, according to that report, and three new commissioners (whose names were not known) had been appointed in addition to the existing higher official staff of the Department.[64]

The press reports and speculation of early February were premature and without foundation, and nothing was done to resolve the difficulties between the rival local government organisations for another few weeks. Cosgrave's tentative first step towards taking control of the LGB took place on 22 February when he sent a hand-written note to Barlas 'for communication to LGB officials' indicating that:

> The Minister of Local Government desires that Mr E. P. McCarron BL be facilitated freely in all respects as regards any information he requires in all matters affecting Local Government. Officials in charge of papers shall submit them for decision at the City Hall and take any necessary directions from Mr McCarron who is authorised by the Minister to receive them.[65]

The original note was annotated and initialled on the following day, indicating that it had been 'read' by Robinson and 'noted' by Sir Edward Coey Bigger, medical commissioner; Charles Hugh O'Conor, junior commissioner; Francis Joseph McCarthy, who occasionally acted as commissioner, and Barlas; typed copies were made and sent to staff in the board's various offices. The selection of 41-year-old Edward McCarron for such a sensitive and critical position must have come as a complete surprise not only to the staff of the LGB but also to those serving in the Dáil Department.[66] He had joined the civil service as a boy clerk in 1896 when still only 15 years old and became an Assistant Clerk in the LGB in 1901. He was promoted to a second division clerkship later that year, to a third-class auditor position in 1911, a second-class auditor post in June

1920 and a first-class auditor post in October 1921. He was assigned on loan to the Chief Secretary's office at Dublin Castle to work with George Chester Duggan in the finance division of that office on preparations for the commencement of the financial clauses of the 1920 act, and was still on loan to the office until his appointment by Cosgrave in February 1922. He had never served in a senior administrative or management position, nor had he any experience of policy or legislative work. Why he was selected by Cosgrave for appointment as his anointed delegate in the LGB, over the heads of more senior LGB officials and instead of any of those who had worked in the Dáil department, is not clear. There is no evidence of any official connection or contact between the two men before 1922, and there is nothing to suggest that McCarron may have secretly assisted Cosgrave in 1921–22 as, for example, Joseph Brennan had assisted Michael Collins. One possible explanation is that some personal contact may have arisen because McCarron's sister, Mary, worked as a professor of music at the Leinster School of Music while Cosgrave's sister, Mary (May), who was roughly the same age, worked as a piano tutor at the same school. Having met Cosgrave in early March, Waterfield (who continued to work at the Castle until late 1922) told Anderson that McCarron was acting as Cosgrave's 'personal secretary and assistant, a position in which he can do most useful work as he of course is familiar with the various financial problems from the Castle point of view, and is both an experienced and trustworthy official'.[68] These comments are consistent with the memoir written years later by Duggan, who recorded that McCarron had been assigned to help him in his work at the Castle and 'had that mastery of detail and clarity of interpretation which goes with the legal mind that has handled administration, added to a gift of humour which it sometimes lacks'.[69]

Although no official announcement of McCarron's appointment as assistant to Cosgrave had been made, the matter was raised in the Dáil on 1 March when Deputy Joseph MacDonagh, brother of one of the executed 1916 leaders and anti-Treaty TD for North Tipperary, asked Cosgrave if he had taken McCarron into his service and made him 'private secretary and liaison officer' between his department and the LGB. In his reply, Cosgrave stated that while McCarron was still on the LGB payroll, he was availing of his services in his capacity as Minister for Local Government, and he was acting 'under my direction and with my authority in all matters affecting all functions of the LGB'. MacDonagh followed up by asking if Cosgrave was aware that McCarron had attested under the Derby Scheme during the war but was declared by Robinson to be indispensable, to which Cosgrave's reply was that he simply did not know as 'I have not the advantage of being in Sir Henry Robinson's confidence.' In response to further questions, Cosgrave said that he did not know whether it was true that McCarron had offered his services to the military in Drogheda during Easter Week, but he acknowledged that McCarron was the auditor who had controversially surcharged the Balrothery board of guardians, arising from payment of the salary of Dr Richard Hayes TD for a period during which the doctor was in gaol. Although the surcharge resulted in the seizure of property from some of the guardians, Cosgrave defended McCarron's action on the grounds that he was an honourable man whose failure to do his duty by making the surcharge would have rendered him liable for instant dismissal. The questions were put in very bad taste, Cosgrave concluded.[70]

Finding a Successor to Robinson

Cosgrave told his ministerial colleagues on 3 March that Barlas, the LGB secretary, had resigned, and a week later he reported that he was taking over the machinery of the LGB, but whether this had any real impact is not clear.[71] His instruction on 22 February that LGB staff should take directions from McCarron did not directly affect Robinson's position and left open the questions of who would succeed him as Vice-President and who would become secretary of the department that was to replace the board on 1 April 1922. One year earlier there had been a new appointment to the board caused by the resignation of Edmund Bourke, who had been a commissioner since 1910; Anderson and Robinson had both proposed to the Chief Secretary on that occasion that impending constitutional changes under the 1920 Act should not deprive Charles Hugh O Conor, the board's most senior inspector, of a promotion to which he might legitimately look forward in the ordinary course, having been acting temporarily as commissioner at intervals since 1916. O'Conor was duly appointed with effect from 14 April 1921, but it was made absolutely clear to him that the promotion would not give him any claim to succeed to the Vice-Presidency.[72]

Robinson would have been due to retire in November 1922 under 'the 65 rule' but he had opted to resign from his permanent position early in 1921, preferring to have his pension arrangements settled before the 1920 act came into operation. In January 1921, in a personal note to Anderson, he wrote:

> I quite see that I would be ill-advised to bump up against the appointed day and come under a new superannuation department.

> After 45 years of exacting work and collar work, nearly all the time danced upon by you d....d Saxons (which of course was hardest of all to bear!) I think I am entitled to go under the old regime. But I don't want to do anything which would be inconvenient to the Government and I would stay on just as long or as short a time as I was wanted if I could resign to the British Government. Would it be possible to let me go, at my pension, and to keep me on at a non-pensionable addition thereto (raising it to my present salary) till such time as the new act was floated and the Government didn't want me anymore? [73]

He followed up by formally offering his resignation to Greenwood with effect from 31 March 1921, telling him that as local government was about to pass under the control of the Irish Parliament, it was right that 'the new ministers should have the nomination and appointment of the permanent civil servant who is to be the head of Irish Local Government'. At the same time, he offered to continue to act temporarily as Vice-President if he could be 'of any use in helping to divide the local administration between the two parliaments and otherwise in assisting the transitory arrangements for handing over the government to the new ministers'.[74] Greenwood was glad to accept Robinson's offer to continue to act for the time being 'as we still have great need of your services', and there was no difficulty in implementing the financial arrangement he had suggested.[75] He was awarded a pension of £1,181 and a lump sum of £4,164, but was to carry on in a temporary capacity with his existing salary of £2,550 'for as long as you really want me', as he told Anderson.[76]

News of Robinson's new status soon leaked out and the *Irish Independent* was able to report that he had consented, at the request of the government, to continue in office until the new parliaments provided for in the 1920 act were set up.[77] Some months later, on 20 June, the *Independent* reported that he was about to retire, but subsequent events, including the Truce and the prolonged negotiations which followed it, led to requests that he should further delay his retirement.[78] On 24 January 1922 the *Independent* reported that one of the first notable resignations following the change of government would be that of Robinson, who had told the newspaper's representative that he had again been asked to remain on pending the setting up of the new southern government and had consented to do so, and while he had not yet seen Cosgrave (disregarding the brief encounter at the Castle on 16 January), he was carrying on the work in accordance with the proclamation issued by the government on that date.[79]

In a memorandum for the provisional government, Waterfield had advised them on 23 January that the Treasury had declined before the appointed day to fill high-level posts which had fallen vacant, giving as an illustration of this the Vice-Presidency of the LGB, which had intentionally been allowed to remain unfilled on a substantive basis.[80] At the beginning of February, after he had 'definitely decided to retire immediately', Robinson was told by Waterfield that it would be extremely embarrassing for the Government to have to appoint a successor at that stage; nevertheless, Waterfield invited him to recommend a possible replacement and advised him to consult his minister about the matter.[81] The reference to embarrassment for the Government was obviously enough to induce Robinson to postpone his departure for a little longer, but he must have regretted this when he had to suffer the humiliating experience of being instructed to take directions from McCarron, who had been a 17-year-old boy clerk in the Custom House in 1898 when Robinson himself had already become Vice-President.

Newspaper speculation about Robinson's position continued in early March when it was reported that while he had been asked to continue in office pending the change of government, arrangements had been made to enable him to retire on 15 March.[82] Robinson had in fact notified Waterfield that he had arranged to step down on that date, but this was still seen to create difficulty because, as Waterfield reported to Anderson on 7 March after 'a very interesting talk with Cosgrave', they did not want Bigger [the medical commissioner] and 'we do not want O'Conor' [the other and more junior commissioner]. The staff of the Dáil department had their own ideas about the succession: the memorial which they submitted on 15 February had described Coey-Bigger as 'leading the die-hards on the staff' but suggested that O'Conor was genuinely anxious to facilitate the transfer and was willing to work under the Dáil.[83] To break the stalemate, it was agreed that Cosgrave would ask Joseph Louis Smith, the board's Assistant Secretary, to see him personally and to invite him to take up the position, but when Smith refused to act, Cosgrave suggested in a phone call to Waterfield that it would be best to let Robinson stay on until 31 March as he didn't want to interfere in the LGB until 1 April.[84] Waterfield then had to revert to Robinson, pleading that it would be a great advantage if he would agree – which he did – to continue until 31 March.[85]

At a late stage, Cosgrave personally intervened to break the impasse which had developed in relation to the appointment of a successor to Robinson, concentrating on the position of accounting officer rather than that of secretary of the new department. On 27 March, in a letter to Collins as chairman of the provisional government, he noted that O'Conor was next in seniority to Robinson, but he had been obliged to allow him six weeks leave due to illness and this would not expire until 3 April. O'Conor, he went on, was an able official, but apart from a general knowledge of his ability and industry, which were unquestionable, he had no knowledge of his suitability for the changed circumstances which must inevitably occur. Given that there was need for 'an official having a correct impression of the psychology of the times', Cosgrave's letter went on to discuss the case for appointing McCarron, specifying his professional qualifications, detailing his twenty-five-year-career in the LGB since his appointment as a boy clerk and noting his usefulness, efficiency, ability, industry and his practice of usually working in the office until 10.00 p.m. 'I have no alternative but to recommend Mr McCarron', he concluded, completely ignoring the possibility of appointing one of the more senior administrative staff of the board, or any of the staff of his own Dáil department. In a subsequent letter on 30 March, Cosgrave insisted that even if he were disposed to do so, he would be unable to suggest an alternative, adding that McCarron had been 'in effect my chief executive officer since 22 February' and would become so in fact from 31 March, when Robinson would relinquish duty. McCarron was duly appointed as accounting officer by letter dated 31 March, and his name appears in a list of accounting officers appointed with effect from 1 April although in a typewritten draft of the list, his name was added in manuscript at the end, confirming that the appointment was a last-minute one.[87]

A carefully choreographed series of parallel actions were taken on both sides of the Irish Sea at the end of March 1922 to give effect to the transfer of functions, services and powers to the provisional government. The Irish Free State (Agreement) Act, 1922 was passed by the Westminster Parliament on 31 March to give the force of law from that date to the Treaty and to authorise the British government to make orders in council transferring powers to the provisional government. On the same day, Public Notice No. 6, approved by the provisional government and subsequently published in *Iris Oifigiúil*, indicated that eight ministries (including a Ministry of Local Government) had been constituted with effect from that date and listed the functions and services assigned to each.[88] Public Notice No. 9, also dated 31 March, named the ministers appointed to head the new ministries, including W. T. Cosgrave at the Ministry of Local Government.[89] Finally, by order in council made in the name of the King on 1 April, 1922, powers were formally transferred on that date to the ministers and departments constituted by the provisional government.[90] In the case of the new Ministry of Local Government, the transferred functions, as listed in the schedule to the order, included all of the functions performed until then by the LGB.

The official heads of several of the important agencies of the pre-1922 Irish administration continued in office after 1 April 1922.[91] However, Robinson's tenure of the Vice-Presidency of the LGB formally ended on that date, although his board colleagues – Sir Edward Coey-Bigger, the medical commissioner, and Charles O'Conor, the junior commissioner – both opted to transfer to the new department under the default provisions of the Treaty and the 1920 Act before being allowed subsequently to retire under Article X of the Treaty.[92] McCarron's ascendancy was clear from April 1922 onwards, but he had not been formally appointed as secretary at that stage: he was apparently one of fifty-nine higher-grade officials interviewed by a board set up by the provisional government in April to recommend civil servants to fill vacancies at the higher levels, and he emerged as one of seven classed as exceptional.[93] While Cosgrave had intended that he should be secretary, McCarron's status was that of acting secretary until 12 September (still receiving his auditor's salary of £700 and an allowance of £300) when the new minister, Earnan de Blaghd (Ernest Blythe), at the request of Cosgrave who had transferred to the Department of Finance two weeks earlier, gave notice to staff that McCarron was appointed secretary, adding that he would 'act as chief administrative officer and will exercise authority generally over the work of the General Local Administration Branch' and the other units of the department, while Michael de Lacy (the senior member of the corps of inspectors assimilated from the 1919–22 Dáil department) would act as principal of that branch.[94] It is clear from Blythe's wording that there was still some sensitivity about the position of de Lacy and other Dáil officials who were now to be subservient to McCarron, whose appointment was deeply resented by many of those who, at some risk to themselves, had served the department at different times from 1920 to 1922. To avoid serious difficulty, McCarron handed Blythe his resignation, which was not accepted, but resentment about his appointment simmered for years and may even have contributed to his removal from office in 1936.[95]

The Break-up of the Local Government Board

When Robinson retired, the organisation he had built up over the previous twenty years was still largely intact. Under the 1920 act, officers of the board whose functions did not relate solely to the north or to the south were to be allocated between the two governments by a civil service committee. However, even after Northern Ireland had become a reality, there had been reluctance on the part of the authorities in London and Dublin to take any action in relation to staffing that might prejudice the negotiations for a conference which were in progress with de Valera. In Belfast, Samuel Watt, the former LGB official who had taken up duty as permanent secretary of the Ministry of Home Affairs in June 1921 was complaining in August of that year that the continuing delay in assigning staff from Dublin could mean that the whole of the northern government would prove to be a farce and that the northern parliament would be nothing more than a debating society.[96] He was still writing to Dublin in November seeking information on the likely composition and number of staff available for, and willing to, transfer from the LGB to his new department – but with little success.[97] After it was decided that transfers of services to the north would take place in November,[98] the LGB was asked to indicate what staff in each grade they proposed to allocate to the north, and what staff would be required to perform the duties which would remain after the transfer, but the reply from Barlas was particularly unhelpful: 'The board have not allocated any staff provisionally to the north as they are advised that they have no authority to do so.'[99]

Under the 1920 act, officers of the LGB who were concerned solely with the administration of services in Northern Ireland automatically became officers of the northern government. This provision affected three auditors whose districts fell entirely within the north as well as Adrian Robinson, son of Sir Henry and the general inspector for the Belfast district. Robinson's transfer from the Cork–Kerry district in February 1921 was justified on the basis that he was the only protestant available with professional qualifications, and that it would not be fair to allocate the district to a man on a lower rate of salary. It must be assumed, however, that the transfer was arranged by his father in the knowledge that the younger Robinson would be liable to serve in the north and in the expectation that his future career prospects there would be better. In the event, Robinson became an Assistant Secretary at the Ministry of Home Affairs in 1935 and was the department's permanent secretary from 1939 to 1957. In advance of any formal transfer arrangements, a small number of other LGB staff had been moving voluntarily to Belfast from June 1921 onwards, and while transfers of this kind were initially suspended by the provisional government, it was subsequently agreed that all of the officials who had volunteered for service in the north would be let go.[100]

Sixteen members of the LGB staff retired on pension between June 1921 and March 1922. These included the board's long-serving legal adviser, Sir George Vanston, Louis E. Deane, the senior architect and Alfred D. Price, a senior engineering inspector. Others who retired during that period included William H. Wilson, a principal clerk who was advised to retire by his medical adviser because his nerves were shattered as a result of the attack on the Custom House, and William Geary, another principal clerk, whose right arm was declared by his surgeon to be useless following a bullet wound which shattered the elbow during the attack.[101] By default, staff who were still on the payroll and who had neither retired nor moved to the north before 1 April 1922 became staff of the provisional government on that date. Surprisingly, those who made this transition pending subsequent discharge via the Wylie committee mechanism included Eddie Saunderson, who had achieved notoriety while acting as private secretary to Lord French between 1918 and 1921, and Alfred Tennyson, Birrell's stepson, both of whom still held substantive positions as local government inspectors.[102] While the *Freeman's Journal* carried reports in February about meetings of the staff presided over by Dr Peter Cowan, the chief engineering inspector, to discuss the issue of transferring to the new government or the alternative of retiring, a significant proportion of them were happy to transfer and to continue in the civil service of the new state.[103] The separate Dáil department continued to function until July when McCarron sent proposals to Gregg in Finance to bring an end to what he described as the recent plurality of control, the consequent inevitable disorganisation and temporary expedients of various kinds. Formal sanction to assimilation proposals (including new gradings and salary scales for each staff member) was conveyed by Finance in September, allowing the Dáil officials to be assigned to pensionable or non-pensionable posts in the new department, depending on whether they had joined the department before or after the Truce. However, although the former department had been one of the successes of the 1919–21 period and had expanded its activities considerably between the Truce and the Treaty, former LGB officials filled most of the more senior positions after 1922. Blythe told the Bureau of Military History in 1954[104] that McCarron's appointment and the relative positions of the two groups of staff had led to the threat of a crisis similar to that which had arisen in the Civic Guards in May 1922 when ex-RIC men had been employed as officers and instructors. He went on to note that:

> Local government authorities throughout the country, under the guidance of the officials of the Dáil Local Government Department, had been fighting and defying the Local Government Board and carrying on the work of the various councils contrary to all the instructions and wishes of the board. In consequence, the LGB was looked upon with some of the hatred with which volunteers looked

upon the headquarters staff of the RIC. Although we proceeded to dismiss the members of the board, like Dr Bigger, practically all the Dáil officials who had been carrying on the fight, were very discontented when they learned that an official of the old board was going to be Secretary of the department and their official superior. A rumour reached me that the Dáil officials had had a meeting and had made up their minds to resign in a body and do their best to carry all the councils in the country over to the anti-Treaty side. Whether everybody was present at such a meeting or not I do not know, but that some such plan was being canvassed I was certain – and it was afterwards admitted.

According to his 1954 statement, Blythe's plan of action against 'the prospective mutineers' was to take the list of salaries which had been fixed for the Dáil officials (but not announced) and without any personal knowledge of the circumstances or qualifications of the officials concerned, to adjust individual salaries upwards or downwards on an arbitrary basis, creating a 'deep and lasting split' among the officials and making concerted action impossible. There is no documentary evidence that such a plan ever existed or that it was implemented, although Blythe did direct in November 1922 that the salaries of a small number of former Dáil staff should be increased. He also directed in January 1923 that Dr Cowan, the board's experienced chief engineering inspector who had opted to continue in the service of the new state, should be summarily dismissed on the spurious ground that this was 'in consequence of the need for reorganising the department'.[106] As Cosgrave recalled it years later, the amalgamation of the two staff groups had 'presented a complication' to Cornelius Gregg and his colleagues in the establishment section of the Ministry of Finance, but the problem was eased to some extent by the fact that some of what he described as 'the British officials' retired and by the assignment of some of the Dáil staff to other departments. However, he gave the impression (which is confirmed by surviving files) that it was left mainly to Gregg, in consultation with McCarron, to sort out the problem as ministers like himself and Blythe were then far too busy with other things to be able to devote much time to staffing issues.[107]

In February 1923, there were still unresolved staffing problems, as is clear from McCarron's letter to the Department of Finance about his department's estimates for 1923/24. His staffing situation was far from satisfactory, he explained, because 'to an extent far exceeding that affecting any of the former departments of government, the staff of the Local Government Board has been dispersed to other ministries, while of those remaining, a substantial number is for political reasons totally or partially disemployed'.[108] Continuing dissatisfaction among former Dáil Éireann officials with the fact that LGB staff held influential positions surfaced again at a meeting of An Choiste Gnótha of Cumann na nGaedheal on 10 October 1924, when the elder brother of Michael Collins, Sean (Johnny) Collins, who had been given a position in the Land Commission, complained about officials in the Department of Local Government who 'were all-powerful and dictate policy'. In response, Blythe, in his usual blunt fashion, argued that the agitation arose 'from disappointed job-hunters or those who failed to get promotion ... the whole thing was only bunkum ... revenue could not meet the added expense of pensioning off all the people to whom objection was made'. Kevin O'Higgins admitted that it would be pleasing to turn out all the unpopular officials and dismiss those who did not have an Irish outlook, but the cost of pensions had to be considered and 'to avoid breaking ourselves we must use these people in the present situation'. When Johnny Collins retorted that 'a man or two at the head of departments is all that need be changed – and the country was willing to pay', Cosgrave joined the debate, pointing out that 'the heads of departments who were appointed as having an Irish outlook were in the majority ... no one who entered the civil service by competitive examination had been dismissed, only some who had entered by patronage or were politically impossible'. He admitted, however, that the civil service was a problem which they had not had time to examine.[109] More than ten years later, civil servants who had served Dáil Éireann before the Treaty were still unhappy at the manner in which they had been dealt with. As they saw it, their interests and claims had received little consideration and instead of being the absorbing body, they were themselves absorbed and denied the status or salary to which their rank in the Dáil civil service entitled them.[110]

'A Somewhat Vague Remnant of the LGB'

Robinson's retirement on 1 April 1922 marked the end of his long association with local government affairs in Ireland, but it was to take more than sixty years after that to wind up the scheme of housing for ex-sailors and soldiers which, as described in chapter XIV, he had pressed ahead enthusiastically during 1921, effectively disregarding the implications of impending constitutional change and without keeping the Chief Secretary's Office and the Treasury fully briefed. In the short term, there were special problems in relation to the large housing scheme at Killester in north Dublin where site development and construction work had been undertaken by the LGB, initially on a direct labour basis. By April 1922 only a small number of dwellings had been completed and it was emerging that the final unit cost would come to more than £1,300, as against about £800 for dwellings erected elsewhere.[111] After his retirement, Robinson was reminded by Waterfield, more in sorrow than in anger, that this made nonsense of the assurances he had provided 'in most emphatic language' about the likely costs of the Killester scheme.[112]

Around the country, relatively few of the 3,672 houses, which had been pledged by the LGB to ex-servicemen, had been completed when the board went out of existence.[113] It was agreed at a conference between British and Irish ministers that funds would be provided by the British government[114] for the continuation of the programme, but Cosgrave made it clear that he did not want to have the work carried out by his new department.[115] Thus, after the LGB was taken over on 1 April by the provisional government, the staff unit dealing with the scheme continued in a limbo-like position, effectively a separate department of the Imperial Government, but Robinson's offer to continue to direct the operation as a representative of that government was not taken up.[116] In November, the two governments agreed to set up a trust with a capital of £1.5 million and a mandate to complete the dwellings which the LGB had undertaken to provide.[117] Subsequently, legislation was enacted in both jurisdictions to set up the Irish Sailors and Soldiers Land Trust[118] as 'a somewhat vague remnant of the LGB'.[119] The trust was staffed in 1923 by seventeen permanent civil servants, some of whom were former LGB staff, as well as temporary clerical staff and inspectors paid by the Colonial Office. With headquarters in London and local offices in Dublin and Belfast, the organisation continued until 1987/88, when it was finally wound up under legislation passed by the British and Irish parliaments, sixty years after Robinson had gone to his grave.[120] His promotion of the scheme – some aspects of which were described by Waterfield as having 'all the ingredients of a pretty scandal'[121] – had resulted in the addition (at the expense of the British government) of several thousand units to the housing stock of the Free State, but the whole episode must be seen as an unfortunate and regrettable conclusion to an otherwise distinguished official career.

NOTES

1   Sir Henry Robinson, *Memories Wise and Otherwise* (London, 1923), pp.295–96.
2   Sir John Ross, *Pilgrim Scrip* (London, 1927), pp.244–45.
3   W. H. Kautt (ed.), *Ground Truths: British Army Operations in the Irish War of Independence* (Sallins, 2014), p.186.

4   Anderson to Chief Secretary, 11 May, 1921, Parliamentary Archives, Lloyd George Papers, LG/F/19/4/10.

5   Paul McMahon, *British Spies and Irish Rebels: British Intelligence and Ireland, 1916–45* (Woodbridge, 2008), p.63.

6   Keith Middlemas (ed.), *Thomas Jones Whitehall Diary* (Vol. III) (London, 1971), p.99–100.

7   Major-General Hugh Tudor had been appointed police adviser to the Irish administration in May 1900.

8   Letter of Aug. 1921, presumed to be addressed to Tom Jones, in *Jones Whitehall Diary*, pp.104–05.

9   Government of Ireland Act: Memorandum by the Chief Secretary for Ireland, C.P. 3369, 6 Oct. 1921, TNA, CAB 24/128.

10 Ireland: Memorandum by the Secretary of State for War, S.F.B. 14, 22 Oct. 1921, TNA, CAB 43/2.

11 Michael Laffan, *The Resurrection of Ireland* (Cambridge, 1999), p.342.

12 Letter of 21 Aug. 1921, NAI, DE 2/475.

13 Dáil Éireann, Official Report, 17 Aug. 1921, 33–36; Minutes of Proceedings, private session, 22 Aug. 1921, 35–38.

14 W.T. Cosgrave, BMH, WS 449, 14 Nov. 1950.

15 Dáil Éireann, Minutes of Proceedings, private session, 25 Jan. 1921, 255.

16 Mary E. Daly, *The Buffer State* (Dublin, 1997), pp.91–2.

17 Irish Office Survey of Present Situation, 27 Apr. 1921, TNA, CO 904/232.

18 Robinson, *Memories*, pp.327–28.

19 *Hansard* V, 140, 4 Apr. 1921, 16–17; the figures include county and county borough councils, urban and rural district councils, the separate boards of guardians and the town commissioners.

20 Relations between Irish Local Authorities and the LGB: Memorandum by Chief Secretary for Ireland C.P. 3230, 16 Aug. 1921, TNA, CAB 24/127.

21 George Chester Duggan (*Periscope*), 'The Last Days of Dublin Castle', *Blackwood's Magazine*, 1282 (Aug. 1922), vol. 212, p.186.

22 Robinson to Anderson, 16 July 1921, NAI, CSORP 1921/2503/8.

23 Exchequer assistance towards payment of compensation for malicious damage in Ireland, Memorandum by the Chief Secretary for Ireland, C.P. 2637, 1 Mar. 1921, TNA, CAB 24/120; Conclusions of a meeting of the Cabinet, no. 14 (21), 22 Mar. 1921, TNA, CAB 23/24.

24 Memorandum by the Chief Secretary for Ireland, C.P. 3012, 3 June 1921, TNA, CAB 24/125; Conclusions of a meeting of the Cabinet no. 49 (21), 14 June 1921, TNA, CAB 23/26.

25 Conclusions of a meeting of the cabinet no. 71 (21), 19 Aug. 1921, TNA, CAB 23/26.

26 Robinson to Greenwood, 10 Aug. 1921, attached to Memorandum by Chief Secretary for Ireland, C.P. 3230, 16 Aug. 1921, TNA, CAB 24/127.

27 *Hansard* V, 150, 15 Feb. 1922, 1005.

28 *Irish Times*, 1 Dec. 1921.

29   Report of the Cabinet Committee appointed to consider what steps should be taken on approval of the Treaty (P.G.I. 18), submitted with memorandum C.P. 3601, 11 Jan. 1922, TNA, CAB 24/132.
30   Heads of Working Arrangements for implementing the Treaty as settled ... in London on 24 Jan. 1922 (C.P. 3648), TNA, CAB 24/132.
31   *Hansard* V, 150, 22 Feb. 1922, 2013–28; 24 Feb. 1922, 2245–49.
32   Seanad Debates, Vol. 3, 24 July 1924, 935.
33   *Compensation (Ireland) Commission, Warrant of Appointment*, 8 May 1922, HC 1922 [Cmd. 1654].
34   R. B. McDowell, *Crisis and Decline: The Fate of the Southern Unionists* (Dublin, 1997), p.109.
35   Robinson's application to the Irish grants committee, 15 Nov. 1926, TNA, CO 762/32/24, No. 478.
36   Robinson to Captain A. F. Hemming, private secretary to Greenwood (no date but probably late Dec.1921), TNA, HO 317/60.
37   Possibly a reference to a statement by Chamberlain in the House of Commons that the government would do its best to secure a chairman 'whose sagacity and impartiality will meet with the acceptance of both sides' (*Hansard* V, 149, 16 Dec. 1921, 357–58).
38   Robinson to Birrell (probably late Jan. 1912), TNA, CO 906/18/1.
39   Robinson, *Memories*, pp.228, 296, 323–4.
40   Minutes of meetings of the Provisional Government, NAI, G 1/1.
41   *Irish Times*, 17 Jan. 1922.
42   Robinson, *Memories*, p.324; Minutes of meetings of the Provisional Government, NAI, G 1/1; Sir John Ross also wrote about 'the surrender of Dublin Castle' – an almost incredible thing, which left loyalists in despair (*Pilgrim Scrip* (London, 1927), p.245).
43   Robinson, *Memories*, pp.325–26, 329.
44   *Irish Times*, 17 Jan. 1922.
45   Dáil Debates, 1 Mar. 1922, 141.
46   Cosgrave to Collins, 19 Aug. 1922, UCDA, Mulcahy MSS, P7/B/29(6).
47   Conference on Ireland: Lionel Curtis, Memorandum on the Provisional Government as contemplated by Article 17 of the Treaty, S. F. (B) 40, 10 Dec. 1921, TNA, CAB 43/2.
48   John McColgan, *British Policy and the Irish Administration 1920–22* (London, 1983), p.97.
49   Robinson to Greenwood, 6 Aug. 1921, attached to Memorandum C.P. 3230 submitted to the Cabinet on 16 Aug. 1921, TNA, CAB 24/127.
50   Department of the Environment and Local Government, Secretary's Office Papers, Folder no. 7.
51   *Irish Times*, 17 Jan. 1922.
52   *Irish Times*, 19 Jan. 1922.
53   *Irish Times*, 23 Jan. 1922.
54   *Irish Times*, 26 Jan. 1922.

55   *Irish Times,* 2 and 17 Mar. 1922.

56   *Iris Oifigiúil,* 21 Mar. 1922, 131–32.

57   T.J. McArdle, BMH, WS 501, 19 Feb. 1951; a list of the staff of the Dáil department serving before 1 April 1922 is included in NAI, DE 5/2/51.

58   McArdle had been a second division clerk in the LGB until 31 October 1918 when he was dismissed for refusing to take the Oath of Allegiance; he joined the staff of the Dáil Department in September 1920.

59   Memorial dated 15 Feb. 1922 addressed by Lorcan Robins to the President of Dáil Éireann, NAI, DE 2/243; copy also in NAI, DE 4/11/60.

60   Minutes of meetings of the Provisional Government, NAI, G 1/1.

61   *Freeman's Journal,* 1 Feb. 1922.

62   Robins had been on the staff of the Dáil department from February 1921 onwards and was elected to the second Dáil in June 1921.

63   The resignation of Barlas was reported to his ministerial colleagues by Cosgrave on 3 March.

64   *Irish Times,* 3 Feb. 1922.

65   Department of the Environment and Local Government, Secretary's Office Files.

66   See biography of McCarron by Brendan O Donoghue, a new entry added to the electronic version of the *Dictionary of Irish Biography,* Dec. 2013.

67   I am grateful to Charles Lysaght for bringing this information to my notice.

68   Waterfield to Anderson, 7 Mar. 1922, TNA, T.158/7.

69   George Chester Duggan, typescript draft of an unpublished book entitled *The Life of a Civil Servant,* pp.20–21, NLI, Leon Ó Broin Papers, MS 31,689.

70   Dáil Éireann, Official Report, 1 Mar. 1922, 141–142.

71   Minutes of meetings of the Provisional Government, 3 and 10 Mar. 1922, NAI, G 1/1.

72   Anderson – Robinson correspondence, Mar.–Apr. 1921, NAI, CSORP 1921/3065.

73   Postscript to letter of 12 Jan. 1921 from Robinson to Anderson, TNA HO 317/62.

74   Robinson to Greenwood, 26 Mar. 1921, NAI, CSORP 1921/3065/2.

75   Greenwood to Robinson, 29 Mar. 1921, NAI, CSORP 1921/3065/2.

76   Robinson to Anderson, 26 Mar. 1921, TNA, CO 904/26.

77   *Irish Independent,* 6 Apr. 1921.

78   *Irish Independent,* 20 June 1921.

79   *Irish Independent,* 24 Jan. 1922.

80   Memorandum for the Provisional Government from Waterfield, 23 Jan. 1922, TNA T.162/85.

81   Waterfield to Robinson, 4 Feb. 1922, TNA, T.158/7; Robinson had suggested to Anderson in January 1921 that Charles O'Conor 'will probably run the southern section of the board' (letter of 12 Jan. 1921, TNA, HO 317/62).

82   *Irish Times,* 8 Mar. 1922; a similar report appeared in the *Irish Independent* on the same date.

83   NAI, DE 2/243.

84   Smith, a native of County Down, had been a higher division clerk in the LGB since 1901 and a senior clerk since 1907; he transferred to the Department of Local Government in 1922.

85 Waterfield to Anderson, 7 Mar. 1922, TNA, T.158/7; Waterfield to Robinson, 9 Mar. 1922, TNA, T.158/8; Waterfield to McCarron and to PMG, 9 Mar. 1922, T.158/8.

86 Letters of 27 and 30 Mar. 1922 from L.T. MacCosgair and letter of appointment dated 31 March 1922, NAI, FIN/1/2658.

87 Joseph Brennan Papers, NLI, MS 26,205.

88 *Iris Oifigiúil*, 4 Apr. 1922, pp.167–180.

89 *Iris Oifigiúil*, 14 Apr. 1922.

90 *London Gazette*, 4 Apr. 1922.

91 At OPW, Sir Philip Hanson was chairman until 1934; Sir J. A. Glynn was chairman of the National Health Insurance Commission until 1933; at DATI, T. P. Gill continued in office until 1923 as did W. L. Micks of the CDB.

92 O'Conor retired at the end of 1923 while Coey-Bigger retired in September 1922 (NAI, Wylie Committee minute book and unsorted boxes of applications to the committee).

93 Martin Maguire, *The Civil Service and the Revolution in Ireland, 1912–38* (Manchester, 2008), p.157, relying on NAI E 75/15, not now available.

94 Department of the Environment and Local Government, Secretary's Office file.

95 Ernest Blythe, BMH, WS 939, 12 Apr. 1954, pp.163–64.

96 Watt's memorandum of 12 Aug. 1921, PRONI, CAB 4/15/1, cited in McColgan, *British Policy and the Irish Administration*, pp.62–63.

97 Letters of 21 Sept. and 18 Nov. 1921, TNA, T.160/220.

98 Circular of 10 Nov. 1921, TNA, T.160/220; NLI, Joseph Brennan Papers, MS 26,203/1.

99 Waterfield to LGB, 26 Nov. 1921 and reply from Barlas, 14 Dec. 1921, TNA, T.162/74.

100 Minutes of the Provisional Government, NAI, G 1/1.

101 Department of the Environment and Local Government, Secretary's Office Papers, Folder No. 5.

102 Department of the Environment and Local Government, Secretary's Office Papers, Folder No.4 containing departmental staff list; Saunderson retired on pension with effect from 1 June 1923, following consideration of his case by the Wylie Committee.

103 *Freeman's Journal*, 1 and 3 Feb 1922.

104 Ernest Blythe, BMH, WS 939, 12 Apr. 1954.

105 McCarron to Gregg, 20 Nov. 1922, NAI, E/48.

106 Blythe to McCarron, Jan. 1923, Dept. of the Environment and Local Government, Secretary's Office File; for biographical information on Cowan, see Brendan O Donoghue, *The Irish County Surveyors: A Biographical Dictionary* (Dublin, 2007), pp.137–143.

107 Letter (ca. 1955) from W. T. Cosgrave in Leon Ó Broin Papers, NLI, MS 31,692.

108 McCarron to Department of Finance, 25 Jan. 1923, NAI, FIN 1/1726.

109 Minutes of meeting of An Choiste Gnótha, 10 Oct. 1924 (copy), NLI, Leon Ó Broin unsorted papers.

110 Statement submitted to the Commission of Inquiry into the Civil Service by the Association of Dáil Civil Servants and Dismissed British Civil Servants, Memoranda of Evidence submitted to the Commission, 1935.

111   Waterfield to Anderson, 1 May 1922, TNA, HO 317/66.

112   Waterfield to Robinson, 4 and 6 Apr. 1922, TNA, T.158/8.

113   Sturgis to Anderson, 3 Nov. 1922, TNA, HO 317/66.

114   Heads of working arrangements for implementing the Treaty (2nd revise, 23 Jan. 1922), NLI, Leon Ó Broin papers, MS 31,666; Memorandum C.P. 3648 of 24 Jan. 1922, TNA, CAB 24/132.

115   Waterfield to Anderson, 7 Mar. 1922, TNA, T.158/7.

116   Robinson to Waterfield and Waterfield to Robinson, 14 and 16 Nov. 1921, TNA, T.160/214.

117   Note of meeting of 9 Nov. 1922 between the Cabinet committee on Irish affairs and ministers of the provisional government, NLI, Joseph Brennan Papers, MS 26,213.

118   Irish Free State (Consequential Provisions) Act, 1922, 13 Geo. 5, ch. 2, session 2, 5 Dec. 1922; Land Trust Powers Act, 1923 (No. 25 of 1923).

119   Browne to Waterfield, 29 Aug. 1923, TNA, T.162/97.

120   The Irish Sailors and Soldiers Land Trust Act, 1987, ch. 48; The Irish Sailors and Soldiers Land Trust Act, 1988 (No. 33 of 1988).

121   Waterfield to Anderson, 1 May 1922, TNA, HO 317/66.

CHAPTER XIX

Family Matters and Final Years, 1922–27

Robinson's Family

On 6 November 1883 Henry Robinson married Harriet Lynch-Blosse, daughter of Sir Robert Lynch-Blosse, 10th Baronet, of Athavallie, near Balla, County Mayo and his wife, Harriet Browne, daughter of the 2nd Marquess of Sligo. The Lynch-Blosse estate of more than 17,500 acres had been the location of some of the earliest mass protests during the first Land War when Davitt, Parnell and other speakers denounced a proposed eviction in November 1879. Athavallie itself was an overnight stop in October 1890 when Arthur Balfour, his Under-Secretary, Sir Joseph West-Ridgeway, and his private secretary, George Wyndham, toured the West.[1] The estate was later sold to the CDB and the house became a convent and girls' school run by the St Louis nuns.

As one of her sons recorded it, 21-year-old Harriet effectively dealt with her grandfather's determination that she should marry a Mayo landowner by slipping out one morning after breakfast while the family were living temporarily at Folkestone (possibly to escape the Land League agitation) to marry Robinson in the local parish church with only his brother Sydney and the verger as witnesses.[2] Reconciliation with Harriet's family was achieved some time later. The Robinsons had three sons, two of whom served in the LGB at different times:

Christopher Henry (later, Sir Christopher Henry Lynch-Robinson), was born on 18 October 1884 and spent his early years at Westport where his father was then based. Educated at Wellington College and at Sandhurst, he was commissioned in the Royal Fusiliers in 1904 and after service in Bermuda and South Africa spent two years in Jamaica as ADC to the governor, Sir Sydney (later Baron) Olivier. Having resigned his commission, he became a temporary assistant inspector in the LGB, was appointed as resident magistrate (RM) in 1912 and was later called to the Bar. With the other RMs, who were still nominally serving in April 1922, he continued in a state of limbo until August when the appointments were formally terminated by the provisional government; his subsequent claim to have been *The last of the Irish R.M.s* (London, 1951) was therefore slightly misleading. Having gone to live in England, he worked for a few years as political private secretary to Lord Dunraven and subsequently worked in a managerial capacity for a food processing company. In February 1947 he assumed the surname *Lynch*, obtained an assignment of the arms of Lynch in addition to those of Robinson and was subsequently known as Sir Christopher Lynch-Robinson. With his brother, Adrian, he wrote *Intelligible Heraldry* (London, 1948). Christopher succeeded his father as second Baronet in 1927 and died at Hove, Sussex, on 22 November 1958

Bryan Arthur, born on 26 October 1889, was commissioned as a temporary second lieutenant in the Royal Army Service Corps on 3 January 1916. He was farming in England in the early 1920s but was described as a retired civil servant when he died without issue in London on 4 November 1963.[3]

Adrian, born in Dublin on 14 April 1892, was educated at Charterhouse, TCD (BA, 1912) and Kings Inns (1912–15) before being called to the Bar in 1915. While still studying, he became a temporary assistant inspector in the LGB and was subsequently appointed to an established position. His assignment to the Belfast district in 1921 meant that he automatically became part of the civil service of the government of Northern Ireland that year. He served initially as general inspector at the Ministry of Home Affairs, became Chief Inspector in 1930, then an assistant secretary, and Permanent Secretary of the Ministry in 1939, becoming in effect a virtual successor to his grandfather and father. When a separate Ministry of Health and Local Government was created in 1944 he became permanent secretary of that ministry and on his retirement in 1957 was the last official serving in Northern Ireland who had begun his career in Dublin. He died in Belfast on 2 December 1975.

In 1901 Henry Robinson and his wife were living at No. 12 Haddington Terrace, a large house on the seafront at Kingstown (now Dun Laoghaire), opposite the East Pier, with their two younger sons and five servants. His mother-in-law, Lady Harriet Lynch-Blosse, aged 74, lived next door at No. 11 with six servants.[4] By 1904, the Robinsons had moved to Lisnacarrig, Brighton Road, Foxrock, where Christopher and Adrian were living with their parents in 1911, with four female servants, including a cook and a ladies maid.[5] A large, attractive, early Victorian house on almost six acres, Lisnacarrig was originally known as Mount Aventine. It was designed by E. H. Carson (the Dublin architect best known as the father of Sir Edward) and was built in the early 1860s for John Bentley, one of the developers of the lands in the Foxrock area.[6] It adjoined Kilteragh – the ninety-acre estate acquired around the turn of the century by Sir Horace Plunkett, Vice-President of DATI, who built a spacious house there in 1905–06. At the time, Foxrock was a relatively undeveloped suburb within easy reach of the city by rail from the nearby station or, for early motorists like Robinson and Plunkett, by the main Bray road.

Freedom from Official Shackles

Unlike some of the senior staff of the board, Robinson had no plans to leave Ireland permanently when the provisional government took up its duties in April 1922. Having attended the official opening by the Lord Lieutenant of the annual RHA exhibition on 3 April,[7] he and his wife, to 'signalize his freedom from official shackles', began a long sea voyage, leaving Liverpool on 7 April in one of the Booth Shipping Company's liners and culminating in a trip on the River Amazon, which he found to be an enthralling experience and one which drowned out any thought of Ireland, past, present and future.[8] He arrived back in England in mid-May and on his return to Dublin, resumed residence at Lisnacarrig. [9] He would obviously have been aware of a document signed on 11 January by Arthur Griffith, as President of Dáil Éireann, outlining an indemnity to be granted by the provisional government to all British government officials and stating that every possible step would be taken to protect such persons and their property in the future.[10] In practice, however, with the civil war raging from the end of June, there was little the government could do to give effect to their good intentions, leaving Robinson and others like him in a vulnerable position.

The *Irish Times* reported on 21 August that armed men had raided Robinson's house on the previous Friday night (18 August) and destroyed a great deal of property, including a valuable collection of rare china, having been kept at bay by Sir Henry and one of his sons with automatic pistols until their ammunition was exhausted. *The Times,* on the same day, also reported the incident, adding that the occupants of the house had put up a fight for half an hour before they were overpowered.[11] In a letter to the *Irish Times* a few days later, Robinson corrected the press reports, stating that after his son Christopher and himself had 'ceased firing and surrendered to the Irregulars to save the house being burned over our heads', the raiders had honoured their undertaking to do no violence to person or property and seemed anxious in making their search for arms, binoculars and other things to avoid doing damage. His real grievance was that 'the two men who broke into the house first to reconnoitre opened fire on us at sight without a word of warning or explanation'.[12] In his 1923 memoirs he stated that the house 'was broken into by armed Irregulars who opened fire upon me and my family and looted everything they wanted' including his notes for a proposed book, his private papers and many of his best photographs.[13] In 1926, when claiming compensation, he presented a still more dramatic picture of the events, noting that the attack involved 'revolver fighting through the passages' and a three and a half hour siege, after which the house was smashed up and valuables stolen.

A more embroidered account of the incident given by Christopher Robinson almost thirty years later tells of a duel within the house between two men with revolvers and the two Robinsons who were armed with automatics, firing at five yards range at most, in which nobody was hit – which seems a rather unlikely story.[14] His account goes on to mention a subsequent parley, which led to a search of the house for arms and the departure of the raiders 'having filled their pockets with loot'. He stated also that the family learned on the day after the raid that the attack had been carried out by local hooligans rather than by the Irregulars, a statement which is consistent with his father's recall of a warning from one of his workmen that an armed gang were 'coming down from the Dublin mountains in the evenings raiding and looting on all sides'.[15] It does appear, however, that Foxrock was an area of considerable low-level republican activity in 1922,[16] to such an extent that Sir Horace Plunkett advised John Dillon on 14 August that he could not use his own motor car, or keep it at his home at Kilteragh, and warned Dillon to come by train to Kilteragh rather than by motor 'as the republicans are in possession of this district'.[17] Plunkett's diary for 22 August records that shots were fired at his house from the plantation of pine trees which surrounded the house during a more determined attack on a neighbour – possibly a reference to the attack on the Robinson home.

Robinson and his son left somewhat conflicting accounts of the events which followed the attack on Lisnacarrig:

- Robinson wrote in 1926 that on the morning after the raid he appealed to the provisional government for assistance and while he received every courtesy from Mr Cosgrave personally, he was told that the most he could do would be to provide the protection of a company of soldiers for a few days while he removed what was left of his property for safe storage elsewhere in Dublin, after which Cosgrave considered that it would be wise for him to get out of the country at once. In due course, Cosgrave sent a detachment of military in armoured cars, one of which was ambushed on the way from Dublin; the military had to fight their way to reach the house and while they were encamped in the grounds they were subjected to heavy rifle-fire from the woods around.[18]
- Christopher, writing in 1951, told of a visit to Lisnacarrig by Michael Collins in an armoured car on the morning after the raid, having survived an ambush on the Stillorgan Road. According to Christopher, it was Collins who advised the family that the government were not in a position to protect anybody and that they 'had much better clear out and come back later on when things had settled down a bit'.[19]

While it is difficult to determine whether one or other of these accounts can be fully believed, the best available evidence is a memorandum dated 19 August 1922 which Henry Robinson presented to W. T. Cosgrave when he called to his office that morning and a subsequent letter from Cosgrave to Collins. Robinson's memorandum recorded that at about 10.00 p.m. the night before, two men had entered the house and ran through the kitchen into the front hall. While Robinson and his family waited on the top landing –

> ...one of the raiders then fired a revolver at us, whereupon my son and I took out our revolvers and fired at the flash. The man was so alarmed at finding us armed that he jumped through the hall window, and the other man got out the back. Shortly afterwards, a good number of men came and surrounded the house and opened fire from all quarters. After a while they called on us to surrender and as our ammunition was nearly all gone, we did so on the understanding that our lives would be spared and no violence done. This they promised and kept their promise. Seven or eight then came into the house, took our three revolvers, shotgun, field glasses, a gold watch and chain, and some jewellery and said they

would do no more. They left me under the impression that their headquarters might take a different view of my conduct.

Following Robinson's visit to his office, Cosgrave, who was then acting chairman of the provisional government, telephoned the office of Michael Collins, as Commander-in-Chief, telling him that Robinson was very anxious about his wife who had suffered severely from shock after the night's happenings and asked that immediate protection should be provided for the family before they left Ireland later that day. [20] In a follow-up letter to Collins, Cosgrave told him that he was impressed by the fact that Robinson had put up a good fight and noted that Sir Henry had 'very powerful influence behind him in England and had been of very great assistance to us since the taking-over; as far back as February last, he gave £1,200 for the relief of distress in the West'. For these reasons he was very anxious to accommodate him in any ordinary matter and much more so in a matter, to him, of life and death. The whole Foxrock district within a radius of two miles around Robinson's house, Cosgrave added, had been infested with Irregulars and thieves for some time past: there had been raids and shootings and Robinson's own motor car had been taken away for some days. Collins and his staff appear to have responded quickly to Cosgrave's plea for protection for the Robinsons: a manuscript note at the foot of his letter records that arrangements had been made for a guard to report at 2.30 p.m. that day.

Reports of Michael Collins' busy round of activities on 18–19 August make no mention of a visit to Lisnacarrig but such a visit is not inconsistent with those reports. After he had apparently been dropped off on 18 August at Greystones, where his fiancée was staying at the Grand Hotel, his car was ambushed near Stillorgan that afternoon on its return to Dublin. Collins sent a note to Desmond Fitzgerald, director of publicity, on the following morning, expressing his disappointment that the ambush had not been reported in the press,[21] and as a result, an official statement was carried on the front page of the *Sunday Independent* on 20 August indicating that 'the Commander-in-Chief's car was ambushed at 1.00 p.m. on Friday [18 August] on the Dublin side of Stillorgan on its way from Greystones'. Collins was not in the car, which was badly damaged by rifle fire and a bomb, and one of the drivers was wounded and taken to hospital.[22]

Richard Mulcahy recalled that Collins had an early breakfast with him at Portobello barracks on Saturday 19 August,[23] while Marjorie Forester recorded that Collins left the barracks that morning on another visit to Greystones.[24] If Christopher Robinson's statements can be relied on, the Collins visit to Lisnacarrig that day must have been one of his last official activities in the Dublin area, fitted in perhaps on his journey to Greystones, on the day before he began the ill-fated tour of inspection to the south which was to lead to his death on 22 August. Around 6.00 p.m. on 19 August, the Crossley touring car in which Collins was travelling was badly damaged in a collision with a vehicle carrying national army troops in York Street, Dun Laoghaire and another car had to be obtained for him.[25] Collins was back again in Foxrock that evening when Elizabeth, Countess of Fingall, recorded that he was brought to supper at Sir Horace Plunkett's house by Sir John and Lady Hazel Lavery, who had been staying at the Salthill Hotel, Monkstown; W. T. Cosgrave and George Bernard Shaw were also there.[26] An entry in Plunkett's diary for 19 August confirms that 'Lady Lavery brought Michael Collins to supper ... he took a risk in coming here without an escort. I fear he is too careless of his life. His car was bombed only yesterday when, luckily, he was not in it.'[27]

After the raid on his house, Robinson lodged a claim for compensation of £325 in respect of malicious damage, but he was apparently awarded only £40 in respect of actual damage to the outside and inside of the house, as no claim could be entertained for stolen jewellery, silver, plate and clothes, and for damage to the flower beds, fruit trees and lawns.[28] Four years later, under pressure from the London-based Southern Irish Loyalist Relief Association and others, the British government established a new Irish Grants Committee to deal, *inter alia*, with claims for compensation from southern Irish loyalists who had suffered loss or damage between the date of the Truce and the end of the civil war in 1923. A claim submitted by Robinson on 3 November – among the first received by the committee – sought recoupment of £1,000 towards the expenses which he incurred by reason of the attack on his house. He was awarded £400 compensation at the end of May, and even though this was only a fraction of the losses for which he had claimed, he wrote – in what may well have been his last official letter – that he was immensely cheered at the knowledge that he was wrong in believing that there was no sympathy in England for people like himself and that the 'English Government had a kindly thought for our tribulations after all.'[29]

Following the incident at his residence, Robinson took the advice he had been given and went to live in England, as Plunkett was to do when his house at Foxrock was mined and fired by republicans in January 1923.[30] For nine months, he travelled with his wife from place to place in England 'living in hotels and trying to get my wife's health and nerves restored after her experience in Ireland'. To meet these expenses, he was obliged to sell stocks and shares to the value of £1,000. The couple spent a week in Dublin in March 1923 before returning to the south of England.[31]

The residue of the furniture and other contents of Lisnacarrig, including prints, 1,000 books, and all outdoor effects, were auctioned at the house in September,[32] but the house itself did not sell for some time – Robinson had to go on paying rent and rates and wages 'to keep the place up' until it passed to Edmund Mooney about 1925.[33] The house was offered for sale in an executor's sale on 13 June 1933 and was on the market again in 1995 when it was sold for £2 million, believed to be the top price paid for a Dublin house until then.[34] Standing in its original grounds of about six acres, Lisnacarrig is still (2015) privately owned and is possibly the last and the finest of the original houses in an area where the curtilages of many of the adjoining properties have been developed for apartments and suburban housing.

In pressing for an early decision on his compensation claim in May 1927, Robinson wrote that the rebels had left him with 'such a legacy of high pressure heart trouble that … I seem never to have got free of illness and nursing homes'.[35] Exactly five months later, on Sunday 16 October 1927, the angina and arterio-sclerosis from which he had suffered led to his death at his home, Highmoor, Kingsbridge Road, Parkstone, a suburb of Poole, Dorset.[36] He was buried on 19 October at Parkstone Cemetery. His wife, Dame Harriet, who survived him, died in England on 14 January 1942 and her ashes were buried at Parkstone two weeks later.[37] Robinson left gross estate of £13,181.[38] His eldest son, Christopher, succeeded to the Baronetcy.

Obituaries

A lengthy *Irish Times* obituary recorded that Robinson had the reputation of having a better understanding of the real Ireland than that possessed by any other administrator and was chosen as the man to acquaint successive chief secretaries with the nature of the country and its people.[39] Although he belonged naturally to the old class of Irish unionists, he served successive governments loyally and was credited at large with a great way of getting his own will with them all. His major part in drafting the 1898 Act and bringing the new local government system into operation was noted, as was his association with the Labourers Acts. An editorial on the same day described him as one of 'the band of able and devoted men' who ruled Ireland under the British regime but had lived to see most of their work undone for better or worse. It went on:

> His knowledge of the problems of local administration and of rural congestion and poverty was profound. He knew the Irish peasant's

character as few men have known it. He loved his country and worked earnestly for it and his patriotism was only half-concealed by a certain cynicism in his outlook on public affairs. For a full generation, Sir Henry Robinson was, perhaps, the most influential citizen of Ireland. Chief secretaries came and went –'transient and embarrassed phantoms' as one of them said – but the Vice-President of the Local Government Board was the permanent power behind the throne. He played the part of Chiron to every new Achilles – at least a score of them, and every one of them, as all soon discovered, with a vulnerable heel. A grand tour of Ireland under Sir Henry's guidance was for every new chief secretary a part of the ritual of government and after that experience, made delightful by his guide's wit and information, every one of them, even the most suspicious liberal, saw Irish affairs largely through Sir Henry's eyes. It was a fortunate thing for Ireland that those eyes, despite their sometimes malicious twinkle, were so knowledgeable and so kind.

The Times obituary asserted that it was universally admitted that Robinson had discharged his onerous responsibility faithfully and efficiently between 1898 and 1922 and noted that his work in drafting and implementing the new local government system in 1898 'may be said to have been the preparation of the Irish democracy for the fuller measure of self-government which it has now to exercise'. It recorded that:

> He knew Ireland from end to end [and] understood his own people as few have ever understood them. He knew every ruse of the local politician and place-hunter and how to counter them with imperturbable good humour and supreme tact. He had many opponents, but even the strongest of them were not his personal enemies. In the latter days of the British administration of Ireland, Sir Henry's unrivalled experience and ripe judgment were an immense asset to the Irish government. It is significant that, when shortly before his assassination [on 10 July 1927] the late Mr Kevin O'Higgins was asked whom of those who had opposed Sinn Féin he had regarded as the most formidable enemy, he replied without hesitation: 'Sir Henry Robinson. He had the brains'... In his private life he was the kindest of men and the most witty of companions, while as a teller of Irish stories he had few, if any, equals.[40]

In a letter to *The Times* a few days after Robinson's death, Alfred Tennyson, grandson of the poet laureate and stepson of Augustine Birrell, who had become an LGB inspector in 1911 paid warm personal tribute to his former boss:

> Might I ... as one of those who served under him, put on record how much he was loved and reverenced by the members of the old Irish Local Government Board. Sir Henry had a naturally adventurous spirit, and all those who served under him found themselves a band of brothers engaged in a gay adventure. There was nothing that 'the V. P.' (as he was affectionately known) could have asked of us that we would not cheerfully have done. He was always accessible, always helpful, always loyal to us all.[41]

Memories Wise and Otherwise

Recalling how the old Local Government Board for Ireland and himself, as its last Vice-President, had passed out of official existence together, Robinson promised himself that when he 'had passed through the troubled waters of these years to a peaceful anchorage', he would find time to write something of all the happenings which had affected his fate and made his intimate association with twenty chief secretaries so full of interest. Writing as he put it under great disadvantages (because his notes, private papers and best photographs had been destroyed at his house in August 1922), he completed a first 350-page volume titled *Memories: Wise and Otherwise* for publication by Cassell and Company Limited in March 1923 and dedicated it to the staff of the LGB. A shorter 261-page second volume was titled *Further Memories of Irish Life* and published by Herbert Jenkins Limited in 1924; this was dedicated to 'the lovers of Ireland who have been driven from their country by stress of circumstances but whose affection for Ireland nothing can wholly obliterate'. Although these volumes include character studies of the different chief secretaries with whom Robinson worked, and some comments on his dealings with them on LGB business, they make no reference to his unofficial advisory role in the various political controversies which raged between 1912 and 1922. There is interesting material relating to some of the main service developments with which the board was concerned, including the introduction of old age pensions in 1908, but the bulk of the text relates to incidents – sometimes amusing – in the west of Ireland. The *Times* review was therefore correct when it noted that *Memories* contains no estimate, critical or otherwise, of British rule or any appreciation of the forces which led to the downfall of the Irish Party and the rise of

Sinn Féin.[42] In the introduction to his second volume Robinson himself warned that the book has no historic value whatever but deals only with 'the lighter aspect of Irish life'.

A review of *Memories* in the *Irish Independent* commented that the book revealed Robinson 'as an able, shrewd and diplomatic official ... whose advice on matters not appertaining strictly to his own department was sought, given and followed' from time to time.[43] Reviews appeared also in the *Irish Times*.[44] The book has been unfairly criticised for presenting a 'stage Irish' picture of a roguish peasantry for the amusement of readers in England or in what to-day would be termed Dublin 4, but the same criticism was made of the popular Somerville and Ross Irish RM stories published between 1898 and 1915 – and which, it is tempting to suggest, may have influenced Robinson.[45] In his memoirs, John Oliver, a one-time permanent secretary in the Northern Ireland civil service, describes Robinson's *Memories* as amusing and obligatory reading in relation to the pre-1922 administration in Dublin and a valuable record of experiences which gave 'some penetrating insight into the workings of the government system'. However, he notes that his copy of the book was annotated by a former colleague of Robinson's (and of his own) who described some of the countless anecdotes of the Somerville and Ross type as 'pure invention' and who criticised what he saw as the representation of the Irish people as ignorant idiots or rogues.[46]

More modern comments on Robinson's memoirs vary. His photographic captions are described by Cormac Ó Gráda as 'wry, sometimes condescending',[47] while Martin Maguire says that the memoirs 'betray his condescension toward the Irish peasantry, whose dependency on his largesse affirmed his own bloated sense of self-importance'.[48] For Mary Daly, his descriptions of particular incidents and individuals smack of considerable embroidery (which is almost certainly true) and demonstrate (which is debatable) an attitude that was racist in that he paints a picture of a people who were simple-minded, ignorant and emotional, prone to deceit and violence, and caricatures them as friendly delightful people who knew little or nothing of what was going on in the outside world.[49] As against this, Fitzpatrick says that *Memories* presents delightful anecdotes and vignettes,[50] while Virginia Crossman wrote that he depicts the Irish as 'charming, child-like creatures whose attempts to exercise any kind of administrative or governmental responsibility required constant monitoring and frequent intervention' ... in low-level public positions, they were simple minded, 'with a perfectly childish reverence for the traditions of the service and a burning desire to follow the law' to ridiculous lengths.[51]

Vale

Robinson's visit to Dublin with his wife in March 1923 may have been his last visit to the city where he had been prominent for over thirty years, but he was kept in touch with developments in the city and in the south in the 1920s by letters from friends and acquaintances, allowing him in 1924 to comment on the situation in Vale, the last chapter of his *Further Memories*. He firmly believed at that stage that if the people of the south had combined to give the Free State a fair start, instead of resorting to civil war, the new government would have made good, particularly because it was made up of men of grit, courage, statesmanship and resourcefulness. And, pointing out that the Free State was for all practical purposes an independent republic, he lamented the fact that idealists and dreamers had not come to realise this but continued to fight to sever the last link with England. On a slightly more optimistic note, he felt that while the shadow of the boundary impasse seemed to darken all hopes, the prospects of peace in the country were improving. But, although he hoped that brighter days might be dawning, he still believed that there seemed to be little prospect of a return to the land of their birth for himself and the other exiles who had not a drop of English blood in their veins, but who had been driven to cast anchor in the quiet waters of English havens.[52] Ireland, for us, he concluded sadly, is *The Isle of Long Ago*.[53]

NOTES

1   George Wyndham to his wife, 24 and 25 Oct. 1890, PRONI, Wyndham Papers, T 3221/1/137 and 138.

2   Sir Christopher Lynch-Robinson, *The Last of the Irish R.M.s* (London, 1951), p.17; a certified copy of an entry of marriage gives Sydney W. Johnson (incorrectly) and Louisa S. Iremonger as witnesses.

3   Certified copy of an entry of death, Chelsea Registration District.

4   Census of Ireland, 1901.

5   Census of Ireland, 1911.

6   *Dublin Builder*, 1 June 1862, p.140.

7   *Irish Times*, 4 Apr. 1922.

8   *Irish Times*, 8 Apr. 1922; Sir Henry Robinson, *Memories: Wise and Otherwise* (London, 1923), p.xii.

9   *Irish Times*, 26 May 1922.

10   NAI, DE/4/11/45.

11   *Irish Times*, 21 Aug. 1922; *The Times*, 21 Aug. 1922.

12   *Irish Times*, 23 Aug. 1922.

13   Robinson, *Memories*, pp.xii, 324.

14   Lynch-Robinson, *The Last of the Irish R.M.s*, pp.17–73.

15 Sir Henry Robinson, *Further Memories of Irish Life* (London, 1924), p.44.
16 Plunkett diary for March to May 1921, quoted in Trevor West, *Horace Plunkett: Co-Operation and Politics, an Irish Biography* (Gerrards Cross, 1986), pp.192 and 199.
17 Plunkett to Dillon, 14 Aug. 1922, quoted in Elizabeth, Countess of Fingall, *Seventy Years Young* (Dublin, 1991), p.408.
18 Letter of 3 Nov. 1926 from Robinson to the Irish Grants Committee, TNA, CO 762/32/24, no. 478.
19 Lynch-Robinson, *The Last of the Irish R.M.s*, p.173.
20 Cosgrave to Collins, 19 Aug. 1922, UCDA, Richard Mulcahy Papers, P7/B/29 (6) and (7).
21 Letter from Collins to Desmond Fitzgerald, 19 Aug. 1922, Kathleen McKenna Napoli Papers, NLI, MS 22,779.
22 *Sunday Independent*, 20 Aug. 1922; *Irish Times*, 21 Aug. 1922; James Scannell, 'Stillorgan Road Assassination Attempt on Michael Collins', *Obelisk*, No. 6, 2011/2012, pp.38–44.
23 Risteárd Mulcahy, *Richard Mulcahy (1886–1971) A Family Memoir* (Dublin, 1999), Appendix 1, pp.351–55.
24 Margery Forester, *Michael Collins: The Lost Leader* (London, 1972), p.333.
25 *Irish Times*, 21 Aug. 1922.
26 Elizabeth, Countess of Fingall, *Seventy Years Young*, pp.408–9.
27 Plunkett diary, entry for 19 Aug., reproduced in Trevor West, *Horace Plunkett*, p.198.
28 *Irish Times*, 7 Sept. 1922.
29 Letter of 30 May 1927 to the Irish Grants Committee, TNA, CO 762/32/24, no. 478.
30 *Irish Times*, 11 Sept. 1922.
31 *Irish Times*, 14 Mar. 1923.
32 *Irish Times*, 7, 25 and 26 Sept. 1923.
33 Valuation Office Dublin, Revision Books.
34 *Irish Times*, 14 Dec. 1995.
35 Letter of 16 May 1927 to the Irish Grants Committee.
36 General Register Office, certified copy of an entry of death.
37 Register of Burials at Parkstone Cemetery.
38 *Irish Times*, 5 Dec. 1927; *Irish Independent*, 3 Dec. 1927.
39 *Irish Times*, 18 Oct. 1922.
40 *The Times*, 18 Oct. 1927.
41 *The Times*, 20 Oct. 1927.
42 Reproduced in *Irish Times*, 23 Mar.1923.
43 *Irish Independent*, 26 Mar. 1923.
44 *Irish Times*, 16 and 23 Mar. 1923.
45 *Some Experiences of an Irish RM* (1999); *Further Experiences of an Irish RM* (1908); *In Mr Knox's Country* (1915).
46 John A. Oliver, *Working at Stormont* (Dublin, 1978), p.233.
47 Cormac Ó Gráda, Preface in Ciara Breathnach (ed.), *Framing the West* (Dublin, 2007), p.xv.
48 Martin Maguire, *The Civil Service and The Revolution in Ireland, 1912–38* (Manchester, 2008), p.22.

49   Mary E. Daly, *The Buffer State* (Dublin, 1997), pp.32–33.
50   David Fitzpatrick, *Politics and Irish Life 1913–1921* (Cork, 1998), p.304.
51   Virginia Crossman, 'Local Government in Nineteenth-Century Ireland' in Terence McDonough (ed.), *Was Ireland a Colony?* (Dublin, 2005), p.112.
52   Robinson, *Further Memories*, pp.10, 260–261.
53   *The Isle of Long Ago* was written by the American poet, Benjamin Franklin Taylor (1819–1887).

CHAPTER XX

Conclusions

In attempting to sum up the career of Sir Henry Augustus Robinson, there is little difficulty in answering 'yes' to the question of whether his work as Vice-President of the Local Government Board for Ireland between 1898 and 1922 had a measurable and beneficial impact. Similarly, the available evidence suggests that the systems and administrative procedures which he put in place within the LGB worked effectively and survived for years after the board itself was swept away in 1922. It is less easy, however (without undertaking a serious exercise in counter-factual history) to assess whether his advice on political issues at different times between 1912 and 1922 was soundly based or to judge whether the outcome in Ireland would have been any different if that advice had been accepted and acted upon.

Robinson's Impact as Head of the Local Government Board

The effect of the Local Government (Ireland) Act 1898 was not far short of revolutionary in social terms.[1] While the Balfour brothers deserve the credit at political level for proposing and carrying the act through, it was Robinson who was primarily responsible for framing, and efficiently and enthusiastically, implementing a particularly complex piece of legislation, which was to provide an invaluable training-ground in democratic self-government for over ten thousand new local councillors, most of them catholic and nationalist. Gerald Balfour publicly acknowledged that the principal burden of implementing the act had fallen on Robinson and asserted that any department of State, English or Irish, might justly be proud of what had been achieved.[2] The reorganisation which was planned and implemented between 1897 and 1899 was undoubtedly a significant achievement for which Robinson, in particular, deserved great credit;

indeed, as noted earlier, the smooth transition has been described as a triumph for his board.[3]

There are good grounds also for accepting that relations between the LGB and the new local councils in the early years of the twentieth century were remarkably harmonious,[4] and there is evidence to support the view of Virginia Crossman that much of the credit for that was due to Robinson.[5] It is less easy, however, in the absence of the files and records of the LGB itself, to assess his personal influence on the development of local services. His work on the financial and procedural clauses of the important Labourers Housing Act of 1906 was clearly significant, as was his recognition of the importance attached by the Irish Party and the Liberal government to the speedy and efficient administration of that programme. But for the outbreak of the First World War in 1914, he might also have succeeded in initiating a major drive to rid Dublin of its notorious slums, building on the momentous report, which was completed expeditiously by a committee of his officials after the 1913 Church Street disaster. And, but for the breaking-off by local councils in 1920 of their relations with his board, the financial and organisational arrangements he put in place in 1919 would almost certainly have made a real impact on urban housing conditions, not just in Dublin, but also throughout the country. While there was little he could have done to offset the preference of local councillors and Irish Party MPs for adoptive health and welfare legislation and their reluctance to finance services which, they argued, were more appropriate to urbanised England, he could perhaps have done more to speed-up the reform of the poor relief/workhouse system by implementing changes on which there was fairly general agreement by 1910. However, in this – as in other cases where complex legislation would have been required – Robinson and the Chief Secretary had to contend with the pressure from other departments and ministers for an allocation of parliamentary time for their own priorities, and with the huge proportion of the time taken up in the House of Commons by the Home Rule Bill between 1912 and 1914.

Judged by the standards of the early twentieth century, Robinson built the LGB into an efficient and effective organisation, and one which proved itself to be capable of taking on new and expanded responsibilities and carrying them out satisfactorily, including the huge job of implementing the Old Age Pensions system in 1908–09. While the organisation was not 'the fountainhead of corruption in Ireland' as Arthur Griffith alleged in 1918,[6] some appointments and promotions at senior levels were undoubtedly made on the basis of patronage, while others involved discrimination on religious or other grounds. Robinson can clearly be criticised for going along with and defending the systems he had inherited, but it would be wrong to assign to him personally all of the blame for the continuation of procedures which allowed unionist and protestant-dominated networks to have an undue and unfair influence, not just in the civil service, but also in business and in some of the professions. Notwithstanding this criticism, however, he deserves to be recognised as one of a small number of officials who made a real difference in Ireland in the first decades of the century.

'The Ireland that We Made'

When asked in 1928 by his niece and first biographer, Blanche Dugdale, what remained of his Irish policy, Arthur Balfour, Chief Secretary from 1887 to 1891, replied: 'Everything. Everything. What was the Ireland the Free State took over? It was the Ireland that we made...'[7] If Henry Robinson had lived into the 1930s and 1940s, would he have been entitled to give a similar response to the same question if it applied to local government administration and local services? For at least twenty-five years before 1922 he had been the dominant personality in shaping the local government, public health, environmental and roads services and the central and local organisations through which these services were provided. In relation to these and other public services, the 1935 commission of inquiry into the civil service reported that the passing of State services generally into the control of a native government entailed, broadly speaking, no immediate disturbance of any fundamental kind ... under changed masters the same main tasks continued to be performed by the same staffs on the same general line of organisation and procedure.[8] It must of course be acknowledged that a very different view of what happened in 1922 was held by Kevin O'Higgins, who declared in October 1924 that 'the provisional government was simply eight young men ... standing amidst the ruins of one administration, with the foundations of another not yet laid ... the wheels of administration hung idle, battered out of recognition by the clash of rival jurisdictions'.[9] Neither Joseph Brennan, who chaired the 1935 commission, nor O'Higgins, was, of course, a detached or unbiased observer, but most historians of the period accept the 'uninterrupted continuity' thesis. Ronan Fanning's *Independent Ireland* (1983), for example, supports the continuity argument, noting that more than 98 per cent of the civil service in the early 1920s had transferred from service under Britain,[10] while Tom Garvin noted that 'the new politicians found themselves dependent on the experience of civil servants who had been trained under the British government'.[11]

Whatever scope there may be for argument about the position in other policy or functional areas, it is clear that continuity was the hallmark of the transition in the local government and public health fields. The central organisation which Robinson had built up in Dublin, and the systems and procedures he had worked hard to develop and implement at both central and local level, continued to form the basis of the new administration, not only in the 1920s, but for decades after that. The primary legislation and detailed codes of secondary legislation that he and his colleagues drafted continued to have effect long after 1922, and much of that body of law was not repealed for up to one hundred years.[12] Continuing the practice initiated in 1898, delegated legislation was heavily relied on for decades by the new Department of Local Government, notwithstanding frequent criticism in the Dáil and the Seanad, and the practice of 'ruling by circular', which also attracted regular criticism, continued to be a feature of the operation of the department for many years. While all large bureaucracies may be disposed to maintain inherited systems and procedures, there is merit in Mary Daly's conclusion that the high degree of continuity in administrative procedures between the LGB and independent Ireland 'cannot be entirely attributed to conservatism or inertia' but to some extent reflected the fact that parts of the old system functioned effectively.[13]

Robinson's influence on the staffing and organisational arrangements of the new Department of Local Government and Public Health was detectable for decades after his retirement. Staff who had joined the LGB during his term of office and had been trained and promoted under his supervision provided most of the senior and middle management of the new department in 1922, and continued to form a large proportion of the staff of the department for years after that, exercising a system of central controls as stringent as any exercised by his board.[14] In 1930 the secretary and five of the department's ten principal officers were former LGB officers; in addition, the chief medical adviser, his deputy and all five medical inspectors had served in the LGB, and so too had the legal adviser, his deputy and the inspector of audits.[15] McCarron, as secretary of the department, was succeeded in 1936 by James Hurson, a former private secretary of Robinson's, and he in turn was succeeded in 1946 by T. J. McArdle, who had served in the LGB from 1901 until 1918 when he was dismissed for failing to take the Oath of Allegiance. Some former LGB officials were still in place in the Custom House into the 1960s, the most senior being P. J. (Paddy) Daly, who was then deputy secretary. Other former LGB officials, Patrick Murray and Patrick Kennedy, served as secretaries of the Department of Health when it was split from Local

Government in 1947, and it is worth noting also that James J. McElligott, whom Robinson reluctantly dismissed from his first division post in the LGB after the 1916 Rising, was the influential secretary of the Department of Finance from 1927 to 1953 and was followed (1953–56) by O. J. Redmond, another former LGB official.

While only a few of the first division men to whom Robinson attached such importance continued to serve in the new department after 1922, steps were soon taken to build up a replacement corps of administrative officers (AOs). One of the six successful candidates at the first AO examination in 1925 (John Garvin, who became secretary in 1947) was assigned to the department and one of three successful candidates at a 1926 competition was also assigned to the Custom House.[16] By the 1930s, the department was again the largest employer of staff in the AO grade outside the Department of Finance, and this continued to be the position into the early 1960s when the present author was one of four AOs employed by the department.

The Unofficial Political Adviser

One of his friends told *The Leader* that 'presidents may come and presidents may go, but Sir Henry [as LGB Vice-President] goes on forever'.[17] Lords lieutenant and chief secretaries did come and go from 1898 to 1922, and there were frequent changes of senior personnel in the Irish administration, but Robinson seemed always to be there, dominating the direction and management of the LGB – the organisation in which he took such pride – at its prestigious headquarters in the Custom House. He clearly possessed what one of his sons described as 'an intimate knowledge of the country and the people', and some nationalist MPs believed that in touring the West with him, chief secretaries imbibed more about the hearts and spirit of the people than by listening to the MPs at Westminster. As one of them colourfully put it in 1917 'the first duty of the chief secretary when he goes to Ireland is to go round the country in a perambulator pushed by Sir Henry Robinson'.[18] A columnist in the *Tuam Herald* in 1918 described these tours as shams, humbugs and a sickening show, and suggested that the chief secretary should be allowed to see the country for himself instead of being led around by Robinson – 'an astute bear leader who was an old hand at the game'.[19]

Robinson's political significance was recognised by D. P. Moran, who wrote in *The Leader* in 1913 that, apart from being the uncrowned king of the LGB, he was 'one of the most dangerous officials to democratic rule in Ireland ... his affability may deceive some simple-minded nationalists, but we know the value of his affability and his so-called official impartiality'.[20] In 1914 the same journal saw him as 'one of the cleverest quick-change artists in Ireland … the ascendancy clique rightly regard him as their most capable official wirepuller and some nationalists, with a simple faith, regard him as toleration personified … perhaps before another year has passed, and in view of Home Rule, Sir Henry may be a corporal in the Irish Volunteers'.[21] *The Leader* was not alone in its assessment of Robinson: Tim Healy considered him to be 'the most plausible opponent the nationalists had',[22] while Kevin O'Higgins believed that because 'he had the brains', he was the 'most formidable enemy' of the independence movement,[23] a view which more or less supports Robinson's own 1926 statement that he was looked on by the revolutionary movement as the most dangerous and formidable ally of the British government in Ireland.[24]

There is some evidence in Robinson's correspondence with Gerald Balfour in the late 1890s, and with Walter Long in the early twentieth century, that he was already willing to deviate from apolitical civil service norms; although Long was then in opposition, he advised him in 1906 that the Liberal government's proposal to set up an elected central council to control the public departments, including his own, would be 'sheer madness' and cause dire embarrassment and trouble for the government.[25] The surviving papers, however, suggest that his emergence as a significant adviser on political matters dates from 1912 when the Home Rule controversy was raging. Although the Ulster unionists had already demonstrated the strength of their opposition to Home Rule, he advised Birrell in January of that year that the Belfast Orangemen should be let screech and yell till they were tired. He was critical of the Orange 'fanatics', questioned their 'so-called loyalty' and, with others, advised that the Ulster unionists were really engaged in a bluffing game – a view which was of course soon shown to be entirely wrong. Two years later, when the Cabinet were considering the exclusion of some northern counties from the Home Rule scheme, he urged Birrell that exclusion was tactically an unsound proposition and put forward his own version of a 'home-rule-within-home-rule' scheme which, if it had been incorporated in the original bill, might have gone a considerable distance towards resolving the deadlock between the northern unionists and the Irish Party. This first effort by Robinson to avert a partitionist solution failed to attract support, and while he subsequently prepared maps at Birrell's request showing how a border might be delineated, he never ceased to criticise the principle of partition.

Ten years after the event, Robinson claimed that when the Easter Rising broke out, he was called upon almost hourly to advise the Lord Lieutenant, the Chief Secretary and occasionally the Prime Minister on the situation but nothing has emerged to support this. He was certainly among those consulted by Asquith in the course of his fact-finding visit to Ireland in May 1916, but his own account of that meeting suggests that nothing of significance was discussed. Similarly, his relationship with Lord Lieutenant Wimborne was such that it seems very unlikely that he was ever called on to advise him on matters of substance. He was more prominent than any other senior civil servant in the process of making good the effects of the Rising on buildings and services in Dublin, but it is difficult to accept his claim that this work alone would have led the revolutionary movement to identify him as a dangerous adversary as he claimed in 1926.

From 1918 onwards Robinson continued to advise the Cabinet on major strategic issues but this would rarely have come to public notice. In his initial comments at a Cabinet meeting on the likely reaction to an announcement about conscription, he completely misjudged the situation and was quickly forced to withdraw his recommendation that the scheme should be pressed ahead. Later that year, however, he provided the Cabinet, in advance of the general election results, with an excellent assessment of the strength of the Sinn Féin movement and the character and competence of its leaders. He was the first, after the election, to urge that the German Plot prisoners, including de Valera and others (some of whom had won seats at the election) should be released; in his view, they were courageous and patriotic and might be able to persuade their more militant colleagues to eschew violence. Unfortunately, those in authority continued to disregard the success of Sinn Féin as a political party and to delay the release of the prisoners. This was another of the occasions on which Robinson's advice, if it had been accepted, would have influenced the history of the following years.

Robinson was happy to accept by 1918 that some form of Home Rule was sooner or later inevitable, but when the drafting of the Government of Ireland Bill was undertaken in 1919–20, he continued to press his anti-partition view. Alone of the officials who made up the Irish administration at the time, he attempted to persuade the Cabinet that a strong Council of Ireland should be provided for in order to enhance the prospect that the north and the south, by working together, would eventually establish a Parliament of Ireland. His proposals were not accepted and the 1920 Act went on to copper-fasten the partition of Ireland – and partition, as he sadly and wisely concluded in 1923, was to become the greatest obstacle to peace and a bar to the fulfilment of the hope of an Irish nation.[26] In the last analysis, therefore, the conclusion must be that although his advice was influential at times, contributing, for example, to the reform of Dublin Castle in May 1920 and to the eventual Cabinet decision to agree a truce in July 1921, it cannot be seen to have had any influence on the eventual settlement of December 1921.

Was Robinson the Best Under-Secretary Ireland Never Had?

If it is acknowledged that Robinson was a competent administrator as head of the Local Government Board, and if it is conceded that his advice to ministers on wider political issues was regularly noted – if not always accepted and acted on – a question naturally arises as to why he was not appointed as Under-Secretary when that position became vacant at different times in the two decades before 1922.

Six men served as Under-Secretary and four others as Assistant Under-Secretary during the critical ten-year period from 1912 onwards. There were eleven different holders of the office of attorney general, some of them drawn from the team of eleven men who served in succession as solicitor general; there were four Lords Chancellor and four Lords Chief Justice, six different army commanders-in-chief, three RIC inspectors general and changes in the senior management of most of the departments which made up the Irish administration. In addition to these changes of personnel, chief secretaries had to contend with the inadequacies of the Dublin Castle administration, which was found by Sir Norman Fisher in 1920 simply to have 'no existence' in the important spheres of informing and advising on policy and in the application of policy.[27] In these circumstances, and with little or no personal staff or advisers, it is difficult not to have a certain sympathy for the four Chief Secretaries who, as virtual strangers to the country, were faced with the problem of what to do about Ireland from 1916 onwards, while also participating in the Cabinet's deliberations on the management of the World War, on the post-war labour and other problems in Britain, and on the major issues outstanding in Europe and the Middle-East after 1918. In these circumstances, too, it was not surprising that some of these men were happy, on occasion, to accept advice from Robinson on major issues, given his uniquely long service in a senior position and his intimate knowledge of the country.

Robinson could never be accused of functioning as a routine clerk as the Under-Secretary did in Fisher's view, nor could he be included in the category of officials described in Fisher's confidential supplementary report as men who were 'almost woodenly stupid ...quite devoid of imagination ... and never seemed to think of the utility of keeping in close touch with opinions of all kinds'.[28] He was certainly not switched off from the current of national life and feeling as Birrell found the Castle administration to be in 1907.[29] He never attempted to hide his own

southern unionist feelings and was never slow to express the strong views
he held on a variety of issues, but he had no difficulty in working with
and supporting ministers like Birrell who were strong supporters of Home
Rule. He had a correct sense of what would be acceptable from the point
of view of different parties and groups, quite unlike some other senior
officials such as Antony MacDonnell, who was noted for his 'disastrous
insensitivity' to the likely political impact of his ideas.[30] Why, in all of these
circumstances, did Robinson's 'long, distinguished and loyal service to his
sovereign and country' not justify his appointment as Under-Secretary –
the natural ambition of every Irish civil servant – as Walter Long put it.[31]
Was he, in fact, the best Under-Secretary Ireland never had – and if he
had been appointed when the position fell vacant in 1902, 1908, 1914,
1916 or 1918, how different would Irish history have been?

Given his ssuccessful civil service career, his management of the
transition to a radically new local government system in 1899 and the
fact that within the Irish civil service his position as Vice-President of the
LGB was second only to that of the Under-Secretary in terms of salary and
status, it was not surprising that rumour and speculation linked Robinson
to the more senior position on every occasion on which a vacancy was
expected to occur. In 1902, he was aware that he was seen as 'first favourite'
when Harrel was expected to retire, and on each subsequent occasion
he would have been aware from newspaper reports and civil service
gossip that his name was being mentioned as the likely new appointee.
Although he wrote afterwards that he did not want the Under-Secretary
post in 1902, he must have been bitterly disappointed on at least some
subsequent occasions to find himself passed over in favour of men whom
he disliked, or men whose competence and fitness for office he strongly
challenged. Dougherty, he wrote, had been 'dragged out of the obscurity
of the presbyterian ministry' and was 'an old man with one year to run' at
the time of his appointment; Chalmers had 'no interest whatever in the
Irish question'; and in 1916 Byrne came 'into the Irish maelstrom too late
in life to be of much help to anyone'.

At political level, Robinson's greatest supporter was Walter Long,
for whom it was a matter of continuing regret that Robinson was not
appointed to the highest official position in Ireland.[32] Throughout the
1916–20 period, while Long was probably the most powerful single voice
in Irish affairs in British government circles,[33] he was in regular contact
with Robinson and used every opportunity to impress on his colleagues
in government that Sir Henry was a man whose advice they should seek
and respect – and, more than once, lobbied to have him appointed as
Under-Secretary. By virtue of this close association with Long – dating

from 1905 if not earlier – and because of the influence which he exercised and the information which he provided to Long and to other policy makers, it is not unreasonable to suggest that although he failed to gain appointment as Under-Secretary, Robinson must be included in any short list of individuals who, on the government side, had a significant effect on Irish affairs in the first decades of the twentieth century. He was respected and admired by a succession of chief secretaries, both conservative and liberal – from Gerald Balfour to Hamar Greenwood – and was spoken of by them in public in terms, which suggested that his advice and opinions carried a great deal of weight. He was well known to most prime ministers of the period (Arthur Balfour, Herbert Asquith and Lloyd George). His views on major issues were occasionally incorporated in memoranda submitted by chief secretaries to the Cabinet, while letters or memoranda of his own were on other occasions submitted directly to the Cabinet. Occasionally he – rather than the Under-Secretary – was called on to attend Cabinet meetings when critically sensitive issues were being discussed.

When he came to write his memoirs in 1923, Walter Long reiterated his admiration for Robinson as 'one of the ablest of the many distinguished men who have from time to time served in the civil service'. It was essential, he wrote, to have Irishmen in the top civil service positions in Ireland and noted that one curious and unfortunate factor (which) has always exercised 'a malign influence' over the future of Ireland was the view of successive governments that 'some brilliant Englishman, selected from one of the great departments of state or from some other branch of public service, would be able to contribute to the better government of Ireland'. This policy has always been followed; he went on – not altogether correctly – although it had never succeeded.[34] W. J. Braithwaite, the able young English civil servant with whom Robinson had worked closely in 1910–11 on the preparation of the national insurance scheme, believed that it was 'disastrous that he was never made Under-Secretary for Ireland, but when it might have come to his turn the Castle, which he had spent much of his time in outwitting, defeated him'.[35] A broadly similar view of the Castle influence was expressed by Long in 1918 when he wrote that opposition to Robinson's promotion derived from 'a long-standing and deplorable jealousy between the Under-Secretary's Office and the Local Government Board', which caused each department to oppose the selection of anybody except from their own men.[36] But while it is true that the LGB was practically a parallel department to that of the Under-Secretary and that Robinson consistently frustrated efforts to bring the activities of his board under the supervision and control of Dublin Castle, that can hardly be accepted as the reason why he was never promoted to the Under-Secretary position but was left to continue in his more limited official position at the Custom House.

The excuse for passing over Robinson which Wyndham gave to Arthur Balfour in 1902 (he lacked initiative and drive) can only be regarded as a fabricated, if not dishonest, one, given that Wyndham had already made up his mind for very different reasons to appoint Antony MacDonnell. In 1908, when Birrell had already come to have a high regard for Robinson, his failure to appoint him can only be ascribed to an unwillingness to risk alienating the Irish Party, some of whose leading members, particularly Dillon and Devlin, would have raised strong objections: Beatrice Webb at that time believed that 'if it were not for politics, undoubtedly Robinson would get the place, but he is reputed a unionist and the Irish nationalists detest him'.[37] However, even Robinson himself accepted that Birrell could not very well have passed over Dougherty on that occasion because of his previous service, even if he had wanted to.[38] In 1914, when Asquith finally decided that 'old Dougherty' should be replaced, he and Lloyd George chose Nathan to replace him, presumably because they believed that an independent outsider could best tackle the task of preparing the administration in Dublin for the transition to the service of an Irish Home Rule parliament; in this instance also Robinson seemed to accept that there was good reason for the appointment because he saw Nathan as a man who came with a fresh mind and no party prejudice.

When the need arose in 1916 to replace Nathan, any possibility that Robinson might succeed had vanished, notwithstanding strong pressure from Walter Long. Wimborne advised against the appointment simply because he was a 'Kildare Street unionist' and because the Irish Party – with Home Rule on the statute book – were already complaining about unionist rule; Nathan, too, believed that his successor, if not Irish, should at least be a catholic and approved the appointment of Sir William Byrne 'an Irishman and a catholic ... which is the right direction'.[39] It is clear that this was the dominant consideration also in the appointment of James MacMahon in 1918, before the functions of the office were effectively taken over by Sir John Anderson in mid-1920. Robinson reserved his strongest criticism for this appointment – MacMahon was a man whom he considered to be in the hands of the Catholic bishops and the AOH and his appointment was 'an exhibition of sheer funk'. He told Walter Long that having served twenty chief secretaries, he knew 'too much of the pitfalls of Irish administration to be a safe person – from the nationalist point of view – to be allowed to work beside the Chief Secretary at the Castle, so I never imagined Shortt [then Chief Secretary] would face the *Freeman* protests which would inevitably follow my appointment'.[40]

Overall, the best explanation for Robinson's failure to be appointed to the top civil service position is provided in a letter that he wrote to Bryce as far back as 1906. Although this letter related to the possibility of his appointment to head the new department of local government which was to be established under the Irish Council Bill, the view he expressed then would apply with even greater force to a possible appointment as Under-Secretary, especially after 1914:

> I have always managed to keep out of politics ... but the Irish Party seem to consider that those who are not entirely with them are against them ... I do not think that individually any of the Irish politicians I am known to would do me an injury if they could avoid it, but collectively ... [they] would feel that to allow a non-catholic official, who had been instrumental in carrying out the hated English government policy under seventeen chief secretaries, to remain at the head of the most important public department in Ireland would be utterly inconsistent ... [41]

Were Redmond, Dillon, Devlin and the other members of the Irish Party wise or unwise in effectively denying Robinson the promotion to the Under-Secretary position which he would almost certainly have gained but for their antagonism? And would events in Ireland, and the outcome generally for Ireland, have been significantly different if Robinson had been appointed Under-Secretary when vacancies arose between 1902 and 1918? In relation to 1902, when MacDonnell was appointed to succeed Harrel, a perfect answer was provided by Robinson himself: 'Things might have been easier for Wyndham if he had appointed me' and the devolution crisis of 1904–05 which 'led to his undoing' would never have occurred. Regarding the Rising of 1916, Maurice Headlam, the Treasury Remembrancer, wrote in 1947 – with the benefit of hindsight – that if Robinson rather than Nathan had been Under-Secretary, Birrell might have been persuaded to pay attention to the warnings of the police and to take measures in time to avert the Rising. While this is debatable, it is certainly reasonable to suggest that events in Ireland in the 1914–16 period would have been quite different if Robinson had been Under-Secretary during those years.

In civil service terms, Robinson might be said to have accepted without protest his passing-over for promotion in 1902, 1908, 1914 and 1916, but the appointment of MacMahon in 1918 infuriated him. MacMahon turned out to be a weak and ineffectual Under-Secretary who allowed himself to be pushed aside without protest in favour of the hard-line combination of the assistant Under-Secretary, Sir John Taylor, with Saunderson and Watt who supported the introduction of the Black and Tans and the Auxiliaries in 1920. If Robinson rather than MacMahon had been appointed in 1918, it is arguable that the status and authority he would have enjoyed as Under-Secretary would have averted not just some of the chaotic and conflicting activities which characterised the French–Short–Macpherson administrations, but also some of the repressive measures that were introduced in 1920. In light of the views he had expressed in 1919 about the strength of the Sinn Féin movement, the calibre of its leaders, and the desirability of releasing de Valera, Griffith, Cosgrave and the other more moderate German Plot internees, it is not unreasonable to suggest also that the descent into violence in 1920–21 might have been delayed, if not entirely avoided.

'He Deserved a Better End at the Hands of Fate'

Shortly after Robinson's death in October 1927, the *Irish Times* reprinted a piece entitled 'Mistakes of Government', which had been written by a correspondent of *The Times* who obviously knew Robinson well and had travelled with him in Ireland. Robinson's exile was considered by the writer to be 'only the last of the blows dealt him by capricious fortune – and cowardly politicians', adding that he bore it 'as gallantly and bravely as he bore his many official disappointments'. Sir Henry, it went on –

> Was head and shoulders above the civil servants of Ireland in intelligence, in experience, in knowledge of the country. At every vacancy for the post of under-secretary, those who loved Ireland said: 'They cannot fail to give it to Henry Robinson this time'. And each time, the Government of the day, whatever its political complexion, gave it to someone else – to an ex-Indian civil servant, to an ex-professor, to a revenue official from London, to a minor official from Dublin, to anyone rather than the one man who might have saved Ireland, but who had incurred the enmity of John Redmond.

> If Redmond had had more vision, if he had realised that with a man of Robinson's calibre in office, the partition of Ireland might have been avoided, would he have withdrawn his ban against a man who, while he loved Ireland no less, knew it infinitely better than himself? ... He carried on loyally under policies which he knew could lead only to chaos. He put his great gifts at the service of those who occupied the office which he might well have felt ought to have

been his own. He met with a jest the condolences of those who felt for him much more bitterly than he did for himself. The world has lost a *preux chevalier* [a gallant knight] and Ireland a devoted friend and servant.[42]

At the risk of being branded as an uncritical hagiographer, the last word is left to Christopher Lynch-Robinson, even if, as an affectionate son, he cannot be regarded as an unbiased observer. Writing about his father in the 1950s, he recorded that:

> It broke his heart to see his life's work smashed, for that was how he felt about it. He loved Ireland devotedly and had worked for her exclusively and unselfishly all his life. In his own way, he had done more than any man of his time to improve the lot of her people and to get the best out of the English hegemony. But ... he never could see Ireland as anything but part of the British Empire and the separatist idea was to him emotionally horrible ... he was, in his own sphere, a really great man of a greatness that was conceded by all who worked with him. He deserved a better end at the hand of fate.[43]

NOTES

1 F. S. L. Lyons, *Ireland since the Famine* (2nd Ed.) (London, 1973), p.212.
2 *Hansard* IV, 73, 30 June 1899, 1226–27.
3 Pauric Travers, 'A Bloodless Revolution: The Democratization of Irish Local Government 1898–9' in Mary E. Daly (ed.) *County & Town* (Dublin, 2001), p.14.
4 R. B. McDowell, 'Administration and the Public Services', *NHI*, VI, p.594.
5 Virginia Crossman, *Sir Henry Augustus Robinson*, DIB 8, pp.536–7.
6 *Nationality*, 16 Mar. 1918.
7 Blanche Dugdale, *Arthur James Balfour*, vol. I (London, 1936), p.181.
8 *Final reports of the Commission of Inquiry into the Civil Service*, vol. I, 3.
9 Address to the Irish Society at Oxford University, 31 Oct. 1924, *Irish Times*, 1 Nov. 1924.
10 Ronan Fanning, *Independent Ireland* (Dublin 1983), pp.60–61.
11 Tom Garvin, *Nationalist Revolutionaries in Ireland 1858–1928* (Dublin, 2005), pp.171–2.
12 Although an officially commissioned compendium of local government law, running to more than 1,500 pages, was published in 1955 (Howard A. Street, *The Law Relating to Local Government*, Stationery Office, Dublin) the volumes compiled by Robinson's legal adviser, Sir George Vanston, between 1892 and 1919 on public health and local government law were still in everyday use in the Custom House into the 1970s when the present author served there.

13   Mary E. Daly, *The Buffer State* (Dublin, 1997), p.46.

14   David Fitzpatrick, *Politics and Irish Life 1913–1921* (Cork, 1980), p.192.

15   *Thom's Directory*, 1930.

16   Civil Service Commissioners, JAO examination, Nov. 1926, NAI, FIN 2/158.

17   *The Leader*, vol. xxvii, no. 13, 8 Nov. 1913, pp. 297–98.

18   *Hansard*, V, 92, 18 Apr. 1917, 1772.

19   *Tuam Herald*, 22 June 1918.

20   *The Leader*, vol. xxvii, no. 13, 8 Nov. 1913, pp.297–98.

21   *The Leader*, vol. xxviii, no. 15, 23 May 1914.

22   T. M. Healy, *Letters and Leaders of my Day* (vol II) (London, 1928), p.585.

23   *Irish Times*, 18 Oct. 1927.

24   Letter of 3 Nov. 1926 from Robinson to the Colonial Office, TNA, CO 762/32/24 No. 478.

25   Robinson to Long (no date but probably Nov. 1906), WRO, Long Papers, WRO 947/126/10.

26   Robinson, *Memories*, p.337.

27   Confidential report of 12 May 1920 entitled 'Dublin Castle' by Sir Warren Fisher, TNA, HO 317/50; copy also in Parliamentary Archives, Lloyd George papers, LG/F/31/1/32.

28   Supplementary report by Sir Warren Fisher, TNA, HO 317/50; copy also in Parliamentary Archives, Lloyd George papers, LG/F/31/1/33.

29   *Hansard* IV, 174, 7 May 1907, 83.

30   Eunan O'Halpin, *The Decline of the Union: British Government in Ireland 1892–1920* (Dublin, 1987), p.49.

31   Walter Long, *Memories* (London, 1923), p.164.

32   Ibid.

33   D.G. Boyce and Cameron Hazlehurst, 'The Unknown Chief Secretary: H.E. Duke and Ireland', *IHS* xx, no. 79 (Mar. 1977), p.301.

34   *Long, Memories*, pp.253–54.

35   William J. Braithwaite (ed. Henry N. Bunbury), *Lloyd George's Ambulance Wagon* (London, 1957), p.148.

36   Long to French 9 July 1918, IWM, French Papers, JDPF 8/3.

37   Beatrice Webb (eds Barbara Drake and Margaret I. Cole), *Our Partnership* (London, 1948), pp.408–09.

38   *Robinson, Memories*, pp.219–220.

39   Nathan to Dorothy Stopford, 23 Oct. 1916, NLI, MS 15341/1.

40   Robinson to Long, 2 July 1918, WRO, Long Papers, WRO 947/332.

41   Robinson to Bryce, 30 Nov. 1906, NLI, James Bryce Papers, MS 11,014(3).

42   *Irish Times*, 21 Oct. 1927.

43   Sir Christopher Lynch-Robinson, *The Last of the Irish R.M.s* (London, 1951), p.174.

Select Bibliography

I – MANUSCRIPT SOURCES

UNIVERSITY COLLEGE, DUBLIN

Diary of J. R. Clark
Ernest Blythe Papers
Kevin O'Higgins Papers
Richard Mulcahy Papers
de Valera Papers
G. C. Duggan Memoir
Belgian Refugees Committee, Minute Book, 1914–15

TRINITY COLLEGE, DUBLIN

John Dillon Papers
Ruttledge Papers
Sir David Harrel, *Recollections and Reflections* (typescript, for private circulation, 1926)

NATIONAL LIBRARY OF IRELAND

A. S. Green Papers
G. C. Duggan: draft of an unpublished book *The Life of a Civil Servant*
Harrington Papers
James Bryce Papers
John Redmond Papers
Joseph Brennan Papers
Leon Ó Broin Papers (including unsorted and unlisted material)
McKenna–Napoli Papers

Stopford-Price Papers
Sweetman Papers
T. P. Gill Papers
Thomas H. Nally Papers
W. L. Micks Papers
Wylie Papers
Wyse Papers

BUREAU OF MILITARY HISTORY, DUBLIN

Witness statements
Alice Cashel
Capt. E. Gerrard
Col. Dan Bryan
Daithí O Donoghue
Daniel Mc Aleese
Ernest Blythe
Frank Robbins
G. C. Duggan
James Kenny
Katherine Barry-Moloney
Michael de Lacey
Michael Knightly
Nancy Wyse-Power
Pádraig Ó Caoimh
Seamus Doyle
Séamus ua Caomhánaigh (James Kavanagh)
Sean Saunders
T. J. McArdle
Tadhg Kennedy
W. T. Cosgrave

NATIONAL ARCHIVES OF IRELAND

Chief Secretary's Office Registered Papers
Dáil Éireann (DE) records, 1919–22
Dáil Éireann Local Government files (DELG)
Minutes of meetings of the Provisional Government, 1922–25

PUBLIC RECORD OFFICE OF NORTHERN IRELAND (PRONI)

Clark Papers
Theresa Lady Londonderry Papers
George Wyndham Papers
Assistant Under-secretary Papers (AUS)
Armour Papers
Saunderson Papers
Carson Papers
Spender Papers
The Stormont Papers

PARLIAMENTARY ARCHIVES, LONDON

Lloyd George Papers
Bonar Law Papers

NATIONAL ARCHIVES OF SCOTLAND

Papers of the Balfour Family

THE NATIONAL ARCHIVES, LONDON (FORMERLY PRO)

Cabinet Papers: Minutes, Conclusions and Memoranda
Balfour Papers
Treasury Files
Treasury Ireland Files
Colonial Office Files
Home Office Files

BODLEIAN LIBRARY, OXFORD

Papers of Sir Matthew Nathan
Papers of Lord MacDonnell of Swinford
Papers of Augustine Birrell
Papers of James Ian Macpherson, Baron Strathcarron
Papers of H. H. Asquith, Earl of Oxford and Asquith
Papers of Andrew Magill
Papers of James Viscount Bryce

IMPERIAL WAR MUSEUM, LONDON

Papers of Field Marshal Lord French

BRITISH LIBRARY

Balfour Papers
J. H. Bernard Papers
Walter Hume Long Papers
Wrench Papers
Campbell-Bannerman Papers
Burns Papers
Viscount Gladstone Papers

WILTSHIRE AND SWINDON ARCHIVES

Walter Hume Long Papers

DURHAM COUNTY RECORD OFFICE

Londonderry Papers

II – NEWSPAPERS AND PERIODICALS

Annual Register
Connacht Tribune
Cork Examiner
Freeman's Journal
Glasgow Herald
Irish Builder
Irish Bulletin
Irish Independent
Irish News
Irish Times
Kildare Observer
Leeds Mercury
Meath Chronicle
Nationalist
Nationality
The Leader
The Times
Tuam Herald

III – PARLIAMENTARY AND OTHER OFFICIAL PAPERS

Annual Reports of the Local Government Board for Ireland
British Parliamentary Papers, 1898–1922
Dáil Éireann, *Minutes of Proceedings of the First Parliament of the Republic of Ireland 1919–1921*
Dáil Debates, 1922–1930
Dublin Gazette
HANSARD – Parliamentary Debates
Iris Oifigiúil
London Gazette

IV – BOOKS AND OTHER PRINTED SOURCES

Aan de Wiel, Jérôme, *The Catholic Church in Ireland, 1914–1918* (Dublin, 2003).

Aberdeen, Ishbel, Marchioness of Aberdeen and Temair, *The Musings of a Scottish Granny* (London, 1936).

Aberdeen, Marquis and Marchioness of, *More Cracks with 'We Twa'* (London, 1929).

Aberdeen, Marquis and Marchioness of, *We Twa: Reminiscences of Lord and Lady Aberdeen* (2 vols) (London, 1925).

Adams, R. J. Q., *Bonar Law* (1999).

Anderson, Malcolm and Eberhard Burt, *The Irish Border: history, politics, culture* (Liverpool, 1999).

Asquith, Herbert Henry (Earl of Oxford and Asquith), *Memories and Reflections, 1852–1927* (London, 1928).

Augusteijn, Joost (ed.), *The Irish Revolution, 1913–1923* (Hampshire, 2002).

Baguley, Margaret (ed.), *World War I and the Question of Ulster: the correspondence of Lilian and Wilfrid Spender* (Dublin, 2009).

Barrington, Ruth, *Health, Medicine and Politics in Ireland, 1900–1970* (Dublin, 1987).

Bellamy, Christine, *Administering Central–Local Relations, 1871–1919* (Manchester, 1988).

Birmingham, George A., *The Lighter Side of Irish Life* (London, 1911).

Birmingham, George A., *Irishmen All* (London, 1913).

Birrell, Augustine, *Things Past Redress* (London, 1937).

Blunt, Wilfrid Scawen, *My Diaries: being a Personal Narrative of Events, 1888–1914* (London, 1919–20).

Bonsall, Penny, *The Irish RMs* (Dublin, 1997).

Borgonovo, John, *The Dynamics of War and Revolution: Cork City, 1916–1918* (Cork, 2013).

Bowman, John, *De Valera and the Ulster Question 1917–1973* (Oxford, 1982).

Bowman, Timothy, *Carson's Army: The Ulster Volunteer Force, 1910–22* (Manchester, 2007).

Boyce D.G. and Cameron Hazlehurst, 'The Unknown Chief Secretary: H.E. Duke and Ireland, 1916–18', *Irish Historical Studies*, xx, 79 (Mar.1977), pp.286–311.

Boyce, D. George and Alan O'Day (eds), *Gladstone and Ireland* (London, 2010).

Boyce, D. George and Alan O'Day (eds), *Ireland in Transition, 1867–1921* (2004)

Boyne, Sean, *Emmet Dalton* (Dublin, 2014).

Breathnach, Ciara (ed.), *Framing the West: Images of Rural Ireland 1891–1920* (Dublin, 2007).

Brennan-Whitmore, W. J., *Dublin Burning: The Easter Rising from behind the Barricades* (2nd edition) (Dublin, 2013).

Brillman, M. L., 'A Crucial Administrative Interlude: Sir Antony MacDonnell's return to Ireland, 1902–04', *New Hibernia Review*, ix, 2 (Summer 2005), pp.65–83.

Brock, Michael and Eleanor (eds), *H. H. Asquith: Letters to Venetia Stanley* (Oxford, 1982).

Buckland, Patrick, *Irish Unionism: One: The Anglo-Irish and the New Ireland, 1885–1922* (Dublin, 1972)

Buckland, Patrick, *Irish Unionism: Two: Ulster Unionism and the origins of Northern Ireland, 1886–1922* (Dublin, 1973).

Buckland, Patrick, *The Factory of Grievances: Devolved Government in Northern Ireland, 1921–39* (Dublin, 1979).

Bull, Philip, 'The UIL and the Reunion of the Irish Parliamentary Party', *Irish Historical Studies*, xxi, 101, May 1988, p.62.

Bunbury, Sir Henry N. (ed.), *Lloyd George's Ambulance Wagon, being the memoirs of William J. Braithwaite, 1911–1912* (London, 1957).

Callanan, Frank, *T. M. Healy* (Cork, 1996).

Campbell, Fergus, *Land and Revolution: Nationalist Politics in the West of Ireland, 1891–1921* (Oxford, 2005).

Campbell, Fergus, *The Irish Establishment 1879–1914* (Oxford, 2009).

Carden, Sheila, *The Alderman: Alderman Tom Kelly (1868–1942) and Dublin Corporation* (Dublin, 2007).

Carroll, F.M. (ed.), *The American Commission on Irish Independence 1919* (Dublin, 1985).

Churchill, Winston S., *The World Crisis, 1911–1918* (London, 1938).

Cole, Margaret I (ed.), *Beatrice Webb's Diaries 1912–1924* (1952).

Colvin, Ian, *The Life of Lord Carson* (London, 1934).

Commission of Inquiry into the Civil Service, Final Reports with appendices (Dublin, 1935).

Connell, Joseph E. A. Jnr., *Dublin in Rebellion* (Dublin, 2009).

Cooney, D. A. L., 'An Englishman in Ireland: Arthur Dean Codling', *Dublin Historical Record*, xlvii (Spring 1994), pp.5–23.

Corlett, Christiaan, *Darkest Dublin: the story of the Church Street disaster and a pictorial account of the slums of Dublin in 1913* (Dublin, 2008).

Cowan, P.C. DSc, *Report on Dublin Housing* (Dublin, 1918).

Crossman, Virginia and Peter Gray (eds), *Poverty and Welfare in Ireland 1838–1948* (Dublin, 2011).

Crossman, Virginia, 'Local Government in Nineteenth-Century Ireland' in McDonough, Terence (ed.), *Was Ireland a Colony?* (Dublin, 2005).

Crossman, Virginia, 'The charm of allowing people to manage their own affairs' in D. George Boyce and Alan O'Day (eds), *Ireland in transition, 1867–1921* (London, 2004).

Crossman, Virginia, *Local Government in Nineteenth-century Ireland* (Belfast, 1994).

Crossman, Virginia, *Politics, Law and Order in Nineteenth-century Ireland* (Dublin, 1996).

Crossman, Virginia, *Politics, Pauperism and Power in late Nineteenth-Century Ireland* (Manchester, 2006).

Crossman, Virginia, *The Poor Law in Ireland 1838–1948* (Dublin, 2006).

Curry, James, *Artist of the Revolution: the Cartoons of Ernest Kavanagh (1884–1916)* (Cork, 2012).

Daly, Mary E. (ed.), *County & Town, One Hundred Years of Local Government in Ireland* (Dublin, 2001).

Daly, Mary E., *The Buffer State: The Historical Roots of the Department of the Environment* (Dublin, 1997).

Daly, Mary E., *The First Department: A History of the Department of Agriculture* (Dublin, 2002).

Dangerfield, George, *The Damnable Question: A study in Anglo-Irish Relations* (London, 1976).

David, Edward (ed.), *Inside Asquith's Cabinet: From the Diaries of Charles Hobhouse* (London, 1977).

Deeny, James, *To Cure & to Care* (Dublin, 1989).

Devine, Francis (ed.), *A Capital in Conflict: Dublin city and the 1913 Lockout* (Dublin, 2013).

Dickinson, Page Lawrence, *The Dublin of Yesterday* (London, 1929).

Doherty, Gabriel (ed.), *The Home Rule Crisis 1912–14* (Cork, 2014).

Dooley, Thomas P., *Irishmen or English Soldiers* (Liverpool, 1995).

Dubois, Louis Paul, *Contemporary Ireland* (Dublin, 1908).

Dugdale, Blanche, *Arthur James Balfour*, vol. I (London, 1936).

Duggan, George Chester (*Periscope*), 'The last days of Dublin Castle', *Blackwood's Magazine*, 1282 (Aug.1922), vol 212.

Dunraven, Earl of, *The Outlook in Ireland: the case for devolution and conciliation* (Dublin, 1907).

Dwyer, T. Ryle, *Michael Collins and the Civil War* (Cork, 2012).

Fair, John D., *British Interparty Conferences* (Oxford, 1980).

Fanning, J.R., 'The unionist party and Ireland 1906–10', *Irish Historical Studies* XV, No. 58 (Sept. 1966).

Fanning, Ronan, *Fatal Path: British Government and Irish Revolution 1910–1922* (London, 2013).

Fanning, Ronan, *Independent Ireland* (Dublin, 1983).

Fanning, Ronan, *The Irish Department of Finance 1922–58* (Dublin, 1978).

Feeney, Brian, *Sinn Fein: A Hundred Turbulent Years* (Dublin, 2002).

Feingold, William L., *The Revolt of the Tenantry: the Transformation of Local Government in Ireland, 1872–86* (Boston, 1984).

Ferriter, Diarmuid, *'Lovers of Liberty'? : Local Government in 20th century Ireland* (Dublin, 2001).

Fingall, Elizabeth Countess of, *Seventy Years Young* (London, 1937).

Fitzpatrick, David, *Politics and Irish Life 1913–1921* (2nd ed.) (Cork, 1998).

Fitzpatrick, David, *The Two Irelands 1912–1939* (Oxford, 1998).

David Fitzpatrick, 'Ireland and the Empire' in Andrew Porter (ed.), *The Oxford History of the British Empire, Vol. III, The Nineteenth Century* (Oxford, 1999), p.496.

Flanagan, Kieran, 'The Chief Secretary's Office, 1853–1914: a bureaucratic enigma', *Irish Historical Studies*, xxiv, 94 (Nov. 1984).

Foley, Caitriona, *The Last Irish Plague: the Great Flu Epidemic in Ireland 1918–19* (Dublin, 2011).

Forester, Margery, *Michael Collins: The Lost Leader* (London, 1971).

Foy, Michael T. & Brian Barton, *The Easter Rising* (2001 edition) (Stroud, 2011).

Fraser, Murray, *John Bull's Other Homes: State Housing and British Policy in Ireland, 1883–1922* (Liverpool, 1996).

Fry, Sir Edward, *James Hack Tuke: a memoir* (1899).

Gailey, Andrew, 'Unionist rhetoric and Irish local government reform, 1895–9', *Irish Historical Studies* xxiv, 93 (May 1984), pp.52–68.

Gailey, Andrew, *Ireland and the death of Kindness: the experience of constructive unionism 1890–1905* (Cork, 1987).

Gallagher, M. J., 'The Fateful Week' (section of an unpublished manuscript), *Administration*, vol. 14, No. 2 (Summer 1966), pp.171–185.

Garvin, Tom, *1922: The Birth of Irish Democracy* (Dublin, 1996).

Garvin, Tom, *Nationalist Revolutionaries in Ireland 1858–1928* (2nd ed.) (Dublin, 2005).

Geary, Laurence M., *Medicine and Charity in Ireland 1718–1851* (Dublin, 2004).

Gogarty, Oliver St J., *As I was going down Sackville Street* (London, 1937).

Gogarty, Oliver St John, *Tumbling in the Hay* (London, 1939).

Gray, Peter and Olwen Purdue (eds), *The Irish Lord Lieutenancy c. 1541–1922* (Dublin, 2012).

Griffith, Arthur, *The Resurrection of Hungary: A Parallel for Ireland* (Dublin, 1904).

Gwynn, Denis, *The History of Partition (1912–1925)* (Dublin, 1950).

Gwynn, Denis, *The Life of John Redmond* (London, 1932).

Haldane, Richard Burdon (Viscount Haldane), *An Autobiography* (London, 1929).

Hand, Geoffrey J. (ed.), *Report of the Irish Boundary Commission 1925* (Shannon, 1969).

Hart, Peter, *Mick: the Real Michael Collins* (London, 2005).

Hart, Peter, *The I.R.A. and its Enemies* (Oxford, 1998).

Hart, Peter, *The I.R.A. at War 1916–1923* (Oxford, 2003).

Hastings, Max, *Catastrophe: Europe goes to War 1914* (London, 2013).

Haydon, Anthony P., *Sir Matthew Nathan: British colonial governor and civil servant* (1976).

Headlam, Maurice, *Irish Reminiscences* (London, 1947).

Healy, T. M., *Letters and Leaders of My Day* (London, 1928).

Hepburn, A. C., 'The Irish Council Bill and the Fall of Sir Antony MacDonnell, 1906–07', *Irish Historical Studies*, xvii, 68 (Sept. 1971), pp.470–498.

Hogan, David, *The Four Glorious Years* (Dublin, 1953).

Holmes, Richard, *The Little Field Marshal: Sir John French* (London, 1981).

Hopkinson, Michael, *The Irish War of Independence* (Dublin, 2002).

Hopkinson, Michael, *The Last Days of Dublin Castle: the diaries of Mark Sturgis* (Dublin, 1999).

Horne, John (ed.), *Our War: Ireland and the Great War* (2008).

Howard, C. H. D., 'Documents relating to the Irish "central board" scheme 1884–5', *Irish Historical Studies* viii, 31 (Mar. 1953), pp.255–57.

Hudson, David R. C., *The Ireland that We Made: Arthur and Gerald Balfour's contribution to the origins of Modern Ireland* (Akron, 2003).

Hughes, J. L. J., 'The Chief Secretaries in Ireland 1566–1921', *Irish Historical Studies*, vii, 29 (Mar.1952), pp.59–72.

Irish Times, *1916 Rebellion Handbook* (Dublin, 1916).

Jackson, Alvin, *Colonel Edward Saunderson: Land and Loyalty in Victorian Ireland* (Oxford, 1995).

Jackson, Alvin, *Home Rule: an Irish History, 1900–2000* (London, 2000).

Jalland, Patricia, 'A liberal chief secretary and the Irish question: Augustine Birrell, 1907–1914', *The Historical Journal*, 19, 2 (1976), pp.421–451.

Jalland, Patricia, *The Liberals and Ireland: The Ulster Question in British Politics to 1914* (Brighton, 1980).

Jalland, Patricia, 'Irish Home Rule Finance: A Neglected Dimension of the Irish Question, 1910–14', *Irish Historical Studies* xxiii, 91 (May 1983), pp.233–253.

Jeffery, Keith (ed.), *The Sinn Féin Rebellion as they saw it* (Dublin, 1999).

Jeffery, Keith, *Field Marshal Sir Henry Wilson* (Oxford, 2006).

Jeffery, Keith, *Ireland and the Great War* (Cambridge, 2000).

Jeffery, Keith, *The GPO and the Easter Rising* (Dublin, 2006).

Jenkins, Roy, *Asquith* (London, 1964).

Jones, Greta and Elizabeth Malcolm (eds), *Medicine, Disease and the State in Ireland, 1650–1940* (Cork, 1999).

Jones, Thomas, *Lloyd George* (Oxford, 1951).

Kautt, W. H. (ed.) *Ground Truths: British Army Operations in the Irish War of Independence* (Dublin, 2014.

Keane, Maureen, *Ishbel: Lady Aberdeen in Ireland* (Dublin, 1999).

Keating, Carla Ruth, *Sir Horace Plunkett and Rural Reform*, thesis submitted for the degree of PhD (UCD, 1984).

Kendle, John, *Ireland and the Federal Solution: the Debate over the United Kingdom Constitution, 1870–1921* (Montreal, 1989).

Kendle, John, *Walter Long, Ireland, and the Union, 1905–1920* (Montreal, 1992).

Keogh, Ann and Dermot Keogh, *Bertram Windle, the Honan Bequest and the Modernisation of University College Cork, 1904–1919* (Cork, 2010).

Laffan, Michael, *Judging W. T. Cosgrave: The Foundation of the Irish Free State* (Dublin, 2014).

Laffan, Michael, *The Partition of Ireland, 1911–1925* (Dundalk, 1983).

Laffan, Michael, *The Resurrection of Ireland: The Sinn Féin Party, 1916–1923* (Cambridge, 1999).

Lawrence, R. J., *The Government of Northern Ireland: public finance and public services 1921–64* (Oxford, 1965).

Lee, Joseph, *The Modernisation of Irish Society 1848–1918* (Dublin, 1973).

Lloyd George, David, *War Memoirs of David Lloyd George* (2 vols.) (London, 1938).

Long, Viscount of Wraxall (Walter Long), *Memories* (London, 1923).

Lowther, James William, Viscount Ullswater, *A Speaker's Commentaries* (vol II) (London, 1925).

Lynch-Robinson, Sir Christopher and Adrian, *Intelligible Heraldry* (London, 1948).

Lynch-Robinson, Sir Christopher, *The Last of the Irish R.M.s* (London, 1951).

Lyons, F. S. L., 'The Irish Unionist Party and the Devolution Crisis of 1904–5', *Irish Historical Studies*, vi, 21 (Mar. 1948), pp.1–22.

Lyons, F. S. L., *The Irish Parliamentary Party,1890–1910* (London, 1951).

Lyons, F. S. L., *Ireland since the Famine* (London, 1971).

Lyons, F. S. L., *John Dillon: a biography* (Chicago, 1968).

Macardle, Dorothy, *The Irish Republic* (London, 1937).

McCarthy, Michael J. F., *Five Years in Ireland 1895–1900* (8th edn) (Dublin, 1902).

Mackail, J. W. and Guy Wyndham, *Life and Letters of George Wyndham* (London, 1925).

MacLellan, Anne, *Dorothy Stopford Price, Rebel Doctor* (Dublin, 2014).

MacLeod, Roy (ed.), *Government and Expertise: Specialists, Administrators and Professionals, 1860–1919* (Cambridge, 1988, 2003).

Macready, General Sir Nevil, *Annals of an Active Life* (2 vols) (London, 1924).

Magill, Charles W. (ed.), *From Dublin Castle to Stormont: the Memoirs of Andrew Philip Magill, 1913–25* (Cork, 2003)

Maguire, Martin, 'Gladstone and the Irish civil service' in Boyce, D. George and Alan O'Day (eds), *Gladstone and Ireland* (London, 2010), 208–232.

Maguire, Martin, *The Civil Service and the Revolution in Ireland, 1912–38* (Manchester, 2008).

Mansergh, Nicholas, *Nationalism and Independence* (Cork, 1997).

Mansergh, Nicholas, *The Irish Question 1840–1921* (third ed.) (1975).

Mansergh, Nicholas, *The Unresolved Question: the Anglo-Irish settlement and its undoing 1912–72* (New Haven and London, 1991).

Martin, F. X. (ed.), *Leaders and Men of the Easter Rising: Dublin 1916* (London, 1967).

Martin. F. X., *The Irish Volunteers 1913–1915* (Dublin, 1963).

Martin, Micheál, *Freedom to Choose: Cork & Party Politics in Ireland 1918–1932* (Cork, 2009).

Maume, Patrick, *The Long Gestation: Irish Nationalist Life 1891–1918* (Dublin, 1999).

McBride, Lawrence W., *The Greening of Dublin Castle* (Washington, 1991).

McCabe, J. F., 'The Design of Dublin', *The Dublin Magazine*, Dec. 1924, pp.342–47; Jan. 1925, pp.387–390.

McCabe, J. F., 'Town and Country', *The Dublin Magazine*, May 1925, pp.675–79.

McCabe, J. F., 'The Irish Ways', *The Dublin Magazine* Apr.-June 1926, pp.34–41.

McCarron, Edward, *Life in Donegal 1850–1900* (Cork, 1981).

McColgan, John, *British Policy and the Irish Administration, 1920–22* (London, 1983).

McConnel, James, 'Jobbing with Tory and Liberal: Irish Nationalist MPs and the Politics of Patronage 1880–1914', *Past and Present*, 188 (2005), pp.105–131.

McConnel, James, *The Irish Parliamentary Party and the Third Home Rule Crisis* (Dublin, 2013).

McCracken, J. L., *Representative Government in Ireland: A Study of Dáil Éireann, 1919–48* (London, 1958).

McDonough, Terence (ed.), *Was Ireland a Colony?* (Dublin, 2005).

McDowell, R. B., *Crisis and Decline: The Fate of the Southern Unionists* (Dublin, 1997).

McDowell, R. B., *The Irish Administration 1801–1914* (London, 1964).

McDowell, R. B., *The Irish Convention 1917–18* (London, 1970).

McDowell, R. B., 'Administration and the public services, 1870–1921' in *NHI* VI, p. 593.

McGarry, Fearghal, *Rebels: Voices from the Easter Rising* (Dublin, 2011).

McGarry, Fearghal, *The Rising, Ireland: Easter 1916* (Oxford, 2010).

McGee, Owen, *The IRB: The Irish Republican Brotherhood from the Land League to Sinn Féin* (Dublin, 2005).

McHugh, Roger (ed.), *Dublin 1916* (London, 1966).

McMahon, Paul, *British Spies and Irish Rebels: British Intelligence and Ireland, 1916–1945* (Woodbridge, 2008).

McMinn, J. R. B. (ed.), *Against the Tide: a calendar of the papers of Rev. J. B. Armour, Irish presbyterian minister and home ruler, 1869–1914* (Belfast, 1985).

Meghen, P. J., 'Irish Local Government and the Robinson Family', *Administration* 9, No. 4, Winter 1961–62.

Meleady, Dermot, *John Redmond: The National Leader* (Sallins, 2014).

Meleady, Dermot, *Redmond: the Parnellite* (Cork, 2008).

Micks, William L., *An Account of the Constitution, Administration and Dissolution of the Congested Districts Board for Ireland from 1891 to 1923* (Dublin, 1925).

Middlemas, Keith (ed.), *Thomas Jones, Whitehall Diary (vol.III): Ireland 1918–25* (Oxford, 1971).

Midleton, Earl of, *Records and Reactions, 1856–1939* (New York, 1939).

Mitchell, Arthur, *Revolutionary Government in Ireland: Dáil Éireann, 1919–22* (Dublin, 1995).

Montgomery, Bob, *An Irish Roadside Camera: Ireland's Earliest Motorists and their Automobiles, 1896–1906* (Dublin, 1997).

Moody, T. W. and Richard Hawkins (eds), *Florence Arnold-Forster's Irish Journal* (Oxford, 1988).

Morley, Viscount John, *Recollections* (New York, 1917).

Morrissey, Thomas S. J., *Patriot and Man of Peace: Laurence O'Neill (1864–1943), Lord Mayor of Dublin* (Dublin, 2014).

Mulcahy, Risteárd, *Richard Mulcahy (1886–1971): A Family Memoir* (Dublin, 1999).

Murphy, James H., *Ireland's Czar: Gladstonian Government and the Lord Lieutenancies of the Red Earl Spencer* (Dublin, 2014).

Murphy, Richard, 'Walter Long and the making of the Government of Ireland Act, 1919–20', *Irish Historical Studies* xxv, 97 (May 1986), pp.82–96.

Murphy, William, *Political Imprisonment and the Irish, 1912–1921* (Oxford, 2014).

Murray, Paul, *The Irish Boundary Commission and its Origins 1886–1925* (Dublin, 2011).

Ó Broin, Leon, *Dublin Castle and the 1916 Rising* (rev. ed.) (London, 1970).

Ó Broin, Leon, *No Man's Man: a biographical memoir of Joseph Brennan* (Dublin, 1982).

Ó Broin, Leon, *The Chief Secretary* (Connecticut, 1970).

Ó Broin, Leon, *The Prime Informer* (London, 1971).

Ó Broin, Leon, *W. E. Wylie and the Irish Revolution, 1916–1921* (Dublin, 1989).

O'Brien, Paul, *Blood on the Streets: 1916 & the Battle for Mount Street Bridge* (Cork, 2008).

O'Brien, R. Barry, *Dublin Castle and the Irish People* (Dublin, 1909).

Ó Cathaoir, Brendan, *John Blake Dillon, Young Irelander (Dublin, 1990).*

O'Connor, Ulick, *Oliver St. John Gogarty* (London, 1964).

O'Day, Alan, *Irish Home Rule 1867–1921* (Manchester, 1998).

O Donoghue, Brendan, 'From Grand Juries to County Councils: the Effects of the Local Government (Ireland) Act 1898' in Felix M. Larkin (ed.), *Librarians, Poets and Scholars* (Dublin, 2007), pp.175–184.

O Donoghue, Brendan, *The Irish County Surveyors, A Biographical Dictionary* (Dublin, 2007).

O'Halpin, Eunan, 'Historical Revision XX: H. E. Duke and the Irish Administration, 1916–18', *Irish Historical Studies* xxii, 88 (Sept. 1981), pp.362–376.

O'Halpin, Eunan, 'Sir Warren Fisher and the Coalition, 1919–1922', *The Historical Journal* 24, 4 (1981), pp.907–927.

O'Halpin, Eunan, 'The Politics of Governance in the Four Countries of the United Kingdom, 1912–1922' in S. J. Connolly (ed.), *Kingdoms United? Great Britain and Ireland since 1950* (Dublin, 1999).

O'Halpin, Eunan, *Head of the Civil Service: A Study of Sir Warren Fisher* (London, 1989).

O'Halpin, Eunan, *The Decline of the Union: British Government in Ireland 1892–1920* (Dublin, 1987).

O'Hegarty, P. S., *The Victory of Sinn Féin* (1998 ed.), Dublin, 1998.

O'Leary, Cornelius, *The Irish Republic and its experiment with Proportional Representation* (Notre Dame, 1961).

O'Leary, Cornelius, *Irish Elections 1918–1977* (Dublin, 1979).

Oliver, John A., *Working at Stormont* (Dublin, 1978).

O' Mahony, Sean, *The Burning of the Custom House in Dublin, 1921* (Dublin, 2000).

Parkinson, Alan F., *Friends in High Places* (Belfast, 2012).

Peden, G. C., *The Treasury and British Public Policy, 1906–1959* (Oxford, 2000).

Pentland, Marjorie, *A Bonnie Fechter: the life of Ishbel Marjoribanks, Marchioness of Aberdeen & Temair* (London, 1952).

Plunkett, Horace, *Ireland in the New Century* (London, 1904).

Plunkett, Sir Horace, *Home Rule and Conscription* (Dublin, 1918).

Prendergast, Elizabeth and Helen Sheridan, *Jubilee Nurse: Voluntary District Nursing in Ireland, 1890–1974* (Dublin, 2012).

Privilege, John, *Michael Logue and the Catholic Church in Ireland, 1879–1925* (Manchester, 2009).

Prunty, Jacinta, *Dublin Slums, 1800–1925* (Dublin, 1999).

Reid, Colin, *The Lost Ireland of Stephen Gwynn* (Manchester, 2011).

Robins, Joseph, *Champagne and Silver Buckles: the Viceregal Court at Dublin Castle 1700–1922* (Dublin, 2001).

Robins, Joseph, *Nursing and Midwifery in Ireland in the Twentieth Century* (Dublin, 2000).

Robins, Joseph, *The Lost Children* (Dublin, 1980).

Robins, Joseph, *Custom House People* (Dublin 1993).

Robinson, Hercules, *Sea Drift* (London, 1858).

Robinson, Sir Henry A., *Further Memories of Irish Life* (London, 1924).

Robinson, Sir Henry, *Memories: Wise and Otherwise* (London, 1923).

Roskill, Stephen, *Hankey: Man of Secrets, vol. 1, 1877–1918* (London, 1970).

Ross, Sir John, *Pilgrim Scrip: More Random Reminiscences* (London, 1927).

Ryan, Meda, *The Day Michael Collins was Shot* (Dublin, 1989).

Sagarra, Eda, *Kevin O'Shiel, Tyrone Nationalist and Irish State-Builder* (Sallins, 2013).

Saunderson, Henry, *The Saundersons of Castle Saunderson* (privately printed, 1936).

Scannell, James, 'Stillorgan Road Assassination Attempt on Michael Collins', *Obelisk*, No. 6, 2011/2012, pp.38–44.

Scholes, Andrew, *The Church of Ireland and the Third Home Rule Bill* (Dublin, 2009).

Shannon, Catherine B., *Arthur J. Balfour and Ireland, 1874–1922* (Washington, 1988).

Shannon, Catherine B., *Local Government in Ireland, the Politics and Administration*, MA Thesis (UCD, 1963).

Shannon, Catherine B., 'Lord Randolph Churchill and Ireland: The Road to and from the Orange Card, 1886–1893', in Robert McNamara (ed.), *The Churchills and Ireland 1660–1965* (Dublin, 2012), p.120.

Shea, Patrick, *Voices and the Sound of Drums* (Belfast, 1981).

Smith, Cornelius F., *The History of the Royal Irish Automobile Club 1901–1991* (Dublin, 1994).

Smith, Jeremy, *The Tories and Ireland* (Dublin, 2000).

Spender, Harold, *Home Rule* (London, 1912).

Stephens, James, *The Insurrection in Dublin* (3rd ed., Dublin, 1966).

Sweeney, Pat, *Liffey Ships & Shipbuilding* (Cork, 2010).

Taylor, Monica, *Sir Bertram Windle, A Memoir* (London, 1932).

Taylor, Rex, *Michael Collins* (London, 1958).

Townshend, Charles, *The British Campaign in Ireland 1919–1921* (Oxford, 1975).

Townshend, Charles, *Political Violence in Ireland: Government and Resistance since 1848* (Oxford, 1983).

Townshend, Charles, *Ireland: The 20th Century* (London, 1999).

Townshend, Charles, *The Republic: The Fight for Irish Independence, 1918–1923* (London, 2013).

Travers, Pauric, *Settlements and Divisions: Ireland 1870–1922* (Dublin, 1988).

Traynor, Oscar, 'The Burning of the Custom House', in *Dublin's Fighting Story 1916–21* (Tralee, 1948).

Urquhart, Diane, *The ladies of Londonderry: women and political patronage* (London and New York, 2007).

Urquhart, Diane, *Women in Ulster Politics, 1890–1940* (Dublin, 2000).

Urquhart, Diane, 'Pillar of Unionism: the Politics of Theresa Sixth Marchioness of Londonderry', in *From the United Irishmen to twentieth-century Unionism: A Festschrift for A.T.Q. Stewart* (Dublin, 2004), p.114.

Ward, Alan J., 'Lloyd George and the 1918 Irish Conscription Crisis', *The Historical Journal*, xvii, 1 (Mar. 1974), 107–129.

Webb, Beatrice (ed. Barbara Drake and Margaret I. Cole), *Our Partnership* (London, 1948).

West, Trevor, *Horace Plunkett: Co-Operation and Politics, an Irish Biography* (Gerrards Cross, 1986).

Wheatley, Michael, *Nationalism and the Irish Party: provincial Ireland 1910–16* (Oxford, 2005).

Wheeler-Bennett, John W., *John Anderson, Viscount Waverly* (London, 1962).

Williams, Basil (ed.), *Home Rule Problems* (London, 1911).

Williams, Desmond (ed.), *The Irish Struggle 1916–1926* (London, 1966).

Wilson, Trevor (ed.), *The Political Diaries of C. P. Scott 1911–1928* (London, 1970).

Wrench, Sir John Evelyn, *Struggle: 1914–1920* (London, 1935).

Yeates, Pádraig, *A City in Turmoil: Dublin 1919–21* (Dublin, 2012).

Yeates, Pádraig, *A City in Wartime: Dublin 1914–18* (Dublin, 2011).

INDEX

Note: Maps, illustrations and plate entries appear in bold, i.e. the first plate is indicated thus: **P1**.